ASIAN ECONOMIC INTEGRATION REPORT 2019/2020

DEMOGRAPHIC CHANGE, PRODUCTIVITY, AND THE ROLE OF TECHNOLOGY

NOVEMBER 2019

ASIAN DEVELOPMENT BANK

ADB

Notes:
In this publication, "$" refers to United States dollars, unless otherwise stated.
All masthead photos are from ADB.

ADB recognizes "China" as the People's Republic of China; "Hongkong" as Hong Kong, China; "Korea" as the Republic
of Korea; and "Vietnam" as Viet Nam.

Cover design by Erickson Mercado.

CONTENTS

Tables, Figures, and Boxes v

Foreword x

Acknowledgments xi

Definitions xii

Abbreviations xiii

Highlights xv

1. TRADE AND GLOBAL VALUE CHAINS 1

Recent Trends in Asia's Trade 1

Asia's Intraregional Trade..3

Progress of Global and Regional Value Chains 5

Trade Conflict and Its Potential Impact 11

Updates on Regional Trade Policy...22

The Role of FTAs in Making Trade Work for All 27

References...32

ANNEX 1a: Impact of Technology on GVC Exports 34

2. CROSS-BORDER INVESTMENT 36

Trends and Patterns of Foreign Direct Investment in Asia 36

Outward Foreign Direct Investment 47

References...50

3. FINANCIAL INTEGRATION 51

Asia's Cross-Border Financial Assets and Liabilities 51

Outward Portfolio Investment 52

Inward Portfolio Investment 56

Subregional Portfolio Investment...58

Bank Holdings 63

Analysis Using Price Indicators..69

References...76

4. MOVEMENT OF PEOPLE 78

Remittances..78

International Tourism and the Movement of Visitors 82

International Tourism Receipts 89

References 95

5.   SUBREGIONAL COOPERATION INITIATIVES **97**
Central and West Asia: Central Asia Regional Economic Cooperation Program 97
Southeast Asia: Greater Mekong Subregion Program 102
East Asia: Support for RCI Initiatives under CAREC and GMS Subregional Programs 106
and Knowledge-Sharing Activities
South Asia: South Asia Subregional Economic Cooperation 109
The Pacific: Partnering with the Private Sector to Expand Energy Access 114
The Asia-Pacific Regional Cooperation and Integration Index 116
Role of Economic Integration in Growth and Development...118
References...123

6.   THEME CHAPTER: DEMOGRAPHIC CHANGE, PRODUCTIVITY, ... **126**
     AND THE ROLE OF TECHNOLOGY
Introduction 126
Population Aging in Asia 128
Workforce Aging, Productivity, and the Role of Technology...143
Technology Options for Graying Asia..155
Assessing the Technology Needs of Countries Based on Age-Education Profiles 171
Turning the Demographic Headwind to a Tailwind-Policy Considerations 181
Background Papers 195
References..196
ANNEX 6a: Demographical Change, Technological Advance, and Growth: A Cross-Country Analysis.................205
ANNEX 6b: Data and Methodology Used in Country Case Studies 208

7.   STATISTICAL APPENDIX..**209**
Regional Groupings..209
Table Descriptions 209

TABLES, FIGURES, AND BOXES

TABLES

1.1	Asian FTAs with Labor Provisions	28
2.1	Top 10 Global and Asian FDI Destinations	37
2.2	Top Sources of FDI in Asia—Greenfield and M&As	39
2.3	Top Destinations of FDI in Asia—Greenfield and M&As	39
2.4	Average Project and Deal Size—Asia	39
2.5	Top Sources of Job Creation in Asia—Greenfield FDI	42
2.6	Top Destinations of Job Creation in Asia—Greenfield FDI	42
2.7	Top 10 Sources of Global and Asian FDI	47
3.1	Destinations of Outward Portfolio Debt Investment—Asia	55
3.2	Destinations of Outward Portfolio Equity Investment—Asia	55
3.3	Sources of Inward Portfolio Debt Investment—Asia	58
3.4	Sources of Inward Portfolio Equity Investment—Asia	59
3.5	Destinations of Cross-Border Bank Claims—Asia	66
3.6	Sources of Cross-Border Bank Liabilities—Asia	66
3.7	Average Simple Correlation of Weekly Total Bond Return Indexes—Asia with Asia and the World	70
3.8	Average Simple Correlation of Stock Price Index Weekly Returns—Asia with Asia and the World	72
4.1	Remittance Inflows by Recipient Region, 2018	79
4.2	Remittance Inflows to Asian Subregions, 2018	80
4.3	Top Outbound Visitors to Asia	86
4.4	Top Destinations of Asian Visitors	88
4.5	Tourism Arrivals and Receipts in Asia by Subregion, 2017	90
5.1	Selected Economic Indicators, 2018—CAREC	97
5.2	Selected Economic Indicators, 2018—Greater Mekong Subregion	102
5.3	Selected Economic Indicators, 2018—SASEC	110
6.1	Aging and Productivity: A Literature Review	150
6.2	Description of Criteria Used to Classify Selected Economies in Asia	173
6.3	Summary Policy Matrix—Technology Needs by Type of Demographic Pattern and Priority	186
6.4	Early and Normal Retirement Ages by Type of Pension Scheme, 2016	190

FIGURES

1.1	Merchandise Trade Volume and Real GDP Growth—Asia and World	1
1.2	Sources of Trade Volume Growth—Asia	2
1.3	Trade Value—Asia and World	2
1.4	Monthly Trade by Value and Volume—Asia	3
1.5	Global Business Confidence and Asia's Trade Volume Growth	3
1.6	Intraregional Trade Share—Asia, EU, and North America	4
1.7	Intraregional Trade Shares by Asian Subregions	5
1.8	Analytical Framework of GVC and RVC Participation	7
1.9	RVC–GVC Intensity—Asia, EU, and North America	7

1.10	RVC–GVC Intensity—Asian Subregions	8
1.11	RVC–GVC Intensity by Major Sector—Asia	9
1.12	Overall RVC and GVC Participation—Selected Asian Economies	10
1.13	Complex RVC and GVC Participation—Selected Asian Economies	11
1.14	Chronology of Tariffs Filed by the PRC and the US	12
1.15	Number of Products with Tariffs Filed by the PRC and the US by Major Category	13
1.16	Bilateral Import Growth Rate Ratio by Sector and Semester—US and PRC	14
1.17	Impact of US Tariff Hikes on PRC Aluminum	15
1.18	Impact of US Tariff Hikes on PRC Transmission Apparatus	15
1.19	Impact of PRC Tariff Hikes on US Soybeans and Miscellaneous Grains and Fruits	16
1.20	Impact of PRC Tariff Hikes on US Cotton—Raw Material, Yarn, and Woven Fabric	17
1.21	Impact of PRC Tariff Hikes on US Automobiles	17
1.22	Export Growth of Selected Asian Economies	18
1.23	Value-Added Decomposition for One Unit of iPhone4	19
1.24	Backward and Forward Linkages of US and PRC Trade on Electrical and Optical Equipment	21
1.25	Backward and Forward Linkages of US and PRC Trade on Textile and Textile Products	22
1.26	Number of Newly Effective Free Trade Agreements—Asia	23
1.27	Number of Proposed and Signed Free Trade Agreements—Asia	23
1.28	Number of Signed Free Trade Agreements—Asia	23
1.29	Number of Signed Free Trade Agreements, Intraregional and Extraregional	24
1.30	Number of SME-Related Provisions in Asian FTAs	29
1.31	Main Areas of SME-Related Provisions in RTAs	30
2.1	Global Inward FDI by Destination	37
2.2	FDI by Mode of Entry—Asia	38
2.3	Total Inward FDI to Asia by Sector	40
2.4	Intra-Asia FDI by Sector	41
2.5	Inward Greenfield FDI Job Creation in Asia by Source	41
2.6	Inward Greenfield FDI Job Creation in Asia by Sector	43
2.7	Global Inward FDI to Asia by Destination Subregion	44
2.8	Intraregional FDI Inflows—Asia	44
2.9	Regional FDI Share—Asia	45
2.10	Global Outward FDI by Source	47
2.11	Asia's Outward FDI by Source	48
2.12	Asia's Outward FDI to the Rest of the World by Sector	49
2.13	Jobs Created by Asian Greenfield FDI by Destination	49
2.14	Total FDI Flows—Asia	49
3.1	Cross-Border Assets—Asia	51
3.2	Cross-Border Liabilities—Asia	52
3.3	Outward Portfolio Investment—Asia	53
3.4	Change in Outward Portfolio Investment—Asia	54
3.5	Inward Portfolio Investment—Asia	56
3.6	Change in Inward Portfolio Investment—Asia	57
3.7	Subregional Portfolio Debt Investment—Asia	59
3.8	Subregional Portfolio Equity Investment—Asia	62
3.9	Global Portfolio Investment—Asia with the Rest of the World	63
3.10	Cross-Border Bank Holdings—Asia	64
3.11	Change in Cross-Border Bank Holdings—Asia	65
3.12	Bank Volatility—Asia	67
3.13	Nonperforming Loan Ratios—Selected Asian Economies	69
3.14	Conditional Correlation of Total Bond Return Indexes—Asia with Select Economies and Regions	71

3.15	Conditional Correlation of Equity Markets—Asia with Select Economies and Regions	72
3.16	Share of Variance in Asian Capital Market Returns, as Explained by Global, Regional, and Domestic Shocks	73
3.17	σ-Convergence of Total Return Bond Indexes—Asia	75
4.1	Remittance Inflows to Asia and the World	78
4.2	Financial Flows to Asia by Type	79
4.3	Top 10 Remittance Recipients in Asia, 2018	80
4.4	Top 10 Remittance-Recipient Economies in Asia, 2018	81
4.5	Global Visitor Arrivals by Region	82
4.6	Intraregional and Extraregional Flows of Visitors from Asia, 2017	83
4.7	Extraregional Visitor Flows to Asia, 2017	86
4.8	Tourism Expenditure by Asian Economies	86
4.9	Tourism Expenditure per Outbound Tourist	87
4.10	Intra-Subregional Tourism Share—Asia	89
4.11	International Tourism Receipts by Region, 2017	89
4.12	Top 10 Recipients of Tourism Receipts, 2017	90
4.13	Tourism Receipts per Arrival	91
4.14	Growth in International Tourist Receipts and Arrivals, 2010–2017	93
5.1	CAREC Investments by Funding Source, as of 31 December 2018	98
5.2	CAREC Investments by Sector, as of 31 December 2018	98
5.3	Progress of Multimodal Corridor Network Development—CAREC	100
5.4	SASEC Investment by Sector and Volume	110
5.5	SASEC Projects by Sector, as of 31 December 2018	110
5.6	SASEC Investment by Sector, Volume, and Finance Partner	111
5.7	Cost of and Access to Electricity	115
5.8	Overall and Dimensional Subindexes—Asia	117
5.9	Overall Indexes—Asian Subregions	117
5.10	Dimensional Subindexes by Asia Subregions, 2017	117
5.11	Dimensional Subindexes by Subregional Cooperation Initiatives, 2017	118
5.12	Regional Integration Index, 2017—Asia versus Other Regions	118
5.13	Intraregional, Extraregional, and Global Economic Integration Indexes	120
5.14	Intraregional, Extraregional, and Global Economic Integration Indexes by Income Level	121
5.15	Global Economic Integration Indexes, by Region	121
5.16	Intraregional, Extraregional, and Global Economic Integration Indexes—Asia	121
6.1	Population by Major Age Group—Asia	128
6.2	Evolution of the Population Pyramid—Asia	129
6.3	Life Expectancy—Asia	129
6.4	Pattern of Fertility Rate Decline—Selected Economies	130
6.5	Speed of Aging—Selected Economies	131
6.6	Income Levels and Share of Older Persons, 1960–2017—Selected Asian Economies	131
6.7	Population Growth, 2000–2019—Asia	132
6.8	Working Age Population—Asia	133
6.9	Average Age of the Working Age Population	133
6.10	Labor Force Participation by Age Group—Asia	134
6.11	Labor Force Participation of Older Workforce—Selected Asian Economies	135
6.12	Sector Distribution of Employment by Age Group—Selected Asian Economies	136
6.13	Task Distribution of Employment by Age Group—Selected Asian Economies	137
6.14	Unemployment Rate by Age Group—Asia	137
6.15	Human Capital Development and Fertility	140
6.16	Mean Years of Schooling of Population Ages 25–64	141
6.17	Mean Years of Schooling by Age Group—Asia	142

6.18   First Demographic Dividend in Selected Asian Economies   143
6.19   Aging Workforce and the Three Factors of Production   144
6.20   Physical Ability and Fitness Level by Age Group: A Case of Japan   145
6.21   Cognitive Ability by Age Group Based on Psychometric Tests   145
6.22   Literacy and Numeracy Skills by Age Group   146
6.23   Walking Speed of Older Persons—Japan   146
6.24   Extension of Healthy Life Span in Asian Economies   147
6.25   Population and Dependency Ratios—Selected Asian Economies   151
6.26   Workforce Aging and Industrial Robot Adoption, 2007–2017   151
6.27   Relative Contribution to Per Capita GDP Growth by Age Cohorts   152
6.28   Relative Contribution to Per Capita GDP Growth by Age Cohorts with Interactions: Life Expectancy   153
6.29   Relative Contribution to Per Capita GDP Growth by Age Cohorts with Interactions: TFP   154
6.30   Framework on Aging and Growth   156
6.31   Ways Technology Enhances Factors of Productivity   157
6.32   Robot Adoption in Selected Economies, 2017   159
6.33   Rates of Telework or ICT-Mobile Work in Selected Countries   161
6.34   Population Distribution by Age and Education—People's Republic of China   172
6.35   Type-1 Population Distribution by Age and Education—Selected Asian Economies   174
6.36   Type-2 Population Distribution by Age and Education—Selected Asian Economies   174
6.37   Type-3 Population Distribution by Age and Education—Selected Asian Economies   175
6.38   Type-4 Population Distribution by Age and Education—Selected Asian Economies   176
6.39   Average Annual Change in Employment Share by Age and Task—Selected Asian Economies   179
6.40   Opportunities and Challenges in Type-1 (Fast-Aging, Above Median Education) Pattern   182
6.41   Opportunities and Challenges in Type-2 (Fast-Aging, Below Median Education) Pattern   183
6.42   Opportunities and Challenges in Type-3 (Slow-Aging, Below Median Education) Pattern   184
6.43   Opportunities and Challenges in Type-4 (Slow-Aging, Above Median Education) Pattern   185
6.44   Regional Demographics and Task Employment—Asia   191
6.45   Technology Adoption by Archetype—Asia   192
6.46   Entry Points for Regional Cooperation Strategies   193

BOXES

1.1   Trade Outlook for Asia   4
1.2   Gravity Model Estimation of Bilateral Exports   5
1.3   Trade Complementarity and Substitutability within ASEAN+3   19
1.4   Impact of Technology on Global Value Chain Exports   25
2.1   Trends of Foreign Direct Investment in the People's Republic of China   45
3.1   Recent Progress in Developing Local Currency Bond Markets in ASEAN+3   60
3.2   Harnessing Regional Cooperation to Address Nonperforming Loans: Lessons from Europe   68
3.3   Fintech and Regional Financial Development and Stability   74
4.1   Relaxing Visa Policies to Boost Tourism in CAREC   84
4.2   Tourism Coverage—A Measure of Net Tourism Earnings   92
5.1   Promoting E-commerce in Greater Mekong Subregion   103
5.2   SASEC as a Platform for Knowledge-Sharing for Enhanced Regional Cooperation   113
5.3   Global Integration and Its Effects on Growth and Inequality   122
6.1   Which Jobs Are More Susceptible to Aging?   138
6.2   Japan's Expanding Labor Force in a Time of Population Contraction   139
6.3   How Do We Define the "Old Age" Group?   148
6.4   Technology Adoption and Its Implications on Economic Growth in Aging Asia: Case Studies   155
       for Japan, the People's Republic of China, and the Republic of Korea

6.5	Artificial Intelligence and Its Application in the Workplace	158
6.6	Case Study of Japan's Shimizu Corporation's Adoption of Industrial Robots	160
6.7	Exoskeleton Use in Vehicle Manufacturing	161
6.8	Autonomous Vehicles: Steering Technology in Favor of Seniors	162
6.9	Skills Development Technologies in Developing Asia	163
6.10	Education and Information and Communication Technology in India and Thailand	164
6.11	Digital Interviews and Artificial Intelligence-Powered Human Resources	167
6.12	A Cloud Job-Matching System for Elderly Workers in Japan	168
6.13	Digital Interventions in Healthcare	170
6.14	Future Aging and Educational Attainment Profile	172
6.15	Level of Aging versus Rate of Aging	177
6.16	Technology and Older Workers	180
6.17	Setting New Directions Toward Lifelong Learning	188
6.18	Initiatives That Promote Business and Academic Collaboration and Business Incubators on Aging Technologies	189

FOREWORD

Regional economic integration is one of the critical elements to maintain strong growth momentum in Asia and the Pacific amid unresolved trade tensions, weakening global demand, and policy uncertainties. While Asia's trade volume growth eased to 4.0% in 2018 from 7.3% in 2017, regional trade linkages remain robust and work as a buffer against external challenges. By value, Asia's intraregional trade share stood at nearly 60% in 2018. Asia's global value chain (GVC) participation increased for the last two consecutive years. Trade tensions generated both negative spillover effects and positive trade redirections through expanded production-sharing networks across Asia.

As to cross-border investments, Asia emerges as a major global investor while it continues to attract sizable foreign direct investment (FDI). In 2018, 43.1% of global inward FDI went to Asia, creating around 900,000 jobs. Asia's share of global outward FDI also rose to 49.4%, its highest thus far. Cross-border bank claims ($4.7 trillion) and liabilities ($2.5 trillion) were also record highs, with lower volatility on intraregional bank claims and liabilities than those on the United States and the European Union. Portfolio investment remains biased toward outside the region. With heightened uncertainties in the global economy, governments need to remain vigilant to all signs of external and domestic financial turbulence.

The *Asian Economic Integration Report (AEIR) 2019/2020* introduces the new Global Economic Integration Index (GEII), which examines the progress of an economy's integration into the world economy. The GEII distinguishes the contributions of intraregional and extraregional integration in driving global economic integration. This new index provides an analytical tool to examine the progress and possible impacts of economic integration at different classification of regions.

The AEIR theme chapter assesses the rapid demographic change enveloping Asia from a novel angle of human capital and technology. While economies will be increasingly dependent on an aging workforce, tomorrow's elders will be different from today's elders; they will be healthier, more educated, and more likely to stay at work longer. Higher educational attainment across the region also suggests a steady supply of quality human capital. As such, the changing population structures and workforce profiles open many windows of opportunity to gain from as long as regional economies design appropriate policy responses. Technological adoption and policy reforms for age-friendly employment will be key. As irreversible as demographic aging is, its economic consequences are not preordained if appropriate technologies and policies are adopted.

To maintain high productivity growth in graying Asia, labor market opportunities and challenges are unique for each economy. Different types of technologies can be leveraged to make labor market participation more adaptive and flexible given the population's age and education profiles. Policies that facilitate the movement of capital, labor, and technology could also help individual countries deal with demographic transition. The region's demographic diversity offers opportunities to discuss the potential regional cooperation in education, skilled labor, and talent.

Yasuyuki Sawada
Chief Economist and Director General
Economic Research and Regional Cooperation Department
Asian Development Bank

ACKNOWLEDGMENTS

The Asian Economic Integration Report (AEIR) 2019/2020 was prepared by the Regional Cooperation and Integration Division (ERCI) of the Economic Research and Regional Cooperation Department (ERCD) of the Asian Development Bank (ADB), under the overall supervision of ERCI Director Cyn-Young Park. Jong Woo Kang coordinated overall production assisted by Mara Claire Tayag. ERCI consultants under Technical Assistance 9657: Asian Economic Integration—Building Knowledge for Policy Dialogue, 2018–2021 (Subproject 1) contributed data compilation, research, and analysis.

Contributing authors include Jong Woo Kang, Paul Mariano, Dorothea Ramizo, and Joshua Anthony Gapay (Trade and Global Value Chains); Jong Woo Kang, Fahad Khan, and Clemence Fatima Cruz (Cross-Border Investment); Junkyu Lee, Peter Rosenkranz, and Ana Kristel Lapid, with data support from Arjan Paulo Salvanera, and with contributions to the boxes from Satoru Yamadera, Alyssa Villanueva, Mikko Diaz, and Monica Melchor (Financial Integration); and Kijin Kim, Aiko Kikkawa Takenaka, and Ma. Concepcion Latoja (Movement of People). The chapter "Subregional Cooperation Initiatives" was consolidated by Paulo Rodelio Halili with data support from Pilar Dayag and based on contributions by regional departments of ADB: Guoliang Wu, Xinglan Hu, and Ronaldo Oblepias (Central Asia Regional Economic Cooperation subsection); Greater Mekong Subregion (GMS) Secretariat (GMS subsection); East Asia Department's Regional Cooperation and Integration team (East Asia subsection); Ronald Antonio Butiong, Jesusito Tranquilino, and Leticia de Leon (South Asia Subregional Economic Cooperation subsection); and Alex Burrell, Anthony Maxwell, and Rommel Rabanal (Pacific subsection). The section on Asia-Pacific Regional Cooperation and Integration Index was contributed by Cyn-Young Park, James Villafuerte, and Racquel Claveria.

Aiko Kikkawa Takenaka coordinated and contributed to the production of the theme chapter, "Demographic Change, Productivity, and the Role of Technology," and Waseem Noor served as the economic editor. Background papers were provided by Rafal Chomik, Suqin Ge, Radhicka Kapoor, Daiji Kawaguchi, Kiho Muroga, Cyn-Young Park, Jinyoung Kim, John Piggott, Kwanho Shin, Aiko Kikkawa Takenaka, and Junsen Zhang. Fahad Khan contributed content on foreign direct investment. Raymond Gaspar provided overall research support, along with Ancilla Inocencio, Aleli Rosario, and Ma. Concepcion Latoja. The theme chapter benefited from comments and suggestions provided by internal peer reviewers (Thomas Abell, Kijin Kim, Valerie Mercer-Blackman, and Meredith Wyse) and the participants of the following workshops and events: "Technology and Aging Workforce: Maximize the Gains from Longevity and Long Working Life" held on 17–18 May 2018 in Asiatic Research Institute, Korea University; "ADB–Asian Think Tank Development Forum 2018: Upgrading Human Capital and Skills Development for Future Asia" held on 22–23 August 2018 at Crawford School of Public Policy, Australian National University; "Expert Workshop for AEIR 2019 Theme Chapter: Population Aging, Productivity, and the Role of Technology in Asia" held on 28 November 2018 in Manila, Philippines; and "ADB–ADBI Conference on Demographic Changes, Productivity, and the Role of Technology" held on 13–14 June 2019 in Tokyo, Japan.

Guy Sacerdoti and James Unwin edited the report. Joseph Manglicmot typeset and produced the layout, Erickson Mercado created the cover design and assisted in typesetting. Tuesday Soriano proofread the report, while Ma. Cecillia Abellar and Pilar Dayag handled the page proof checking. Carol Ongchangco helped in proofreading. Support for AEIR 2019/2020 printing and publishing was provided by the Printing Services Unit of ADB's Office of Administrative Services and by the Department of Communications. Carol Ongchangco, Pia Asuncion Tenchavez, Maria Criselda Aherrera, and Marilyn Parra provided administrative and secretarial support, and helped organize the AEIR workshops, launch events, and other AEIR-related seminars. Karen Lane and Ami Takagawa of the Department of Communications and Harumi Kodama, Representative of Japan Representative Office coordinated the launch and dissemination of AEIR 2019/2020.

DEFINITIONS

The economies covered in the *Asian Economic Integration Report 2019/2020* are grouped by major analytic or geographic group.

- Asia refers to the 49 Asia and the Pacific members of the Asian Development Bank, which includes Japan and Oceania (Australia and New Zealand) in addition to the 46 developing Asian economies.

- Subregional economic groupings are listed below:

  - Central Asia comprises Armenia, Azerbaijan, Georgia, Kazakhstan, the Kyrgyz Republic, Tajikistan, Turkmenistan, and Uzbekistan.
  - East Asia comprises the People's Republic of China; Hong Kong, China; Japan; the Republic of Korea; Mongolia; and Taipei,China.
  - South Asia comprises Afghanistan, Bangladesh, Bhutan, India, Maldives, Nepal, Pakistan, and Sri Lanka.
  - Southeast Asia comprises Brunei Darussalam, Cambodia, Indonesia, the Lao People's Democratic Republic, Malaysia, Myanmar, the Philippines, Singapore, Thailand, and Viet Nam.
  - The Pacific comprises the Cook Islands, the Federated States of Micronesia, Fiji, Kiribati, the Marshall Islands, Nauru, Niue, Palau, Papua New Guinea, Samoa, Solomon Islands, Timor-Leste, Tonga, Tuvalu, and Vanuatu.
  - Oceania includes Australia and New Zealand.

Unless otherwise specified, the symbol "$" and the word "dollar" refer to United States dollars, and percent changes are year-on-year.

ABBREVIATIONS

ADB	Asian Development Bank
AEIR	Asian Economic Integration Report
AI	artificial intelligence
ARCII	Asia-Pacific Regional Cooperation and Integration Index
ASEAN	Association of Southeast Asian Nations (Brunei Darussalam, Cambodia, Indonesia, the Lao People's Democratic Republic, Malaysia, Myanmar, the Philippines, Singapore, Thailand, and Viet Nam)
BIS	Bank for International Settlements
BEZ	border economic zone
BOP	balance of payments
CAGR	compounded annual growth rate
CAREC	Central Asia Regional Economic Cooperation
CITA 2030	CAREC Integrated Trade Agenda 2030
CPIS	Coordinated Portfolio Investment Survey
CPTPP	Comprehensive and Progressive Trans-Pacific Partnership Agreement
CWRD	Central and West Asia Department
DCC	dynamic conditional correlations
DMC	developing member country
DVA	domestic value added
EARD	East Asia Department
ECD	economic corridor development
EEII	Extraregional Economic Integration Index
EU	European Union (Austria, Belgium, Bulgaria, Croatia, Cyprus, Czech Republic, Denmark, Estonia, Finland, France, Germany, Greece, Hungary, Ireland, Italy, Latvia, Lithuania, Luxembourg, Malta, the Netherlands, Poland, Portugal, Romania, Slovak Republic, Slovenia, Spain, Sweden, and the United Kingdom)
FDI	foreign direct investment
FTA	free trade agreement
GDP	gross domestic product
GEII	Global Economic Integration Index
GFC	global financial crisis
GMS	Greater Mekong Subregion
GVC	global value chain
GWh	gigawatt-hours
HS	harmonized system
ICT	information and communication technology
IEII	Intraregional Economic Integration Index
ILO	International Labour Organization
IMF	International Monetary Fund
IPP	independent power producer

km	kilometer
KNOMAD	Global Knowledge Partnership on Migration and Development
Lao PDR	Lao People's Democratic Republic
LCY	local currency
LPG	liquefied petroleum gas
M&As	mergers and acquisitions
NIEs	newly industrialized economies (Hong Kong, China; the Republic of Korea; Singapore; and Taipei,China)
NPL	nonperforming loan
OECD	Organisation for Economic Co-operation and Development
PARD	Pacific Regional Department
PRC	People's Republic of China
PREP	Pacific Renewable Energy Program
RCEP	Regional Cooperation Economic Partnership
RCI	regional cooperation and integration
RKSI	Regional Knowledge-Sharing Initiative
ROW	rest of the world
RSAP	Rolling Strategic Action Plan
RVC	regional value chain
SARD	South Asia Department
SASEC	South Asia Subregional Economic Cooperation
SASEC OP	SASEC Operational Plan
SMEs	small and medium-sized enterprises
SEZ	special economic zone
SPS	sanitary and phytosanitary
UK	United Kingdom
US	United States
UNWTO	United Nations World Tourism Organization
VR	virtual reality
WTO	World Trade Organization

HIGHLIGHTS

Trade and Global Value Chains

- **Asia's trade growth is expected to decelerate further in 2019, amid persistent global trade tensions.**
  In 2018, Asia's trade (by volume) grew by 4.0%, slower than the 7.3% growth in 2017. This came in tandem with the slowdown in global trade growth from 4.6% to 3.0%. Continued trade tensions and a weakening of global demand pose key downside risks to the region's trade and growth outlook. Ongoing trade frictions between the United States (US) and the People's Republic of China (PRC) since early 2018 are affecting global and regional trade growth. PRC imports from the US declined 31.0% (year-on-year) in the second half of 2018, particularly among the sectors affected by the tariff hikes such as soybeans and other agricultural products. US imports from the PRC fell 12.6% for the first 8 months of 2019. Persistent trade tensions could dampen business confidence and weaken investments globally, casting a shadow over global economic prospects.

- **Asia's intraregional trade share—measured by value—remained a robust 57.5% in 2018, above the average 56.3% during 2012–2017.** Asia's global value chain (GVC) participation grew further in 2018 following its 2017 rebound, though at a slower pace. Regional production sharing networks across Asia have also deepened and expanded. Spillover effects of international trade tensions will cascade into a broader set of economies, either positive or negative, through the region's supply chains. For example, as supply chain integration boosted trade complementarity, particularly among economies in East Asia and Southeast Asia, a decrease in PRC exports to the US may have negative spillovers to other Asian economies. However, many of these economies also have similarities in their exports. High export competition among these economies suggests potential gains from either substitution or trade redirection. The net effect of higher US tariffs on PRC exports will be based on each economy's trade position in either a substitute or a complementary relationship with the PRC within GVCs. For example, Viet Nam and Taipei,China saw net gains in their exports in electronics and machinery while PRC exports fell. On the other hand, those whose exports complement PRC exports in the regional supply chains will likely experience net losses.

Cross-Border Investment

- **Inward foreign direct investment to Asia continues to grow despite a decline in the world's total inward FDI.** Estimates of global inward foreign direct investment (FDI) in 2018 was $1.3 trillion, a 13.4% contraction from $1.5 trillion in 2017. In contrast, inward FDI to Asia rose by 6.3% to $559.7 billion in 2018. Intraregional investment linkages also strengthened in 2018, rising 2.8% from $262.7 billion in 2017. After a sharp contraction in 2017, intraregional greenfield FDI rebounded in 2018 with manufacturing leading the recovery. FDI in services continued to rise in 2018, with one-third of it intraregional—mainly through mergers and acquisitions—in business, communications, finance, software and information technology, and transportation services. Greenfield FDI into Asia in 2018 was estimated to have created around 900,000 jobs in total, 56.9% from regional projects.

- **Asia's share of the world's total outward FDI rose to 49.4%, its highest thus far.** Over the years, Asia has cemented its status as a major international investor. Japan became the top source of global FDI with $143 billion invested in 2018, while tax reforms in the US caused a repatriation of its overseas investment and thus a significant drop in its outward FDI. The PRC's outward FDI fell below inward FDI in 2018 after 3 consecutive years of net FDI outflows. This reversal was largely due to the decline in outward FDI to the US and the European Union (EU), while inward FDI held up strongly in sectors such as automobiles, chemicals, semiconductors, and communications. In 2018, greenfield investments from the region were estimated to have generated some 850,000 jobs—36.0% of all jobs created globally—in real estate, textiles, automotive original equipment manufacturing, and electronic components, among others. Around two-thirds of the jobs were created within Asia, with the largest number in the PRC, India, and Viet Nam. Outside the region, the US, the Russian Federation, and the United Kingdom are the top three beneficiaries of Asia's greenfield FDI in terms of job creation.

Financial Integration

- **Outward portfolio debt investment by Asian economies continued to increase in 2018, though at a slower pace compared with 2017. However, outward portfolio equity investment contracted in 2018 after a surge in 2017.** Asia's outward portfolio debt investment increased by $108.1 billion in 2018 compared with an increase of $278.2 billion in 2017. Portfolio equity investment contracted by $293.6 billion in 2018 compared with an increase of $930.1 billion in 2017. The majority of Asia's portfolio investment remains invested outside the region, resulting in moderate intraregional shares for portfolio debt investment (16.8% for both 2018 and 2017) and portfolio equity investment (18.0% in 2018 from 18.1% in 2017). Despite large fluctuations over time, Asia's non-regional equity investment grew rapidly. Between 2013 and 2018, while the non-regional portfolio debt investment increased by $253.9 billion, Asian investors increased their non-regional equity investment by $1.5 trillion.

- **In 2018, while inward portfolio debt investment growth slowed, inward equity investment fell amid increasing concerns over Asia's economic prospects associated with rising global trade tensions.** Inward portfolio debt outstanding increased by $103.7 billion in 2018, driven by modest increases from the US. However, inward equity investment outstanding decreased by $691.5 billion in 2018 from a year ago. A fall in equity investment from the US accounted for nearly half of the decrease, while the EU accounted for about 36.0%. The decline may partly reflect stock market corrections across developing Asia, due to concerns over the PRC's growth moderation and possible spillovers to other Asian economies. The intraregional share of inward portfolio debt remained around 25.6% in 2018, and that of inward portfolio equity rose to 16.1% in 2018, slightly higher than in 2017.

- **Asia's cross-border banking activities continue to rise; foreign bank claims in 2018 reached $4.7 trillion and foreign bank liabilities hit $2.5 trillion, both records.** On the liability side, EU bank lending to Asia in 2018 was a major driver behind the increase in foreign bank liabilities. However, Asian bank borrowing from the US has declined since 2015, amid US monetary policy normalization. The volatilities of intraregional cross-border bank claims and liabilities have fallen since the 2008/09 global financial crisis and are lower than those of Asian banks' claims and liabilities to the EU and the US. The volatile nature of cross-border bank claims and liabilities calls for close monitoring of the foreign exposures of Asian banks in case the global liquidity cycle reverses.

Movement of People

- **Remittance inflows to Asia reached a record $302.1 billion in 2018, up from $278.7 billion a year ago.** Improved economic and job market conditions in the US, a rebound in outward remittances from the Middle East, and the economic recovery of the Russian Federation boosted remittances to the region. Higher oil prices and a strengthening of the Russian ruble also appear to have contributed. Except for Central Asia and Oceania, all Asian subregions saw a pickup in remittance inflows. South Asia received around $132 billion of the region's remittance inflows, followed by East Asia ($79 billion). India, the PRC, and the Philippines were the top three remittance recipients, accounting for 59.5% of remittances to Asia and 26.3% of global inflows. Remittances remain a vital and relatively stable source of foreign exchange income for many countries in developing Asia, especially ADB's Pacific developing member countries (DMCs) and Central Asian countries—remittances continued to be significant in per capita terms ($1,776 for Tonga and $793 for Samoa) and as a proportion of gross domestic product (38% for Tonga and 33% for the Kyrgyz Republic).

- **Tourist arrivals in Asia grew faster than anywhere else in the world with international tourism receipts hitting a record $368 billion in 2017.** Inbound tourists from both Asia (up by 10.3% from 2016) and non-Asia (up by 8.2%) contributed to the high growth in Asian tourism. Asia attracted 23.4% (310.7 million tourists) of global tourist arrivals in 2017, up from 20.5% (195.4 million) in 2010. Intraregional tourists accounted for nearly 80% of tourists to Asia. The largest number of tourists came from Hong Kong, China and the PRC. Outside Asia, the US and the Russian Federation had the largest number of tourists to the region. The PRC, Japan, and Thailand were the most popular destinations for Asian tourists. Steady income growth across the region continues to boost the number of Asian tourists and their travel expenditures. Total expenditures by Asian tourists doubled between 2010 and 2017, led by the PRC, reaching $495.3 billion in 2017. Each outbound tourist from Asia spent $1,231 on average in 2017. Asia earned $1,097 per tourist in 2017 ($951 for Europe), although tourism receipts per arrival varied widely across subregions and countries. Tourism receipts remain a key source of income for many Pacific DMCs and Southeast Asian countries, while the region's top three beneficiaries are Thailand ($62 billion); Australia ($44 billion); and Hong Kong, China ($38 billion).

Regional and Global Economic Integration

- **Regional economic cooperation remains strong in Asia and the Pacific, providing a buffer against any cascading effect of rising global trade tensions.** Latest estimates of the Asia-Pacific Regional Cooperation and Integration Index (ARCII) based on 2017 data show a broadly steady pace of Asian integration. The index declined slightly in 2017, driven by a smaller contribution from the money and finance dimension. This was partly offset by increases in infrastructure and connectivity, the movement of people, and institutional and social integration dimensions. By subregion, East Asia remains the most regionally integrated while Central Asia the least. Relative to other regions globally, Asia came second to the EU in overall integration, but stayed even with the EU in terms of trade and investment integration.

- **This report introduces a new measure of global economic integration to complement the ARCII with the region's integration with outside economies.** The Global Economic Integration Index distinguishes the contributions of intraregional and extraregional integration for each economy's integration with the world. Between the two, intraregional integration contributes more to a higher degree of global economic integration than extraregional integration. Analyses also show that while global integration promotes economic growth, it may widen income inequality. Moreover, high-income countries appear to take better advantage of the overall positive effects of globalization, while low-income countries benefit more from intraregional integration.

Demographic Change, Productivity, and the Role of Technology

- **The Asia and Pacific region is facing rapid demographic change, with several countries aging dramatically; but tomorrow's elderly will be different from today's.** The ongoing demographic transition will leave many of the region's economies increasingly dependent on an aging workforce, posing a challenge to sustaining potential growth for both advanced and many developing economies. However, with large improvements in educational attainment across the region, most economies are expected to enjoy a continuous supply of quality human capital even as they age. Older workers are now healthier and more educated than in the past. The average healthy life span (expectancy) increased by nearly 7 years from 57.2 to 63.8 years between 1990 and 2017 for the economies in Asia and the Pacific. The average years of education among 55 to 64 year-olds also increased from 4.6 in 1990 to 7.8 in 2015.

- **The changing workforce age and education profiles open multiple windows of opportunity for the region's economies to gain from the demographic transition.** Aside from the "first" demographic dividend based on contributions from a young and growing population for economic growth, ongoing changes in workforce age and education profile offer opportunities for new demographic dividends, arising from (i) improved human capital (the "second" demographic dividend), and (ii) extended longevity (the "third" or "silver" dividend). Improved health and longevity also encourage a relatively younger segment of older workers (aged 55-64) to stay in or reenter the labor force. Simulation analysis shows that longer life expectancy leads to an increase in productive contributions of older workers. Countries with expanding working age populations have more years to reap from productive cohorts, while making technology and policy adjustments before the workforce share begins to decline.

- **Technological progress, applying science, and research and development may also help mitigate the downside economic impact of aging.** Historically, an aging workforce was seen as an impediment to an economy's innovative capacity, which is an important engine of economic growth. However, recent studies suggest potentially positive impacts of a maturing and aging workforce on labor force productivity, because aging and a shrinking workforce can induce rapid adoption of labor-saving technologies. Fourth Industrial Revolution technologies may also complement and augment physical labor, raising labor force participation of seniors. There are ways adopting technology can support economic growth by positively affecting the use of enhanced human capital. It categorizes the types of technologies into five broad groups: those that (i) substitute labor and skills; (ii) complement labor and skills; (iii) aid education, skills development, and lifelong learning; (iv) better match workers with jobs and tasks; and (v) extend healthy life and overall life expectancy.

- **While the demographic transition may be irreversible, its economic impact depends on policy and behavioral responses, including ways by which countries adopt and apply technologies.** There are four distinct types of countries in Asia and the Pacific, based on the projected distribution in 2050 of economically active populations in countries by age (fast or slow aging) and education (above or below the median of the share of those with post-secondary education). These are based on the trajectories of past economic development and education attainment. Also, employment trends across population subsegments per country type can be tracked, identifying varying patterns of the rise and fall of employment across age/education types over time. Together, these group-specific patterns of the demographic transition and education profiles of labor forces help identify appropriate solutions for each country type.

Conclusions and Policy Recommendations

- **Unique labor market opportunities and challenges arise for each country depending on the age and education profile of its population.** There are a specific set of technologies suggested for each of the four country types: Type-1 (fast aging and above median education), Type-2 (fast aging and below median education), Type-3 (slow aging and below median education), and Type-4 (slow aging and above median education). Regardless of an economy's position in terms of population aging and level of post-secondary education penetration, there is an urgent need for rethinking education and skills training policy, combined with mainstreaming lifelong learning. The unprecedented speed of technological progress is rapidly eroding some older worker skills. This calls for strategic reforms to improve learning and training opportunities for older workers. Governments and their agencies should encourage adopting and applying new technologies to facilitate economic adjustments to population aging with supplementary policies that induce behavioral change among workers and employers.

    - **Fast aging economies (Type-1 and Type-2) will need to prioritize technology adoption that fosters professional and foundational skills and improves job matching for workers, given the general difficulties faced by older workers in finding jobs.** Technologies that aim to boost health and longevity are also beneficial. In addition, fast aging and above median education countries (Type-1) will need to promote automation to mitigate the challenges of an undersupply of older primary-educated and younger secondary-educated workers. In contrast, fast aging and below median education countries (Type-2) need to prioritize policies that build the base of a high-educated workforce and reskill older primary-educated workers.

    - **Slow aging economies (Type-3 and Type-4) will need to prioritize technologies and policies that take advantage of a young and still-expanding workforce—while addressing challenges that impact both older and younger workforces—to meet the future demand for skilled labor.** Slow aging and below median education countries (Type-3) will grasp the opportunity arising from an expanding supply of younger and older secondary-educated workers. The gains can be maximized by adopting technologies that give them better foundational and professional skills and job matching. But a Type-3 country will face a limited supply of high-educated workers, which requires policies to aid education and lifelong learning. Slow aging and above median education countries (Type-4), on the other hand, can adopt technologies that leverage their younger and older-skilled workforce.

- **Across the region, economies need to consider policies that connect the right technologies to the changing nature of the workforce and bring greater flexibility in labor market participation.** Policy priorities in three areas may be considered. The first set of policies should promote technological adoption, diffusion, and application that can transform work and workspace—to allow greater labor force participation by older workers through subsidies and tax incentives targeting firms and industry–academia consortia. The second area is instituting labor market laws and regulations that meet the diverse and flexible working styles of employees, such as encouraging reform in mid-career employment, work-sharing, and options for gradual retirement. The third set of policies should be directed at reforming social security and tax systems so as not to penalize or disincentivize older workers from participating in the labor force. These policies would range from raising the statutory retirement age to embracing the concept of "pensionable age," one that allows a flexible and personalized approach to maintaining work–life balance throughout a worker's life.

- **Developing economies across Asia and the Pacific can benefit from the demographic diversity accompanied by varying demographic trends in the region**. Policies that facilitate the movement of capital, labor, and technology across countries could help alleviate particular challenges facing individual countries at different stages of demographic transition and technological adoption. Outward FDI can help companies from Type-1 (fast aging and high technology adoption) tap the large supply of secondary-educated workers in the other types. Migration can alleviate challenges associated with the lack of primary-educated workers in some countries and the absence of post-secondary-educated workers in others. Technology transfer can speed up the adoption of appropriate technologies for the needs of specific types. To encourage these movements, establishing regional cooperation frameworks and appropriate action plans in these areas would help. Examples include mutual skills recognition and social security agreements that encourage increased labor mobility between countries.

1 Trade and Global Value Chains

Recent Trends in Asia's Trade

Asia's trade growth moderated in 2018 amid persistent trade tensions and moderation in global economic growth momentum.[1]

After a strong 7.3% growth recovery in 2017, Asia's merchandise trade volume grew a slower 4.0% in 2018 (Figure 1.1a). Ongoing trade tensions between the United States (US) and the People's Republic of China (PRC), along with slowing global economic growth, curbed the upward trajectory of the region's trade growth, which fell below the 4.6% output growth. The expansion of global trade volume also slowed from 4.6% in 2017 to 3.0% in 2018, falling slightly below the 3.1% global economic

growth (Figure 1.1b). Other regions also saw trade growth decelerating: the European Union (EU) (1.6% in 2018 from 3.1% in 2017), Latin America and the Caribbean (3.5% from 4.1%), and the Middle East (0.6% from 2.9%). In contrast, trade growth accelerated in North America (4.7% from 4.1%) and Africa (3.5% from 2.1%).

Several Asian economies recorded slower export growth due to weaker external demand from developed countries and the potential negative effect from persisting trade tensions, which largely offset gains in commodity-exporting countries from higher global commodity prices. The region's export volume growth declined to 3.5% in 2018 from 6.8% in 2017. Meanwhile, import volume expanded at 4.7% in 2018, down from 8.1% in 2017. Strong

Figure 1.1: Merchandise Trade Volume and Real GDP Growth—Asia and World (%, year-on-year)

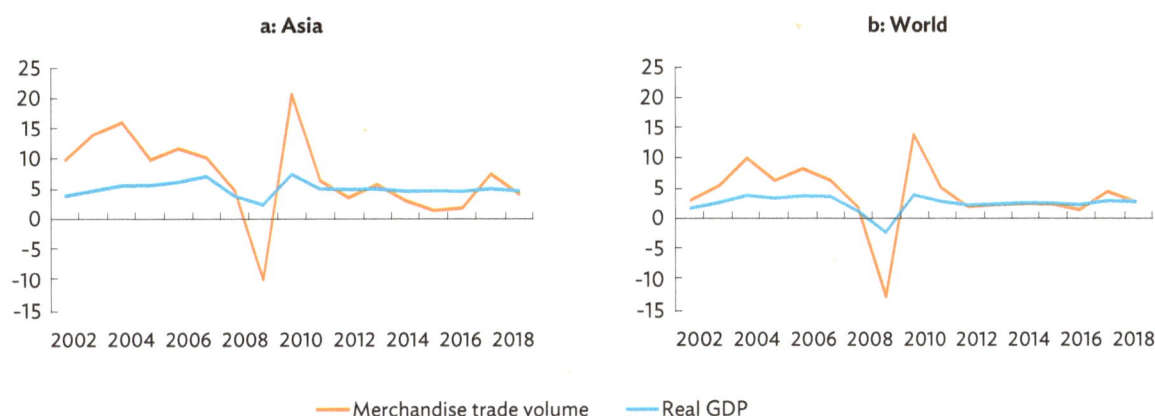

a: Asia

b: World

Merchandise trade volume — Real GDP

GDP = gross domestic product.

Note: Real GDP growth is weighted using market-exchange rates.

Sources: ADB calculations using data from International Monetary Fund. World Economic Outlook April 2019 Database. https://www.imf.org/external/pubs/ft/weo/2019/01/weodata/index.aspx (accessed October 2019); and World Trade Organization. Statistics Database. http://stat.wto.org/Home/WSDBHome.aspx (accessed April 2019).

---

[1]   Asia refers to the 49 Asia and Pacific members of the Asian Development Bank (ADB), which includes Japan and Oceania (Australia and New Zealand) in addition to the 46 developing Asian economies.

domestic demand, mostly from net-importing countries, continued to support import, even if growth was slightly restrained by the commodity price increase.

As in previous years, the PRC remained the key driver of Asia's trade expansion, accounting for 41.3% of trade growth (Figure 1.2). Other top contributors to export growth were Japan; the Republic of Korea; Viet Nam; and Taipei,China. On the other hand, top contributors on import growth were Hong Kong, China; Viet Nam; Indonesia; and Singapore.

Figure 1.2: Sources of Trade Volume Growth—Asia
(percentage points)

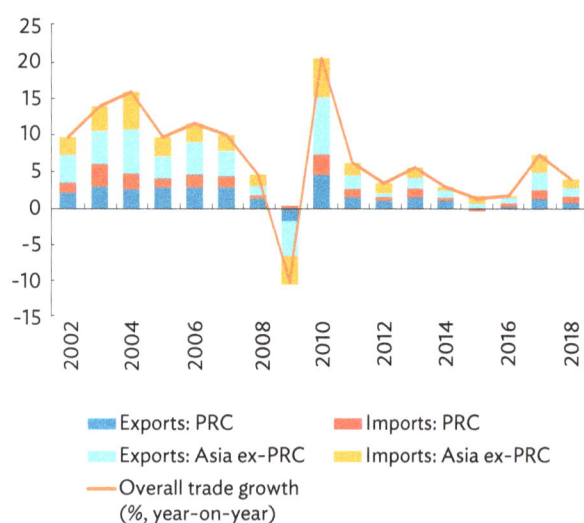

Exports: PRC
Imports: PRC
Exports: Asia ex-PRC
Imports: Asia ex-PRC
Overall trade growth (%, year-on-year)

PRC = People's Republic of China.

Source: ADB calculations using data from World Trade Organization. Statistics Database. http://stat.wto.org/Home/WSDBHome.aspx (accessed April 2019).

Asia's trade value growth also decelerated, albeit marginally.

In contrast to trade volume, Asia's trade value growth remained strong at 10.5% in 2018, comparable to the 12.8% recorded in 2017 (Figure 1.3). The increase in global commodity prices largely offset the slow growth in trade volume. Oil prices, in particular, rose by about 30%, contributing to higher commodity prices. This helped augment trade revenues of commodity-exporting countries such as Mongolia and some Central Asian economies.

Figure 1.3: Trade Value—Asia and World

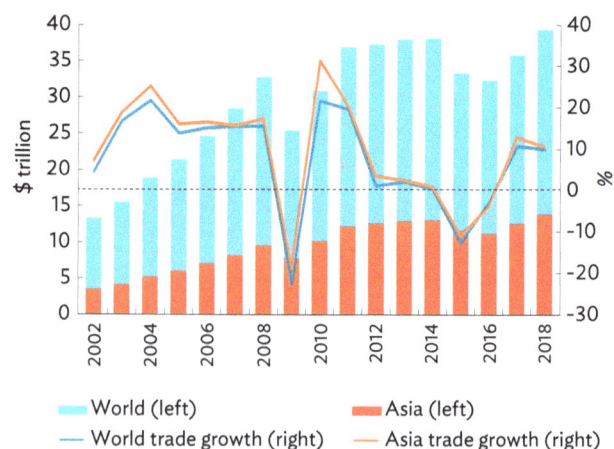

World (left)
Asia (left)
World trade growth (right)
Asia trade growth (right)

Source: ADB calculations using data from World Trade Organization. Statistics Database. http://stat.wto.org/Home/WSDBHome.aspx (accessed April 2019).

Asia's trade growth in recent months has faltered as trade policy uncertainties in key economies weigh in.

The region's trade volume growth peaked in early 2017 during the global trade recovery, and continued until the first half of 2018 (Figure 1.4). In tandem with the escalating US–PRC trade tensions and the softening of global industrial activity, however, trade growth began moderating in Q3 2018. Despite a temporary pause in tariff hikes in December 2018 (as agreed by the US and the PRC), the first 7 months of 2019 saw both the volume and value of trade growth decrease—affected by declining business and investment confidence. Asia's export and import volume growth trend largely follows the trajectory of global business confidence (Figure 1.5).

The slowdown in trade growth is projected to continue through the rest of 2019 and stabilize in 2020 (Box 1.1). Downside risks remain as trade frictions among major economies might not be resolved in the foreseeable future. The implemented US and PRC tariffs against each other, as of September 2019, equal to about $491.8 billion of bilateral imports (ADB 2019)—equivalent to 2.5% of total global imports. Global output is estimated to decline by 0.19%, and could further decrease by up to 0.55% if the trade conflict further escalates (ADB 2019). This could affect economic growth of Asian economies, as most are closely integrated

Figure 1.4: Monthly Trade by Value and Volume—Asia

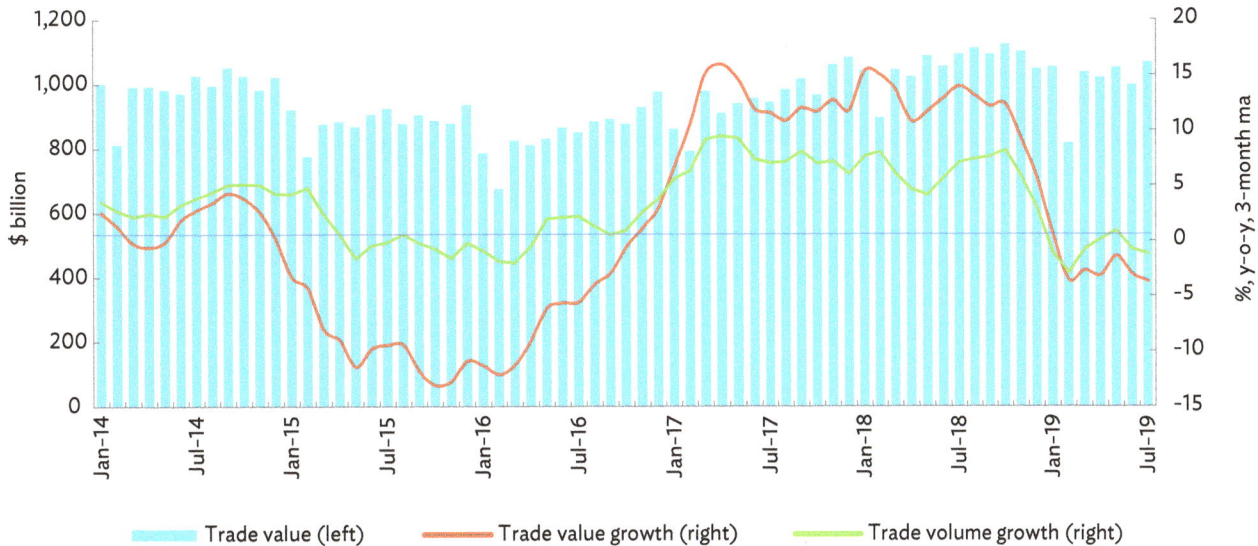

Trade value (left)   Trade value growth (right)   Trade volume growth (right)

ma = moving average, y-o-y = year-on-year.

Notes: Trade volume growth rates were computed using volume indexes. For each period and trade flow type (i.e., imports and exports), available data include indexes for Japan and the People's Republic of China, and an aggregate index for selected Asian economies, which include Hong Kong, China; India; Indonesia; Malaysia; Pakistan; the Philippines; the Republic of Korea; Singapore; Taipei,China; Thailand; and Viet Nam. To come up with an index for Asia, trade values were used as weights. Trade value levels and growth rates were computed by aggregating import and export values of the same Asian economies.

Sources: ADB calculations using data from CEIC; and CPB Netherlands Bureau for Economic Policy Analysis. World Trade Monitor. https://www.cpb.nl/en/worldtrademonitor (both accessed October 2019).

Figure 1.5: Global Business Confidence and Asia's Trade Volume Growth

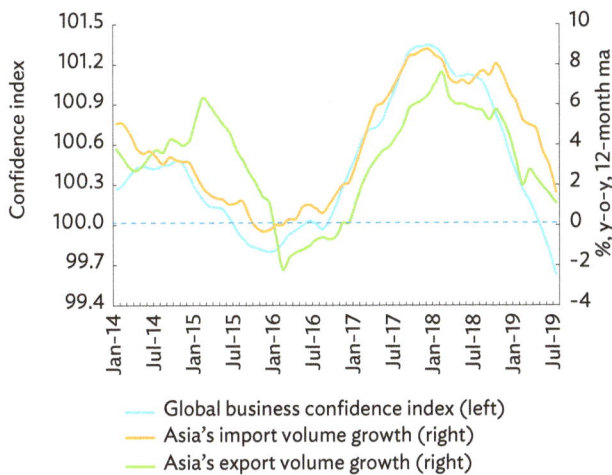

Global business confidence index (left)
Asia's import volume growth (right)
Asia's export volume growth (right)

ma = moving average, y-o-y = year-on-year.

Notes: Export and import volume growth rates were computed using volume indexes. For each period and trade flow type, available data include indexes for Japan and the People's Republic of China, and an aggregate index for selected Asian economies, which include Hong Kong, China; India; Indonesia; Malaysia; Pakistan; the Philippines; the Republic of Korea; Singapore; Taipei,China; Thailand; and Viet Nam. To come up with an index for Asia, export and import values were used as weights. Global business confidence index represents Organisation for Economic Co-operation and Development economies.

Sources: ADB calculations using data from CEIC; CPB Netherlands Bureau for Economic Policy Analysis. World Trade Monitor. https://www.cpb.nl/en/data; and Organisation for Economic Co-Operation and Development. Database. https://data.oecd.org/ (all accessed October 2019).

into global value chains (GVCs) across various industries. Although some Asian economies may benefit from trade diversion in the near term as the US and the PRC may resort to trade with other countries that offer close substitutes of the goods targeted, no country would be immune eventually from the negative impact of trade tensions.

Asia's Intraregional Trade

Despite ongoing trade tensions, Asia sustained its strong intraregional trade linkages.

The region's intraregional trade share by value remained at 57.5% in 2018, above the 56.3% average during 2012–2017 (Figure 1.6). Asia's intraregional trade remained higher than North America (40.5%), while lower than the EU (63.8%). The stronger trade linkages of Asian economies can be a buffer for the potential trade growth slowdown due to the persistent trade conflict. Asia's intraregional trade expanded by 10.4% in 2018—slightly below the 14.0% recorded in 2017, but far higher than the 5-year average of 1.5% from 2012 to 2017. Growth of Asia's extraregional trade accelerated further to 11.7% in 2018.

Box 1.1: Trade Outlook for Asia

World trade growth (by volume) is expected to slow—from 3.0% in 2018 to 1.8% in 2019—as a result of the persistent trade conflict between the United States (US) and the People's Republic of China (PRC).

Since January 2018, export growth by volume eased across the board, reflecting the combined effects of the US–PRC trade tensions, slowing global economic activity, and moderating PRC growth. Export volume growth recovered briefly midyear, possibly due to more anticipated tariff hikes, but moderated again in October 2018. There was some recovery in early 2019 as a temporary truce in the US–PRC trade tensions offered some respite to trade policy uncertainty. The deceleration in export volume growth was more evident in developing Asia.

Developing Asia's trade growth is expected to decelerate further. Trade growth (by volume) will likely decline from the 4.3% estimate in 2018 to 3.5% in 2019 (Box Figure).[a]

Notwithstanding the less favorable prospect for 2019, the PRC continues to lead developing Asia's trade growth, with the four newly industrialized economies (NIEs) (Hong Kong, China; the Republic of Korea; Singapore; and Taipei,China) and the four middle-income Association of Southeast Asian Nations (ASEAN) economies (Indonesia, Malaysia, the Philippines, and Thailand) providing a boost.

Trade Volume Growth (%, year-on-year)

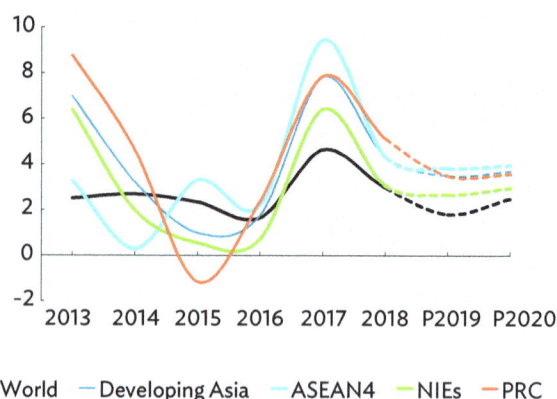

— World — Developing Asia — ASEAN4 — NIEs — PRC

ASEAN = Association of Southeast Asian Nations, NIEs = newly industrialized economies, P = projected, PRC = People's Republic of China.

Notes: ASEAN4 includes Indonesia, Malaysia, the Philippines, and Thailand. NIEs include Hong Kong, China; the Republic of Korea; Singapore; and Taipei,China. Trade volume growth projections are calculated using trade volume growth rates of all economies generated using each economy's elasticity-to-real gross domestic product (GDP) (for imports) and elasticity-to-real GDP of top trading partners (for exports).

Sources: ADB calculations using data from International Monetary Fund (IMF). Direction of Trade Database. https://www.imf.org/en/Data (accessed September 2019); IMF. World Economic Outlook April 2019 database. https://www.imf.org/external/pubs/ft/weo/2017/01/weodata/index.aspx (accessed October 2019).

[a] Developing Asia refers to the 46 developing member economies of ADB. Asia refers to developing Asia plus Australia, Japan, and New Zealand.

Source: ADB staff.

Figure 1.6: Intraregional Trade Share—Asia, EU, and North America (%)

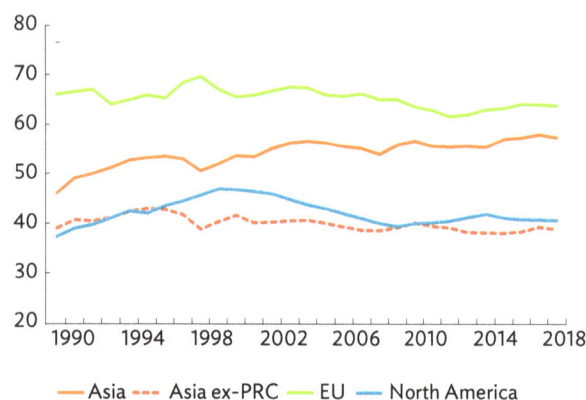

— Asia --- Asia ex-PRC — EU — North America

EU = European Union, PRC = People's Republic of China.

Notes: Values expressed as percentage of the region's total merchandise trade (sum of exports and imports). EU refers to the aggregate of 28 members. North America covers Canada, Mexico, and the United States.

Source: ADB calculations using data from International Monetary Fund. Direction of Trade Statistics. https://www.imf.org/en/Data (accessed September 2019).

Intraregional trade linkages continued to deepen across subregions.

Intraregional trade shares increased across all subregions in 2018 from 2010. The Pacific and Oceania continues to hold the highest intraregional trade share (71.7%) in 2018, followed by Southeast Asia (69.3%) and East Asia (55.5%) (Figure 1.7). Central Asia's intraregional trade share increased the most (33.3% in 2018 from 28.1% in 2010), followed by South Asia (40% from 35.4%). Moreover, East Asia still holds the highest intra-subregional trade share (35.5%) in 2018. Trade intensities of subregions estimated using gravity models show the same results (Box 1.2).

Figure 1.7: Intraregional Trade Shares by Asian Subregions (%)

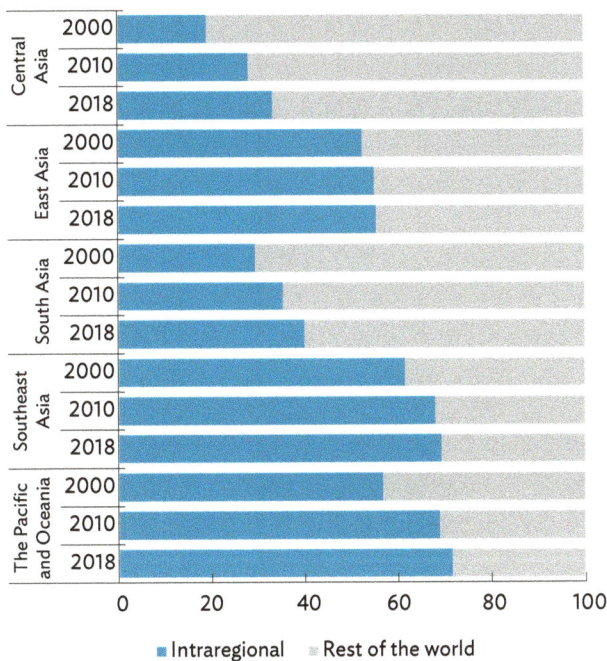

■ Intraregional   ▨ Rest of the world

Source: ADB calculations using data from International Monetary Fund. Direction of Trade Statistics. https://www.imf.org/en/Data (accessed September 2019).

Progress of Global and Regional Value Chains

Trade ties within Asia have considerably increased due to growing regional value chain linkages.

A new framework for understanding GVC and regional value chain (RVC) participation is introduced here to better track Asia's progress in its global and regional trade linkages. The world's gross exports can be divided into two: (i) exports that cross border once as final goods (represented by the blue area in Figure 1.8a); and (ii) exports that go through two or more economies for further production or "GVC exports" (yellow area in Figure 1.8a). World GVC is the share of the world's total GVC exports to its gross exports. Asia-to-world GVC is the share of Asia's total GVC exports to its gross exports. Asia-to-Asia gross RVC is the share of Asia's intraregional GVC exports to its intraregional gross exports, excluding all non-Asian third economies.[2] Asia-to-Asia net RVC is similar to gross RVC, except that its denominator, total intraregional exports, includes non-Asian third economies.

Box 1.2: Gravity Model Estimation of Bilateral Exports

The progress in Asia's regional trade integration can also be tracked using gravity model estimation of bilateral exports. An advantage of using this method is that factors such as multilateral trade resistances (cost of trading), and unobserved trade frictions are controlled. Intraregional trade intensity in Asia can be measured by the estimated coefficient of a dummy variable for "both in Asia" (if both pair of countries belong to the region) in the gravity models. The estimation is done using 5-year rolling panel regression on annual data covering 2014–2018 and 2013–2017.

Results show that intensity in intraregional trade in Asia continued to be higher on capital goods, followed by consumption goods (although the coefficients are not significant) (Box Table 1, columns 2 and 4). On the other hand, Asia's trade of intermediate goods has higher intensity outside the region (Box Table 1, column 3). This implies that Asia is an important supplier of intermediate goods to the countries outside the region.

Among subregions, East Asia's intra-subregional trade intensity remained the highest, albeit slightly declining (Box Table 2). Southeast Asia follows with a similar declining trend, while intra-subregional trade intensity increased in Central Asia. South Asia continues to trade significantly more with other subregions within Asia, although its inter-subregional bias weakened slightly.

continued on next page

---

2   Third economies are those that indirectly participate in a GVC transaction. For example, Singapore exports intermediate goods used by the PRC to produce and export final goods to Malaysia. From Singapore's point of view, the PRC is the direct partner, while Malaysia is the third economy.

Box 1.2: Gravity Model Estimation of Bilateral Exports (continued)

1: Gravity Model Estimation Results, 2014–2018
Dependent Variable: Log(Bilateral Exports)

Variables	All Goods	Capital Goods	Consumption Goods	Intermediate Goods
	(1)	**(2)**	**(3)**	**(4)**
Log(distance)	-1.65***	-1.62***	-1.74***	-1.71***
	(0.02)	(0.02)	(0.02)	(0.02)
Colonial relationship dummy	0.82***	0.85***	0.95***	0.85***
	(0.04)	(0.09)	(0.10)	(0.10)
Common language dummy	1.00***	0.91***	1.05***	0.90***
	(0.10)	(0.04)	(0.04)	(0.04)
Contiguity dummy	1.03***	1.23***	1.22***	1.11***
	(0.10)	(0.10)	(0.11)	(0.11)
Regional dummies (base: Asia to ROW)				
Both in Asia dummy	0.04 [0.47]	0.14 [0.22]	0.04 [0.44]	-0.42 [-0.11]
	(0.33)	(0.32)	(0.42)	(0.35)
Importer in Asia dummy	0.70	-1.32**	0.01	0.64
	(0.57)	(0.65)	(0.42)	(0.66)
Both in ROW dummy	0.31	-1.80***	-0.51	0.71
	(0.40)	(0.52)	(0.44)	(0.49)
Rho (sample selection term)	0.13***	0.41***	0.21***	0.21***
Sample size	260,970	212,447	239,491	243,020
Censored observations	151,052	106,842	129,573	133,102
Uncensored observations	109,917	105,605	109,918	109,918

*** = significant at 1%, ** = significant at 5%, * = significant at 10%, ROW = rest of the world. Estimates for 2013–2017 are in brackets. Robust standard errors in parentheses.

Notes: Time-varying economy dummies are included but not shown for brevity. Heckman sample selection estimation was used to account for missing bilateral economy-pair data and zero bilateral trade. Data cover 229 economies, of which 46 are from Asia. Trade data are based on Broad Economic Categories.

Sources: ADB calculations using data from Centre d'Études Prospectives et d'Informations Internationales (the French Research Center in International Economics). GeoDist Database. http://www.cepii.fr/CEPII/en/cepii/cepii.asp; and United Nations. Commodity Trade Database. https://comtrade.un.org (both accessed August 2019).

2: Gravity Model Estimation Results, 2014–2018: Intra- and Inter-Subregional Trade (All Goods)

Variables	Central Asia	East Asia	South Asia	Southeast Asia	The Pacific and Oceania
Intra-subregional trade dummy	4.45***	6.03***	0.06	4.82***	0.92
	[4.10***]	[6.59***]	[0.52]	[5.21***]	[1.42*]
Inter-subregional trade dummy	-0.47	-0.09	3.71***	0.22***	-0.15
	[-0.07]	[0.32]	[4.60***]	[-0.15]	[-0.41]

*** = significant at 1%, ** = significant at 5%, * = significant at 10%. Estimates for 2013–2017 are in brackets.

Notes: Base category (benchmark) is the subregion's trade with economies outside Asia. The usual gravity model variables and time-varying economy dummies are included but not shown for brevity. Heckman sample selection estimation was used to account for missing bilateral economy-pair data and zero bilateral trade. Data cover 229 economies, of which 46 are from Asia. Trade data are based on Broad Economic Categories.

Sources: ADB calculations using data from Centre d'Études Prospectives et d'Informations Internationales (the French Research Center in International Economics). GeoDist Database. http://www.cepii.fr/CEPII/en/cepii/cepii.asp; and United Nations. Commodity Trade Database. https://comtrade.un.org (both accessed August 2019).

Source: ADB staff.

Using the framework shows that at the global level, participation to cross-border production networks have increased since 2000 (Figure 1.8b). Asia's participation in GVCs continued to be strong. Measured by the share of value-added content in gross exports used for further processing through cross-border production networks, the region's GVC participation rate was 68.1% in 2018 (Figure 1.8b).

Asian economies' participation in RVCs—which only involves production networks within the region—increased from 46.6% in 2000 to 49.4% in 2010 and hovered around 48.3%–49.5% since (Figure 1.8b). GVC participation appears higher than RVC participation. Nonetheless, the region's intensity of participation in RVC with respect to GVC participation (the ratio of the two rates) has been increasing in general over the past decades (Figure 1.9). This implies that a relatively larger portion of production is being finalized within the loop of the regional production networks.

Figure 1.9: RVC–GVC Intensity—Asia, EU, and North America

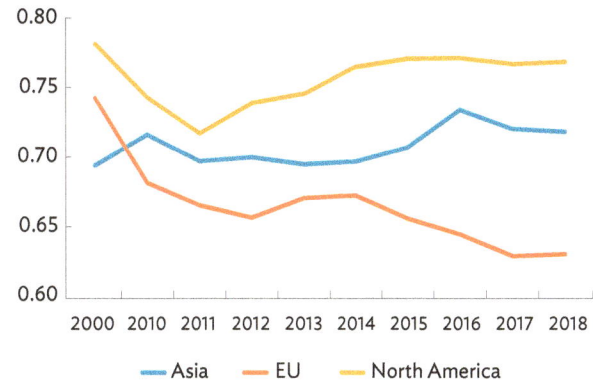

EU = European Union, GVC = global value chain, RVC = regional value chain.

Note: RVC–GVC intensity is the ratio of RVC participation and GVC participation rates.

Sources: ADB calculations using data from ADB. Multi-Regional Input-Output Tables; and methodology by Wang, Wei, and Zhu (2014).

Figure 1.8: Analytical Framework of GVC and RVC Participation

a: Analytical Framework

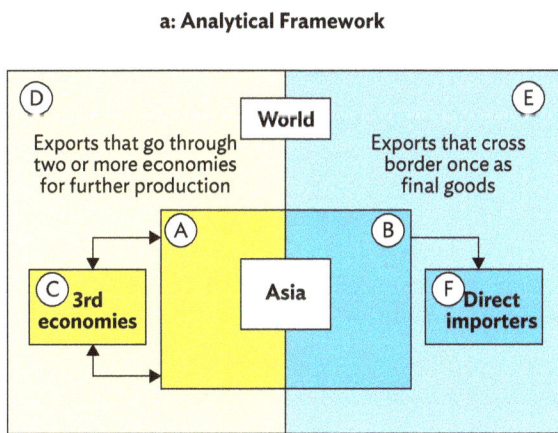

Participation Rates:

(1)   World GVC $= \dfrac{A + C + D}{A + B + C + D + E + F}$

(2)   Asia-to-World GVC $= \dfrac{A + C}{A + B + C + F}$

(3)   Asia-to-Asia Gross RVC $= \dfrac{A}{A + B}$

(4)   Asia-to-Asia Net RVC $= \dfrac{A}{A + B + C}$

b: GVC and RVC Participation Rates (%)

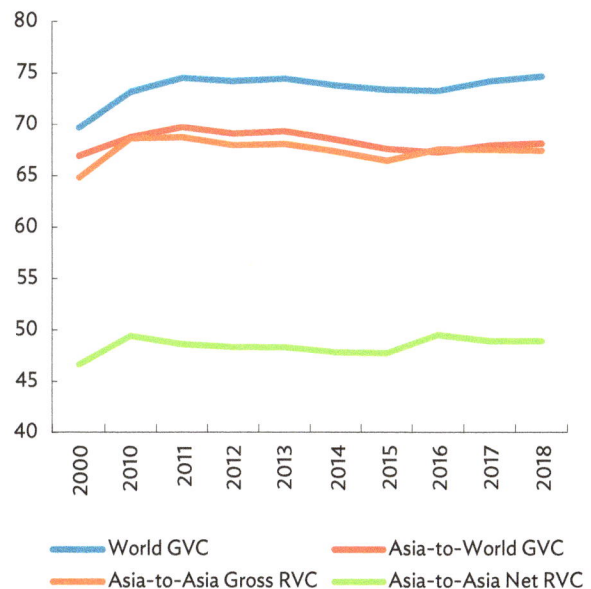

GVC = global value chain, RVC = regional value chain.

Notes: The GVC participation rate is the share of gross exports that involves production in at least two countries using cross-border production networks. The RVC participation rate, on the other hand, is the same as that of GVC, except that it only involves countries of the same region.

Sources: ADB calculations using data from ADB. Multi-Regional Input–Output Tables; and methodology by Wang, Wei, and Zhu (2014).

Asia's RVC-to-GVC participation was higher than the EU beginning in 2010, but remained lower than North America (Figure 1.9). The EU's RVC–GVC intensity is generally declining as the region's trade networks expand outside the region. On the other hand, its GVC participation rate became stronger, gradually increasing from 72.1% in 2010 to 74.8% in 2018. In North America, the RVC linkage between the US and Canada continued to strengthen. The RVC participation in North America has been increasing gradually: from 52.5% in 2010 to 55.4% in 2018, while its GVC participation also increased from 70.6% to 72.1% during the same period.

Inter-subregional value chain linkages are stronger than intra-subregional linkages.

Meanwhile, RVCs of Asia subregions showed signs of deepening (Figure 1.10a). The Pacific and Oceania has consistently shown strong integration with the region, both in terms of trade value shares and RVC–GVC partipation intensity, which generally increased from 2011

to 2017. Central Asia was second, recording higher intesity scores than East Asia and Southeast Asia from 2010 to 2016. However, in 2017 to 2018, East Asia overtook Central Asia, given a rapid increase in the intensity ratio. The Pacific and Oceania and Central Asia are deeply involved in the regional production network (especially with East Asia) through exports of raw materials, metals, and minerals than outside of the region.

The relative importance of trade linkages within subregions vary considerably across subregions. The intensity ratio of subregional value chain participation rate and GVC participation rate varies from 0.24 to 0.62 (Figure 1.10b). East Asia has the highest intensity scores, reflecting the strong production networks in manufacturing within the subregion. On the other hand, Southeast Asia recorded low levels of intensity, reflecting its deep value chain linkage with East Asia in manufacturing product assembly, such as electrical machineries and transport equipment. Although South Asia has shown lower scores in intraregional value chain and GVC intensity, its trade linkages within the subregion

Figure 1.10: RVC–GVC Intensity—Asian Subregions

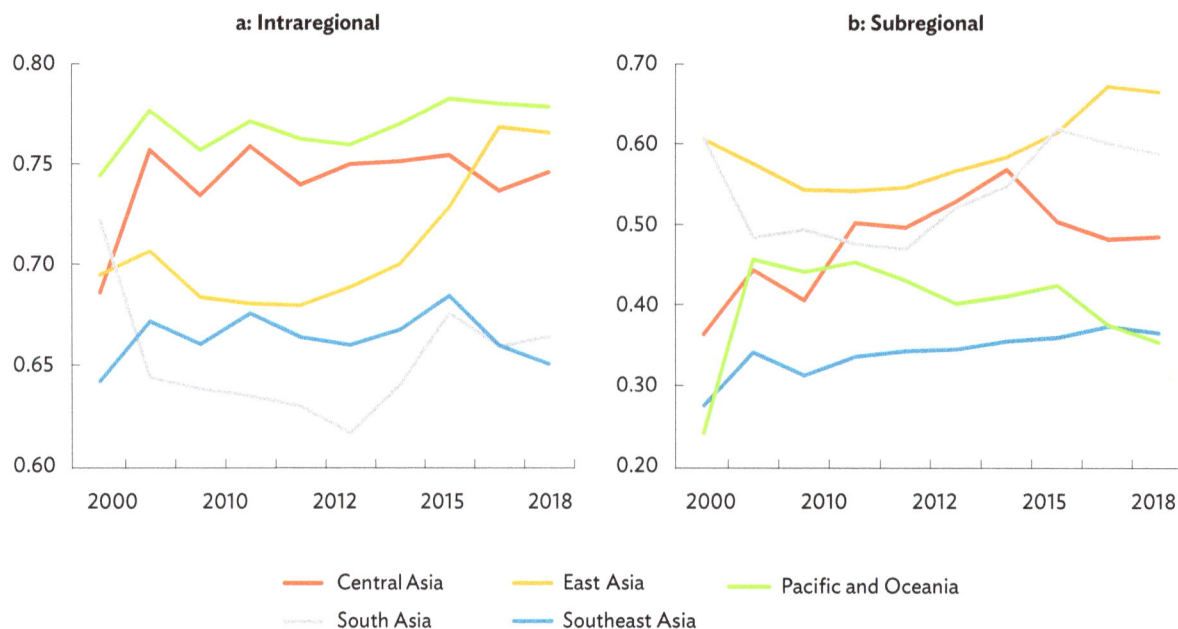

GVC = global value chain, RVC = regional value chain.

Notes: RVC–GVC intensity is the ratio of RVC participation and GVC participation rates. Central Asia only includes Kazakhstan and the Kyrgyz Republic. Southeast Asia excludes Myanmar. South Asia excludes Afghanistan. The Pacific and Oceania only includes Australia and Fiji.

Sources: ADB calculations using data from ADB. Multi-Regional Input-Output Tables; and methodology by Wang, Wei, and Zhu (2014).

is stronger compared with other subregions. Central Asia saw increasing instensity scores from 2000 to 2014, reflecting their faster increase in subregional value chain linkages than GVC linkages.

Asia still has much room to enhance RVC linkages in top tier sectors.

Across sectors in Asia, the primary sector—which includes agriculture along with mining and quarrying—had the highest RVC participation rate in 2018 (72.1%). It also had the highest GVC participation rate (92.4%) (Figure 1.11). This gives the primary sector one of the highest intensity scores. Although the low technology sector held the highest RVC-GVC intensity ratio across sectors, it merely reflects a faster increase in the RVC participation rate than GVC participation rate. In absolute terms, it had one of the lowest RVC (41.2% in 2018) and GVC (51.1%) participation rates.

In contrast, the region's trade linkage was slow to rise in medium and high technology, and business services. In these sectors, GVC participation rates were around 69% to 70% in 2017, while RVC participation rates were only from 41% to 49%. This implies that some Asian economies likely have more room to move up in the RVC by increasing their value chain linkages within the region. Policies that can strengthen capacities and relax trade and investment restrictions would help to further deepen an economy's participation in GVCs and RVCs.

Across Asian economies, the degree of RVC and GVC participation varies considerably.

Across Asian economies, Bangladesh has the highest intensity ratio, exceeding 1 which indicates stronger trade linkages with RVCs than GVCs (Figure 1.12). It was followed by Nepal with an intensity score of 0.88 and Pakistan at 0.87. These countries highly specialize in the textiles and textile products sector, and leather and footwear sector. Their production networks are mostly linked subregionally with India and intraregionally with the PRC. Despite higher intensities, these countries have relatively lower RVC and GVC participation rates, indicating a large portion of their exports of final goods are purely domestically produced. For instance, Bangladesh's RVC participation rate was only 44% in 2018, while its GVC participation was 40.6%.

Figure 1.11: RVC–GVC Intensity by Major Sector—Asia

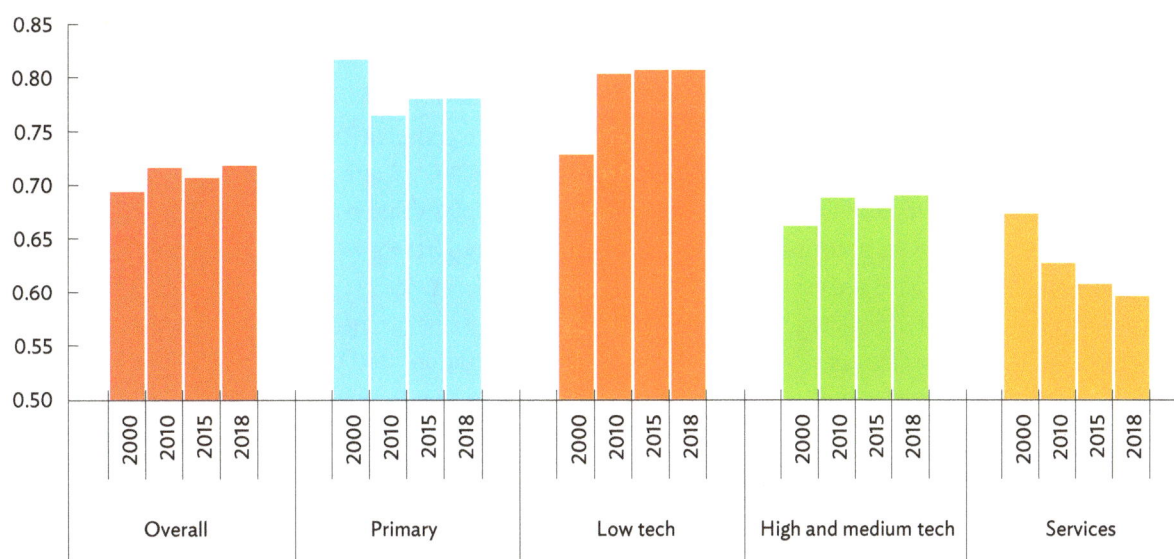

GVC = global value chain, RVC = regional value chain.

Notes: RVC–GVC intensity is the ratio of RVC participation and GVC participation rates. Sectoral classification is based on ADB (2015).

Sources: ADB calculations using data from ADB. Multi-Regional Input-Output Tables; and methodology by Wang, Wei, and Zhu (2014).

Figure 1.12: Overall RVC and GVC Participation—Selected Asian Economies

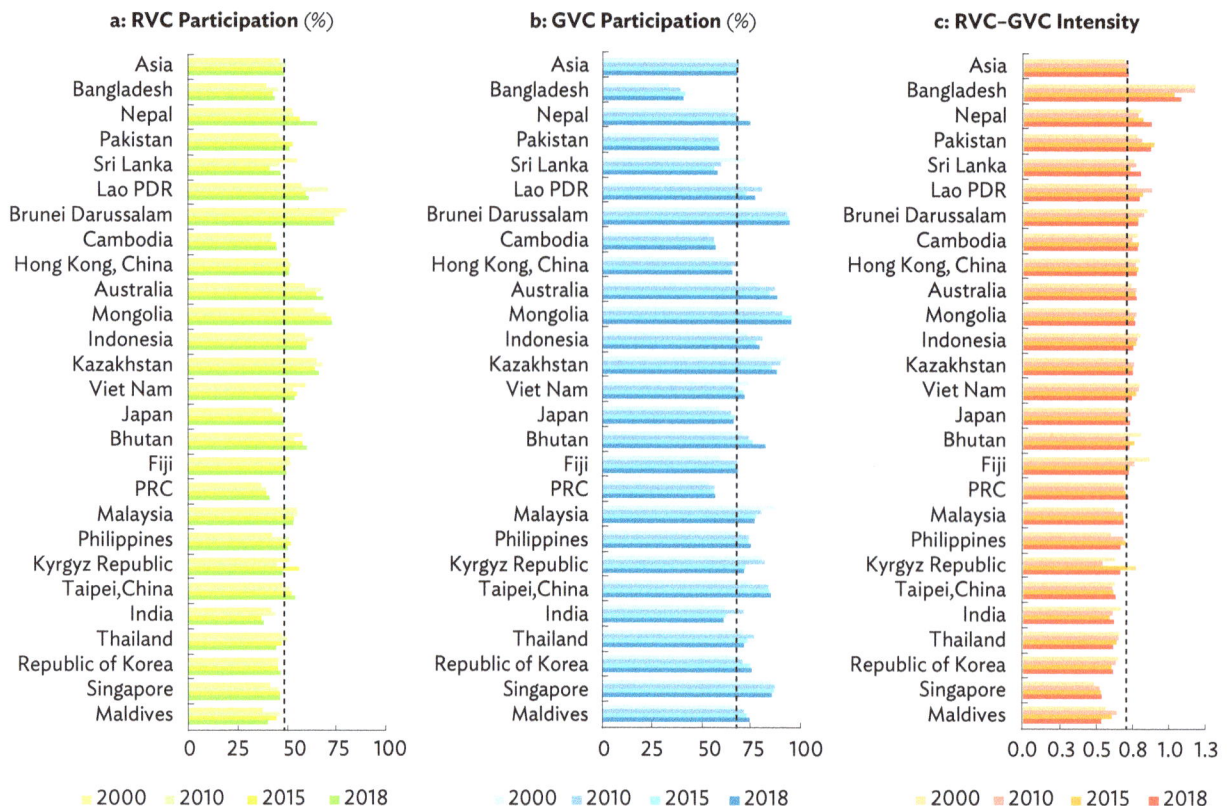

GVC = global value chain, Lao PDR = Lao People's Democratic Republic, PRC = People's Republic of China, RVC = regional value chain.

Notes: RVC–GVC intensity is the ratio of RVC participation and GVC participation rates. The overall GVC participation rate is the share of gross exports that involves production in at least two economies using cross-border production networks. The overall RVC participation rate is the same as that of GVC, except that it only involves economies of the same region.

Sources: ADB calculations using data from ADB. Multi-Regional Input-Output Tables; and methodology by Wang, Wei, and Zhu (2014).

Commodity-exporting economies—such as Indonesia, the Lao People's Democratic Republic (Lao PDR), Brunei Darussalam, Kazakhstan, Mongolia, and Australia— tend to have both high GVC and RVC participation rates. Most of the commodity-exports are used as raw materials for the production of intermediate and final goods, which translates into these countries' high value chain participation at upstream. For example, Brunei Darussalam exports most of its fuel and natural gas to Malaysia and Singapore, which are used by these countries in export production. This also applies to Mongolia, which exports minerals to the PRC; the Lao PDR, which exports electricity to Thailand; and Kazakhstan, which exports fuel and metals to the PRC.

Looking at the complex RVC and GVC participation rates, and RVC–GVC intensity ratios show a different picture. Complex value chain linkages include part of the gross exports for which the production entails border-crossing twice or more. Economies like Hong Kong, China; Taipei,China; Japan; the Republic of Korea; Malaysia; Singapore; and Viet Nam have relatively high RVC–GVC intensity scores (Figure 1.13). These economies are highly embedded into the deeper manufacturing production networks in electrical and optical equipment, and transport and equipment, which involve complex GVCs and RVCs.

Figure 1.13: Complex RVC and GVC Participation—Selected Asian Economies

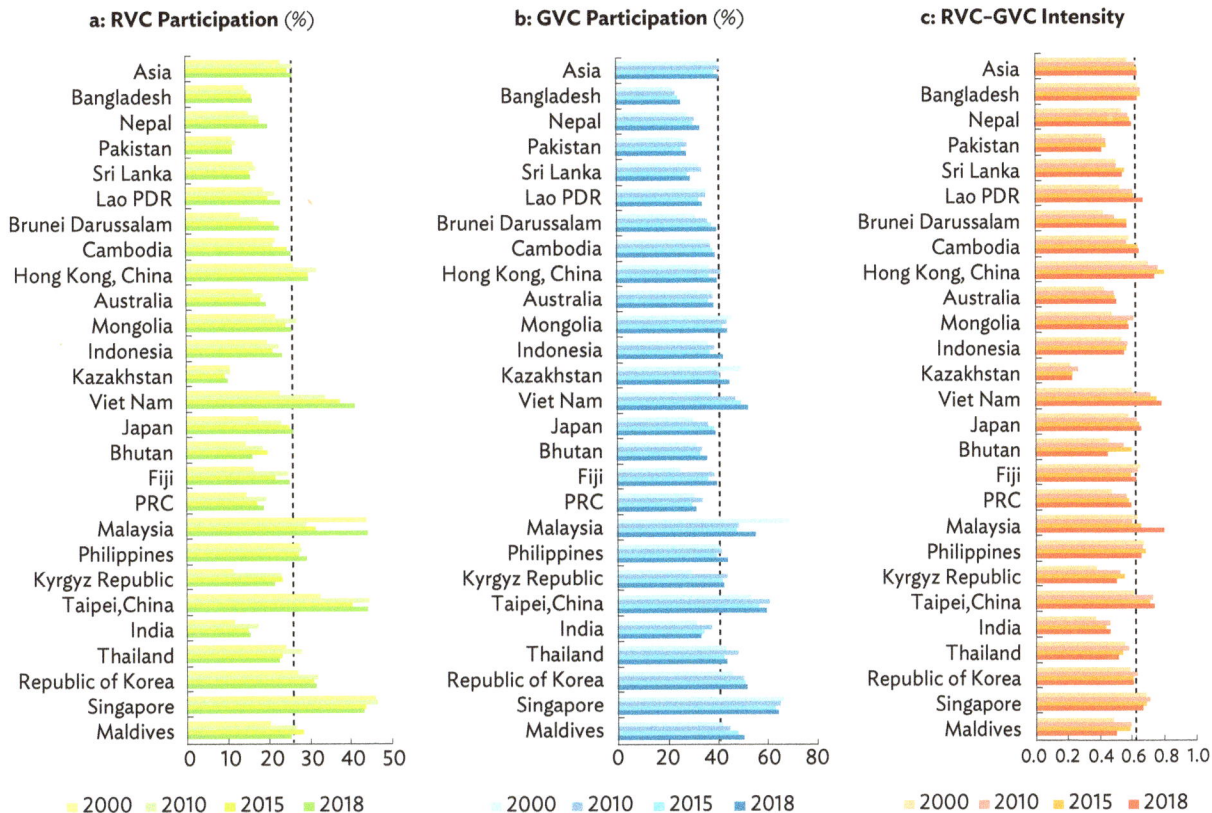

GVC = global value chain, Lao PDR = Lao People's Democratic Republic, PRC = People's Republic of China, RVC = regional value chain.

Notes: RVC–GVC intensity is the ratio of RVC participation and GVC participation rates. The complex GVC participation rate is the share of gross exports that involves production in at least two economies using cross-border production networks. The complex RVC participation rate, on the other hand, is the same as that of GVC, except that it only involves economies of the same region. Both complex GVC and RVC participation includes only part of the gross exports for which the production entails border crossing twice or more. The straight vertical lines indicate the value for Asia in 2018.

Sources: ADB calculations using data from ADB. Multi-Regional Input-Output Tables; and methodology by Wang, Wei, and Zhu (2014).

Trade Conflict and Its Potential Impact

Protracted trade tensions between the US and the PRC will likely affect the trade landscape globally as well as regionally.

The recovery from the global trade slowdown in 2017 is losing momentum in tandem with protracted US–PRC trade tensions. This poses a constant risk to Asia's trade performance. Aside from being the two largest economies in the world, the US and the PRC are also top traders—accounting for a quarter of global trade. They are also major, if not the main, trading partners for most Asian economies—in 2018, the US had a 9.8% share of Asia's total trade (excluding the PRC), while the PRC accounted for 24%.

Beginning January 2018, the US implemented higher tariffs on all imports (regardless of country source, but with some exceptions) on solar panel imports, washing machines, steel, and aluminum (Office of the US Trade Representative 2018). The PRC retaliated by imposing higher tariffs on 128 products (Ministry of Commerce of the PRC 2018). The two countries then released initial tariff plans against each other with lists of products covered. As one adjusts their lists, the other party answers with a revised list of their own. The tariff plan implementation in 2018 occurred in three rounds—July 2018, August 2018, and September 2018—with the US initiating and the PRC retaliating. By September 2018, it is estimated that $260 billion worth of imports from the PRC and $113 billion worth of imports from the US were affected by the tariff hikes (Figure 1.14).

The number of tariff hikes and the value of affected imports continue to grow as the US and the PRC recently revived plans to hike rates. Both countries have implemented the first batch of the fourth round of tariff hikes in in September 2019. The PRC plans to implement its second batch in December 2019, while the US plans to raise tariffs on $250 billion worth of imported goods from the PRC to 30% on 15 October 2019 and then implement its second batch in December 2019. However, on 11 October 2019, the US announced its delay of the 15 October 2019 tariff hikes, amid the crafting of the "Phase 1" trade deal between the US and the PRC (Ching 2019). As of September 2019, the US had imposed higher tariffs on 9,956 PRC products at Harmonized System (HS) 8-digit code, while the PRC raised tariffs on 6,667 US products (Figure 1.14). The basic metal, minerals, and chemicals sector has the most number

of products with tariff hikes (Figure 1.15). By the end of 2019, affected imports from the PRC would reach about $536.1 billion, while around $120.5 billion worth of imports from the US will be affected.

By industry, the import growth of many subsectors, particularly in the PRC, softened in the second half of 2018.

After the July 2018 first round, bilateral trade growth in both countries began moderating. The PRC import sectors targeted by tariff hikes experienced slowing import growth. Figure 1.16 plots the ratios of growth rates (year-on-year) of the subsector at HS 4-digit code to the growth rate of the total bilateral imports between

Figure 1.14: Chronology of Tariffs Filed by the PRC and the US

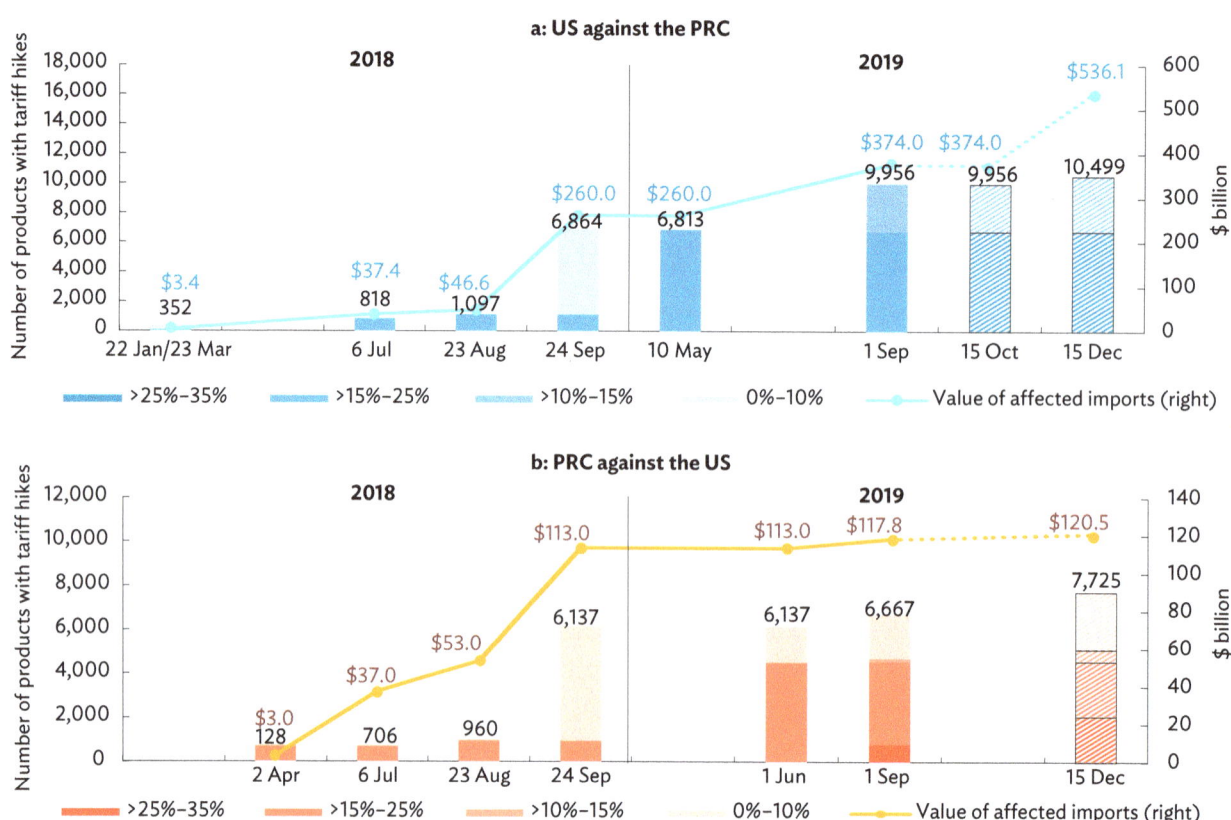

a: US against the PRC

b: PRC against the US

PRC = People's Republic of China, US = United States.

Notes: The number of products is based on the number of Harmonized System 8-digit codes with tariff lines. The broken lines and bars with striped colors refer to tariffs that are announced but not yet implemented. The plans of the US to raise tariffs on 15 October 2019 were not implemented after the US announced its delay on 11 October 2019, while the "Phase 1" trade deal between the US and the PRC is under negotiation.

Sources: ADB calculations using data from ADB (2019); Federal Register. The Daily Journal of the US Government. https://www.federalregister.gov; Ministry of Finance of the PRC. Policy Release. http://gss.mof.gov.cn; Office of the US Trade Representative. PRC Section 301—Tariff Actions and Exclusion Process. https://ustr.gov/issue-areas/enforcement/section-301-investigations/tariff-actions; and World Trade Organization. Tariff Download Facility. http://tariffdata.wto.org (all accessed September 2019).

Figure 1.15: Number of Products with Tariffs Filed by the PRC and the US by Major Category

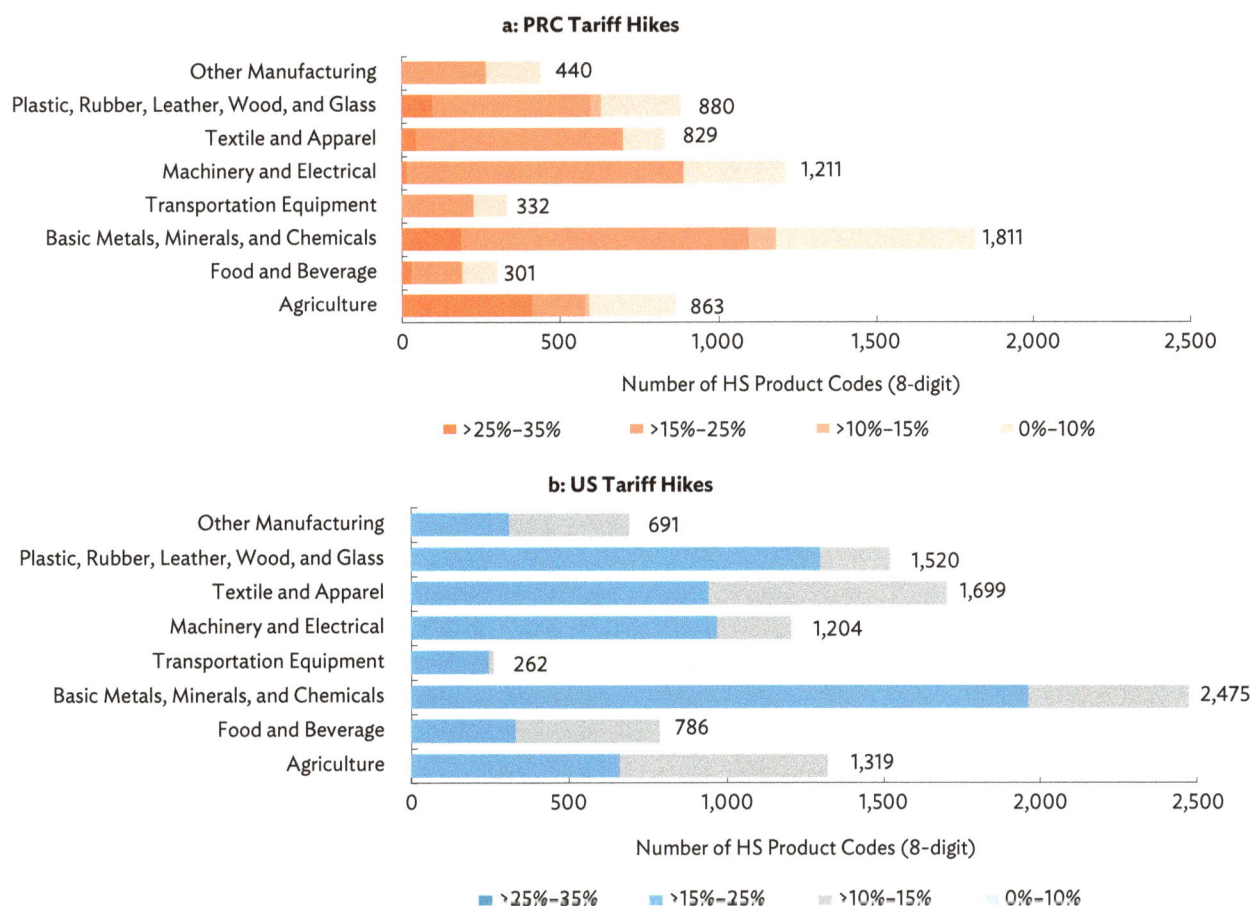

a: PRC Tariff Hikes

Other Manufacturing	440
Plastic, Rubber, Leather, Wood, and Glass	880
Textile and Apparel	829
Machinery and Electrical	1,211
Transportation Equipment	332
Basic Metals, Minerals, and Chemicals	1,811
Food and Beverage	301
Agriculture	863

Number of HS Product Codes (8-digit)

■ >25%–35%   ■ >15%–25%   ■ >10%–15%   0%–10%

b: US Tariff Hikes

Other Manufacturing	691
Plastic, Rubber, Leather, Wood, and Glass	1,520
Textile and Apparel	1,699
Machinery and Electrical	1,204
Transportation Equipment	262
Basic Metals, Minerals, and Chemicals	2,475
Food and Beverage	786
Agriculture	1,319

Number of HS Product Codes (8-digit)

■ >25%–35%   ■ >15%–25%   ■ >10%–15%   0%–10%

HS = Harmonized System, PRC = People's Republic of China, US = United States.

Note: The number of products is based on the number of HS 8-digit codes with tariff lines, which have been implemented as of September 2019.

Sources: ADB calculations using data from Federal Register. The Daily Journal of the US Government. https://www.federalregister.gov; Ministry of Finance of the PRC. Policy Release. http://gss.mof.gov.cn; Office of the US Trade Representative. PRC Section 301—Tariff Actions and Exclusion Process. https://ustr.gov/issue-areas/enforcement/section-301-investigations/tariff-actions; and World Trade Organization. Tariff Download Facility. http://tariffdata.wto.org (all accessed September 2019).

the US and the PRC, comparing H2 2018 with H2 2017. A great number of points fall below the 45-degree line, indicating slower expansion or a decrease in imports. Sectors subject to tariffs are the most affected. For instance, the PRC tariff hikes on US products have affected 1,046 out of 1,087 US sectors at the HS 4-digit level codes, leaving only 41 sectors unaffected. Among the affected sectors, 615 experienced lower export growth rates to the PRC in H2 2018. Concurrently, out of 1,104 PRC sectors at the HS 4-digit level codes, the US tariff hikes have affected 864 sectors in which 368 have incurred decreasing export growth rates to the US in H2 2018.

An analysis of bilateral imports and exports of the US and the PRC on selected sectors provides a snapshot of how trade directions are adjusting.

One of the direct effects is trade diversion, which in general refers to shifting trade from one trade partner to another. It is usually a response to increasing trade costs. In the case of the US and the PRC, rising tariffs increases the cost of importing targeted goods, inducing the two countries to find trade partners that produce or import close substitute goods. This trade diversion effect could benefit some Asian economies in the short run through an increase in exports.

Figure 1.16: Bilateral Import Growth Rate Ratio by Sector and Semester—US and PRC

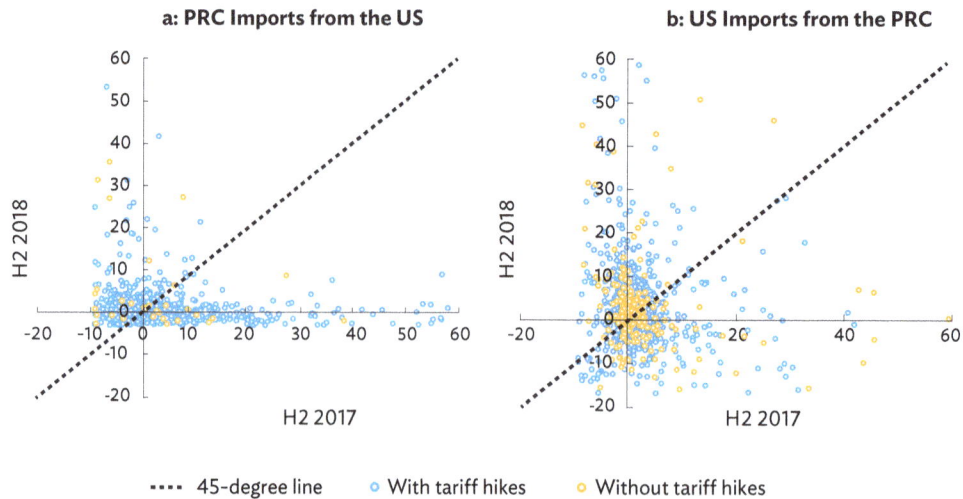

a: PRC Imports from the US

b: US Imports from the PRC

- - - - 45-degree line   ○ With tariff hikes   ○ Without tariff hikes

H2 = second half, PRC = People's Republic of China, US = United States.

Note: Each point in the figure represents the ratio of the growth rate of the subsector at Harmonized System 4-digit code to the growth rate of total bilateral imports between the US and the PRC, comparing the second half of 2018 to the same period of 2017.

Sources: ADB calculations using data from Ministry of Finance of the PRC. Policy Release. http://gss.mof.gov.cn/; Office of the US Trade Representative. PRC Section 301—Tariff Actions and Exclusion Process. https://ustr.gov/issue-areas/enforcement/section-301-investigations/tariff-actions; and United Nations. Commodity Trade Database. https://comtrade.un.org (all accessed July 2019).

For instance, as the US imposed higher tariffs on aluminum (beginning the first round), the country's imports from the PRC declined by 19.8% in H2 2018—equivalent to $347.9 million. Moreover, with the PRC as the second top supplier of aluminum to the US (next to Canada), its share of US aluminum imports decreased from 13.6% in H2 2017 to 10.9% in H2 2018 (Figure 1.17a). Despite the large decline, the sector still saw an expansion of imports, albeit very minimal at 0.4% in H2 2018 compared with the twofold increase in H2 2017. The US has imported aluminum products from other countries. Australia, India, Indonesia, Japan, the Republic of Korea, and Viet Nam increased their aluminum product exports to the US (Figure 1.17a). In the meantime, the PRC increased its exports of aluminum to other European and Latin American countries (Figure 1.17b).

US imports of transmission apparatus were also affected by the tariff hike increase in August 2018. The products under this sector are the top 86th most traded globally (according to Observatory of Economic Complexity) and are produced through a wide cross-border production network. They are usually components necessary for

radios, cellphones, wireless computers, and Bluetooth-enabled devices. Around the world, the PRC is the top exporter in this sector, while the US is one of its key trading partners. The US implementation of the second round tariff list caused a large decline on US transmission apparatus imports from the PRC of about $116.4 million in H2 2018 (or 24.3%). However, some US imports moved to Mexico, some to EU countries (Germany, France, and Belgium), and some to Asian countries (Thailand, the Philippines, Viet Nam, and Malaysia) (Figure 1.18a). Nonetheless, this trade shift generated only around $68 million and was unable to offset the decline from the PRC. The PRC, on the other hand, diverted its exports to other countries such as Mexico, Brazil, the Russian Federation, some EU countries, Japan, the Philippines, and Myanmar (Figure 1.18b).

Beginning July 2018, the PRC discouraged buying soybeans from the US, as a retaliation to US tariff hikes. The PRC tapped other countries to sustain its soybean imports. Brazil, for example, saw a large increase in share of PRC soybean imports (from 49% in H2 2017 to 74.8% in H2 2018), and Canada's share also increased (from 5.8% to 13.5%) (Figure 1.19a).

Figure 1.17: Impact of US Tariff Hikes on PRC Aluminum

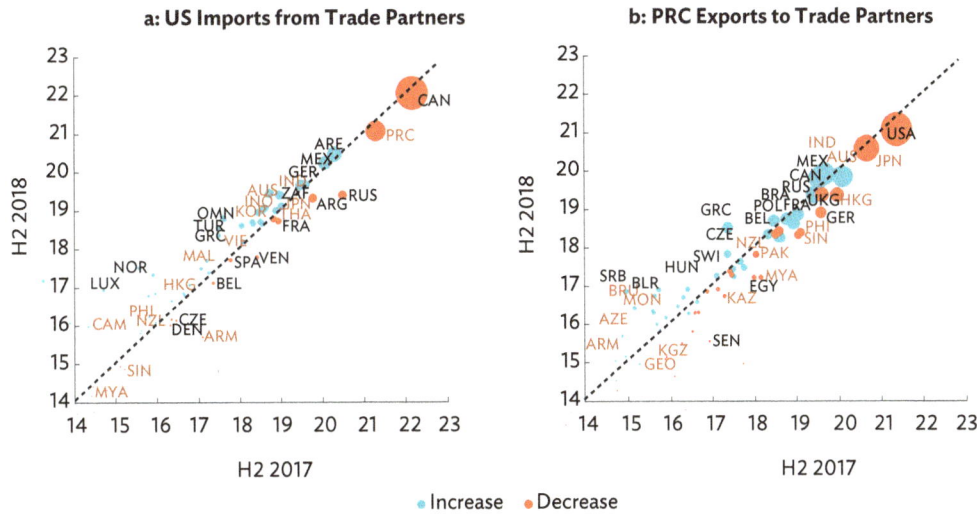

a: US Imports from Trade Partners

b: PRC Exports to Trade Partners

• Increase   • Decrease

H2 = second semester; ARE = United Arab Emirates; ARG = Argentina; ARM = Armenia; AUS = Australia; AZE = Azerbaijan; BEL = Belgium; BLR = Belarus; BRA = Brazil; BRU = Brunei Darussalam; CAM = Cambodia; CAN = Canada; CZE = Czech Republic; DEN = Denmark; EGY = Egypt; FRA = France; GEO = Georgia; GER = Germany; GRC = Greece; HKG = Hong Kong, China; HUN = Hungary; IND = India; INO = Indonesia; JPN = Japan; KAZ = Kazakhstan; KGZ = Kyrgyz Republic; KOR = Republic of Korea; LUX = Luxembourg; MAL = Malaysia; MEX = Mexico; MON = Mongolia; MYA = Myanmar; NOR = Norway; NZL = New Zealand; OMN = Oman; PAK = Pakistan; PHI = Philippines; POL = Poland; PRC = People's Republic of China; RUS = Russian Federation; SEN = Senegal; SIN = Singapore; SPA = Spain; SRB = Serbia; SWI = Switzerland; THA = Thailand; TUR = Turkey; UKG = United Kingdom; US or USA = United States; VEN = Venezuela; VIE = Viet Nam; ZAF = South Africa.

Notes: Asian economy codes are marked in orange. The figures compare the natural log of the import values from second half of 2017 to the same period in 2018. Each point represents a trade partner. The size of the points indicates the share to PRC imports or US exports. The line in each figure is the 45-degree line, which separates the economies experiencing a decline or increase in trade. Red points below the line indicate decline in trade in 2018, while blue points indicate increase in trade.

Source: ADB calculations using data from United Nations. Commodity Trade Database. https://comtrade.un.org (accessed July 2019).

Figure 1.18: Impact of US Tariff Hikes on PRC Transmission Apparatus

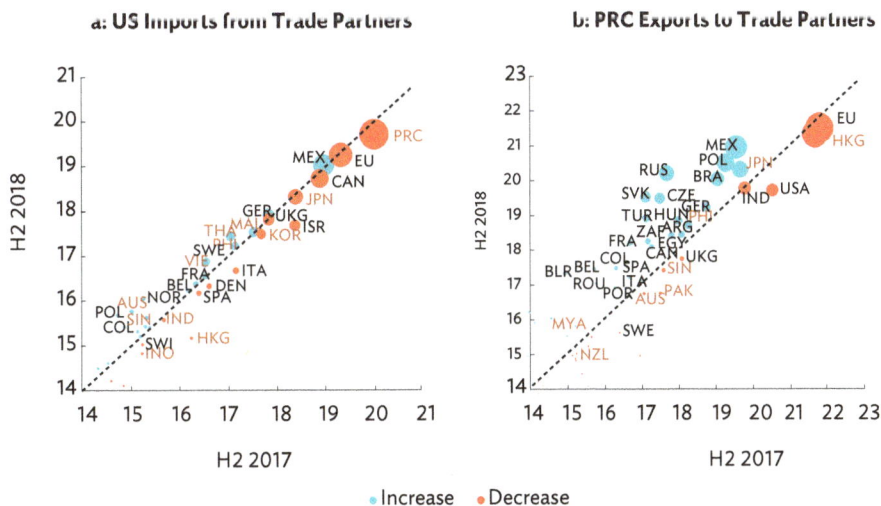

a: US Imports from Trade Partners

b: PRC Exports to Trade Partners

• Increase   • Decrease

H2 = second semester; ARG = Argentina; AUS = Australia; BEL = Belgium; BLR = Belarus; BRA = Brazil; CAN = Canada; COL = Colombia; CZE = Czech Republic; DEN = Denmark; EGY = Egypt; EU = European Union; FRA = France; GER = Germany; HKG = Hong Kong, China; HUN = Hungary; IND = India; INO = Indonesia; ISR = Israel; ITA = Italy; JPN = Japan; KOR = Republic of Korea; MAL = Malaysia; MEX = Mexico; MYA = Myanmar; NOR = Norway; NZL = New Zealand; PAK = Pakistan; PHI = Philippines; POL = Poland; POR = Portugal; PRC = People's Republic of China; ROU = Romania; RUS = Russian Federation; SIN = Singapore; SPA = Spain; SVK = Slovak Republic; SWE = Sweden; SWI = Switzerland; THA = Thailand; TUR = Turkey; UKG = United Kingdom; US or USA = United States; VIE = Viet Nam; ZAF = South Africa.

Notes: Asian economy codes are marked in orange. The figures compare the natural log of the import values from second half of 2017 to the same period in 2018. Each point represents a trade partner. The size of the points indicates the share to PRC imports or US exports. The line in each figure is the 45-degree line, which separates the economies experiencing a decline or increase in trade. Red points below the line indicate decline in trade in 2018, while blue points indicate increase in trade.

Source: ADB calculations using data from United Nations. Commodity Trade Database. https://comtrade.un.org (accessed July 2019).

Among Asian economies, Myanmar saw its soybean exports to the PRC grow fivefold (from $16.9 million to $115.7 million), while Pakistan (52.6%) and Hong Kong, China (23.5%) also recorded higher growth. Meanwhile, some Asian countries—Bangladesh, Indonesia, Japan, Malaysia, Pakistan, the Philippines, the Republic of Korea, Thailand, and Viet Nam—also benefited from the reallocation of US soybean exports (Figure 1.19b). The countries received a combined share to US total soybean exports of 26.2% in H2 2018, an increase from 17.1% in H2 2017 (equivalent to $584 million).

Large declines in PRC imports from the US also occurred in cotton, particularly on yarns used as intermediate goods. US bilateral cotton exports declined by 27.1% in H2 2018 ($89.5 million) (Figure 1.20a). The PRC also reduced its imports from Pakistan, Australia, Japan, Italy, and Turkey (worth $385.3 million). However, this was more than offset by large exports of $534.9 million from India; Hong Kong, China; and Kazakhstan, and $388.1 million from Brazil. The US, on the other hand, diverted $163.4 million in cotton exports to the top Asian textile and garment exporters—Viet Nam, Pakistan,

and Bangladesh (Figure 1.20b). The ASEAN5 countries (Indonesia, Thailand, Malaysia, the Philippines, and Singapore) also received higher exports from the US.

The PRC raised the tariffs on US automobile imports to 40% in the first round. As a result, bilateral imports decreased by about 49.2% in H2 2018, equivalent to $3.7 billion. However, overall, automobile imports by the PRC declined by 38.4% as it reduced its imports by $12.5 billion from its major trading partners—Japan, Germany, the United Kingdom, and Italy (Figure 1.21a). This more than offset the increase in PRC imports from Hong Kong, China; Singapore; India; the Philippines; and Armenia (worth $263 million). The US, however, had just a 5.5% decline in automobile exports in H2 2018. Asian countries increased demand worth $552 million, with large increased purchases from Australia, the Republic of Korea, Japan, Georgia, Singapore, Cambodia, and Mongolia (Figure 1.21b). The decline in US automobile exports to the PRC is expected to taper slightly in 2019. In December 2018, the PRC indicated it would cut tariffs for US-made automobiles to 15%, and suspend 5% on selected auto parts.

Figure 1.19: Impact of PRC Tariff Hikes on US Soybeans and Miscellaneous Grains and Fruits

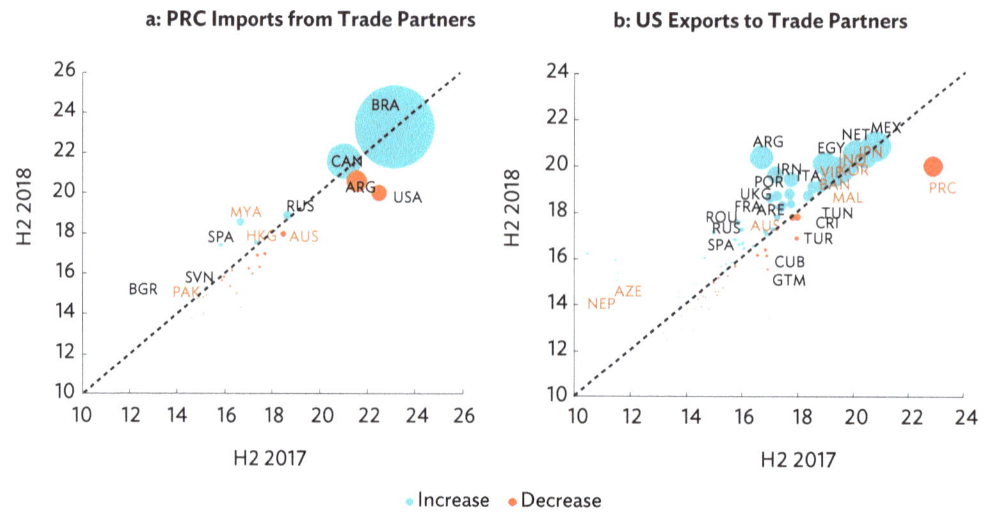

a: PRC Imports from Trade Partners

b: US Exports to Trade Partners

● Increase ● Decrease

H2 = second semester; ARE = United Arab Emirates; ARG = Argentina; AUS = Australia; AZE = Azerbaijan; BAN = Bangladesh; BRA = Brazil; BGR = Bulgaria; CAN = Canada; CRI = Costa Rica; CUB = Cuba; EGY = Egypt; FRA = France; GTM = Guatemala; HKG = Hong Kong, China; INO = Indonesia; IRN = Islamic Republic of Iran; ITA = Italy; JPN = Japan; KOR = Republic of Korea; MAL = Malaysia; MEX = Mexico; MYA = Myanmar; NEP = Nepal; NET = Netherlands; PAK = Pakistan; POR = Portugal; PRC = People's Republic of China; ROU = Romania; RUS = Russian Federation; SVN = Slovenia; SPA = Spain; TUN = Tunisia; TUR = Turkey; UKG = United Kingdom; US or USA = United States; VIE = Viet Nam.

Notes: Asian economy codes are marked in orange. The figures compare the natural log of the import values from second half of 2017 to the same period in 2018. Each point represents a trade partner. The size of the points indicates the share to PRC imports or US exports. The line in each figure is the 45-degree line, which separates the economies experiencing a decline or increase in trade. Red points below the line indicate decline in trade in 2018, while blue points indicate increase in trade.

Source: ADB calculations using data from United Nations. Commodity Trade Database. https://comtrade.un.org (accessed July 2019).

Figure 1.20: Impact of PRC Tariff Hikes on US Cotton—Raw Material, Yarn, and Woven Fabric

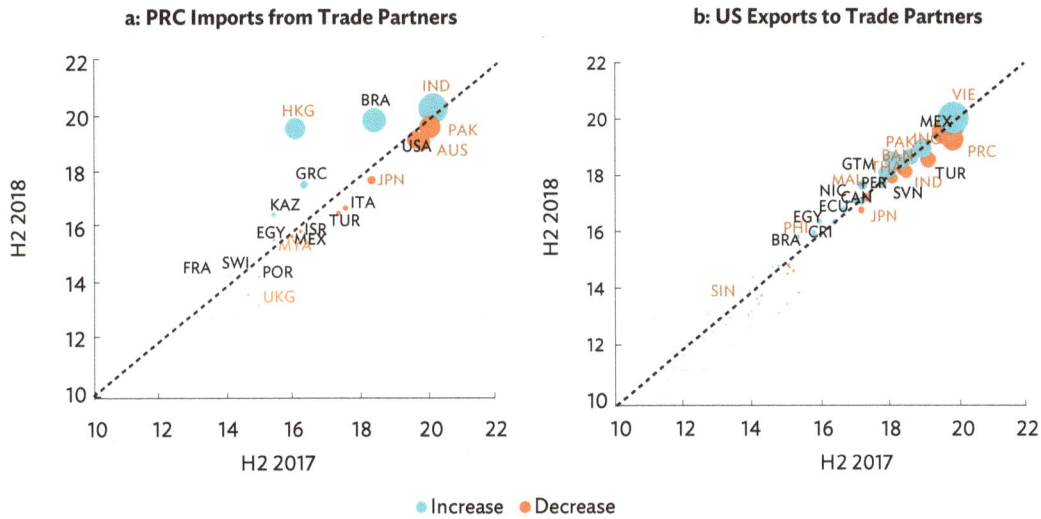

a: PRC Imports from Trade Partners

b: US Exports to Trade Partners

● Increase   ● Decrease

H2 = second semester; AUS = Australia; BAN = Bangladesh; BRA = Brazil; CAN = Canada; CRI = Costa Rica; ECU = Ecuador; EGY = Egypt; FRA = France; GRC = Greece; GTM = Guatemala; HKG = Hong Kong, China; IND = India; INO = Indonesia; ISR = Israel; ITA = Italy; JPN = Japan; KAZ = Kazakhstan; MAL = Malaysia; MEX = Mexico; MYA = Myanmar; NIC = Nicaragua; PAK = Pakistan; PER = Peru; PHI = Philippines; POR = Portugal; PRC = People's Republic of China; SIN = Singapore; SVN = Slovenia; SWI = Switzerland; THA = Thailand; TUR = Turkey; UKG = United Kingdom; US or USA = United States; VIE = Viet Nam.

Notes: Asian economy codes are marked in orange. The figures compare the natural log of the import values from second half of 2017 to the same period in 2018. Each point represents a trade partner. The size of the points indicates the share to PRC imports or US exports. The line in each figure is the 45-degree line, which separates the economies experiencing a decline or increase in trade. Red points below the line indicate decline in trade in 2018, while blue points indicate increase in trade.

Source: ADB calculations using data from United Nations. Commodity Trade Database. https://comtrade.un.org (accessed July 2019).

Figure 1.21: Impact of PRC Tariff Hikes on US Automobiles

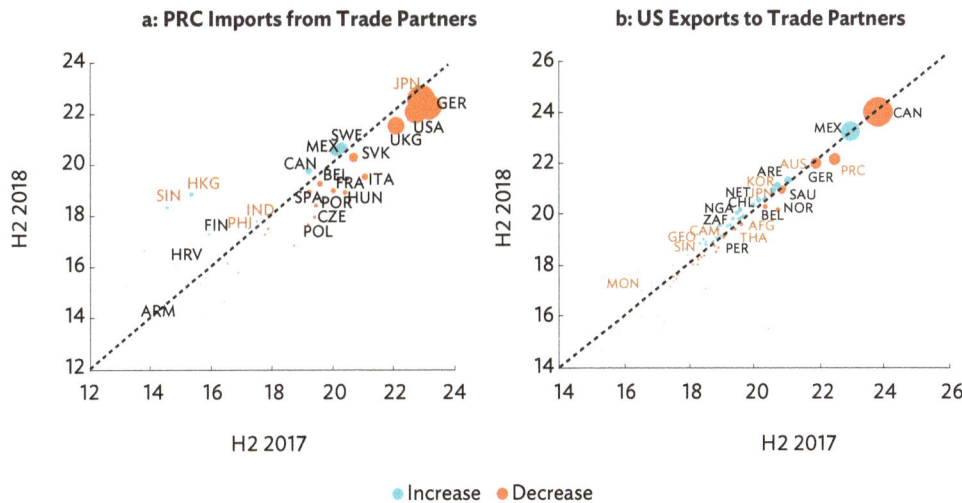

a: PRC Imports from Trade Partners

b: US Exports to Trade Partners

● Increase   ● Decrease

H2 = second semester; AFG = Afghanistan; ARE = United Arab Emirates; ARM = Armenia; AUS = Australia; BEL = Belgium; CAM = Cambodia; CAN = Canada; CHL = Chile; CZE = Czech Republic; FIN = Finland; FRA = France; GEO = Georgia; GER = Germany; HKG = Hong Kong, China; HRV = Croatia; GEO = Georgia; HUN = Hungary; IND = India; ITA = Italy; JPN = Japan; KOR = Republic of Korea; MEX = Mexico; MON = Mongolia; NET = Netherlands; NGA = Nigeria; NOR = Norway; PER = Peru; PHI = Philippines; POL = Poland; POR = Portugal; PRC = People's Republic of China; SAU = Saudi Arabia; SIN = Singapore; SPA = Spain; SVK = Slovak Republic; SWE = Sweden; THA = Thailand; UKG = United Kingdom; US or USA = United States; ZAF = South Africa.

Notes: Asian economy codes are marked in orange. The figures compare the natural log of the import values from second half of 2017 to the same period in 2018. Each point represents a trade partner. The size of the points indicates the share to PRC imports or US exports. The line in each figure is the 45-degree line, which separates the economies experiencing a decline or increase in trade. Red points below the line indicate decline in trade in 2018, while blue points indicate increase in trade.

Source: ADB calculations using data from United Nations. Commodity Trade Database. https://comtrade.un.org (accessed July 2019).

Recent trends point to sluggish export growth across Asia, in particular exports to the PRC.

Amid trade tensions, most Asian economies saw overall export growth slow in H1 2019. In H2 2018, exports by Hong Kong, China; India; Malaysia; and Viet Nam to the PRC showed relatively higher growth than other Asian economies on year-on-year basis. Yet the growth of exports to the PRC moderated across the board in H1 2019, with India; Japan; Indonesia; the Philippines; the Republic of Korea; Singapore; Taipei,China; and Viet Nam contracting (Figure 1.22a). PRC imports from the US continued to decline in H1 2019. Asian exports to the US were relatively more resilient in H2 2018. But in H1 2019, the export outcome became more varied across economies, with Australia; India; the Republic of Korea; Taipei,China; and Viet Nam showing relatively higher growth rates in bilateral exports to the US (Figure 1.22b).

Although trade diversion or the redirection effect could benefit some Asian economies, there is no guarantee the benefits would be sustainable in the long run. Furthermore, if uncertainties surrounding international trade persist and continue to dampen business and investment confidence, there could be a significantly negative impact on global economic growth and international trade.

The net effect of higher US tariffs on the PRC exports will be based on each economy's trade position in either a substitute or a complementary relationship with the PRC in exports (Box 1.3).

The spillover impact of higher trade barriers may move beyond trade partners due to backward and forward industrial value chain linkages.

Production network across borders has involved multiple countries. For example, Apple's iPhone assembled in the PRC requires various intermediate goods from other countries, including the US (Figure 1.23).

Figure 1.22: Export Growth of Selected Asian Economies (%)

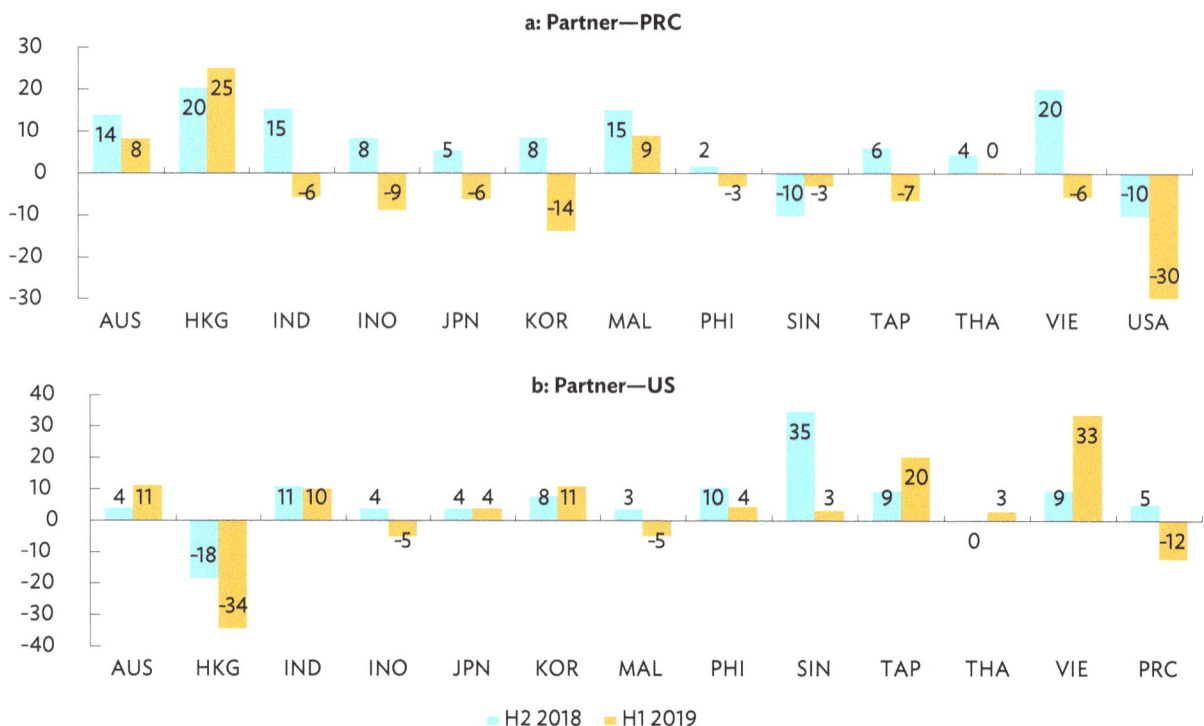

AUS = Australia; H1 = 1st semester; H2 = 2nd semester; HKG = Hong Kong, China; IND = India; INO = Indonesia; JPN = Japan; KOR = Republic of Korea; MAL = Malaysia; PHI = Philippines; PRC = People's Republic of China; SIN = Singapore; TAP = Taipei,China; THA = Thailand; US or USA = United States; VIE = Viet Nam.

Source: ADB calculations using data from CEIC.

Figure 1.23: Value-Added Decomposition for One Unit of iPhone4

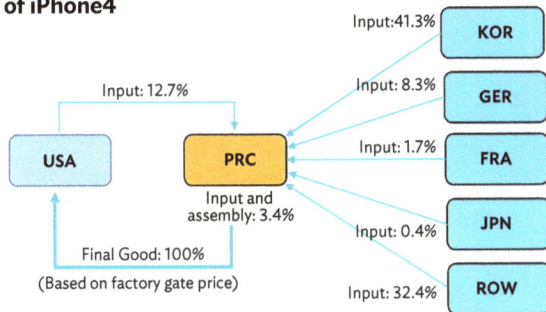

FRA = France, GER = Germany, JPN = Japan, KOR = Republic of Korea, PRC = People's Republic of China, ROW = Rest of the World, USA = United States.

Source: De Backer (2011).

The impact of US tariff hikes against the PRC in the electrical and optical equipment, and textile product sectors can be depicted through network charts of GVC linkages. The charts provide information on how much other economies are involved in the backward linkages of value chains (represented by the size of the circles in Figures 1.24a and 1.25a), as well as in the forward linkages (size of the circles in Figures 1.24b and 1.25b). The charts also describe the magnitude and direction of the flow of goods between economies (represented by the thickness of the lines and the direction of arrows in Figures 1.24 and 1.25). The greater the involvement of

Box 1.3: Trade Complementarity and Substitutability within ASEAN+3

Spillover effects of the international trade tensions will cascade into a broader set of economies through the region's supply chains. While the supply chain integration has boosted trade complementarity particularly among economies in East Asia and Southeast Asia, exports of many of these economies demonstrate increased substitutability. High export substitutability (i.e. high competitive pressures for exports) suggests potential gains from trade redirection for some economies. Impact of the PRC's export decline on other Asian countries'

export performance will be dependent upon the net effects of these two factors.

Box Tables 1 and 2 indicate degrees of bilateral export substitutability and trade complementarity among ASEAN+3 economies, where data are available. With respect to the PRC, Thailand; Viet Nam; and Hong Kong, China show the greatest export substitutability in export structure. On the other hand, Singapore, Malaysia, and the Republic of Korea have the highest degree of trade complementarity with the PRC.

1: Export Substitutability by ASEAN+3 Trade Partner, 2017

Reporter	Partner													
	BRU	CAM	LAO	MYA	VIE	INO	MAL	PHI	THA	SIN	PRC	HKG	JPN	KOR
BRU		0.017	0.016	0.235	0.043	0.101	0.125	0.041	0.040	0.054	0.042	0.037	0.052	0.043
CAM	0.017		0.187	0.214	0.271	0.157	0.076	0.090	0.134	0.060	0.165	0.105	0.061	0.058
LAO	0.016	0.187		0.207	0.302	0.216	0.228	0.241	0.269	0.214	0.275	0.298	0.193	0.202
MYA	0.235	0.214	0.207		0.231	0.261	0.177	0.144	0.168	0.098	0.175	0.125	0.096	0.121
VIE	0.043	0.271	0.302	0.231		0.330	0.374	0.358	0.422	0.303	0.554	0.405	0.300	0.334
INO	0.101	0.157	0.216	0.261	0.330		0.414	0.252	0.340	0.218	0.323	0.214	0.261	0.258
MAL	0.125	0.076	0.228	0.177	0.374	0.414		0.436	0.468	0.520	0.470	0.496	0.474	0.526
PHI	0.041	0.090	0.241	0.144	0.358	0.252	0.436		0.418	0.542	0.392	0.420	0.424	0.400
THA	0.040	0.134	0.269	0.168	0.422	0.340	0.468	0.418		0.387	0.503	0.416	0.496	0.504
SIN	0.054	0.060	0.214	0.098	0.303	0.218	0.520	0.542	0.387		0.376	0.553	0.471	0.527
PRC	0.042	0.165	0.275	0.175	0.554	0.323	0.470	0.392	0.503	0.376		0.516	0.474	0.497
HKG	0.037	0.105	0.298	0.125	0.405	0.214	0.496	0.420	0.416	0.553	0.516		0.426	0.497
JPN	0.052	0.061	0.193	0.096	0.300	0.261	0.474	0.424	0.496	0.471	0.474	0.426		0.658
KOR	0.043	0.058	0.202	0.121	0.334	0.258	0.526	0.400	0.504	0.527	0.497	0.497	0.658	

= "low" similarity, export similarity index (ESI) of below 0.3;   = "medium" similarity, ESI between 0.3 and 0.5;   = "high" similarity, ESI above 0.5 and below 1.0; ASEAN = Association of Southeast Asian Nations; BRU = Brunei Darussalam; CAM = Cambodia; HKG = Hong Kong, China; INO = Indonesia; JPN = Japan; KOR = Republic of Korea; LAO = Lao People's Democratic Republic; MAL = Malaysia; MYA = Myanmar; PHI = Philippines; PRC = People's Republic of China; SIN = Singapore; THA = Thailand; VIE = Viet Nam.

Notes: Export substitutability is measured by the ESI, which captures the degree of similarity of the export patterns between two economies. The index is between 0 and 1, where 1 indicates perfect overlap in the export profile and 0 indicates no overlap. It is computed by taking the sum over all commodities of the smaller export shares—based from the comparison of the export shares between two economies. In mathematical form the index for countries, i and j is $ESI_{ij} = \sum_{\forall c} \min[x_{ic}, x_{jc}]$, where each $x_{\bullet c}$ is the commodity c's share to the respective total exports of each economy. The summation over commodity groupings is at the level 4 of the Standard International Trade Classification.

Sources: ADB calculations using United Nations. Commodity Trade Database. https://comtrade.un.org (accessed October 2019); and methodology by Finger and Kreinin (1979).

continued on next page

Box 1.3: Trade Complementarity and Substitutability within ASEAN+3 (continued)

2: Trade Complementarity by ASEAN+3 Trade Partner, 2017

Reporter	BRU	MYA	VIE	INO	MAL	PHI	SIN	PRC	HKG	JPN	KOR
BRU		0.255	0.142	0.274	0.227	0.199	0.321	0.237	0.091	0.314	0.332
MYA	0.262		0.219	0.381	0.335	0.278	0.363	0.331	0.155	0.433	0.402
VIE	0.390	0.340		0.408	0.588	0.517	0.532	0.521	0.600	0.519	0.493
INO	0.431	0.539	0.383		0.507	0.471	0.503	0.507	0.273	0.626	0.589
MAL	0.488	0.550	0.713	0.611		0.695	0.770	0.736	0.595	0.664	0.680
PHI	0.421	0.353	0.616	0.426	0.648		0.624	0.588	0.746	0.519	0.516
SIN	0.468	0.473	0.663	0.567	0.769	0.699		0.749	0.643	0.614	0.643
PRC	0.541	0.461	0.685	0.562	0.698	0.645	0.628		0.575	0.595	0.595
HKG	0.327	0.273	0.544	0.358	0.561	0.482	0.604	0.506		0.432	0.437
JPN	0.561	0.515	0.562	0.560	0.591	0.649	0.538	0.567	0.422		0.599
KOR	0.539	0.566	0.749	0.628	0.748	0.733	0.684	0.690	0.554	0.560	

☐ = "low" complementarity, with trade complementarity index (TCI) of below 0.3; ☐ = "medium" complementarity, with TCI between 0.3 and 0.5; ☐ = "high" complementarity, with TCI above 0.5 and below 1.0; ASEAN = Association of Southeast Asian Nations; BRU = Brunei Darussalam; HKG = Hong Kong, China; INO = Indonesia; JPN = Japan; KOR = Republic of Korea; MAL = Malaysia; MYA = Myanmar; PHI = Philippines; PRC = People's Republic of China; SIN = Singapore; VIE = Viet Nam.

Notes: Trade complementarity is measured using an index that ranges from 0 and 1, where 1 indicates perfect complementarity and 0 indicates no complementarity. The index provides information how one economy's export pattern matches another economy's import pattern. It is computed as: $TCI_{ij} = 1 - \sum_{vc} |m_{ic} - x_{jc}|/2$, where m_{ic} is commodity c's share to economy i's total imports and x_{jc} is commodity c's share to economy j's exports.

Source: Data from World Bank. World Integrated Trade Solutions. https://wits.worldbank.org/ (accessed September 2019).

Source: ADB staff.

an economy in value chains, the more susceptible it is to one country's tariff rate hikes against the other.

In the backward linkages, the intermediate goods that the economies export would eventually be imported by the PRC (represented by green thick lines in Figures 1.24a and 1.25a), and then processed to be exported to the US as final goods (thickest dark green line in Figures 1.24a and 1.25a). Moreover, the PRC also imports intermediate goods from other economies, which were produced by using intermediate goods that were also initially imported from other economies. In terms of the GVC framework, these initial intermediate goods are domestic value added (DVA) of primary economies to the US–PRC linkage (thin light green lines in Figures 1.24a and 1.25a). The charts also take into account US-returned DVA in imported final goods via third economies (thin light orange lines in Figures 1.24a and 1.25a), and returned DVA in imported final goods directly from the PRC (orange line in Figures 1.24a and 1.25a).

Consequently, in the forward linkages, the PRC's intermediate exports (represented by the thickest dark green line in Figures 1.24b and 1.25b) are used by the US to produce either intermediate or final goods for other economies (green thick lines in Figures 1.24b and 1.25b). US intermediate exports would then be used by the third economies to produce final goods to be exported to another economy (thin light green lines in Figures 1.24b and 1.25b), while some may go back to the US (thin yellow lines in Figures 1.24b and 1.25b). The charts also consider economies' returned DVA in imported final goods via the PRC and the US (thin orange line in Figure 1.24b).

In the case of electrical and optical equipment, the Republic of Korea and Taipei,China are found to be affected the most through their direct backward value chain linkages with the PRC. The gross impact— combining both the direct impact and indirect impact through third economies—is likely to be greater in Japan;

Figure 1.24: Backward and Forward Linkages of US and PRC Trade on Electrical and Optical Equipment

a: Backward Linkages

b: Forward Linkages

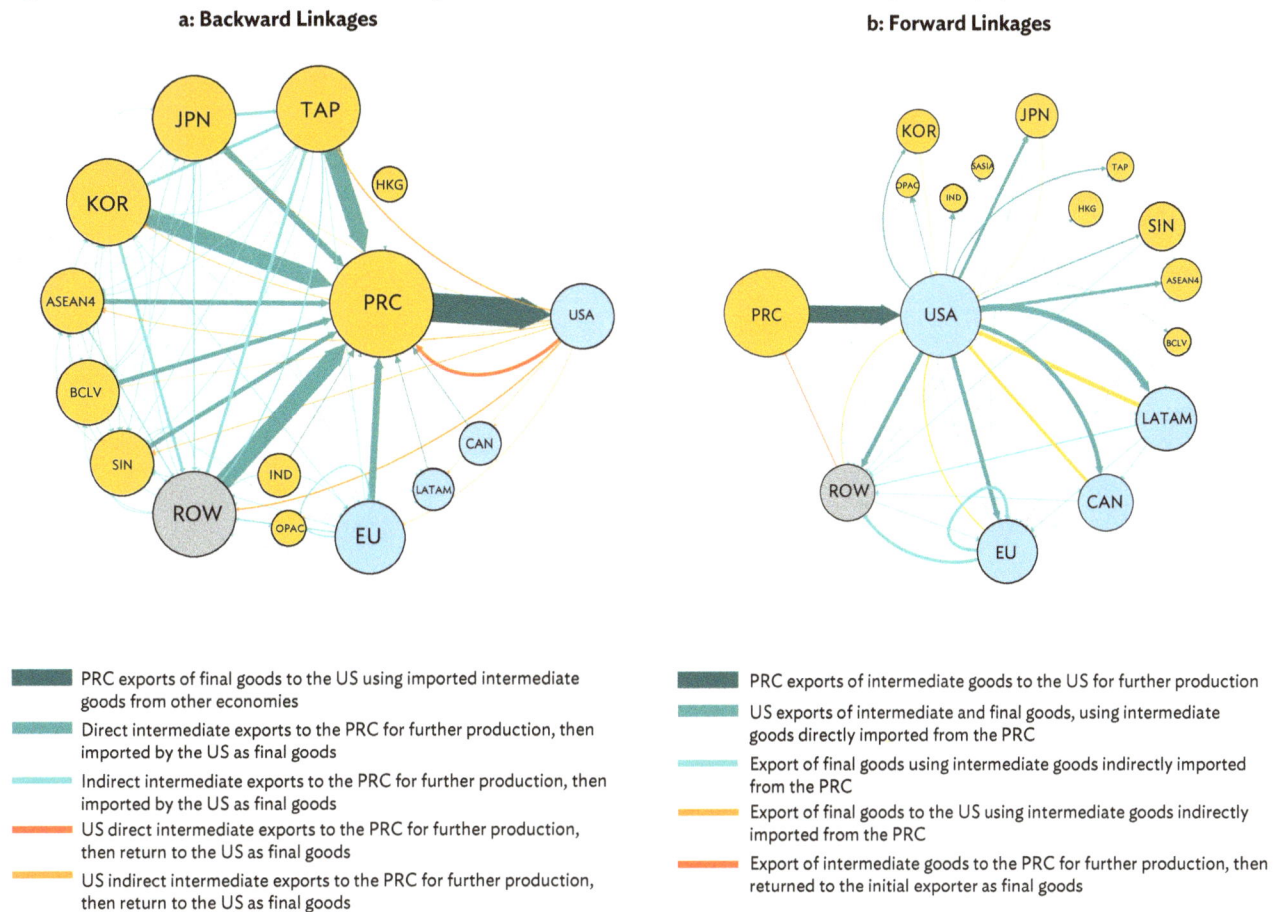

PRC exports of final goods to the US using imported intermediate goods from other economies

Direct intermediate exports to the PRC for further production, then imported by the US as final goods

Indirect intermediate exports to the PRC for further production, then imported by the US as final goods

US direct intermediate exports to the PRC for further production, then return to the US as final goods

US indirect intermediate exports to the PRC for further production, then return to the US as final goods

PRC exports of intermediate goods to the US for further production

US exports of intermediate and final goods, using intermediate goods directly imported from the PRC

Export of final goods using intermediate goods indirectly imported from the PRC

Export of final goods to the US using intermediate goods indirectly imported from the PRC

Export of intermediate goods to the PRC for further production, then returned to the initial exporter as final goods

ASEAN4 = Indonesia, Malaysia, the Philippines, and Thailand; BCLV = Brunei Darussalam, Cambodia, the Lao People's Democratic Republic, and Viet Nam; CAN = Canada; EU = European Union; HKG = Hong Kong, China; IND = India; JPN = Japan; KOR = Republic of Korea; LATAM = Latin America (Brazil and Mexico); OPAC = the Pacific and Oceania (Australia and Fiji); PRC = People's Republic of China; ROW = Rest of the world; SASIA = South Asia (Bangladesh, Bhutan, Maldives, Nepal, Pakistan, and Sri Lanka); SIN = Singapore; TAP = Taipei,China; US or USA = United States.

Notes: Indirect intermediate exports to the PRC refer to an economy's export of intermediate goods, which is used by another economy for the production of intermediate exports to the PRC, while direct intermediate exports refer to an economy's export of intermediate goods directly to the PRC. Indirect intermediate imports from the PRC refer to an economy's import of intermediate goods from another economy which has used intermediate imports from the PRC for production. Orange circles refer to Asian economies, while blue circles refer to non-Asia. In the backward linkages figure, the size of the circles represents the magnitude of the economy's direct and indirect export of intermediate goods processed by the PRC to be exported to the US as final goods. In the forward linkages, the size of the circles represents the economy's export value of intermediate and final goods using processed direct and indirect imports from the PRC. For both figures, the thickness of the lines linking the economies represent the value of the flow of intermediate and final goods between them.

Sources: ADB calculations using data from ADB. Multi-Regional Input-Output Tables; and methodology by Wang, Wei, and Zhu (2014).

the Republic of Korea; and Taipei,China than in others (Figure 1.24a). In the forward value chain linkages, economies like those in Latin America, Canada, the EU, Japan, and some ASEAN economies (to a lesser extent) are expected to be affected relatively more in case US imports of electrical and optical equipment are affected by its tariff hikes against the PRC (Figure 1.24b).

For textile and textile products, those most affected through direct backward value chain linkages with the PRC are likely

to be the Republic of Korea and South Asian economies (except for India) as a group, plus India; Japan; Taipei,China; and the EU to a lesser extent. The gross impact—with direct and indirect impact combined—could be greater in the Republic of Korea and South Asian economies (Figure 1.25a). For forward linkages, economies in Latin America, Canada, and the EU are likely to be affected most through both direct and indirect value chain linkages, while other East Asian and Southeast Asian economies will also be affected to a lesser extent (Figure 1.25b).

Figure 1.25: Backward and Forward Linkages of US and PRC Trade on Textile and Textile Products

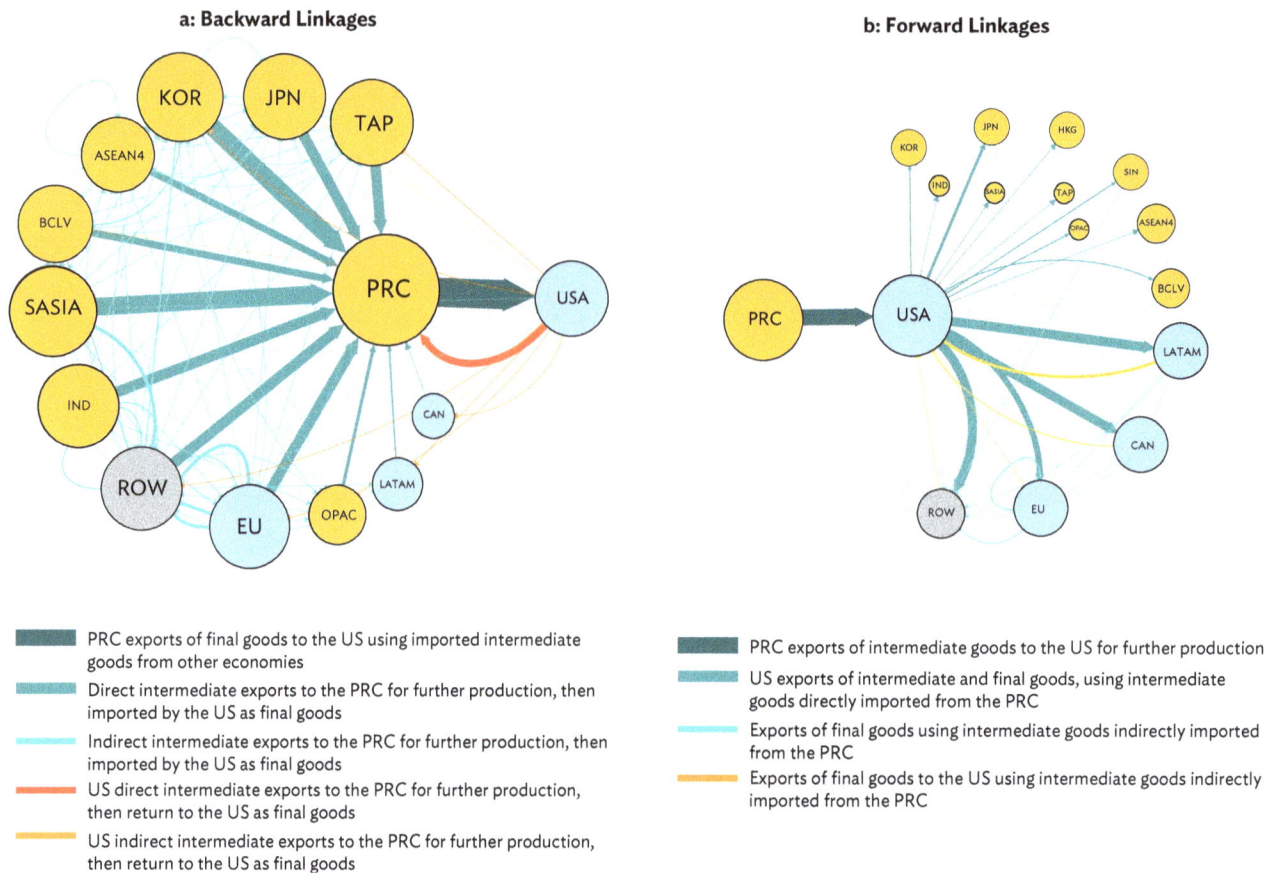

a: Backward Linkages

b: Forward Linkages

Legend for backward linkages:
- PRC exports of final goods to the US using imported intermediate goods from other economies
- Direct intermediate exports to the PRC for further production, then imported by the US as final goods
- Indirect intermediate exports to the PRC for further production, then imported by the US as final goods
- US direct intermediate exports to the PRC for further production, then return to the US as final goods
- US indirect intermediate exports to the PRC for further production, then return to the US as final goods

Legend for forward linkages:
- PRC exports of intermediate goods to the US for further production
- US exports of intermediate and final goods, using intermediate goods directly imported from the PRC
- Exports of final goods using intermediate goods indirectly imported from the PRC
- Exports of final goods to the US using intermediate goods indirectly imported from the PRC

ASEAN4 = Indonesia, Malaysia, the Philippines, and Thailand; BCLV = Brunei Darussalam, Cambodia, the Lao People's Democratic Republic, and Viet Nam; CAN = Canada; EU = European Union; HKG = Hong Kong, China; IND = India; JPN = Japan; KOR = Republic of Korea; LATAM = Latin America (Brazil and Mexico); OPAC = the Pacific and Oceania (Australia and Fiji); PRC = People's Republic of China; ROW = Rest of the world; SASIA = South Asia (Bangladesh, Bhutan, Maldives, Nepal, Pakistan, and Sri Lanka); SIN = Singapore; TAP = Taipei,China; US or USA = United States.

Notes: Indirect intermediate exports to the PRC refer to an economy's export of intermediate goods, which is used by another economy for the production of intermediate exports to the PRC, while direct intermediate exports refer to an economy's export of intermediate goods directly to the PRC. Indirect intermediate imports from the PRC refer to an economy's import of intermediate goods from another economy which has used intermediate imports from PRC for production. Orange circles refer to Asian economies, while blue circles refer to non-Asia. In the backward linkages figure, the size of the circles represents the magnitude of the economy's direct and indirect export of intermediate goods processed by the PRC to be exported to the US as final goods. In the forward linkages, the size of the circles represents the economy's export value of intermediate and final goods using processed direct and indirect imports from the PRC. For both figures, the thickness of the lines linking the economies represent the value of the flow of intermediate and final goods between them.

Sources: ADB calculations using data from ADB. Multi-Regional Input-Output Tables; and methodology by Wang, Wei, and Zhu (2014).

Updates on Regional Trade Policy

With a steep resurgence in the number of signed Asian free trade agreements, the region's trade agreement landscape is moving toward greater trade liberalization.

The rise in the number of signed Asian free trade agreements (FTAs) is a welcome development—given that rules-based trade can help strengthen the stability and predictability in the international trading system. It also sends an encouraging signal to the world that Asia remains committed to trade openness.

According to the World Trade Organization (WTO) Regional Trade Agreements database, all FTAs that came into force in 2018 involve Asian economies (Figure 1.26). This is a huge jump compared with the 33% share of Asian FTAs in 2017. The number of signed Asian FTAs increased from 8 to 13 (Figure 1.27), also reflected in the rise in the cumulative number of signed FTAs (Figure 1.28).

Figure 1.26: Number of Newly Effective Free Trade Agreements—Asia

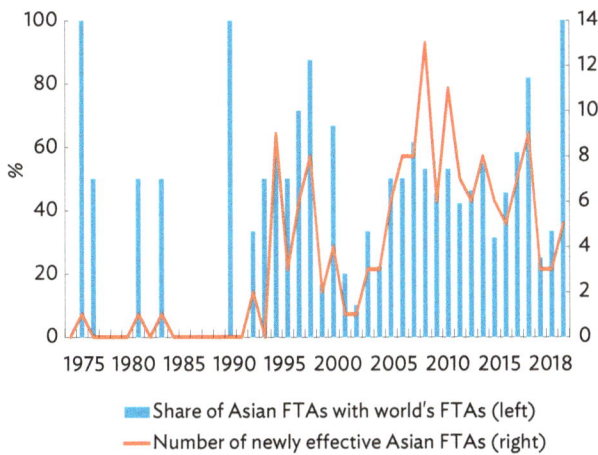

Share of Asian FTAs with world's FTAs (left)
Number of newly effective Asian FTAs (right)

FTA = free trade agreement.

Sources: ADB calculations using data from ADB. Asia Regional Integration Center FTA Database. https://aric.adb.org/fta (accessed September 2019); and World Trade Organization. Regional Trade Agreement Information System. http://rtais.wto.org (accessed August 2019).

Figure 1.27: Number of Proposed and Signed Free Trade Agreements—Asia

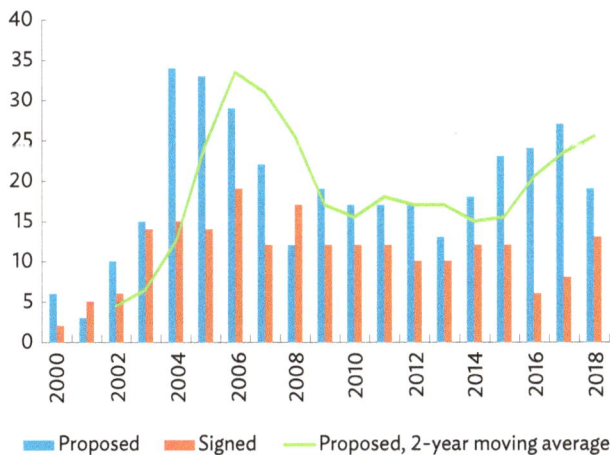

Proposed   Signed   Proposed, 2-year moving average

FTA = free trade agreement.

Notes: Includes bilateral and plurilateral FTAs with at least one of ADB's 49 regional members as signatory. "Signed" includes FTAs that are signed but not yet in effect, and those signed and in effect. "Proposed" includes FTAs that are (i) proposed (the parties consider an FTA, governments or ministries issue a joint statement on the FTA's desirability, or establish a joint-study group and joint-task force to conduct feasibility studies); (ii) framework agreements signed and under negotiation (the parties, through ministries, negotiate the contents of a framework agreement that serves as a framework for future negotiations); and (iii) under negotiation (the parties, through ministries, declare the official launch of negotiations, or start a first round of negotiations).

Source: ADB. Asia Regional Integration Center FTA Database. https://aric.adb.org/fta (accessed September 2019).

Figure 1.28: Number of Signed Free Trade Agreements—Asia (cumulative since 1975)

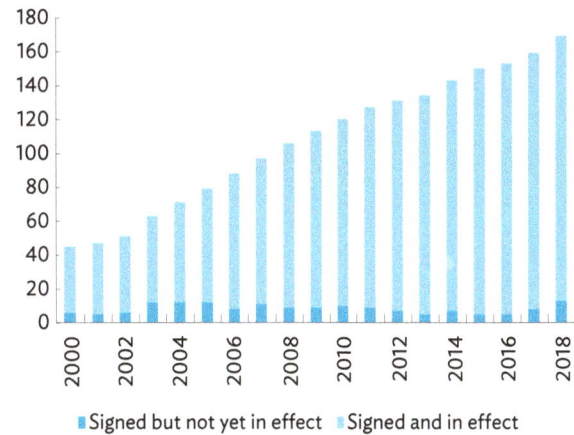

Signed but not yet in effect   Signed and in effect

FTA = free trade agreement.

Notes: Includes bilateral and plurilateral FTAs with at least one of ADB's 49 regional members as signatory. "Signed" includes FTAs that are signed but not yet in effect, and those signed and in effect.

Source: ADB. Asia Regional Integration Center FTA Database. https://aric.adb.org/fta (accessed September 2019).

Some key trends characterize Asia's FTA landscape. Asia continues to push for stronger trade ties and greater market access with economies outside the region (Figure 1.29). Eleven of the 13 signed Asian FTAs (85%) involve non-Asian partners. Except for bilateral FTAs between Australia and Peru; Hong Kong, China and Georgia; the PRC and Georgia; and Taipei,China and Paraguay, the rest of signed Asian FTAs involve multiple FTA partners outside the region. Foremost among these is the Comprehensive and Progressive Trans-Pacific Partnership Agreement (CPTPP), a mega trade deal composed of 11 economies representing 495 million people and a combined gross domestic product (GDP) of $13.5 trillion. It was signed on 8 March 2018 and came into force in December 2018 between Australia, Canada, Japan, Mexico, New Zealand, and Singapore. The CPTPP entered into force for Viet Nam on 14 January 2019.

The ambitious scope and high quality of standards and rules of the CPTPP makes it a novel trade agreement which can influence the rules on economic integration and shape the future direction for businesses. To illustrate, the CPTPP is currently the most advanced trade agreement shaping the international trade policy discourse on the

Figure 1.29: Number of Signed Free Trade Agreements, Intraregional and Extraregional (cumulative since 1975)

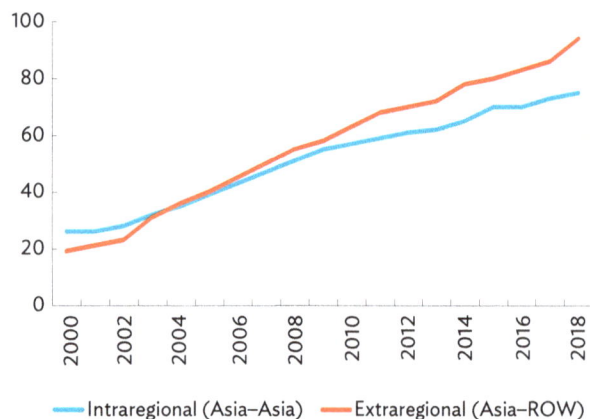

FTA = free trade agreement, ROW = rest of the world.

Notes: Includes bilateral and plurilateral FTAs with at least one of ADB's 48 regional members as signatory. "Signed" includes FTAs that are signed but not yet in effect, and those signed and in effect.

Source: ADB. Asia Regional Integration Center FTA Database. https://aric.adb.org/fta (accessed September 2019).

digital economy. It will introduce new rules to address the high costs of international mobile roaming (Australian Government, Department of Foreign Affairs and Trade 2016). Because internet connectivity is the backbone of the digital economy, lower international mobile roaming charges will make the internet more accessible, creating positive impacts not only in the digital economy but also on GVC exports (Box 1.4).

The digital economy will benefit from zero duties on every single part and component of information and communication technology goods. For instance, a smartphone manufacturer has the opportunity to procure materials from across the CPTPP members including screens from Japanese firms, semiconductor chips manufactured in Malaysia, and chassis made in Singapore, without paying duties on any of these items.[3] The smartphone, assembled in Viet Nam, can be transported to consumers in CPTPP markets, also without duties (Asian Trade Centre 2018). The free flow of information and communication technology products across CPTPP members can enhance the availability of latest technologies, which is an important factor affecting GVC exports (see Box 1.4).

Meanwhile, another mega trade deal, Regional Comprehensive Economic Partnership (RCEP), presents an opportunity for Asian economies to further enhance trade liberalization within the region. The 16 RCEP nations account for 32% of global GDP, 28% of global trade, and a population of 3.5 billion. Although some challenges have yet to be resolved in the negotiations, RCEP negotiations have reached a critical milestone as the deadline for reaching an agreement. RCEP member economies recognize the urgency of successfully concluding the RCEP to strengthen the rules-based international trading system and enhance certainty in the market, which are key elements of a vibrant trade and investment environment in the region.

Another mega trade deal signed in 2018 is the Economic Partnership Agreement (EPA) between Japan and the EU, which represents almost a third of the world's GDP. The EPA entered into force on 1 February 2019, effectively creating new markets of 635 million people. Four years after the conclusion of the negotiations, the Singapore–EU FTA was finally signed on 18 October 2018, making Singapore the first Southeast Asian country to seal a trade deal with the EU. The Philippine–European Free Trade Area (EFTA) FTA also took effect in 2018. Other plurilateral FTAs signed in 2018 include the Eurasian Economic Union's bilateral FTAs with the Islamic Republic of Iran and the PRC, the Indonesia–EFTA FTA, and the Republic of Korea–Central America FTA.

The plurilateral ASEAN–Hong Kong, China FTA (AHK FTA), which became effective 11 June 2019, is ASEAN's first FTA to come into force in almost a decade. According to the Trade and Industry Department of Hong Kong, China (2019), under the AHK FTA, Hong Kong, China and Singapore will eliminate all tariffs upon entry into force of the agreement. Hong Kong, China will enjoy tariff-free access on 85% of products traded with four ASEAN economies namely, Brunei Darussalam, Malaysia, the Philippines, and Thailand. These economies will reduce another 10% of tariff lines on exports from Hong Kong, China within 14 years. Indonesia and Viet Nam will grant tariff-free access to 75% of their products within 10 years and reduce another 10% of tariff lines within 14 years. Cambodia, the Lao PDR, and Myanmar will remove tariffs for 65% of their products within 15 years and cut back another 20% of tariff lines within 20 years.

---

[3]   Smartphone is an advanced technology not covered by existing multilateral agreement for electronics products, the Information Technology Agreement.

Australia signed bilateral FTAs with Indonesia and Hong Kong, China in 2019. Viet Nam has also inked a trade deal with the EU. On 7 October 2019, the US and Japan, which together account for approximately 30% of world GDP, signed a trade deal granting tariff reductions on agricultural and industrial goods, including commitments on digital trade. The two economies expressed intent to commence trade talks on a more comprehensive deal after the entry into force of the initial agreement, which is expected to be on 1 January 2020 (Congressional Research Service 2019).

The PRC continues to upgrade FTAs with trade partners. It upgraded bilateral FTAs with Hong Kong, China and Macau, China coming into force on 1 January 2019, with Chile on 1 March 2019, and with the signing of the protocol upgrading its FTA with Pakistan on 28 April 2019. It also concluded FTA upgrade negotiations with Singapore and launched another with Peru. On 26 February 2019, ASEAN and Japan signed the protocol that will amend the existing ASEAN–Japan FTA to incorporate chapters on trade in services, movement of natural persons, and investment. Overall, 13 Asian FTAs are currently in different stages of the upgrading process.

Box 1.4: Impact of Technology on Global Value Chain Exports

Rapid technological advancements, particularly in information and communication technology (ICT), have revolutionized the production of goods and services. ICT infrastructure includes fixed, mobile, and broadcast networks that enhance the connectivity of devices, people, and objects—leading to the expansion of the digital economy. These developments allow production processes in both manufacturing and services to have a finer degree of specialization, allowing them to be more fragmented than in the past—known as global value chains (GVCs).

Although technology has been widely recognized as an important driving force behind GVC trade, empirical studies have mostly focused on the role of technology as enabler of gross exports. Here, the role of technology, in particular including different components of ICT as a determinant of GVC exports, is examined using the following empirical specifications based on Ang et al. (2015):

(1) $\ln GVC_{it} = \delta_0 + \delta_1 \ln TWI_{it} + \delta_2 \ln tar_{it} + \delta_3 \ln P_{it}^{ex} + \delta_4 \ln LC_{it}^{MW}$

$+ \delta_5 \ln LC_{it}^{ME} + \delta_6 \ln TECH_{it}^x + CD_i + \varepsilon_{1,it}$

(2) $\ln GVC_{it} = \lambda_0 + \lambda_1 \ln TWI_{it} + \lambda_2 \ln tar_{it} + \lambda_3 \ln P_{it}^{ex} + \lambda_4 \ln LC_{it}^{MW}$

$+ \lambda_5 \ln LC_{it}^{ME} + \lambda_6 \ln TECH\_L_{it}^x + CD_i + \varepsilon_{2,it}$

where $\ln GVC_{it}$ is the natural log of GVC exports of country i at year t, TWI_{it} is the natural log of GVC-weighted real income of importing countries,[a] $\ln tar_{it}$ is the natural log of GVC-weighted simple average tariff,[b] P_{it}^{ex} is the natural log of GVC export price competitiveness where an increase in P_{it}^{ex} denotes a deterioration of the exporter's price competitiveness.[c] In LC_{it}^{MW} is the natural

log of labor cost competitiveness using the minimum wage as a measure of labor cost.[d] In LC_{it}^{ME} is the natural log of labor cost competitiveness using monthly earnings as a measure of labor cost.[e] In $TECH_{it}^x$ is the natural log of technology competitiveness for the technology variable x.[f] In $TECH\_L_{it}^x$ is the natural log of the technology variable x in levels. CD represents a set of country dummies, and ε is the stochastic error term.

Foreign income and GVC exports price competitiveness are significant determinants of GVC exports (Ang et al. 2015). The coefficients of GVC exports price competitiveness are statistically significant in all cases for both technology variables in levels and index. As expected, importing countries' income exert positive impact on GVC exports, while price competitiveness of export countries has a negative impact. GVC-weighted simple tariff coefficients manifest the expected negative sign and are statistically significant. Coefficients of the labor cost competitiveness index using monthly earnings exhibit negative relationship with GVC exports. In the meantime, minimum wage shows positive impact on GVC exports.

When technology variables in levels are considered, international internet bandwidth (kilobits per second)—being positive and statistically significant—emerges as the most important technological factor affecting GVC exports. A 10% increase in international internet bandwidth or data speed supported by a network connection leads to a 0.29% rise in GVC exports (Annex Table 1a.1, column 4). To determine whether the relationship between technology and GVC exports is nonlinear, a square of log-transformed technology variables is included in the regression (Annex Table 1a.1, columns 5–8). The exercise shows that while the technological readiness index and the percentage of

continued on next page

Box 1.4: Impact of Technology on GVC Exports *(continued)*

individuals using the internet positively affects GVC exports, the square of these variables are negative and statistically significant, which means that the positive impact on GVC exports of further improvements in these technological factors will be lessened.

Employing a 1-year lag of the values of the technology variables to control for endogeneity reinforces the result that international internet bandwidth is an important technological factor in increasing GVC exports. A 10% increase in the lag value of this technological variable raises GVC exports by 0.31% (Annex Table 1a.1, column 12).

The technology competitiveness of the exporting country relative to the rest of the world was also considered. An improvement in the availability of latest technologies (ALT) of an exporting country compared with all other importers has a positive effect on GVC exports. A unit increase in technology competitiveness in terms of ALT will increase GVC exports by 0.37% (Annex Table 1a.2, column 2).

Moreover, as the exporter's ALT competitiveness further improves, the positive impact of ALT on GVC exports becomes stronger as the squared of log-transformed ALT is positive and statistically significant (Annex Table 1a.2, column 9). While a unit increase in the 1-year lag of ALT competitiveness results in a smaller increase in GVC exports (0.18%) compared with the contemporaneous value of ALT (Annex Table 1a.2, column 10), this further highlights that relative ALT competitiveness plays an important role in enhancing GVC exports.

Meanwhile, a unit increase in the 1-year lag of foreign direct investment (FDI) and technology transfer (FTT) competitiveness decreases GVC exports by 0.24% (Annex Table 1a.2, column 11). Conversely, when the FTT of the rest of the importers is higher than the FTT of the exporter, the FTT competitiveness of the exporter will lead to higher GVC exports, which highlights the relative importance of the absorptive capacity of importing countries.

[a] TWI_{it} is the GVC weighted real income of importing countries and is computed as follows:

$$(1)\ TWI_{it} = \sum_{j=1}^{n} \frac{GVC_{jit}\,Y_{jt}}{GVC_{it}},\ \ i \neq j$$

   GVC_{jit} = GVC exports of home country i to destination country j at year t

   Y_{jt} = real income of destination country j

   Real income (real GDP) for each country is normalized to have a mean of 1.

[b]   GVC weighted simple average tariff of importing countries is computed similar to TWI_{it}, replacing Y_{jt} with tar_{jt}.

[c]   GVC exports price competitiveness is constructed using bilateral GVC weights as follows:

$$(2)\ P_{it}^{ex} = \frac{P_{it}}{\sum_{j=1}^{n} \frac{GVC_{jit}\,e_{ijt}\,P_{jt}}{GVC_{it}}},\ \ i \neq j$$

   P_i and P_j are exports unit values (export prices) of country i and destination country j at year t.

   e_{ijt} = bilateral exchange rate between country j and i

[d]   Labor cost competitiveness using minimum wage is constructed using bilateral GVC weights as follows: $LC_{it}^{MW} = \frac{MW_{it}}{\sum_{j=1}^{n} \frac{GVC_{ijt}\,MW_{jt}}{GVC_{it}}}\ \ i \neq j$

   MW_{it} and MW_{jt} are minimum wages of source country i and destination country j at year t.

[e]   Labor cost competitiveness using monthly earnings is constructed similar to LC_{it}^{MW} replacing MW_{it} with ME_{it}.

[f]   Technology competitiveness is computed similar to LC_{it}^{MW} with $TECH_{it}^{x}$ replacing MW_{it}. $TECH_{it}^{x}$ is the technology variable x of country i at year t. Technology variable x takes the following indicators: (1) technological readiness index; (2) availability of latest technologies; (3) firm-level technology absorption; (4) foreign direct investment and technology transfer; (5) % of individuals using the internet; (6) fixed broadband internet subscription; (7) international internet bandwidth, kb/s; (8) mobile broadband subscription/100 population; (9) mobile telephone subscription; (10) fixed telephone lines; and (11) ICT use. Technological readiness index is comprised of items (2) – (11) while ICT use covers items (5)–(10).

Sources: ADB calculations using Ang et al. (2015) and data from ADB. Multi-Regional Input–Output Tables; CEIC; United Nations. Commodity Trade Database. https://comtrade.un.org; World Bank. World Development Indicators. https://databank.worldbank.org/source/world-development-indicators; World Bank. World Integrated Trade Solutions. https://wits.worldbank.org; and World Economic Forum. The Global Competitiveness Index Dataset 2007-2017. https://www.weforum.org; (all accessed February 2019); and methodology by Wang, Wei, and Zhu (2014).

The region continues to pursue trade liberalization by forging more plurilateral trade deals outside the region and by deepening existing FTA commitments. These efforts are expected to help create new trade and business opportunities against the backdrop of global trade policy uncertainties.

The Role of FTAs in Making Trade Work for All

The last 3 decades saw an unprecedented rise in cross-border flows of goods and services, capital, technology, information, and people. The widely accepted belief is that breaking down economic, cultural, and geographic barriers result in higher productivity, increased economic opportunities, and overall improvement in living standards. While this belief is true to a certain extent, it obscures the fact that not everyone benefits from free trade. Indeed, free trade has left many behind, particularly the most vulnerable segments of society such as unskilled labor, small businesses, women, and indigenous people.

As the linkages between trade policy, development, and equitable distribution of gains from trade become increasingly clear, the role of trade instruments such as FTAs in making trade work for all becomes more evident as well. FTAs have increasingly included commitments in areas that are outside WTO obligations, such as protection of cultural heritage and traditional knowledge of indigenous people, which lie outside the WTO Agreement on Trade-Related Intellectual Property Rights. FTAs can also induce structural reforms in the economies involved by including provisions that set a standard on working conditions, create a favorable environment for small businesses, and promote gender equality.

Labor

The International Labour Organization (ILO) defines labor provisions as "any standard which addresses labour relations or minimum working terms or conditions, mechanisms for monitoring or promoting compliance, and/or a framework for cooperation" (ILO 2016). This broad definition reflects the heterogeneity of labor provisions in Asian FTAs and their extensive scope.[4] Two key principles underpin the core functions of labor provisions: (i) outline a set of standards or commitments, and (ii) stipulate a mechanism to ensure compliance. Asian FTAs with labor provisions are relatively new, with the oldest (Singapore–US FTA) entering into force in 2004. Out of 142 active FTAs with available full text, almost a quarter (35 FTAs) contains some form of labor provisions.

The most commonly referenced baseline for standards and commitments in Asian FTAs is the 1998 ILO Declaration on fundamental principles and rights at work and its follow-up (Table 1.1). It expects every member country to respect fundamental rights merely by virtue of membership and explicitly mentions that "labour standards should not be used for protectionist trade purposes" (ILO 1998).[5] Another ILO convention cited in FTAs is the 2006 Economic and Social (ECOSOC) Declaration that supports the ratification of additional conventions, in particular those "concerning the employment rights of women, youth, persons with disabilities, migrants and indigenous people" (Engen 2017). More than a quarter of Asian FTAs with labor provisions (26%) include this standard, while 17% cover the 2008 ILO Declaration, which includes four labor-empowerment goals.[6]

One-fifth of Asian FTAs with labor provisions further explicitly promote non-fundamental ILO conventions. For

---

[4]   Asian FTAs involve at least one partner from Asia and the Pacific.

[5]   These fundamental rights, also known as the Core Labour Standards, include (i) freedom of association and the effective recognition of the right to collective bargaining, (ii) the elimination of all forms of forced or compulsory labor, (iii) the effective abolition of child labor, and (iv) the elimination of discrimination with respect to employment and occupation.

[6]   (i) Promoting employment; (ii) developing measures of social protection; (iii) promoting social dialogue; and (iv) respecting, promoting, and realizing the fundamental principles and rights at work.

Table 1.1: Asian FTAs with Labor Provisions

Labor Provisions in FTAs	Number of FTAs	Share in Total Number of Active FTAs with Available Full Text (%)	Share in Total Number of FTAs with Labor Provisions (%)
International Standards			
ILO 1998	25	17.2	71.4
ECOSOC 2006	9	6.3	25.7
ILO 2008	6	4.2	17.1
ILO Convention	7	4.9	20.0
Commitments			
Enforce own standards	21	14.8	60.0
Not encourage trade or investment through weakening of labor laws	25	17.6	71.4
Compliance Mechanism			
Enforcement (DSM)	25	17.6	71.4
Legally binding arbitration	5	3.5	14.3
Normal agreement DSM	4	2.8	11.4
Consultation only, no enforcement	16	11.3	45.7
No (purely cooperational)	10	7.0	28.6
Cooperation on Labor Issues	31	22.5	88.6
Monitoring			
Civil society involvement	15	11.3	42.9
FTAs with labor provisions	35	24.7	
Active FTAs with available full text	142		

DSM = Dispute Settlement Mechanism, ECOSOC 2006 = 2006 Economic and Social (ECOSOC) Declaration, FTA = free trade agreement, ILO = International Labour Organization.

Sources: ADB calculations using data from ADB. Asia Regional Integration Center FTA Database. https://aric.adb.org/fta (accessed May 2019); and official FTA texts.

instance, the EU–Georgia FTA urges member economies to "reaffirm their commitment to effectively implement in their law and practice the fundamental, the priority, and other ILO conventions ratified."[7] The ILO is responsible for monitoring adherence to ILO conventions. As a result, the use of ILO conventions as the international standard is beneficial to both parties, because linking commitments to externally monitored and relatively unambiguous standards can help evaluate compliance as well as provide legitimacy to a ruling in disputes (Engen 2017). The most common commitment is the prohibition of lowering labor rights to encourage trade or investment (71%). Provisions prohibiting the non-enforcement of domestic labor laws are present in 21 FTAs (60%). In terms of enforcement, most agreements include consultations and dialogue only (46%), while only a few agreements feature legally binding arbitration (14%). The labor provisions of Asian FTAs ascribe heavy emphasis on cooperation. With the exception of three Japanese agreements with labor provisions in their investment, cooperation provisions are found in all the agreements reviewed. In general, monitoring is not the strongest point of Asian FTA labor provisions. On the one hand, the provisions in the FTAs reviewed allow for some kind of labor committee or subcommittee, or at the minimum, contact points for both partners. On the other hand, most provisions do not indicate the monitoring responsibilities of these committees or any semblance of a time frame or schedule for assessment. Only 16 agreements (46%) mention civil society participation, and even less when the context of monitoring is considered.

Small and Medium-Sized Enterprises

Small and medium-sized enterprises (SMEs) in Asia have much to gain from participating in GVCs and international trade. This includes the opportunity to

---

7   European Union, *Association Agreement between the European Union and the European Atomic Energy Community and their Member States, of the one Part, and Georgia, of the other Part.*

improve productivity and achieve economies of scale through increased exports to more markets. Participation in GVCs and collaboration within a network of upstream and downstream industries create positive spillover effects on SMEs—through more learning opportunities, introducing new business models and advanced technologies, leading to the expansion of SME growth horizons.

While SMEs have much to gain from increased internationalization, only a few are involved in international trade (Harvie 2010). FTAs can help SMEs plug into GVCs by reducing or eliminating tariff and nontariff barriers, simplifying customs procedures, promoting electronic commerce, and fostering technology transfer. Moreover, while the number of FTAs continues to grow, FTA utilization of SMEs remains low. This means SMEs may not be reaping the full benefits from FTAs (Tambunan and Chandra 2014). SME-related

provisions in FTAs—such as enhancing information exchange on trade-related domestic laws and financial access—may help improve FTA utilization of SMEs.

The analysis shows that out of 142 FTAs with Asian partners reviewed, only 60 incorporate at least one provision explicitly mentioning SMEs. The 2000s saw a tremendous increase in the number of FTAs with SME-related provisions (Figure 1.30). In addition, the quantity and quality of details of these SME-related provisions in FTAs have also improved considerably.

The goal of strengthening institutional support to SMEs and enhancing their participation in international trade cuts through a wide range of concerns. This explains why SME-related provisions are scattered across different locations in FTAs and cover distinct areas. As presented in Figure 1.31, SME-related provisions pertain mostly to cooperation on SMEs.

Figure 1.30: Number of SME-Related Provisions in Asian FTAs

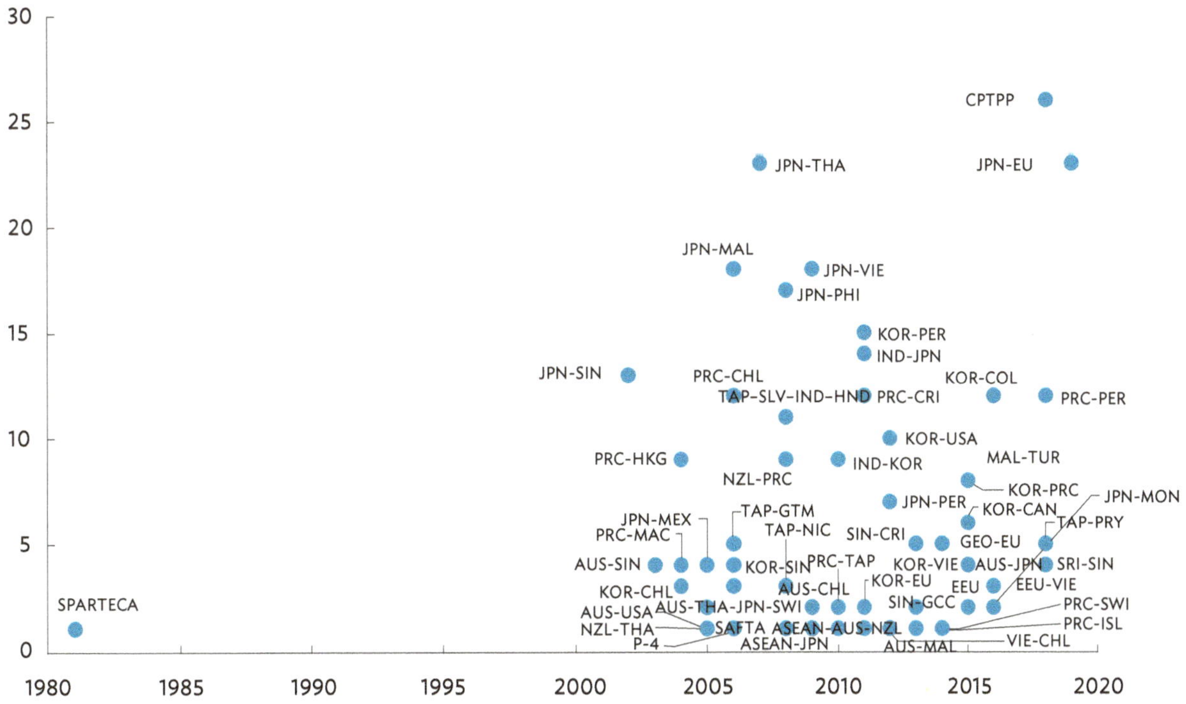

ASEAN = Association of Southeast Asian Nations; AUS = Australia; CAN = Canada; CHL = Chile; COL = Colombia; CPTPP = Comprehensive and Progressive Agreement for Trans-Pacific Partnership; CRI = Costa Rica; EEU = Eurasian Economic Union; EU = European Union; FTA = foreign trade agreement; GCC = Gulf Cooperation Council; GEO = Georgia; GTM = Guatemala; HKG = Hong Kong, China; HND = Honduras; IND = India; ISL = Iceland; JPN = Japan; KOR = Republic of Korea; MAC = Macau, China; MAL = Malaysia; MEX = Mexico; MON = Mongolia; NIC = Nicaragua; NZL = New Zealand; P-4 = Trans-Pacific Strategic Economic Partnership Agreement; PER = Peru; PHI = Philippines; PRC = People's Republic of China; PRY = Paraguay; SIN = Singapore; SLV = El Salvador; SAFTA = South Asia Free Trade Area; SME = small and medium-sized enterprise; SPARTECA = South Pacific Regional Trade and Economic Co-operation Agreement; SRI = Sri Lanka; SWI = Switzerland; TAP = Taipei,China; THA = Thailand; TUR = Turkey; USA = United States; VIE = Viet Nam.

Sources: ADB calculations using ADB. Asia Regional Integration Center FTA Database. https://aric.adb.org/fta (accessed May 2019); and official FTA texts.

Figure 1.31: Main Areas of SME-Related Provisions in RTAs

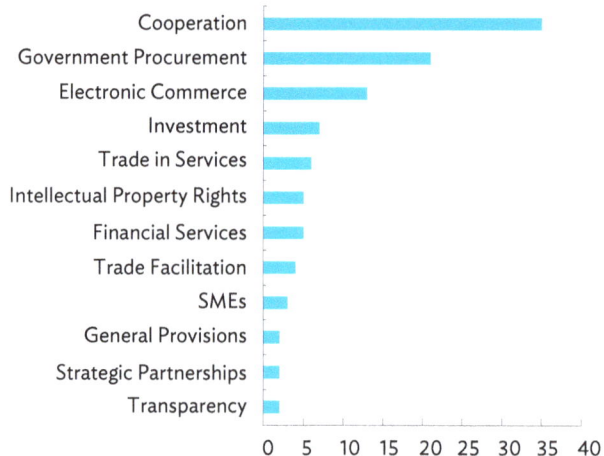

FTA = free trade agreement, RTA = regional trade agreement, SME = small and medium-sized enterprise.

Sources: ADB calculations using ADB. Asia Regional Integration Center FTA Database. https://aric.adb.org/fta (accessed May 2019); and official FTA texts.

The extent and areas of cooperation relating to SMEs differ across FTAs. While some FTAs merely identify SMEs as a specific area for cooperation, others include more specific language. Promoting a favorable environment for SME development and engendering capacity-building programs for SMEs are among the most covered issues in cooperation provisions of Asian FTAs. Other key matters addressed in cooperative activities include development of opportunities for business partnerships, formation of information networks, export promotion, and encouragement of innovation and technology transfers. Several FTAs also contain provisions on improving information exchange on access to finance for SMEs and the development of financial intermediaries.

Other types of SME-related provisions are found in the following areas: (i) government procurement, (ii) electronic commerce, (iii) investment, (iv) services, (v) intellectual property, and (vi) financial services. Of the 60 Asian FTAs with SME-related provisions, only three—all involving Japan—have a chapter dedicated to SMEs. Similar to labor provisions, SME-related provisions are remarkably heterogeneous and vary considerably

in terms of language, scope, and commitments. Most SME-related provisions are couched in best endeavor language in contrast with strong stipulations that give rise to mandatory obligations. The two most common categories are stipulations (i) promoting cooperation in SMEs, and (ii) specifying that SMEs are excluded from certain FTA obligations.

Women and Gender

The prevailing assumption for decades has been that free trade, combined with the liberalization of investment and financial systems, is a "gender-neutral" policy that would facilitate the process of sustained economic growth, leading to more employment opportunities and higher standards of living for both men and women. Recent statistics on gender inequality, however, cast doubts on this long-held notion. Women remain more vulnerable to deprivation in terms of less access to food, health care, and education. Women also remain underrepresented in international trade, with only 13.6% of women-led firms in developing Asia engaged directly or indirectly as exporters (World Bank Enterprise Surveys).

One way to make trade policy work for women is through trade instruments addressing gender inequality. The inclusion of gender-related provisions in FTAs is a welcome step toward raising the profile of gender equality challenges in the trade discourse. As of present, only a handful of Asian FTAs in force includes gender-related provisions.[8] These provisions are located in different parts or chapters—such as the preamble; labor; cooperation and capacity-building; trade and sustainable development; and employment, social policy, and equal opportunities. Gender-related provisions also differ according to language, scope, and commitment, although most stipulations are couched in best endeavor terms.

Cooperation provisions on gender are the most prevalent type of gender-related provision in Asian FTAs. These provisions focus on the elimination of discrimination in

---

[8]   (i) Australia–US FTA; (ii) Taipei,China–Nicaragua FTA; (iii) CPTPP; (iv) Georgia–EU Deep and Comprehensive FTA; (v) Viet Nam–Chile FTA; and (vi) PRC–Peru FTA.

respect of employment and occupation, and providing capacity-building programs for women. For instance, the preamble of the CPTPP explicitly reaffirms commitment to gender equality. It also identifies promotion of gender equality as an area of cooperation in the context of labor and capacity building. CPTPP's chapter on development has specific provisions for women and economic growth. It aims to increase opportunities for women by providing advice or training in the form of (i) programs aimed at helping women build skills and capacity, and enhance their access to markets, technology and financing; (ii) developing women's leadership networks; and (iii) identifying best practices related to workplace flexibility.

On the multilateral level, 123 of 164 WTO member states and observers backed the groundbreaking Joint Declaration on Trade and Women's Economic Empowerment. Though nonbinding, the declaration provides a framework for WTO members to adopt "gender-responsive" trade policies. The declaration says that both developed and developing countries acknowledge that "improving women's access to opportunities and removing barriers to their participation in national and international economies contributes to sustainable economic development." This joint declaration may pave the way for gender equality issues to form part of mainstream trade policy discourse and for gender-neutral trade rules to become regular features of well-established trade instruments such as FTAs.

Indigenous People

While the free flows of goods, services, people, and ideas have undoubtedly improved the standards of living of many and brought about modern conveniences, it has also challenged cultural norms and threatened the age-old traditional knowledge and practices that indigenous people and native communities have developed from their intimate ties to land.

Protection of traditional knowledge, indigenous cultural expressions, and heritage from commercialization and cultural appropriation is one of the key issues of indigenous groups over trade. These concerns are addressed in some FTAs, particularly those involving New Zealand; Australia; and Taipei,China.[9] These FTAs include an explicit statement that "nothing in this Agreement shall be construed to prevent the adoption or enforcement by a Party of measures necessary... to support creative arts," which includes indigenous traditional practices.

FTAs such as the CPTPP and PRC–Peru also include a specific article recognizing the role of traditional knowledge in environment preservation by considering "the importance of respecting, preserving, and maintaining knowledge and practices of indigenous and local communities embodying traditional lifestyles that contribute to the conservation and sustainable use of biological diversity."

---

[9]   (i) New Zealand–Taipei,China Economic Cooperation Agreement; (ii) CPTPP; (iii) New Zealand–Malaysia FTA; (iv) New Zealand–PRC FTA; (v) New Zealand–Taipei,China Economic Cooperation Agreement; (vi) Trans-Pacific Strategic Economic Partnership Agreement; (vii) ASEAN–Australia and New Zealand FTA;(viii) Australia–US FTA; (ix) Taipei,China–Guatemala FTA; (x) Taipei,China–Nicaragua FTA; (xi) Taipei,China–Panama FTA; (xii) PRC–Peru FTA; (xiii) Australia–Chile FTA; and (xiv) Australia–Chile FTA.

References

Ang, J., B. Jakob, B. Madsen, and P. Robertson. 2015. Export Performance of the Asian Miracle Economies: The Role of Innovation and Product Variety. *The Canadian Journal of Economics*. 48 (1). pp. 273-309.

Asian Development Bank (ADB). Asia Regional Integration Center Free Trade Agreement Database. https://aric.adb.org/fta (accessed May 2019 and September 2019).

———. Multi-Regional Input-Output Tables.

———. 2015. *Key Indicators for Asia and the Pacific 2015 46th Edition*. Manila.

———. 2019. *Asian Development Outlook 2019 Update: Fostering Growth and Inclusion in Asia's Cities*. Manila. https://www.adb.org/publications/series/asian-development-outlook (accessed September 2019).

Asian Trade Centre. 2018. Ten Benefits of the Comprehensive and Progressive Trans-Pacific Partnership (CPTPP). https://static1.squarespace.com/static/5393d501e4b0643446abd228/t/5aa1042aec212dcf8e6fc2aa/1520501823014/CPTPP+Benefits+Digital+final.pdf (accessed 2 October 2019).

Australian Government, Department of Foreign Affairs and Trade. 2016. *Trans-Pacific Partnership Agreement Chapter Summary: Telecommunications*. https://dfat.gov.au/trade/agreements/in-force/cptpp/summaries/Documents/telecommunications.pdf.

Centre d'Études Prospectives et d'Informations Internationales (the French Research Center in International Economics). GeoDist Database. http://www.cepii.fr/CEPII/en/cepii/cepii.asp. (accessed August 2019).

Ching, N. 2019. US, China Reach Partial Trade Deal; Avoid Tariff Increase. *Voice of America*. 11 October. https://www.voanews.com/usa/us-politics/us-china-reach-partial-trade-deal-avoid-tariff-increase.

Congressional Research Service. 2019. US-Japan Trade Agreement Negotiations. https://crsreports.congress.gov/product/pdf/IF/IF11120

CPB Netherlands Bureau for Economic Policy Analysis. World Trade Monitor. https://www.cpb.nl/en/data (accessed October 2019).

De Backer, K. 2011. *Global Value Chains: Preliminary Evidence and Policy Issues.* Report prepared for the meeting of the Committee on Industry, Innovation, and Entrepreneurship (CIIE) under the Directorate for Science, Technology, and Industry (DSTI). 31 March–1 April. https://unstats.un.org/unsd/trade/globalforum/publications/gvc/n%20-%20OECD%20-%202011%20-%20GVCs%20-%20Preliminary%20Evidence%20-%20Policy%20Issues_March%204.pdf (accessed October 2019).

Engen, L. 2017. Labour Provisions in Asia-Pacific Free Trade Agreements. Background paper for the project, Enhancing the Contribution of Preferential Trade Agreements to Inclusive and Equitable Trade. *Background Paper*. No. 1/2017. Bangkok: United Nations Economic and Social Commission for Asia and the Pacific.

European Union. *Association Agreement between the European Union and the European Atomic Energy Community and their Member States, of the one part, and Georgia, of the other part.* O.J. L261/4. 2014. https://eur-lex.europa.eu/legal-content/EN/TXT/?uri=uriserv:OJ.L_.2014.261.01.0004.01.ENG&toc=OJ:L:2014:261:TOC (accessed July 2019).

Federal Register. The Daily Journal of the US Government. https://www.federalregister.gov (accessed July 2019 and September 2019).

Finger, J., and M. E. Kreinin. 1979. A Measure of 'Export Similarity' and Its Possible Uses. *The Economic Journal*. 89 (356). pp. 905–912.

Harvie, C. 2010. East Asian Production Networks—the Role and Contribution of SMEs. *International Journal of Business and Development Studies*. 2 (1). pp. 27–62.

International Labour Organization. 1998. *Declaration on Fundamental Principles and Rights at Work.* Geneva.

———. 2016. *Studies on Growth with Equity: Assessment of Labour Provisions in Trade and Investment Arrangements.* Geneva.

International Monetary Fund. Direction of Trade Database. https://www.imf.org/en/Data (accessed September 2019).

———. World Economic Outlook April 2019 Database. https://www.imf.org/external/pubs/ft/weo/2019/01/weodata/index.aspx (accessed October 2019).

Ministry of Commerce of the People's Republic of China. 2018. The Spokesperson of the Ministry of Commerce Makes Remarks on China's Release of a List of Discontinuation Concessions against the U.S. Steel and Aluminum Imports under Section 232. http://english.mofcom.gov.cn/article/newsrelease/policyreleasing/201803/20180302723376.shtml (accessed July 2019 and September 2019).

Ministry of Finance of the People's Republic of China. Policy Release. http://gss.mof.gov.cn (accessed September 2019).

Office of the United States Trade Representative. People's Republic of China Section 301—Tariff Actions and Exclusion Process. https://ustr.gov/issue-areas/enforcement/section-301-investigations/tariff-actions (accessed September 2019).

———. 2018. President Trump Approves Relief for U.S. Washing Machine and Solar Cell Manufacturers. https://ustr.gov/about-us/policy-offices/press-office/press-releases/2018/january/president-trump-approves-relief-us (accessed September 2019).

Observatory of Economic Complexity. Product Profile of Transmission Apparatus for Radio-Broadcasting or Television, Whether or Not Incorporating Reception Apparatus or Sound Recording or Reproducing Apparatus; Television Cameras, Digital Cameras and Video Camera Recorders. https://oec.world/en/profile/hs07/8525/ (accessed July 2019).

Organisation for Economic Co-operation and Development (OECD). OECD Data. https://data.oecd.org/ (accessed October 2019).

Tambunan, T. and A. Chandra. 2014. *Maximizing the Utilization of ASEAN-Led Free Trade Agreements: The Potential Roles of Micro, Small, and Medium-Sized Enterprises.* Manitoba: International Institute for Sustainable Development.

Trade and Industry Department (Hong Kong, China). Free Trade Agreement between Hong Kong, China and the Association of Southeast Asian Nations. https://www.tid.gov.hk/english/ita/fta/hkasean/index.html (accessed July 2019).

United Nations. Commodity Trade Database. https://comtrade.un.org (accessed February 2019, July 2019, and October 2019).

Wang, Z., S. J. Wei, and K. Zhu. 2014. Quantifying International Production Sharing at the Bilateral and Sector Levels. *NBER Working Paper.* No. 19677. Cambridge, MA: National Bureau of Economic Research.

World Bank. World Development Indicators. https://databank.worldbank.org/source/world-development-indicators (accessed February 2019).

———. Enterprise Surveys. http://www.enterprisesurveys.org (accessed February 2019).

———. World Integrated Trade Solutions. https://wits.worldbank.org/ (accessed February 2019 and September 2019).

World Economic Forum. The Global Competitiveness Index Dataset 2007-2017. https://www.weforum.org (accessed February 2019).

World Trade Organization. Statistics Database. http://stat.wto.org/Home/WSDBHome.aspx (accessed April 2019).

———. Regional Trade Agreement Information System. http://rtais.wto.org (accessed August 2019).

———. Tariff Download Facility. http://tariffdata.wto.org (accessed September 2019).

ANNEX 1a: Impact of Technology on GVC Exports

Annex Table 1a.1: Panel Ordinary Least Squares Using Technology Variables in Levels
Dependent Variable: Log(GVC Exports$_{it}$)

Variables	(1)	(2)	(3)	(4)	(5)	(6)	(7)	(8)	(9)	(10)	(11)	(12)
	Technology Variables in Levels											
	TR	ALT	IUT	IIB	TR	ALT	IUT	IIB	TR	ALT	IUT	IIB
Log(GVC weighted income)	0.052**	0.065***	0.048**	-0.00009	0.071***	0.060***	0.064***	-0.0005	0.011	0.015	0.007	-0.023
	(0.025)	(0.017)	(0.024)	(0.028)	(0.019)	(0.017)	(0.025)	(0.030)	(0.033)	(0.028)	(0.035)	(0.041)
Log(GVC weighted simple tariff)	-0.015*	-0.017**	-0.012	0.002	-0.013*	-0.018*	-0.010*	0.002	0.005	0.005	0.004	0.006
	(0.009)	(0.009)	(0.007)	(0.007)	(0.007)	(0.010)	(0.006)	(0.007)	(0.008)	(0.007)	(0.008)	(0.008)
Log(Price Competitiveness Index)	-0.065***	-0.062***	-0.064***	-0.053***	-0.060***	-0.061***	-0.053***	-0.053***	-0.053***	-0.053***	-0.050***	-0.045***
	(0.019)	(0.018)	(0.019)	(0.017)	(0.015)	(0.018)	(0.017)	(0.017)	(0.017)	(0.017)	(0.016)	(0.016)
Log(Labor Cost Competitiveness Index) - Monthly Earnings	-0.025**	-0.022*	-0.025***	-0.024***	-0.028**	-0.024**	-0.025**	-0.024***	-0.028***	-0.026***	-0.028***	-0.022**
	(0.010)	(0.012)	(0.009)	(0.007)	(0.012)	(0.012)	(0.011)	(0.007)	(0.009)	(0.009)	(0.009)	(0.011)
Log(Labor Cost Competitiveness Index) - Minimum Wage	0.031	0.028	0.033	0.035**	0.047**	0.029	0.041**	0.035**	0.038**	0.036**	0.039**	0.034
	(0.021)	(0.019)	(0.021)	(0.017)	(0.021)	(0.018)	(0.021)	(0.018)	(0.017)	(0.016)	(0.017)	(0.020)
Log(Technology Variable)	0.249	0.556	0.196	0.029***	7.453***	5.512	4.74*	0.032				
	(0.335)	(0.364)	(0.219)	(0.007)	(1.817)	(4.782)	(2.52)	(0.037)				
[Log(Technology Variable)]^2					-2.402***	-1.516	-0.584*	-0.0003				
					(0.596)	(1.403)	(0.321)	(0.003)				
Lag[Log(Technology Variable)]									0.057	0.211	0.081	0.031**
									(0.179)	(0.225)	(0.213)	(0.015)
Constant	11.99***	11.41***	11.56***	12.26***	6.742***	7.423*	2.907	12.26***	12.32***	12.03***	12.06***	12.25***
	(0.590)	(0.673)	(0.965)	(0.034)	(1.387)	(4.067)	(4.901)	(0.110)	(0.311)	(0.422)	(0.944)	(0.082)
Observations	113	113	113	107	113	113	113	107	107	107	107	98
Country Fixed Effect	Yes	Yes	Yes	Yes	Yes	Yes	Yes	Yes	Yes	Yes	Yes	Yes
Exporter	All Countries	All Countries	All Countries	All Countries	All Countries	All Countries	All Countries	All Countries	All Countries	All Countries	All Countries	All Countries
Overall R-squared	0.998	0.998	0.998	0.999	0.998	0.998	0.998	0.999	0.998	0.998	0.998	0.998

*** = significant at 1%, ** = significant at 5%, * = significant at 10%. Robust standard errors in parentheses.

ALT = availability of latest technologies; GVC = global value chain; IIB = international internet bandwidth, kb/s; IUT = % of individuals using the internet; TR = Technological Readiness Index.

Sources: ADB calculations using data from ADB. Multi-Regional Input–Output Tables; CEIC; United Nations. Commodity Trade Database. https://comtrade.un.org; World Bank. World Development Indicators. https://databank.worldbank.org/source/world-development-indicators; World Bank. World Integrated Trade Solutions. https://wits.worldbank.org; and World Economic Forum. The Global Competitiveness Index Dataset 2007-2017. https://www.weforum.org; (all accessed February 2019); and methodology by Wang, Wei, and Zhu (2014).

Annex Table 1a.2: Panel Ordinary Least Squares Using Technology Variables Index

Dependent Variable: Log(GVC Exports$_{it}$)

Variables	(1) TR	(2) ALT	(3) FTT	(4) ICT	(5) TR	(6) ALT	(7) FTT	(8) ICT	(9) TR	(10) ALT	(11) FTT	(12) ICT
	Technology Variables Index											
Log(GVC weighted income)	0.067***	0.072***	0.071***	0.067***	0.066***	0.066***	0.071***	0.067***	-0.008	0.009	0.020	-0.006
	(0.021)	(0.017)	(0.023)	(0.022)	(0.020)	(0.014)	(0.022)	(0.022)	(0.025)	(0.033)	(0.032)	(0.026)
Log(GVC weighted simple tariff)	-0.014*	-0.025**	-0.014*	-0.014*	-0.015*	-0.027***	-0.015	-0.014*	0.010	0.006	0.006	0.009
	(0.008)	(0.011)	(0.008)	(0.008)	(0.008)	(0.010)	(0.009)	(0.008)	(0.006)	(0.011)	(0.012)	(0.007)
Log(Price Competitiveness Index)	-0.061***	-0.056**	-0.064***	-0.059***	-0.059***	-0.042*	-0.056**	-0.059***	-0.052***	-0.059***	-0.058***	-0.057***
	(0.017)	(0.024)	(0.021)	(0.017)	(0.017)	(0.022)	(0.022)	(0.017)	(0.014)	(0.020)	(0.017)	(0.015)
Log(Labor Cost Competitiveness Index) – Monthly Earnings	-0.029**	-0.023*	-0.024**	-0.027*	-0.026*	-0.023	-0.018	-0.026	-0.025**	-0.022**	-0.031***	-0.020*
	(0.014)	(0.014)	(0.012)	(0.015)	(0.015)	(0.015)	(0.012)	(0.016)	(0.010)	(0.009)	(0.011)	(0.011)
Log(Labor Cost Competitiveness Index) – Minimum Wage	0.018	0.033*	0.031	0.021	0.019	0.031*	0.027	0.020	0.035*	0.031*	0.041**	0.031*
	(0.021)	(0.020)	(0.023)	(0.023)	(0.021)	(0.017)	(0.021)	(0.025)	(0.019)	(0.016)	(0.018)	(0.019)
Log(Technology Variable)	(0.021)	0.026*	0.004	0.015	0.026	0.048***	0.010	0.016				
	0.014	(0.014)	(0.017)	(0.027)	(0.037)	(0.017)	(0.018)	(0.032)				
[Log(Technology Variable)]^2					0.008	0.010**	0.013	0.004				
					(0.012)	(0.005)	(0.009)	(0.031)				
Lag[Log(Technology Variable)]									-0.018	0.012**	-0.017**	-0.023
									(0.014)	(0.006)	(0.007)	(0.014)
Constant	12.45***	12.43***	12.44***	12.44***	12.44***	12.41***	12.42***	12.44***	12.42***	12.42***	12.45***	12.42***
	(0.021)	(0.025)	(0.030)	(0.024)	(0.023)	(0.019)	(0.034)	(0.024)	(0.016)	(0.022)	(0.022)	(0.019)
Observations	107	101	97	106	107	101	97	106	95	96	94	95
Country Fixed Effect	Yes	Yes	Yes	Yes	Yes	Yes	Yes	Yes	Yes	Yes	Yes	Yes
Exporter	All Countries	All Countries	All Countries	All Countries	All Countries	All Countries	All Countries	All Countries	All Countries	All Countries	All Countries	All Countries
Overall R-squared	0.998	0.998	0.998	0.998	0.998	0.998	0.998	0.998	0.999	0.998	0.999	0.999

*** = significant at 1%, ** = significant at 5%, * = significant at 10%. Robust standard errors in parentheses.

ALT = availability of latest technologies; FTT = foreign direct investment and technology transfer; GVC = global value chain; ICT = information and communication technology; TR = Technological Readiness Index.

Sources: ADB calculations using data from ADB. Multi-Regional Input–Output Tables; CEIC; United Nations. Commodity Trade Database. https://comtrade.un.org; World Bank. World Integrated Trade Solutions. https://wits.worldbank.org; and World Economic Forum. The Global Competitiveness Index Dataset 2007-2017. https://www.weforum.org; (all accessed February 2019); and methodology by Wang, Wei, and Zhu (2014).

2 Cross-Border Investment

Trends and Patterns of Foreign Direct Investment in Asia

Global foreign direct investment continued to slide in 2018.

Global foreign direct investment (FDI) inflows fell for the third consecutive year in 2018, estimated at $1.3 trillion, a 13.4% contraction from 2017. Tax reforms in the United States (US) in late 2017 led to a repatriation of foreign earnings by US-based multinationals, which consequently affected global FDI as outward investment from the US declined to just –$63.6 billion from $300.4 billion in 2017.

Despite the global slowdown, Asia continued as a prime destination, with inward FDI to the region growing 6.3% over 2017, attracting 43.1% of the 2018 global total.[10] A considerable amount of inward FDI to Asia went to the People's Republic of China (PRC) and other financial hubs such as Hong Kong, China and Singapore. The region also continued as a major source of FDI, with 49.4% of global outward FDI originating from Asia. Japan; the PRC; and Hong Kong, China were top investors. While 2019 may show some global recovery, it will likely be modest, as the underlying trend in inward FDI continues to be feeble. In addition, headwinds such as trade tensions may further dampen foreign investment activity.[11]

Updates on Global Inward FDI to Asia

Asia's inward FDI proved bullish in 2018, despite dipping global trends.

For a third year, total inward FDI slipped (Figure 2.1). Global estimates for 2018 total $1.3 trillion, a 13.4% contraction from the $1.5 trillion in 2017. Much of the decline was due to the continued drop in investment to developed economies—particularly those in Europe—and to transition economies. Meanwhile, multinational firms based in the US repatriated funds in 2018 due to the 2017 tax cuts, which had considerable impact on global inward investment.[12]

Asia, however, showed resilience amid the declining global inward FDI. Foreign investment to the region picked up in 2018, growing by 6.3% compared with the previous year's 1.1%. This amounted to $559.7 billion, representing 43.1% of the global inward FDI. As a share of gross domestic product (GDP), estimates for Asia remained broadly stable between 2017 and 2018 at 1.9%. Across economies, Hong Kong, China (31.9%) and Singapore (21.5%) had the highest FDI as a percentage of GDP. Mongolia (16.7%), Cambodia (12.7%), and Maldives (10.4%) were also among the highest.

The PRC and Hong Kong, China emerged as the top destinations in Asia (Table 2.1). The PRC received

---

[10] Asia refers to the 49 Asia and Pacific members of the Asian Development Bank (ADB) with available data, which includes Japan and Oceania (Australia and New Zealand) in addition to the developing Asian economies.

[11] The World Investment Report excludes the Caribbean financial centers from the total. These include Anguilla, Antigua and Barbuda, Aruba, the Bahamas, Barbados, British Virgin Islands, the Cayman Islands, Curaçao, Dominica, Grenada, Montserrat, Saint Kitts and Nevis, Saint Lucia, Saint Vincent and the Grenadines, Sint Maarten, and the Turks and Caicos Islands.

[12] The first half of 2018 saw the largest amounts of funds repatriated; however, the amount dropped sharply afterward. Fund repatriation will likely drop further in the future. See Reuters (2018) and Bloomberg (2018).

Figure 2.1: Global Inward FDI by Destination

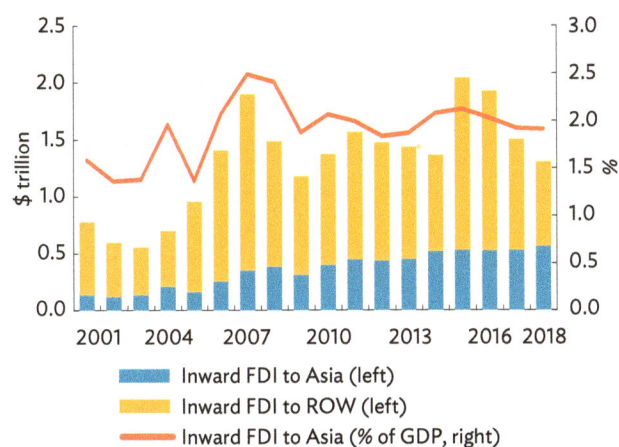

FDI = foreign direct investment, GDP = gross domestic product, ROW = rest of the world.

Sources: ADB calculations using data from Association of Southeast Asian Nations Secretariat. ASEANstats Data Portal. https://data.aseanstats.org/ (accessed July 2019); CEIC; Eurostat. Balance of Payments. https://ec.europa.eu/eurostat (accessed July 2019); International Monetary Fund. World Economic Outlook April 2019 database. https://www.imf.org/external/pubs/ft/weo/2019/01/weodata/index.aspx (accessed April 2019); and United Nations Conference on Trade and Development. World Investment Report 2019 Statistical Annex Tables. http://unctad.org/en/Pages/DIAE/World%20Investment%20Report/Annex-Tables.aspx (accessed June 2019).

$139.0 billion (24.8% of total inward FDI to Asia), while Hong Kong, China received $115.7 billion (20.7%). Meanwhile, 13.9% of total investment to Asia went to Singapore, followed by 10.8% to Australia. Outside the region, investors flocked to the US, as the country attracted over a third of investment to non-Asian economies.

Firm-level data on greenfield FDI and mergers and acquisitions (M&As) for 2018 show a recovery in global committed investments in Asia, after a slump in 2017 (Figure 2.2b).[13] Total committed spending and deal value reached $640.2 billion in 2018, up 70.6% from 2017 estimates. While the majority still originated outside Asia, the intraregional share picked up to 45.3% in 2018 from 42.8% in 2017. The number of projects and deals in Asia rose further in 2018, from 7,500 in 2017 to 8,800 (Figure 2.2a).

Greenfield FDI and M&A deal values from both intraregional and extraregional sources drove the $265.0 billion increase in 2018, with intraregional activity rebounding by 80.5% and extraregional activity by 63.2%.

Table 2.1: Top 10 Global and Asian FDI Destinations ($ billion)

Global	2018	2017	2013	Asia	2018	2017	2013
United States	251.8	277.3	201.4	China, People's Republic of	139.0	134.1	123.9
China, People's Republic of	139.0	134.1	123.9	Hong Kong, China	115.7	110.7	74.3
Hong Kong, China	115.7	110.7	74.3	Singapore	77.6	75.7	56.7
Singapore	77.6	75.7	56.7	Australia	60.4	42.3	56.8
Netherlands	69.7	58.2	51.1	India	42.3	39.9	28.2
United Kingdom	64.5	101.2	51.7	Indonesia	22.0	20.6	18.8
Brazil	61.2	67.6	59.1	Viet Nam	15.5	14.1	8.9
Australia	60.4	42.3	56.8	Korea, Republic of	14.5	17.9	12.8
Spain	43.6	20.9	37.4	Thailand	10.5	6.5	15.5
India	42.3	39.9	28.2	Japan	9.9	10.4	2.3

FDI = foreign direct investment.

Source: ADB calculations using data from United Nations Conference on Trade and Development. World Investment Report 2019 Statistical Annex Tables. http://unctad.org/en/Pages/DIAE/World%20Investment%20Report/Annex-Tables.aspx (accessed June 2019).

[13] Data on greenfield FDI are from fDi Markets and cover cross-border investment in new physical projects, as well as expansion of existing projects that results in new jobs and capital investment. Data on M&As are from the Zephyr M&A database and cover completed and confirmed deals in the specified period (calendar year 2018). Deals refer to M&As, while projects refer to greenfield FDI.

Figure 2.2: FDI by Mode of Entry—Asia

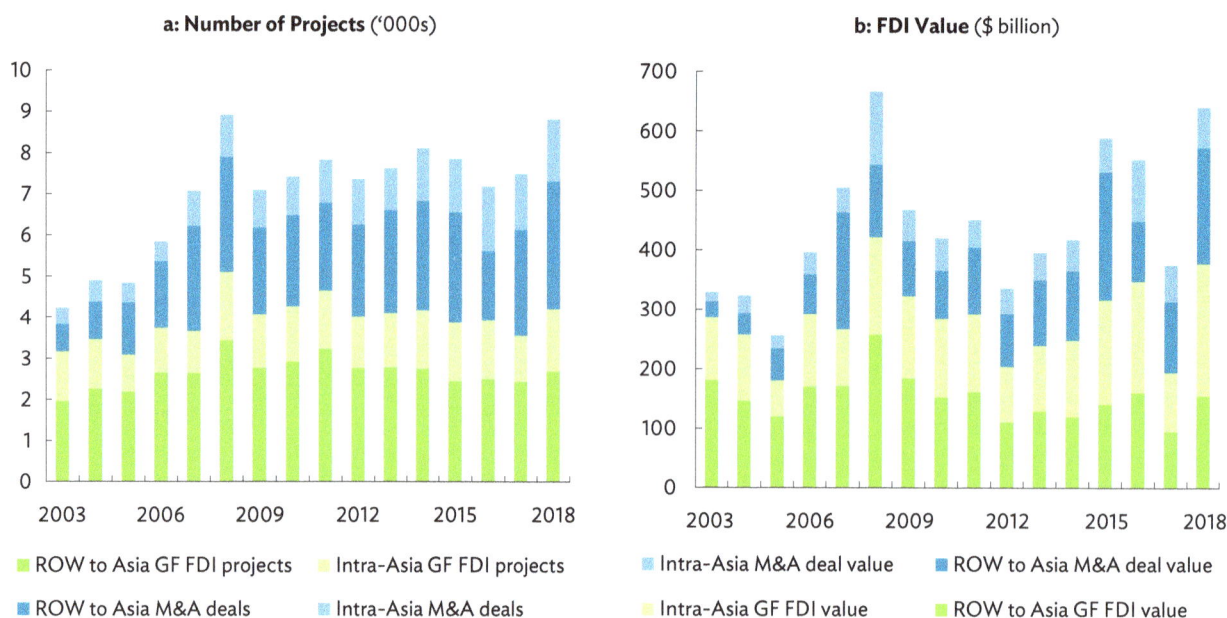

a: **Number of Projects** ('000s)

b: **FDI Value** ($ billion)

- ■ ROW to Asia GF FDI projects
- ■ Intra-Asia GF FDI projects
- ■ ROW to Asia M&A deals
- ■ Intra-Asia M&A deals

- ■ Intra-Asia M&A deal value
- ■ ROW to Asia M&A deal value
- ■ Intra-Asia GF FDI value
- ■ ROW to Asia GF FDI value

FDI = foreign direct investment, GF = greenfield, M&A = mergers and acquisitions, ROW = rest of the world.

Sources: ADB calculations using data from Bureau van Dijk. Zephyr M&A Database; and Financial Times. fDi Markets.

The US served as the foremost source of commitments into Asia, accounting for 20.6% of total allocations (Table 2.2). Greenfield investment from the US almost doubled between 2017 and 2018, while US M&A deals rose in value by roughly 50.0%. Other countries outside the region such as the Cayman Islands (7.0% of total), France (5.8%), Germany (5.2%), and the United Kingdom (UK) (4.5%) are also among those that directed the most committed investment in Asia.

Within the region, the PRC emerged as the top source of committed investment to Asia. The country accounted for 12.1% of Asia's inward investment, putting the PRC next to the US as the largest source. Greenfield FDI from the PRC nearly tripled in 2018, driving its overall contribution upward. Other financial giants such as Japan (8.6% of total) and Singapore (5.0%) were also among top Asian investors.

Chief among beneficiaries of investment in the region is the PRC, which received 29.3% of Asia's inward investment (Table 2.3). India and Australia were also popular FDI destinations in 2018. Capital and deal allocations in India accounted for 12.0% of the total,

while those in Australia accounted for 11.7%. Meanwhile, increased commitments in Indonesia, the Philippines, and Malaysia are worth noting. These countries experienced significant growth in inward investment, largely owing to higher greenfield FDI.

FDI in Indonesia almost quadrupled in 2018 due to the $22.0 billion investment from the PRC—much of which was in the renewable energy sector—$6.0 billion from the Republic of Korea, and $3.7 billion from Japan. FDI also more than quadrupled in the Philippines, with an influx of investment from the PRC in the metals industry ($7.9 billion) and from Thailand in the hotels and tourism industry ($3.1 billion). In Malaysia, FDI almost tripled, with the Philippines as the largest investor. The country invested $3.5 billion in Malaysia's coal, oil, and gas sector and $0.4 billion in the real estate sector.

Increased greenfield project sizes across all sectors and M&A deal sizes in manufacturing and services helped offset the decline in the average M&A deal size in the primary sector (Table 2.4). This resulted in a 45.1% increase in overall project and deal size, from $50.0 million in 2017 to $72.6 million in 2018.

Table 2.2: Top Sources of FDI in Asia—Greenfield and M&As

Source	$ billion		Y-o-Y Change (%)	Share in Total, 2018 (%)
	2018	2017		
United States	132.0	79.5	66.0	20.6
China, People's Republic of	77.3	29.8	159.1	12.1
Japan	55.1	31.3	75.7	8.6
Cayman Islands	44.8	26.6	68.4	7.0
France	37.4	8.0	367.9	5.8
Germany	33.4	16.4	103.8	5.2
Singapore	31.7	29.3	8.3	5.0
Taipei,China	30.9	13.2	133.2	4.8
United Kingdom	28.7	13.9	106.9	4.5
Hong Kong, China	27.5	14.8	86.0	4.3

FDI = foreign direct investment, M&As = mergers and acquisitions, Y-o-Y = year-on-year.

Sources: ADB calculations using data from Bureau van Dijk. Zephyr M&A Database; and Financial Times. fDi Markets.

Table 2.3: Top Destinations of FDI in Asia—Greenfield and M&As

Destination	$ billion		Y-o-Y Change (%)	Share in Total, 2018 (%)
	2018	2017		
China, People's Republic of	187.9	95.7	96.3	29.3
India	77.1	61.9	24.6	12.0
Australia	75.1	47.7	57.5	11.7
Indonesia	42.6	13.0	226.3	6.6
Viet Nam	40.9	22.4	82.5	6.4
Singapore	40.3	34.2	17.8	6.3
Hong Kong, China	26.9	14.0	92.5	4.2
Philippines	22.4	5.0	348.0	3.5
Malaysia	20.4	7.5	170.9	3.2
Japan	19.4	20.8	(7.0)	3.0

( ) = negative, FDI = foreign direct investment, M&As = mergers and acquisitions, Y-o-Y = year-on-year.

Sources: ADB calculations using data from Bureau van Dijk. Zephyr M&A Database; and Financial Times. fDi Markets.

Table 2.4: Average Project and Deal Size—Asia ($ million)

Period	GF	M&As	Total	Greenfield			M&As			Total		
				MFG	PRI	SRV	MFG	PRI	SRV	MFG	PRI	SRV
2017	54.8	45.7	50.0	77.7	287.9	28.1	52.0	195.2	35.7	67.5	219.0	32.7
2018	89.8	56.9	72.6	127.7	480.8	38.0	67.4	72.4	51.7	103.8	207.1	46.1

GF = greenfield, M&As = mergers and acquisitions, MFG = manufacturing, PRI = primary, SRV = services.

Notes: Average project and deal size equals greenfield project value and M&A deal value in Asia divided by number of projects and deals. Asia refers to the regional members of ADB with available data.

Sources: ADB calculations using data from Bureau van Dijk. Zephyr M&A Database; and Financial Times. fDi Markets.

Greenfield FDI in manufacturing nearly doubled between 2017 and 2018, while M&As grew by 66.6% in services, translating into strong FDI activity across most sectors in 2018.

The rise in greenfield FDI in manufacturing, coupled with a similar trend in M&As in services, helped reverse the downturn in 2017 investment (Figure 2.3a). Greenfield FDI in manufacturing increased by $124.5 billion in 2018, accounting for 67.8% of the $183.6 billion increase. Likewise, greenfield FDI to the primary sector and services rose, each accounting for roughly 16.0% of the total. Meanwhile, M&A deals in services accounted for 78.4% of the $82.7 billion increase in the total value of M&A deals, followed by manufacturing, which accounted for over a third of the total increase. High turnout for both sectors cushioned the $13.3 billion decline in the value of deals in the primary sector (Figure 2.3b).

Intraregional activity reinforced these sectoral trends. Much of the increase in intraregional FDI was due to the rise in manufacturing greenfield FDI and M&A deals in services (Figure 2.4a, b). Intraregional greenfield investment in manufacturing rose by $82.5 billion, accounting for two-thirds of the $123.6 billion increase. Much of the higher greenfield FDI in manufacturing came from the PRC (up $28.1 billion); Japan ($15.0 billion); Taipei,China ($9.9 billion); and Singapore ($9.1 billion). Greenfield FDI to services ($22.3 billion) and the primary sector (up $18.8 billion) also rose, but modestly compared with manufacturing. M&A deals in services (up $16.3 billion) and manufacturing (up $1.4 billion) offset the sharp decrease in the primary sector (down $12.1 billion).

Nearly 1 million jobs were committed in Asia in 2018, a new high after a slide in 2017.

The strong influx of greenfield FDI to Asia also revitalized the associated job creation. Jobs created in 2018 due to greenfield investment, both actual and planned, reached 989,293—a 46.8% increase over 2017 levels. Jobs associated with intraregional greenfield FDI reached 562,658, which is a marked improvement from the 308,439 jobs committed in 2017 (Figure 2.5a).

Figure 2.3: Total Inward FDI to Asia by Sector ($ billion)

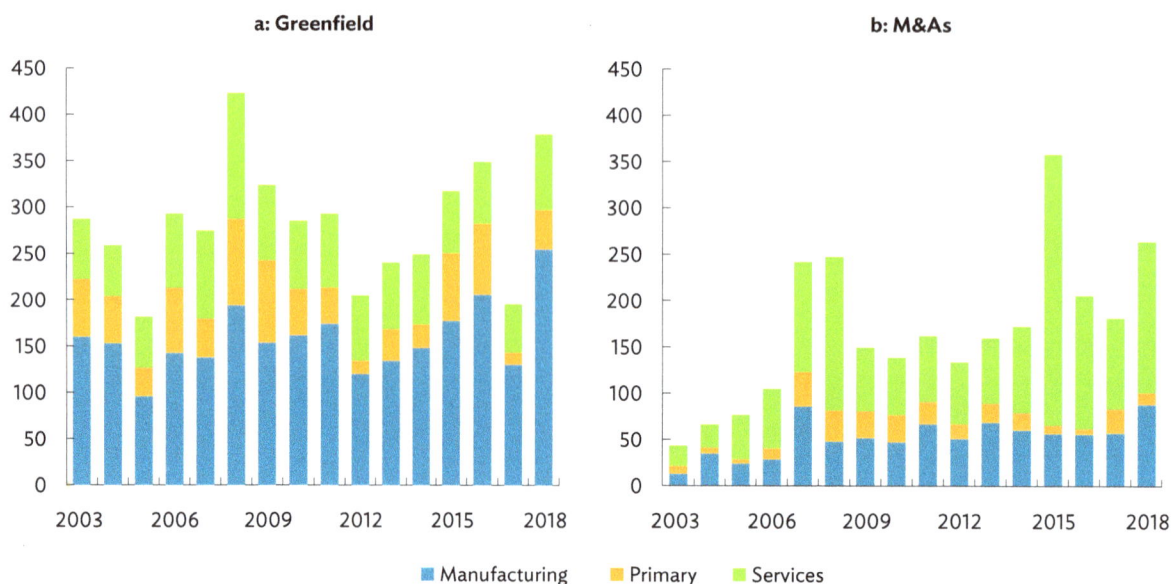

a: Greenfield

b: M&As

■ Manufacturing   ■ Primary   ■ Services

FDI = foreign direct investment, M&As = mergers and acquisitions.

Sources: ADB calculations using data from Financial Times. fDi Markets; and Bureau van Dijk. Zephyr M&A Database.

Figure 2.4: Intra-Asia FDI by Sector ($ billion)

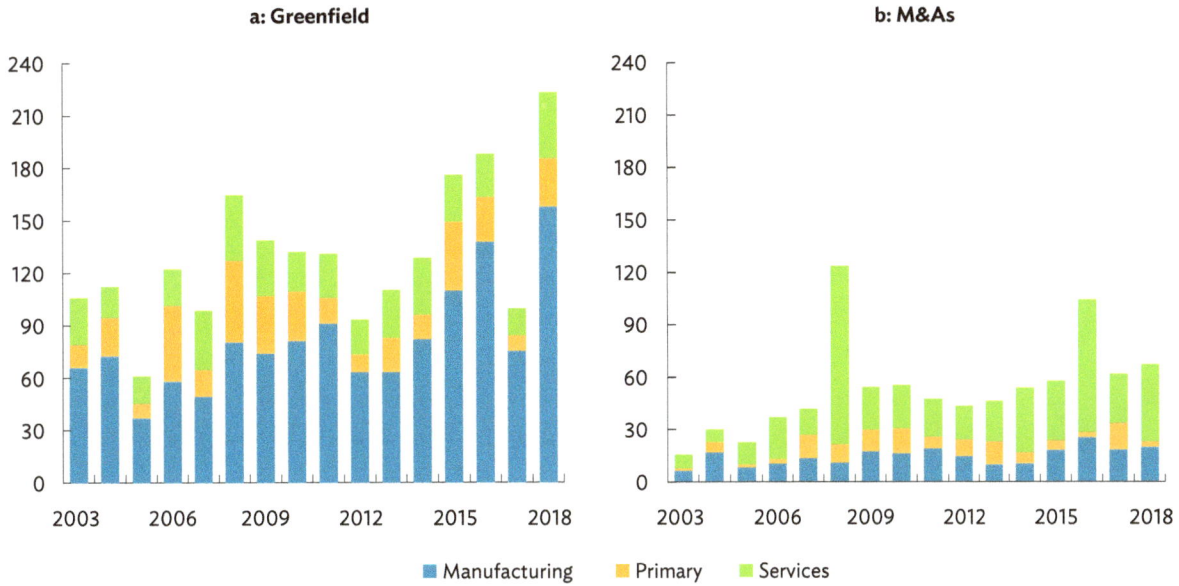

a: Greenfield

b: M&As

■ Manufacturing   ■ Primary   ■ Services

FDI = foreign direct investment, M&As = mergers and acquisitions.

Sources: ADB calculations using data from Bureau van Dijk. Zephyr M&A Database; and Financial Times. fDi Markets.

Figure 2.5: Inward Greenfield FDI Job Creation in Asia by Source

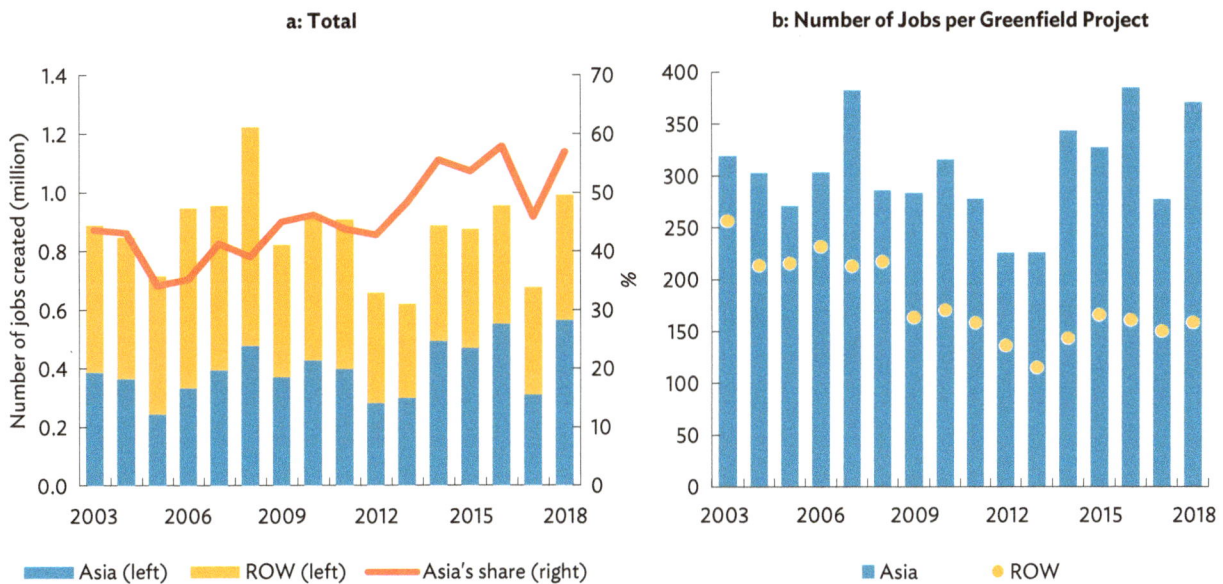

a: Total

b: Number of Jobs per Greenfield Project

■ Asia (left)   ■ ROW (left)   — Asia's share (right)

■ Asia   ● ROW

FDI = foreign direct investment, ROW = rest of the world.

Source: ADB calculations using data from Financial Times. fDi Markets.

In 2018, each greenfield project generated more jobs (Figure 2.5b). The average number of jobs created per project increased to 235 overall compared with 190 in 2017. Projects from intraregional sources generated more jobs on average, with 370 jobs per project in 2018. In turn, Asian countries are also among top sources of total greenfield jobs in Asia (Table 2.5). Greenfield investment from Japan had 123,687 jobs committed in 2018,

Table 2.5: Top Sources of Job Creation in Asia—Greenfield FDI

Destination	Number of Jobs Created ('000)		Y-o-Y Change (%)	Share in Total, 2018 (%)
	2018	2017		
United States	174.2	142.1	22.6	17.6
Japan	123.7	84.0	47.2	12.5
China, People's Republic of	108.1	47.3	128.5	10.9
Singapore	88.5	27.7	219.3	8.9
Hong Kong, China	65.0	22.7	187.0	6.6
Republic of Korea	62.1	43.0	44.5	6.3
Germany	58.2	59.2	(1.6)	5.9
Taipei,China	42.2	42.7	(1.1)	4.3
United Kingdom	38.5	31.7	21.3	3.9
France	24.3	23.7	2.6	2.5

( ) = negative, FDI = foreign direct investment, Y-o-Y = year-on-year.

Source: ADB calculations using data from Financial Times. fDi Markets.

Table 2.6: Top Destinations of Job Creation in Asia—Greenfield FDI

Destination	Number of Jobs Created ('000)		Y-o-Y Change (%)	Share in total, 2018 (%)
	2018	2017		
India	266.2	169.4	57.1	26.9
China, People's Republic of	235.9	154.3	52.9	23.8
Viet Nam	105.2	81.2	29.6	10.6
Philippines	53.5	37.4	43.2	5.4
Indonesia	38.0	20.3	87.6	3.8
Thailand	35.1	26.6	31.7	3.5
Singapore	32.0	30.5	4.7	3.2
Australia	31.1	24.5	27.0	3.1
Malaysia	29.9	23.4	27.8	3.0
Japan	26.7	19.2	39.1	2.7

FDI = foreign direct investment, Y-o-Y = year-on-year.

Source: ADB calculations using data from Financial Times. fDi Markets.

followed by investment from the PRC (108,132 jobs); Singapore (88,529); Hong Kong, China (65,007); the Republic of Korea (62,140); and Taipei,China (42,213). Investment from the US generated the most in 2018, with 174,249 jobs. Other top extraregional sources were Germany (58,230), the UK (38,516), and France (24,300).

India and the PRC gained many new jobs in 2018, as committed jobs in those countries accounted for 50.8% of the total jobs created in Asia (Table 2.6). Southeast Asia also benefited from the high job creation. Together, jobs in Viet Nam, the Philippines, Indonesia, Thailand, Singapore, and Malaysia accounted for 29.7% of jobs created in Asia.

Job creation rebounded across all sectors, with much of the new jobs in manufacturing (Figure 2.6a). New manufacturing jobs reached 727,763, accounting for 73.6% of total for 2018. Greenfield FDI in services generated 248,649 jobs, a 22.0% increase from 2017.

Figure 2.6: Inward Greenfield FDI Job Creation in Asia by Sector

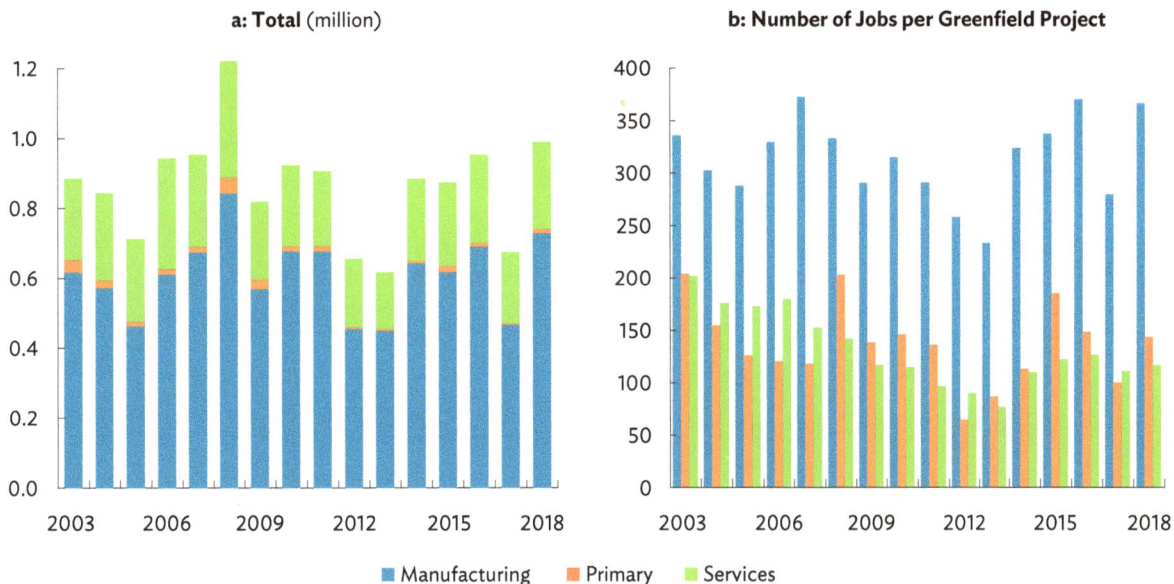

a: Total (million)

b: Number of Jobs per Greenfield Project

■ Manufacturing   ■ Primary   ■ Services

FDI = foreign direct investment.

Source: ADB calculations using data from Financial Times. fDi Markets.

Though the primary sector had the smallest share, job creation in the sector nearly tripled in 2018 from 4,688 to 12,881. Investment projects in manufacturing also continued to be the most job intensive, averaging 366 jobs per project, well above those in the primary sector (143 jobs) and services (117 jobs) (Figure 2.6b).

Updates on Regional Trends

Global and intraregional investors continue to invest largely in East Asia. Over half of the world's investment to Asia, as well as that of intraregional investment, headed toward the subregion.

Based on standard balance of payments data, FDI to Asia increased by $33.1 billion in 2018 to $559.7 billion, from $526.6 billion in 2017. Developing Asia hosted $488.0 billion, 3.5% higher than 2017. Meanwhile, FDI to developed Asia grew by 29.7% to $71.7 billion in 2018, reversing the 16.7% decline in 2017. East Asia continues to host over 50.0% of global FDI to Asia, largely due to investment in the PRC and Hong Kong, China

(Figure 2.7). Southeast Asia also attracted a fair amount of investment, with four countries from the region (Singapore, Indonesia, Viet Nam, and Thailand) among the top 10 Asian destinations for global FDI

Investment rebounded in almost all subregions, particularly in East Asia and the Pacific and Oceania. Total FDI to East Asia increased by $10.3 billion to $288.2 billion in 2018, with the increase originating mainly outside the region. The UK, the US, and Germany were the top sources of higher investment. A 42.9% increase in Australia's inward FDI was behind the recovery in investment to the Pacific and Oceania. Increased investment from Canada, the PRC, and Germany helped buoy FDI to the subregion.

Inward FDI also increased in Southeast Asia (up $4.5 billion) and South Asia (up $3.4 billion) in 2018. Thailand (up $4.0 billion) and Singapore (up $1.9 billion) largely benefited from increased investment. Luxembourg; Japan; and Hong Kong, China had the largest increases in FDI to Southeast Asia in 2018. In South Asia, India (up $2.4 billion) and Bangladesh (up $1.5 billion) received most of the increased investment,

Figure 2.7: Global Inward FDI to Asia by Destination Subregion ($ billion)

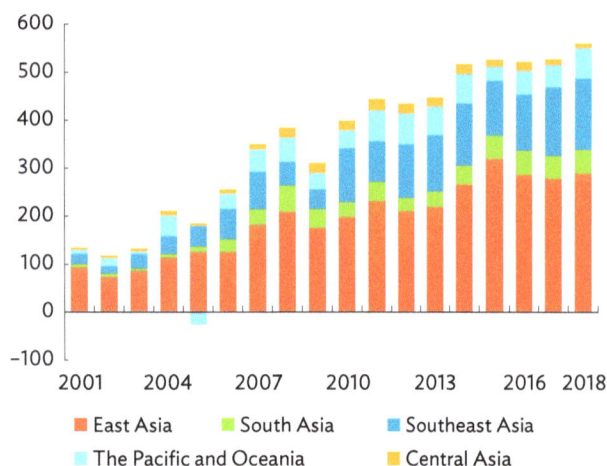

FDI = foreign direct investment.

Sources: ADB calculations using data from Association of Southeast Asian Nations Secretariat. ASEANstats Data Portal. https://data.aseanstats.org/ (accessed July 2019); CEIC; Eurostat. Balance of Payments. https://ec.europa.eu/ eurostat (accessed July 2019); International Monetary Fund. World Economic Outlook April 2019 database. https://www.imf.org/external/pubs/ft/weo/2019/01/ weodata/index.aspx (accessed April 2019); and United Nations Conference on Trade and Development. World Investment Report 2019 Statistical Annex Tables. http://unctad.org/en/Pages/DIAE/World%20Investment%20Report/Annex-Tables.aspx (accessed June 2019).

Figure 2.8: Intraregional FDI Inflows—Asia

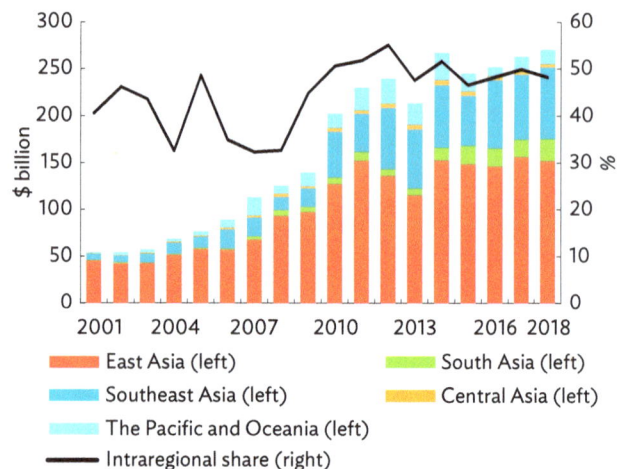

FDI = foreign direct investment.

Note: Based on balance of payments data. Due to limited availability of bilateral FDI data, missing values were imputed with gravity model estimates.

Sources: ADB calculations using data from Association of Southeast Asian Nations Secretariat. ASEANstats Data Portal. https://data.aseanstats.org/ (accessed July 2019); CEIC; Eurostat. Balance of Payments. https://ec.europa.eu/ eurostat (accessed July 2019); International Monetary Fund. World Economic Outlook April 2019 database. https://www.imf.org/external/pubs/ft/weo/2019/01/ weodata/index.aspx (accessed April 2019); and United Nations Conference on Trade and Development. World Investment Report 2019 Statistical Annex Tables. http://unctad.org/en/Pages/DIAE/World%20Investment%20Report/Annex-Tables.aspx (accessed June 2019).

with increased FDI to the subregion originating primarily from Asian countries such as Singapore, Japan, and the Republic of Korea.

Meanwhile, global investment to Central Asia continued to decline in 2018, from $12.0 billion in 2017 to $9.5 billion in 2018. Azerbaijan (down $1.5 billion) and Kazakhstan (down $0.9 billion) were most affected by the fall.

Asia's intraregional linkages continued to grow in 2018 (Figure 2.8). Intraregional FDI rose 2.8% from $262.7 billion in 2017 to $270.1 billion in 2018—a 48.2% share of inward FDI to Asia. Intraregional investors continued to favor East Asia, with 56.2% of intraregional investment heading toward the subregion. Asian investors also favored Southeast Asia, with the subregion attracting 28.2% of intraregional investment.

Investment grew across most subregions, particularly in South Asia. Asian FDI to South Asia grew by 26.9% in

2018, reversing a 2017 decline. FDI to Southeast Asia from Asian countries also increased in 2018 by 9.9%. Meanwhile, Asia's FDI to East Asia contracted by 2.6%.

Firm-level data also show a recovery in intraregional greenfield and M&A commitments, with 2018 estimates reaching $289.9 billion from $160.6 billion in 2017. While intraregional deal values increased by 9.3% in 2018 from $61.2 billion in 2017, the bulk of the increase was due to increased intraregional greenfield FDI. This more than doubled in 2018, from $99.4 in 2017 to $223.0 billion.

The PRC continued to be an active investor and an attractive destination of FDI (Box 2.1). The country was both the largest investor and largest recipient of intraregional greenfield investment in 2018. The country invested $58.1 billion in Asia in 2018, the largest in Indonesian renewable energy. The PRC's Sinohydro Corporation committed $17.8 billion to an Indonesian project in April 2018, with 1,029 new jobs expected.

The PRC received $48.0 billion in Asian greenfield investment. Taipei,China was the largest investor in the PRC, with $12.0 billion in committed capital expenditures. Electronics manufacturer Foxconn allotted $9.0 billion for PRC semiconductors, making it the largest source of greenfield FDI from Taipei,China to the PRC.

Intraregional share has remained stable since 2010 and has fluctuated around 50.0% over the past 9 years (Figure 2.9). Intraregional activity relies in large part on investment within subregions. In 2018, 28.8% of total inward FDI to Asia was intra-subregional investment. However, investment across subregions has regained traction since 2015, with the share of inter-subregional investment increasing to 19.4% in 2018.

Figure 2.9: Regional FDI Share—Asia (%)

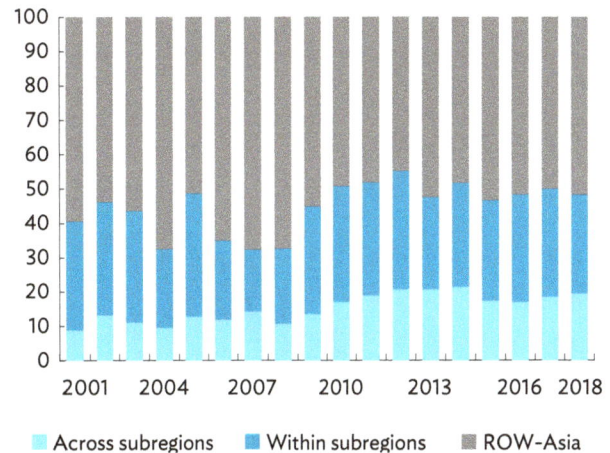

FDI = foreign direct investment, ROW = rest of the world.

Sources: ADB calculations using data from Association of Southeast Asian Nations Secretariat. ASEANstats Data Portal. https://data.aseanstats.org/ (accessed July 2019); CEIC; Eurostat. Balance of Payments. https://ec.europa.eu/eurostat (accessed July 2019); International Monetary Fund. World Economic Outlook April 2019 database. https://www.imf.org/external/pubs/ft/weo/2019/01/weodata/index.aspx (accessed April 2019); and United Nations Conference on Trade and Development. World Investment Report 2019 Statistical Annex Tables. http://unctad.org/en/Pages/DIAE/World%20Investment%20Report/Annex-Tables.aspx (accessed June 2019).

Box 2.1: Trends of Foreign Direct Investment in the People's Republic of China

The People's Republic of China (PRC) has been an attractive destination and a formidable source of foreign direct investment (FDI), with its high economic growth over recent decades. According to standard balance of payments data, its share of global and Asian investment continued to increase between 2001 and 2018. In fact, the PRC accounted for more than 10% of the world's inward or outward investment in 2018, while accounting for roughly 25% of Asia's outward FDI (Box Figure 1).

Investment to the PRC tripled between 2001 and 2018, reaching $139.0 billion. The PRC's investment appetite increased much faster over the years, reaching a peak in 2016 of $196.1 billion. Since 2016, however, the country's outward investment has moderated.

FDI Flows in the PRC

Asia has continuously been the largest source of FDI to the PRC, with over half of the country's FDI coming from within the region (Box Figure 2). Since 2013, roughly 75% of the PRC's inward FDI was from Asian investors, with the intraregional share peaking at 82.1% in 2017. Hong Kong, China has consistently been the top investor in the PRC, with its average share over 66% of Asia's FDI

1: Inward and Outward FDI—People's Republic of China

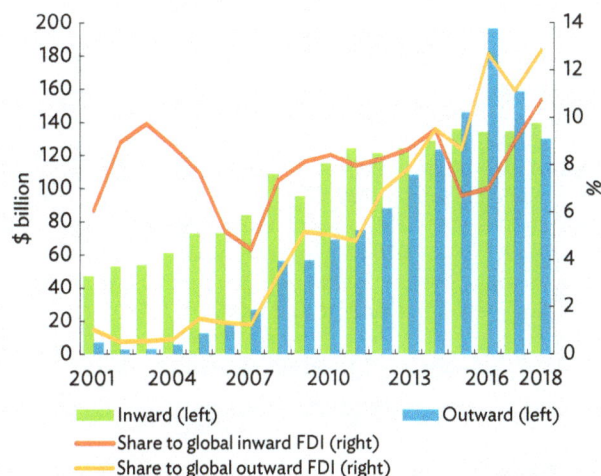

FDI = foreign direct investment.

Source: ADB calculations using data from United Nations Conference on Trade and Development. World Investment Report 2019 Statistical Annex Tables. http://unctad.org/en/Pages/DIAE/World%20Investment%20Report/Annex-Tables.aspx (accessed June 2019).

continued on next page

Box 2.1: Trends of Foreign Direct Investment in the People's Republic of China (*continued*)

2: Inward FDI by Source Region—People's Republic of China ($ billion)

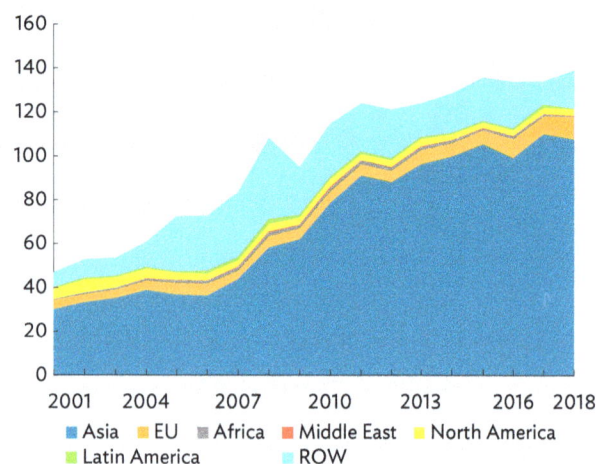

EU = European Union, FDI = foreign direct investment, ROW = rest of the world.

Note: FDI is based on balance of payments definition.

Sources: ADB calculations using data from Association of Southeast Asian Nations Secretariat. ASEANstats Data Portal. https://data.aseanstats.org/ (accessed July 2019); CEIC; Eurostat. Balance of Payments. https://ec.europa.eu/eurostat (accessed July 2019); International Monetary Fund. World Economic Outlook April 2019 database. https://www.imf.org/external/pubs/ft/weo/2019/01/weodata/index.aspx (accessed April 2019); and United Nations Conference on Trade and Development. World Investment Report 2019 Statistical Annex Tables. http://unctad.org/en/Pages/DIAE/World%20Investment%20Report/Annex-Tables.aspx (accessed June 2019).

to the PRC. In 2018, Hong Kong, China accounted for 83.5% (or $89.9 billion) of Asia's investment in the PRC. Singapore is a distant second ($5.2 billion), followed by the Republic of Korea ($4.7 billion), Japan ($3.8 billion), and Samoa ($1.6 billion).

Outside Asia, the British Virgin Islands ($4.7 billion), the Cayman Islands ($4.1 billion), and Germany ($3.7 billion) were among the top sources of FDI to the PRC. FDI from the United States (US) increased to $2.7 billion in 2018 from $2.6 billion in 2017, despite growing trade tensions. However, the 1.5% growth was well below the increases in preceding years (14.2% in 2016 and 11.0% in 2017).

Greenfield FDI and M&As in the PRC

Based on firm-level data, approximately 40.0% of the greenfield FDI in 2018 went to automotive original equipment manufacturers (OEM) and chemicals, with about 20.0% apiece. Capital expenditure from US-based Tesla Motors was the largest contributor in the PRC's automotive OEM sector, with $5.2 billion in investment during May and July 2018. German company BASF directed $10.3 billion in the chemicals sector. The PRC also benefited from capital from Taipei,China's Foxconn, which invested $9.0 billion in semiconductors, as well as from Hong Kong, China's Hongkong Land Holdings, which invested approximately $3 billion in real estate.

Mergers and acquisitions (M&As) in the PRC also increased in 2018. Over half the 2018 amount went to communications, which garnered $42.2 billion in M&A deals. Many of these were in data processing, hosting, and related services, the largest of which was a stake gained by the US-based Carlyle Group LP in the Ant Financial Services group ($14.0 billion). Alibaba's holding company based in the Cayman Islands also contributed to the PRC communications sector when it acquired Shanghai Lazhasi Information Technology Co., LTD for $5.4 billion and increased its capital in Ant Financial Services Group by $5.0 billion.

A considerable amount of the PRC's outward greenfield investment went to alternative and renewable energy. The largest project—and overall from the PRC—was Sinohydro Corporation's $17.8 billion investment in Indonesia in April 2018. The PRC also invested in metals, the largest two in the Philippines. Hesteel Group invested $4.4 billion in December 2018, while a project from the Panhua Group generated $3.5 billion in June 2018.

In 2018, the PRC's outward FDI was redirected considerably within the region, as East Asia and Southeast Asia benefited the most with the PRC investment almost quadrupling in amount (Box Table). Southeast Asia accounted for more than a quarter of total PRC outward investment, and East Asia more than a tenth. The PRC's investment outside the region fell to $79 billion in 2018 from $142 billion in 2017.

Outward FDI— People's Republic of China ($ million, % share of total in parentheses)

Destination	2010–2016 Annual Average		2017		2018	
Central Asia	1,213.9	(1.3)	4,309.8	(2.5)	6,180.1	(3.9)
East Asia	12,368.7	(12.8)	4,304.5	(2.5)	18,954.1	(12.1)
South Asia	6,660.9	(6.9)	6,872.8	(4.0)	6,502.2	(4.2)
Southeast Asia	12,701.2	(13.1)	9,183.9	(5.3)	41,702.5	(26.6)
The Pacific and Oceania	3,853.9	(4.0)	5,165.0	(3.0)	3,969.4	(2.5)
Rest of the World	60,024.5	(62.0)	142,101.8	(82.6)	79,282.6	(50.6)

FDI = foreign direct investment.

Note: Outward FDI includes greenfield FDI and mergers and acquisitions.

Sources: ADB calculations using data from Bureau van Dijk. Zephyr M&A Database; and Financial Times. fDi Markets.

Source: ADB staff.

Outward Foreign Direct Investment

Global outward FDI contracted in 2018, mainly due to lower investment from developed countries.

In 2018, outward FDI from developed countries totaled $558.4 billion—a 39.6% decline from 2017 estimates (Figure 2.10). This drove the share of FDI from developed countries down from 62.1% in 2017 to 55.1% of global outward FDI, its lowest thus far. The US, which was the top source of global FDI in 2017, took a back seat in 2018 in favor of repatriated funds of foreign multinationals due to the tax overhaul, leading to a negative $63.6 billion in 2018, a reversal from its $300.4 billion outward investment in 2017. Consequently, global outward FDI from the world declined by 28.9% in 2018 to $1.0 trillion from $1.4 trillion in 2017.

Asia's investment to the world declined by 7.4% in 2018 to $500.6 billion. Higher outward investment from other Asian countries was not enough to offset the decline in outward FDI from powerhouses such as the PRC (–$28.5 billion), Japan (–$17.3 billion), and Singapore (–$6.6 billion).

Figure 2.10: Global Outward FDI by Source

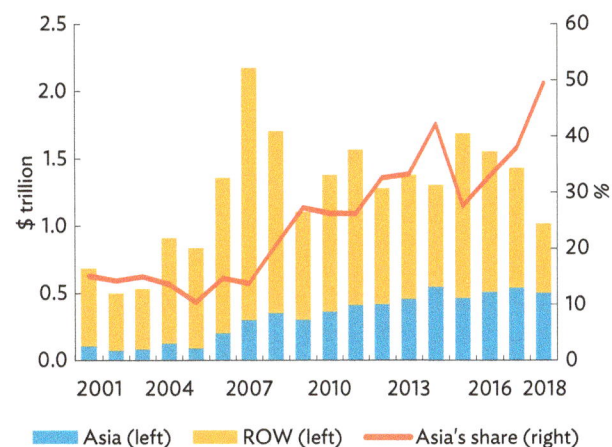

FDI = foreign direct investment, ROW = rest of the world.

Source: ADB calculations using data from United Nations Conference on Trade and Development. World Investment Report 2019 Statistical Annex Tables. http://unctad.org/en/Pages/DIAE/World%20Investment%20Report/Annex-Tables.aspx (accessed June 2019).

Over the years, Asia has cemented its status as a major source of global investment. Asia's share in global outward FDI rose to 49.4% in 2018, its highest thus far. Both Japan and the PRC overtook countries outside the region as top sources of outward FDI (Table 2.7). In 2018, Japan invested $143.2 billion globally, while the PRC invested $129.8 billion. France ($102.4 billion); Hong Kong, China ($85.2 billion); and Germany

Table 2.7: Top 10 Sources of Global and Asian FDI ($ billion)

Global				Asia				
2018		2017		2018		2017		
Japan	143.2	United States	300.4	Japan	143.2	Japan	160.4	
PRC	129.8	Japan	160.4	PRC	129.8	PRC	158.3	
France	102.4	PRC	158.3	Hong Kong, China	85.2	Hong Kong, China	86.7	
Hong Kong, China	85.2	United Kingdom	117.5	Korea, Republic of	38.9	Singapore	43.7	
Germany	77.1	Germany	91.8	Singapore	37.1	Korea, Republic of	34.1	
Netherlands	59.0	Hong Kong, China	86.7	Taipei,China	18.0	Thailand	17.1	
British Virgin Islands	56.0	Canada	79.8	Thailand	17.7	Taipei,China	11.6	
Canada	50.5	British Virgin Islands	54.7	India	11.0	India	11.1	
United Kingdom	49.9	Singapore	43.7	Indonesia	8.1	Malaysia	5.6	
Cayman Islands	40.4	France	41.3	Malaysia	5.3	Australia	3.3	

FDI = foreign direct investment, PRC = People's Republic of China.

Source: ADB calculations using data from United Nations Conference on Trade and Development. World Investment Report 2018 Statistical Annex Tables. http://unctad.org/en/Pages/DIAE/World%20Investment%20Report/Annex-Tables.aspx (accessed June 2019).

($77.1 billion) were also among the top five sources of global investment. In Asia, the Republic of Korea ($38.9 billion) and Singapore ($37.1 billion) were among the top.

Despite the 8.0% contraction in 2018, East Asia continued as the largest source of FDI from Asia (Figure 2.11). Investment from the subregion accounted for 82.9% of Asia's outward FDI. Apart from consistently large investment from Japan; the PRC; Hong Kong, China; and the Republic of Korea, investment from Taipei,China grew by 56.0% from $11.6 billion in 2017 to $18.0 billion in 2018.

Southeast Asia remains the second-largest source, with a 13.9% share. Increased investment from Thailand, Indonesia—whose global investment nearly quadrupled between 2017 and 2018—and Viet Nam helped cushion contractions from Singapore and Malaysia. This resulted in a moderate 1.7% decline. Global outward investment also declined from South Asia (down 2.4%) and Central Asia (down 73.2%). Meanwhile, investment from the Pacific and Oceania grew 19.3% in 2018, mostly due to increased investment from Australia (up 9.5%) and a positive reversal in New Zealand's investment.

Figure 2.11: Asia's Outward FDI by Source ($ billion)

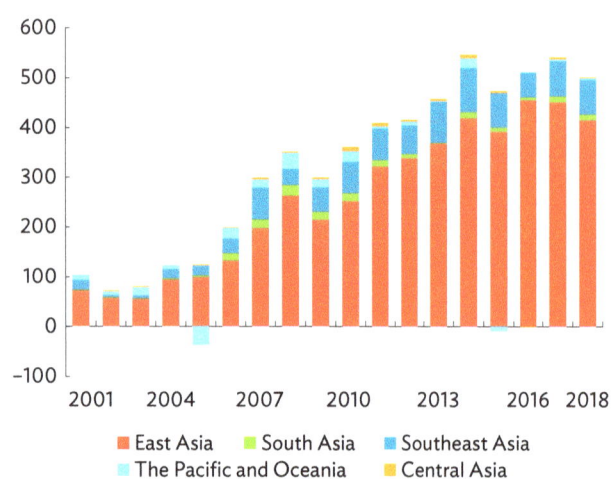

FDI = foreign direct investment.

Source: ADB calculations using data from United Nations Conference on Trade and Development. World Investment Report 2018 Statistical Annex Tables. http://unctad.org/en/Pages/DIAE/World%20Investment%20Report/Annex-Tables.aspx (accessed June 2019).

Combined greenfield and M&A FDI from Asia to the rest of the world dipped in 2018 in contrast to inward FDI (Figure 2.12). Though Asia's outward greenfield FDI increased by $21.4 billion, this was not enough to offset a $75.5 billion decline in M&As, due mostly to a fall in manufacturing M&As (–$67.3 billion). Overall, FDI activity based on firm-level data slid by $54.0 billion in 2018. FDI from Asia declined largely in destinations outside the region, particularly Switzerland (–$43.8 billion), the US (–$28.8 billion), the UK (–$12.2 billion), and Czech Republic (–$10.5 billion).

Asia's extraregional greenfield investment is primarily in manufacturing, with a 65.6% share in 2018 (Figure 2.12). However, recent years have seen a relatively gradual increase in the share of the primary sector and services. In 2018, 18.2% of Asia's extraregional greenfield FDI was directed toward projects in the primary sector, while 16.3% went into services. The majority of Asia's M&As outside the region were in services. In 2018, the sector's share reached 57.2%. Manufacturing M&As followed at 34.7%.

Higher intraregional deal and project values in 2018 (up $129.4 billion to $289.9 billion) cushioned the decline in extraregional ones, resulting in an increase in overall outward greenfield investment and M&As (up $74.8 billion to $559.0 billion). In turn, jobs due to greenfield FDI from Asia recovered in 2018 (Figure 2.13). Actual and planned jobs created by Asian greenfield FDI reached 848,840. This surpassed the 2016 level of 810,315.

The majority of the jobs created were due to intraregional investment (66.3% or 562,658), with jobs generated in the PRC (125,514), India (117,656), and Viet Nam (76,439) accounting for over half of intraregional new jobs. Outside the region, the US emerged on top with 55,363 jobs generated from Asia's greenfield FDI, followed by the Russian Federation (22,822), the UK (19,928), and Mexico (17,477).

Greenfield FDI from Asia's strong economies—such as the PRC, Japan, and Singapore—generated the most jobs in 2018. Over 57.0% of total jobs generated by Asian greenfield FDI came from those countries, with the PRC accounting for 207,816 jobs; Japan, 181,706 jobs; and Singapore, 101,869 jobs.

Figure 2.12: Asia's Outward FDI to the Rest of the World by Sector ($ billion)

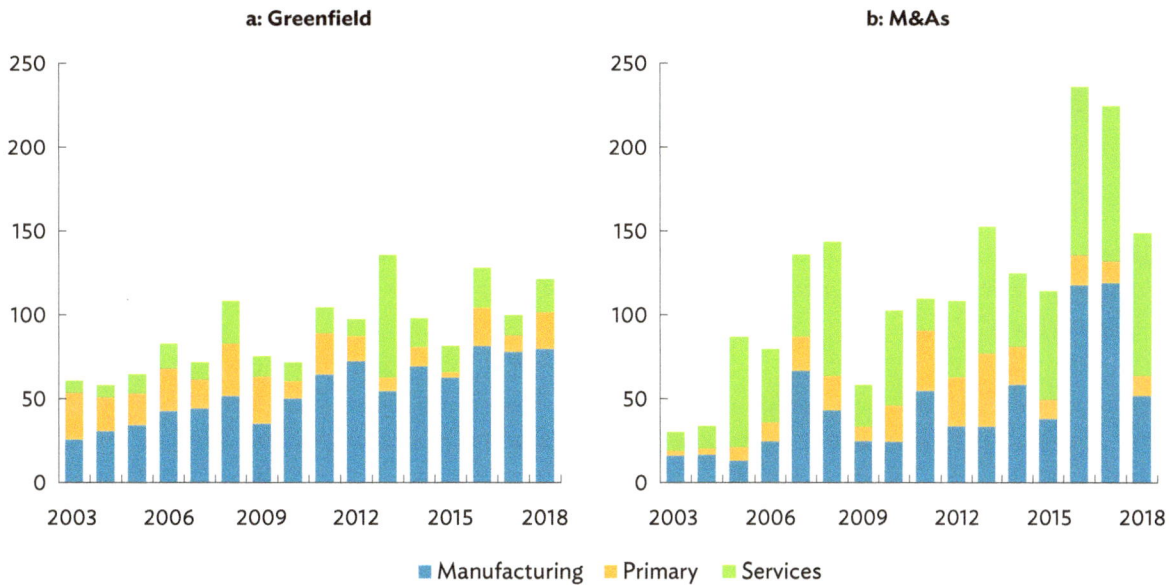

a: Greenfield

b: M&As

■ Manufacturing   ■ Primary   ■ Services

FDI = foreign direct investment, M&A = mergers and acquisitions.

Sources: ADB calculations using data from Bureau van Dijk. Zephyr M&A Database; and Financial Times. fDi Markets.

Figure 2.13: Jobs Created by Asian Greenfield FDI by Destination

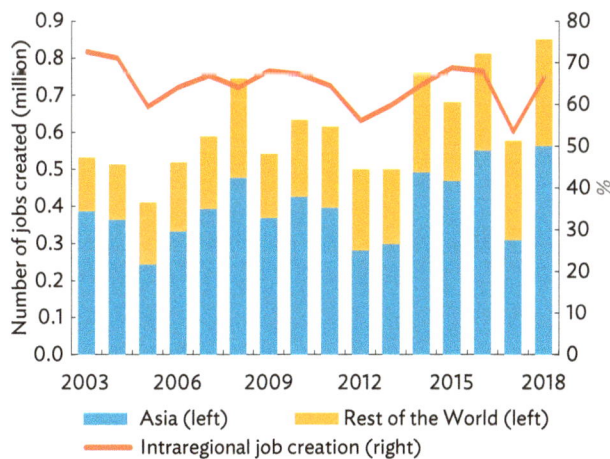

■ Asia (left)   ■ Rest of the World (left)
— Intraregional job creation (right)

FDI = foreign direct investment.

Source: ADB calculations using data from Financial Times. fDi Markets.

Figure 2.14: Total FDI Flows—Asia ($ billion)

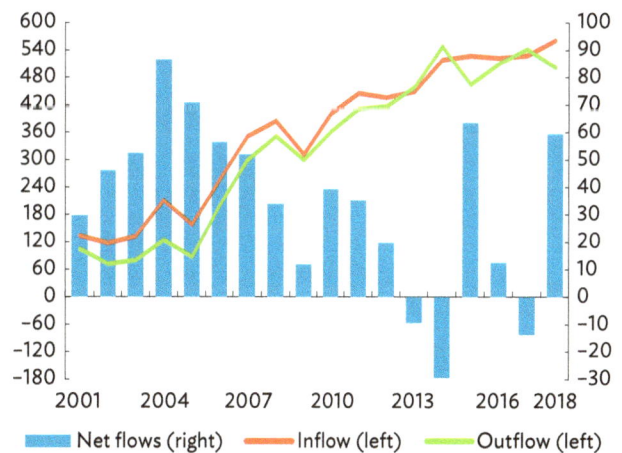

■ Net flows (right)   — Inflow (left)   — Outflow (left)

FDI = foreign direct investment.

Sources: ADB calculations using data from Association of Southeast Asian Nations Secretariat. ASEANstats Database. https://www.aseanstats.org/ (accessed July 2019); and United Nations Conference on Trade and Development. World Investment Report 2019 Statistical Annex Tables. http://unctad.org/en/Pages/DIAE/World%20Investment%20Report/Annex-Tables.aspx (accessed June 2019).

After first turning negative in 2013, Asia's net FDI flows have generally fluctuated between positive and negative (Figure 2.14). Larger investment came to Asia in 2015 and 2016, while 2017 saw higher outward than inward investment. In 2018, a dip in Asia's outward investment and an increase in inward FDI resulted in positive net investment flows.

References

Association of Southeast Asian Nations Secretariat. ASEANstats Database. https://www.aseanstats.org/ (accessed July 2019).

Bloomberg. 2018. U.S. Cash Repatriation Plunges 50%, Defying Trump's Tax Forecast. 19 December. https://www.bloomberg.com/news/articles/2018-12-19/u-s-offshore-repatriated-cash-fell-almost-50-in-third-quarter.

Eurostat. Balance of Payments. http://ec.europa.eu/eurostat/web/balance-of-payments/data/database (accessed July 2019).

International Monetary Fund. World Economic Outlook, April 2019 database. https://www.imf.org/external/pubs/ft/weo/2018/01/weodata/download.aspx (accessed April 2019).

Reuters. 2018. U.S. Companies Repatriate Over Half a Trillion Dollars in 2018, but pace slows. 31 December. https://www.reuters.com/article/us-us-repatriation-companies/u-s-companies-repatriate-over-half-a-trillion-dollars-in-2018-but-pace-slows-idUSKCN1OU0ME.

United Nations Conference on Trade and Development. 2019. *World Investment Report 2019: Special Economic Zones.* Geneva.

———. Bilateral FDI Statistics. http://unctad.org/en/Pages/DIAE/FDI%20Statistics/FDI-Statistics-Bilateral.aspx (accessed June 2019).

———. World Investment Report 2019 Statistical Annex Tables. https://unctad.org/en/Pages/DIAE/World%20Investment%20Report/Annex-Tables.aspx (accessed June 2019).

3 Financial Integration

Asia's Cross-Border Financial Assets and Liabilities

Asia's cross-border financial linkages continue to grow and strengthen, with a pronounced increase in outward foreign direct investment (FDI) and equity. FDI grew from $3.2 trillion in 2013 to $4.2 trillion in 2017, while equity expanded from $2.5 trillion in 2013 to $4.2 trillion in 2018. Between 2013 and

2018, Asia's cross-border assets increased by $3.7 trillion, with a significant contribution of the increase coming from cross-border portfolio equity holdings.[14]

Asia's cross-border assets increased by a compounded annual growth rate (CAGR) of 4.9%—from $13.7 trillion in 2013 to $17.4 trillion in 2018. Asia's intraregional share remained broadly stable at 24.0% in 2018 (24.2% in 2013) (Figure 3.1).[15]

Figure 3.1: Cross-Border Assets—Asia

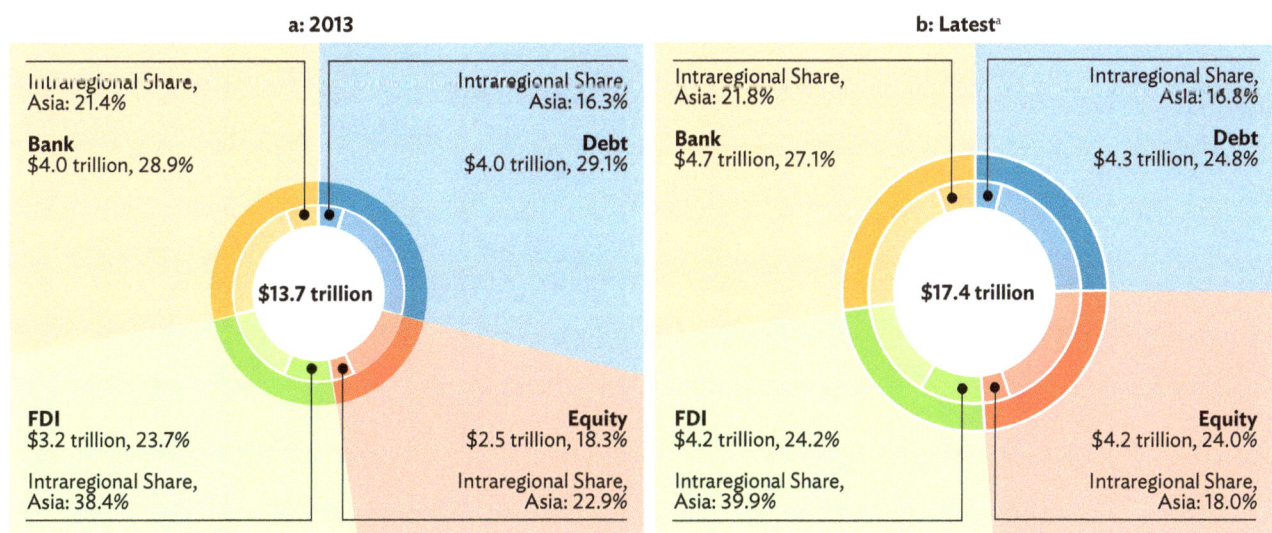

a: 2013

Intraregional Share, Asia: 21.4%
Bank $4.0 trillion, 28.9%

Intraregional Share, Asia: 16.3%
Debt $4.0 trillion, 29.1%

$13.7 trillion

FDI $3.2 trillion, 23.7%
Intraregional Share, Asia: 38.4%

Equity $2.5 trillion, 18.3%
Intraregional Share, Asia: 22.9%

b: Latest[a]

Intraregional Share, Asia: 21.8%
Bank $4.7 trillion, 27.1%

Intraregional Share, Asia: 16.8%
Debt $4.3 trillion, 24.8%

$17.4 trillion

FDI $4.2 trillion, 24.2%
Intraregional Share, Asia: 39.9%

Equity $4.2 trillion, 24.0%
Intraregional Share, Asia: 18.0%

FDI = foreign direct investment.

Notes: FDI assets refer to outward FDI holdings. Bank assets refer to bank claims of reporting Asian economies. Asia includes ADB regional members for which data are available.

[a] As of December 2018 for Bank, Debt, and Equity, and as of December 2017 for FDI.

Sources: ADB calculations using data from Bank for International Settlements. Locational Banking Statistics. https://www.bis.org/statistics/bankstats.htm (accessed September 2019); International Monetary Fund (IMF). Coordinated Direct Investment Survey. http://data.imf.org/CDIS (accessed May 2019); and IMF. Coordinated Portfolio Investment Survey. http://data.imf.org/CPIS (accessed September 2019).

---

14   There is a slight difference between the figures presented for 2017 in AEIR 2018 and AEIR 2019/2020 due to data revisions.

15   Throughout this chapter, Asia's cross-border asset holdings refer to the stock of outward portfolio debt, portfolio equity, FDI, and bank claims. Asia's cross-border liabilities refer to the stock of inward portfolio debt, portfolio equity, FDI, and bank liabilities.

The increase in cross-border portfolio debt was benign. However, increases in bank claims ($0.7 trillion), FDI ($1.0 trillion), and cross-border portfolio equity ($1.7 trillion) were more pronounced by their sheer size. The intraregional share for FDI increased to 39.9% from 38.4%, bank claims grew to 21.8% from 21.4%, and cross-border portfolio debt to 16.8% from 16.3%. However, the intraregional share for cross-border portfolio equity declined to 18.0% from 22.9%.

Between 2013 and 2018, Asia's cross-border liabilities also increased, largely due to a substantial increase in inward FDI holdings and portfolio equity investment.

Asia's cross-border liabilities increased by a CAGR of 4.5%, from $14.4 trillion in 2013 to $18.0 trillion in 2018, while Asia's intraregional share declined from 31.4% to 30.9% (Figure 3.2). FDI holdings grew by $1.6 trillion, while the intraregional share declined to 42.9%. Inward

cross-border portfolio debt increased by $0.6 trillion and cross-border portfolio equity investment outstanding rose by $1.1 trillion. But the intraregional share of cross-border portfolio debt declined to 25.6% from 29.2% and cross-border portfolio equity investment outstanding increased slightly to 16.1% from 16.2%. Outstanding bank liabilities increased moderately by $0.1 trillion from 2013 to 2018, with a considerable increase in the intraregional share from 19.8% in 2013 to 26.2% 2018.

Outward Portfolio Investment[16]

Asian portfolio debt and equity investors continue to prefer investing outside the region, apparent from their moderate, stable intraregional share. Asia's outward portfolio debt investment outstanding was $4.3 trillion in 2018, up from $4.2 trillion in 2017, while outward portfolio equity investment was $4.2 trillion in 2018, down from $4.5 trillion in 2017.

Figure 3.2: Cross-Border Liabilities—Asia

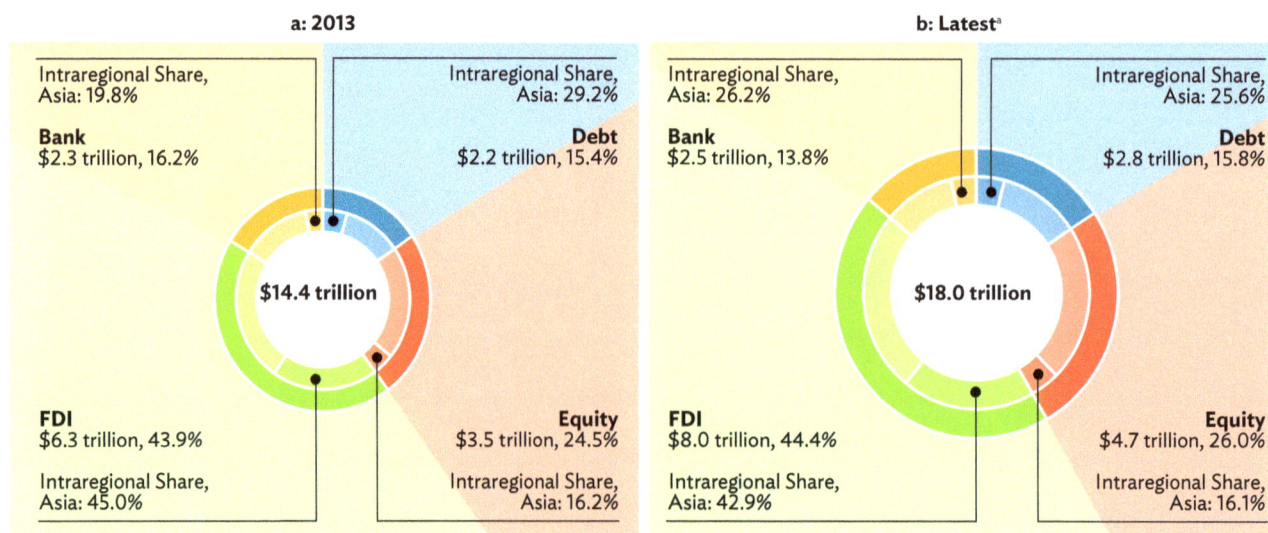

a: 2013

Intraregional Share, Asia: 19.8%
Bank $2.3 trillion, 16.2%

Intraregional Share, Asia: 29.2%
Debt $2.2 trillion, 15.4%

$14.4 trillion

FDI $6.3 trillion, 43.9%
Intraregional Share, Asia: 45.0%

Equity $3.5 trillion, 24.5%
Intraregional Share, Asia: 16.2%

b: Latest[a]

Intraregional Share, Asia: 26.2%
Bank $2.5 trillion, 13.8%

Intraregional Share, Asia: 25.6%
Debt $2.8 trillion, 15.8%

$18.0 trillion

FDI $8.0 trillion, 44.4%
Intraregional Share, Asia: 42.9%

Equity $4.7 trillion, 26.0%
Intraregional Share, Asia: 16.1%

[a] As of December 2018 for Bank, Debt, and Equity; and as of December 2017 for FDI.

FDI = foreign direct investment.

Notes: FDI liabilities refer to inward FDI holdings. Asia includes ADB regional members for which data are available.

Sources: ADB calculations using data from Bank for International Settlements. Locational Banking Statistics. https://www.bis.org/statistics/bankstats.htm (accessed September 2019); International Monetary Fund (IMF). Coordinated Direct Investment Survey. http://data.imf.org/CDIS (accessed May 2019); and IMF. Coordinated Portfolio Investment Survey. http://data.imf.org/CPIS (accessed September 2019).

[16]   Portfolio investment data are based on stock data from the Coordinated Portfolio Investment Survey of the International Monetary Fund. Asia's reporting economies include Australia; Bangladesh (data beginning 2014); Hong Kong, China; India (data beginning 2003); Indonesia; Japan; Kazakhstan; Malaysia; Mongolia (data beginning 2010); New Zealand; Pakistan (data beginning 2002); Palau (data beginning 2014); Singapore; Thailand; the Philippines; the Republic of Korea; and Vanuatu (data from 2001–2005). The People's Republic of China is excluded due to lack of comparable data for 2001–2014.

Asia's outward portfolio debt investment increased from $4.2 trillion in 2017 to $4.3 trillion in 2018, with intraregional share hovering at 16.8% in 2018 (Figure 3.3a). The year-on-year growth rate of outward portfolio debt investment in 2018 was 2.6% and is close to its CAGR of 1.6% between 2013 and 2018. Asia's outward portfolio equity investment, however, declined for the first time since 2011, from $4.5 trillion in 2017 to $4.2 trillion in 2018. Asia's intraregional outward portfolio equity investment share remained stable at 18.0% in 2018 (Figure 3.3b). Despite contracting by 6.6% in 2018, it has grown by a CAGR of 10.8% between 2013 and 2018.

Asia's outward portfolio debt investment continued to increase in 2018, though at a slower pace compared with 2017. However, outward portfolio equity investment fell by 6.6% in 2018 after a 26.3% surge in 2017.

In 2018, outward portfolio debt investment increased by $108.1 billion or 2.6% from 2017 (Figure 3.4a).

It was primarily driven by increased investment in debt securities issued in the European Union (EU), which rose by $100.5 billion in 2018. As Japanese investors searched for higher-yielding assets, holdings of United States (US) portfolio debt securities contracted by $18.0 billion (Greifeld 2018).

After an increase by almost $1.0 trillion in 2017, portfolio equity investment declined by $293.7 billion in 2018, given the subdued performance in equity markets and depreciating Asian currencies against the US dollar (Figure 3.4b). This large drop could also be attributed to a contraction in Asia's equity investment to the rest of the world (ROW) excluding the EU and the US, by $243.8 billion in 2018 after increasing $578.7 billion in 2017. From Australia alone, investment declined by $86.3 billion, after increasing by $111.0 billion in 2017. Hong Kong, China's combined equity investment in Bermuda and the Cayman Islands increased by $262.5 billion in 2017, but contracted by $174.0 billion in 2018. Japan's equity investment to the Cayman Islands increased by $121.2 billion in 2017, but only by $28.0 billion

Figure 3.3: Outward Portfolio Investment—Asia

a: Outward Portfolio Debt Investment

b: Outward Portfolio Equity Investment

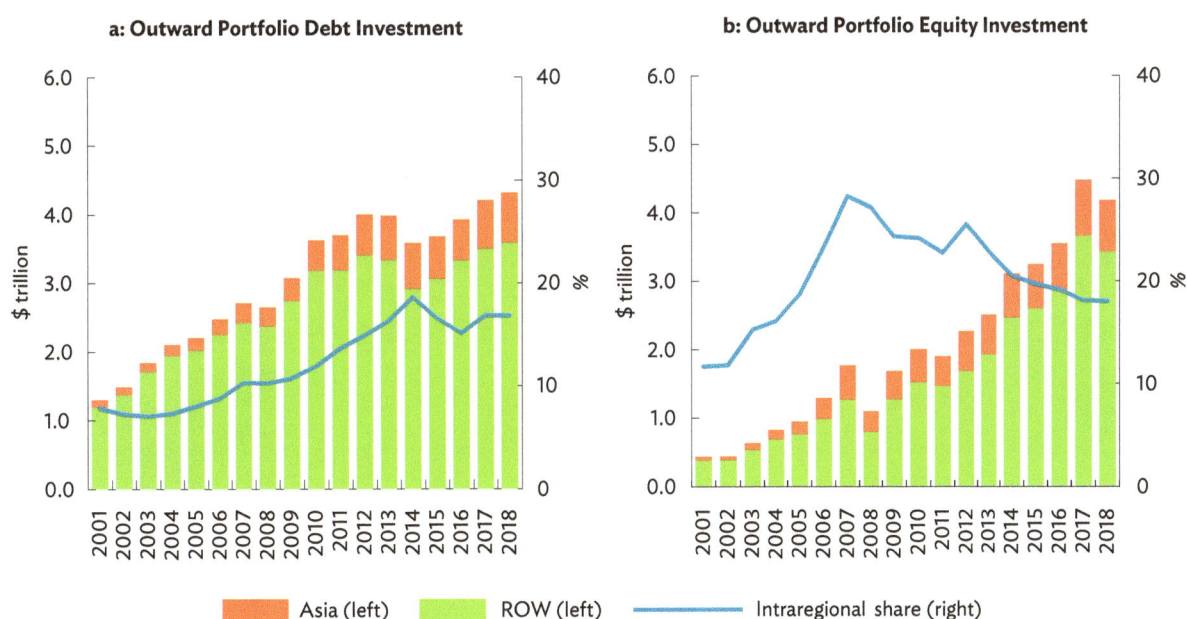

Asia (left)   ROW (left)   Intraregional share (right)

ROW = rest of the world.

Note: Asia includes ADB regional members for which data are available.

Source: ADB calculations using data from International Monetary Fund. Coordinated Portfolio Investment Survey. http://data.imf.org/CPIS (accessed September 2019).

in 2018. Additionally, intraregional portfolio equity investment declined, particularly from Hong Kong, China (–$20.1 billion); Japan (–$19.0 billion); Australia (–$9.1 billion); and Singapore (–$8.4 billion). The decline in intraregional equity investment could also be driven by valuation effects, as the Hong Kong dollar depreciated against the US dollar by 0.8% and the Singapore dollar by 4.0% in 2018.

Portfolio debt securities issued in Australia, the People's Republic of China (PRC), and Japan remained the most preferred by Asian cross-border investors (Table 3.1). Amid heightened trade tensions, the share of portfolio debt investment into the PRC declined from 5.2% to 4.4%, while the share of portfolio debt investment to Japan increased from 0.7% to 1.7%. Given the trade tensions and a slowdown in growth in the PRC, investors may have shifted their portfolio debt investment to Japan.

Between 2013 (the period of the "taper tantrum") and 2018 (ongoing US monetary policy normalization),

Asian investors' holdings of US portfolio debt securities increased by 6.1% CAGR, as treasury security yields moved up from zero. The share of portfolio debt investment to the US grew from 29.6% to 36.8%. Negative bond yields in the EU have made the region less attractive to regional investors, prompting the share of portfolio debt investment to the EU to fall from 30.1% in 2013 to 26.1% in 2018. Nonetheless, the region remained one of the most preferred destinations.

The PRC, Japan, and Australia remained the most preferred equity markets for Asian investors, although intraregional share declined from 22.9% in 2013 to 18.0% in 2018 (Table 3.2). This mirrors the fact that Asian investors increased their non-regional equity investment by 77.3% between 2013 and 2018, reaching $1.5 trillion and underpinning the region's appetite for global equities. Japan contributed significantly to the increase in portfolio equity investment from Asia to the Cayman Islands between 2013 and 2018—both by value and in share. Investment to the Cayman Islands grew more than three times between 2013 and 2018,

Figure 3.4: Change in Outward Portfolio Investment—Asia ($ billion)

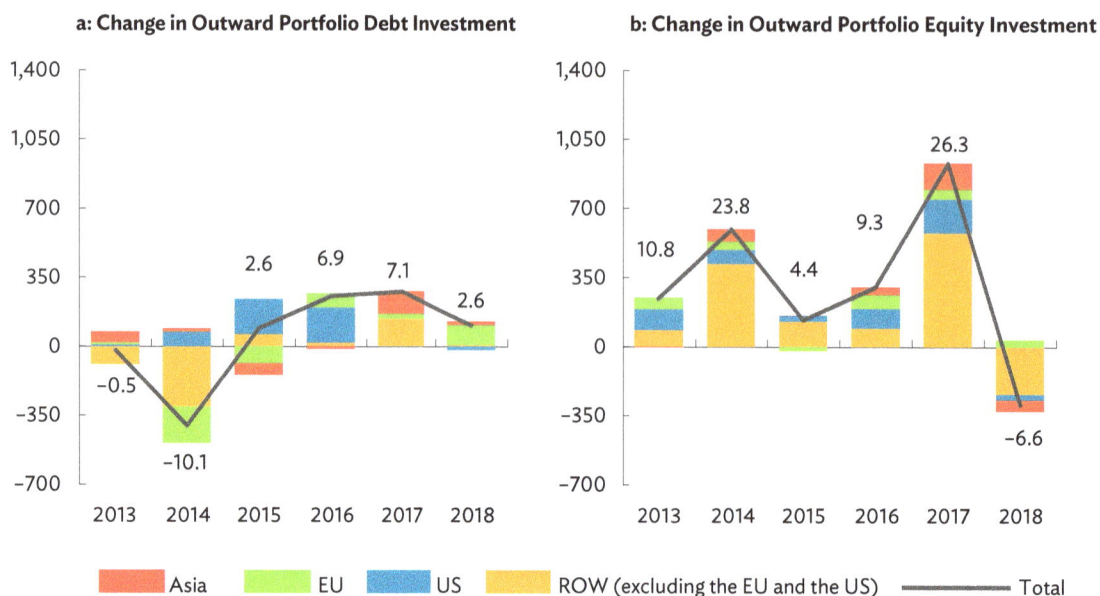

a: Change in Outward Portfolio Debt Investment

b: Change in Outward Portfolio Equity Investment

Legend: Asia | EU | US | ROW (excluding the EU and the US) | Total

EU = European Union, ROW = rest of the world, US = United States.

Notes: Asia includes ADB regional members for which data are available. Labels refer to year-on-year percentage change in outward portfolio investment data.

Source: ADB calculations using data from International Monetary Fund. Coordinated Portfolio Investment Survey. http://data.imf.org/CPIS (accessed September 2019).

Table 3.1: Destinations of Outward Portfolio Debt Investment—Asia

	2013		2018		**
	$ billion	% share	$ billion	% share	
Asia					
Australia	166	4.2	197	4.6	▲
People's Republic of China	205	5.2	191	4.4	▼
Japan	26	0.7	73	1.7	▲
Other Asia	252	6.3	263	6.1	▼
Asia's outward portfolio debt investment to Asia	649	16.3	724	16.8	▲
Non-Asia					
United States	1,177	29.6	1,583	36.8	▲
European Union	1,197	30.1	1,126	26.1	▼
Cayman Islands	457	11.5	239	5.5	▼
Other non-Asia	498	12.5	635	14.7	▲
Asia's outward portfolio debt investment to non-Asia	3,329	83.7	3,583	83.2	▼
Asia total outward portfolio debt investment	**3,978**	**100.0**	**4,307**	**100.0**	

** = direction of change in % share, ▼ = decrease, ▲ = increase.

Source: ADB calculations using data from International Monetary Fund. Coordinated Portfolio Investment Survey. http://data.imf.org/CPIS (accessed September 2019).

Table 3.2: Destinations of Outward Portfolio Equity Investment—Asia

	2013		2018		**
	$ billion	% share	$ billion	% share	
Asia					
People's Republic of China	248	9.9	311	7.4	▼
Japan	59	2.4	91	2.2	▼
Australia	58	2.3	65	1.6	▼
Other Asia	206	8.3	284	6.8	▼
Asia's outward portfolio equity investment to Asia	573	22.9	751	18.0	▼
Non-Asia					
Cayman Islands	351	14.0	1,170	28.0	▲
United States	741	29.6	1,082	25.9	▼
European Union	445	17.8	621	14.9	▼
Other non-Asia	393	15.7	548	13.1	▼
Asia's outward portfolio equity investment to non-Asia	1,929	77.1	3,420	82.0	▲
Asia total outward portfolio equity investment	**2,502**	**100.0**	**4,171**	**100.0**	

** = direction of change in % share, ▼ = decrease, ▲ = increase.

Source: ADB calculations using data from International Monetary Fund. Coordinated Portfolio Investment Survey. http://data.imf.org/CPIS (accessed September 2019).

as Japanese investors looked for riskier—albeit higher yielding—assets. The world's largest pension fund, Japan's Government Pension Fund, has started to engage in riskier assets in recent years, which can explain, in part, the trend to invest in equities issued outside of Asia, such as in the Cayman Islands (Huckle 2018).

Inward Portfolio Investment

In 2018, while inward portfolio debt investment growth slowed, inward equity investment actually fell amid rising concerns over Asia's economic prospects associated with rising global trade tensions.

In 2018, Asia's inward portfolio debt investment outstanding was $2.8 trillion, while inward portfolio equity investment was $4.7 trillion. After considerable increases in 2017, inward portfolio equity investment declined in 2018, from $5.4 trillion in 2017, amid tightening global financial conditions, less favorable equity market performance in the region, and depreciating regional currencies. Inward portfolio debt investment slightly increased from $2.7 trillion in 2017 (Figure 3.5a). This contrasts to the longer-term trend since 2013, during which portfolio debt investment increased by 5.0% CAGR and inward equity investment increased by 5.7% CAGR.

After a surge in cross-border equity investment into Asia between 2013 and 2017—from $3.5 trillion to $5.4 trillion—it declined to $4.7 trillion in 2018

(Figure 3.5b). Despite a 7% decline in intraregional portfolio equity investment, the intraregional share still rose from 15.1% in 2017 to 16.1% in 2018, as inward portfolio equity investment outstanding from non-Asian economies even declined by 14.0%. The intraregional share of inward portfolio debt investment declined slightly—from 25.9% in 2017 to 25.6% in 2018.

In 2018, inward portfolio equity investment declined by a considerable 12.9%. While to some extent this may reflect rebalancing after a surge of 32.8% in 2017, it also mirrors tighter global financial market conditions in general in the same year.

Inward portfolio debt outstanding increased by 3.8% or $103.7 billion in 2018, down from 18.6% in 2017, driven by smaller increases from the US and the ROW (excluding the EU and the US). Amid rising US interest rates, investment from the US only grew by $19.9 billion in 2018 compared with $128.3 billion in 2017, while investment from the ROW (excluding the EU and the US) grew $61.4 billion in 2018 compared with

Figure 3.5: Inward Portfolio Investment—Asia

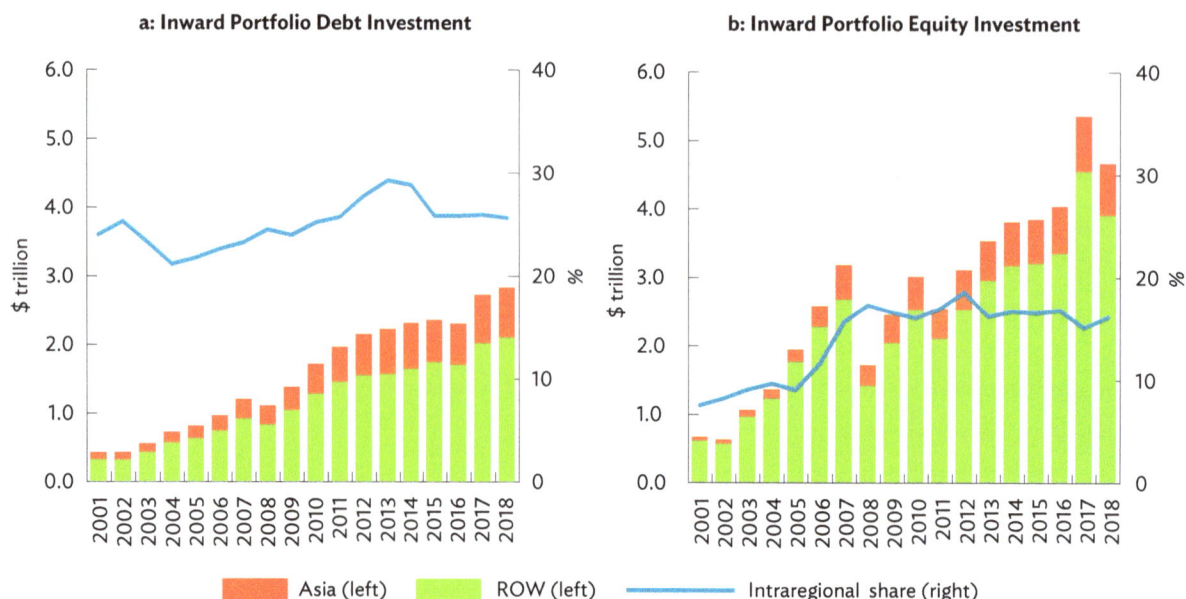

a: Inward Portfolio Debt Investment

b: Inward Portfolio Equity Investment

Asia (left)   ROW (left)   Intraregional share (right)

ROW = rest of the world.

Note: Asia includes ADB regional members for which data are available.

Source: ADB calculations using data from International Monetary Fund. Coordinated Portfolio Investment Survey. http://data.imf.org/CPIS (accessed September 2019).

$154.5 billion in 2017 (Figure 3.6a). US investment into Japanese portfolio debt increased by only $1.6 billion in 2018 after increasing by $75.0 billion in 2017. One of the reasons could be decreasing yields on Japanese debt in 2018, while US government bond yields increased in tandem with rising US interest rates in 2018.

There was a sharper drop in inward portfolio investment outstanding in equities in 2018. After a $1,323.2 billion increase in 2017, inward portfolio investment dropped by as much as $691.5 billion in 2018, with inward equity investment from the US contracting by $344.3 billion and by $249.3 billion from the EU (Figure 3.6b). The large reversals in investment from the US were most pronounced in Japan (from $206.9 billion in 2017 to –$126.8 billion in 2018), the Republic of Korea (from $87.7 billion in 2017 to –$34.9 billion in 2018), and Singapore (from $42.8 billion in 2017 to –$89.5 billion in 2018), reflecting tighter global financial conditions and the tepid performance of regional equity markets in 2018. For instance, equity markets in the PRC declined by 24.6%

in 2018 after a 6.6% increase in 2017. The same trend occurred in the equity markets of Hong Kong, China (from 36.0% to –13.6%); the Republic of Korea (from 21.8% to –17.3%); Malaysia (from 9.4% to –5.9%); the Philippines (25.1% to –12.8%); and Singapore (18.1% to –9.8%). Portfolio equity investment from the ROW (excluding the EU and the US) also dropped by $41.0 billion in 2018.

While Hong Kong, China; Japan; and Singapore remained the top sources of intraregional inward portfolio debt investment, their combined share declined from 91.5% in 2013 to 83.4% in 2018 (Table 3.3). This was primarily due to increased intraregional investment from the Republic of Korea, from $6.5 billion to $29.2 billion—a 352.8% increase. Hong Kong, China continued to invest heavily in the PRC. In 2018, 50.2% of its intraregional portfolio debt investment was to the PRC, while 15.7% went to Japan. In 2018, 62.2% of Japan's intraregional debt investment was to Australia. Singapore invested heavily in PRC portfolio debt ($33.4 billion), the Republic of Korea ($19.6 billion), and Australia ($19.1 billion).

Figure 3.6: Change in Inward Portfolio Investment—Asia ($ billion)

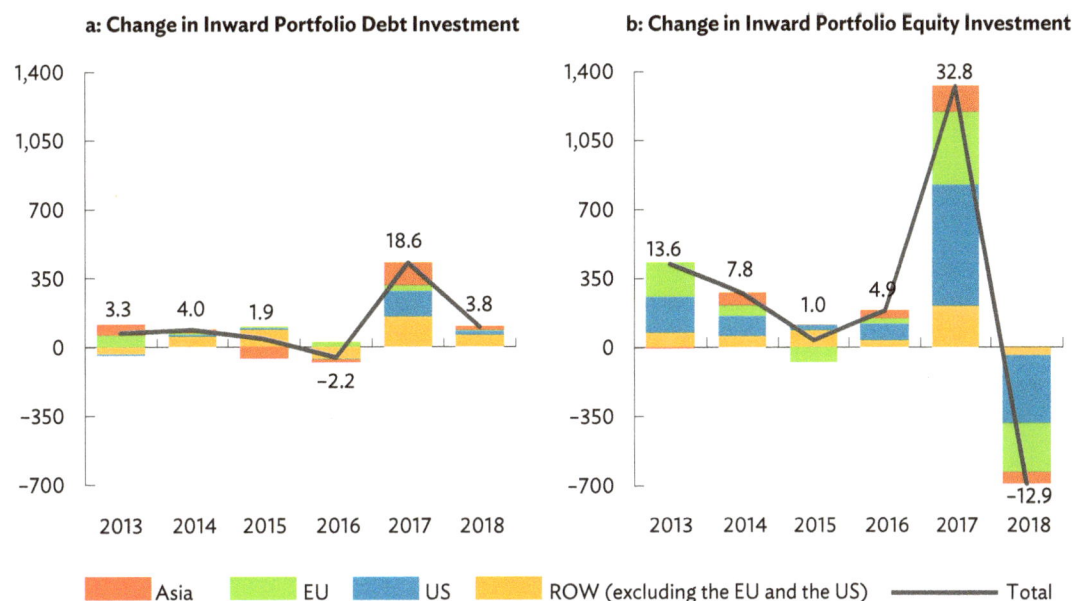

a: Change in Inward Portfolio Debt Investment

b: Change in Inward Portfolio Equity Investment

Asia   EU   US   ROW (excluding the EU and the US)   ——— Total

EU = European Union, ROW = rest of the world, US = United States.

Notes: Asia includes ADB regional members for which data are available. Labels refer to year-on-year percentage change in inward portfolio investment data.

Source: ADB calculations using data from International Monetary Fund. Coordinated Portfolio Investment Survey. http://data.imf.org/CPIS (accessed September 2019).

Table 3.3: Sources of Inward Portfolio Debt Investment—Asia

	2013		2018		**
	$ billion	% share	$ billion	% share	
Asia					
Hong Kong, China	272	12.2	271	9.6	▼
Japan	168	7.6	196	6.9	▼
Singapore	154	6.9	137	4.9	▼
Other Asia	55	2.5	120	4.2	▲
Asia's inward portfolio debt investment to Asia	649	29.2	724	25.6	▼
Non-Asia					
European Union	688	31.0	761	26.9	▼
United States	401	18.1	566	20.0	▲
International organizations	282	12.7	394	13.9	▲
Other non-Asia	199	9.0	384	13.6	▲
Asia's inward portfolio debt investment to non-Asia	1,571	70.8	2,104	74.4	▲
Asia total inward portfolio debt investment	**2,219**	**100.0**	**2,828**	**100.0**	

** = direction of change in % share, ▼ = decrease, ▲ = increase.

Source: ADB calculations using data from International Monetary Fund. Coordinated Portfolio Investment Survey. http://data.imf.org/CPIS (accessed September 2019).

Outside the region, the EU, the US, and international organizations remained the top sources of portfolio debt investment into the region. Japan was a popular destination for the top three sources. Inward investment from the EU into Australia and Japan accounted for 63.9% of its total portfolio debt investment into Asia. The US also invested in Japan, which absorbed 40.3% of its debt investment to Asia. In addition, 72.8% of international organizations' debt investment into the region went to Japan.

Financial hubs in the region—Hong Kong, China; Singapore; and Japan—remained the top sources of inward intraregional portfolio equity investment (Table 3.4). Other Asian economies increasing investment in the region were Australia ($52.1 billion), the Republic of Korea ($46.9 billion), and Malaysia ($27.9 billion). Though from a low base, other Association of Southeast Asian Nations (ASEAN) economies also increased activity in cross-border intraregional equity investment—investment from Thailand increased by 249.2% and Indonesia by 150.3%.

Outside the region, the US, the EU, and Canada remained top investors in Asia. The increase in share of other non-Asian investors—from 9.0% in 2013 to 13.6% in 2018—was buoyed by the increased participation of the Cayman Islands. In particular, investment from the Cayman Islands into Japan increased from $4.0 million to $43.9 billion over the same period. Investment from outside the region also came from Mauritius to India, increasing by more than 30% and amounting to $90.7 billion in 2018.

Subregional Portfolio Investment

East Asia continued to drive inter- and intra-subregional portfolio debt investment. Most intraregional linkages strengthened in East Asia, Southeast Asia, and Oceania.

As a source, East Asia's share of intraregional portfolio debt investment hovered around 68.5% between 2013 and 2018 (Figure 3.7), with Hong Kong, China's investment to the PRC strengthening East Asia's intra-subregional portfolio debt investment. Despite the strong inter-subregional linkages of Japan and the Republic of Korea, East Asia's share as a destination

Table 3.4: Sources of Inward Portfolio Equity Investment—Asia

| | 2013 | | 2018 | | ** |
	$ billion	% share	$ billion	% share	
Asia					
Hong Kong, China	196	5.6	246	5.3	▼
Singapore	183	5.2	246	5.3	▲
Japan	66	1.9	97	2.1	▲
Other Asia	127	3.6	162	3.5	▼
Asia's inward portfolio equity investment to Asia	573	16.2	751	16.1	▼
Non-Asia					
United States	1,497	42.4	1,976	42.4	—
European Union	1,044	29.6	1,169	25.1	▼
Canada	110	3.1	166	3.6	▲
Other non-Asia	306	8.7	601	12.9	▲
Asia's inward portfolio equity investment to non-Asia	2,958	83.8	3,911	83.9	▲
Asia total inward portfolio equity investment	**3,530**	**100.0**	**4,662**	**100.0**	

** = direction of change in % share, ▼ = decrease, ▲ = increase, — = no change.

Source: ADB calculations using data from International Monetary Fund. Coordinated Portfolio Investment Survey. http://data.imf.org/CPIS (accessed September 2019).

Figure 3.7: Subregional Portfolio Debt Investment—Asia

a: 2013

Total = $648.6 billion

b: 2018

Total = $724.4 billion

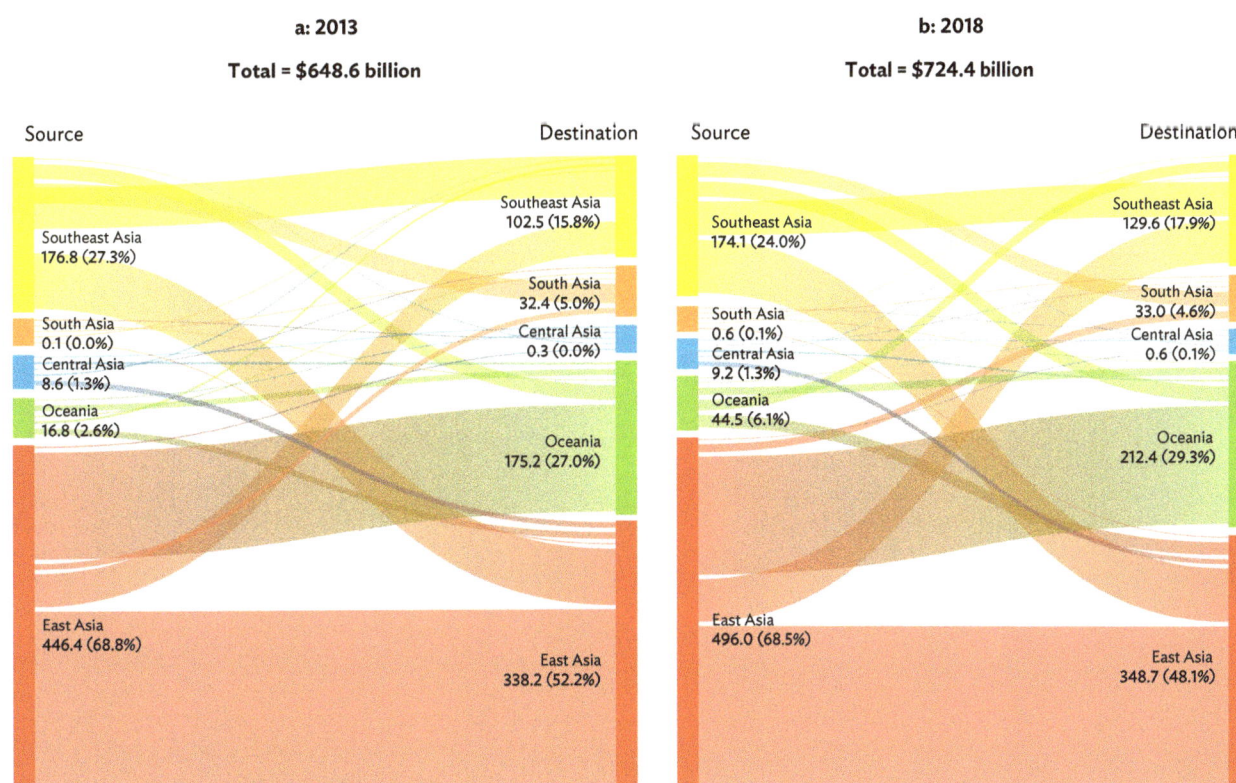

Notes: Figures in parentheses indicate the percent share of the total. Source economies for subregions are as follows: Central Asia includes Kazakhstan. East Asia includes Hong Kong, China; Japan; Mongolia; and the Republic of Korea. Oceania includes Australia and New Zealand. South Asia includes Bangladesh, India, and Pakistan. Southeast Asia includes Indonesia, Malaysia, the Philippines, Singapore, and Thailand. Asia includes Central Asia, East Asia, Oceania, South Asia, and Southeast Asia.

Source: ADB calculations using data from International Monetary Fund. Coordinated Portfolio Investment Survey. http://data.imf.org/CPIS (accessed September 2019).

declined from 52.2% in 2013 to 48.1% in 2018. The increased inter-subregional portfolio debt investment into Singapore reinforced Southeast Asia's inter-subregional linkages, with its share as a destination increasing from 15.8% to 17.9%. Oceania's linkage as source economy also grew from 2.6% to 6.1%, with rising portfolio debt investment to Japan and Singapore.

While South Asia's participation declined, Central Asia remained more or less isolated. ASEAN; Hong Kong, China; Japan; the PRC; and the Republic of Korea's (ASEAN+3) progress to promote local currency bond markets may provide further opportunities for intraregional portfolio debt investment (Box 3.1).

Box 3.1: Recent Progress in Developing Local Currency Bond Markets in ASEAN+3

Regional financial cooperation in Asia is designed to jointly meet development challenges. While local currency (LCY) bond market development is largely national, regional arrangements can support and often complement these efforts. ADB has been working closely with the Association of Southeast Asian Nations (ASEAN) plus Japan; the People's Republic of China; and the Republic of Korea (ASEAN+3) to develop LCY bond markets and promote regional bond market integration under the Asian Bond Markets Initiative (ABMI). ABMI was formed following the 1997/98 Asian financial crisis to offer alternative financing options in the bank-dominated region. There have been several recent developments.

Expanding ABMI beyond ASEAN+3 to Share Experiences and Lessons Learned

Since the ABMI was established in 2002, LCY bond markets in ASEAN+3 economies have grown steadily, and today are comparable in size to the United States (US) Treasury and euro-denominated bonds issued by residents in the euro area (Box Figure 1).

Since 2018, ASEAN+3 has agreed to allow officials from non-ASEAN+3 economies to attend as observers to the ASEAN+3 Bond Market Forum (ABMF). The ABMF was established in 2010 under ABMI as a platform for dialogue between ASEAN+3 financial authorities, regional and global market participants and experts to promote the harmonization of regulatory standards and market practices. As the first non-ASEAN+3 official, Mongolia's Ministry of Finance joined the 28th ABMF meeting in June 2018 in Fukuoka, Japan.

In May 2019, ADB published *Good Practices for Developing a Local Currency Bond Market: Lessons from the ASEAN+3 Asian Bond Markets Initiative* at the ASEAN+3 Finance Ministers and Central Bank Governors' Meeting on the sidelines of the ADB annual meeting in Fiji (ADB 2019). Though every market has its own unique features—there is no "one-size-fits-all" approach—sharing experiences and lessons learned from the ABMI can help foster the process of LCY bond market development across developing Asia.

1: Size of Local Currency Bond Markets
(amount outstanding, $ billion)

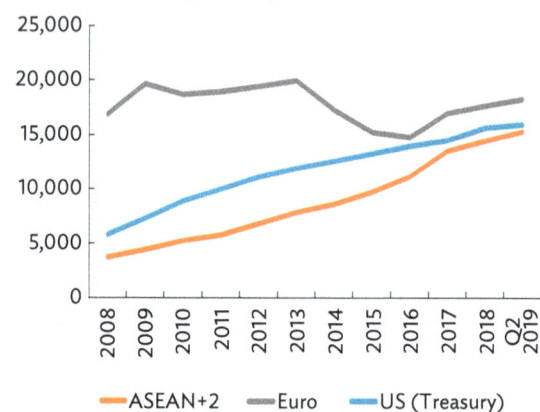

ASEAN = Association of Southeast Asian Nations, Q2 = second quarter, US = United States.

Notes: ASEAN+2 refers to ASEAN plus the Republic of Korea; Hong Kong, China; and the People's Republic of China. Euro refers to euro-denominated debt securities issued by euro area residents. US (Treasury) includes bills, notes, bonds, treasury inflation-protected securities, and floating rate notes.

Sources: AsianBondsOnline, CEIC, European Central Bank, International Monetary Fund, and Securities Industry and Financial Markets Association.

ASEAN+3 Multi-Currency Bond Issuance Framework

The ASEAN+3 Multi-Currency Bond Issuance Framework (AMBIF) is an ABMI policy initiative designed to help facilitate intraregional transactions by standardizing bond and note issuance, along with investment processes (Box Figure 2). This can help facilitate the process of recycling savings within the region more pragmatically and efficiently. AMBIF helps intraregional bond and note issuance and investment by creating common market practices; utilizing a common document for submission—the single submission form (SSF); and highlighting transparent issuance procedures documented in implementation guidelines for participating markets.

continued on next page

Box 3.1: Recent Progress in Developing Local Currency Bond Markets in ASEAN+3 *(continued)*

Under the AMBIF, an issuer can apply for bond issuance and make an offer under multiple jurisdictions using the SSF, which uses English as a common language. The AMBIF supports local funding of corporates that operate in various ASEAN+3 markets. It also facilitates intraregional bond investment as investors do not have to translate local documents.

Since 2018, use of the AMBIF has been gradually increasing (Box Table), due to the shift in corporate funding needs from US dollars to local currencies—as ASEAN+3 continues to transform from a production base to a consumer market. As the AMBIF allows multiple listings in different jurisdictions, it aims to support flexible funding needs in different currencies when needed.

Market integration offers various benefits—such as economies of scale, lower capital costs, more opportunities for risk sharing, and stronger political influence in global discussions. While ASEAN+3 recognizes these merits, it is pursuing development differently from the European Union, which is based on top-down leadership with strong cohesion and harmonization. ASEAN+3 integration efforts, however, operate on an open, multitrack, bottom-up and market-friendly approach, based on pragmatism—given the region's diversity in market and economic development. Therefore, ASEAN+3 focuses more on standardization than harmonization. Standardization tries to ensure conformity, while harmonization attempts to eliminate differences. Standardization can ensure

2: Combining Professional Markets to Build an ASEAN+3 Multi-Currency Bond Issuance Framework

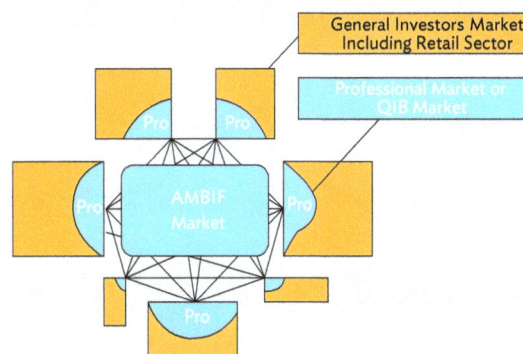

ASEAN = Association of Southeast Asian Nations; ASEAN+3 = ASEAN plus the People's Republic of China, Japan, and the Republic of Korea; AMBIF = ASEAN+3 Multi-Currency Bond Issuance Framework; QIB = qualified institutional buyer.

Source: ADB (2019).

interoperability among different systems under different jurisdictions, while harmonization tries to implement the same system across all jurisdictions. ASEAN+3's "open regionalism" approach can be shared and transferred across other Asian subregions. Multilateral development banks like ADB can help facilitate and promote standards that provide a basis for regional cooperation and market integration. As an "honest broker," it can help ensure the specific aims of each member economy are considered, and help bring all stakeholders together as part of a regional arrangement.

Selected Cases of Bond Issuance Based on AMBIF

No.	Issuer	Sector	Currency and Amount	Tenure	Issuance Date
1	Mizuho Bank, Ltd.	Financials (Banking)	B3 billion	3 years	28 September 2015
2	Hattha Kaksekar Limited	Financials (Consumer Finance)	KR120 billion	3 years	14 November 2018
3	AEON Credit Services (Philippines) Inc.[a]	Financials (Consumer Finance)	₱900 million	3 years	16 November 2018
			₱100 million	5 years	16 November 2018
4	CJ Logistics Asia Pte. Ltd.[a]	Logistics	S$70 million	5 years	26 March 2019

AMBIF = ASEAN+3 Multi-Currency Bond Issuance Framework.
[a] Guaranteed by the Credit Guarantee and Investment Facility.
Source: ADB (2019).

Source: Asian Development Bank.

With Hong Kong, China as the top source for intraregional portfolio equity investment, further buoyed by Japan and the Republic of Korea, East Asia's share of intraregional portfolio equity investment increased from 50.9% to 52.0% from 2013 to 2018 (Figure 3.8). It also remained the most preferred destination, receiving 70.3% of intraregional equity investment. Aside from East Asia,

Southeast Asia and Oceania continued to drive inter-subregional equity investment. Apart from Singapore, other ASEAN economies such as Indonesia, Malaysia, and Thailand invested more in regional equities in 2018. New Zealand also bolstered its contribution to inter-subregional equity investment.

Figure 3.8: Subregional Portfolio Equity Investment—Asia

a: 2013

Total = $572.6 billion

b: 2018

Total = $751.0 billion

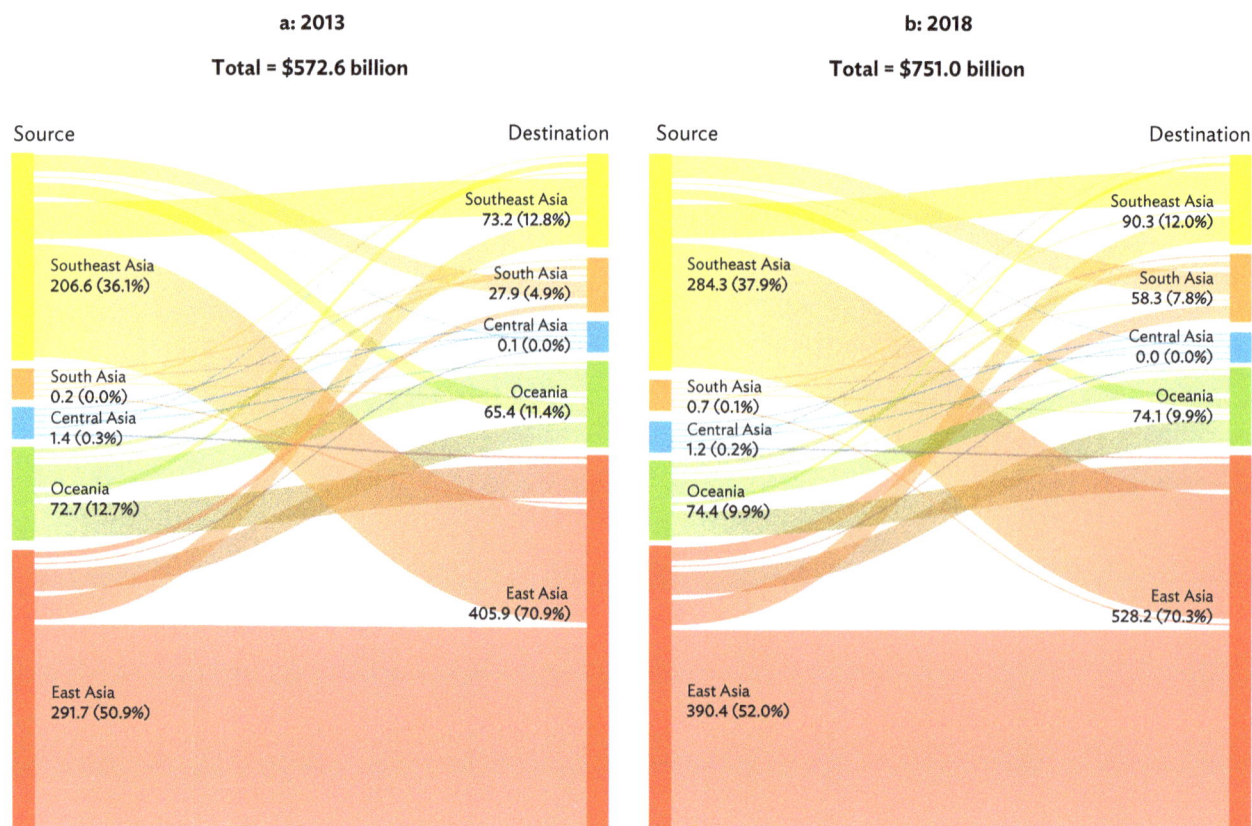

Notes: Figures in parentheses indicate the percent share of the total. Source economies for subregions are as follows: Central Asia includes Kazakhstan. East Asia includes Hong Kong, China; Japan; Mongolia; and the Republic of Korea. Oceania includes Australia and New Zealand. South Asia includes Bangladesh, India, and Pakistan. Southeast Asia includes Indonesia, Malaysia, the Philippines, Singapore, and Thailand. Asia includes Central Asia, East Asia, Oceania, South Asia, and Southeast Asia.

Source: ADB calculations using data from International Monetary Fund. Coordinated Portfolio Investment Survey. http://data.imf.org/CPIS (accessed September 2019).

Asia's global portfolio investment outstanding continued to grow, underpinning the region's increasing importance as both an attractive investment destination and global portfolio investor. In net terms, Asia remains a net portfolio debt investor and a net equity issuer globally.

Amid rather limited intraregional shares of portfolio investment, Asia steadily increased its global portfolio investment position, while global investors likewise continued to enlarge their portfolio investment in Asia. This pattern reflects both the preference of Asian investors to invest outside the region and global investor appetite for Asian debt and equities.

Asian investors hold more portfolio debt outside the region than global investors invest in debt securities issued in Asia (Figure 3.9a). As a result, the region is a net portfolio debt investor globally. Considering only extraregional cross-border portfolio investment, Asian investors held 17.8% or $3.6 trillion of the global total in 2018. The main global portfolio debt investors are Japan; Hong Kong, China; and Singapore. But the Republic of Korea's investment has also grown strong, as it shifted from being a net debt issuer to a net debt investor. Global investors in turn invested 10.4% or $2.1 trillion of the global total in 2018 in Asia, with Oceania increasingly becoming a net debt issuer. In 2018, the largest portion of Asian extraregional portfolio debt investment outstanding was invested in US debt securities, whereas

Figure 3.9: Global Portfolio Investment—Asia with the Rest of the World ($ trillion)

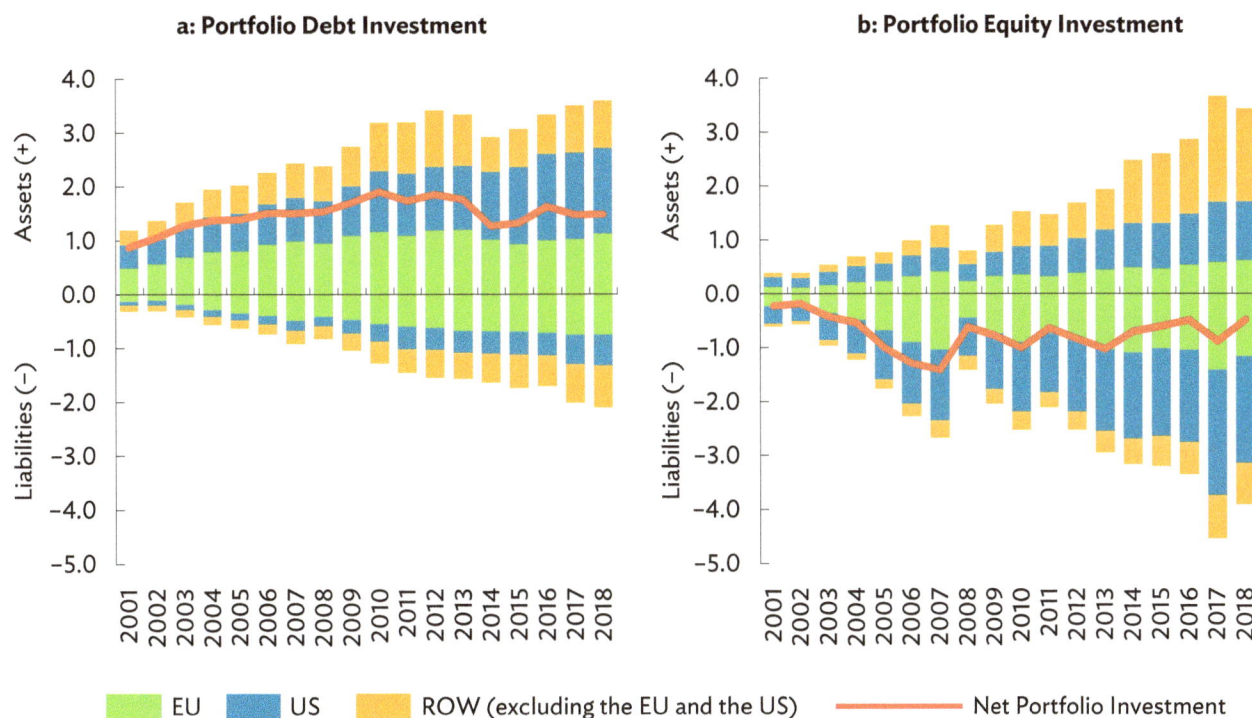

a: Portfolio Debt Investment

b: Portfolio Equity Investment

EU   US   ROW (excluding the EU and the US)   —— Net Portfolio Investment

EU = European Union, ROW = rest of the world, US = United States.

Note: Asia includes ADB regional members for which data are available.

Source: ADB calculations using data from International Monetary Fund. Coordinated Portfolio Investment Survey. http://data.imf.org/CPIS (accessed September 2019).

the ROW (excluding the EU and the US) was the primary investor in Asian debt securities.

The pattern is different for global portfolio equity investment, with Asia remaining a net equity issuer (Figure 3.9b). Global investors placed 18.9% or $3.9 trillion of the global total extraregional portfolio equity investment in 2018 in Asia, exceeding Asia's global equity investment—$3.4 trillion or 16.5% of the global total. India, the Republic of Korea, and ASEAN4 economies are significant net equity issuers, while Hong Kong, China and Singapore have increasingly become net equity investors.[17] Australia shifted from being a net equity issuer to an investor in 2011. In 2018, the US was the main global investor in Asian equities, whereas Asia's equity investment to the ROW (excluding the EU and the US) increased considerably over recent years, and was the largest in 2018.

Bank Holdings[18]

Asia's cross-border bank credit continues to soar, with cross-border bank claims reaching a record $4.7 trillion in 2018 and liabilities hitting $2.5 trillion, also a record. Bank claims on borrowers outside the region increased, while intraregional bank credit fell from $1.1 trillion in 2017 to $1.0 trillion.

Asia's cross-border bank claims rose to $4.7 trillion in 2018 from $4.6 trillion in 2017, despite the decline in intraregional bank claims to $1.0 trillion from $1.1 trillion (Figure 3.10a). The share of intraregional bank claims thus fell to 21.8% from 22.7%. Asia's cross-border bank liabilities rose to $2.5 trillion in 2018 from $2.4 trillion in 2017, but the intraregional share declined slightly from

---

[17]   ASEAN4 economies comprise Indonesia, Malaysia, the Philippines, and Thailand.

[18]   Bank holdings are based on the Locational Banking Statistics from the Bank for International Settlements. Asia's reporting economies include Australia; Japan; the Republic of Korea (data beginning 2005); the Philippines (data beginning 2016); and Taipei,China. Hong Kong, China is excluded due to lack of comparable data for 2001–2013.

Figure 3.10: Cross-Border Bank Holdings—Asia

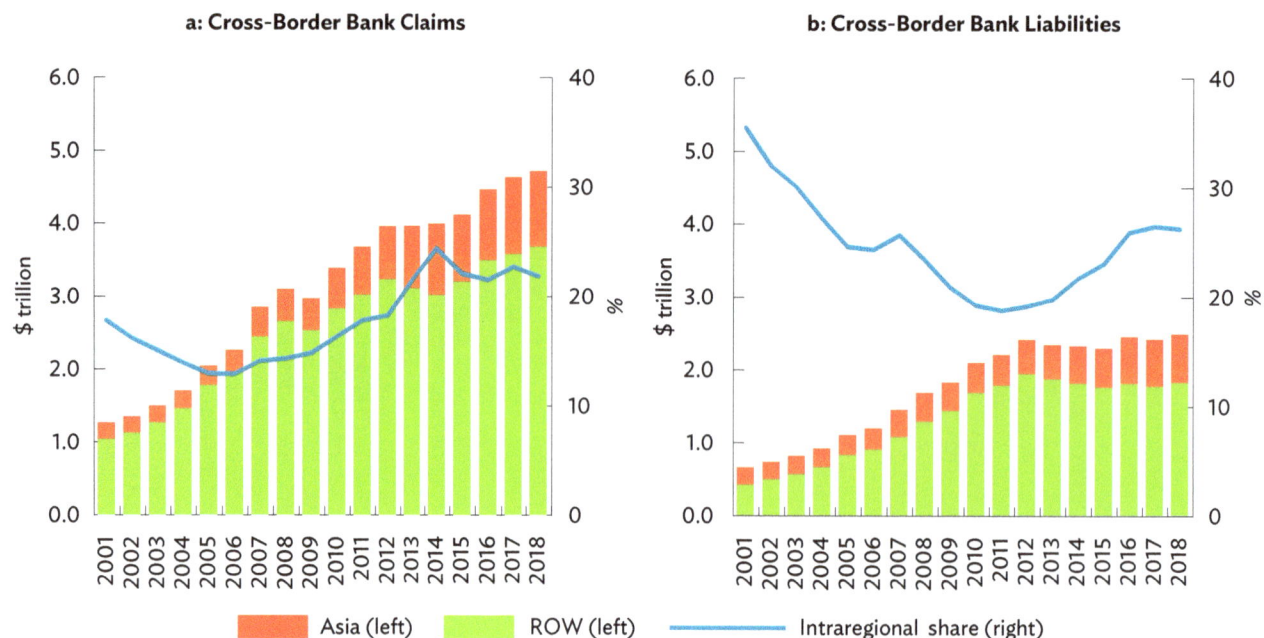

a: Cross-Border Bank Claims

b: Cross-Border Bank Liabilities

Asia (left)   ROW (left)   Intraregional share (right)

ROW = rest of the world.

Note: Asia includes ADB regional members for which data are available.

Source: ADB calculations using data from Bank for International Settlements. Locational Banking Statistics. https://www.bis.org/statistics/bankstats.htm (accessed September 2019).

26.5% to 26.2% (Figure 3.10b). The majority of Asia's bank claims and liabilities remain on countries outside the region, while both shares of intraregional bank claims and liabilities fell during 2017–2018.

Asia's cross-border bank claims on the ROW (excluding the EU and the US) and liabilities on the EU were behind the rise in cross-border bank claims in 2018, while Asia's bank liabilities on the US have continued to decline since 2016. Asia's bank claims within the region fell by $21.3 billion while those on the ROW (excluding the EU and the US) rose by $63.5 billion.

Both Asia's bank claims and liabilities on the EU rose in 2018, while intraregional bank claims declined. The region increased its bank claims on the ROW (excluding the EU and the US) by 5.8% or $63.5 billion, possibly driven by a search for higher returns in an otherwise low

interest rate environment. Japan still accounts for the major share of the region's overall cross-border banking activity.

The increase in Asia's cross-border bank claims declined from $169.7 billion in 2017 to $82.5 billion in 2018, with the change in intraregional bank claims accounting for much of the drop (Figure 3.11a), as it fell from $91.5 billion in 2017 to –$21.3 billion in 2018. The combined change in bank claims on the PRC; Hong Kong, China; and Japan was –$35.7 billion. Asia's bank claims on the EU, however, increased from $1.7 billion in 2017 to $45.8 billion in 2018, with bank claims on the United Kingdom (UK) accounting for much of the increase ($51.0 billion).

The change in Asia's bank liabilities increased significantly—to $68.6 billion in 2018 from –$37.0 billion in 2017—with Asia and the EU driving the increase (Figure 3.11b). The change in Asia's bank liabilities with the EU increased from –$25.6 billion to $88.3 billion,

Figure 3.11: Change in Cross-Border Bank Holdings—Asia ($ billion)

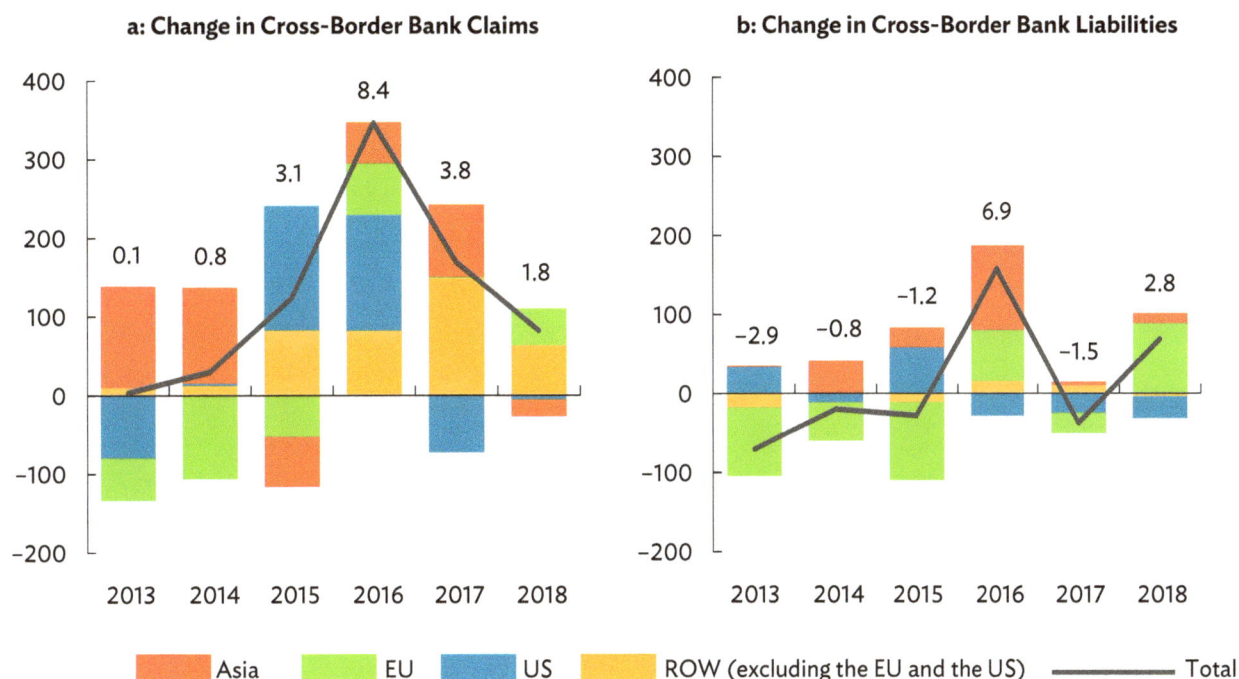

a: Change in Cross-Border Bank Claims

b: Change in Cross-Border Bank Liabilities

Asia   EU   US   ROW (excluding the EU and the US)   Total

EU = European Union, ROW = rest of the world, US = United States.

Notes: Asia includes ADB regional members for which data are available. Labels refer to year-on-year percentage change in bank holdings data.

Source: ADB calculations using data from Bank for International Settlements. Locational Banking Statistics. https://www.bis.org/statistics/bankstats.htm (accessed September 2019).

with Asia's bank liabilities on France, Germany, and the UK accounting for $80.7 billion. Asia's intraregional bank liabilities also picked up by $11.9 billion in 2018, compared with only $3.8 billion in 2017, during which bank liabilities with Hong Kong, China increased by $13.5 billion.

With increased cross-border banking linkages between Australia and the PRC, the PRC has overtaken both Singapore and Hong Kong, China as the most preferred destination for intraregional bank claims (Table 3.5). Australia's bank claims on the PRC more than doubled from $20.1 billion in 2013 to $41.6 billion in 2018, as they forged closer ties (Cranston 2019). The increasing proportion of intraregional bank claims on other Asian economies could specifically be attributed to Asia's rising bank claims on Japan and India.

Despite the contraction in Asia's bank claims on the US in 2017 and 2018, the US remained the most preferred destination in 2018 in terms cross-border bank claims outstanding. While bank claims on the EU declined

between the 2013 taper tantrum and the US monetary policy normalization period, they have increased again. The increase in Asia's bank claims on the Cayman Islands stands out, as Japan's bank claims almost doubled from $396.0 billion in 2013 to $759.3 billion in 2018—the Cayman Islands is Japan's second largest counterparty for cross-border bank claims. This could be attributed to a search for higher returns by Japanese investors amid the low domestic interest rate environment and associated challenges for large institutional investors, such as pension funds. Australia's bank claims on the Cayman Islands also increased substantially, from $1.0 billion in 2013 to $27.8 billion in 2018.

In the aftermath of the global financial crisis (GFC), Asia's cross-border bank liabilities outside the region fell in tandem with the rising trend of its intraregional share, from 19.8% in 2013 to 26.2% in 2018 (Table 3.6). Hong Kong, China; Singapore; and the PRC remained the region's top sources of cross-border bank liabilities,

Table 3.5: Destinations of Cross-Border Bank Claims—Asia

	2013		2018		**
	$ billion	% share	$ billion	% share	
Asia					
People's Republic of China	166	4.2	214	4.5	▲
Singapore	196	5.0	213	4.5	▼
Hong Kong, China	186	4.7	210	4.5	▼
Other Asia	300	7.6	393	8.3	▲
Asia's cross-border bank claims on Asia	849	21.4	1,029	21.8	▲
Non-Asia					
United States	1,049	26.5	1,279	27.1	▲
European Union	1,288	32.6	1,242	26.4	▼
Cayman Islands	409	10.3	808	17.2	▲
Other non-Asia	363	9.2	353	7.5	▼
Asia's cross-border bank claims on non-Asia	3,109	78.6	3,682	78.2	▼
Asia's total cross-border bank claims	**3,958**	**100.0**	**4,711**	**100.0**	

** = direction of change in % share, ▼ = decrease, ▲ = increase.

Source: ADB calculations using data from Bank for International Settlements. Locational Banking Statistics. https://www.bis.org/statistics/bankstats.htm (accessed September 2019).

Table 3.6: Sources of Cross-Border Bank Liabilities—Asia

	2013		2018		**
	$ billion	% share	$ billion	% share	
Asia					
Hong Kong, China	165	7.0	272	11.0	▲
Singapore	127	5.4	149	6.0	▲
People's Republic of China	25	1.1	70	2.8	▲
Other Asia	147	6.3	160	6.4	▲
Asia's cross-border bank liabilities to Asia	463	19.8	651	26.2	▲
Non-Asia					
European Union	997	42.6	976	39.3	▼
United States	706	30.2	673	27.1	▼
Cayman Islands	54	2.3	54	2.2	▼
Other non-Asia	121	5.2	130	5.2	—
Asia's cross-border bank liabilities to non-Asia	1,878	80.2	1,833	73.8	▼
Asia's total cross-border bank liabilities	**2,341**	**100.0**	**2,484**	**100.0**	

** = direction of change in % share, ▼ = decrease, ▲ = increase., — = no change.

Source: ADB calculations using data from Bank for International Settlements. Locational Banking Statistics. https://www.bis.org/statistics/bankstats.htm (accessed September 2019).

accounting for more than three-quarters of total intraregional bank liabilities. The EU, the US, and the Cayman Islands remain the region's main sources of bank liabilities from outside the region.

The volatility of intraregional bank claims and liabilities tends to be lower than those with the US and the EU. The volatility with the US has increased steadily, especially

since the onset of US monetary policy normalization in 2016. Asia's bank liabilities with the EU have been more volatile than those with the US, Asia, and the ROW (excluding the EU and the US).

From December 1998 until the GFC period, Asia's cross-border bank claims on the EU were the most volatile compared with others. Since the post-GFC and US monetary policy normalization periods, Asia's bank claim volatility with the US has risen rapidly, but still remains lower than the peak volatility with the EU during the GFC period (Figure 3.12a). On the liability side, while the EU was the largest counterpart of Asia's bank liabilities, they were also the most volatile, illustrating the associated risks of financial volatility (Figure 3.12b).

The volatilities of intraregional cross-border bank claims and liabilities have fallen since the 2008/09 GFC and are lower than those in the EU and the US, suggesting that intraregional banking activities are less responsive to external shocks compared with others. Therefore, in recent years, there has been a need for Asian policy makers to closely monitor Asia's bank credit exposure to the global banking network—such as the EU and the US. Appropriate macroprudential and capital flow management measures—such as limiting short-term bank debt—could be used to lessen systemic concern and mitigate volatilities of cross-border bank credits if needed. The volatile nature of cross-border bank claims and liabilities calls for close monitoring of Asian banks' foreign exposures in case the global liquidity cycle reverses.

Ensuring the stability of the banking sector—the major source of credit in Asia—is more crucial in the face of recently increasing nonperforming loans (NPLs) and their ratios in selected Asian economies. NPL ratios for these economies increased in recent years and remain elevated (Figure 3.13). With Asia's financial markets becoming increasingly integrated, addressing NPLs swiftly remains critical to safeguard regional financial stability and development. Since the European sovereign debt crisis, Europe has taken great efforts regionally to address the systemic challenges associated with NPLs—which have grown and persisted—offering important lessons for Asia's forward-looking policy options (Box 3.2).

Figure 3.12: Bank Volatility—Asia (change in bank holdings to GDP, standard deviation)

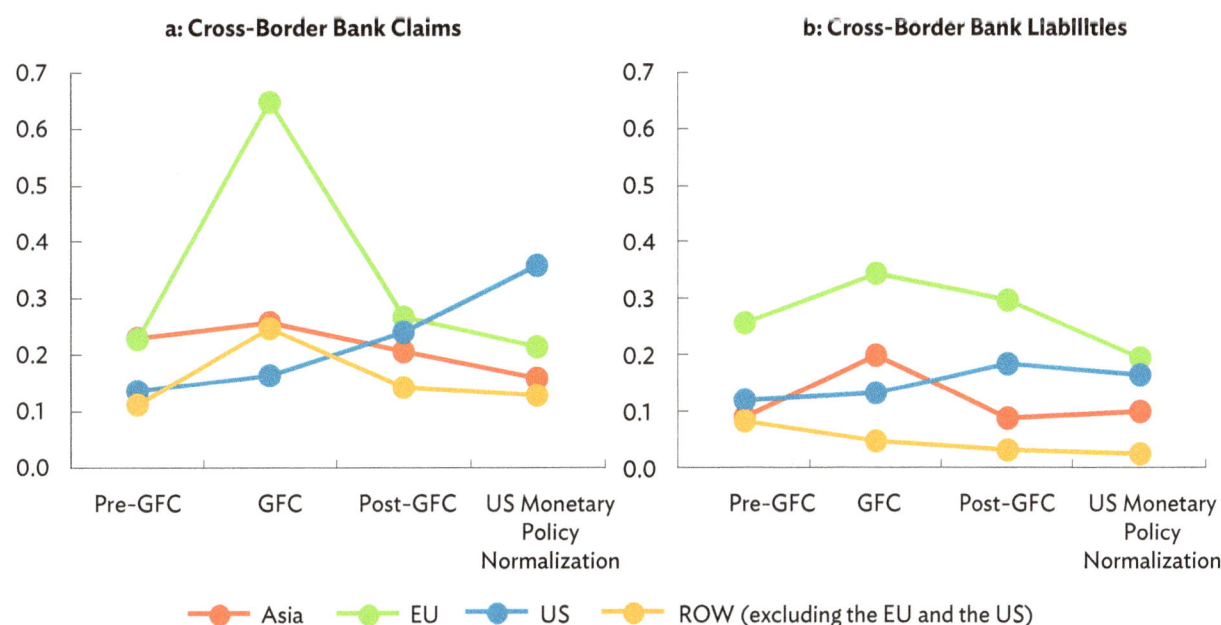

a: Cross-Border Bank Claims

b: Cross-Border Bank Liabilities

Asia   EU   US   ROW (excluding the EU and the US)

EU = European Union, GDP = gross domestic product, GFC = global financial crisis, ROW = rest of the world, US = United States.

Pre-GFC = December 1998 to September 2007, GFC = October 2007 to June 2009, Post-GFC = July 2009 to December 2015, US Monetary Policy Normalization = January 2016 to December 2018.

Notes: Asia includes ADB regional members for which data are available. Volatility is measured as the standard deviation of the 4-quarter moving average of the change in bank holdings to GDP.

Source: ADB calculations using data from Bank for International Settlements. Locational Banking Statistics. https://www.bis.org/statistics/bankstats.htm (accessed May 2019).

Box 3.2: Harnessing Regional Cooperation to Address Nonperforming Loans: Lessons from Europe

Previous financial crises have demonstrated the long-lasting negative impact nonperforming loans (NPLs) can have on financial stability and the economy, as the effects of elevated NPL levels persist beyond crisis periods. Even after the recovery of economic growth, there is a tendency for NPLs to continue to rise unless appropriate measures are taken. Mongolia is the latest example of an economic recovery with persisting high NPLs. High and rising NPL levels are a cause for concern, as they are a result of weak macroeconomic conditions and prompt harmful feedback effects on the overall economy. Empirical analysis examining the macrofinancial implications of NPLs illustrates how a rising NPL ratio decreases gross domestic product (GDP) growth and credit supply while increasing unemployment (Lee and Rosenkranz 2019).

This lesson is particularly relevant for Asia, with its increasingly integrated financial markets. Risks of contagion and spillover of financial instability can potentially spread across sectors and economies. Its significance is underscored by the important role banking plays across Asia's financial systems. Bank financing comprises by far the largest share of corporate financing in emerging Asia, accounting for 123.6% of corporate financing (as a percentage of GDP) in the region in 2018.[a]

NPLs increased in several Asian economies in recent years, constituting cause for concern for policy makers and highlighting that swift action is critical for safeguarding regional financial stability and economic development (see Figure 3.13). Hence, an appropriate mix of national and regional policies should become a part of crisis management and prevention toolkits.

The European Response to the NPL Problem

The euro area's recent experience with mounting NPLs vividly illustrates the systemic and negative impact NPLs have on all economies in the region. In the absence of a banking union—alongside insufficient transnational supervisory and regulatory structures governing banks and other financial institutions—failures of banks that also operate across borders can easily be transmitted across a highly financially integrated single market.

In response to the European sovereign debt crisis, Europe has taken great strides toward establishing a European banking union, putting in place mechanisms and facilities for integrated banking supervision and resolution. First, the Single Supervisory Mechanism was established to strengthen the European Central Bank's supervisory capabilities over important financial institutions and enhance its ability to monitor compliance with capital,

leverage, and liquidity requirements. Second, the Single Resolution Mechanism was set up in 2014 to ensure the protection of depositors and public funds, secure the continuity of essential banking operations, and more broadly enhance financial stability.

Despite extensive efforts to strengthen banking sector stability and resilience in the euro area, the region still suffers from high NPL levels in some countries, and NPL resolution—while gaining in momentum—has been slow (European Central Bank 2019). As of the third quarter of 2018, gross NPLs and advances as a percentage of total gross loans and advances for the six euro area economies[b] most plagued by NPLs during the height of the crisis averaged 16.8%; the corresponding figure for the European Union (EU) as a whole was 3.3% (European Commission 2019).

Consequently, European policy makers have been determined to act in recent years to address the NPL challenge—identified as a key area to reduce risk in European banking—which has systemic implications for the region's banking sector as a whole. A comprehensive response was the EU's Action Plan to Tackle NPLs in Europe (Action Plan), which was announced in July 2017. It is grounded in four areas—(i) insolvency frameworks, (ii) supervision, (iii) secondary markets, and (iv) macroprudential approaches. The Action Plan is close to being fully implemented[c] (European Commission 2019) and includes measures ranging from the review of national insolvency frameworks, data harmonization, and provisioning requirements; to more innovative solutions such as a blueprint for creating national asset management companies (AMCs), or the potential creation of regional NPL transaction platforms (European Commission 2018a).

As part of the Action Plan, the European Commission (2018b) outlined factors to be considered in establishing EU-wide transaction platforms to bolster NPL market development, particularly secondary markets. A European NPL platform would be an electronic marketplace and data warehouse facilitating the exchange of NPLs between banks and investors and providing a facility for the efficient and timely disposal of NPLs. To maximize effectiveness and stem the buildup of NPLs on financial institutions' future balance sheets, the platform should (i) be broad in scope, (ii) ensure data sharing and a high degree of data standardization, and (iii) serve as a price discovery mechanism and intermediary between investors and third-party service providers (European Commission 2018b). Asian policy makers should closely monitor these developments and draw on any relevant lessons.

continued on next page

Box 3.2: Harnessing Regional Cooperation to Address Nonperforming Loans: Lessons from Europe (continued)

Lessons for Asia

As seen in Europe, increasing financial integration highlights the possible systemic implications of NPLs. This underscores the need for regional cooperation to safeguard financial stability and resilience. Against the backdrop of Europe's NPL experience—and the recent rise of NPLs in Asia—it is an increasingly important issue for stability in predominantly bank-based Asia. Regional cooperation can help bolster NPL resolution and promote secondary NPL market development.

Regional efforts to address growing NPL levels and stem any future NPL buildup must deal with Asia's heterogeneous legal frameworks, lack of a standardized definition of NPLs, and less data harmonization relative to Europe. Asian policy makers need to take concerted action to strengthen legal structures—such as collateral or insolvency frameworks—enhance data transparency and harmonization, and facilitate knowledge exchange, all while taking into account specifics in each economy.

The option of creating a public AMC has long existed in several Asian economies. It is a viable option as a (i) NPL resolution mechanism, and (ii) facilitator for NPL market development. Public AMCs in Indonesia, Malaysia, the Republic of Korea, and Thailand helped banks recover in

the aftermath of the 1997/98 Asian financial crisis (AFC). A mix of policy options in the aftermath of the AFC, including AMC operations with strengthened legal and institutional reforms, contributed to building financial market resilience which helped Asian financial markets weather the GFC. Asia's experience illustrates the efficiency in reducing NPLs by combining a market-friendly resolution approach with a clearly defined role for a centralized public AMC. Furthermore, Asia's experience has demonstrated how public AMCs can simultaneously facilitate crisis resolution while enhancing financial resilience between crises.

NPL transaction platforms in Asia could also help deepen Asian NPL markets, possibly across borders, thereby eventually strengthening the regional financial safety net. The platform could facilitate data consolidation and standardization, bridge investors and sellers through a centralized contact point, guarantee transparency and fairness in the exchange of NPLs (Manca, Böschenbröker, and Navarra 2019), and contribute to fostering banking sector stability. NPL transaction platforms remain an innovative policy option that can help overcome implementation challenges. Such platforms could be developed using fintech developments—including big data, a robo-advisor on distressed assets, and payment and settlement.

[a] Emerging Asia includes India, Indonesia, Malaysia, the People's Republic of China, the Philippines, the Republic of Korea, Thailand, and Viet Nam. Data taken from CEIC; International Monetary Fund, World Economic Outlook, www.imf.org/en/Data; and national sources (all accessed August 2019).

[b] These are Cyprus, Greece, Ireland, Italy, Portugal, and Slovenia.

[c] Of the 14 initiatives subsumed under the Action Plan, 11 were accomplished as of 12 June 2019; two were categorized as ongoing, and one imminent (European Commission 2019).

Source: Asian Development Bank.

Figure 3.13: Nonperforming Loan Ratios—Selected Asian Economies (% of gross loans)

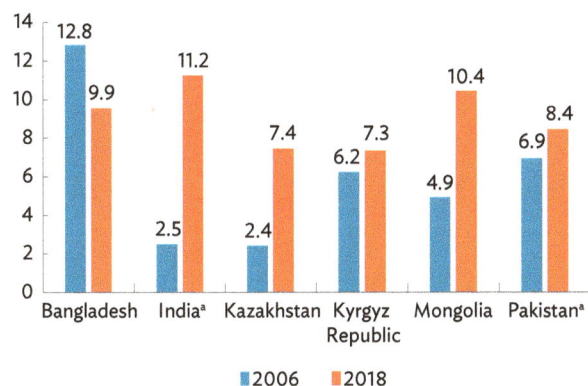

[a] Latest available data as of 2017.

Source: ADB calculations using data from the Bank of Mongolia; CEIC; and World Bank. World Development Indicators. https://databank.worldbank.org/source/world-development-indicators (accessed July 2019).

Analysis Using Price Indicators

Debt

The intraregional correlation of Asia's bond market returns and correlation of Asia's bond markets with global markets increased between 2016 and 2019—the period of US monetary policy normalization. The correlation with global markets exceeded the intraregional correlation, coinciding with the limited intraregional shares for outstanding portfolio debt investment discussed earlier.

Between the post-GFC and US monetary policy normalization periods, the correlation of Asia's bond returns with the global markets increased considerably, both within the region and the world (Table 3.7). The increasing correlation between Asia and the world can be attributed to the increasing correlation between Asian and US bond market returns. By subregion, markets in East Asia, Southeast Asia, and South Asia contributed to this increased correlation. Central Asia's bond markets correlation with external markets also increased significantly, while Oceania's markets remained negatively correlated with global markets.

The average intraregional bond return correlation increased from 0.19 to 0.34, illustrating the increased integration of the region's bond markets. Bond returns in the PRC and Japan have become increasingly correlated with Asia's bond returns. Central Asia, East Asia, Southeast Asia, and South Asia also drove this increased correlation, while Oceania's bond market returns became negatively correlated with Asia's bond returns.

The correlation of Asia's bond returns with global markets increased considerably between the post-GFC and US monetary policy normalization periods. By subregion, the markets of East Asia, Southeast Asia, and South Asia

contributed to this trend. The correlation of Central Asia's bond markets with external markets significantly increased, while Oceania's markets remained negatively correlated with global markets.

The dynamic conditional correlation of Asia's bond returns remained highest with global markets, followed by the US markets.

A dynamic conditional correlation (DCC) analysis of Asia's bond returns shows similar patterns to the analysis of simple correlation—Asia's bond market returns tend to co-move more with global markets than with those within the region. For Asia's DCCs with the world and the US, as well as intraregionally, there were peaks during the 2016 US presidential election as well as US interest rate hikes and the PRC–US trade tension onset in 2018, suggesting that these events had a considerable influence on the region's bonds market returns (Figure 3.14). By contrast, during US interest rate hikes, the DCC with the PRC fell into a trough. Asia's bond return DCC with the US picked up considerably since the period of US monetary policy normalization in 2016, while Asia's bond return DCC with EU markets hovered below zero.

Table 3.7: Average Simple Correlation of Weekly Total Bond Return Indexes—Asia with Asia and the World

| Region | Asia | | | World | | |
	Post-GFC	US Monetary Policy Normalization	**	Post-GFC	US Monetary Policy Normalization	**
Central Asia	0.12	0.32	▲	0.15	0.35	▲
East Asia	0.25	0.42	▲	0.41	0.53	▲
Southeast Asia	0.26	0.54	▲	0.35	0.55	▲
South Asia	0.03	0.27	▲	0.18	0.23	▲
Oceania	0.01	-0.34	▼	-0.21	-0.24	▼
Asia	**0.19**	**0.34**	▲	**0.27**	**0.39**	▲

** = direction of change in simple correlation between post-GFC and US monetary policy normalization, ▼ = decrease, ▲ = increase, GFC = global financial crisis, US = United States.

Post-GFC = July 2009 to December 2015, US Monetary Policy Normalization = January 2016 to August 2019.

Notes: (i) Values refer to the average of pair-wise correlations. Weekly returns are computed as the natural logarithm difference between weekly average of daily total bond return index for the current week, and the weekly average of the daily total bond return index from the previous week. World returns are calculated from Bloomberg Barclays Global Treasury Total Return Index Value Unhedged USD. (ii) Central Asia includes Kazakhstan. East Asia includes Hong Kong, China; Japan; the People's Republic of China; the Republic of Korea; and Taipei,China. Oceania includes Australia and New Zealand. South Asia includes India. Southeast Asia includes Indonesia, Malaysia, the Philippines, Singapore, and Thailand. Asia includes Central Asia, East Asia, Oceania, South Asia, and Southeast Asia.

Sources: ADB calculations using data from Bloomberg; CEIC; and World Bank. World Development Indicators. https://data.worldbank.org/indicator/ny.gdp.mktp.cd (accessed September 2019).

Figure 3.14: Conditional Correlation of Total Bond Return Indexes—Asia with Select Economies and Regions

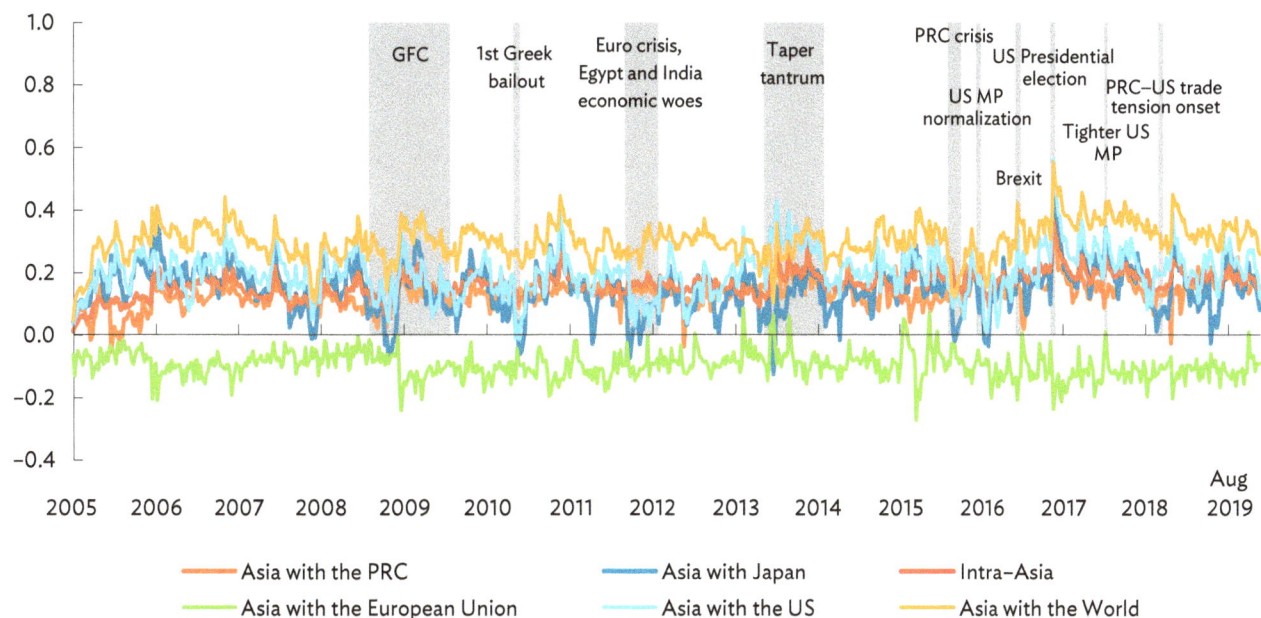

GFC = global financial crisis, MP = monetary policy, PRC = People's Republic of China, US = United States.

Note: Asia includes Australia; Hong Kong, China; India; Indonesia; Japan; Kazakhstan; Malaysia; New Zealand; the People's Republic of China; the Philippines; the Republic of Korea; Singapore; Taipei,China; and Thailand.

Source: ADB calculations using data from Bloomberg; and methodology by Hinojales and Park (2010).

Equity

Asia's equity returns continue to be more correlated globally than regionally, with increasing intraregional correlations. While the increased correlation in bond returns is more pronounced, average equity return correlations still exceed those of bond returns, suggesting that Asia's equity markets are more integrated than its bond markets.

Asia's intraregional equity return correlation increased in the US monetary policy normalization period, driven primarily by East Asia and Southeast Asia, suggesting progress in integrating the region's equity markets. In particular, Japan's equity return correlation with East Asia has increased since 2016 (Table 3.8).

Asia's equity return correlation with world equity returns has increased slightly from 0.33 to 0.37. By subregion, there has been a slight decline in Oceania and a notable increase in East Asia. The increase suggests a rising degree of integration of the PRC and Hong Kong, China equity markets globally.

Asia's equity return DCC, both intraregional and global, peaked toward the end of 2018, suggesting that escalating trade tensions were triggering equity market volatility. In line with Asia's pronounced portfolio equity investment globally, DCC with the world and US markets remain highest.

Asia's DCC with the world remained higher than the intraregional DCC (Figure 3.15). Asia's intraregional equity return DCC remained buoyed by the elevated equity return DCC with Japan. During crisis episodes and other important events, intraregional equity returns move in the same direction as Japan's. Asia's equity return DCC, however, moves in the opposite direction of the PRC's equity returns. However, after Asia's DCC peaked in October 2018—a period during which PRC–US trade tensions intensified—Asia's intraregional equity return DCC increased.

Table 3.8: Average Simple Correlation of Stock Price Index Weekly Returns—Asia with Asia and the World

Region	Asia			World		
	Post-GFC	US Monetary Policy Normalization	**	Post-GFC	US Monetary Policy Normalization	**
Central Asia	0.13	0.16	▲	0.12	0.16	▲
East Asia	0.52	0.61	▲	0.49	0.60	▲
Southeast Asia	0.37	0.44	▲	0.46	0.47	▲
South Asia	0.18	0.18	—	0.15	0.19	▲
Oceania	0.07	0.03	▼	0.18	0.13	▼
Asia	0.31	0.36	▲	0.33	0.37	▲

** = direction of change in simple correlation between post-GFC and US monetary policy normalization, ▼ = decrease, ▲ = increase, — = no change, GFC = global financial crisis, US = United States.

Post-GFC = July 2009 to December 2015, US Monetary Policy Normalization = January 2016 to August 2019.

Notes: (i) Values refer to the average of pair-wise correlations. Weekly returns are computed as the natural logarithm difference between weekly average of daily stock price index for the current week, and the weekly average of the daily stock price index from the previous week. World returns are calculated from the MSCI All-Country World Index. (ii) Central Asia includes Georgia, Kazakhstan, and the Kyrgyz Republic. East Asia includes Hong Kong, China; Japan; Mongolia; the People's Republic of China; the Republic of Korea; and Taipei,China. Oceania includes Australia and New Zealand. South Asia includes Bangladesh, India, Nepal, Pakistan, and Sri Lanka. Southeast Asia includes Indonesia, the Lao People's Democratic Republic, Malaysia, the Philippines, Singapore, Thailand, and Viet Nam. Asia includes Central Asia, East Asia, Oceania, South Asia, and Southeast Asia.

Sources: ADB calculations using data from Bloomberg; CEIC; Stooq. Stooq Online. https://stooq.com/q/?s=^sti; and World Bank. World Development Indicators. http://data.worldbank.org/data-catalog/world-development-indicators (all accessed September 2019).

Figure 3.15: Conditional Correlation of Equity Markets—Asia with Select Economics and Regions

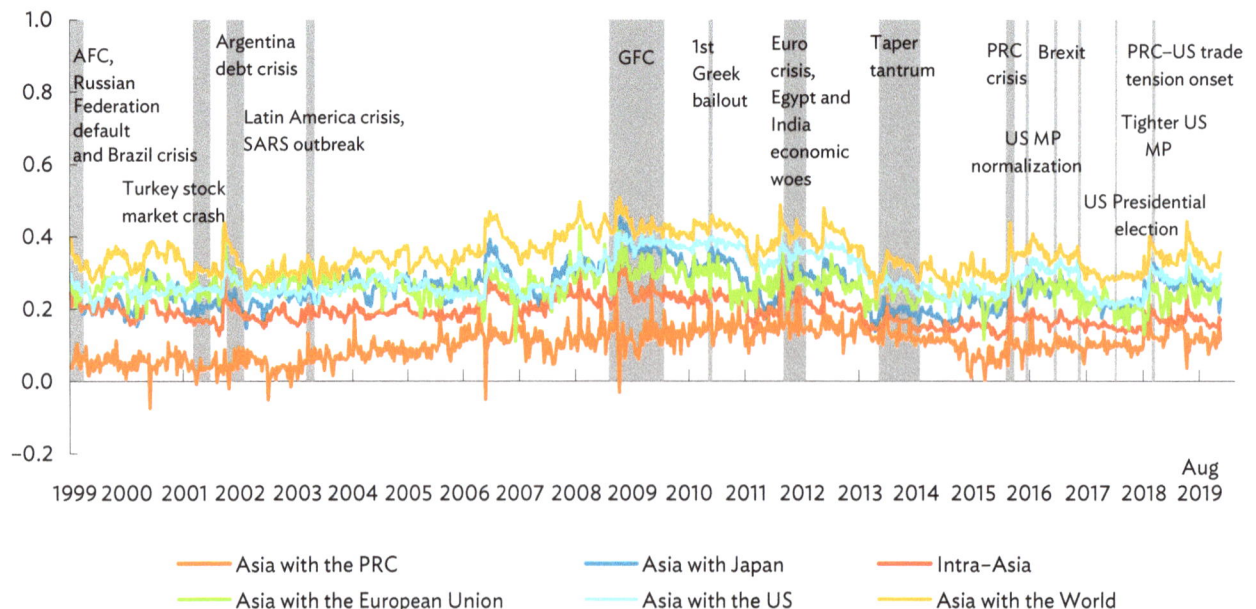

AFC = Asian financial crisis, GFC = global financial crisis, MP = monetary policy, PRC = People's Republic of China, SARS = severe acute respiratory syndrome, US = United States.

Note: Asia includes Australia; Bangladesh; Georgia; Hong Kong, China; India; Indonesia; Japan; Kazakhstan; the Kyrgyz Republic; the Lao People's Democratic Republic; Malaysia; Mongolia; Nepal; New Zealand; Pakistan; the People's Republic of China; the Philippines; the Republic of Korea; Singapore; Sri Lanka; Taipei,China; Thailand; and Viet Nam.

Sources: ADB calculations using Bloomberg; CEIC; Stooq. Stooq Online. http://stooq.com/q/d/_s=^sti (accessed September 2019); and methodology by Hinojales and Park (2010).

Financial Spillovers

Since the US monetary policy normalization—including the onset of trade tensions in 2018—the sensitivity of Asian bond and equity market returns to global shocks has risen, while their sensitivity to regional shocks has declined. These patterns suggest that Asia's financial markets continue to be more exposed to global markets than those within the region.

Between post-GFC and US monetary policy normalization periods, Asia's bond return sensitivity to global shocks increased, from 8.5% to 12.2% (Figure 3.16a). Substantial increases were in Oceania (7.1% to 11.4%) and Southeast Asia (9.0% to 17.4%). At the same time, their sensitivity to regional shocks declined, with only 4.5% of their variances explained by regional shocks during the period of US monetary policy normalization.

As illustrated by the correlation analyses, the region's equity markets are more integrated regionally and globally than their bond market counterpart. This in turn could result in equity markets being more sensitive to shocks in external markets than bond markets. In particular, Asia's equity market sensitivity to global shocks increased—from 20.2% during the post-GFC period to 22.4% since 2016 (Figure 3.16b). East Asia, South Asia, and Southeast Asia contributed to this increase. At the same time, Asia's equity market sensitivity to regional shocks decreased from 11.4% to 6.0%, with substantial declines in East Asia, South Asia, and Southeast Asia. This pattern mirrors the declining intraregional share of outward portfolio equity investment.

Recent developments in fintech and its potential implications for the region's financial stability could affect the region's exposure to financial spillovers (Box 3.3).

Figure 3.16: Share of Variance in Asian Capital Market Returns, as Explained by Global, Regional, and Domestic Shocks (%)

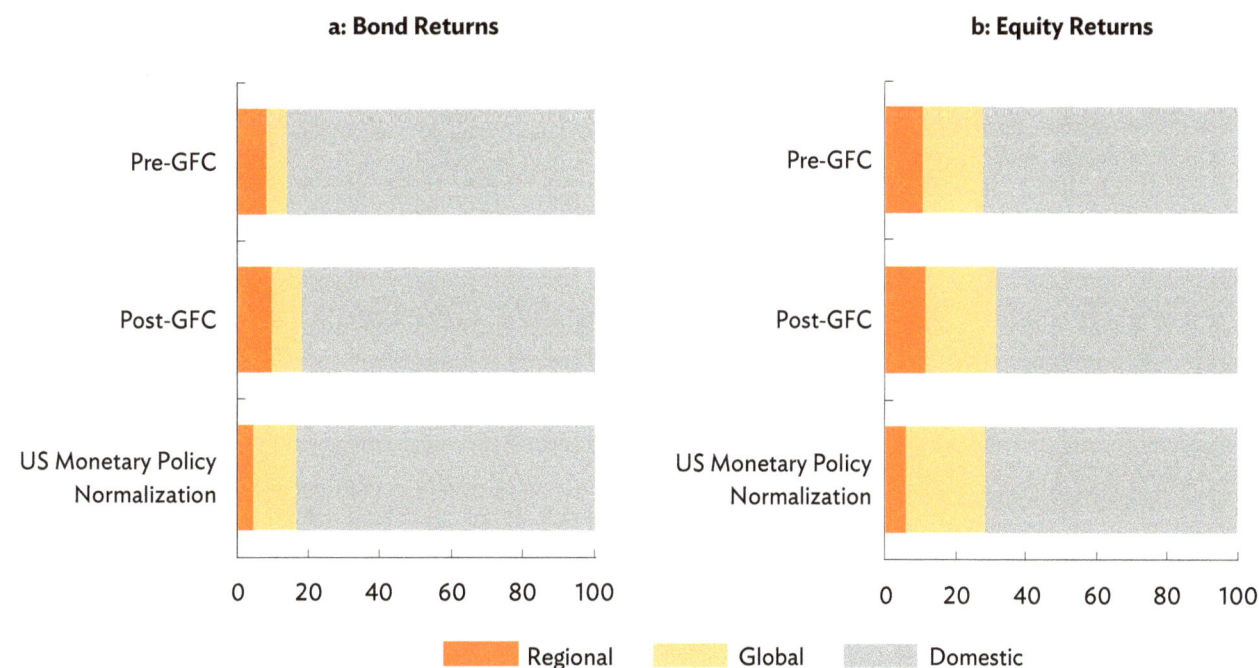

a: Bond Returns

b: Equity Returns

Regional   Global   Domestic

GFC = global financial crisis, US = United States.

Pre-GFC = January 1999 to September 2007, Post-GFC = July 2009 to December 2015, US Monetary Policy Normalization = January 2016 to August 2019.

Notes: Asia includes Australia; *Bangladesh*; *Georgia*; Hong Kong, China; India; Indonesia; Japan; Kazakhstan; *the Kyrgyz Republic*; *the Lao People's Democratic Republic*; Malaysia; *Mongolia*; *Nepal*; New Zealand; *Pakistan*; the People's Republic of China; the Philippines; the Republic of Korea; Singapore; *Sri Lanka*; *Taipei,China*; Thailand; and *Viet Nam*. Italicized names indicate they are included only in equity returns.

Sources: ADB calculations using data from Bloomberg; CEIC; Stooq. Stooq Online. http://stooq.com/q/d/_s=^sti (accessed September 2019); World Bank. World Development Indicators. https://data.worldbank.org/indicator/ny.gdp.mktp.cd (accessed September 2019); and methodology by Lee and Park (2011).

Box 3.3: Fintech and Regional Financial Development and Stability

Currently, innovations in financial technology (fintech) can offer a "leapfrog" development opportunity for developing Asian economies. Financial innovation offers new solutions to solving financial system frictions by increasing the efficiency, accessibility, and the provision of financial services. However, there are also concerns over possible risks to regional financial stability.

Fintech can benefit both users of traditional banking services and new, previously unbanked consumers. Mobile banking and mobile cross-border remittances using fintech services can enhance consumer welfare, creating a virtuous cycle of better services at lower cost. Low-hanging fruit can be enjoyed by filling the gaps between traditional banking services and consumers' increasing needs—such as lowering remittance costs by using technology in financial services.

New solutions built on the cloud, digital platforms, and distributed ledger technologies covering mobile payments and peer-to-peer (P2P) applications have appeared, filling gaps brought about by legacy systems (GSMA 2018). Mobile money and mobile payments—which provide significant benefits such as lower fees, time savings, and reduced travel costs—have increased customer activity rates over the years. Total global transaction value grew by 21% from $26 billion in 2016 to $31.5 billion in 2017, while registered accounts grew 18.4% from $285.9 million in 2016 to $338.4 million in 2017 (GSMA 2018).

 Among all economies, the People's Republic of China (PRC) has the largest mobile payment market—dominated by BigTech companies such as Ant Financial (Alipay) and Tencent (WeChat Pay), which account for 94% of the PRC mobile payments market (Frost et al. 2019).[a] BigTech companies have been a major source of financial innovation. Traditionally starting with mobile payments to facilitate their core business, BigTech companies can leverage network effects and data into other business lines such as credit, insurance, and savings and investment products (Frost et al. 2019). Overall, fintech investment saw explosive growth in 2018 (KPMG 2019), while fintech credit has had steadily increasing growth since 2013 (Frost et al. 2019).

Though fintech has the capacity to increase financial inclusion, increased access to credit could lead to potential financial instability if left unchecked. In the PRC, the lack of regulation has led to significant growth in domestic P2P lending, which was accompanied by growth in fraudulent activities—leading to an estimated failure of one-third of all P2P lenders (UNSGSA FinTech Working Group and CCAF 2019). Operational risks such as cybersecurity and anti-money laundering/combating the financing of terrorism

issues also rise with increasing reliance on decentralized digital solutions, brought about by financial innovation. Fintech could facilitate financial contagion caused by new forms of cross-border financial flows such as tokenized securities, blockchain bonds, or cross-border crowdfunding activities (IMF and World Bank Group 2019).

Financial innovation has blurred the lines between fintech firms and traditional financial service providers. This potential transition could lead to many financial service providers with greater incentives for risk-taking activities—due to their licenses falling outside the regulatory perimeter. Lai and Van Order (2017) indicate that fintech and BigTech firms that engage in deposit-taking and loan-provision activities are essentially unregulated and uninsured shadow banks.

Adding to the risks presented by fintech activities, fintech regulation remains challenging. This is due to numerous factors: (i) fintech firms benefit from regulatory arbitrage due to the limited scope of existing financial regulation—while fintech firms increasingly diversify reach and essentially provide banking and other financial services, fintech firms have less reporting and regulatory requirements as licenses are subject to less stringent monitoring; (ii) limited regulatory experience results in difficulty understanding and assessing fintech's regulatory implications; (iii) resource constraints, especially for emerging and developing economies, limit adequate responses to fintech risks; and (iv) the focus on domestic financial landscape increases risks for cross-border regulatory arbitrage.

Faced with the risks brought about by financial innovation, regulators have responded with similar regulatory innovations. Challenges posed by regulatory arbitrage and limited knowledge of fintech activities can be solved with innovation offices and regulatory sandboxes. Innovation offices provide an avenue for regulator–innovator engagement. Engaging with the fintech industry helps regulators understand key trends and the potential issues and risks of innovative financial services and their implications for regulatory policy.

Resource constraints for emerging and developing economies, though not directly addressed, can be mitigated through regional knowledge-sharing and policy dialogue, such as the ASEAN+3 Economic Review and Policy Dialogue. Efficient and effective policies and regulations can be implemented directly using the experience of more developed economies or through other knowledge-sharing policy platforms. Tangentially, the coordination provided by regional knowledge-sharing and policy dialogue may reduce the potential for regulatory arbitrage by creating uniform international best practices in formulating policies and regulations.

---

[a] BigTech companies offer financial products as one component of a much broader business line while fintech companies operate primarily in financial services.

Source: Asian Development Bank.

Since 2006, there have been several episodes of pronounced bond return divergence—the GFC, the 2013 taper tantrum, and the 2015 steep decline in world commodity prices—while current levels are comparably low. However, since 2018 there have been some signs of divergence.

Amid a steep decline in world commodity prices, bond returns in developing Asia diverged significantly in 2015, driven by Kazakhstan's tightening economic and financial conditions as a commodity price exporter. While this has eased, Asian economies total bond return indexes have signaled divergence since the onset of the PRC–US trade

tensions in 2018 (Figure 3.17a), both intraregionally and within subregions, though being at more moderate levels compared with earlier crisis periods.

Outside the region, the Asia–World sigma-convergence remains lower than intra-Asia's sigma-convergence, indicating a stronger convergence with global markets than within Asia (Figure 3.17b). Recent signs of divergence, particularly with US bond returns, could be driven by deviating economic outlooks and financial conditions among emerging and developed economies. While financial conditions in advanced economies have remained rather accommodative, conditions have tightened in emerging economies.

Figure 3.17: σ-Convergence of Total Return Bond Indexes—Asia

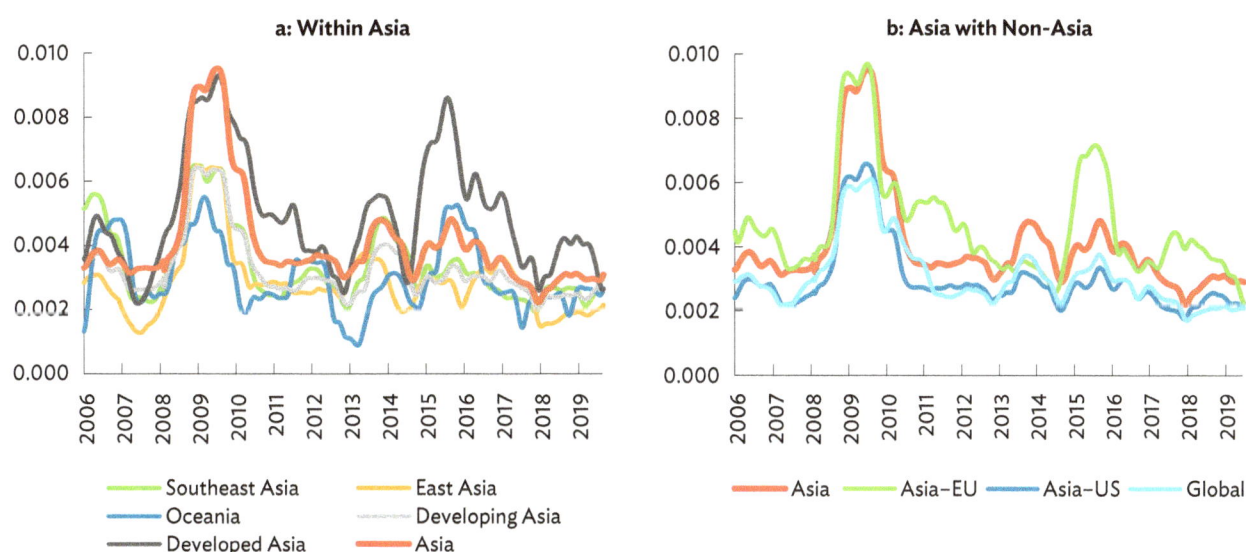

EU = European Union, US = United States.

Notes:

(i)   Values refer to the unweighted mean of an individual economy's σ-convergence included in the subregion. Each economy's σ-convergence is the simple mean of all its pairwise standard deviations. Data are filtered using the Hodrick-Prescott method.

(ii) East Asia includes Hong Kong, China; Japan; the People's Republic of China; the Republic of Korea; and Taipei,China. Oceania includes Australia and New Zealand. Southeast Asia includes Indonesia, Malaysia, the Philippines, Singapore, and Thailand. Developed Asia includes Japan and Oceania. Developing Asia includes East Asia excluding Japan, India, Kazakhstan, and Southeast Asia. Asia includes developed and developing Asia. World σ-convergence calculated from Bloomberg Barclays Global Treasury Total Return Index Value Unhedged USD.

Sources: ADB calculations using data from Bloomberg; CEIC; and methodology by Espinoza, Prasad, and Williams (2010), and Park (2013).

References

Asian Development Bank (ADB). 2019. *Good Practices for Developing a Local Currency Bond Market – Lessons from the ASEAN+3 Asian Bond Markets Initiative*. Manila.

Bank for International Settlements. Locational Banking Statistics. https://www.bis.org/statistics/bankstats.htm (accessed May 2019 and September 2019).

Cranston, M. 2019. Chinese Banks Lend More to Australia than the US. *Financial Review*. 12 June. https://www.afr.com/policy/economy/chinese-banks-lend-more-to-australia-than-the-us-20190612-p51wrl.

Espinoza, R., A. Prasad and O. Williams. 2010. Regional Financial Integration in the GCC. *IMF Working Paper No. 10/90*. Washington, DC: International Monetary Fund.

European Central Bank. 2019. *Financial Stability Review*. Frankfurt.

European Commission. 2018a. *Second Progress Report on the Reduction of Non-Performing Loans and Further Risk Reduction in the Banking Union*. Brussels.

____. 2018b. *Third Progress Report on the Reduction of Non-Performing Loans and Further Risk Reduction in the Banking Union*. Brussels.

____. 2019. *Fourth Progress Report on the Reduction of Non-Performing Loans and Further Risk Reduction in the Banking Union*. Brussels.

Frost, J., L. Gambacorta, Y. Huang, H. S. Shin, and P. Zbinden. 2019. BigTech and the Changing Structure of Financial Intermediation. *BIS Working Papers*. No. 779. Basel: Bank for International Settlements.

Greifeld, K. 2018. As Japan Dumps Treasuries, It's Buying Riskier U.S. Assets. *Think Advisor*. 5 July. https://www.thinkadvisor.com/2018/07/05/as-japan-dumps-treasuries-its-buying-riskier-u-s-a/.

GSMA. 2018. *2017 State of the Industry Report on Mobile Money*. London.

Hinojales, M. and C. Y. Park. 2010. Stock Market Integration: Emerging East Asia's Experience. In M. Devereaux, P. Lane, C. Y. Park, and S. J. Wei, eds. *The Dynamics of Asian Financial Integration: Facts and Analytics*. London and New York: Routledge.

Huckle, J. 2018. How a Change in Strategy is Putting Cayman on the Map for Japanese Institutional Investors. *Ogier*. 4 September. https://www.ogier.com/publications/how-a-change-in-strategy-is-putting-cayman-on-the-map-for-japanese-institutional-investors.

International Monetary Fund (IMF). Coordinated Direct Investment Survey. http://data.imf.org/CDIS (accessed May 2019).

____. Coordinated Portfolio Investment Survey. http://data.imf.org/CPIS (accessed September 2019).

IMF and World Bank Group. 2019. *FinTech: The Experience So Far*. Washington, DC.

KPMG. 2019. *The Pulse of Fintech 2018*. Zurich.

Lai, R.N., and R. Van Order. 2017. Fintech Finance and Financial Fragility: Focusing on China. https://www.researchgate.net/publication/321185322_Fintech_Finance_and_Financial_Fragility-Focusing_on_China.

Lee, J. and P. Rosenkranz. 2019. Nonperforming Loans in Asia: Determinants and Macrofinancial Linkages. *ADB Economics Working Paper. No. 574*. Manila: ADB.

Lee, J. W. and C. Y. Park. 2011. Financial Integration in Emerging Asia: Challenges and Prospects. *Asian Economic Policy Review*. 6 (2). pp. 176–198.

Manca, G., H. Böschenbröker, and P. Navarra. 2019. Banking Hub by zeb. *NPL Transaction Platforms: A Solution to the NPL Rebus?* https://www.bankinghub.eu/banking/operations/npl-rebus.

Park, C. Y. 2013. Asian Capital Market Integration: Theory and Evidence. *ADB Economic Working Paper Series*. No. 351. Manila: ADB.

Stooq. Stooq Online. http://stooq.com/q/d/_s=^sti (accessed September 2019).

UNSGSA FinTech Working Group and CCAF. (2019). *Early Lessons on Regulatory Innovations to Enable Inclusive FinTech: Innovation Offices, Regulatory Sandboxes, and RegTech*. New York, NY and Cambridge, UK: Office of the UNSGSA and CCAF.

World Bank. World Development Indicators. https://data.worldbank.org/indicator/ny.gdp.mktp.cd (accessed July 2019 and September 2019).

4 Movement of People

Remittances

Remittance inflows to Asia continue to climb, reaching a record $302.1 billion in 2018.

Global remittances (inflows) grew 7.6% to $682.6 billion in 2018 (Figure 4.1).[19] Remittances to Asia grew 8.4%, above the global rate, adding $23.4 billion to the

Figure 4.1: Remittance Inflows to Asia and the World

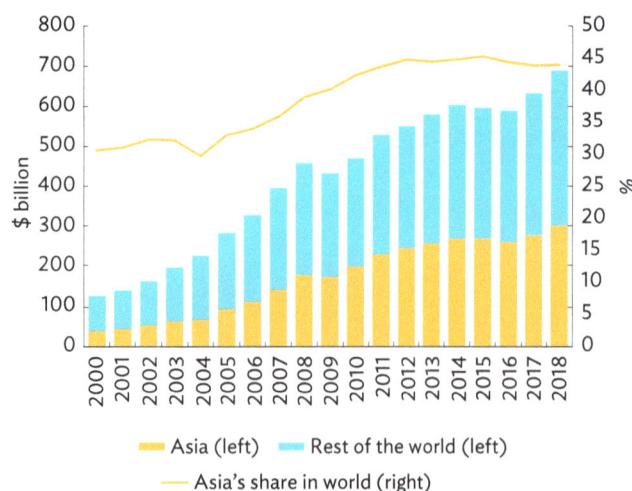

Asia (left)   Rest of the world (left)
Asia's share in world (right)

Source: ADB calculations using data from Global Knowledge Partnership on Migration and Development. http://www.knomad.org/data/remittances (accessed October 2019).

2017 level. The growth was attributed to improved economic performance and job market conditions in the United States (US), the rise in oil prices, a rebound in remittances from Middle East economies and improved economic activity in the Russian Federation (World Bank 2019).

Remittances are a key, stable source of income for many countries in developing Asia. On average, remittance inflows were 10 times the level of official development assistance (ODA) since 2012 and are significant contributors to national output (Figure 4.2). They bolster foreign exchange reserves and directly provide for the consumption, investment, and savings needs of household beneficiaries. As immediate financial flows, remittances help ease the conditions of the poor, particularly in recipient countries with high rates of poverty.[20]

Remittance inflows across all major geographic regions increased in 2018, except the Middle East. Inflows to Asia expanded by 8.4%.

Remittance inflows increased across all global subregions, except the Middle East (World Bank 2019).

---

[19] The World Bank defines personal remittances as the sum of personal transfers and compensation of employees. Personal transfers include all current transfers in cash or in kind between resident and nonresident individuals, independent of the source of income of the sender (and regardless of whether the sender receives income from labor, entrepreneurial or property income, social benefits and any other types of transfers, or disposed assets) and the relationship between the households (regardless of whether they are related or unrelated individuals). Compensation of employees refers to the income of border, seasonal, and other short-term workers who are employed in an economy where they are not resident and of residents employed by nonresident entities.

[20] Yoshino, Taghizadeh-Hesary, and Otsuka (2017) found that a 1% increase in international remittances as a percentage of gross domestic product (GDP) can lead to a 22.6% decline in the poverty gap ratio and a 16.0% decline in the poverty severity ratio in the sample of 10 developing Asian countries from 1981 to 2014. The poverty gap ratio indicates how far below the poverty line the average poor household's income or expenditure falls. Poverty severity (or squared poverty gap index) is measured by averaged squares of the poverty gaps relative to the poverty line.

Figure 4.2: Financial Flows to Asia by Type ($ billion)

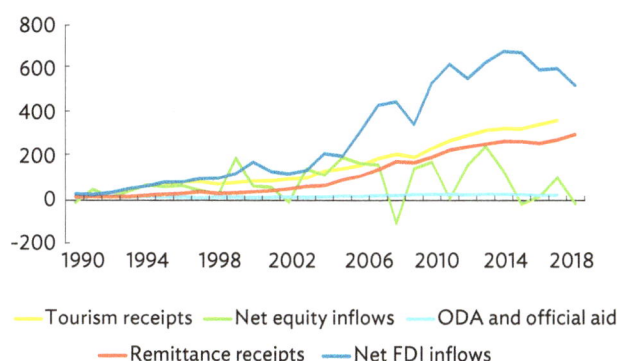

FDI = foreign direct investment, ODA = official development assistance.

Sources: ADB calculations using data from Global Knowledge Partnership on Migration and Development. http://www.knomad.org/data/remittances; and World Bank. World Development Indicators. https://databank.worldbank.org/source/world-developmentindicators (both accessed October 2019).

By absolute value, Asia was highest at $302.1 billion, up by $23.4 billion (Table 4.1). The region benefited from strong oil prices, which improved flows from the Middle East, and the sustained strength of the US labor market. The Middle East hosts significant proportions of migrant workers from South Asia and Southeast Asia and has been a primary remittance source for these subregions. In 2017, around 59% of remittance inflows to South Asia came from Middle East economies; in Southeast Asia, the Middle East accounted for about one-fourth.[21]

Inflows to Europe rose by $11.3 billion to $171.4 billion, driven by sustained economic activities in major European outflow countries such as Poland, the Russian Federation, and Spain. Brisk outflows from the US kept remittances to Latin America and the Caribbean robust at $89.9 billion, a 9.5% jump facilitated by increases in migration and amounts remitted (The Dialogue 2019).

With the exception of Central Asia and Oceania, remittance inflows to all subregions in Asia grew (Table 4.2). South Asia continued to be the lead subregion for remittances, accounting for at least 40% of Asia's total remittances; inflows increased by 12.7%. Local currency depreciation in South Asia contributed to the greater volume of inflows. Inflows to India, the world's top recipient country, gained momentum in 2018—growing by 14.0%, outpacing the 9.9% growth in 2017. In Bangladesh, remittances grew to a record $15.6 billion after contracting in 2016 and 2017. Remittances to Southeast Asia rose by 7.8%, with East Asia inflows rising by 5.0% over 2017—inflows to both subregions increased by more than $5.0 billion. Remittances to Mongolia spiked 61.2% to $440.6 million due to migrant remittances from the Republic of Korea and the Russian Federation. In Southeast Asia, higher inflows from land- and sea-based overseas Filipino workers and the 5.3% depreciation of the peso against the US dollar led remittance flows to the Philippines to reach $33.8 billion, making it the

Table 4.1: Remittance Inflows by Recipient Region, 2018

Region	Share of Total (%)	Amount ($ billion)	Change over 2017 ($ billion)	Growth Rate (%)
Asia	44.3	302.1	23.4	8.4
Europe	25.1	171.4	11.3	7.1
Latin America and the Caribbean	13.2	89.9	7.8	9.5
Middle East	3.6	24.4	-0.1	-0.3
North America	1.2	8.0	0.6	7.7
Africa	12.1	82.8	5.4	7.0

Source: ADB calculations using data from Global Knowledge Partnership on Migration and Development. http://www.knomad.org/data/remittances (accessed October 2019).

---

[21] Saudi Arabia's campaign of labor nationalization (*Nitaqat*) had already resulted in reduced migrant inflows from South Asia, specifically Bangladesh, India, and Pakistan. The *Nitaqat* campaign to increase Saudis in the workforce (launched in September 2011) is a system that combines incentives that encourage firms to hire Saudis and sanctions for those noncompliant. Since its inception, *Nitaqat* has phased out expatriates from a growing number of activity sectors and positions, now restricted solely to Saudi nationals. A decree effective October 2018 bans foreign laborers from 12 more retail sectors. Contracts of expatriates employed in government bodies and ministries are also to be terminated within 3 years and, since 2017, the validity of expatriate work visas for private sector employees has been reduced from 2 years to 1 year (De Bel-Air 2018).

Table 4.2: Remittance Inflows to Asian Subregions, 2018

Subregion	Amount ($ billion, % share of total in parentheses)	Change over 2017 ($ billion, % growth in parentheses)	Economy Within Subregion with Highest Growth (% y-o-y growth in parentheses)
Central Asia	13.0 (4.3%)	-0.6 (-4.5%)	Georgia (13.4%)
East Asia	79.4 (26.3%)	3.8 (5.0%)	Mongolia (61.2%)
South Asia	132.0 (43.7%)	14.9 (12.7%)	Bhutan (34.8%)
Southeast Asia	74.7 (24.7%)	5.4 (7.8%)	Indonesia (24.7%)
Oceania	2.3 (0.8%)	-0.1 (-5.2%)	New Zealand (3.7%)
Pacific	0.8 (0.3%)	0.01 (1.0%)	Solomon Islands (20.3%)

y-o-y = year-on-year.

Source: ADB calculations using data from Global Knowledge Partnership on Migration and Development. http://www.knomad.org/data/remittances (accessed October 2019).

fourth-largest remittance recipient globally. Remittances to Indonesia grew by 24.7% and brought in $2.2 billion in additional receipts in 2018. Indonesia saw the outflow of workers rise by 11.7% between 2016 and 2017—those in elementary occupations increased by 16.8% but the number of managers rose by 29.8% and professionals by 32.0% (International Labour Organization 2018). In New Zealand, the 3.7% rise in remittances reversed the falling inflow trend since 2015. Meanwhile, Australia's downward streak of remittance flows continued in 2018. Pacific developing member countries (DMCs), with smaller populations relative to other regions, received the least remittances.

Remittances remain a vital income source for many countries in developing Asia.

In 2018, the top three remittance recipients—India, the People's Republic of China (PRC), and the Philippines—accounted for 59.5% ($179.8 billion) of all remittances to Asia and 26.3% of remittances globally ($682.6 billion) (Figure 4.3). In 2018, remittances increased in South Asia (12.7%), Southeast Asia (7.8%), and East Asia (5.0%). Together, the three subregions received 94.7% of inflows to Asia and 41.9% of global remittances.

Figure 4.3: Top 10 Remittance Recipients in Asia, 2018 ($ billion)

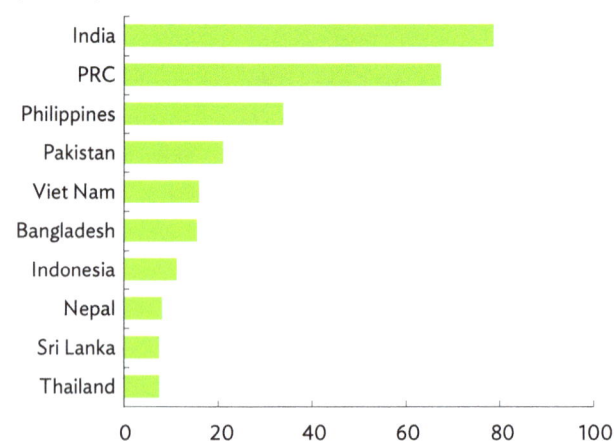

PRC = People's Republic of China.

Source: ADB calculations using data from Global Knowledge Partnership on Migration and Development. http://www.knomad.org/data/remittances (accessed October 2019).

Pacific DMCs and countries in Central Asia received smaller amounts of remittances, but inflows represent a significant proportion of gross domestic product (GDP). In Tonga, for example, remittances are significant both in per capita terms and in proportion to GDP (Figures 4.4a and 4.4b). Shortages of agricultural land, and limited educational and work opportunities drive

Figure 4.4: Top 10 Remittance-Recipient Economies in Asia, 2018

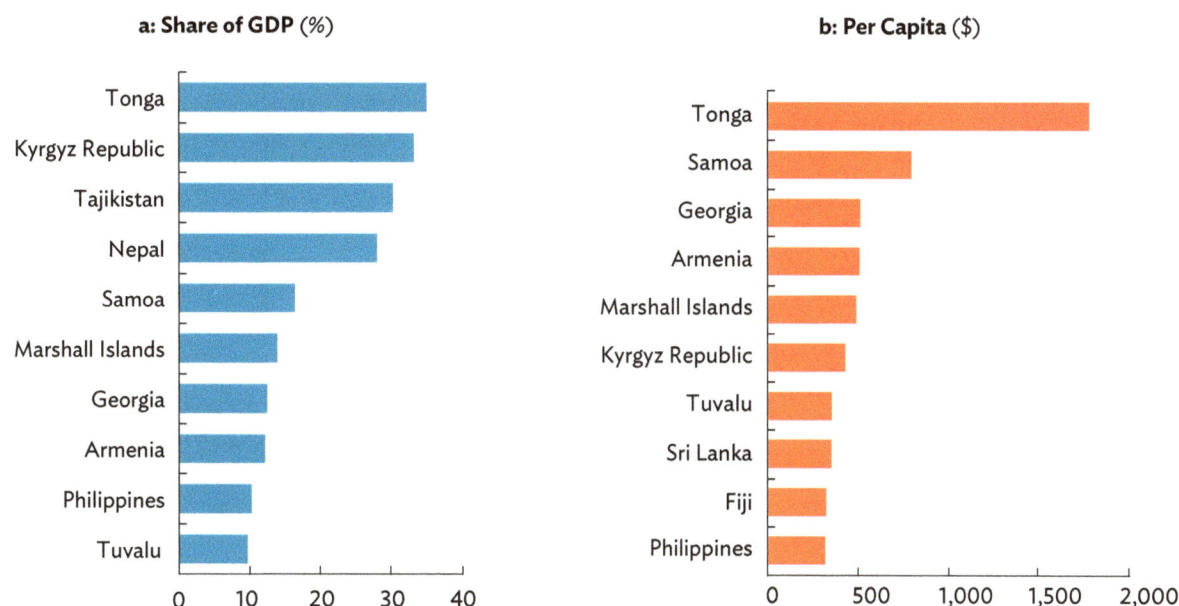

a: Share of GDP (%)

b: Per Capita ($)

GDP = gross domestic product.

Sources: ADB calculations using data from Global Knowledge Partnership on Migration and Development. http://www.knomad.org/data/remittances (accessed October 2019); International Monetary Fund. World Economic Outlook October 2019 Database. https://www.imf.org/external/pubs/ft/weo/2019/02/weodata/index.aspx (accessed October 2019); and United Nations. Department of Economic and Social Affairs, Population Division. World Population Prospects 2019. https://population.un.org/wpp/Download/Standard/Population/ (accessed August 2019).

around 50% of adult Tongans to work abroad—mostly in New Zealand, Australia, and the US (International Finance Corporation 2018). Around 90% of Tongan households rely on remittances as an income source (Fonua 2012). In Central Asia, remittance inflows are equivalent to some 33.0% of GDP for the Kyrgyz Republic and Tajikistan, and around 12.0% of GDP in Georgia and Armenia. In the Pacific, remittances equal around 10.0% of GDP in Tuvalu and Kiribati. In the Philippines, remittances remain a vital source of monetary inflows. As vital as remittance inflows are, the cost of sending money to home countries remains a pervasive constraint to maximizing the benefit of remittances to developing Asian economies.[22]

Remittance inflows are projected to sustain its growth momentum as new labor migration opportunities are created amid a moderate global economic growth outlook for most host countries.

Despite migration policies taking a more restrictive trend in some major host countries—and global growth expected to remain moderate—the Global Knowledge Partnership on Migration and Development (2019) estimates global remittances will grow by 3.5% and 4.6% in 2019 and 2020, respectively; compared with the 7.6% growth in 2018. During this period, inflows to Asia should expand by 4.6% and 4.4% to $315.8 billion

[22]   ADB calculations using data from the World Bank's Remittance Prices Worldwide database indicate that the global average cost of sending remittances (expressed as a percentage of remitted amount) declined to 6.9% in the first quarter (Q1) of 2019; though it varies considerably across Asian subregions. For example, the average cost of sending $200 in cash via a bank in Oceania to Samoa was 12.5% in Q1 2019, more than half of what it used to cost in Q1 2017 (26.7%). Sending the same amount to Tonga cost 9.6% in Q1 2019, lower than 11.2% in the same period in 2017. Although these average costs are lower than 2017 rates, they remain far above the 6.9% global average in Q1 2019 and still far from the Sustainable Development Goal (SDG) target of 3% by 2030.

and $329.7 billion, respectively. Traditional migrant host countries such as the US issued fewer immigrant (down by 4.6%) and nonimmigrant visas (down by 6.8%) in 2018. Employment-preference visas rose by 14.8% to 27,345 in 2018—69.7% of which went to workers from Asia.[23] In the Middle East, the collective aim to reduce dependence on foreign labor will likely reduce the flow of low-skilled and retail workers to the region. However, their aim to develop the technology sector and become a regional digital hub implies an increase in demand for foreign digital investors, high-skilled workers, and information technology technicians. For example, to support their digital development goal, the United Arab Emirates and Saudi Arabia have established privileged visa processes to ease the flow of high-quality foreign workers and technology entrepreneurs into the region.[24] Additionally, some migrant host countries in Asia have begun to relax migration policies, driven by labor market needs amid rapidly aging populations. Japan passed a law in December 2018 that allows the entry of 345,000 workers within the next 5 years. This is expected to generate higher remittances to priority countries identified in the law—Cambodia, Indonesia, Mongolia, Myanmar, Nepal, the PRC, the Philippines, Thailand, and Viet Nam. The Republic of Korea is also planning to host 56,000 foreign workers to ease its low-skilled labor shortage.

International Tourism and the Movement of Visitors

International tourism remained robust in 2017, as 1.3 billion visitors traveled to various parts of the globe. The share of global arrivals to Asia rose to 30.5% in 2017 from 26.3% in 2010.

Global tourism has been growing at a sustained rate since 2010, as the liberalization of air travel market, the emergence of budget airlines, and innovations in digital and mobile technology revolutionized bookings for accommodations and airfares. The number of international visitors grew by 5.2% in 2017—from 1.3 billion in 2016—as economic growth continued to fuel demand for international travel.[25]

Tourism is important in many countries in Asia where it significantly contributes to economic growth and development.[26] International travelers to Asia expanded rapidly to 407.6 million in 2017 from 251.4 million in 2010, clear evidence of the region's success in showcasing itself as a hub of premier destinations (Figure 4.5). By 2017, the region had captured about a third (30.5%) of the total

Figure 4.5: Global Visitor Arrivals by Region

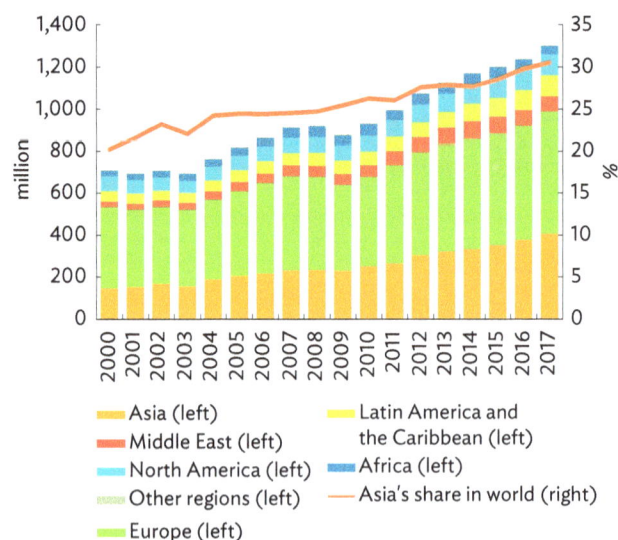

Asia (left)
Middle East (left)
North America (left)
Other regions (left)
Europe (left)
Latin America and the Caribbean (left)
Africa (left)
Asia's share in world (right)

Source: ADB calculations using data from United Nations World Tourism Organization. Tourism Satellite Accounts. http://statistics.unwto.org/ (accessed April 2019).

---

[23] According to the US Department of State Bureau of Consular Affairs, the US issued 533,557 immigrant visas in 2018. The number declined across all immigrant visa categories except for the employment preference category, which increased to 27,345 in 2018 from 23,814 in 2017. This was the most employment category visas issued since 2005.

[24] In May 2019, Saudi Arabia approved its "Privileged Iqama" residency scheme that allows expatriates to live and work without the need of sponsorship by a Saudi national. The United Arab Emirates's "Gold Card" are 5- and 10-year residency permits in three broad categories for investors, entrepreneurs, and special talents.

[25] According to the 2008 Recommendations for Tourism Statistics (United Nations Statistical Commission 2007), *tourism* refers to the activity of *visitors*. A *visitor* is a traveler taking a trip to a main destination outside his/her usual environment, for less than a year, for any purpose (business, leisure or other personal purpose) other than to be employed by a resident entity in the country or place visited. A *visitor* is classified as a *tourist* (or overnight visitor), if his/her trip includes an overnight stay, or as a *same-day visitor* (or excursionist) otherwise. There are no significant differences between the numbers of visitors and tourists in many countries except for the PRC where some 60% of visitors are same-day visitors arriving from Hong Kong, China and Macau, China.

[26] For example, tourism accounted for some 14% of the Thai economy in 2017 with its development direction included in the Twelfth National Economic and Social Development Plan (2017–2021). In Cambodia, tourism is the third-largest economic sector after agriculture and garments, and the second-highest income earner. Growth of Viet Nam's tourism is one of the fastest in the world and, as early as 2011, the government released its *Strategy on Vietnam's Tourism Development until 2020, Vision to 2030* to promote the industry. In Fiji, tourism remains a priority area with a target income goal of $2.21 billion by 2021.

number of global travelers, up from 26.3% in 2010. During the same period, the number of international visitors to Asia grew at an average annual rate of 7.1%, surpassing the world average, as the region hosted 29.5 million more travelers in 2017. Europe, which historically draws the largest number of arrivals (580.9 million visitors in 2017) and the largest share of the global total (43.9% on average since 2010) posted 6.8% growth in 2017, lower than Asia. North America drew 97.7 million visitors, 1.4% higher than 2016,[27] despite an 8.8% decline in the number of B1/B2 visas issued.[28] Even the Middle East posted a modest growth of 1.0% after security challenges resulted in 2 consecutive years in which arrivals contracted (2015 and 2016).

Movement of Visitors in Asia

Visitor arrivals to Asia grew by 7.8% in 2017 to 407.6 million due to robust growth in the number of intraregional visitors (up by 8.0%) as well as extraregional visitors (up by 7.2%).

Intraregional visitors in Asia reached 319.6 million, an increase of 23.6 million from 2016.[29] East Asia and Southeast Asia had the strongest pull in intraregional arrivals, attracting 11.4 million and 7.6 million in additional arrivals, respectively. Extraregional arrivals (87.9 million), on the other hand, continued its upward trend since 2015, with robust growth averaging 7.5% in 2016 and 2017.

Greater tourism cooperation in the region drove intraregional arrivals to a record high as 23.6 million more Asian visitors traveled within the region from 2016 (Figure 4.6). Large numbers of Asian travelers headed to East Asia (59.0% of intraregional Asian visitors) and Southeast Asia (30.9%). The number of intraregional arrivals grew across all Asian subregions, with Central Asia registering the highest growth (22.3%) as 2.8 million more Asian visitors traveled to Central Asian countries. Initiatives to ease travel among Central Asian countries have started under the

Figure 4.6: Intraregional and Extraregional Flows of Visitors from Asia, 2017

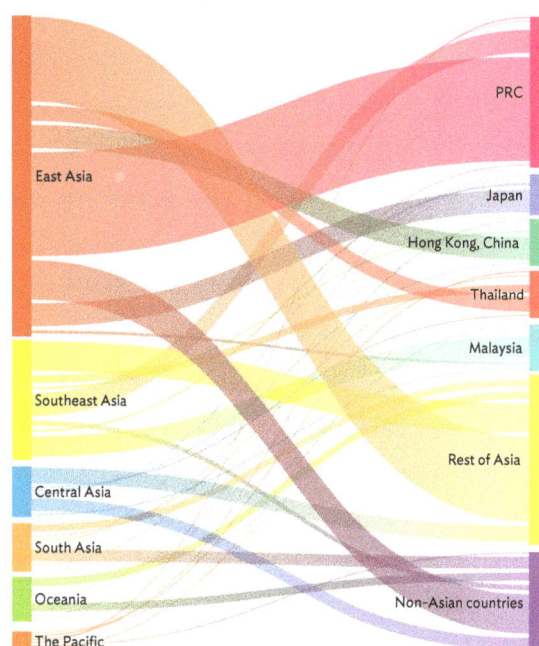

PRC = People's Republic of China.

Source: ADB calculations using data from United Nations World Tourism Organization. Tourism Satellite Accounts. http://statistics.unwto.org/ (accessed April 2019).

Central Asia Regional Economic Cooperation (CAREC) Program. Improved visa facilitation measures have been initiated in line with reviving and promoting tourism among countries along the Silk Road (Box 4.1). South Asia also had double-digit growth (17.8%) in intraregional travel with 7.1 million intraregional visitors in 2017.

More extraregional visitors also traveled to Asia, reaching 87.9 million in 2017, up from 82.0 million in 2016 (Figure 4.7). Europe (41.5%), North America (18.6%), and the Middle East (7.1%) were the top three source regions. East Asia and Southeast Asia were the preferred subregional destinations for Europe and North America, while visitors from the Middle East primarily traveled to Central Asia and Southeast Asia. On average, extraregional visitors traveling to Asia grew by 3.8% annually from 2010 to 2016—and by 7.2% in 2017.

---

[27] However, 60.7% of this increase was due to 826,443 more visitors to Canada. In 2017, the number of visitors to the US grew 0.7% relative to 2016. Visitors to the US from the Middle East fell sharply since 2016, when growth rates contracted 2.5% after rising 11.8% in 2015; and contracted further by 12.7% in 2017.

[28] The US Bureau of Consular Affairs issues B1 visas for business visits to the US, while B2 visas are for tourism. A B1/B2 visa may be used for either purpose. In 2017, 6.3 million B1/B2 visas were issued, 8.8% lower than the 6.9 million visas issued in 2016. In 2018, the number of B1/B2 visas declined further by 9.1% to 5.7 million.

[29] In terms of tourists, Asia attracted 23.4% (310.7 million) of global tourist arrivals in 2017, up from 24.0% (305.4 million) in 2016. Inbound tourists from both Asia (up by 10.3% from 2016) and non-Asia (up by 8.2%) contributed to the high growth in Asian tourism. Intraregional tourists accounted for nearly 80% of tourists to Asia.

Box 4.1: Relaxing Visa Policies to Boost Tourism in CAREC

Tourism development is one of the operational priorities under the Central Asia Regional Economic Cooperation (CAREC) Program's CAREC 2030 strategy. As the subregion's premier economic and social cooperation platform, CAREC seeks to connect people, policies, and projects for shared and sustainable development. In October 2018, a workshop was held in Tashkent, Uzbekistan to assess opportunities and challenges for regional tourism cooperation. It led to the publication of a scoping study on promoting regional tourism cooperation under CAREC 2030 (ADB 2019). At ADB's 52nd annual meeting in Fiji, a high-level session underscored CAREC's regional approach to tourism development by facilitating travel between its 11 members and promoting multicountry experiences that could reap greater socioeconomic benefits for each. With a combined population of 1.8 billion producing 16.6% of global gross domestic product in 2018, the regional initiative holds much tourism potential.[a] International arrivals to the subregion grew 23.8% in 2017 to 177.8 million, up from 143.6 million in 2010.[b] Tourism receipts reached $42.8 billion in 2017.[c] Natural and cultural resource diversity is one of CAREC's main attractions. But several major challenges must be overcome, especially in both hard and soft infrastructure. Transport facilities and existing border control arrangements to manage tourists moving in, out, and around CAREC countries are still below international standards.

Visa policies play an important role in ensuring a destination's capacity to carry out and control tourism demand—through immigration control and managing the entry, duration of stay, or activities of travelers; generating revenue; and applying reciprocity measures (UNWTO 2013). However, bothersome visa requirements can reduce a tourist's desire to visit another country. Within CAREC, there are heterogenic visa policies. Afghanistan, Mongolia, the People's Republic of China (PRC), and Turkmenistan mostly require visas from

tourists in other CAREC countries, while Azerbaijan, Georgia, and Uzbekistan have eased border restrictions with varying visa-free arrangements (Box Table 1). Bilateral reciprocity of visa policies is not necessarily observed. For example, a visa is required for Central Asian tourists going to the PRC, but PRC tourists visiting Georgia, Kazakhstan, the Kyrgyz Republic, Tajikistan, and Uzbekistan can obtain e-visas. ADB (2019) finds that visa openness supports visa reciprocity between members within regional blocs; and that facilitation can help strategic policy formulation, triggering improved visa policies for visitors between regional members.

Harmonizing visa policies across CAREC can only improve tourism numbers. Intra-CAREC visitor arrivals grew by 23.4% to 16.4 million tourists in 2017, a marked improvement from the tepid 2.6% growth in 2016 (Box Figure).[d] Within Central Asia, Kazakhstan, the Kyrgyz Republic, and Uzbekistan had the largest increase in intra-CAREC arrivals, accounting for around 70% of the increase from 2016. These three countries also have relatively visa-free policies and e-visa facilities compared to other CAREC countries. However, even if arrivals growth rates rose from 5.2% in 2010 to 9.7% in 2017, intra-CAREC tourism remains weak, accounting for less than 10% of total arrivals in the subregion. By comparison, tourism within the Association of Southeast Asian Nations (ASEAN) more than doubled during the same period (Box Figure). There were 46.6 million intra-ASEAN arrivals in 2017, equivalent to 38.7% of total tourism in Southeast Asia. In the Greater Mekong Subregion (GMS), intra-GMS tourism accounted for 20.2% of total international arrivals.

Visa entry arrangements also differ significantly for tourists from non-CAREC countries (Box Table 2). Georgia, Kazakhstan, the Kyrgyz Republic, and Uzbekistan have more visa-free arrangements with the sample of source countries within and outside Asia. Mongolia's visa policy

1: Visa-Entry Arrangements among CAREC Members

| Origin Country | Destination | | | | | | | | | | |
	AFG	AZE	GEO	KAZ	KGZ	MON	PAK	PRC	TAJ	TKM	UZB
Afghanistan		vr	ev	vr	ev	vr	vr	vr	ev	vr	ev
Azerbaijan	vr		vf-360	vf-30	VF	vr	voa	vr	vf-90	vr	VF
Georgia	vr	vf-90		vf-90	VF	vr	ev	vr	VF	vf-90	VF
Kazakhstan	vr	vf-90	vf-360		VF	vf-90	ev	vr	VF	vr	VF
Kyrgyz Republic	vr	vf-90	vf-360	vf-90		vf-90	ev	vr	VF	vr	vf-60
Mongolia	vr	vr	ev	vf-90	vf-90		ev	vf-30	voa/ev-45	vr	vf-30
Pakistan	vr	ev	ev	vr	ev	vr		vr	ev	vr	ev
PRC	vr	voa-ev	ev	ev	ev	vr	ev		ev	vr	ev-30
Tajikistan	vr	vf90	vf-360	vf-30	VF	vr	voa/ev-90	vr		vr	vf-30
Turkmenistan	vr	ev	vf-360	ev	ev	vr	ev	vr	voa/ev-45		ev
Uzbekistan	vr	vf90	vf-360	vf-30	vf60	vr	ev	vr	vf-30	vr	

VF = visa-free, vf-360 = visa-free for 360 days, vf-90 = visa-free for 90 days, vf-30 = visa-free for 30 days

ev = e-visa, ev-30 = e-visa for 30 days, ev-90 = e-visa for 90 days, ev-45 = e-visa for 45 days

voa = visa on arrival, vr = visa required

AFG = Afghanistan, AZE = Azerbaijan, GEO = Georgia, KAZ = Kazakhstan, KGZ = Kyrgyz Republic, MON = Mongolia, PAK = Pakistan, PRC = People's Republic of China, TAJ = Tajikistan, TKM = Turkmenistan, UZB = Uzbekistan.

Source: Arton Capital's PassportIndex.org database (electronic). http://www.passportindex.org (accessed August 2019).

continued on next page

Box 4.1: Relaxing Visa Policies to Boost Tourism in CAREC (continued)

is also more open to non-CAREC countries. Given the considerable weight of tourism traffic from non-CAREC countries, accelerating simpler and more accessible visa arrangements (such as visa-on-arrival and online visa applications) and lower visa costs would help portray the region as more tourist friendly. Pakistan wants to introduce a single visa for tourists visiting the CAREC subregion, to both facilitate tourist movement and increase the likelihood of tourists doing multicountry visits, increasing the average time of stay and spending per tourist.[e] In strengthening intrasubregional ties, this would also help CAREC "brand" itself better as a future tourist destination for visitors from other countries in Asia—which make up at least 60% of its market.

Intrasubregional Tourism Shares—CAREC, ASEAN, and GMS (%)

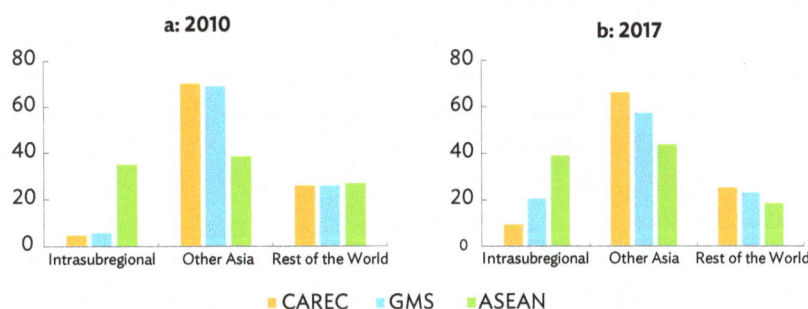

ASEAN = Association of Southeast Asian Nations, CAREC = Central Asia Regional Economic Cooperation Program, GMS = Greater Mekong Subregion.

Note: Calculations are based on arrivals data for Azerbaijan, Georgia, Kazakhstan, the Kyrgyz Republic, Mongolia, the People's Republic of China (PRC), Tajikistan, and Uzbekistan for CAREC; Brunei Darussalam, Cambodia, Indonesia, the Lao People's Democratic Republic (Lao PDR), Malaysia, Myanmar, the Philippines, Singapore, Thailand, and Viet Nam for ASEAN; and Cambodia, the Lao PDR, Myanmar, the PRC, Thailand, and Viet Nam for GMS.

Source: ADB calculations using data from United Nations World Tourism Organization Tourism Satellite Accounts. http://statistics.unwto.org/ (accessed April 2019).

2: Visa-Entry Arrangements for Tourists from Outside CAREC

Origin Country	Destination										
	AFG	AZE	GEO	KAZ	KGZ	MON	PAK	PRC	TAJ	TKM	UZB
Australia	vr	ev	vf-360	vf-30	vf-60	vr	ev	vr	voa/ev-45	vr	vf-30
Canada	vr	ev	vf-360	vf-30	vf-60	vf-30	ev	vr	voa/ev-45	vr	vf-30
Germany	vr	ev	vf-360	vf-30	vf-60	vf-30	voa/ev-90	vr	voa/ev-45	vr	vf-30
Japan	vr	voa/ev-30	vf-360	vf-30	vf-60	vf-30	voa/ev-90	vf-15	voa/ev-45	vr	vf-30
Korea, Rep. of	vr	voa/ev-30	vf-360	vf-30	vf-60	vr	voa/ev-90	vr	voa/ev-45	vr	vf-30
New Zealand	vr	ev	vf-360	vf-30	vf-60	vr	voa/ev-90	vr	voa/ev-45	vr	vf-30
Russian Federation	vr	vf-90	vf-360	vf-90	VF	vf-30	ev	vr	VF	vr	VF
Singapore	vr	voa/ev-30	vf-360	vf-30	vf-60	vf-30	voa/ev-90	vf-15	voa/ev-45	vr	vf-30
United Kingdom	vr	ev	vf-360	vf-30	vf-60	vr	ev	vr	voa/ev-45	vr	vf-30
United States	vr	ev	vf-360	vf-30	vf-60	vf-90	ev	vr	voa/ev-45	vr	ev-30

VF visa-free   vf-360 visa-free for 360 days   vf-90 visa-free for 90 days   vf-30 visa-free for 30 days

ev e-visa   ev-30 e-visa for 30 days   ev-90 e-visa for 90 days   ev-45 e-visa for 45 days

voa visa on arrival   vr visa required

AFG = Afghanistan, AZE = Azerbaijan, GEO = Georgia, KAZ = Kazakhstan, KGZ = Kyrgyz Republic, MON = Mongolia, PAK = Pakistan, PRC = People's Republic of China, TAJ = Tajikistan, TKM = Turkmenistan, UZB = Uzbekistan.

Source: Arton Capital's PassportIndex.org database (electronic). http://www.passportindex.org (accessed August 2019).

[a] International Monetary Fund. World Economic Outlook October 2019 Database. https://www.imf.org/external/pubs/ft/weo/2019/02/weodata/index.aspx (accessed October 2019).

[b] United Nations World Tourism Organization. Tourism Satellite Accounts. http://statistics.unwto.org/ (accessed April 2019).

[c] World Bank. World Development Indicators. https://databank.worldbank.org/source/world-development-indicators (accessed October 2019).

[d] Based on ADB computations using data from United Nations World Tourism Organization. Tourism Satellite Accounts. http://statistics.unwto.org/ (accessed April 2019).

[e] Kazakhstan and Uzbekistan are in the process of preparing a visa common to both countries. Dubbed as the "Silk Visa," it would allow tourists with a valid visa from either country to visit both.

Source: ADB staff.

Figure 4.7: Extraregional Visitor Flows to Asia, 2017

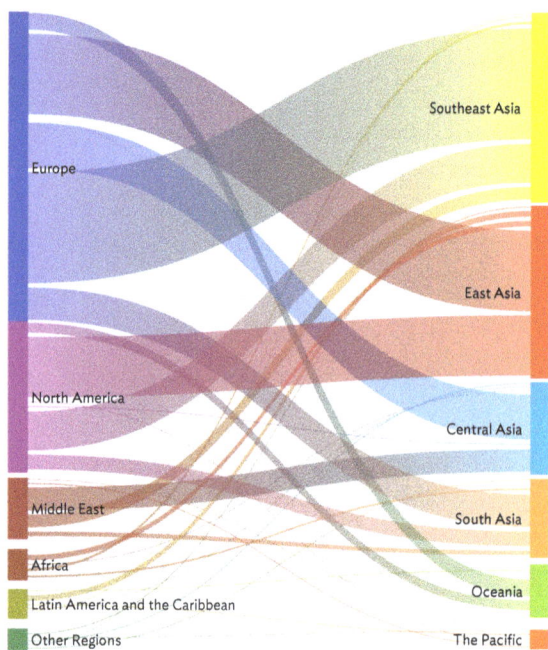

Source: ADB calculations using data from United Nations World Tourism Organization. Tourism Satellite Accounts. http://statistics.unwto.org/ (accessed April 2019).

Among Asian economies, the greatest number of visitors to Asia in 2017 came from Hong Kong, China and the PRC. Between 2010 and 2017, Asian tourist expenditures doubled, led by the PRC, reaching $495.3 billion in 2017.

The top three visitors to Asia came from Hong Kong, China; the PRC; and the Republic of Korea (Table 4.3). Steady income growth regionally continues to boost the number of tourists and travel expenditures (Figure 4.8). Tourism expenditures from Asia (led by outbound tourists from the PRC, Australia, and the Republic of Korea) doubled between 2010 and 2017 reaching $495.3 billion in 2017. East Asia's tourism spending per outbound tourist nearly doubled, from $790 to $1,343

Figure 4.8: Tourism Expenditure by Asian Economies

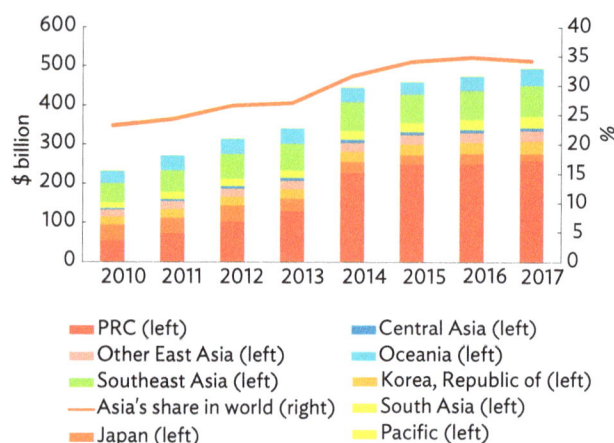

- PRC (left)
- Other East Asia (left)
- Southeast Asia (left)
- Asia's share in world (right)
- Japan (left)
- Central Asia (left)
- Oceania (left)
- Korea, Republic of (left)
- South Asia (left)
- Pacific (left)

PRC = People's Republic of China.

Source: United Nations World Tourism Organization (2019a); and World Bank. World Development Indicators. https://databank.worldbank.org/source/world-development-indicators (accessed August 2019).

Table 4.3: Top Outbound Visitors to Asia

Top Sources in 2017	Number (million, % share of total in parentheses)	Top Sources in 2010	Number (million, % share of total in parentheses)
Within Asia		**Within Asia**	
Hong Kong, China	86.3 (21.2%)	Hong Kong, China	82.0 (32.6%)
PRC	61.3 (15.0%)	PRC	22.2 (8.8%)
Korea, Republic of	21.8 (5.4%)	Japan	12.4 (4.9%)
Singapore	19.1 (4.7%)	Korea, Republic of	10.9 (4.3%)
Taipei,China	15.1 (3.7%)	Taipei,China	9.1 (3.6%)
Outside Asia		**Outside Asia**	
United States	13.1 (3.2%)	United States	9.0 (3.6%)
Russian Federation	10.0 (2.4%)	Russian Federation	6.0 (2.4%)
United Kingdom	6.9 (1.7%)	United Kingdom	5.2 (2.1%)
Germany	4.3 (1.0%)	Germany	3.0 (1.2%)
France	3.6 (0.9%)	France	2.6 (1.0%)

PRC = People's Republic of China.

Source: ADB calculations using data from United Nations World Tourism Organization. Tourism Satellite Accounts. http://statistics.unwto.org/ (accessed April 2019).

Figure 4.9: Tourism Expenditure per Outbound Tourist ($ '000)

a: Asian Subregions

b: Selected Asian Economies

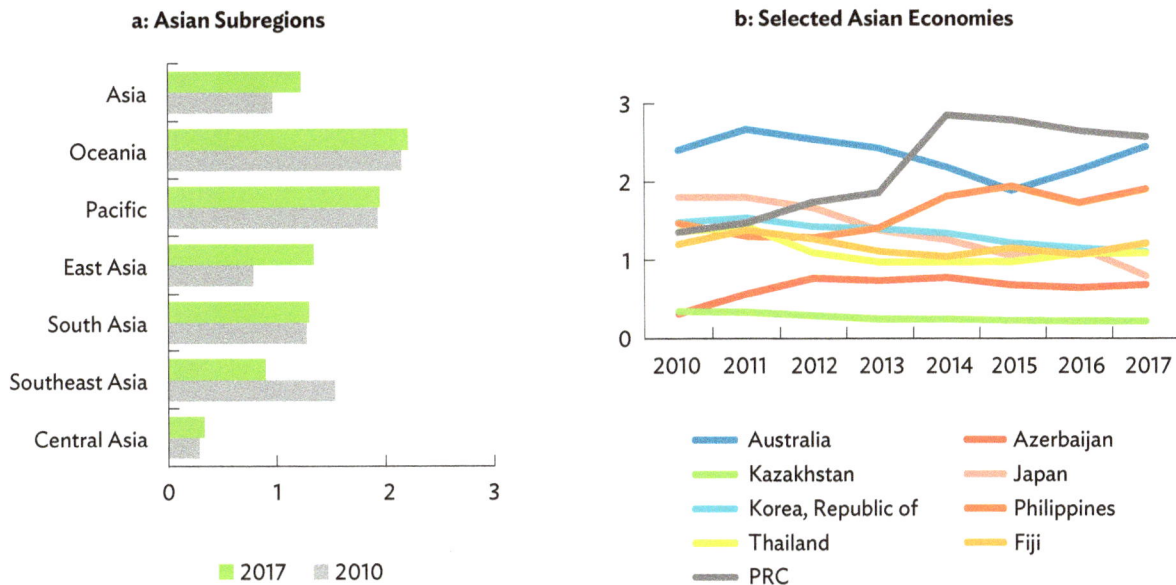

2017   2010

Australia   Azerbaijan
Kazakhstan   Japan
Korea, Republic of   Philippines
Thailand   Fiji
PRC

PRC = People's Republic of China.

Sources: ADB calculations using data from United Nations World Tourism Organization. Tourism Satellite Accounts. http://statistics.unwto.org/ (accessed April 2019); and World Bank. World Development Indicators. https://databank.worldbank.org/source/world-development-indicators (accessed August 2019).

(Figure 4.9a), with country-level data showing it was mostly driven by the PRC (Figure 4.9b).

The PRC and the Republic of Korea are good examples of economies with a rising propensity for tourism spending. In 2000, there were just 9.4 million international Chinese visitors. But increased per capita income and rising household wealth as the PRC continued its robust economic growth helped catapult its place up the global tourism ranks—in 2017, the PRC was the third top source of international arrivals, with 100.3 million outbound visitors, of which 61.1% traveled to Asia. The PRC remains a strong market mover, both as a tourist source and as destination. In 2017, tourists from the PRC spent $258 billion on travel, more than six times the spending of Australian tourists ($39.5 billion), for example, and almost eight times the spending of tourists from the Republic of Korea ($33.4 billion). By 2028, the PRC's tourism sector is forecast to contribute 12.9% to GDP growth and contribute 116.5 million to total employment (World Travel and Tourism Council 2018). In the Republic of Korea, improved prosperity that accompanied its transformation to a high-income

country afforded more people to travel. Ranked as the 8th largest supplier of international visitors to the world, the number of arrivals from the Republic of Korea grew fivefold from 5.9 million in 2000 to 30.4 million in 2017. Around 70% of Korean visitors travel within Asia.

The PRC remained the most-visited country by Asian visitors in 2017, followed by Japan and Thailand.

In 2010, the PRC (39.6%); Hong Kong, China (6.7%); Singapore (3.7%); Thailand (3.7%); and the Republic of Korea (2.7%) were the most popular destinations for visitors from Asia (Table 4.4). The US (3.2%) and the Russian Federation (3.4%) were the only two non-Asian countries among the top 10 destinations of visitors from Asia—but only the US was among the top 10 in 2017. The PRC remained the most-visited country intraregionally—drawing 118 million visitors in 2017, up 16.9% from 2010. Japan had around 4 times as many visitors from Asia in 2017 (25.1 million) as in 2010 (6.7 million)—while its rank rose from 8th to 2nd most

Table 4.4: Top Destinations of Asian Visitors

Top Destinations in 2017	Number (million, % share of total in parentheses)	Top Destinations in 2010	Number (million, % share of total in parentheses)
Within Asia		**Within Asia**	
PRC	117.9 (27.7%)	PRC	100.9 (39.6%)
Japan	25.1 (5.9%)	Hong Kong, China	17.1 (6.7%)
Thailand	25.1 (5.9%)	Singapore	9.5 (3.7%)
Hong Kong, China	24.8 (5.8%)	Thailand	9.4 (3.7%)
Malaysia	24.2 (5.7%)	Korea, Republic of	6.9 (2.7%)
Outside Asia		**Outside Asia**	
United States	13.8 (3.2%)	Russian Federation	8.6 (3.4%)
Russian Federation	8.8 (2.1%)	United States	8.1 (3.2%)
Saudi Arabia	6.7 (1.6%)	Turkey	2.8 (1.1%)
Turkey	5.2 (1.2%)	United Kingdom	2.5 (1.0%)
United Kingdom	3.6 (0.8%)	France	1.7 (0.7%)

PRC = People's Republic of China.

Source: ADB calculations using data from United Nations World Tourism Organization. Tourism Satellite Accounts. http://statistics.unwto.org/ (accessed April 2019).

visited country. Japan adopted several travel facilitation measures to attract more international visitors, especially from the region. In the second half of 2018, Japan eased its travel visa requirements for India and the Philippines.

Intra-Subregional Tourism

Intraregional tourism in Asia rose during 2010–2017, while intra-subregional tourism varied.

In 2017, the share of intraregional visitors in Asia (against visitors globally) increased to 78.4% from 74.0% in 2010. Comparing intra-subregional tourism shares in 2010 and 2017 suggest that it has improved in Central Asia, South Asia, and Southeast Asia (Figure 4.10). Intra-subregional tourism share in Central Asia grew to 60.7% from 53.0% in 2010, as countries in the region began improving border control policies to support the easier movement of people, goods, and services, and promote stronger tourism. Kazakhstan, Tajikistan, and Uzbekistan reformed visa requirements and immediately saw an improvement in arrivals—intra-subregional arrivals grew

23.8% in Kazakhstan, 42.3% in Tajikistan, and 34.7% in Uzbekistan. Globally, Central Asia hosted 4.3 million more visitors in 2017—a 19-percentage point increase over the 2016 growth rate. South Asia received around 3.8 million intra-subregional visitors in 2017, with arrivals to India, Maldives, and Nepal climbing 32.7% over 2016. India's tourism strategy targets 15 million international tourists by 2025. Pakistan has recently introduced changes to its visa policy—50 countries are eligible to apply for a visa-on-arrival under the tourist category, while its online visa system is open to 175 countries.[30] Visitors from Southeast Asia have become more Asian-centric. Its shares of intra-subregional (38.7%) and inter-subregional (43.4%) tourism have grown relative to 2010. Intra-subregional visitors increased by around half a million in 2017, while inter-subregional arrivals recorded brisk growth (7.2 million visitors more than in 2016), especially Myanmar and Viet Nam. Meanwhile, countries in the Pacific have proportionally stronger tourism links with other Asian countries (particularly Oceania) rather than within the Pacific itself. In 2017, around 95% of the increase in arrivals to the Pacific were from Australia and New Zealand.

---

[30]   Government of Pakistan, Ministry of Interior. https://visa.nadra.gov.pk/ (accessed July 2019).

Figure 4.10: Intra-Subregional Tourism Share—Asia
(% of total tourist arrivals to each subregion)

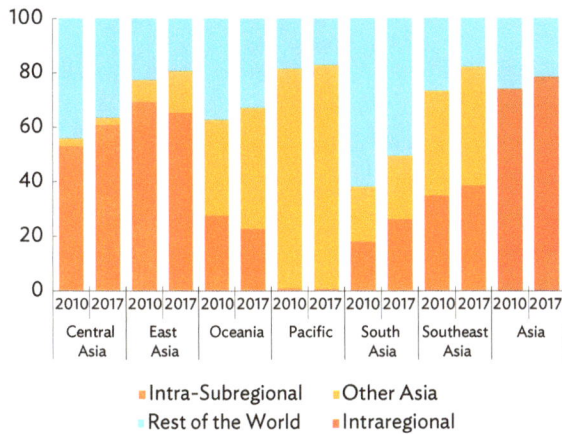

Source: ADB calculations using data from United Nations World Tourism Organization. Tourism Satellite Accounts. http://statistics.unwto.org/ (accessed April 2019).

International Tourism Receipts

Asia's international tourism receipts grew 5.4% to a record $368 billion in 2017, mirroring the steady growth of visitors to the region; significant tourism receipts make it a key source of income for many Pacific DMCs and Southeast Asian countries.

Tourism's most visible economic impact is the significant financial inflows it generates—around $1.5 trillion in visitor spending in 2017. It boosts physical and digital infrastructure investment, strengthens people-to-people linkages, promotes entrepreneurship, and stimulates employment, especially in emerging markets and developing Asia. In 2017, global tourism brought in $1.5 trillion in international tourism receipts, a 7.3% growth over 2016. Globally, the largest share of tourism receipts went to Europe (36.2%), but in terms of year-on-year growth, Africa's 18.9% increase was a vast improvement—$10.3 billion more than 2016 (Figure 4.11). Asia's 24% share remained steady in 2017, but tourism receipts grew 5.4% to $368.0 billion.

The two Asian subregions that accounted for the largest shares of international arrivals also recorded the largest share of the region's tourism dollars—Southeast Asia (37.7%) and East Asia (34.0%) (Table 4.5). However, tourism receipts to East Asia fell by 8.7%, as the PRC and the Republic of Korea earned $11.8 billion and $4.2 billion less than in 2016. Central Asia, South Asia, Southeast Asia, and Oceania had double-digit growth rates in tourism receipts, as improved infrastructure, enhanced travel connectivity, and better travel facilitation measures continued to fan travel demand to the region.

Figure 4.11: International Tourism Receipts by Region, 2017 (Total receipts = $1.53 trillion)

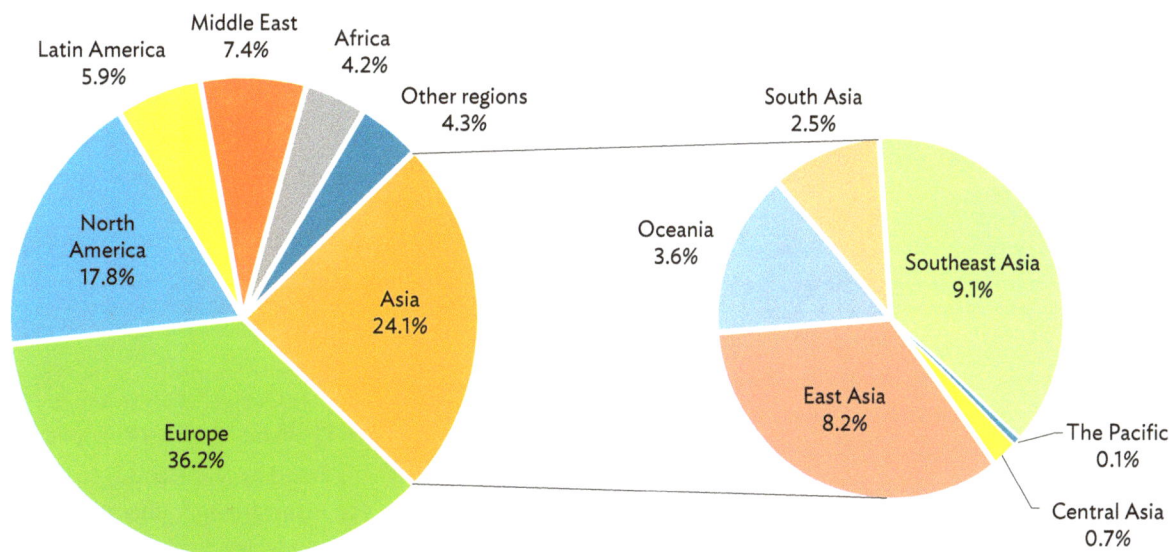

Sources: ADB calculations using data from United Nations World Tourism Organization (2019b); and World Bank. World Development Indicators. https://databank.worldbank.org/source/world-development-indicators (accessed October 2019).

Table 4.5: Tourism Arrivals and Receipts in Asia by Subregion, 2017

Subregion	International Tourism Receipts		International Arrivals	
	$ million	% of Asia's total tourism receipts	million	% of international tourist arrivals to Asia
Central Asia	9,967	2.7	24.6	6.0
East Asia	125,096	34.0	234.0	57.4
Oceania	54,565	14.8	12.5	3.1
South Asia	37,902	10.3	14.4	3.5
Southeast Asia	138,820	37.7	120.4	29.5
The Pacific	1,693	0.5	1.6	0.4
Total	**368,042**	**100.0**	**407.6**	**100.0**

Sources: ADB calculations using data from United Nations World Tourism Organization. Tourism Satellite Accounts. http://statistics.unwto.org/ (accessed April 2019); and World Bank. World Development Indicators. https://databank.worldbank.org/source/world-development-indicators (accessed October 2019).

Figure 4.12: Top 10 Recipients of Tourism Receipts, 2017

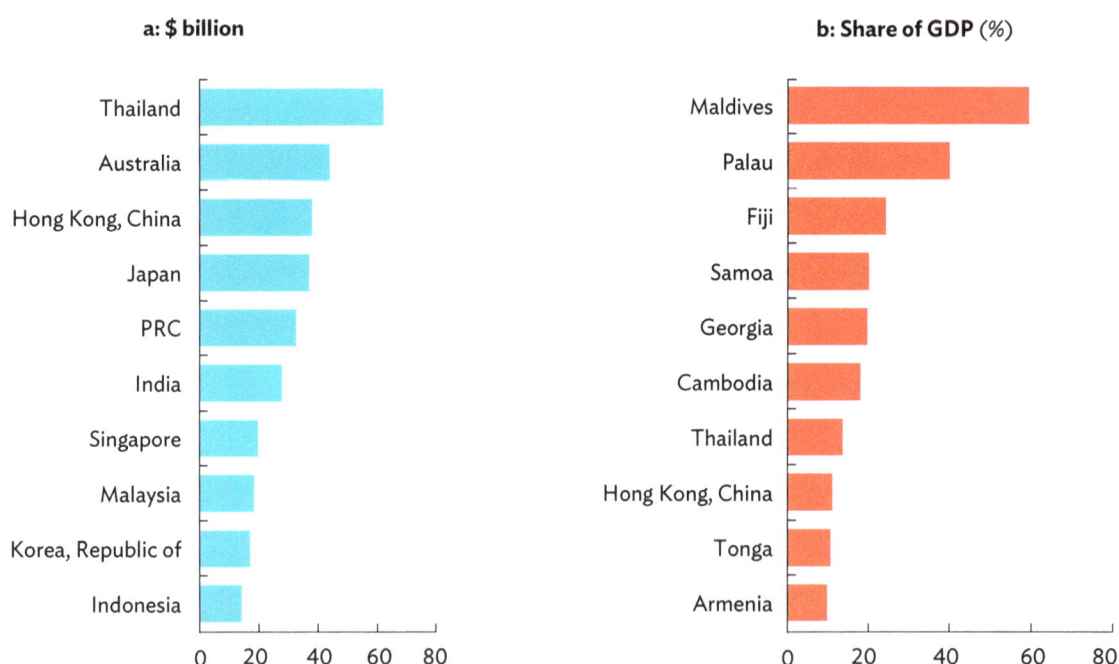

a: $ billion

b: Share of GDP (%)

GDP = gross domestic product, PRC = People's Republic of China.

Note: 2017 data were not available for some economies with substantial tourist receipts (as share of GDP and in per capita terms).

Sources: ADB calculations using data from International Monetary Fund. World Economic Outlook October 2019 Database. https://www.imf.org/external/pubs/ft/weo/2019/02/weodata/index.aspx (accessed October 2019); United Nations World Tourism Organization. Tourism Satellite Accounts. http://statistics.unwto.org/ (accessed April 2019); and World Bank. World Development Indicators. https://databank.worldbank.org/source/world-development-indicators (accessed October 2019).

By value, Thailand; Australia; and Hong Kong, China were the top recipients (Figure 4.12a). Thailand is the third most visited country by tourists from Asia, generating the most tourism income ($62.2 billion) among countries in the region. Between 2016 and 2017,

the number of tourists to Thailand from the Republic of Korea and the PRC increased by 17.2% and 11.6%, respectively. Australia's tourism strategy generated nearly 20% more in international tourism receipts, making it the second largest recipient in 2017. Australia's

2017–2021 tourism strategy targets overnight visitor expenditure to reach $115 billion in 2020 (Tourism Australia 2016). Japan's tourism receipts grew 10.6% in 2017 to $37.0 billion. In recent years, Japan has been using tourism as a revitalization strategy for its economy, leveraging its culture and history, diverse environment and cuisine—it has targeted 40 million tourists by 2020 and 60 million by 2030 (Government of Japan, Ministry of Land, Infrastructure, Transport and Tourism 2016).

For several Pacific DMCs and countries in Southeast Asia and Central Asia, tourism is an important income source. Maldives tops the list—deriving 59.4% of its GDP from tourism (Figure 4.12b) and generating the highest tourism receipts per capita. Fiji and Samoa earned one-fifth of its GDP from tourism and were among the top 10 countries with the highest tourism receipts per capita. Cambodia's tourism income as a proportion of GDP has grown considerably—to 18.1% in 2017—from about 3% of GDP in the mid-1990s. Central Asian countries Georgia and Armenia counted on tourism income for 19.7% and 9.9% of GDP, respectively. The economic contribution of tourism can also be assessed by comparing it to outbound tourism expenditure as an indicator of net tourism earnings (Box 4.2).

Asia earned $903 per international visitor in 2017, while tourism receipts per arrival varied widely across subregions.

Asia earned $903 per international visitor in 2017 (Figure 4.13a).[31] By subregion, Oceania earned the most per arrival in 2017 at $4,370, about 5 times the average for Asia.[32] Second was South Asia at $2,392 per arrival, higher by 9.1% compared with 2010. Earnings per arrival in Central Asia were lowest, reflecting the subregion's nascent tourist industry. The steady average annual growth rate of 2.4%, higher than other subregions, could provide additional impetus to promote tourism in Central Asia. In East Asia, earnings per arrival declined, despite the large numbers of arrivals in the PRC, Japan, and the Republic of Korea (Figure 4.13b). Tourism receipts per arrival also rose in countries where tourism revenues matter most (both as a % of GDP and in per capita terms), especially in the Pacific.

Figure 4.13: Tourism Receipts per Arrival ($ '000)

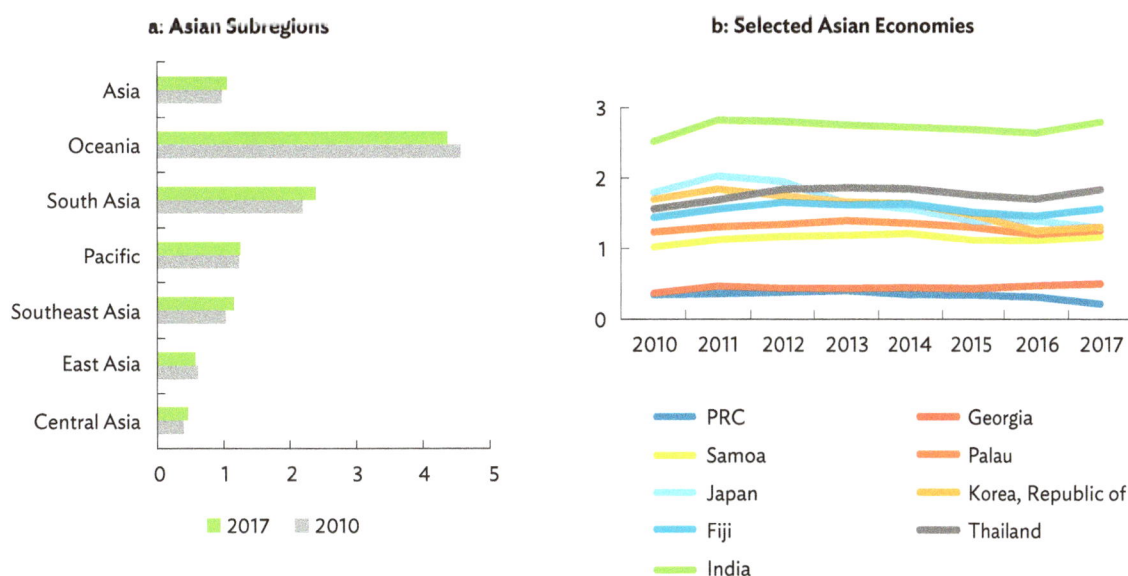

a: Asian Subregions

b: Selected Asian Economies

PRC = People's Republic of China.

Sources: ADB calculations using data from United Nations World Tourism Organization (UNWTO). Tourism Satellite Accounts. http://statistics.unwto.org/ (accessed March 2019); UNWTO (2019b); and World Bank. World Development Indicators. https://databank.worldbank.org/source/world-development-indicators (accessed August 2019).

[31] Tourism receipts per tourist in Asia is estimated to be $1,097 when only tourists (overnight visitors) are counted among inbound visitors to the PRC.

[32] The high level of tourism receipts per arrival in Oceania can be explained mainly by the many long-haul visitors who tend to stay longer and spend more. Higher prices in Australia and New Zealand are also a factor contributing to the high nominal level.

Box 4.2: Tourism Coverage—A Measure of Net Tourism Earnings

Tourism is increasingly used as an economic growth and development platform for its multiple economic impacts. As people visit another country, opportunities to earn from the exchange of goods, services, and money are set in motion. With growth and development from tourism comes greater average income, enabling households in a given economy the means to also experience outbound tourism. Eventually, economies that earn significant tourism revenues also spend for tourism—and over time, possibly spending as much, if not more, on their own tourism. The Box Figure on tourism coverage gives an overview of the extent to which foreign revenue inflows (from tourism receipts) cover for domestic revenue outflow (from outbound tourism). Computed as the proportion (expressed in %) of inbound international tourist expenditures to outbound tourist expenditures in foreign economies, a value higher than 100% means inbound tourism indirectly finances more than all outbound visitor expenditures.

For example, Sri Lanka's tourism coverage in 2017 suggests that it earned $2.1 from inbound tourism for every dollar it spent on outbound tourism. Caution is required, however, in interpreting tourism coverage as a simple indicator of net gains from tourism. Analyzing tourism coverage in the proper context requires knowledge of the state of development of an economy's tourism industry. The Republic of Korea's tourism coverage is 51%, which suggests that the country's tourism expenditures exceeded its tourism receipts, but this is due to its robust outbound tourism industry—Koreans were among the most traveled in 2017. On the other hand, Tajikistan's coverage is 1066%, primarily because its outbound tourism market remains underdeveloped. Nonetheless, most economies with high tourism coverage rates are also those where tourism comprises a significant share of gross domestic product as well as high levels of tourism per capita, underscoring the importance of net tourism earnings.

Tourism Coverage, 2017—Asia (%)

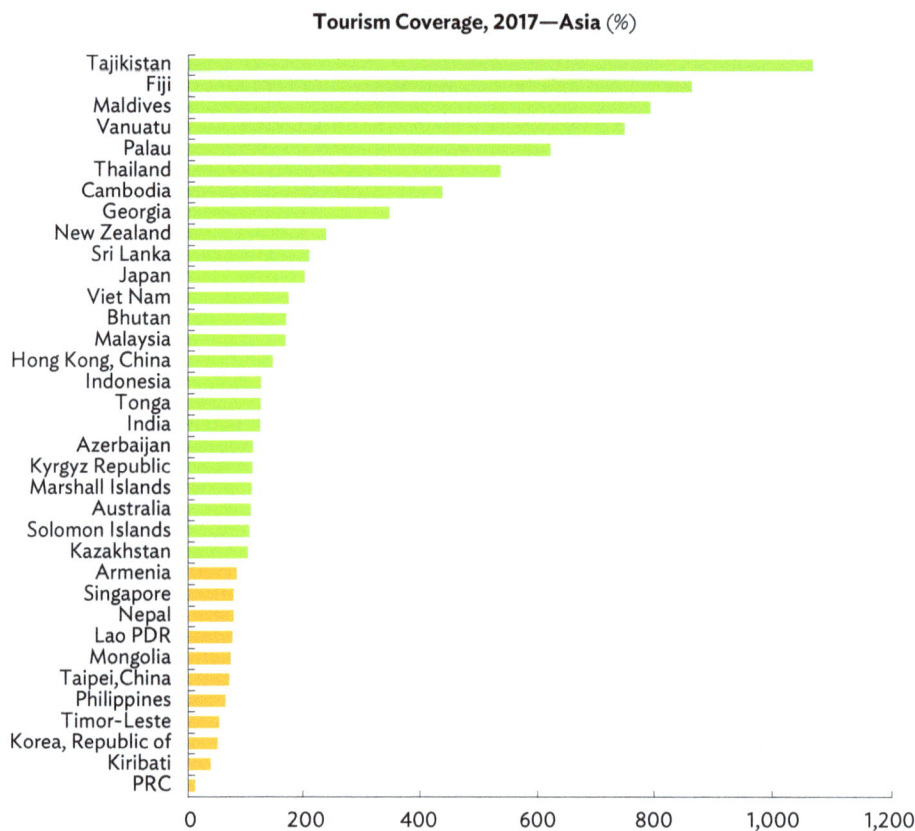

Lao PDR = Lao People's Democratic Republic, PRC = People's Republic of China.

Note: Tourism coverage gives an overview of the extent to which foreign revenue inflows (from tourism receipts) cover for domestic revenue outflow (from outbound tourism).

Source: United Nations World Tourism Organization (2019a).

The most visited countries are not necessarily those that earn most. National tourism strategies can focus more on maximizing visitor experience by offering high-value, quality experiences.

Boosting tourist arrivals and maximizing tourism receipts are often simultaneous targets in national tourism plans but may not be achieved at the same time. Comparing the average annual growth rate of tourism receipts and international arrivals suggests the most-visited countries may not necessarily experience the same degree of growth in tourism earnings (Figure 4.14). For example, arrivals to Sri Lanka and Japan grew by almost the same rate from 2010 to 2017, but Sri Lanka's growth (25.4%)

in tourism earnings outpaced Japan's (13.4%). Average arrival growth in high-traffic countries such as the PRC and the Republic of Korea also exceeded the growth in their receipts, while in Indonesia and Cambodia receipts and arrivals grew at the same rate.

Tourism strategies that primarily target the development of hard infrastructure—such as aviation and mass transport, public facilities, and technology that eases immigration procedures—tend to attract more tourists as soon as the infrastructure are in place.[33] More airports and better public transport could make a country more accessible to tourists and cause arrivals to increase. But whether better infrastructure and greater tourism traffic translate into greater tourism gains depends on many

Figure 4.14: Growth in International Tourist Receipts and Arrivals, 2010–2017

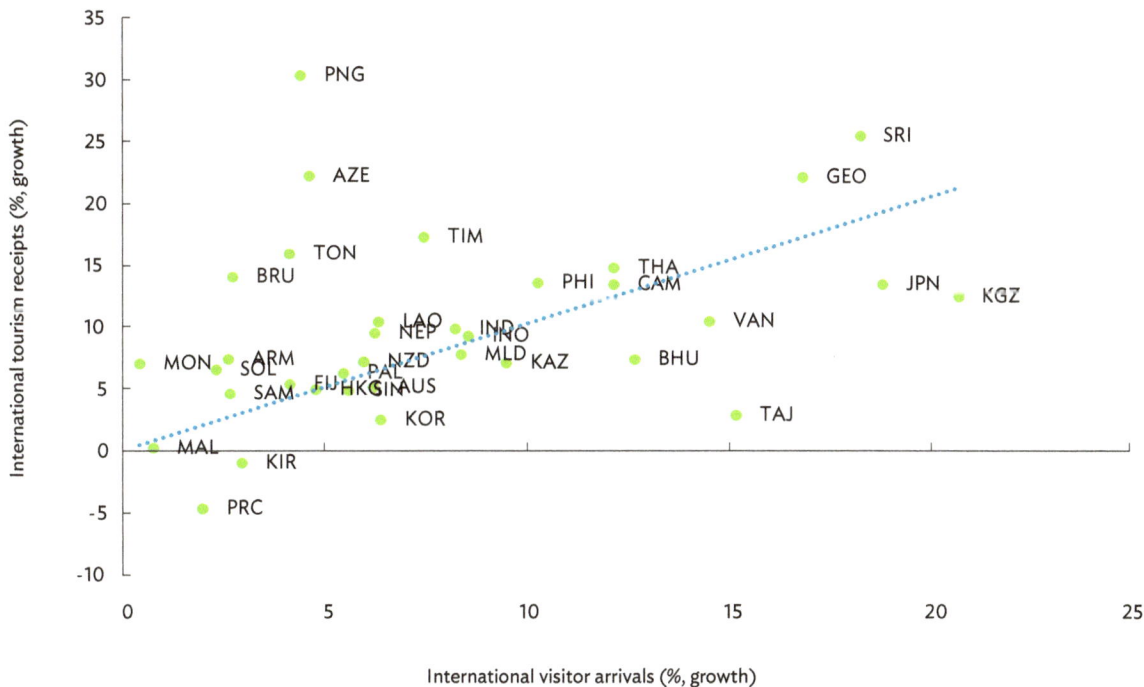

ARM = Armenia; AUS = Australia; AZE = Azerbaijan; BHU = Bhutan; BRU = Brunei Darussalam; CAM = Cambodia; FIJ = Fiji; GEO = Georgia; HKG = Hong Kong, China; IND = India; INO = Indonesia; JPN = Japan; KAZ = Kazakhstan; KGZ = Kyrgyz Republic; KIR = Kiribati; KOR = Republic of Korea; LAO = Lao, People's Democratic Republic; MAL = Malaysia; MLD = Maldives; MON = Mongolia; NEP = Nepal; NZL = New Zealand; PAL = Palau; PNG = Papua New Guinea; PRC = People's Republic of China; PHI = Philippines; SAM = Samoa; SIN = Singapore; SOL = Solomon Islands; SRI = Sri Lanka; TAJ = Tajikistan; THA = Thailand; TIM = Timor-Leste; TON = Tonga; VAN = Vanuatu.

Note: Data represent the average annual growth rate for 2010–2017.

Sources: ADB calculations using data from United Nations World Tourism Organization. Tourism Satellite Accounts. http://statistics.unwto.org/ (accessed April 2019); United Nations World Tourism Organization (2019b); and World Bank. World Development Indicators. https://databank.worldbank.org/source/world-development-indicators (accessed August 2019).

---

[33]   UNWTO and GETRC (2016) reported that most countries in Asia enjoyed healthy growth in international arrivals, supported by increased capacity, air connectivity, and infrastructure development. In the Philippines, Catudan (2016) found infrastructure development directly related to an increase in tourist arrivals. In Singapore, infrastructure development has been a key component of its tourism master plans (Centre for Liveable Cities Singapore 2015). ADB has been supporting various climate-resilient and urban infrastructure projects to boost tourist arrivals and tourism investment across the region. For example, in Mongolia, it approved a $38 million project in May 2019 to develop ecotourism in Khuvsgul Lake National Park and Onon-Balj National Park to serve as models for sustainable tourism, that is economically inclusive development and conservation.

factors. Tourism growth depends on the interaction of (i) tourism policy, regulatory environment, and strategy; (ii) infrastructure; (iii) human resources; and (iv) marketing and product development. It must consider the interests of multiple stakeholders—both public and private—and in other industries such as agriculture and transportation (ADB 2018). Cohesive execution of tourism strategies is key to maximizing tourism gains and ensuring sustainability.

New areas of regional cooperation could strengthen Asia's competitive advantage in tourism.

Tourism's potential can be realized by attracting related investments, hastening rural infrastructure development, enhancing small and medium-sized enterprise business activity and expanding local employment. Regional tourism groups within the Association of Southeast Asian Nations (ASEAN) and the Greater Mekong Subregion (GMS)—stalwarts of tourism cooperation—are deeply committed to joint initiatives to expand tourism categories and travel packages that can sustainably support local community development and help induce tourism's poverty-reducing multiplier effects. ASEAN members have liberalized air services under the ASEAN Single Aviation Market and the harmonization of air traffic operations via the Seamless ASEAN Sky to underscore support for promoting ASEAN as a single sustainable, inclusive, and balanced tourism destination (ASEAN 2019).[34] In the GMS Southern Economic Corridor (including Cambodia, the Lao People's Democratic Republic, Thailand, and Viet Nam), a key component of tourism cooperation is the development of private sector-driven community-based tourism models—promoted jointly and marketed using multicountry thematic routes and collaborative social media campaigns (ADB 2010 and Thraenhart 2018). CAREC countries—following in the footsteps of existing regional tourism cooperation bodies in Asia—have begun to streamline and harmonize visa regimes investigating a possible single CAREC visa, an idea floated to support tourism. As Asian economies continue to host more diverse groups of travelers from a variety of age groups, regional cooperation and integration measures may be modeled to encourage a multigenerational and sustainable focus on tourism—one that promotes shared prosperity, is shaped by modern technology, provides greater access to more efficient infrastructure, and attracts the growing number of people with the desire and means for seeing and experiencing the world.

---

[34]   See the official ASEAN tourism website (www.aseantravel.com) for end-to-end information on different types of travel experiences across ASEAN's 10 members.

References

Asian Development Bank (ADB). 2010. *Strategy and Action Plan for the Greater Mekong Subregion Southern Economic Corridor.* Manila.

———. 2018. *Tourism as a Driver of Growth in the Pacific.* Manila.

———. 2019. *Promoting Regional Tourism Cooperation Under CAREC 2030 A Scoping Study.* Manila.

Association of Southeast Asian Nations (ASEAN). 2019. Chairman's Statement of the 34th ASEAN Summit Bangkok, 23 June 2019: Advancing Partnership for Sustainability. https://www.asean2019.go.th/en/news/chairmans-statement-of-the-34th-asean-summit-bangkok-23-june-2019-advancing-partnership-for-sustainability/.

Arton Capital. PassportIndex.org Database (electronic). https://www.passportindex.org (accessed August 2019).

Catudan, J. M. 2016. The Impact of Tourist Arrivals, Physical Infrastructures, and Employment, on Regional Output Growth. *Procedia Social and Behavioral Sciences.* 219. pp: 175-184.

Centre for Liveable Cities Singapore. 2015. *Planning for Tourism: Creating a Vibrant Singapore. Urban System Studies.* Singapore.

De Bel-Air, F. 2018. Demography, Migration and Labour Market in Saudi Arabia. *Explanatory Note - Gulf Labour Markets, Migration and Population!.* GLMM EN 5/2018. European University Institute and Gulf Research Center.

Fonua, S. 2012. Developing Tonga's Economy. *The Parliamentarian.* Issue One. http://www.cpahq.org/CPAHQ/CMDownload.aspx?ContentKey=07c9d75d-2cba-4183-ae63-1f06c34e1ea1&ContentItemKey=738ad7e6-fe69-4577-a25d-2f646f6e779f .

Global Knowledge Partnership for Migration and Development (KNOMAD). 2019. Migration and Remittances: Recent Developments and Outlook. *Migration and Development Brief.* 31. April. https://www.knomad.org/sites/default/files/2019-04/Migrationanddevelopmentbrief31.pdf.

———.http://www.knomad.org/data/remittances (accessed October 2019).

Government of Japan, Ministry of Land, Infrastructure, Transport and Tourism. 2016. *New Tourism Strategy to Invigorate the Japanese Economy.* https://www.mlit.go.jp/common/001172615.pdf.

Government of Pakistan, Ministry of Interior. https://visa.nadra.gov.pk/ (accessed July 2019).

International Finance Corporation. 2018. *For Tongans, a Secure Way to Send Money Home is Priceless.* https://www.ifc.org/wps/wcm/connect/news_ext_content/ifc_external_corporate_site/news+and+events/news/impact-stories/tonga-remittances.

International Labour Organization. 2018. *International Labour Migration Statistics Database in ASEAN.* Version VI. June. http://apmigration.ilo.org/asean-labour-migration-statistics.

International Monetary Fund. World Economic Outlook October 2019 Database. https://www.imf.org/external/pubs/ft/weo/2019/02/weodata/index.aspx (accessed October 2019).

The Dialogue. 2019. Fact Sheet: Family Remittances to Latin America and the Caribbean in 2018. 8 Feb. https://www.thedialogue.org/analysis/fact-sheet-family-remittances-to-latin-america-and-the-caribbean-in-2018/.

Thraenhart, J. 2018. *Mekong Tourism Regional Tourism Strategy and Initiatives.* Presented at the CAREC Regional Workshop—Promoting Regional Tourism Cooperation under CAREC 2030 in Tashkent, Uzbekistan. https://www.carecprogram.org/uploads/2a.-Presentation_GMS.pdf.

Tourism Australia. 2016. *Tourism Australia Corporate Plan 2017-18 to 2021-22*. http://www.tourism.australia.com/content/dam/assets/document/1/6/x/6/a/2002546.pdf.

United Nations Statistical Commission. 2007. *2008 International Recommendations for Tourism Statistics*. New York/Madrid.

United Nations World Tourism Organization (UNWTO). 2013. *Visa facilitation: Stimulating Economic Growth and Development through Tourism*. Madrid.

———. 2018. *UNWTO Tourism Highlights, 2018 Edition*. Madrid.

———. 2019a. *Compendium of Tourism Statistics Dataset* (electronic). Madrid.

———. 2019b. *World Tourism Barometer*. 17 (3). September. Madrid.

———. Tourism Satellite Accounts. http://statistics.unwto.org/ (accessed April 2019).

UNWTO and Global Tourism Economy Research Centre (GETRC). 2016. *Annual Report on Asia Tourism Trends – 2016 Edition, Executive Summary*. Madrid.

United Nations. Department of Economic and Social Affairs, Population Division. International Migrant Stock: The 2017 Revision. http://www.un.org/en/development/desa/population/migration/data/estimates2/estimates17.shtml (accessed August 2019).

United States Department of State, Bureau of Consular Affairs. Visa Statistics. https://travel.state.gov/content/travel/en/legal/visa-law0/visa-statistics.html (accessed July 2019).

World Bank. World Development Indicators. https://databank.worldbank.org/source/world-development-indicators (accessed August and October 2019).

———. 2019. Record High Remittances Sent Globally in 2018. Press release. 8 April. https://www.worldbank.org/en/news/press-release/2019/04/08/record-high-remittances-sent-globally-in-2018.

World Travel and Tourism Council. 2018. *Travel and Tourism Economic Impact China*. https://www.wttc.org/-/media/files/reports/economic-impact-research/cities-2018/city-travel--tourism-impact-2018final.pdf.

Yoshino, N., F. Taghizadeh-Hesary, and M. Otsuka. 2017. International Remittances and Poverty Reduction. Evidence from Asian Developing Countries. *ADBI Working Paper Series*. No. 759. Tokyo: Asian Development Bank Institute.

5 Subregional Cooperation Initiatives

Central and West Asia: Central Asia Regional Economic Cooperation Program[35]

The Central Asia Regional Economic Cooperation (CAREC) Program includes Afghanistan, Azerbaijan, the People's Republic of China (PRC), Georgia, Kazakhstan, the Kyrgyz Republic, Mongolia, Pakistan, Tajikistan, Turkmenistan, and Uzbekistan. The group

is advancing cooperation under the CAREC 2030 strategy adopted in October 2017, which builds on the solid progress achieved in nearly 2 decades of cooperation—particularly in transport, energy, trade facilitation, and trade policy (Table 5.1). CAREC 2030 has a broader agenda which focuses on five operational clusters: (i) economic and financial stability; (ii) trade, tourism, and economic corridors; (iii) infrastructure and economic connectivity; (iv) agriculture and water; and (v) human development.

Table 5.1: Selected Economic Indicators, 2018—CAREC

	Population (million)	Nominal GDP ($ billion)	GDP Growth (2014 to 2018, average, %)	GDP per Capita (current prices, $)	Trade Openness (total trade, % of GDP)
Afghanistan	37.2	19.4	2.4	521	85.7
Azerbaijan	9.9	46.9	0.4	4,721	65.9
China, People's Republic of	1,392.7	13,608.2	6.9	9,771	34.1
Georgia	3.7	16.2	4.0	4,345	77.0
Kazakhstan	18.3	170.5	2.9	9,331	54.5
Kyrgyz Republic	6.3	8.1	4.1	1,281	80.8
Mongolia	3.2	13.0	4.7	4,104	99.1
Pakistan	212.2	312.6	4.7	1,473	26.7
Tajikistan	9.1	7.5	6.8	827	69.2
Turkmenistan	5.9	40.8	7.1	6,967	30.2
Uzbekistan	33.0	50.5	6.3	1,532	56.5
CAREC	**1,731.5**	**14,293.7**	**6.7**	**8,255**	**34.5**

CAREC = Central Asia Regional Economic Cooperation, GDP = gross domestic product.

Notes: CAREC's average GDP growth rate is weighted using nominal GDP. Total trade refers to the sum of exports and imports.

Sources: ADB calculations using data from Asian Development Bank. 2019. *Asian Development Outlook 2019*. Manila; CEIC; International Monetary Fund. Direction of Trade Statistics. http://data.imf.org; and World Bank. World Development Indicators. http://databank.worldbank.org/ (all accessed October 2019).

---

[35] Contributed by Guoliang Wu, senior regional cooperation specialist, Central and West Asia Department (CWRD); Xinglan Hu, senior regional cooperation specialist, CWRD; and Ronaldo Oblepias, CAREC consultant, CWRD, Asian Development Bank (ADB).

Overview

A new CAREC is envisaged as the subregion expands into new horizons of cooperation.

From six transport projects in 2001 valued at $247 million, CAREC investments reached $34.5 billion as of December 2018, covering 196 regional projects (Figure 5.1). Of this amount, $12.8 billion has been financed by the Asian Development Bank (ADB), $13.8 billion by other development partners, and $7.9 billion by CAREC governments. Of these investments, transport has the biggest share, with about 75%, or $26.1 billion; energy accounts for 23%, or $7.8 billion; and trade accounts for 2%, or $0.6 billion (Figure 5.2). CAREC 2030 aims for far greater shared and sustainable prosperity through increased joint endeavors and engagement in the five operational clusters.

Figure 5.2: CAREC Investments by Sector, as of 31 December 2018 ($ billion)

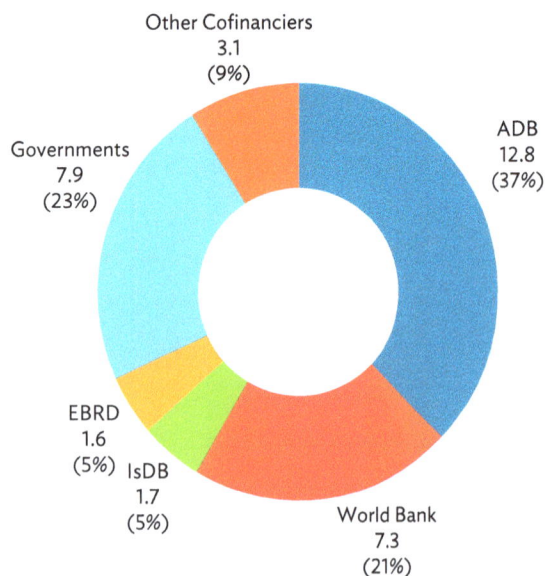

Trade
$0.58 billion
(2%)

Energy
$7.83 billion
(23%)

Transport
$26.09 billion
(75%)

CAREC = Central Asia Regional Economic Cooperation.
Source: ADB. CAREC Program Portfolio.

Central Asia is witnessing dynamic and fast changes. Regional cooperation is seen to continue to expand, capitalizing on new regional dynamics that open opportunities for CAREC agenda across the five operational clusters—in both traditional and new sectors. One key opportunity is a more open Uzbekistan and the improving relationships among neighboring countries.

CAREC's future embraces more than greater openness and expanded sectors. It also opens the door for greater policy dialogue on issues of regional significance, including economic diversification, debt sustainability, capital market development, and new financing mechanisms for infrastructure, among others. The more open and inclusive approach of CAREC is attracting new development partners that extend support to the CAREC Program particularly in new priority areas, such as tourism, education, health, agriculture, transboundary water issues, and disaster risk management.

Figure 5.1: CAREC Investments by Funding Source, as of 31 December 2018 ($ billion)

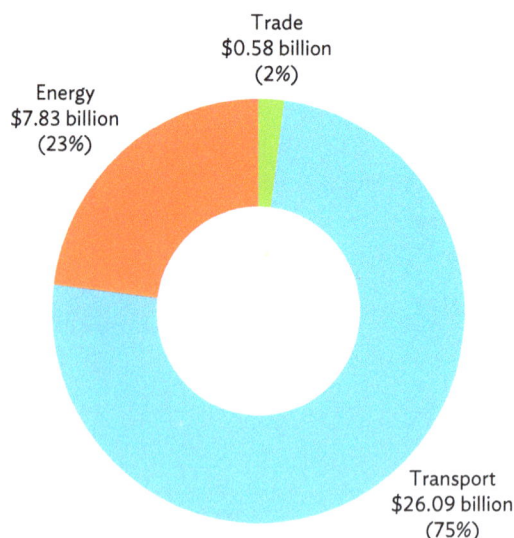

Other Cofinanciers
3.1
(9%)

Governments
7.9
(23%)

ADB
12.8
(37%)

EBRD
1.6
(5%)

IsDB
1.7
(5%)

World Bank
7.3
(21%)

ADB = Asian Development Bank, CAREC = Central Asia Regional Economic Cooperation, EBRD = European Bank for Reconstruction and Development, IsDB = Islamic Development Bank.
Source: ADB. CAREC Program Portfolio.

Performance and Progress over the Past Year

Under CAREC 2030, rapid progress is made in the operational areas.

Economic and Financial Stability. Following the first CAREC High-Level Forum on Macroeconomic Policies for Economic and Financial Stability in 2018, the ADB, International Monetary Fund (IMF), and the World Bank organized another forum in Nur-Sultan, Kazakhstan in May 2019, where CAREC central bank governors, ministers, and other high-level attendees discussed infrastructure financing, fiscal constraints, debt sustainability, and how to attract more private sector investment. In August 2019, the First CAREC Capital Market Regulators' Forum was convened with co-sponsorship of the Securities and Exchange Commission of Pakistan, where senior officials from CAREC member countries and business leaders discussed reforms promoting financial access and private sector development through strengthened regional cooperation and integration in capital markets.

CAREC Integrated Trade Agenda (CITA) 2030. Since endorsement of CITA 2030 in November 2018, good progress has been achieved in the trade sector. Institutional mechanisms such as the CAREC customs cooperation committee and the regional trade group were strengthened. A new regional sanitary and phytosanitary (SPS) working group, comprising high-level representatives from national SPS working groups, was established in June 2019. Sector-specific mechanisms for cooperation in plant and animal health and the CAREC regional food safety network are being conceptualized. These regional initiatives complement country action plans to modernize SPS measures and help CAREC countries align SPS measures with the World Trade Organization (WTO) SPS Agreement and international standards. Ongoing efforts to assist CAREC customs administrations in complying with obligations under the WTO Trade Facilitation Agreement (TFA) were strengthened, with particular focus on developing a CAREC cross-border transit system. CAREC has also published the *Modernizing Sanitary and Phytosanitary Measures in CAREC: An Assessment and the Way Forward* (ADB 2019a) and the *CAREC Corridor Performance Measurement and Monitoring Annual Report 2018* (ADB 2019e). Initiatives to promote economic diversification such as in services trade, investment facilitation and e-commerce, began to take shape under CITA 2030's Rolling Strategic Action Plan (RSAP) 2019–2021.

Infrastructure and Economic Connectivity. Under the CAREC Transport and Trade Facilitation Strategy 2020, CAREC aims to (i) complete 7,800 kilometers (km) of road construction and rehabilitation; (ii) 1,800 km of new railways; and (iii) 2,000 km of renovated, electrified, or signalized railway track. The 2020 targets have already been surpassed. These include (i) 10,462 km of road constructed or rehabilitated; and (ii) 6,028 km of rail track newly built, renovated, electrified, or signaled (Figure 5.3). Progress also continues in other transport subsectors. Two major projects including the expansion of Aktau Port and the construction of the new international seaport in Turkmenistan were completed in 2018. The logistics centers which integrated with the international seaport in Tukmenistan were also completed in 2018, while the construction of the Zamiin-Uud logistics center (Mongolia) is expected to be completed by 2019.

In the energy sector, the flagship Turkmenistan–Uzbekistan–Tajikistan–Afghanistan–Pakistan power interconnection framework and Central Asia—South Asia Electricity Transmission and Trade Project continue to progress. Also, the Turkmenistan–Afghanistan–Pakistan–India (TAPI) Natural Gas Pipeline Investment Agreement was signed among pipeline shareholders in 2016, and investment for the first phase of TAPI project is under discussion. Electricity trade flows within the Central Asian Power System—Kazakhstan, the Kyrgyz Republic, Tajikistan, and Uzbekistan—increased from 583 gigawatt-hours (GWh) to 2,659

Figure 5.3: Progress of Multimodal Corridor Network Development—CAREC (kilometers)

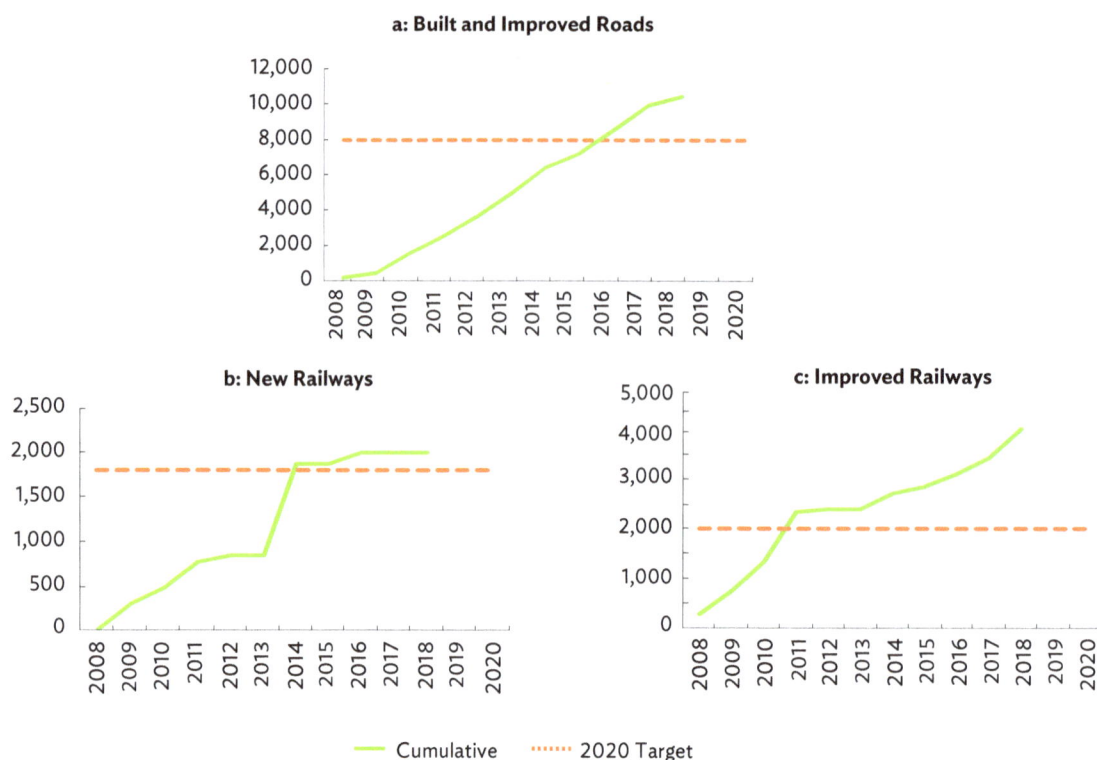

a: Built and Improved Roads

b: New Railways

c: Improved Railways

—— Cumulative   ········ 2020 Target

CAREC = Central Asia Regional Economic Cooperation.

Source: ADB (2019b).

GWh from 2016 to 2018. The first CAREC Energy Ministers' Dialogue held in September 2019 in Tashkent, Uzbekistan discussed regional priorities and strategic issues on CAREC energy sector development and cooperation.

Tourism and Education. Opportunities and challenges including the way forward in developing regional tourism in CAREC were discussed at a workshop held between members and development partners in October 2018 in Tashkent, in a scoping study published in March 2019, and at a high-level panel session during the 52nd ADB Annual Meeting in Fiji in May 2019. Building on the findings from the scoping study, a $2 million regional technical assistance has been approved by ADB in August 2019 to support the development of a CAREC tourism strategy toward 2030 and a regional tourism investment framework over 2021–2025. Findings of a scoping study on education cooperation were

also discussed at a workshop on enhancing regional cooperation in education and skills under CAREC conducted in March 2019 in Bishkek, which laid basis for future directions for education cooperation in CAREC.

CAREC Economic Corridor Development (ECD).
The pilot Almaty-Bishkek Economic Corridor (ABEC) gained new momentum when the prime ministers of both countries created a Kazakhstan–Kyrgyz Republic ABEC Subcommittee in 2017 to oversee the implementation of ABEC. Since then, project preparation to modernize their agricultural wholesale markets and a joint plan for tourism development have been undertaken. A second pilot ECD initiative—the Shymkent-Tashkent-Khujand Economic Corridor— was conceptualized to support an assessment of ECD potential among targeted cities and neighboring oblasts (provinces) in Kazakhstan, Uzbekistan, and Tajikistan.

Prospects

Sector strategies recalibrated under CAREC 2030.

In 2018, CAREC ministers endorsed the CITA 2030 to support growth across the subregion and improve living standards. This needs to be realized through (i) trade expansion from increased market access; (ii) greater diversification; and (iii) stronger trade institutions (ADB 2019d).

The CAREC Transport Strategy 2030 being formulated builds on the Transport and Trade Facilitation Strategy 2020, and aligns with the Strategy 2030 infrastructure agenda. It shifts emphasis from construction and rehabilitation of transport corridors to improving connectivity and sustainability of the regional transport systems through prioritizing multimodal connectivity, quality, and sustainability of transport projects and assets, and development of demand-driven knowledge products. The CAREC Energy Strategy 2030 is also being prepared. Its main building blocks include (i) better energy security through regional interconnections, (ii) more investments through market liberalization reforms, and (iii) enhanced climate mitigation for a sustainable energy system. Energy efficiency and clean energy solutions will be the main drivers to reduce carbon emissions in the high energy-intensive subregion. Both new strategies are finalized for endorsement at the 2019 CAREC Ministerial Conference on 14 November.

Policy Challenges

Facilitating economic diversification through regional integration. Regional integration supports economic diversification by expanding markets, improving resource allocation and facilitating risk-sharing. Most countries in the CAREC region, particularly oil and gas exporting economies, are insufficiently diversified, making them more vulnerable to global and regional economic downturns and commodity price shocks.

CAREC efforts at improving physical connectivity, addressing regional energy demand and supply gaps, and facilitating trade support diversification efforts of member countries. CAREC 2030 strategy's new initiative in the area of strengthening agricultural trade and value chains, including through upgrading SPS systems, and supporting the establishment of regional wholesale markets, can help diversify economies in the agricultural sphere and build their competitiveness. The development of agriculture and horticulture value chains through establishing modern agro-logistics centers in Uzbekistan and modern agriculture wholesale centers development in the Kyrgyz Republic exemplify such endeavors. Likewise, developing the tourism potential of CAREC countries represents a significant opportunity for diversification of economies into the service and hospitality sectors and with potential to generate large-scale tourism-related employment for the workforce of member countries. CITA 2030 and its accompanying RSAPs provide a comprehensive framework to promote economic diversification through promoting e-commerce, trade in services, and the development of special economic zones and industrial parks.

Overall, strong regional cooperation will promote greater economic diversification. Using ADB's regional cooperation and integration (RCI) index to measure integration on a 0 to 1 normalized scale along six dimensions, CAREC is more integrated with Asia on regional value chain and infrastructure and connectivity dimensions while its integration with Asia lags in movement of people and money and finance dimensions (Figure 5.11, please refer to this chapter's section on Asia-Pacific Regional Cooperation and Integration Index). The World Bank's *Doing Business 2019: Training for Reform* puts all but four CAREC countries below the median in "Trading Across Borders." Challenges continue to exist in multimodal connectivity, border-crossing point infrastructure and services, and simplifying customs procedures and harmonization (ADB 2019e).

Southeast Asia: Greater Mekong Subregion Program[36]

Cambodia, the PRC (Yunnan Province and Guangxi Zhuang Autonomous Region), the Lao People's Democratic Republic (Lao PDR), Myanmar, Thailand, and Viet Nam comprise the Greater Mekong Subregion (GMS). ADB houses the GMS Program secretariat. Since 1992, GMS has created an interconnected subregion that improves economic growth with enhanced connectivity and competitiveness (Table 5.2). By the end of 2018, GMS governments and multilateral and bilateral development partners have approved $22.7 billion for 99 investment projects. ADB contributed $9.5 billion, GMS governments $6.0 billion, and other development partners $7.3 billion. The projects built, upgraded, or improved over 11,000 km of roads and 500 km of railway, and constructed 3,000 km of power transmission and distribution lines, adding 1,570 GWh and some 200,000 households to the grid.

Overview

The GMS Program supports subregional projects in transport, transport and trade facilitation, energy, tourism, urban development, health and human resources development, agriculture, and environmental protection. Although the subregion's gross domestic product (GDP) growth slowed marginally—from 6.1% (2013–2017) to 6.0% (2014–2018)—the growth rate remained strong the last 3 years in Cambodia, Viet Nam, and Yunnan Province, as well as Thailand (which recovered from 1% growth in 2014 to 4.1% in 2018). Growth in the subregion is bolstered by growing intraregional trade and tourism has helped, along with strong growth in foreign direct investment in Cambodia, Myanmar, Thailand, and Viet Nam. Intraregional trade as a share of overall trade continues to increase, growing from 5.1% in 2008 to 9.8% in 2018, while value increased from $416 billion in 2016 to $555 billion in 2018. Trade openness is high in Cambodia and Viet Nam, and is growing in Myanmar. GMS tourism

Table 5.2: Selected Economic Indicators, 2018—Greater Mekong Subregion

	Nominal GDP ($ billion)	GDP Growth (2014 to 2018, average, %) and Trend[a]	GDP per Capita (current prices, $)	Trade Openness (total trade, % of GDP)	% Change in FDI (2015 to 2018)[b]	FDI Openness (total FDI Inflows, % of GDP)[c]
Cambodia	25	7.1 ■	1,512	129	70.2	12.6
Guangxi, PRC	307	7.6↓	6,228	21	−34.8	0.4
Yunnan, PRC	270	8.8↓	5,581	11	−64.5	0.4
Lao PDR	18	7.1↓	2,649	73	18.0	7.3
Myanmar	73	6.8↓	1,377	46	25.9	4.9
Thailand	505	3.1↑	7,604	95	86.6	2.1
Viet Nam	245	6.6↑	2,593	196	31.4	6.3
GMS	**1,442**	**6.0↓**	**4,312**	**79**	**29.6**	**2.5**

↑ = Increase from 2013–2017 average, ↓ = Decrease, ■ = Unchanged.

FDI = foreign direct investment, GDP = gross domestic product, GMS = Greater Mekong Subregion, Lao PDR = Lao People's Democratic Republic, PRC = People's Republic of China.

[a] Average GDP growth rate for Greater Mekong Subregion is weighted using nominal GDP. Total trade refers to the sum of exports and imports.
[b] 2015 to 2017 for Guangxi and Yunnan, PRC.
[c] 2017 for Guangxi and Yunnan, PRC.

Sources: GMS Statistical Database. www.greatermekong/statistics; CEIC; International Monetary Fund. World Economic Outlook April 2019 Database. https://www.imf.org/external/pubs/ft/weo/2019/01/weodata/index.aspx; and United Nations Conference on Trade and Development. UNCTADstat. https://unctadstat.unctad.org (all accessed October 2019).

---

[36]   Contributed by the GMS Secretariat, Southeast Asia Department, ADB.

is booming, with 78.8 million tourist arrivals in 2018 generating more than $90 billion. Intraregional tourism grew from 22.2 million arrivals in 2014 to 45.2 million in 2017, or 21.1 % of the subregion's total. For example, tourism receipts account for as much as 18% of GDP in Cambodia.

Performance and Progress over the Past Year

GMS connectivity has strengthened, paving the way for more dynamic subregional economic integration.

The Ha Noi Action Plan 2018–2022. GMS leaders adopted the Ha Noi Action Plan 2018–2022 (ADB 2018a) at the 6th GMS Leaders' Summit in March 2018—establishing strategic directions and operational priorities for GMS integration. It comprises four key elements: (i) a spatial strategy of a network of economic corridors; (ii) refinements in sector strategies; (iii) improvements in planning, programming, and monitoring systems and processes; and (iv) enhancements in institutional arrangements and partnerships. The plan uses a Regional Investment Framework 2022 (RIF 2022) to identify a medium-term pipeline of priority projects to be regularly monitored and updated. The RIF 2022: First Progress Report and Update for 2018 was endorsed by GMS ministers in April 2019, and showed progress on 247 investment and technical assistance projects—the expanded pipeline is valued at $80.9 billion (GMS Secretariat 2019).

In early 2019, GMS leaders directed the development of a new long term strategic framework 2030 in response to the changing global environment. The GMS secretariat supported GMS members, development partners, the private sector, and subregional think tanks in this work. The GMS Strategic Framework 2030 will be discussed at the 23rd GMS Ministerial Meeting for further adoption at the 7th GMS Leaders' Summit in 2020.

Cross-Border Transport Connectivity and Economic Corridor Development. The GMS Transport Sector Strategy 2030 boosts investments in RIF 2022 in railways and ports under construction to increase multimodal transport in non-road transport modes— including the Yuxi–Mohan Railway, Vientiane–Boten Railway, and the Laem Chabang Port Development Project. The Greater Mekong Railway Association has an investment program for priority rail links—some of which have already started, for example the Vientiane, Lao PDR-Boten, PRC line, and the Hekou, Viet Nam–Lao Cai, PRC line. The Poipet-Aranyaprathet Border Railway Bridge between Cambodia and Thailand has been completed. Under the GMS Transport Sector Strategy 2030, a study on GMS road safety regimes identified key challenges and offered ways to better collect data, conduct diagnostics, and formulate effective policies that promote road safety. Country-specific road safety studies are planned.

A study was completed in 2018 to assess existing GMS economic corridors. And while the study focused on the physical condition of transport infrastructure, it also assessed the economic potential of several corridor

---

Box 5.1: Promoting E-commerce in Greater Mekong Subregion

With its tremendous economic potential, particularly for small and medium-sized enterprises, GMS members established a framework for cross-border e-commerce cooperation at its 7th Economic Corridors Forum in Kunming, People's Republic of China, in 2015. Since then, an e-commerce business alliance was established and capacity building and regular dialogues have been conducted to share knowledge on cross-border

e-commerce best practices, policies, and standards. The GMS e-commerce platform also encourages members to foster innovation and entrepreneurship; and promote dialogue on industrial standards, transaction processes, information systems, logistics supply chains, and business opportunities. Progress is reported annually at the GMS Economic Corridors Forum.

GMS = Greater Mekong Subregion, PRC = People's Republic of China.
Source: ADB.

areas. It provided a baseline for monitoring the progress of economic corridor development by identifying gaps and the corresponding required interventions. Cross-border e-commerce cooperation is also being promoted to unlock the economic potential a digital economy offers (Box 5.1).

Transport and Trade Facilitation. An "Early Harvest" of the GMS Cross-Border Transport Facilitation Agreement (CBTA) was launched in August 2018. Cambodia, the Lao PDR, the PRC, Thailand, and Viet Nam (with Myanmar joining in 2020) offer GMS transport permits to be issued and accepted along specified routes and border crossings. Several GMS members have issued these permits and Temporary Admission Documents (TADs) to commercial vehicles (buses and trucks) to expedite cross-border transport. Others are preparing to do so. In March 2019, the Joint Committee for the CBTA agreed to extend Early Harvest implementation for an additional 2 years—until 31 May 2021. It also agreed that Myanmar will initially join through bilateral agreements with neighboring countries. The negotiations for the expansion of corridors, routes and border crossings covered under the CBTA Protocol 1 were concluded in early 2019 and are expected to come into effect soon.

ADB continues to provide technical assistance to improve trade through time release studies with regional customs agencies to identify how to improve border procedures and support SPS arrangements in Cambodia and the Lao PDR, with Myanmar discussions ongoing.

Energy. The Regional Power Trade Coordination Committee (RPTCC) continues to accelerate regional power trade. Working groups on (i) performance standards and grid codes, and (ii) regulatory issues help to harmonize subregional power trade policies. In 2018, the RPTCC focused on determining national transmission charges and a draft GMS Regional Grid Code. Previously planned and ongoing bilateral and through-power trade is increasing. For example, the Lao PDR began exporting power to Malaysia through Thailand—trading 17 GWh in 2018. In March 2019, they agreed to expand up to 100 GWh annually. Also in March, the Lao PDR and Cambodia agreed to a power

purchase agreement of up to 200 megawatts from the Lao PDR to support Cambodia's rising energy demand. Pre-feasibility studies are underway for a Lao PDR–Myanmar interconnection. Discussions for the establishment of a GMS Regional Power Coordination Center continue. Several studies in 2018 focused on integrating strategic environmental assessments into Viet Nam's power development planning to illustrate how strategic environmental assessments can help GMS members build sustainable national power development plans.

Tourism. Subregional tourism continues to increase, thanks to better connectivity, rising incomes, streamlined tourist visa requirements, and easy access to travel information. GMS members, led by the PRC's 19 million visitors to other GMS countries in 2018, were the main source markets. To better cope with steeply rising tourism numbers, the Tourism Working Group (TWG) is prioritizing secondary destination infrastructure, sustainable tourism, environmental management, digital marketing to promote secondary destinations, and human resources development.

The second GMS Tourism Sector Strategy 2016–2025 is being implemented with guidance from the GMS TWG and the Mekong Tourism Coordinating Office (2017). ADB supports two ongoing projects on GMS Tourism Infrastructure for Inclusive Growth in Cambodia, the Lao PDR, and Viet Nam. The first project helps accelerate inclusive economic growth along segments of GMS economic corridors by improving tourism-related access infrastructure and environmental conditions at cross-border tourism centers, and by strengthening the capacity of tourism organizations. The second helps improve urban–rural connectivity, environmental services, and the capacity to manage tourism growth in secondary destinations along GMS economic corridors. It also supports implementation of the Association of Southeast Asian Nations (ASEAN) Tourism Standards. Development partners in the TWG and GMS members also help develop tourism infrastructure and support services, strengthen tourism vocational training institutions and business support services, and expand digital tourism marketing and promotion.

Urban and Border Area Development. In 2018, ADB approved two projects to develop corridor towns in Myanmar, the Lao PDR, and Cambodia. They focus on building urban environment services and strengthening institutional capacity, private sector engagement, information and communication technology (ICT)-based public management systems, developing regional tourism, and supporting city master plans for regional economic connectivity. ADB also approved funding to support projects in the border areas of Guangxi, PRC–Viet Nam and Yunnan, PRC–Myanmar—both with high volumes of trade and human mobility. The Guangxi, PRC–Viet Nam project supports cross-border trade, investment, and financial transactions, particularly for small and medium-sized enterprises (SMEs); developing infrastructure and trade-related services; and improving connectivity and policy coordination. The Yunnan, PRC–Myanmar project supports cross-border trade, border connectivity, and urban and social development issues in Lincang Prefecture in Yunnan, and offers benefits to Myanmar nationals who trade, work, and use social services in Lincang.

ADB is leading a study on spatial planning along the GMS North–South Economic Corridor between Myanmar and the PRC. ADB also published a study examining the role special economic zones (SEZs) play in strengthening the competitiveness of economic corridors in the GMS.

Health and Other Human Resources Development. A GMS Health Cooperation Strategy 2019–2023 was endorsed in early 2019. The strategy focuses on three pillars: (i) improving health systems; (ii) strengthening protection for health impacts of regional integration; and (iii) enhancing human capacity to respond to health issues (ADB 2019c). The GMS Health Security Project for Cambodia, the Lao PDR, Myanmar, and Viet Nam is strengthening public health security against communicable diseases; improving public health security systems; and boosting national and regional capacity for disease surveillance and response, risk assessment, case management, and subregional collaboration. A regional capacity development initiative for government officials under the B-I-G Capacity Building Program for Connectivity (B-I-G Program) helps enhance capacity in developing policies, programs, and projects that support physical, institutional, and people-to-people connectivity in Southeast Asia and the PRC.[37] In 2018, training programs and knowledge events were conducted on economic corridors, SEZs, project management, transport, health assessment in SEZs, e-commerce, trade facilitation, and poverty reduction and social development.

Agriculture. Technical assistance to support a GMS Sustainable Agriculture and Food Security Program is being prepared to help implement the Strategy for Promoting Safe and Environment-Friendly Agro-Based Value Chains and Siem Reap Action Plan for 2018–2022 (ADB 2018b). The program will focus on areas such as climate-smart and gender-conscious agricultural value chains, food safety and quality, and the water–food–energy nexus through activities for (i) greening agribusiness supply chains; (ii) inclusive and gender-conscious food value chains; (iii) financing climate-friendly agribusinesses; (iv) food safety and quality standards, certification, and traceability; (v) cross-border animal health and value chain development; (vi) water for food security in a changing climate; and (vii) agricultural adaptation in the context of the water–food–energy nexus.

In 2018, ADB approved a Climate-Friendly Agribusiness Value Chain Sector Project for Cambodia, the Lao PDR, and Myanmar with cofinancing from the Green Climate Fund and the Global Agriculture Food Security Program. The project will help develop pro-poor agribusiness value chains, focusing on rehabilitating critical production and post-harvest infrastructure to link farming communities and urban centers along GMS corridors.

---

[37]   The Brunei Darussalam–Indonesia–Malaysia–Philippines East ASEAN Growth Area (BIMP-EAGA), the Indonesia–Malaysia–Thailand Growth Triangle (IMT-GT), and the GMS or B-I-G Capacity Building Program for Connectivity is a regional capacity development initiative that provides opportunities for knowledge and experience-sharing between and among the three subregional programs given their unique roles as building blocks for Asian integration. It is funded by ADB and the governments of the Republic of Korea and the PRC. Its activities include training programs, knowledge events, and an internet-based information repository.

Environment. Several activities have been completed under the GMS Core Environment Program Phase II, involving the Green Freight Initiative, land use planning simulation modeling, environmental and air pollution assessments, a study on transboundary wildlife habitat and migration routes, and policy briefs on (i) Breaking Down Barriers to Green Freight Investments, and (ii) How to Promote Investments in Natural Capital in the GMS, among others.

A regional technical assistance on the GMS Climate Change and Environmental Sustainability Program is being prepared to support implementation of the GMS Core Environment Program Strategic Framework for 2018–2022 (GMS Environment Operations Center 2017). The assistance will focus on enabling conditions to leverage investments in green technologies and sustainable infrastructure, ecosystem services and climate resilience, and disaster risk management. Activities will support (i) green technologies for climate action and environmental sustainability; (ii) financing sustainable infrastructure and low-carbon, climate-resilient technologies; (iii) pollution control and sustainable waste management; (iv) climate-smart ecosystem landscapes; (v) decarbonization of agriculture, energy, and transport sectors; and (vi) climate change adaptation and disaster risk management.

Prospects

Tourism and trade will continue to drive GMS growth.

In the short and medium term, the GMS Program will be guided by the Ha Noi Action Plan; the RIF 2022 project pipeline; and sector strategies covering transport, health, tourism, the environment, and agriculture. Over the long term, once adopted, the GMS Strategic Framework 2030 will provide a GMS vision and build on past GMS strengths, while taking into account the rapidly changing global and regional contexts.

Increased multi-sector coordination and intervention is needed in spatial planning, border area development, and other areas under the GMS Program.

Although GMS growth has been strong generally, it has been driven by tourism and trade. To foster sustainable and inclusive tourism, the GMS Tourism Working Group has begun prioritizing promotion of secondary destinations, infrastructure and environmental management, and human resources development. On trade, despite the potential slowdown in global trade, GMS remains a dynamic subregion and could improve trade competitiveness with more efficient logistics and trade procedures.

Policy Challenge

Cooperation for customs and border procedures needs to keep up with growing cross-border movement of goods and people.

As subregional connectivity improves and the flow of goods and people continue to increase across the GMS, members will be challenged to ensure customs and border procedures are efficient and have systems in place to facilitate cross-border trade, especially but not limited to, trade in agriculture and livestock to meet SPS requirements. Members must also cooperate on cross-border health issues, from communicable diseases to animal health, to cross-border labor migration and mobile populations that require access to cross-border health services.

East Asia: Support for RCI Initiatives under CAREC and GMS Subregional Programs and Knowledge-Sharing Activities[38]

ADB continues to help the PRC and Mongolia participate in subregional cooperation programs through CAREC and GMS. It does this mainly through

---

[38]   Contributed by the ADB East Asia Department (EARD) RCI team.

strategically aligned investments and capacity development in cross-border development areas to bring economic spillover benefits to other CAREC and GMS members. Cooperation in knowledge- and experience-sharing between CAREC and GMS members is coordinated through the PRC-based Regional Knowledge Sharing Initiative (RKSI) and CAREC Institute.

Performance and Progress over the Past Year

ADB continues to support projects in Mongolia and the PRC related to CAREC and GMS.[39]

ADB continues to promote active engagement of Yunnan Province and the Guangxi Zhuang Autonomous Region, PRC in GMS by supporting border economic zones (BEZs) and creating effective RCI linkages between the PRC and ASEAN. For example, Tranche 2 of ADB's multitranche financing facility (MFF) for the Guangxi RCI Promotion Investment Program— approved in 2018 for $180 million—helps strengthen key logistics infrastructure and services in the BEZs of the PRC, building roads both within BEZs and those leading to border-crossing points (BCPs). These BEZs also support development of cross-border e-commerce platforms, including an electronic business data center and cross-border trade exhibition center, together with software systems and advisory services. SMEs are being strengthened by providing a business development service information center and ASEAN vocational training facilities to provide SME-related training to students from the PRC and ASEAN.

The 2018-approved $250 million Yunnan Lincang Border Economic Cooperation Zone Development Project assists border towns in Lincang Prefecture, PRC, to improve cross-border trade-related infrastructure and connectivity, and strengthen the competitiveness of urban centers, logistics and industrial parks, and land

ports. Urban populations will benefit from upgraded roads, schools, and medical facilities, together with improved social infrastructure and services. The project helps RCI in Yunnan Province under the GMS Program by further developing economic corridors.

Additional financing of $27 million was approved in September 2019 for Mongolia's Regional Improvement of Border Services (RIBS) project. The project, which began in 2016, will scale up and include two additional BCPs: Bichigt, bordering the PRC in eastern Mongolia; and Borshoo, bordering the Russian Federation in western Mongolia. The RIBS project envisages rehabilitating BCP facilities and introducing ICT-based customs systems. Ongoing work includes improving infrastructure at Altanbulag (connecting with the Russian Federation) and supporting ICT development in Bichigt and Zamiin-Uud. As Bichigt and Borshoo become increasingly functional gateways for Mongolia's bilateral trade with the PRC and the Russian Federation, the additional financing will improve infrastructure and facilities at both BCPs for border clearance and immigration protection standards.

ADB knowledge-sharing platforms will build more effective RCI.

ADB and the CAREC Institute organized a series of trade and RCI-related activities during 2018–2019. Following the endorsement of CITA 2030, a workshop on SEZs (November 2018 in Shenzhen, PRC) emphasized their increasing potential as catalysts for industrialization and drivers of CAREC economic growth—and for Shenzhen, a test of structural reforms. Another jointly organized workshop promoted SME trade finance through cross-country learning in the CAREC region (December 2018 in Xiamen, PRC). In partnership with the Asia-Pacific Finance and Development Institute, a workshop on environmental readiness for e-commerce (December 2018 in Shanghai, PRC) showed how to promote cross-border e-commerce. ADB and the CAREC Institute will continue to work closely to enhance linkages between policies and research, initially in e-commerce regulatory

---

[39] EARD is responsible for implementing CITA 2030, and provides direct support for Mongolia's participation in CAREC. It also supports loans and technical assistance projects in PRC provinces and autonomous regions within CAREC and GMS.

framework and potentially with mutual recognition—and acceptance of paperless SPS certificates during 2019–2020. The 4th CAREC Think Tanks Development Forum (August 2019 in Xi'an, PRC) focused on Trading for Shared Prosperity, underscoring the need to bridge trade policy discussions with knowledge work.

The RKSI was jointly established by the PRC and ADB in 2012 to exchange development knowledge among ADB developing member economies.[40] Drawing largely on the PRC's experience over the past 40 years promoting economic growth and social transformation, RKSI organized 56 events (workshops, conferences, and training) benefiting some 5,000 participants from ADB developing member countries as of the end of June 2019—focusing on the four broad themes of inclusive growth, urbanization, environment and climate change, and RCI.

During 2018–2019, RKSI continued to share knowledge among DMCs. For example, in collaboration with the International Poverty Reduction Center in the PRC, RKSI organized the Sixth and Eighth ASEAN+3 Village Leaders Exchange Program, and the Twelfth and Thirteenth ASEAN-PRC Forum on Social Development and Poverty Reduction. The Village Leader Program is designed specifically to strengthen the role of village leaders in rural development and helps them learn at ground-level from successful poverty alleviation projects and initiatives. In 2018, the Sixth Program focused on human capital development through improved community development, while the Eighth Program in 2019 addressed rural industrial development, agricultural value chains, and rural tourism. Partnering with the Asia-Pacific Finance Development Institute, RKSI also supported SEZ training for ASEAN and PRC officials, sharing the PRC's experience in using SEZs for economic development. The annual event—jointly organized with ADB's Southeast Asia Department—more broadly discusses concepts, trends, good practices, lessons learned for SEZ design, implementation and management, and identifies avenues for cross-border e-commerce development and cooperation.

ADB also supports inter-subregional forums: EARD's Public Management, Financial Sector, and Regional Cooperation Division partnered with both RKSI and the CAREC Institute for the inter-subregional knowledge- and experience-sharing forum on trade facilitation modernization and reform, held in October 2019, in Tbilisi, Georgia. Senior customs officials from the CAREC and South Asia Subregional Economic Cooperation (SASEC) countries worked to identify critical success factors to promote efficient and effective trade flows, resource allocation, and improved regional cooperation, while also supporting national efforts to adopt international best practices and complying with international commitments such as the WTO TFA.

Prospects

ADB supports cross-border economic zone development.

A $30 million ADB loan to Mongolia is being prepared to assist the government to operationalize the Zamiin-Uud free zone and support development of the cross-border economic zone (CBEZ) between Mongolia and the PRC at the Zamiin-Uud–Erenhot border crossing into the PRC's Inner Mongolia Autonomous Region. The project includes construction of infrastructure and facilities in the Zamiin-Uud free zone, strengthened management and operation of the Zamiin-Uud free zone, and establishing a coordination mechanism for Zamiin-Uud–Erenhot CBEZ port of entry.

On the PRC side of the CBEZ, a counterpart project supports construction of an inspection area, with smart port inspection also under preparation. This is part of a broader $420 million ADB-financed MFF under preparation for the PRC's Inner Mongolia RCI Promotion Investment Program. It will support the Inner Mongolia Autonomous Region in promoting RCI between the PRC, Mongolia, and other CAREC members. Enhanced cooperation between the PRC and Mongolia under CAREC will bring high regional spillover economic and

---

[40]   The RKSI website is available at http://www.rksi.org/.

social benefits to Mongolia by improving connectivity, increasing cross-border trade, and expanding Mongolia's access to the PRC and other CAREC markets. The MFF will contribute to reduced poverty and inequality, while supporting rural development through improved infrastructure and increased trade. Program design and implementation is closely coordinated with Mongolia's ADB-financed CBEZ and RIBS projects. Such parallel and coordinated investment approaches between the PRC and Mongolia helps achieve national priorities and promotes RCI through cooperation agreements. It could serve as a model for similar border-related projects and particularly, for CAREC's landlocked countries.

ADB is also assisting the Xinjiang Uygur Autonomous Region, PRC, to develop a $490 million MFF for the Xinjiang RCI Promotion Investment Program, to expand economic opportunities in Xinjiang's border areas. It will increase transport and trade efficiency along CAREC transport corridors and provide better business opportunities to SMEs and local populations. Logistics and other trade-related infrastructure and facilities will help the emerging BEZs' physical expansion and provide international health care facilities for the PRC, Kazakhstan, and other CAREC members. Last-mile road linkages will connect the BEZs more rapidly and effectively with BCPs into Kazakhstan and Mongolia. Road networks within the BEZs will help expand and develop productive capacity. Physical infrastructure and business development services will be designed to provide access to SMEs and local training to improve employment opportunities as the BEZs expand.

Policy Challenges

Subregional trade and transport corridors require effective transit arrangements to promote trade.

With the PRC and Mongolia focusing investment on building better cross-border trade infrastructure and facilities—and reducing transaction costs through the WTO's TFA—there is a growing need to develop more

effective CAREC and GMS cross-border transit trade policy. Current arrangements for multicountry transit trade from East Asia to markets in Central Asia, South Asia, and Europe can be expensive and cumbersome; with the plethora of bilateral transit agreements limited in scope. Subregional transit arrangements, such as those being prepared for a pilot phase under the CAREC trade sector, should be encouraged and supported.

South Asia: South Asia Subregional Economic Cooperation[41]

In 2018, the South Asia Subregional Economic Cooperation (SASEC) Program agreed to fund two transport connectivity projects in India and Nepal valued at $564.2 million to improve international trade corridors, along with a $20 million energy project in Nepal to raise power transmission capacity. Since 2001, ADB has helped finance 52 SASEC projects worth $11.36 billion, with about $6.52 billion in ADB financing. SASEC members—Bangladesh, Bhutan, India, Maldives, Myanmar, Nepal, and Sri Lanka—are following the SASEC Operational Plan 2016–2025 to prioritize gaps in transport and energy networks across the subregion.

Overview

In 2018, SASEC focused on reducing gaps in multimodal connectivity to boost RCI among its members.

Bangladesh, Bhutan, India, and Nepal established SASEC in 2001 to strengthen subregional economic cooperation and address development challenges—such as persistent poverty and demographic growth (Table 5.3). Maldives and Sri Lanka joined in 2014, followed by Myanmar in 2017, expanding opportunities to enhance cross-border connectivity, intraregional trade, and RCI. ADB is lead financier and home to the SASEC secretariat.

---

[41]   Contributed by Director Ronald Antonio Butiong of ADB's South Asia Department (SARD) and SARD consultants Jesusito Tranquilino and Leticia de Leon.

Table 5.3: Selected Economic Indicators, 2018—SASEC

	Population (million)	Nominal GDP ($ billion)	GDP Growth (%, 2014–2018, average)	GDP per Capita (current prices, $)	Trade Openness (total trade, % of GDP)
Bangladesh	166.4	288.4	7.0	1,733.7	30.9
Bhutan	0.8	2.6	5.9	3,160.3	122.0
India	1,354.1	2,718.7	7.5	2,007.8	30.6
Maldives	0.4	5.3	6.4	12,000.0	59.0
Myanmar	53.9	68.7	6.8	1,275.0	52.7
Nepal	29.6	29.0	5.0	980.3	46.9
Sri Lanka	21.5	88.9	4.2	4,128.0	38.0
SASEC	**1,626.7**	**3,201.7**	**7.3**	**1,968.2**	**31.6**

GDP = gross domestic product, IMF = International Monetary Fund, SASEC = South Asia Subregional Economic Cooperation.

Notes: Average GDP growth rate for Myanmar is for 2017 and 2018. SASEC average GDP growth rate is weighted using nominal GDP, based on IMF staff estimates. Total trade refers to the sum of exports and imports.

Sources: ADB (2019f); IMF. Direction of Trade Statistics. https://www.imf.org; IMF. World Economic Outlook October 2019 Database. https://www.imf.org/external/pubs/ft/weo/2019/02/weodata/index.aspx; and World Bank. Population Estimates and Projections. https://datacatalog.worldbank.org/dataset/population-estimates-and-projections (all accessed October 2019).

Figure 5.4: SASEC Investment by Sector and Volume ($ million)

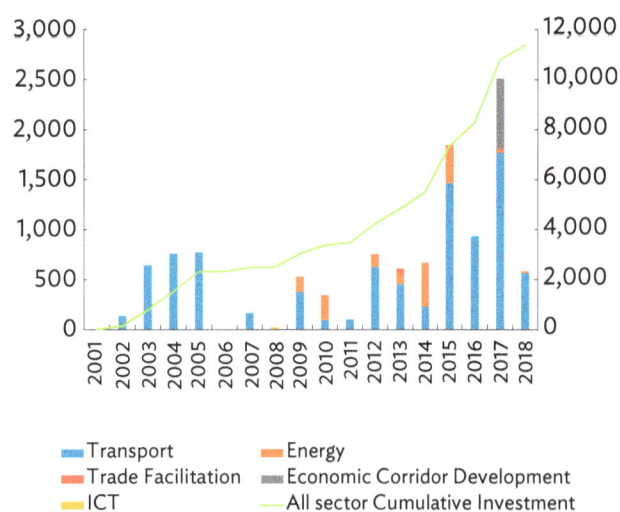

ICT = information and communication technology, SASEC = South Asia Subregional Economic Cooperation.

Source: ADB (2019g).

Figure 5.5: SASEC Projects by Sector, as of 31 December 2018

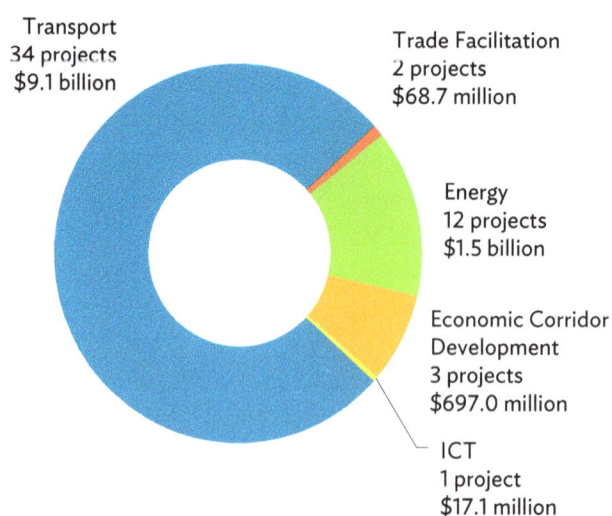

ICT = information and communication technology, SASEC = South Asia Subregional Economic Cooperation.

Source: ADB (2019g).

By the end of 2018, 52 ADB-financed projects worth $11.36 billion had been committed (Figure 5.4), with an additional $106.44 million in 81 technical assistance grants. Infrastructure connectivity investments held the largest share (34 projects, $9.08 billion), with power generation, transmission, and cross-border electricity trade second (12 projects, $1.50 billion). Investments in

economic corridor development, trade facilitation, and ICT development amounted to $782.74 million (Figure 5.5). ADB financed $6.52 billion in investments ($4.31 billion from ordinary capital resources and $2.21 billion in concessional finance), while SASEC members and cofinanciers contributed $4.84 billion (Figure 5.6).

Figure 5.6: SASEC Investment by Sector, Volume, and Finance Partner ($ million)

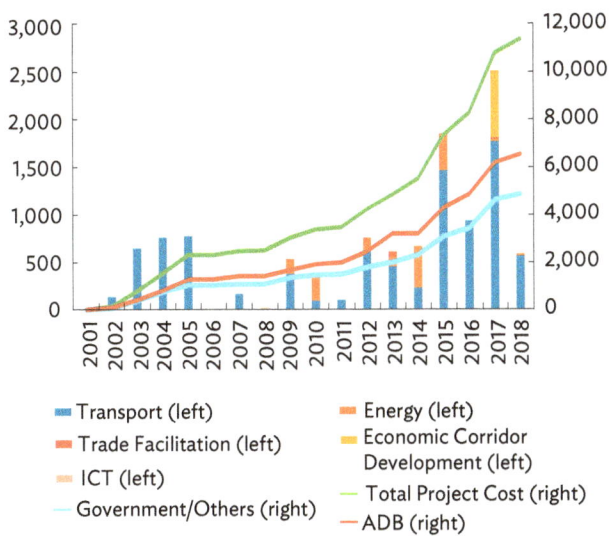

ADB = Asian Development Bank, ICT = information and communication technology, SASEC = South Asia Subregional Economic Cooperation.

Source: ADB (2019g).

The SASEC Operational Plan 2016–2025 (SASEC OP) refocused SASEC's operational priorities with greater emphasis on enhancing multimodal transport networks, developing railways and seaports, land and maritime-based trade facilitation and logistics, promoting regional energy trade and cleaner energy, and reinforcing value chains within economic corridors. The 2017 SASEC Vision (ADB 2017a) aims to transform the subregion into a growth engine by leveraging resource-based industries, expanding regional value chains, and strengthening gateways and hubs. Energy cooperation has been widened to include oil and gas.

Performance and Progress over the Past Year

SASEC nodal officials and working groups met in Singapore in March 2018 to update the SASEC OP, adopting a clearer basis for prioritizing projects: (i) defining which projects comprised transport and energy networks; (ii) conducting a comprehensive list of completed and ongoing projects; and (iii) identifying future priority projects.

Transport. Filling gaps in identified multimodal transport networks that link main industry centers with key ports, airports, and logistics centers are priorities. The SASEC OP update identified six SASEC corridors that address the modal development needs, promoting multifaceted development along routes. These include (i) the Nepal-Kolkata Trade Corridor, (ii) Bay of Bengal Highway, (iii) India-ASEAN East-West Corridor, (iv) Nepal-Bhutan-Bangladesh North-South Corridor, (v) North Bangladesh-India Connector, and (vi) Sri Lanka Port Highway. Two 2018 ADB projects help address these: Nepal's SASEC Highway Improvement ($256.4 million) will support capacity, quality, and safety improvements of the East-West Highway—Nepal's main trade corridor linking to Dhaka and Chittagong through India (within SASEC corridor 4); and India's SASEC Road Connectivity Investment Program Tranche 2 ($307.8 million), will upgrade links between Manipur state and Myanmar (SASEC corridor 3), and develop last-mile connectivity for an international bridge between India and Nepal.

Bangladesh's railway projects, many financed by ADB, are designed to better link India's Mongla and Chattogram ports with Bhutan, Nepal, and Northeast India. Current development on ports and airports—mostly along SASEC corridors—will increase capacity. India's port development stresses improving container handling for port-led industrialization along the East-Coast Economic Corridor—the Bay of Bengal Highway (SASEC corridor 2). Sri Lanka's Colombo port investment helps meet demand for container transshipment and related logistics for international markets.

Trade Facilitation. The SASEC OP allowed more time for its Trade Facilitation Strategic Framework (TFSF) 2014–2018 (ADB 2014) to reach international best practices on clearances. ADB's trade facilitation assistance will focus on (i) simplifying trade documentation, (ii) promoting automation in border agencies and the development of national single windows, (iii) strengthening national conformance bodies to better address SPS measures and other technical barriers to trade, (iv) developing and implementing motor vehicle agreements, (v) developing trade-related infrastructure in ports and land border crossings, and (vi) building trade facilitation capacity and coordination (ADB 2016). Current ADB assistance focuses on (i) support for the SASEC Customs Subgroup—national and subregional projects on exchange of trade documents and transit automation, among others, including capacity building in international customs best practices, (ii) improve cross-border facilities,[42] largely integrated in SASEC road connectivity projects, and (iii) facilitate more efficient movement of people, goods, and vehicles using a multi-track approach.[43]

Energy. Promoting subregional power trade is a SASEC Vision flagship initiative and a priority in the SASEC OP. It provides more reliable, cheaper, and cleaner energy (mainly hydropower) from Bhutan and Nepal to SASEC members Bangladesh, India, and Sri Lanka. India already has a bilateral power trade arrangement individually with Bangladesh, Bhutan, Nepal, and Myanmar. ADB has been supporting hydropower projects in Bhutan and transmission projects in Bangladesh and Nepal to enable power trading,[44] which will continue through the SASEC Cross-Border Power Trade Working Group (SPT-WG).

Two flagship initiatives involve trade in oil and gas: (i) a pipeline corridor between Bangladesh and India for crude oil imports and product supply; and (ii) using Sri Lanka as a liquid petroleum gas (LPG) transshipment and storage hub. The first is progressing via Bangladesh-India discussions within their hydrocarbon partnership framework—recently agreeing to construct a 130 km oil pipeline between Siliguri (India) and Partbatipur (Bangladesh) with a 1 million metric ton annual capacity. ADB will support studies on developing the Sri Lanka LPG Hub as well as establishing LPG and liquid natural gas infrastructure to meet emerging demand. The SASEC oil and gas supply chain was discussed at the SASEC Regional Gas and Petroleum Working Group (RGP-WG), established in late 2018.

Economic Corridor Development. After projects in India and Nepal in 2017, ADB expanded its ECD work through studies on (i) Multimodal Logistics Parks in India's Karnataka and Assam states, (ii) India's Chennai-Kanyakumari Industrial Corridor, (iii) the Southwest Bangladesh Economic Corridor, and (iv) the Colombo-Trincomalee Economic Corridor (CTEC) in Sri Lanka. A 2018 CTEC workshop in Colombo presented a comprehensive development plan for CTEC, laying out the framework and strategy for the corridor's development. ADB also financed a workshop on SEZs and ECD, held in Shanghai, PRC in June 2018, to better understand and share experiences in promoting SEZs, ECD, and defining the role logistics plays.

Prospects

The updated 2018 SASEC OP identified 77 projects ($45.6 billion) to be financed by SASEC members, ADB, and other development partners. Transport remains the bulk (53 projects, $34.0 billion), indicating that SASEC members continue to address their connectivity gaps and build needed links with Southeast Asia and East Asia.

An integrated and holistic approach under the SASEC OP will expand regional trade markets.

Priority transport projects under the updated SASEC OP will expand trade along the defined SASEC road and rail corridors—either by completing missing links to gateways or upgrading of road and rail capacity where congestion exists. Gateway ports and airports are also prioritized for capacity upgrading and removing operational bottlenecks. In trade facilitation, the holistic approach combines both hard and soft components to expedite processes and improve border clearance procedures, with most

---

[42] An ADB study on coordinated border infrastructure development—covering nine land customs stations pairings—examined infrastructural, institutional, procedural, ICT, and other issues that need to be addressed and emphasized the need for better coordination to synchronize investments and software.

[43] The multitrack approach involves (i) expanding pilots for electronic cargo tracking systems for better cargo security and revenue protection, (ii) finding soutions for cross-border routes or border point, and (iii) continuing support for finalizing Bangladesh-Bhutan-India-Nepal motor vehicle agreements.

[44] Nepal's SASEC Power System Expansion project (additional financing) will augment two earlier projects to build power transmission lines and substations to equip the Nepal grid with necessary capacity for future hydropower exports.

pipeline project cost dominated by investments in trade infrastructure, including conformance with SPS and Technical Barriers to Trade issues. By number, the majority of projects will streamline trade documentation, border agency automation, national single windows, and capacity building in trade facilitation best practices. In energy, the comprehensive approach involves broadening cooperation from power to oil and gas, emphasizing (i) power trading, with the SPT-WG promoting priority hydropower and transmission interconnection projects that address power resource imbalances, and (ii) oil and gas trading, with the RGP-WG tasked to look into prospects for enhancing the gas and fuel supply chain, such as setting up LPG and liquid natural gas transshipment and logistics.

Policy Challenges

SASEC countries need to intensify efforts to reduce poverty further.

The poverty rate in South Asia has declined remarkably—from 38.6% in 2002 to 12.4% in 2015. But it remains above the 10% global average. To meet the Sustainable Development Goal of ending all forms of poverty by 2030, SASEC countries would need to do more to reduce poverty and inequality, especially as it faces the dual challenges

of rising populations and employment-reducing effects of new technology and innovation (ADB 2018c). Under ADB's Strategy 2030, eliminating poverty remains the primary development target (ADB 2018d). ADB will use all possible means to address poverty, including greater financial inclusion, creation of quality jobs, access for SMEs, women empowerment, and more support for rural-based agribusiness value chains. To counter future job losses from automation, ADB supports education, vocational training, and labor policies that engender occupational shifts.

SASEC contributes to poverty alleviation by improving market access through enhanced transport connectivity, more seamless cross-border flows of people and goods through trade facilitation, and raising revenues to fund socioeconomic projects of hydropower exporters, while giving importers more secure and affordable power supply. However, there is no guarantee that these RCI initiatives promote greater equity. Other RCI platforms in South Asia—such as the Bay of Bengal Initiative for Multi-Sectoral Technical and Economic Cooperation and the South Asian Association for Regional Cooperation can provide knowledge-sharing on good practices to avoid any regressive RCI effects—incorporating inclusive policies for regional connectivity initiatives, with special attention to capacity building of the rural poor, women, and SMEs. Box 5.2 elaborates

---

Box 5.2: SASEC as a Platform for Knowledge-Sharing for Enhanced Regional Cooperation

The SASEC Vision estimates that the rise in the share of working age population in the subregion by 2025 can become either a "demographic dividend" or a liability, depending on SASEC members' ability to provide avenues for growth (ADB 2017a). The SASEC Vision aims to tap into this potential through cooperative efforts of members, ensuring cohesive policies and programs that harness each country's strengths, creating economic synergies. ADB knows that serious risks can hamper this vision—such as trade tensions, debt and systemic financial issues, climate change, and automation technology.

Overall, however, technology and innovation can provide the means for stronger growth. Regional cooperation can provide a platform for knowledge exchange in new technologies that can accelerate growth and job creation. In energy, knowledge-sharing in state-of-the-art transmission

technology under the SASEC Cross-Border Power Trade Working Group (SPT-WG), for example, can foster better grid interconnectivity where more robust power trade can take place. The SPT-WG will additionally examine sharing suitable renewable energy and more efficient energy technologies that can lead to more climate-friendly energy use. In oil and gas, the SASEC Regional Gas and Petroleum Working Group plans to look into technological advances that can enhance the fuel supply chain, ensure more stable and affordable fuel for importers. In trade facilitation, SASEC's promotion of electronic cargo tracking systems technology is helping realize safer, more secure and efficient cross-border transit between members, and is aligned with the Bangladesh-Bhutan-India-Nepal (BBIN) motor vehicle agreement to create a seamless flow of passenger, personal, and cargo vehicular traffic between BBIN countries.

ADB = Asian Development Bank, SASEC = South Asia Subregional Economic Cooperation.

Source: Asian Development Bank.

further on SASEC serving as a platform for knowledge sharing.

The Pacific: Partnering with the Private Sector to Expand Energy Access[45]

The Pacific Renewable Energy Program (PREP) uses a regional approach to encourage expanded private sector participation in the power sector. Through an innovative blend of financing support, the program aims to surmount current barriers to private investment by boosting the creditworthiness of power utilities. Sustained private sector involvement will help reduce reliance on grants and subsidies from the public sector. Over the longer term, the program will promote sustainable renewable energy generation that ultimately helps close gaps in electricity access.

Overview

Private sector participation in renewable energy may be bolstered with development partner financing support.

Pacific economies share similar development challenges—including small, often isolated populations, limited resources, remoteness, disasters, and vulnerability to external shocks. Power generation across the subregion is shifting from a reliance on fossil fuels to renewable energy sources. This will lower costs, reduce greenhouse gas emissions, and improve energy security. But to work efficiently, it needs the private sector to increasingly own and operate these renewable energy facilities.

Currently, power utilities lack the renewable energy technical capacity to manage grids that are rapidly shifting from relatively simple single-source generation systems (such as diesel) to grids with multiple intermittent renewable energy sources (available wind, solar, and hydropower). More sophisticated integration systems with strong technical expertise can be provided or transferred from experienced private operators. And, of course, this structural shift entails significant investment. Private sector participation can help fill current investment gaps and supplement human capacity.

The private sector currently relies on sovereign guarantees to backstop the offtake obligations of power utilities. However, some ADB DMCs in the Pacific cannot provide guarantees due to sovereign debt ceilings or the preference to use access to direct borrowing. ADB recently approved an umbrella facility designed to work within these constraints. It encourages private sector investment by using development partner financing to backstop payment obligations of power utilities. Each project under the facility will involve one—or a combination of—partial risk guarantees, direct loans, letters of credit, and technical assistance.

The Pressing Need to Expand Access to Electricity

Latest data show less than a third of the Pacific's population has access to electricity (ADB 2018e). At the country level, while at least 90% of households in eight Pacific countries have access to electricity, households located in larger economies tend to have much lower access rates (Figure 5.7). This is mainly due to amplified geographic constraints and other issues, which contribute to complex logistical barriers to expand coverage. For example, in Papua New Guinea (PNG), Solomon Islands, and Vanuatu, collectively, only less than a quarter of households has access, implying that many households remain dependent on less reliable and inefficient substitutes for electricity—such as

---

[45]   Contributed by Alix Burrell, principal investment specialist, Private Sector Operations Department; Anthony Maxwell, principal energy specialist, Pacific Regional Department (PARD); and Rommel Rabanal, public sector economist, PARD, ADB. In this section, Pacific economies include the Cook Islands, the Federated States of Micronesia, Fiji, Kiribati, the Marshall Islands, Nauru, Niue, Palau, Papua New Guinea, Samoa, Solomon Islands, Tonga, Tuvalu, and Vanuatu.

kerosene lamps. And electricity costs are higher in the larger economies with less electricity access. Costs in PNG, Solomon Islands, and Vanuatu averaged $0.70 per kilowatt-hour, compared with the subregional average of $0.44 per kilowatt-hour.

Bridging the gaps in electricity access will require new investment initiatives. There are ways to simultaneously improve access while bringing down costs. They stem from expanding private sector participation in renewable energy generation. This both shifts away from the reliance on expensive diesel imports and supports sustainable energy production.

Figure 5.7: Cost of and Access to Electricity

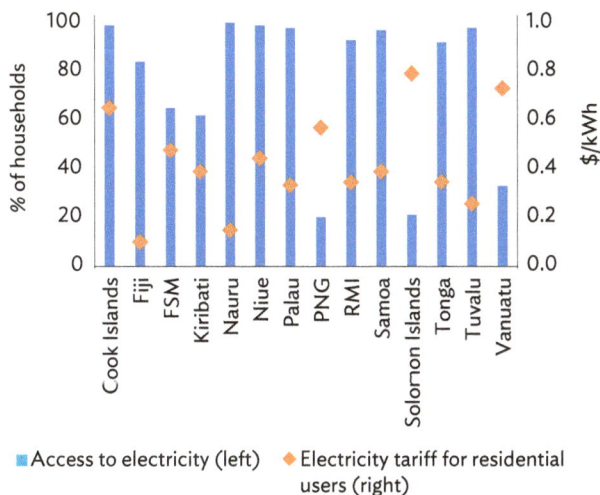

■ Access to electricity (left)   ◆ Electricity tariff for residential users (right)

FSM = Federated States of Micronesia, kWh = kilowatt-hour, PNG = Papua New Guinea, RMI = Republic of the Marshall Islands.

Note: Chart reflects latest available data.

Source: Pacific Region Infrastructure Facility (2016).

Barriers to Private Sector Participation

Commercial and public sector funding for power utilities in the Pacific are inadequate. Most Pacific countries are actively seeking investments from independent power producers (IPPs). However, investment is restricted by the lack of government credit support for paying power utility obligations, as most countries cannot provide guarantees:

(i)   Governments are reluctant to provide guarantees because the obligation will be counted as a

contingent liability and will contribute to national debt.

(ii)   Often, Pacific countries have mandated debt ceilings or would prefer to utilize available headroom for direct borrowing.

(iii)   The small scale of many transactions makes transaction costs for guarantees prohibitive.

Private investment is also hampered by a lack of bankable power purchase agreements (PPAs), uncertainties over foreign currency availability and convertibility, and perceived political risks. These factors have constrained the spread of successful partnerships with IPPs across the subregion.

Breaking Barriers: The Pacific Renewable Energy Program

In March 2019, ADB approved an umbrella facility of up to $100 million that will help finance loans, guarantees, and letters of credit to overcome constraints to private sector investment in Pacific renewable power projects. The PREP can support possibly five renewable energy projects in the Pacific over a 5-year period.

PREP is designed to overcome critical constraints and encourage private sector investment through an innovative blend of direct private sector lending, guarantees for commercial bank lenders, and development partner finance to backstop payment obligations of power utilities. More specifically, each project under the program will include one or more of the following forms of financing support:

• A partial risk guarantee (PRG) covering standard political risks and breaches of contract under a PPA— including coverage of failure by the utility to make a termination payment in the event of full default by the power utility, as set out in the PPA. Payment for breach of contract is made under the PRG upon arbitral award.

• A direct loan supporting a private sector IPP borrower. If ADB cannot fund a loan in local currency, then an ADB partial credit guarantee benefiting one or more local lenders to the project may be offered to the IPP instead of a direct loan.

- A letter of credit covering short-term liquidity risk, drawn down by the IPP to cover payments due under the PPA over a specific period. ADB may arrange for a maximum 24 months of PPA payments per project. The letter of credit will cover the risk that a power utility fails to make payments to the project in accordance with the terms of the PPA, and it will be reinstated once the utility has restored outstanding payments. The letter of credit, if provided, will be fully funded by development partner funds.
- Technical assistance for transaction advisory support and streamlined processes to reduce high transaction costs associated with the relatively small transactions in the Pacific, and to assist with capacity building in environmental and social safeguards.

These support mechanisms will help remove barriers to investment by enhancing the creditworthiness of power utilities and mitigating the perceived political risk for lenders. Providing ways to enhance credit to hedge against key risks will help increase private investment in power. Using this approach, PREP is expected to lower the cost of financing and encourage financing with longer tenors, which will feed through to lower power tariffs and attract new investors and lenders to the Pacific, where they might not otherwise invest.

PREP fulfills the Pacific Renewable Energy Investment Facility's (PREIF) identification of a development partner-backed guarantee program as a key means of promoting private investment in energy. PREIF supports ADB investments in sovereign renewable energy projects in the smallest 11 Pacific countries and assists in sector reform.[46]

Looking Ahead to a Sustainably Powered Future

PREP aims to spur self-sustaining private sector development and, over time, reduce reliance by power utilities on grants and subsidies. Currently, ADB is the largest investor in the Pacific energy sector. PREP is leveraging established relations with an extensive network of Pacific power utilities to identify potential transactions in its early stage. Technical assistance will also help Pacific power utilities and governments improve the quality of doing business with the private sector, build capacity for energy expansion, and further raise private sector interest in the subregion.

The first project proposed under the program has already been identified and a financing plan is under discussion. Participating projects will be required to adopt environmental and social standards and to demonstrate gender parity in energy and related community projects.

The Asia-Pacific Regional Cooperation and Integration Index

Regional Integration Trends in Asia

The Asia-Pacific Regional Cooperation and Integration Index shows that Asia's integration has been broadly steady.

Introduced in 2017 and refined further in 2018 to cover panel data, the Asia-Pacific Regional Cooperation and Integration Index (ARCII) measures the extent to which each economy is integrated into the region. It identifies strengths and weaknesses of multiple regional integration drivers, and comprehensively and systematically tracks progress over time. Given the complex nature of regional integration, the ARCII combines 26 indicators categorized into six regional cooperation and integration dimensions: (i) trade and investment; (ii) money and finance; (iii) regional value chains; (iv) infrastructure and connectivity; (v) movement of people; and (vi) institutional and social integration. It covers ADB's members in Asia (46 developing member economies plus Australia, Japan, and New Zealand), where data are available (ADB 2017b, 2018f).[47]

---

[46]   Formerly the Pacific Islands Renewable Investment Program as approved in May 2017. PREIF was featured in the Pacific section of the Subregional Cooperation Initiatives chapter of AEIR 2017.

[47]   See ADB. Asia Regional Integration Center. ARCII. https://aric.adb.org/database/arcii for ARCII database, methodology, and other related resources.

The pace of regional integration measured by ARCII has been broadly steady during 2006–2017. But latest ARCII estimates show that regional integration in Asia weakened in 2017, driven largely by a decline in the pace of money and finance integration (Figure 5.8). Regional integration in dimensions of (a) trade and investment, and (b) regional value chain also weakened slightly. Meanwhile, the infrastructure and connectivity dimension strengthened together with movement of people and institutional and social integration.

Figure 5.8: Overall and Dimensional Subindexes—Asia

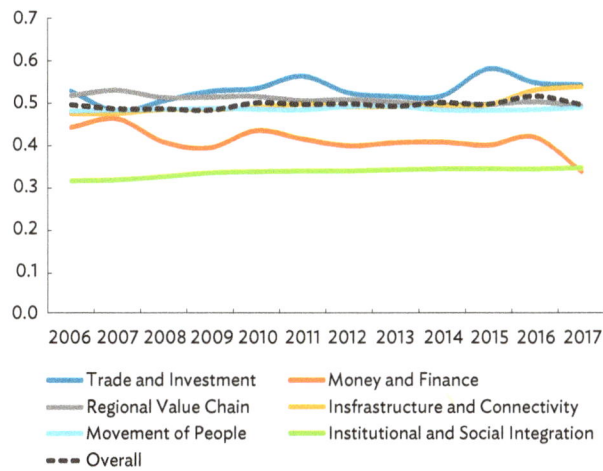

Source: ADB calculations using methodologies of Huh and Park (2018) and Park and Claveria (2018).

Figure 5.9: Overall Indexes—Asian Subregions

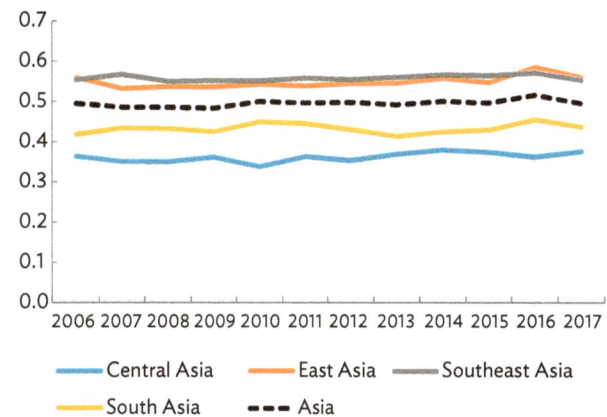

Sources: ADB calculations using methodologies of Huh and Park (2018) and Park and Claveria (2018).

Figure 5.10: Dimensional Subindexes by Asia Subregions, 2017

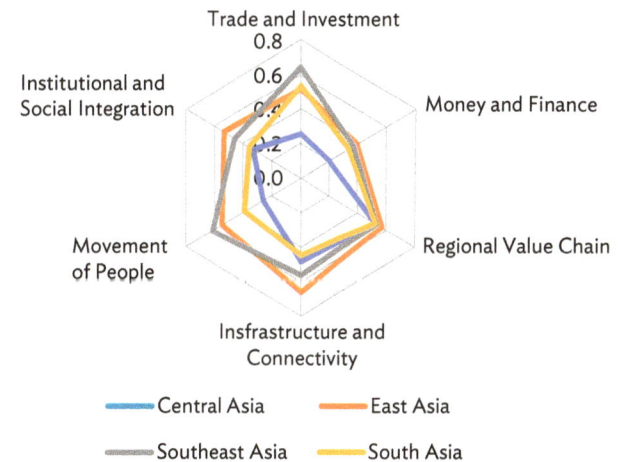

Source: ADB calculations using methodologies of Huh and Park (2018) and Park and Claveria (2018).

Across subregions, East Asia and Southeast Asia appear most integrated with Asia as a whole (Figure 5.9). Central Asia and South Asia scored below the average regional integration.

Subregional results vary across dimensions (Figure 5.10). For example, East Asia scored highest in the dimensions of money and finance, infrastructure and connectivity, regional value chain, and institutional and social integration. Southeast Asia outperformed other subregions in trade and investment and movement of people. South Asia and Central Asia trailed the other subregions in most dimensions.

The ARCII likewise shows the degrees of regional cooperation and integration in Asia's subregional initiatives across the six RCI dimensions. ASEAN exhibits the highest degree of subregional cooperation

and integration with an overall ARCII score of 0.553, particularly strong in the areas of trade and investment and movement of people (Figure 5.11). These two dimensions are also strongest in GMS and SASEC, while the main drivers for CAREC's integration with Asia are regional value chain and infrastructure and connectivity. Regional integration in money and finance seems to be one of the weakest dimensions across the four subregional initiatives. Movement of people is also weakest in CAREC, while institutional and social integration is also weak in ASEAN and SASEC.

Figure 5.11: Dimensional Subindexes by Subregional Cooperation Initiatives, 2017

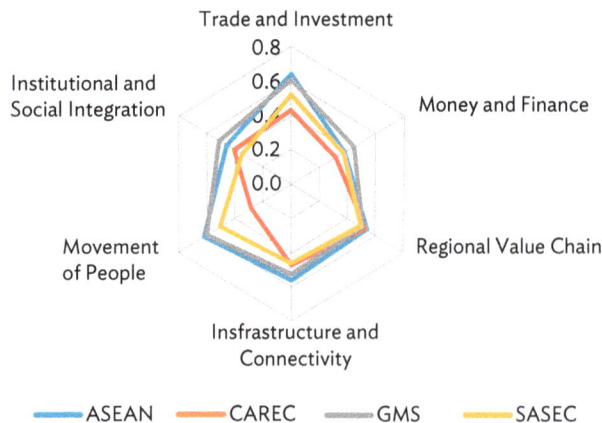

ASEAN = Association of Southeast Asian Nations, CAREC = Central Asia Regional Economic Cooperation, GMS = Greater Mekong Subregion, SASEC = South Asia Subregional Economic Cooperation.

Sources: ADB calculations using methodologies of Huh and Park (2018) and Park and Claveria (2018).

Figure 5.12: Regional Integration Index, 2017—Asia versus Other Regions

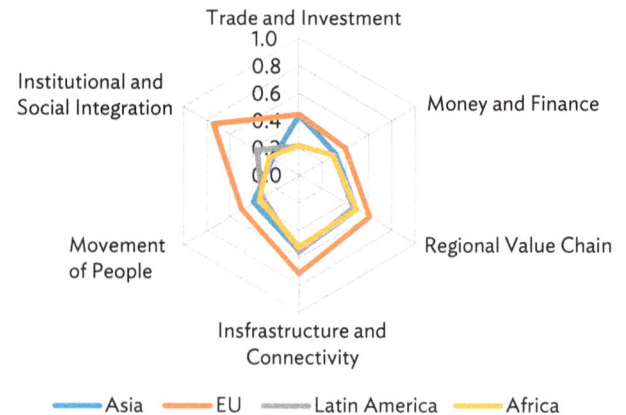

EU = European Union.

Sources: ADB calculations using methodologies of Huh and Park (2018) and Park and Claveria (2018).

The index can be applied to all countries around the globe. To allow global comparison, worldwide normalization is applied to the ARCII. In 2017, Asia was second to the European Union (EU) in overall integration relative to other regions. It remained equal to the EU in trade and investment integration (Figure 5.12). The EU outperformed all other regions in the remaining dimensions. It was strongest in institutional and social integration, given its economic and monetary union institutions.

Role of Economic Integration in Growth and Development

Economic integration can offer substantial economic benefits through efficiency gains, increases in market size, cost-sharing in regional production and cross-border infrastructure, as well as noneconomic benefits.

Economic integration—the process of creating common markets, establishing production sharing networks and promoting the free flow of goods, capital, and labor—promotes economic growth and development

by harnessing efficiency through scale economies. Integration also facilitates positive spillover effects from technology diffusion, investment in knowledge and skills, as well as increased productivity through specialization and production sharing.[48] For example, opening markets, sharing production networks, and allowing the free flow of goods and capital—resources can be more efficiently reallocated—increase incomes, raises economic growth, and improves development outcomes. Technology and knowledge spillovers also hasten the convergence process as less-developed countries leapfrog development stages—using innovation, new technologies, and improved knowledge.

This process of economic integration, particularly through open trade and investment, benefited many Asian economies—including the PRC, the newly industrialized economies (NIEs), ASEAN4, and Viet Nam—achieve remarkable economic growth.[49] Open trade, gradually adopting flexible exchange rates and freer capital accounts (together with market-friendly policies) allowed them to attract foreign direct investment and access technology, management knowhow, and other specialized inputs that facilitated stronger linkages with global production networks.

---

[48]   Economic integration, as defined here, can take several forms of varying degrees of integration. These are free-trade areas, customs unions, common markets, economic unions, and complete economic integration.

[49]   NIEs comprise Hong Kong, China; Singapore; the Republic of Korea; and Taipei,China. ASEAN4 comprises Indonesia, Malaysia, the Philippines and Thailand.

Numerous studies show that the process of economic integration brings significant and positive effects on income and economic growth. For instance, endogenous growth models show that economic integration has positive effects on both output and growth (Grossman and Helpman 1991, Rivera-Batiz and Romer 1991, Walz 1998, Baldwin 1989). Several other studies also show a positive relationship between trade openness and economic growth (Dollar 1992, 2005; Dollar and Kraay 2002; Edwards 1992, 1993; Frankel and Romer 1996; Harrison 1996; Harrison and Hanson 1999; Sachs and Warner 1995)—although results were often subject to serious econometric (often endogeneity or missing variable) issues and data problems.

Another debate concerns the impact of economic integration on income inequality. Trade benefits are not uniform across all economies or all segments within any economy. Some gain from trade openness, but others lose. Fierce competition for resources and markets may contribute to economic and social inequality among individuals or economies, widening income gaps and political polarization which potentially undermine social and cultural cohesion. In addition, economic subordination of underdeveloped countries, marginalization of socioeconomically vulnerable groups, and the loss of sociocultural diversity are cited as legitimate concerns over public policy.

Economic literature also suggests uneven effects of global economic integration on income inequality. For example, Potrafke (2014) found that while some studies suggested that economic integration contributes to increased income, poverty reduction, and gender equality; it also increased income inequality within countries. Gozgor and Ranjan (2017) suggested that while globalization increased redistribution, it also increased inequality through subtle and ambiguous movements in trade, capital, and labor.

Seshanna and Decornez (2003) showed the global economy has become more unequal and polarized amid rapid globalization. Kanbur (2000) and Attanasio, Goldberg, and Pavcnik (2004) conclude that increased openness from globalization coincided with widening income inequality in developing countries. Some European countries, amid increased international competition, have also tried to reduce welfare programs, while shifting the tax burden from mobile capital to immobile labor (Gaston and Nelson 2004, Tanzi 1995). Arguments like these imply globalization worsens income inequality. By contrast, Bordo, Eichengreen, and Irwin (1999) and Rodrik (1998) argue that large welfare states adjust government aid and tax systems in ways that minimize the adverse consequences of globalization, such as income inequality. Mahler (2001) finds little evidence of a systematic relationship between the main modes of globalization and distribution of household income in developed countries. Collier and Dollar (2001) estimate the decline in income inequality for developing countries.

This report introduces a new measure of global economic integration that distinguishes intraregional and extraregional economic integration.

To help measure integration levels and assess their impact on economic growth and development, a globalization (GEII), intraregional (IEII), and extraregional (EEII) integration indexes have been constructed based on 25 indicators that represent the key socioeconomic components of global integration. These indicators are grouped into six dimensions: (i) trade and investment; (ii) money and finance; (iii) value chains; (iv) infrastructure and connectivity; (v) the movement of people; and (vi) institutional and social integration. The study covers 158 economies across Africa, Asia, the EU, Latin America, and North America. The indexes were calculated initially from 2006 to 2014, which is the latest year for which all required data are available. All indicators were normalized based on z-score[50], making each indicator follow a normal distribution with the mean equal to zero for the basis year of 2006. Therefore, a positive index score would generally indicate a higher than average degree of integration, while a negative score shows the opposite.

When the GEII is split into its components, the relative contributions of IEII and EEII to a country's full economic

---

[50]   A z-score is a numerical measurement used in statistics of a value's relationship to the average of a group of values, measured in terms of standard deviations from the mean.

integration (with the global economy) vary by country, for both 2006 and 2014. However, it appears that the IEII contributes more to the degree of global economic integration than the EEII. There are some exceptions, with the United Kingdom and the four major Asian manufacturing economies—the PRC, Japan, the Republic of Korea, and Malaysia—have higher EEII scores, meaning integration with extraregional partners contributed more than intraregional partners to their global economic integration.

The GEII—averaged over all economies—shows an upward trend over time, suggesting globalization has increased (Figure 5.13). However, the global economic integration index fell during the global financial crisis and in 2011/12 during the eurozone debt crisis. The IEII and EEII follow the GEII pattern, rising over time but falling sharply during the two downturns. Between the two subcomponents, the EEII shows a larger variation than the IEII over time, suggesting that intraregional integration is a stabilizing factor for global economic integration.

High-income countries show a higher degree of globalization compared with other income groups driven by both intraregional and extraregional integration.

The level of global economic integration is higher among high-income countries than among other income groups (Figure 5.14). Upper-middle and lower-middle income

Figure 5.13: Intraregional, Extraregional, and Global Economic Integration Indexes (averaged over all economies in the sample)

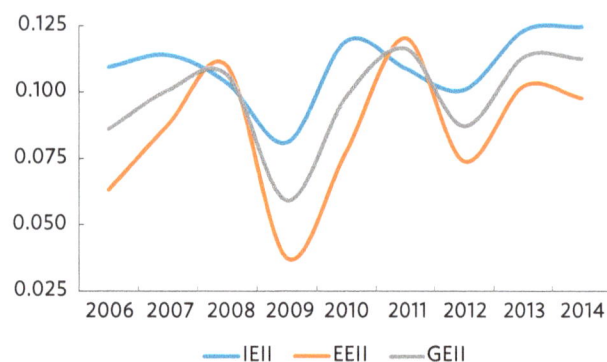

EEII = extraregional economic integration index, GEII = global economic integration index, IEII = intraregional economic integration index.

Source: Huh and Park (2019).

countries generally follow high-income countries, with low-income countries the least globally integrated. Also, high-income countries have higher IEII scores than those of the EEII, reflecting the inclusion of most EU countries in the high-income group. The order is reversed, however, in all other income groups.

By region, the GEII ranks North America highest and the EU second (Figure 5.15). This is in line with the findings in Figure 5.14, as all countries in North America and the EU (aside from Bulgaria and Romania) belong to the high-income group. Asia ranks third, although there is a considerable gap between this region and the first two groups. Latin America comes fourth with Africa the least globalized region.

Asia is not as globally integrated as the global average— its low integration partly comes from its relatively low intraregional integration compared with North America and Europe. Figure 5.16 presents the difference between Asia's index scores and the average index scores of all regional groups. Therefore, the negative score of intraregional integration indicates that Asia is below the regional group average. On the other hand, Asia maintains a higher than average extraregional integration score, reflecting the region's outward orientation in terms of trade, investment, and migration.

While globalization promotes economic growth, it may widen income inequality.

The new index of economic integration can be used to assess the impact of global economic integration on growth and income inequality. Growth regression analysis for the new globalization index shows that globalization promotes economic growth (Box 5.3). Between the two drivers of overall economic integration, extraregional integration appears to be mainly responsible—as against intraregional integration which has a small and insignificant effect. The other explanatory variables—per capita income, years of schooling, government transfers and subsidies, government expenditure, government effectiveness, and labor market regulation—also show significant effects consistent with expectations. Income inequality lessens with increases in GDP per capita, mean years of schooling, government payments of transfers and subsidies, government expenditure on education, government effectiveness, and labor market regulations.

Figure 5.14: Intraregional, Extraregional, and Global Economic Integration Indexes by Income Level

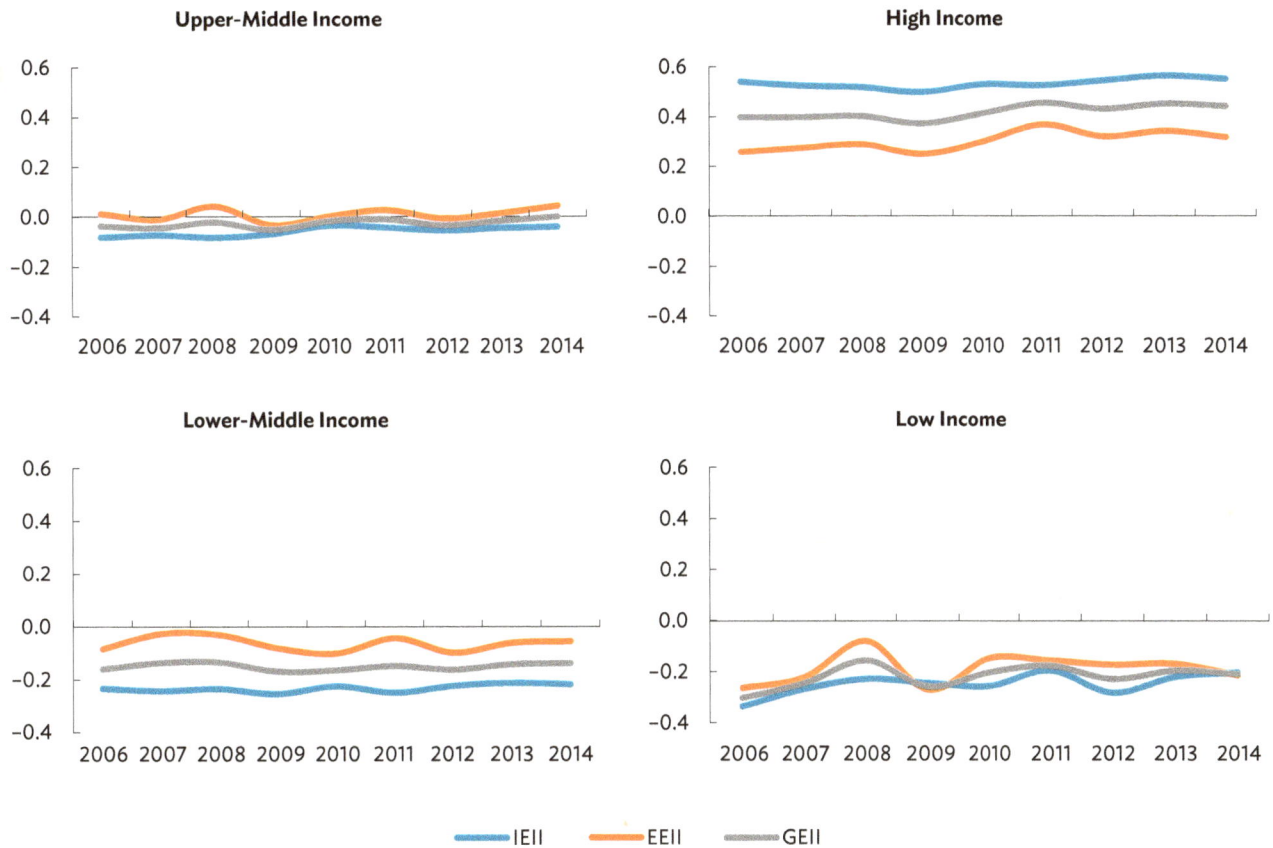

Upper-Middle Income

High Income

Lower-Middle Income

Low Income

IEII   EEII   GEII

EEII = extraregional economic integration index, GEII = global economic integration index, IEII = intraregional economic integration index.

Source: Huh and Park (2019).

Figure 5.15: Global Economic Integration Indexes, by Region

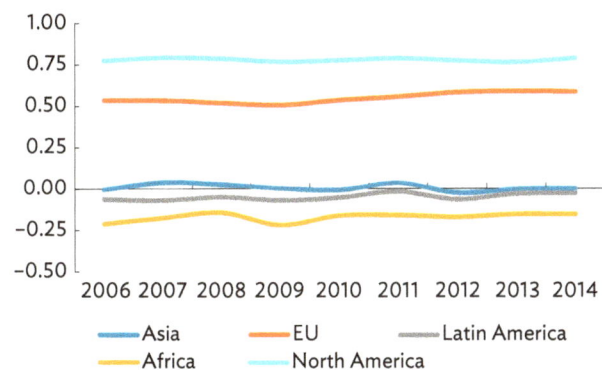

Asia   EU   Latin America
Africa   North America

EU = European Union.

Source: Huh and Park (2019).

Figure 5.16: Intraregional, Extraregional, and Global Economic Integration Indexes—Asia

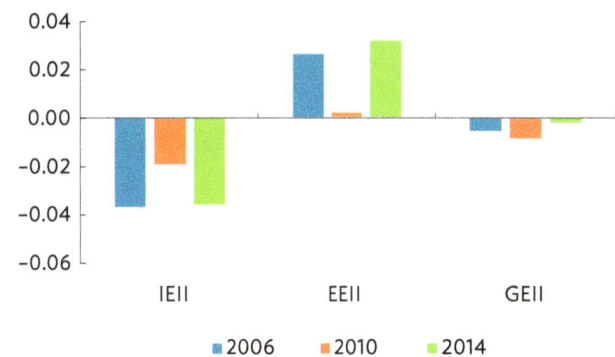

IEII   EEII   GEII

2006   2010   2014

EEII = extraregional economic integration index, GEII = global economic integration index, IEII = intraregional economic integration index.

Source: Huh and Park (2019).

Box 5.3: Global Integration and Its Effects on Growth and Inequality

The box table presents the panel regression results for the relationship between economic growth and globalization. A 0.1 percentage point increase in global economic integration index (GEII) expands gross domestic product (GDP) per capita growth by 0.57 percentage points. Both the intraregional (IEII) and extraregional (EEII) economic integration indexes scores contribute to economic growth with the increase in GDP per capita higher for IEII (0.40) than EEII (0.22). The results for other explanatory variables are consistent with expectations: a higher level of lagged GDP per capita, higher government consumption, and higher fertility rates are associated with lower growth rates. On the other hand, growth rates are higher with more years of schooling, longer life expectancy, larger investments, better rule of law, and greater political stability. Inflation has the expected negative coefficient, but is statistically insignificant.

However, when the regression analysis is done for different income groups, the results are mixed. For high-income economies, only IEII effects are statistically significant, suggesting that higher intraregional integration scores lead to higher economic growth. For upper-middle income countries, on the other hand, only GEII scores are significant, suggesting higher globalization is associated with higher growth rates. For lower-middle-income countries, none of the three scores matter for economic growth, although the small sample could explain this negative result.

To address the small sample issue, income groups are further collapsed into only two groups: upper-income groups (combining the high-income and upper-middle-income) and low-income groups (combining the lower-middle-income and the low-income groups). As expected, the GEII and IEII significantly leads to higher economic growth for the upper-income group. Yet none of the three scores affect economic growth rates. Other explanatory variables are as expected, except for political stability and inflation, which are not significant.

Globalization's positive effect on economic growth is strongest for high-income countries. Due to data limitations, the analysis of the effects of GEII, IEII, and EEII scores on inequality by income group can only be done on high-income and middle-income groups (combining upper- and lower-middle income groups). Results show that while globalization exacerbates income inequality significantly for middle-income countries, they do not affect inequality in high-income countries; again in this case, extraregional economic integration remains the main driver responsible for income inequality.

Regression Results on Globalization and Its Effects on Economic Growth and Income Inequality

	All Countries		High Income		Middle Income	
a: Dependent variable = Growth rate of GDP per capita						
GEII	**0.568**		0.404		0.320	
	(0.00)		(0.15)		(0.25)	
IEII		**0.400**	**0.320**			0.272
		(0.02)	(0.09)			(0.44)
EEII		**0.220**	0.029			0.124
		(0.07)	(0.89)			(0.47)
a: Dependent variable = Gini Index as proxy of income inequality						
GEII	**0.367**		0.115		**0.513**	
	(0.00)		(0.52)		(0.02)	
IEII		0.014	-0.285			0.409
		(0.93)	(0.13)			(0.31)
EEII		**0.244**	**0.302**			**0.232**
		(0.00)	(0.04)			(0.07)

EEII = extraregional economic integration index, GDP = gross domestic product, GEII = global economic integration index, IEII = intraregional economic integration index.

Notes: Figures in parentheses are the marginal significance levels (p-value) of the t-test statistics for the null hypothesis that the coefficient is equal to 0. Figures highlighted in bold are statistically different from zero at the 10% level of significance.

Source: Huh and Park (2019).

Source: Huh and Park (2019).

References

Asian Development Bank. CAREC Program Portfolio.

———. 2014. *South Asia Subregional Economic Cooperation Trade Facilitation Strategic Framework 2014–2018*. Manila.

———. 2016. *South Asia Subregional Economic Cooperation Operational Plan 2016–2025*. Manila.

———. 2017a. *SASEC Powering Asia in the 21st Century*. Manila.

———. 2017b. *Asian Economic Integration Report 2017: The Era of Financial Interconnectedness—How Can Asia Strengthen Financial Resilience?* Manila.

———. 2018a. *The Ha Noi Action Plan 2018–2022*. Manila.

———. 2018b. *Strategy for Promoting Safe and Environment-Friendly Agro-Based Value Chains in the Greater Mekong Subregion and Siem Reap Action Plan, 2018–2022*. Manila.

———. 2018c. *Asian Development Outlook 2018: How Technology Affects Jobs*. Manila.

———. 2018d. *Strategy 2030: Achieving a Prosperous, Inclusive, Resilient, and Sustainable Asia and the Pacific*. Manila.

———. 2018e. *Pacific Energy Update 2018*. Manila.

———. 2018f. *Asian Economic Integration Report 2018: Toward Optimal Provision of Regional Public Goods in Asia and the Pacific*. Manila.

———. 2019a. *Modernizing Sanitary and Phytosanitary Measures in CAREC: An Assessment and the Way Forward*. Manila.

———. 2019b. *CAREC Transport Sector Progress Report and Work Plan 2019–2021*. June.

———. 2019c. *Greater Mekong Subregion Health Cooperation Strategy 2019–2023*. Manila.

———. 2019d. *CAREC Integrated Trade Agenda*. Manila.

———. 2019e. *CAREC Corridor Performance Measurement and Monitoring Annual Report 2018*. Manila.

———. 2019f. *Asian Development Outlook 2019 Update: Fostering Growth and Inclusion in Asia's Cities*. Manila.

———. 2019g. SASEC Project Portfolio 2019.

Attanasio, O., P. K. Goldberg, and N. Pavcnik. 2004. Trade Reforms and Wage Inequality in Colombia. *Journal of Development Economics*. 74 (2). pp. 331–366.

Baldwin, R. 1989. On the Growth Effects of 1992. *Economic Policy*. 4 (9). pp. 247–281.

Bordo, M., B. Eichengreen, and D. Irwin. 1999. Is Globalization Today Really Different from Globalization a Hundred Years Ago? *Brookings Trade Forum*. pp. 1–72.

Bussolo, M., J. Koettl, and E. Sinnott. 2015. *Golden Aging: Prospects for Healthy, Active, and Prosperous Aging in Europe and Central Asia*. Washington, DC: World Bank.

CEIC Database. https://cas.ceicdata.com (accessed July 2019).

Collier, P., and D. Dollar. 2001. Can the World Cut Poverty in Half? How Policy Reform and Effective Aid Can Meet International Development Goals. *World Development*. 29 (11). pp. 1787–1802.

Dollar, D. 1992. Outward-Oriented Developing Countries Really Do Grow More Rapidly: Evidence from 95 LDCs, 1976–85. *Economic Development and Cultural Change*. 40 (3). pp. 523–544.

———. 2005. Globalization, Poverty, and Inequality since 1980. *World Bank Research Observer*. 20 (2). pp. 145–175.

Dollar, D., and A. Kraay. 2002. Growth is Good for the Poor. *Journal of Economic Growth*. 7 (3). pp. 195–225.

Edwards, S. 1992. Trade Orientation, Distortions and Growth in Developing Countries. *Journal of Development Economics*. 39 (1). pp. 31–57.

———. 1993. Openness, Trade Liberalization, and Growth in Developing Countries. *Journal of Economic Literature*. 31 (3). pp. 1358–1393.

Frankel, J. A., and D. Romer. 1996. Trade and Growth: An Empirical Investigation. *NBER Working Paper Series*. 5476. Cambridge, MA: National Bureau of Economic Research.

Gaston, N., and D. Nelson. 2004. Structural Change and the Labour Market Effects of Globalization. *Review of International Economics*. 12 (5). pp. 769–792.

Gozgor, G., and P. Ranjan. 2017. Globalisation, Inequality and Redistribution: Theory and Evidence. *The World Economy*. 40 (12). pp. 2704–2751.

Greater Mekong Subregion Economic Cooperation Program (GMS) Secretariat. 2019. *Regional Investment Framework 2022: First Progress Report and Update*. Manila.

GMS Environment Operations Center. 2017. *Greater Mekong Subregion Core Environment Program Strategic Framework and Action Plan 2018–2022*. Bangkok.

GMS Statistical Database. www.greatermekong/statistics (accessed October 2019).

Grossman, G., and E. Helpman. 1991. Trade, Knowledge Spillovers and Growth. *European Economic Review*. 35 (2–3). pp. 517–526.

Harrison, A. 1996. Openness and Growth: A Time-Series, Cross-Country Analysis for Developing Countries. *Journal of Development Economics*. 48 (2). pp. 419–447.

Harrison, A., and G. Hanson. 1999. Who Gains from Trade Reform? Some Remaining Puzzles. *Journal of Development Economics*. 59 (1). pp. 125-154.

Huh, H. S., and C. Y. Park. 2018. Asia-Pacific Regional Integration Index: Construction, Interpretation, and Comparison. *Journal of Asian Economics*. 54 (February). pp. 22–38.

———. 2019. A New Index of Globalization: Measuring Impacts of Integration on Economic Growth and Income Inequality. *ADB Economics Working Paper Series*. 587. Manila: ADB.

International Monetary Fund (IMF). Direction of Trade Statistics. https://www.imf.org (accessed October 2019).

———. World Economic Outlook (WEO) April 2019 Database. https://www.imf.org/external/pubs/ft/weo/2019/01/weodata/index.aspx (accessed October 2019).

———. WEO October 2019 Database. https://www.imf.org/external/pubs/ft/weo/2019/02/weodata/index.aspx (accessed October 2019).

Kanbur, R. 2000. Income Distribution and Development. In A.B. Atkinson and F. Bourguignon, eds. *Handbook of Income Distribution*. Vol. 1. pp. 791–841. Amsterdam: Elsevier North-Holland.

Mahler, V. A. 2001. Economic Globalization, Domestic Politics and Income Inequality in the Developed Countries: A Cross-National Analysis. *Luxembourg Income Study Working Paper*. 273. Luxembourg: LIS Cross-National Data Center.

Mekong Tourism Coordinating Office. 2017. *Greater Mekong Subregion Tourism Sector Strategy 2016–2025*. Bangkok.

Pacific Region Infrastructure Facility. 2016. *2016 Pacific Infrastructure Performance Indicators*. Sydney.

Park, C. Y. and R. Claveria. 2018. Constructing the Asia-Pacific Regional Cooperation and Integration Index: A Panel Approach. *ADB Economics Working Paper Series*. No. 544. Manila: ADB.

Potrafke, N. 2014. The Evidence on Globalization. *CESifo Working Paper Series*. 4708. Munich: Center for Economic Studies and Ifo Institute.

Rivera-Batiz, L., and P. Romer. 1991. Economic Integration and Endogenous Growth. *The Quarterly Journal of Economics*. 106 (2). pp. 531–55.

Rodrik, D. 1998. Who Needs Capital-Account Convertibility? In S. Fischer, et. al., eds. Should the IMF Pursue Capital Account Convertibility? *Essays in International Finance*. No. 207. pp. 55–65. Princeton: Princeton University.

Sachs, J.D., and A. Warner. 1995. Economic Reform and the Process of Global Integration. *Brookings Papers on Economic Activity*. 26 (1). pp. 1–118.

Seshanna, S., and S. Decornez. 2003. Income Polarization and Inequality across Countries: An Empirical Study. *Journal of Policy Modeling*. 25 (4). pp. 335–358.

Tanzi, V. 1995. *Taxation in an Integrating World*. Washington, DC: Brookings Institution.

United Nations Conference on Trade and Development Statistics. https://unctadstat.unctad.org/wds/TableViewer/tableView.aspx?ReportId=96740 (accessed October 2019).

Walz, U. 1998. Does an Enlargement of a Common Market Stimulate Growth and Convergence? *Journal of International Economics*. 45 (2). pp. 297–321.

World Bank. Population Estimates and Projections. https://datacatalog.worldbank.org/dataset/population-estimates-and-projections (accessed October 2019).

———. World Development Indicators. https://data.worldbank.org/indicator/?tab=all (accessed October 2019).

———. 2019. *Doing Business 2019: Training for Reform*. Washington, DC.

6 Theme Chapter: Demographic Change, Productivity, and the Role of Technology

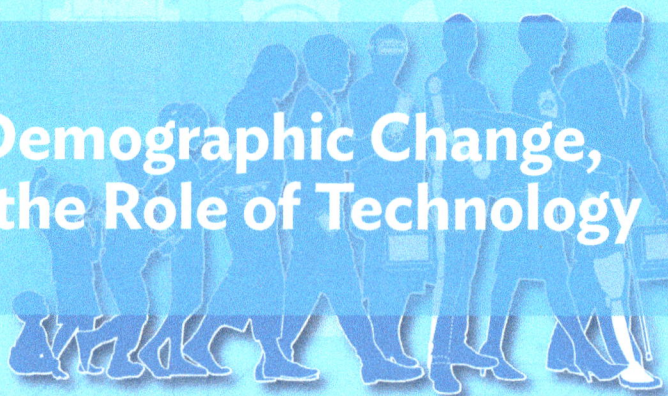

Introduction

The Asia and Pacific region, home to more than half of the world's population, is undergoing rapid demographic changes. Access to better medical and public health services was realized in the early stages of development, which led to a precipitous fall in mortality and fertility rates in many countries. With extended life expectancy following increased healthy years of life, countries are needing to adapt to a changing labor market shaped by a growing share of the elderly population and a fall in the percentage of younger cohorts. This means that Asia will progressively depend more on older workers.[51]

Older people are already staying active in the labor market longer for financial and nonfinancial reasons. Their prolonged stay and reentry is seen in the agriculture and services sectors, which absorb a large share of the workforce. A significant share of older workers is involved in part-time and self-employed jobs and perform nonroutine manual tasks. Even though some countries in Asia are still relatively young, similar aging trends will likely show up in their labor markets over the coming decades.

Meanwhile, developing countries in Asia are experiencing strong human capital development thanks to increases in per child investment. Today, more children are staying longer at school and then going on to attain higher education. This improvement will steadily produce more educated elderly workers. In countries where educational attainment increased rapidly in a short period, however, the gap in schooling between younger and older populations remains wide.

Population aging presents a challenge to maintaining strong and inclusive growth in the region. Historically, population growth is closely linked to the rate at which an economy grows, with benefits reaped from the so-called "demographic dividend." Fewer Asian economies are expected to gain from a demographic dividend as the share of the working age population in the region peaks in 2015–2020. In the coming decades, some countries' working age group will shrink gradually, yet significantly. Aging of working members of the population is inevitable in most countries. Mature and older workers are not necessarily unproductive, and they may perform continuously well in certain types of work, but their productivity in others may naturally decline. In addition, the scarcity of young-to-middle-aged workers could drag down the pace of innovation and technology adoption.

The rich pool of economic literature on how population aging affects economic growth presents mixed results. While many studies argue that the growing elderly populations could slow growth, some studies highlight the positive effects of aging through the formation of a mature workforce. The most recent literature emphasizes how the relative dependency on an aging workforce induces technology adoption in the workplace, and may help mitigate (or reverse) the negative effects of aging on economic growth.

---

[51] Asia refers to the 49 Asia and Pacific members of the Asian Development Bank (ADB), which includes Japan and Oceania (Australia and New Zealand) in addition to the 46 developing Asian economies.

This theme chapter reviews the trend of demographic transition across Asia and examines the effects of aging on productivity and economic growth. In particular, it investigates how technologies alter the aging effects on an economy and discusses policy options highlighting the role of technologies where possible. Experience from economies in advanced stages of aging suggests that population aging can induce innovation and adoption of technologies, and so promote productivity and sustained growth. But there is no guarantee that all aging societies stand to benefit from the same types of technology. For example, automation and artificial intelligence may reduce the demand for certain types of jobs. This may drive older workers out of the workforce instead of complementing them. While digitization and smart devices can improve worker productivity and workplace efficiency, older workers may be discouraged from participating in the workforce if the digital divide is not effectively addressed.

A variety of technologies that offer unique solutions to an aging workforce will be introduced and discussed. This chapter highlights five categories of technologies that (i) substitute labor and skills (such as industrial and service robots); (ii) complement labor and skills (remote office, collaboration tools); (iii) aid education, skills development, and lifelong learning (such as through online learning platforms); (iv) improve the matching of worker with job and task (through job portals and cloud sourcing platforms); and (v) extend life and healthy life expectancy (with digital therapeutics and bioinformatics).

Given that countries are at different stages of demographic transition, with varying age–education population mixes, the policy priorities and strategies for technology adoption and skills development necessarily differ across the region. For example, countries that are aging quickly but have made large improvements in education need different technology and skills development than countries with a relatively younger population and lower educational attainment. Nevertheless, a common need exists for policies that support technology adoption and lifelong learning. Countries should seek to adopt technologies befitting their demographic transition and to facilitate learning across all age groups and skills. Government policy can help create broader learning ecosystems, where learning environments (teachers, peers, pedagogy that fits well with technology) and a culture of learning are fostered internally and across countries.

Policies that leverage technology to improve workforce efficiency and provide greater flexibility in labor market participation should be put in place across Asia. Three areas of investment can be encouraged. First are policies that provide funding for research and development and help the diffusion, adoption, and application of technological innovation. Specific government policy could focus on encouraging application of breakthrough technologies through multi-stakeholder collaboration that makes them more accessible to elderly populations. Second is promoting labor laws that adapt to employees' diverse and flexible working styles, such as those encouraging mid- and late-career employment, work-sharing, and gradual retirement. The third policy area is restructuring social security and tax systems so they do not disincentivize elderly workers from staying in or returning to work. These policies would involve revisiting the concepts of "pensionable age" rather than "retirement age," and encourage workers to invest in retaining, upgrading, and acquiring new skills.

Asian economies can also benefit from regional cooperation for more efficient use of the diverse demographic profiles and input resources. This could take the form of encouraging capital, labor, and technology to move across borders, and include support for foreign direct investment that creates jobs for middle-skilled workers. Labor migration can help alleviate bottlenecks in the supply of low-skilled workers in some countries and the shortage of high-skilled workers in others, while technology transfers between countries of different demographic and technology adoption levels can speed up technology diffusion. To encourage these movements, proper regional frameworks need to be established. These could include mutual skills recognition along with other mechanisms that promote the mobility of labor across borders.

Population Aging in Asia

Asia is undergoing rapid demographic change. The share of the region's working age population has started to decline, and several economies imminently face aging populations. This transition leaves many economies progressively depending on older workers, whose challenges may differ from their younger counterparts. On the positive side, better lifestyles, advanced healthcare and medical technologies, and improvements in educational attainment imply that tomorrow's older workers will be healthier and more educated than today's older workers. Nevertheless, without appropriate action, the aging and shrinking workforce could profoundly impact the ability to innovate and sustain high economic growth.

Asia's Demographic Trajectory

Asia is home to 4.3 billion people, or 55% of the world's population in 2019.

Since the turn of the century, population growth in the region averaged 1% per year, well below the 1.7% annual growth from 1980 to 1999. The region's population is expected to peak at 4.85 billion between 2055 and 2060, with its share of world population falling to 48.7%.

Amid slowing population growth, the share of the working age population will plateau around 70%, while the share of the older population is rising.

About 379 million Asians were of ages 65 and above in 2019.[52] This represents 8.9% of the region's total population, and a 3-percentage-point increase from 5.9% (208 million) in 2000. The proportion of old people in Asia is projected to rise more steeply, so that by the end of 2050, the 888 million old individuals will comprise 18.3% of the population (Figure 6.1).

Figure 6.1: Population by Major Age Group—Asia

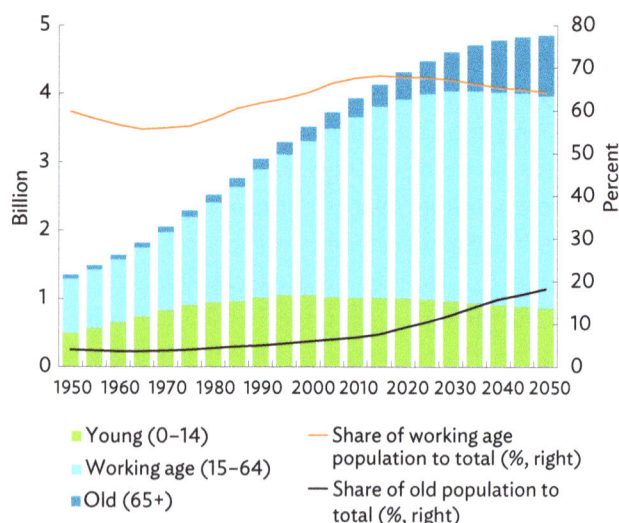

Source: ADB calculations using data from United Nations Department of Economic and Social Affairs, Population Division. Population Database. https://population.un.org/wpp/Download/Standard/Population/ (accessed June 2019).

The region's working age population (between ages 15 and 64) stood at 2.9 billion in 2019. It is expected to peak at 3.1 billion by 2045 and then fall 0.6% (equivalent to a 20 million workforce) by 2050 because of subdued expansion in the young population cohort. As a share to Asia's total population, the working age population peaks at 68% in 2015. The changing shares of varied age cohorts will gradually reshape the age and sex distribution of the region's population from a pyramid to a vase (Figure 6.2).

On average, Asians are healthier and living longer.

Life expectancy across the region grew from 62 years in 1980 to 73 years in 2017 (Figure 6.3). In those 4 decades, increases were largest in Cambodia (41.8 years) and Timor-Leste (34.8 years). Bhutan, Maldives, Nepal, and Afghanistan all extended life expectancy by more than 20 years. It was prolonged even in economies in advanced stages of population aging: Australia extending by 8.2 years; Hong Kong, China by 10.0 years; Japan by 8.0 years; New Zealand by 8.8 years; and Singapore by

---

[52]   In this section, old persons are defined as those of age 65 and above.

Figure 6.2: Evolution of the Population Pyramid—Asia

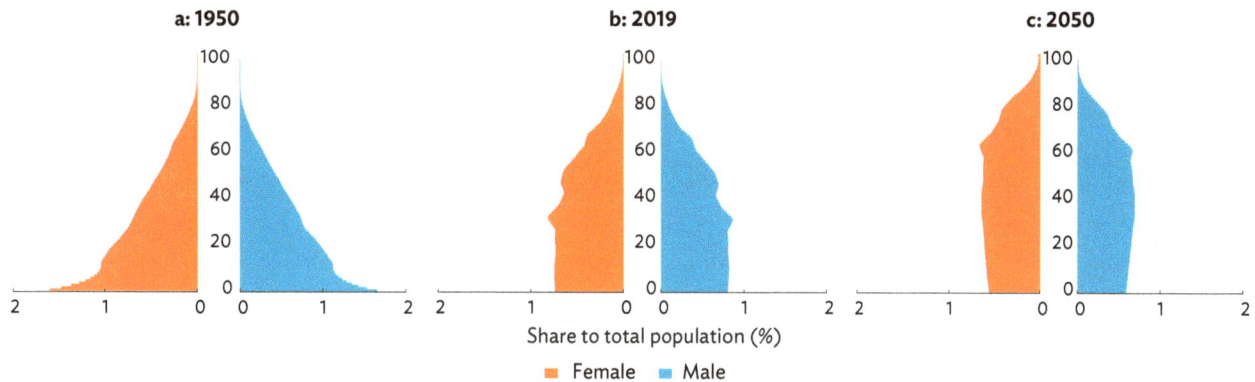

Note: Age of the population in y-axis follows a continuous data format.

Source: ADB calculations using data from United Nations Department of Economic and Social Affairs, Population Division. Population Database. https://population.un.org/wpp/Download/Standard/Population/ (accessed June 2019).

Figure 6.3: Life Expectancy—Asia (number of years)

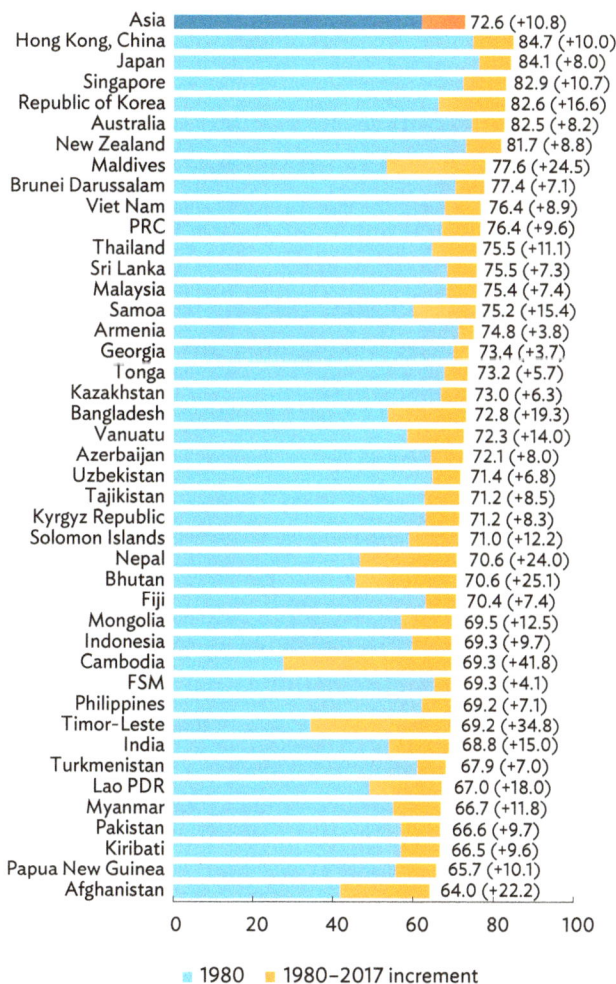

FSM = Federated States of Micronesia, Lao PDR = Lao People's Democratic Republic, PRC = People's Republic of China.

Note: Data labels refer to the life expectancy at birth in 2017, and the increment from 1980 is in parentheses.

Source: ADB calculations using data from World Bank. World Development Indicators. https://databank.worldbank.org/source/world-development-indicators (accessed July 2019).

10.7 years. Consequently, the number of centenarians in the region is expected to increase from 245,000 in 2019 to 1.65 million by 2050. By that time, 5 years is expected to be added to the average life expectancy of Asians (at 78 years), with one-third of economies in the region reaching life expectancy of more than 80 years.

A precipitous fall in mortality and fertility rates explains the extension of life expectancy and a growing share of the older population.

The drastic reduction in infant mortality—from 88 per 1,000 births in 1970 to 21 in 2017—is one significant force behind the drop in the overall mortality rate in the region. Increased chances of infant survival also contributed to the decline of fertility rates (measured by births per woman), sliding to 2.5 in 2017 from 5.5 in 1970. Fertility rates have dropped remarkably fast. While it took more than 50 years for advanced economies to fall below the present replacement level fertility rate of 2.1 births per woman from 4.0 births per woman (Figure 6.4a), some developing Asian economies have made this change in less than 20 years (Figure 6.4b). Among other factors, improvements in public health and medical services, the spread of education, increased women's economic participation, and family planning programs played critical roles in reducing mortality and fertility rates.

Figure 6.4: Pattern of Fertility Rate Decline—Selected Economies

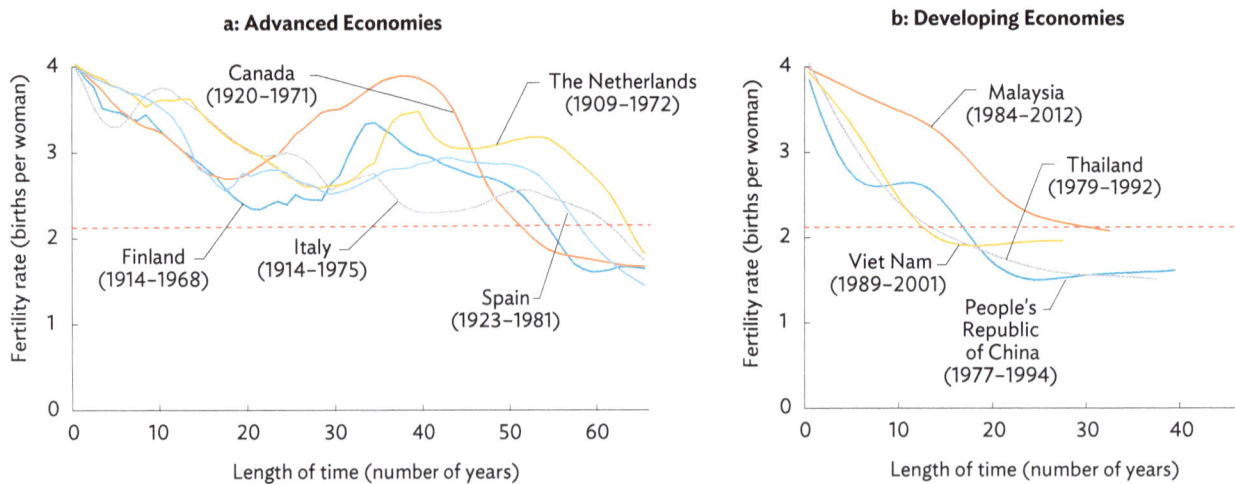

Notes: Fertility rate refers to the number of births per woman. The red-dashed line indicates the current global replacement level of 2.1 births per woman.

Sources: ADB calculations using data from Chesnais (1992); and World Bank. World Development Indicators. https://databank.worldbank.org/source/world-development-indicators (accessed July 2019).

Many economies in Asia are aging at an accelerated rate.

Following the United Nations definition, a country transitions to different phases of economic aging based on the share of old individuals to its total population. An economy is classified as "aging" when the share to total population of people of ages 65 and above reaches 7%, "aged" once the share reaches 14%, and ultimately "super-aged" when it exceeds 21%. It has taken several decades to more than a century for some Western nations to shift from aging to super-aged societies. That transition has taken place over 160 years in France, 135 years in Sweden, 110 years in Australia, and 100 years in the United Kingdom (Figure 6.5).

In Asia, population aging is occurring at a much faster pace. It is strikingly fast in Japan, where the old population share grew from 7% to 14% in only 25 years to 1995, and increased to 21% 20 years later. The pace of graying in Japan will be mirrored in other Asian countries, with some expected to reach "super-aged" in even shorter periods. It is anticipated to take no more than 40 years for the share of old persons in the People's Republic of China (PRC) to increase from 7% to 21%, and 35 years for the Republic of Korea. Thailand will make the same transition in less than 35 years and it will

happen in Viet Nam over 40 years. Meanwhile, the shift to "super-aged" will be slower in India, at 60 years, and will take 55 years in Indonesia.

Fast-paced population graying may pose inadvertent risks particularly among the developing economies.

Figure 6.6 presents contemporaneous population aging and incremental per capita gross domestic product (GDP) (at constant 2010 prices) relative to 1960 for select Asian economies. Japan, for example, experienced a $10,000 per capita income rise when the older population comprised 7% of its population. The same is true for the Republic of Korea and Hong Kong, China that show similar trajectory while Singapore's aging was met by a much higher income rise. In contrast, the per capita income of developing countries currently exhibiting quick demographic transition—such as Armenia, the PRC, Georgia, Sri Lanka, and Thailand—has only witnessed a per capita increment below $4,000 (at constant 2010 prices) when the share of the old reached 7% of their populations. These newly aging countries have seen fiscal expenditure for healthcare and pensions increase, while still allocating resources to build basic and large-scale economic infrastructure necessary to promote and sustain growth.

Figure 6.5: Speed of Aging—Selected Economies

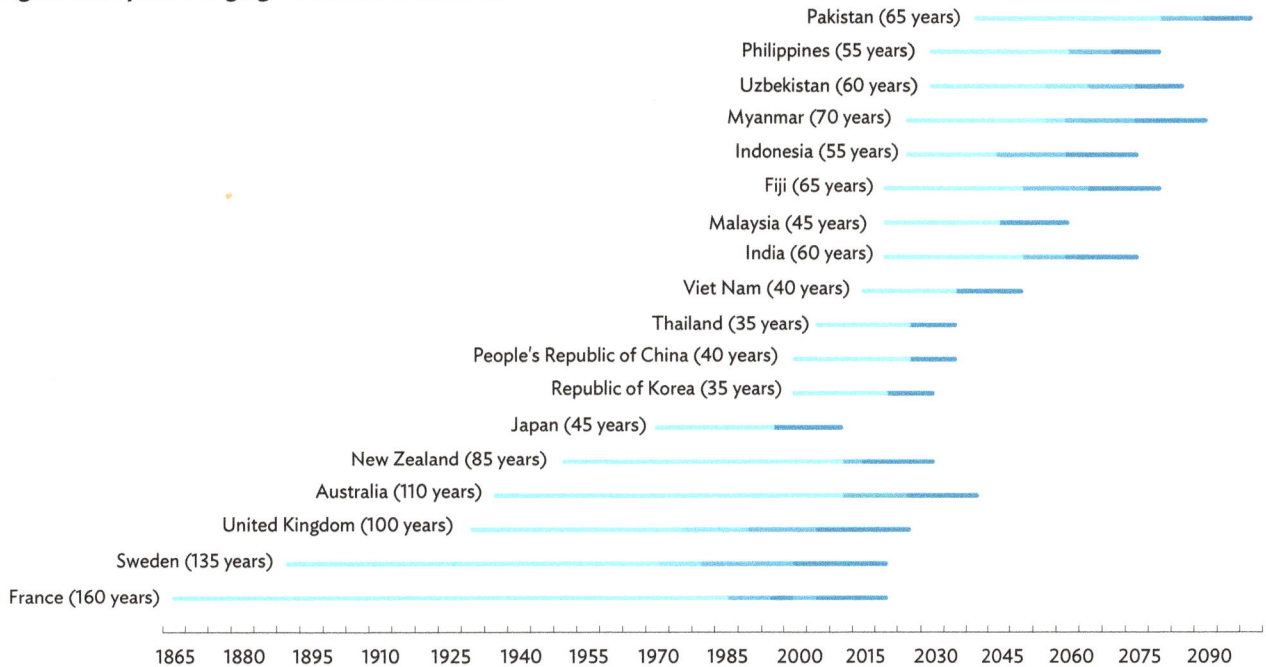

Pakistan (65 years)
Philippines (55 years)
Uzbekistan (60 years)
Myanmar (70 years)
Indonesia (55 years)
Fiji (65 years)
Malaysia (45 years)
India (60 years)
Viet Nam (40 years)
Thailand (35 years)
People's Republic of China (40 years)
Republic of Korea (35 years)
Japan (45 years)
New Zealand (85 years)
Australia (110 years)
United Kingdom (100 years)
Sweden (135 years)
France (160 years)

1865 1880 1895 1910 1925 1940 1955 1970 1985 2000 2015 2030 2045 2060 2075 2090

Note: The lines refer to the number of years for the share of the population of age 65 and above to increase from 7% to 21%, with light blue indicating 7% to 14% movement.

Source: ADB calculations using data from United Nations Department of Economic and Social Affairs, Population Division. Population Database. https://population.un.org/wpp/Download/Standard/Population/ (accessed June 2019).

Figure 6.6: Income Levels and Share of Older Persons, 1960–2017—Selected Asian Economies

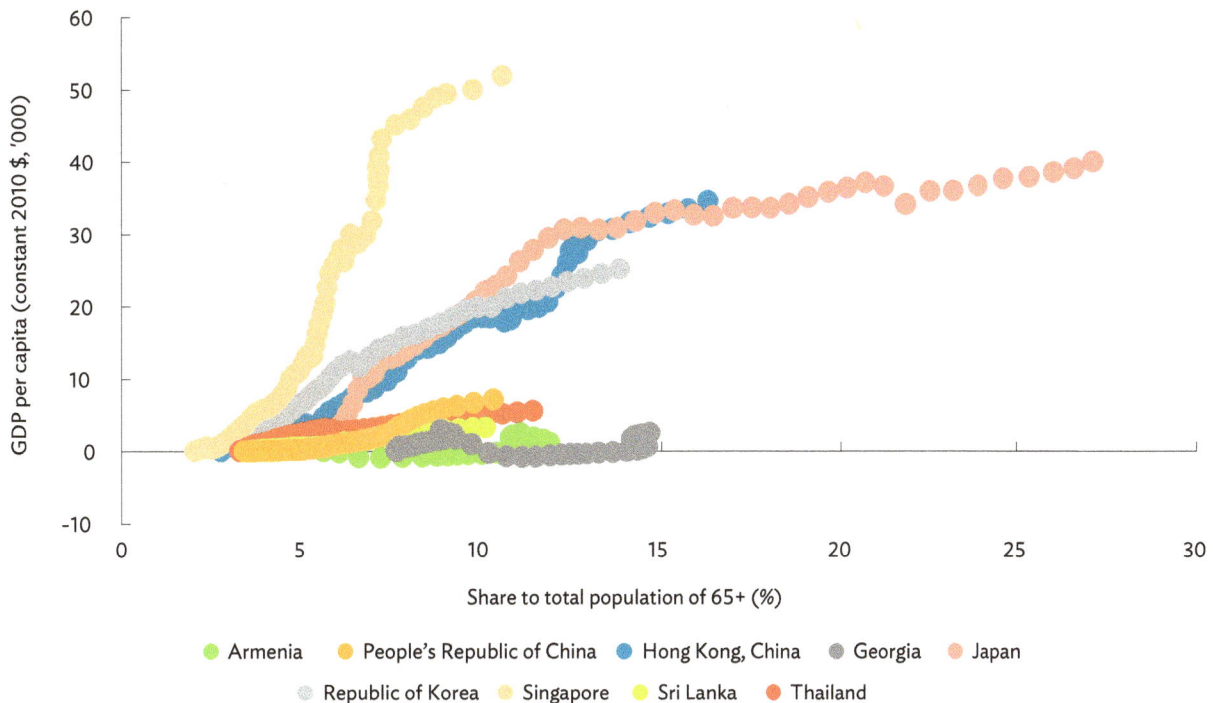

GDP per capita (constant 2010 $, '000)

Share to total population of 65+ (%)

● Armenia   ● People's Republic of China   ● Hong Kong, China   ● Georgia   ● Japan
● Republic of Korea   ● Singapore   ● Sri Lanka   ● Thailand

GDP = gross domestic product.

Note: GDP per capita is normalized to zero during the earliest period of availability.

Sources: ADB calculations using data from United Nations Department of Economic and Social Affairs, Population Division. Population Database. https://population.un.org/wpp/Download/Standard/Population/ and World Bank. World Development Indicators. https://databank.worldbank.org/source/world-development-indicators (both accessed June 2019).

Economies in Asia are undergoing different phases of demographic transition and are feeling the impact of aging at different points in time.

An aging population poses an immediate policy concern in the region overall, but country-specific trends leave room to tackle the diverse challenges. In 2019, the populations of Armenia, Georgia, and Japan were smaller than in 2000, while the rest of the economies in the region experienced an expansion of population (Figure 6.7). In Japan, this decline is explained by fluctuating yet sustained below-replacement births per woman. Population decline in Armenia and Georgia is due to sizable emigration of labor (Cancho, Facusse, and Berenice 2019; and Badurashvili and Nadareishvili 2012). Varying degrees of population expansion are observed in other countries.

Figure 6.7: Population Growth, 2000–2019—Asia (%)

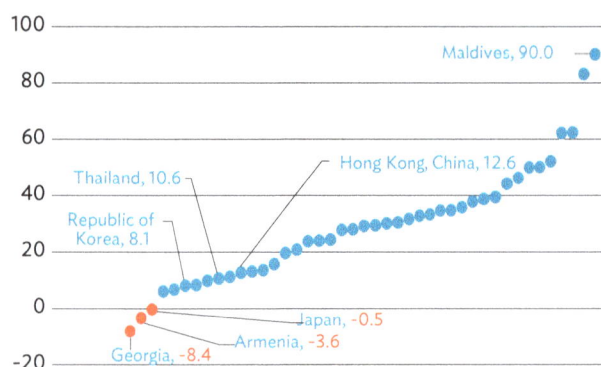

Source: ADB calculations using data from United Nations Department of Economic and Social Affairs, Population Division. Population Database. https://population.un.org/wpp/Download/Standard/Population/ (accessed June 2019).

Population Aging and the Labor Supply

Ongoing demographic transition leads to a decline in the working age population among aging economies.

Between 2020 and 2050, economies in an advanced stage of aging such as Japan; the Republic of Korea;

and Taipei,China will show the most rapid contraction in working age population (Figure 6.8a). The potential workforce is also projected to decline in Armenia; Brunei Darussalam; the PRC; Georgia; Hong Kong, China; Maldives; Singapore; Sri Lanka; and Thailand. These economies account for 41.8% of the region's working age population in 2019, but the shrinkage is expected to reduce this share to 31.9% by 2050. In contrast, further increases in the working age population will occur across many economies over the same period. The largest expansions are expected in Afghanistan, Solomon Islands, and Vanuatu, while the other 30 Asian economies will see more moderate growth. Overall, the region's working age population is expected to decline after reaching a peak of about 3.13 billion between 2045 and 2050.

More importantly, the workforce will age in most economies.

Figure 6.8b shows that the economies whose working age populations will fall by 2050 have a larger share of workers of aged 55 and above. This age group made up at least 17% of the total working age population in the PRC; Georgia; Hong Kong, China; Japan; the Republic of Korea; Singapore; Taipei,China; and Thailand. But workforce aging is common across economies, including ones with younger populations. The working age population from the rapidly aging economies of Hong Kong, China; Japan; the Republic of Korea; Singapore; Taipei,China; and Thailand will have an average age of 40 and above in 2020 (Figure 6.9). By 2050, Armenia, Azerbaijan, Bhutan, Brunei Darussalam, the PRC, Maldives, and Nepal will also have average workforce ages of at least 40. Notably, the aging trend will even be more pronounced in countries such as Bangladesh (+4.7 years) and the Lao People's Democratic Republic (Lao PDR) (+4.4 years).[53]

---

[53]   Actual average age of the workforce is potentially underestimated by exclusion of workers of ages 65 and above who, by definition, are not included in the working age population of those between ages 15 to 64.

Figure 6.8: Working Age Population—Asia

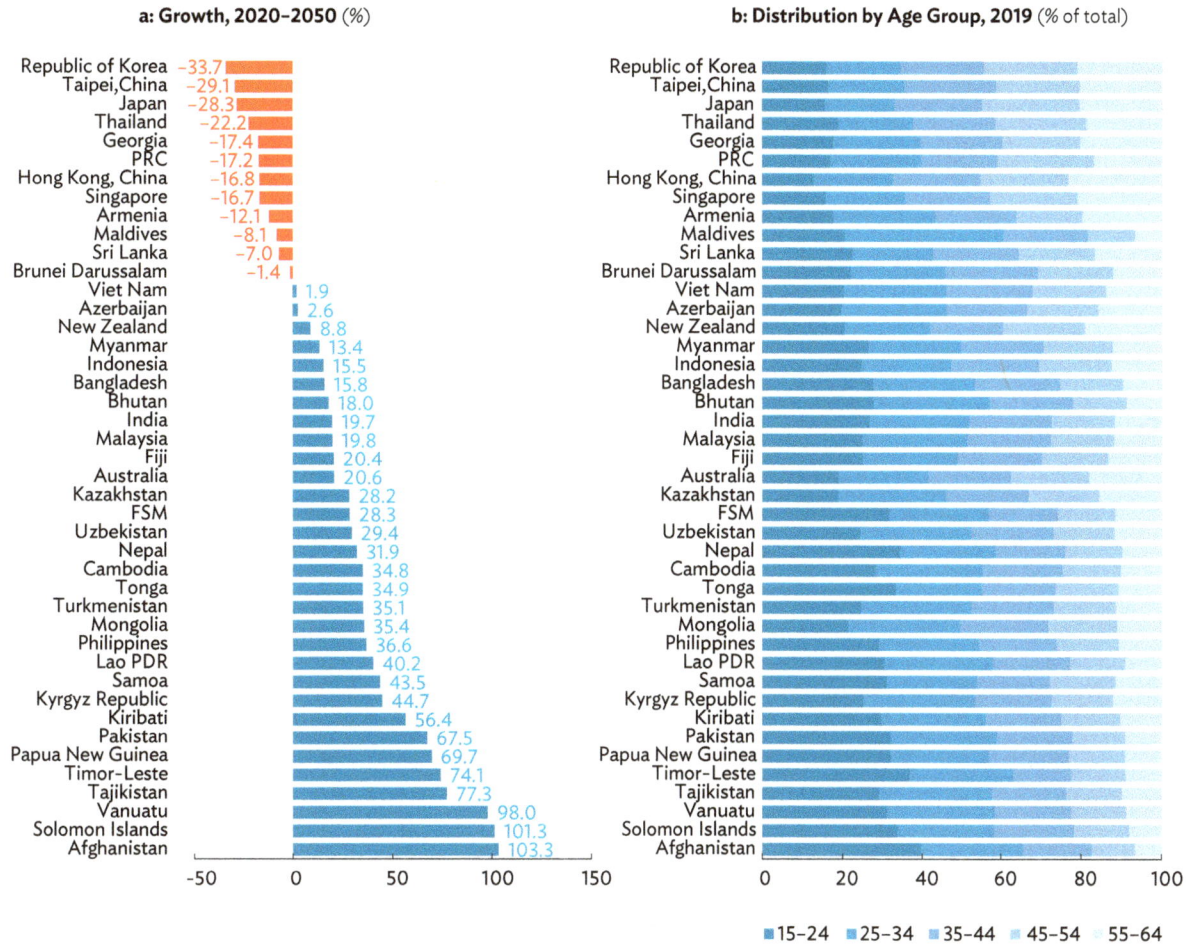

a: Growth, 2020–2050 (%)

Republic of Korea	−33.7
Taipei,China	−29.1
Japan	−28.3
Thailand	−22.2
Georgia	−17.4
PRC	−17.2
Hong Kong, China	−16.8
Singapore	−16.7
Armenia	−12.1
Maldives	−8.1
Sri Lanka	−7.0
Brunei Darussalam	−1.4
Viet Nam	1.9
Azerbaijan	2.6
New Zealand	8.8
Myanmar	13.4
Indonesia	15.5
Bangladesh	15.8
Bhutan	18.0
India	19.7
Malaysia	19.8
Fiji	20.4
Australia	20.6
Kazakhstan	28.2
FSM	28.3
Uzbekistan	29.4
Nepal	31.9
Cambodia	34.8
Tonga	34.9
Turkmenistan	35.1
Mongolia	35.4
Philippines	36.6
Lao PDR	40.2
Samoa	43.5
Kyrgyz Republic	44.7
Kiribati	56.4
Pakistan	67.5
Papua New Guinea	69.7
Timor-Leste	74.1
Tajikistan	77.3
Vanuatu	98.0
Solomon Islands	101.3
Afghanistan	103.3

b: Distribution by Age Group, 2019 (% of total)

■ 15–24 ■ 25–34 ■ 35–44 ■ 45–54 ■ 55–64

FSM = Federated States of Micronesia, Lao PDR = Lao People's Democratic Republic, PRC = People's Republic of China.

Source: ADB calculations using data from United Nations Department of Economic and Social Affairs, Population Division. Population Database. https://population.un.org/wpp/Download/Standard/Population/ (accessed June 2019).

Figure 6.9: Average Age of the Working Age Population (number of years)

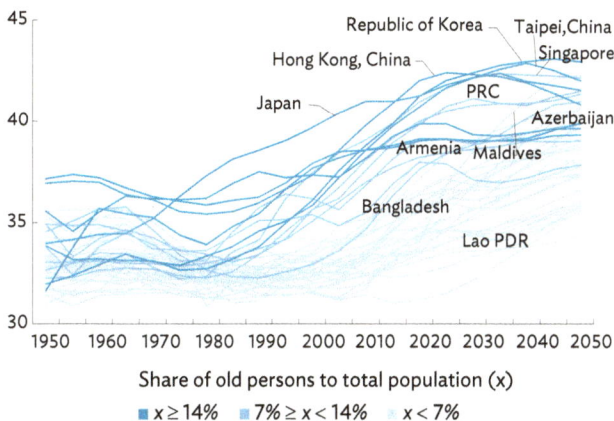

Share of old persons to total population (x)

■ x ≥ 14%   ■ 7% ≥ x < 14%   x < 7%

Lao PDR = Lao People's Democratic Republic, PRC = People's Republic of China.

Note: The color gradient refers to the share to total population of people of ages 65 and above in 2019.

Source: ADB calculations using data from United Nations Department of Economic and Social Affairs, Population Division. Population Database. https://population.un.org/wpp/Download/Standard/Population/ (accessed June 2019).

For various reasons, age remains critical in influencing decisions to take part in the labor market.

Generally, labor force participation increases with age, especially during the early years, and peaks during a person's forties, then declines gradually, following an inverted-U pattern shown in Figure 6.10. The young cohorts have low participation, with an increasing share of youth pursuing further education and advanced degrees. Participation rates gradually decline among older cohorts for many different reasons, including health and retirement. On average, economies at a more advanced phase of population aging have higher participation rates across all ages, including the older ones. Gender differences exist in how age affects

Figure 6.10: Labor Force Participation by Age Group—Asia (%)

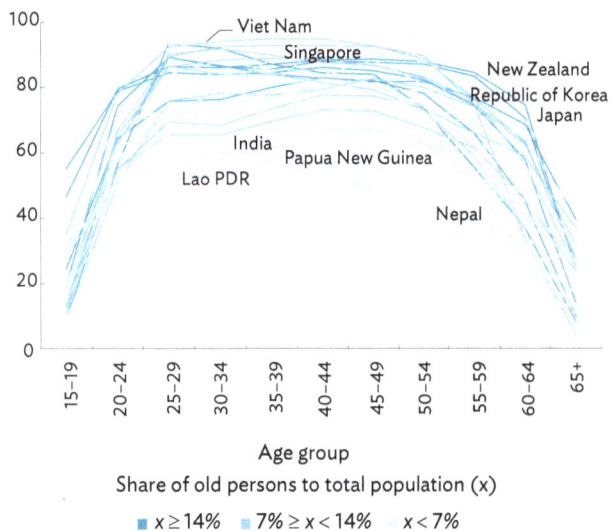

Lao PDR = Lao People's Democratic Republic.

Note: The color gradient refers to the share to total population of people of ages 65 and above in 2019.

Source: ADB calculations using data from the International Labour Organization. ILOSTAT. https://www.ilo.org/ilostat (accessed June 2019).

labor force participation. The likelihood of joining the workforce fluctuates more with age for women than men as they often take a greater share of responsibility in managing the household and providing care to family members. For example, women tend to retreat from the labor market more gradually starting from their early fifties, often to take a more active role in raising grandchildren (Ko and Hank 2014).

A growing share of older people stay in the labor market.

Figure 6.11 shows growing labor participation among workers of ages 60 and above within economies undergoing rapid aging. The rising share of people in the 70–74 cohort who are working way past retirement age is notable. In contrast, the rate remains much more stable in economies, such as India and Indonesia, with youth populations that are still growing. Shifts from agriculture to other sectors and shifts toward wage employment that brings more rigidity to job structures, including the enforcement of the statutory retirement age, might explain the retreat of older workers in these countries,

especially in urban areas. Labor force surveys in some countries exclude older workers from the sample, which makes it difficult to assess their employment status and working conditions.

Financial and nonfinancial drivers help explain extension and reentry of older workers in the labor market.

Social security reforms and the necessity to earn a living influence the labor participation of older persons. In Japan, like many other advanced economies, the labor force participation of older cohorts is highly sensitive to aging-related policies, including the statutory retirement age and the pension system. Oshio, Usui, and Shimizutani (2018) show that labor participation decisions among older workers are strongly associated with changes in social security incentives, such as the rise in pensionable age. Inadequate retirement savings programs and expected cost of living upon retirement are major factors motivating older workers to remain in—or return to—the workplace. Active labor market policy may also influence participation. Singapore introduced a reemployment program in 2017 to boost the employment rate of older residents.

Nonfinancial factors such as the desire to pursue an active professional life and self-fulfillment by connecting with other people at work remain important in motivating older people to remain in the workplace. Most importantly, the participation of older workers greatly depends on their capacity to handle workplace tasks; accordingly, improved health conditions are among the major drivers for old individuals to seek employment or remain in work beyond retirement age.

The confluence of work preferences of older people and labor market demand leads to older workers being more concentrated in certain sectors.

A large share of workers of ages 60 and above is generally observed in agriculture, and holds true in real estate, transportation, and construction. Workers age

Figure 6.11: Labor Force Participation of Older Workforce—Selected Asian Economies (%)

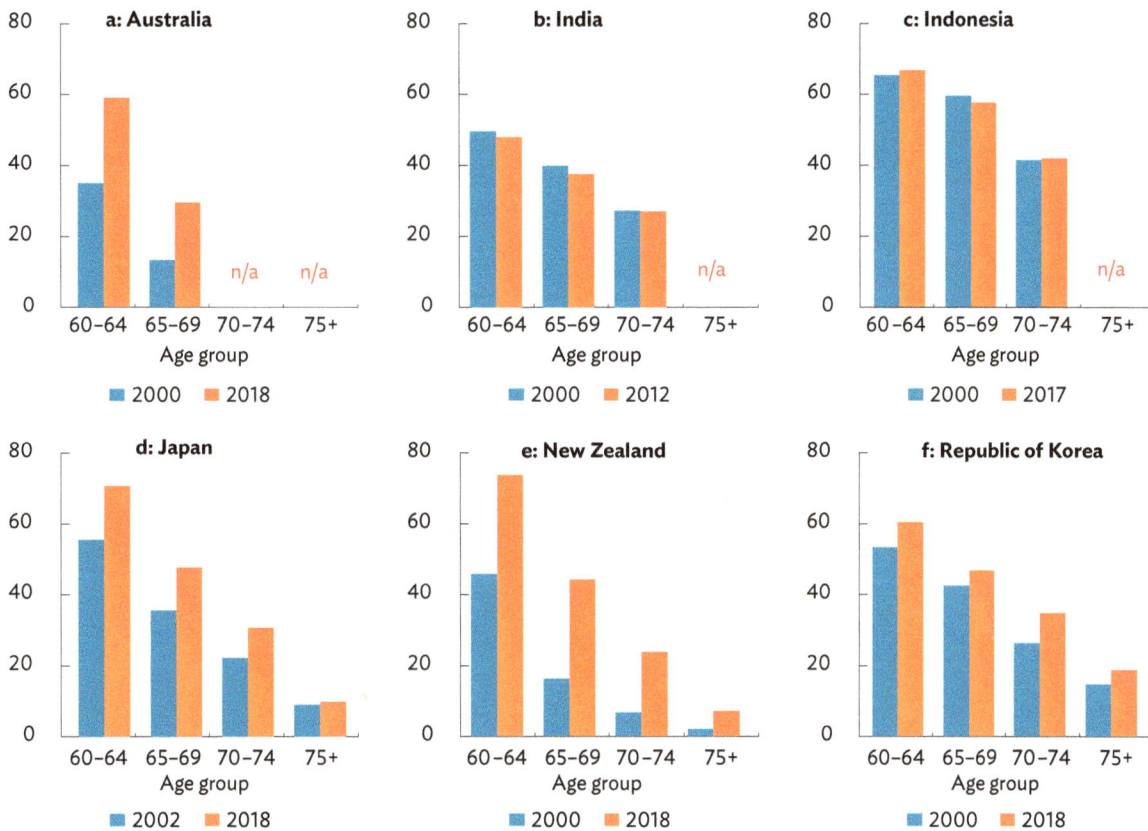

n/a = data not available.

Note: Latest available data for India are 2012, while those for Indonesia are 2017.

Source: ADB calculations using data from Organisation for Economic Co-operation and Development (OECD). OECD Stat Database. https://stats.oecd.org/ (accessed June 2019).

60 and above account for as high as 61% of agricultural workforce in Japan and 65% in the Republic of Korea (Figure 6.12). Agriculture offers some advantages for older workers. First, it does not usually impose strict retirement ages. Second, it provides more flexibility in working hours, especially given the prevalence of family-owned farms. Third, with increasing mechanization, farming becomes less physically demanding. Aside from agriculture, real estate also attracts older workers. In Japan, employees of ages 60 and above comprise 35% of staff in the real estate sector. Older workers also seek wage employment in real estate, for example as brokers, for flexibility in working hours.

Given abilities decline with age, along with other factors, older workers prefer occupying less physically demanding jobs; adoption of technology may enable them to handle more routine-oriented tasks.

Compared with routine tasks, occupations involving nonroutine manual tasks are less physically demanding. These include service jobs requiring human interactions, and this partly explains the large share of workers age 60 and above performing jobs with nonroutine manual tasks (Figure 6.13). This group has the highest share of workers over the age of 60—25% of the total employed

Figure 6.12: Sector Distribution of Employment by Age Group—Selected Asian Economies (%)

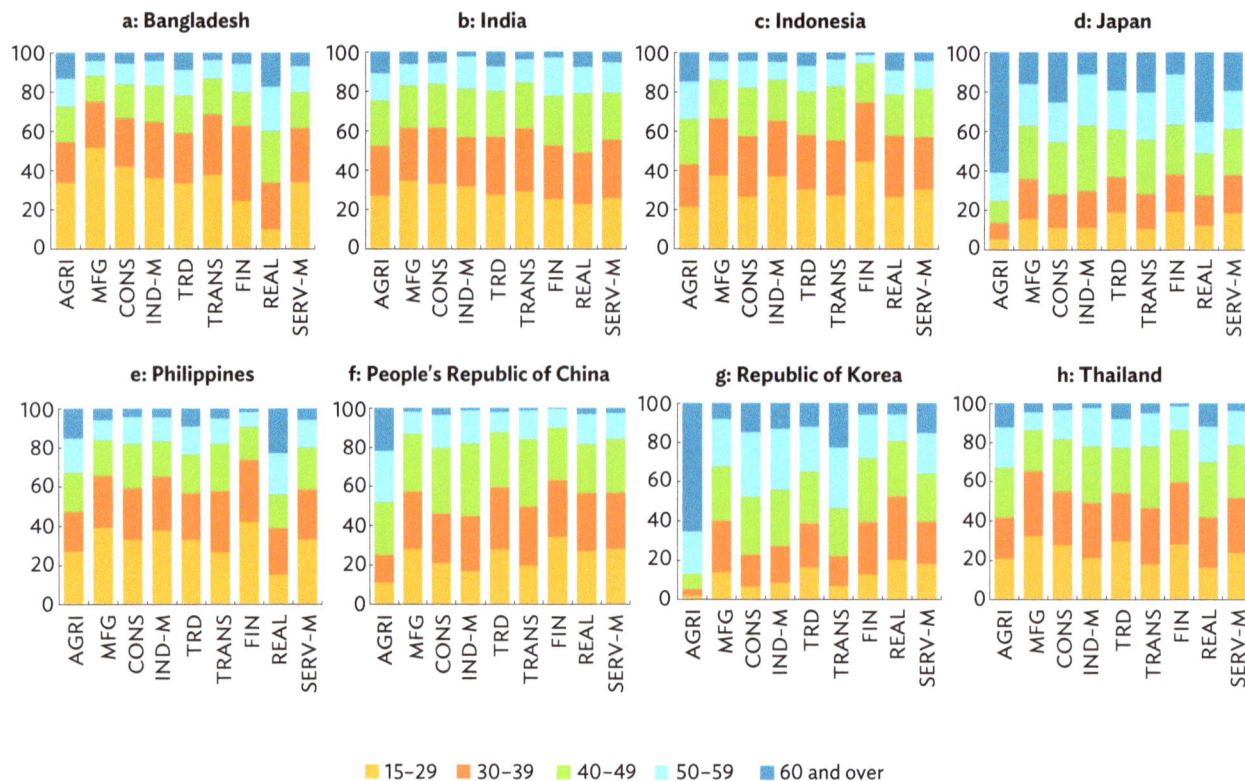

AGRI = agriculture, CONS = construction, FIN = finance, IND-M = other industries, MFG = manufacturing, REAL = real estate, SERV-M = other services, TRANS = transportation, TRD = wholesale and retail trade.

Note: Employment data for the People's Republic of China refer to urban employment only.

Sources: ADB calculations using data from Government of the People's Republic of China, Ministry of Human Resources and Social Security. China Labour Statistical Yearbook 2016. http://www.mohrss.gov.cn/2016/indexeh.htm (accessed June 2019); Korean Statistical Information Service. https://kosis.kr/eng/ (accessed June 2019); Statistics Bureau of Japan. Employment Status Survey 2018. https://www.stat.go.jp/english/data/index.html (accessed June 2019); and respective labor force surveys for other economies.

in nonroutine tasks in Japan and 23% for the Republic of Korea, and this is also the case in younger economies, including India and the Philippines.

In some countries, however, adoption of industrial robots and other automation capital makes it easier to retain and involve older workers in handling routine and manual tasks, which traditionally require physical ability and dexterity. This possibly explains the large share of older workers in routine jobs in Japan, the Republic of Korea, and the PRC. Technology use at the workplace may change the landscape of how susceptible jobs and tasks are to workforce aging, which at present varies across occupations (Box 6.1).

While unemployment is low among the elderly, selection bias potentially masks real labor market conditions.

It is not surprising that unemployment is higher among youth than for middle-aged or older workers because youth try different career paths. The median unemployment rate of workers of ages 15–19 across the 35 Asian economies with available data is 14.6%, and 11.9% for ages 20–24 (Figure 6.14). The reported unemployment declines with age, falling to as low as 1% among workforce older than 65. However, low unemployment among older workers does not necessarily indicate that their labor market situation is better. Official unemployment figures do not capture discouraged older jobseekers, leaving the job market for

Figure 6.13: Task Distribution of Employment by Age Group—Selected Asian Economies (%)

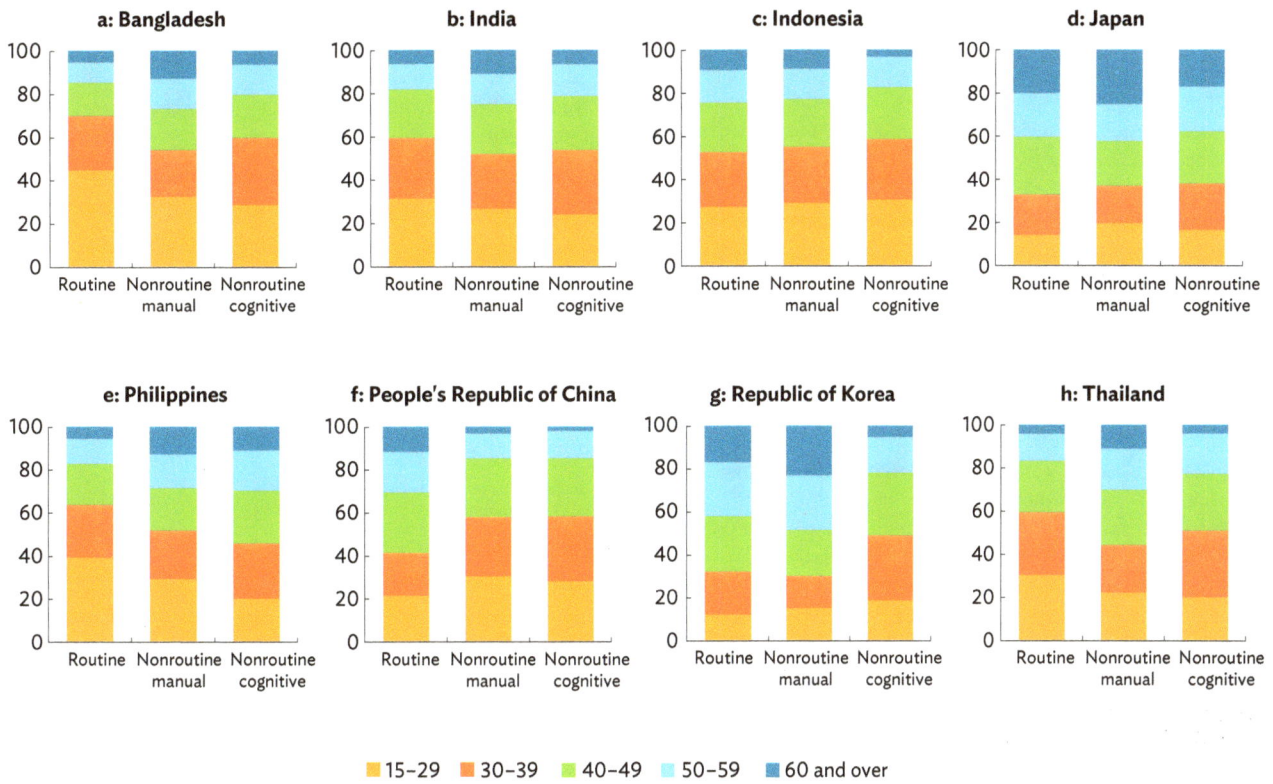

Legend: ■ 15–29   ■ 30–39   ■ 40–49   ■ 50–59   ■ 60 and over

Notes: Task categories follow the International Labour Organization's classification of occupations. Routine occupations include clerical support workers, craft and related trades workers, plant and machine operators and assemblers, and elementary occupations. Nonroutine manual includes services and sales workers, and skilled agriculture workers. Nonroutine cognitive includes managers, professionals, and technicians.

Sources: ADB calculations using data from Government of the People's Republic of China, Ministry of Human Resources and Social Security. China Labour Statistical Yearbook 2016. http://www.mohrss.gov.cn/2016/indexeh.htm (accessed June 2019); Korean Statistical Information Service. https://kosis.kr/eng/ (accessed June 2019); Statistics Bureau of Japan. Employment Status Survey 2018. https://www.stat.go.jp/english/data/index.html (accessed June 2019); and respective labor force surveys for other economies.

involuntary reasons besides declining health and their ability to collect a pension.

Older workers tend to face more difficulty than young ones in finding a new job when they become unemployed.

In Australia, workers of ages 55 and above who found new jobs did so on average 15.9 months after becoming unemployed, double the average 7 months of unemployment for workers of ages 15–24. Extended job searches partially explain the lower labor participation rates among older workers. Rones (1983) pointed out that older unemployed workers are less likely to find jobs than the younger cohorts, and that they are more likely to leave the labor market involuntarily after a prolonged spell of unemployment. Job markets tend to be less responsive to the needs and

Figure 6.14: Unemployment Rate by Age Group—Asia (%)

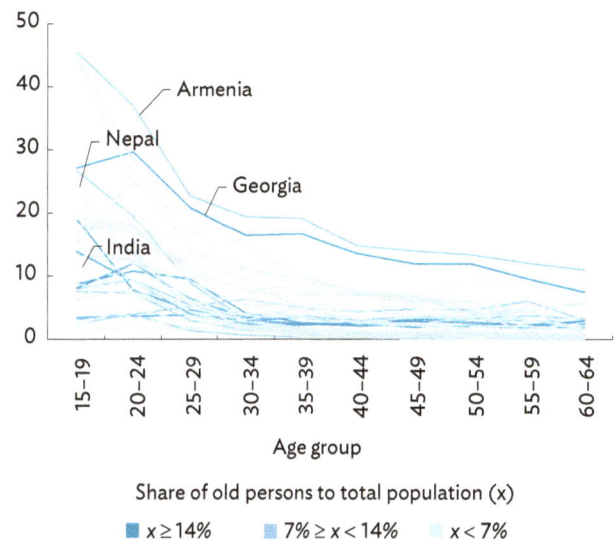

Share of old persons to total population (x)

■ x ≥ 14%   ■ 7% ≥ x < 14%   ■ x < 7%

Note: The color gradient refers to the share to total population of people of ages 65 and above in 2019.

Source: ADB calculations using data from the International Labour Organization. ILOSTAT. https://www.ilo.org/ilostat (accessed June 2019).

Box 6.1: Which Jobs Are More Susceptible to Aging?

Different occupations require different skills and abilities. Since these abilities decline with age at different tempos, the direction and extent of impact of aging can vary substantially across occupations. Belbase, Sanzenbacher, and Gillis (2015) developed a Susceptibility Index that systematically assesses the physical and cognitive skills required for each occupation and the tendency of such skills to decline with age.[a] The study first identifies the cognitive and physical abilities that decline by early to mid-sixties (Box Table).

Occupations are then indexed based on the number of abilities and their importance to the job, where a higher index indicates that the job relies on many abilities that tend to decline early. The index therefore reflects how susceptible an occupation is to declines in ability, and it is found to predict early retirement. The Box Figure shows selected occupations and their susceptibility index percentiles. Interestingly, it shows that some white collar occupations are just as susceptible as blue collar occupations to early ability declines in work. However, blue collar occupations are especially susceptible to early ability declines, such that workers in these occupations are less likely to be able to work to full retirement age as it increases to 67.

Susceptibility Index Percentiles—Selected Occupations

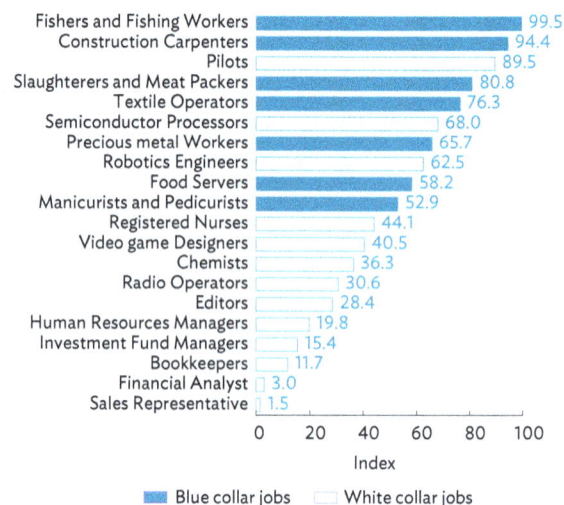

Occupation	Index
Fishers and Fishing Workers	99.5
Construction Carpenters	94.4
Pilots	89.5
Slaughterers and Meat Packers	80.8
Textile Operators	76.3
Semiconductor Processors	68.0
Precious metal Workers	65.7
Robotics Engineers	62.5
Food Servers	58.2
Manicurists and Pedicurists	52.9
Registered Nurses	44.1
Video game Designers	40.5
Chemists	36.3
Radio Operators	30.6
Editors	28.4
Human Resources Managers	19.8
Investment Fund Managers	15.4
Bookkeepers	11.7
Financial Analyst	3.0
Sales Representative	1.5

Blue collar jobs   White collar jobs

Source: Center for Retirement Research at Boston College. Susceptibility Index. http://crr.bc.edu/wp-content/uploads/2016/04/Susceptibility Index_April-2016.pdf (accessed July 2019).

Abilities that Show Early Decline

Cognitive	Psychomotor	Physical strength	Sensory
Fluency of ideas	Arm–hand steadiness	Explosive strength	Night vision
Inductive reasoning	Manual dexterity	Dynamic strength	Peripheral vision
Deductive reasoning	Finger dexterity	Extent flexibility	Depth perception
Memorization	Reaction time	Dynamic flexibility	Glare sensitivity
Information ordering	Wrist-finger speed	Gross body coordination	Sound localization
Speed closure	Speed of limb movement	Gross body equilibrium	
Perceptual closure			
Spatial orientation			
Visualization			
Time sharing			

Source: Belbase, Sanzenbacher, and Gillis (2015).

[a] The Occupational Information Network (O*NET), a free online database owned and maintained by the United States Department of Labor that contains occupational definitions, was used to evaluate occupations. After indexing, the Health and Retirement Study (HRS)—a model of early retirement—was used to estimate the likelihood of early retirement for individuals in certain occupations. Read the full paper for deeper explanation of the susceptibility index.

Source: Belbase, Sanzenbacher, and Gillis (2015).

preferences of the older workers who might lack necessary skills and training, among other attributes for employment. Employers are expected to have less desire to take on older workers because their hiring and training costs tend to outweigh the shorter tenure they can expect compared with younger workers (Munnell, Sass, and Soto 2006).

Aside from preference, labor market bias against the older workforce also explains the large representation of older cohorts in casual jobs and self-employment.

Based on the 2018 Labor Force Survey in Japan, 37% of nonagriculture sector employees aged more than 54 were involved in part-time and temporary employment, compared with 24% among the 15–34 cohort. Self-employment is also common among older individuals: 54% in agriculture and 13% in non-agricultural activities. In contrast, in ages 15–34, 13% in agriculture and 2% in nonagricultural activities are self-employed. Data from the 2016 China Labour Statistical Yearbook suggests a very similar pattern in the PRC, with 14.3% of workers of ages 65 and above working less than 20 hours a week, compared with 2.6% for workers aged 20–24. Self-employment is also relatively high among old people, at 8.8% of the employed of ages 65 and above, compared with 3.7% for ages 20–24.

Tapping the latent workforce can offer huge benefits during demographic transition in Asia.

The region, especially among economies at advanced stages of aging, could reap benefits from breaking barriers for women and the older workforce to reenter the labor market (Box 6.2 highlights the case of Japan). Efforts focus

---

Box 6.2: Japan's Expanding Labor Force in a Time of Population Contraction

The share of the productive-age (15 to 64 years) population in Japan peaked in the middle of the 1990s and has been declining since. It is projected to drop by 28.3% (about 21 million) between 2020 and 2050. Contrary to the demographic scenario, Japan's labor force has grown in recent years. This growth is largely explained by the steadfast rise of older workforce (ages 55 and above) alongside increasing number of female and foreign workers (Box Figure).

Change in Japan Labor Force (in 10,000s)

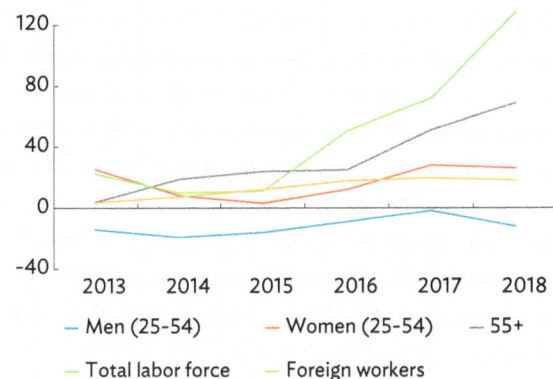

Note: Labor force data is inclusive of foreign workers.

Source: ADB calculations using Japan Labour Force Surveys (2012-2018) data from e-Stat (Portal Site of Official Statistics of Japan). https://www.e-stat.go.jp/ (accessed August 2019).

The more mature workforce of ages 55 and above has increased from 1.9 million in 2013 to 2 million in 2018. Better health, longer lives, higher education levels, and working in less physically demanding jobs all contributed to their greater participation in the labor force. However, the key drivers behind such trend are major policy reforms: reduced social security benefits and an increase in the eligibility age from 60 to 65. For workers past retirement age, data show that they continue working part-time, and more women do so than men.

Increased female participation can also be explained by policies such as Prime Minister Abe's "Womanomics," aimed at encouraging women, especially mothers with young children, to continue to work. These include programs such as establishing childcare facilities, increasing childcare leave, and enforcing options for shorter working hours. The share of women who continued to work after having a child significantly increased from 15.3% in 2000 to 28.3% in 2014 (Government of Japan, Ministry of Health, Labour, and Welfare).

With labor demand exceeding supply, foreign workers have filled job vacancies largely in construction from 2015 and in nursing-care from 2017. In April 2018, Japan introduced new visa categories for manual workers and skilled blue collar workers, hoping to attract more than 300,000 foreign workers within 5 years. Data from the Ministry of Health, Labour, and Welfare show that the number of foreign workers has increased from 720,000 in 2013 to 1.46 million in 2018.

Sources: Gale (2018); Ip (2019); Nagase (2018); Oshio, Usui, and Shimizutani (2018); and Sato (2019).

at balancing work and family life and other personal needs to incentivize their labor force participation. The size of the untapped older workforce can potentially be large. Using the population-based 2016 Comprehensive Survey of the Living Conditions, Oshio (2018) estimates that about 6.7 million workers of ages 60–74 could have been added to the labor supply, equivalent to 10% of Japan's total labor force in 2016.

The unemployed younger population of some countries belies a need for action on workforce aging.

Several policy agenda items need to be tackled for young economies to better prepare for the inevitable demographic transition to a more mature population. For one, these economies have particularly high youth unemployment, which is even more prevalent among the highly educated. Prolonged unemployment early in a career may render people less employable. Bell and Blanchflower (2011) found that it imposes costs later in their careers including lower pay and higher risk of displacement.

Education Trends and Human Capital

Factors shaping demographic change also influence the level and pattern of human capital development in the region.

The recorded drop in the fertility rate over 4 decades has translated to higher investment in improving children's welfare and potential. Parents decide on the number of children they want to raise in consideration of expected spending on their offspring's education and health, given the potential family income and the availability and quality of the public welfare system. Figure 6.15 gives a broad view of the quantity–quality trade-off that was put forward by Becker (1960), as economies with lower fertility rates spend more on human capital investment per child.

Children are staying in school longer and the gender gap in education has largely closed.

Increased public and private expenditure on education per child, along with other factors, has led to an expansion in schooling years. Between 1980 and 2015,

Figure 6.15: Human Capital Development and Fertility

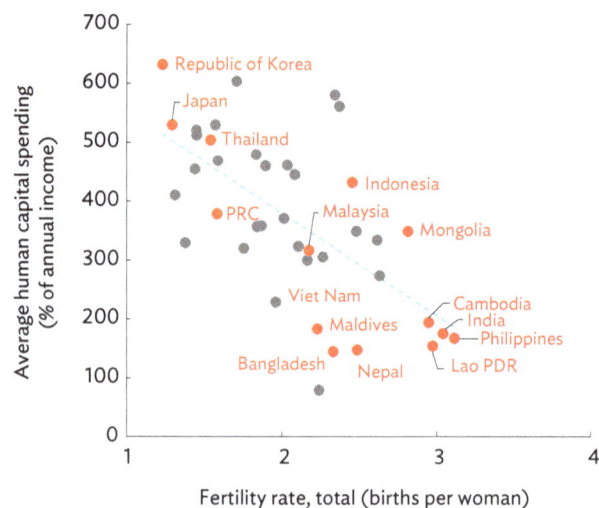

Lao PDR = Lao People's Democratic Republic, PRC = People's Republic of China.

Notes: Red dots refer to Asian economies with available data; gray dots to non-Asian economies. Human capital spending refers to the combined public and private spending per child given per capita health spending for children age 0–17 and per capita education spending for children age 3–26. Total fertility rate refers to births per woman in 2017.

Sources: ADB calculations using data from East–West Center. National Transfer Accounts Data Sheet 2016. https://www.ntaccounts.org (accessed July 2019); and World Bank. World Development Indicators. ttps://databank.worldbank.org/source/world-development-indicators (accessed June 2019).

the average years of schooling among the economically active population (ages 25–64) across Asia increased from 5.2 to 9.0 years (Figure 6.16a). More than half the economies observed 10 or more years of increment in schooling. Another notable pattern of change is the closing of the gender gap in education. Figure 6.16b clearly illustrates how schooling years of females reached the same as males in many economies. In 1980, for ages 25–64, males had had an average of 1.3 years more schooling than females. By 2015, the gap narrowed to 0.7 years, reflecting improvements in Kiribati and Mongolia. Significant change also came about in the Republic of Korea; Singapore; and Taipei,China. This trend is expected to translate into a further reduction in fertility.

Improved schooling among younger cohorts leads to a decline in the share of a less-educated older population.

Figure 6.17 shows the mean years of schooling across all age cohorts in the region in 1980 and in 2015. During the

Figure 6.16: Mean Years of Schooling of Population Ages 25–64 (Number of years)

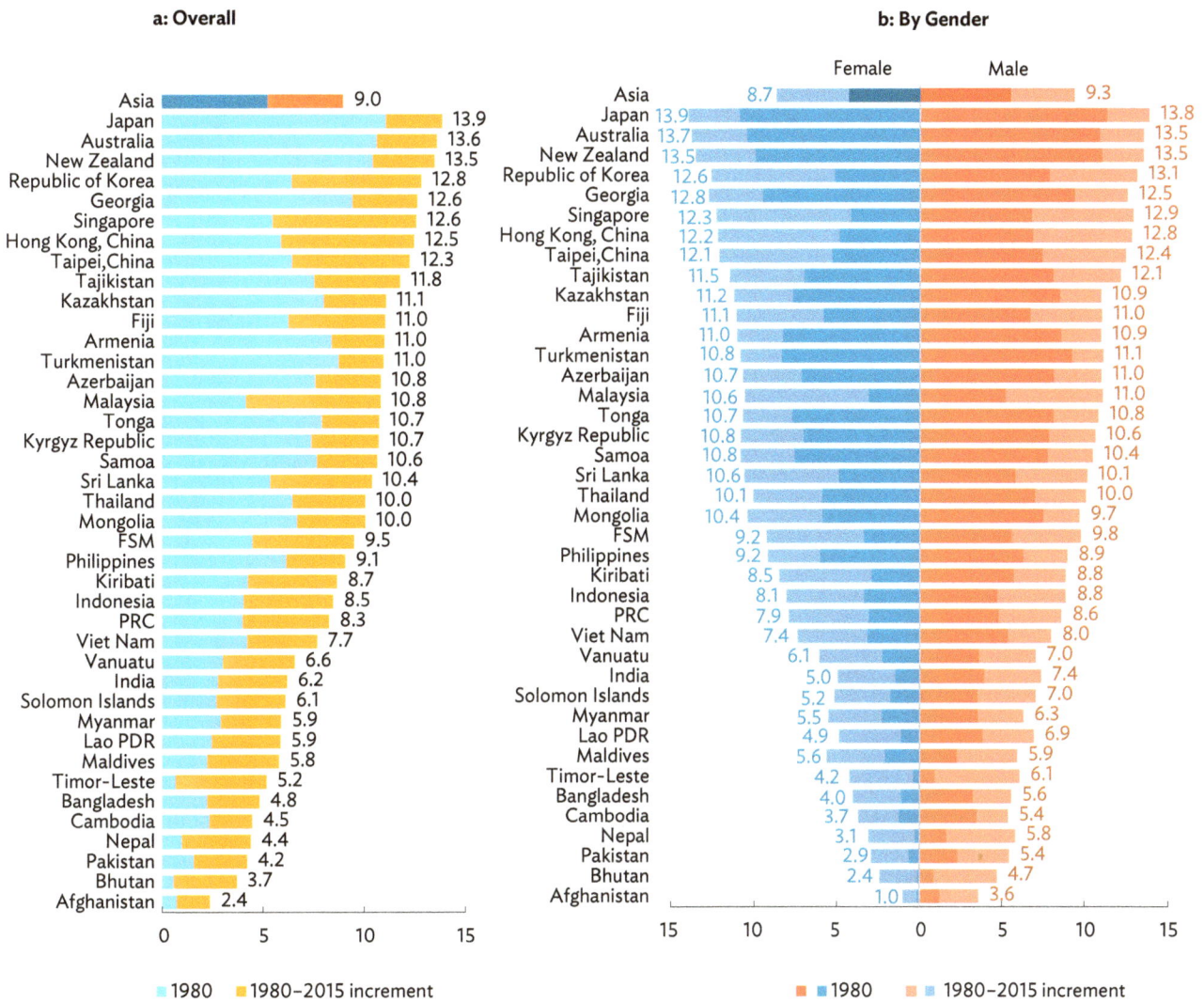

a: Overall

Country	2015 value
Asia	9.0
Japan	13.9
Australia	13.6
New Zealand	13.5
Republic of Korea	12.8
Georgia	12.6
Singapore	12.6
Hong Kong, China	12.5
Taipei,China	12.3
Tajikistan	11.8
Kazakhstan	11.1
Fiji	11.0
Armenia	11.0
Turkmenistan	11.0
Azerbaijan	10.8
Malaysia	10.8
Tonga	10.7
Kyrgyz Republic	10.7
Samoa	10.6
Sri Lanka	10.4
Thailand	10.0
Mongolia	10.0
FSM	9.5
Philippines	9.1
Kiribati	8.7
Indonesia	8.5
PRC	8.3
Viet Nam	7.7
Vanuatu	6.6
India	6.2
Solomon Islands	6.1
Myanmar	5.9
Lao PDR	5.9
Maldives	5.8
Timor-Leste	5.2
Bangladesh	4.8
Cambodia	4.5
Nepal	4.4
Pakistan	4.2
Bhutan	3.7
Afghanistan	2.4

■ 1980   ■ 1980–2015 increment

b: By Gender

Country	Female	Male
Asia	8.7	9.3
Japan	13.9	13.8
Australia	13.7	13.5
New Zealand	13.5	13.5
Republic of Korea	12.6	13.1
Georgia	12.8	12.5
Singapore	12.3	12.9
Hong Kong, China	12.2	12.8
Taipei,China	12.1	12.4
Tajikistan	11.5	12.1
Kazakhstan	11.2	10.9
Fiji	11.1	11.0
Armenia	11.0	10.9
Turkmenistan	10.8	11.1
Azerbaijan	10.7	11.0
Malaysia	10.6	11.0
Tonga	10.7	10.8
Kyrgyz Republic	10.8	10.6
Samoa	10.8	10.4
Sri Lanka	10.6	10.1
Thailand	10.1	10.0
Mongolia	10.4	9.7
FSM	9.2	9.8
Philippines	9.2	8.9
Kiribati	8.5	8.8
Indonesia	8.1	8.8
PRC	7.9	8.6
Viet Nam	7.4	8.0
Vanuatu	6.1	7.0
India	5.0	7.4
Solomon Islands	5.2	7.0
Myanmar	5.5	6.3
Lao PDR	4.9	6.9
Maldives	5.6	5.9
Timor-Leste	4.2	6.1
Bangladesh	4.0	5.6
Cambodia	3.7	5.4
Nepal	3.1	5.8
Pakistan	2.9	5.4
Bhutan	2.4	4.7
Afghanistan	1.0	3.6

■ ■ 1980   ■ ■ 1980–2015 increment

FSM = Federated States of Micronesia, Lao PDR = Lao People's Democratic Republic, PRC = People's Republic of China.

Note: Data labels denote the mean years of schooling in 2015.

Source: ADB calculations using data from Wittgenstein Centre for Demography and Global Human Capital. Wittgenstein Centre Data Explorer Version 2.0. www.wittgensteincentre.org/dataexplorer (accessed June 2019).

period, the years of schooling of population of ages 25–34 increased from 7.1 years to 10.2 years. Greater improvement is witnessed among the old. The years of schooling among older cohorts of age 55–64 have extended from 3.4 years in 1980 and 4.6 years in 1990 to 7.8 years in 2015, reflecting expansion of basic education in their youth. Correspondingly, the share of people ages 55–64 with highest attainment of primary schooling decreased from 89.1% in 1980 to 58.1% in 2015.

Nevertheless, the schooling gap between the young and old remains wide and visible.

This is particularly true among economies that have quickly climbed the education ladder. In 2015, Singapore and Taipei,China both exhibited a 7 years gap in average years of schooling between the age groups 25–29 and people in their seventies. The education gap also remains high in countries that have increased enrollment in primary to secondary education, such as Timor-Leste

Figure 6.17: Mean Years of Schooling by Age Group—Asia (number of years)

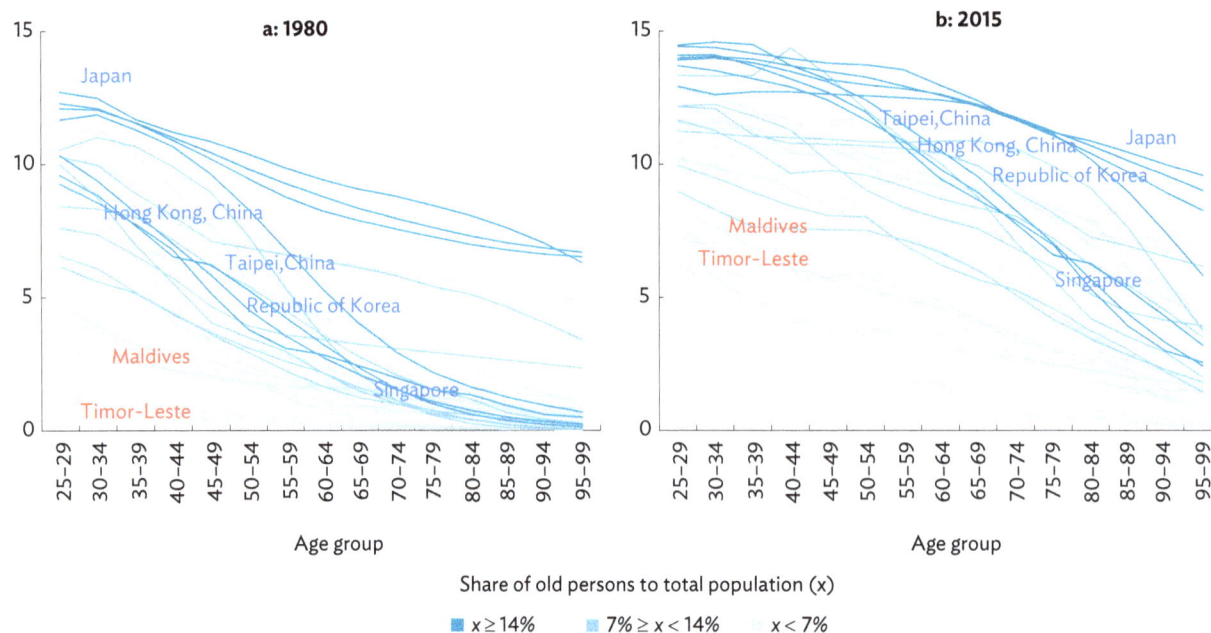

Note: The color gradient refers to the share to total population of people of ages 65 and above in 2019.

Source: ADB calculations using data from Wittgenstein Centre for Demography and Global Human Capital. Wittgenstein Centre Data Explorer Version 2.0. www.wittgensteincentre.org/dataexplorer (accessed June 2019).

(8 years) and Maldives (6 years). In addition, a considerable gap remains in economies with highly educated adults, including the Republic of Korea showing a gap in schooling of 6 years. This trend is apparent in many of the region's economies, and differs only in the extent and speed of such progress. This implies that adult learning will be essential for the older cohorts to remain economically active, especially when the nature of work is rapidly changing with the advancement of technology.

Aging Demographics and Growth Potential

Demographic changes and population growth are historically linked to the speed at which an economy grows, reaping the so-called demographic dividend from labor abundance.

This is especially evident in Asia, where foreign investment boosted growth of strategically targeted countries with an ample supply of workforce. Bloom and Williamson (1998) estimated that workforce expansion

explains around a third of the rapid economic growth experienced by the East Asian tiger economies. Bloom and Canning (2004) also validated the positive and significant relationship between rising shares in the working age population and economic growth.

The first demographic dividend is realized when the working population expands at a faster rate than the total.

A growing supply of workers boosts production and income while stimulating consumption and market expansion. Taxes on labor income support public investment and government services that build social and economic infrastructures. For many countries in Asia, a window of opportunity to gain from the first demographic dividend will remain open for several more years before eventually closing. Estimates proxying the dividend with the ratio of producers to consumers, suggest that out of 18 Asian economies, 9 will remain at the stage of reaping the first demographic dividend for 20 years from 2015 (Figure 6.18). These countries are Bangladesh, India, Indonesia, the Lao PDR, Malaysia,

Maldives, Nepal, the Philippines, and Timor-Leste (East-West Center 2017). By 2055, the number will fall to three: Indonesia, the Lao PDR, and Timor-Leste.

Figure 6.18: First Demographic Dividend in Selected Asian Economies (Effective number of producers per 100 consumers)

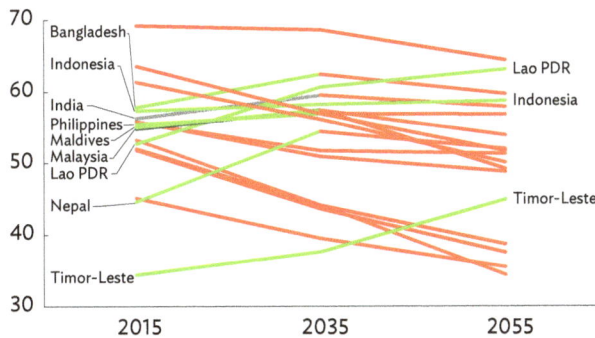

Lao PDR = Lao People's Democratic Republic.

Note: Green line indicates increasing trend, while red line indicates a fall in income per effective consumer.

Source: ADB calculations using data from National Transfer Accounts. Data Sheet 2016. https://www.ntaccounts.org (accessed July 2019).

As countries in the region start experiencing a gradual decline in the share of working age population, their ability to sustain high growth will be challenged.

The transitory bonus from the first demographic dividend should be turned into sustainable assets and investment, realizing a "second demographic dividend." Potential growth relies heavily on labor productivity, which calls for investing in raising the quality of human and physical capital. Such investment can be sourced from accumulated savings and increased demand for wealth in preparation for longer years of retirement amid extending longevity. Lee and Mason (2011) estimate that population aging in developing Asia could lead to substantial capital deepening, where pension assets are expected to rise from 1.2 times total labor income in 2010 to 2.7 times in 2050. For Japan, the study also found that longer life expectancy was accompanied by increasing life cycle pension wealth in the postwar period.

The sequential gain from a demographic dividend does not need to end at the second harvest.

Potential sources of growth in an aging society (the "third" or "silver" dividend) is longevity and longer working life. Harvesting the gain requires tapping previously untapped talents, including those of old men and women, and encouraging continuous learning and upgrading or acquiring new skills. Using the Japanese Study of Aging and Retirement, a longitudinal survey of people of ages 50–70, and considering the extension in years of good health among the old, Matsukura et al. (2018) estimated that more than 11 million Japanese of ages 60–79 years are untapped for the labor force, and they could have contributed 4.5% more in Japan's real GDP in 2010. Households and individuals, facing dramatic extension in healthy life spans over the years, have incentive to invest in human capital—not only in early education, but in lifelong education. The next section takes a close look at how population and workforce aging affect productivity growth and explores ways in which technology can help to reignite growth.

Workforce Aging, Productivity, and the Role of Technology

With rapidly changing demographics, Asia faces contraction in the working age population share, and the growth potential of some economies may be at imminent risk. Aging restricts economic growth in multiple ways, but the biggest concern is slowing productivity (e.g., Maestas, Mullen, and Powell 2016; Aiyar, Ebeke, and Shao 2016). Although economic literature generally points to negative economic impacts of aging, new technologies can help maintain productivity growth and skill augmentation for aging populations.

Aging Effects on the Factors of Production Growth

An aging workforce impacts overall economic productivity.

A changing age profile of the population can affect productivity in many ways. Aging populations can impact inputs into production, which in turn affects overall productivity and future economic growth (Chomik and Piggott 2018). Productivity growth, commonly measured by the growth of output per unit of input, is driven particularly by (i) an increase in the quantity and quality of labor inputs (due to better health and education outcomes, experience, and skills); (ii) increased or technology-enhanced capital (machinery, and equipment, factories, and infrastructure); and (iii) other factors such as technological advance that affect all factors combined (Figure 6.19).

Human abilities and skills change over the life cycle, affecting the quantity and quality of labor.

Population aging is believed to have direct and indirect effects on the quantity and quality of labor, subject to the changes in the age and skill composition of the workforce. The biological effect of aging on physical strength and fitness is somewhat obvious. A range of physical ability and fitness measures such as balance, agility, and muscle strength all fall with age. Figure 6.20 shows that balance and instantaneous power are the fastest to deteriorate in both sexes, though at varying speed. For jobs and industries that require these abilities,

productivity can be at risk if the dependence on older workers is growing.

But knowledge-based intelligence is sustained until very old age.

Drawing from a population-based study of 291 individuals of ages 6 to 89, Li et al. (2004) find that fluid intelligence, like problem-solving and pattern recognition skills, goes into steep decline as early as in the twenties (Figure 6.21). Crystalized intelligence, which relates to accumulated knowledge, strategic skills, empathy, and big-picture perspective, is more resilient, and declines only marginally between ages 40 and 60 and beyond (vocabulary, for instance, is shown to continue increasing into very old age). These patterns are broadly consistent across cultures, including in Asia (Park, Nisbett, and Hedden 1999).

Essential work-related skills such as numeracy and literacy decline with age.

Adult skills in numeracy and literacy show an inverted U-shaped pattern over the life cycle, peaking at middle-

Figure 6.19: Aging Workforce and the Three Factors of Production

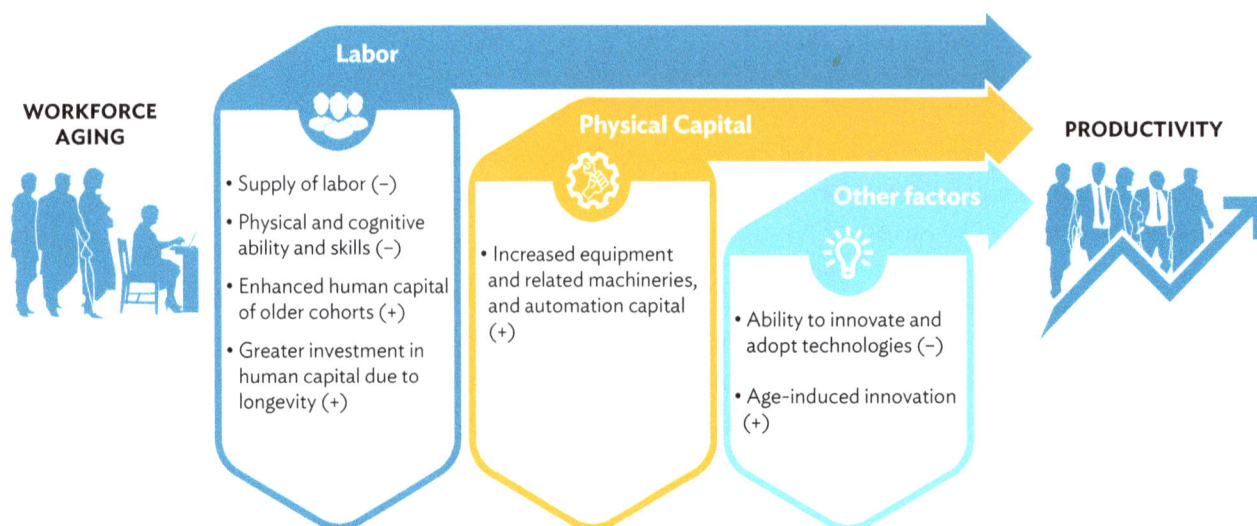

+ = positive contributor to productivity growth, – = negative contributor to productivity growth.

Source: Asian Development Bank.

Figure 6.20: Physical Ability and Fitness Level by Age Group: A Case of Japan

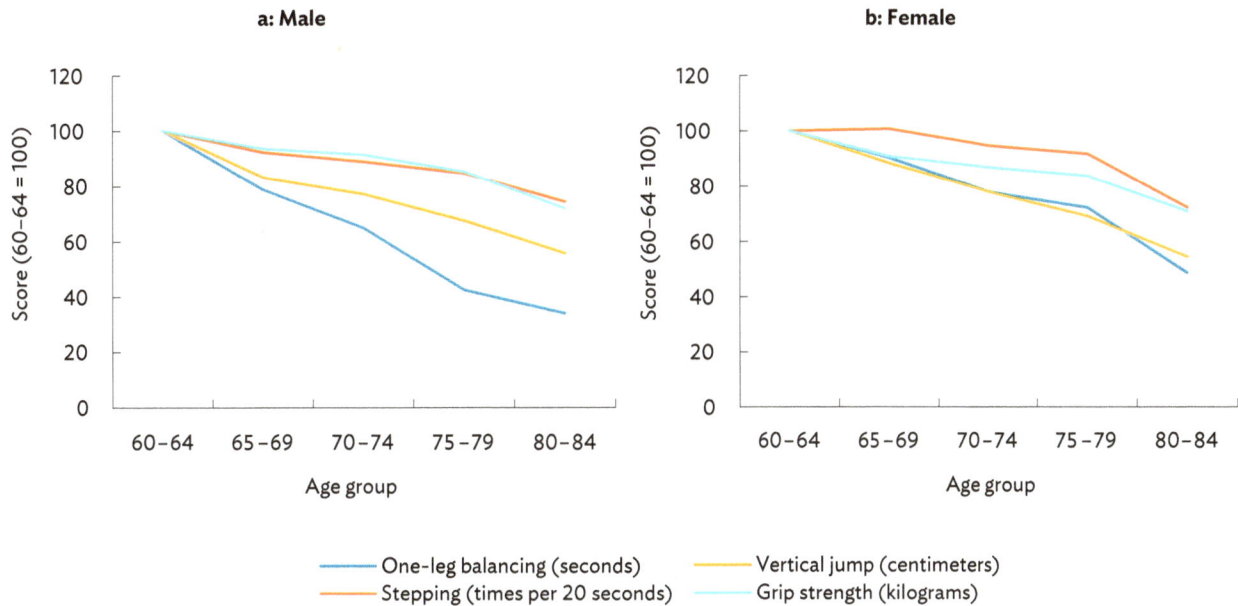

Notes: Scores are obtained from a battery of fitness tests including one-leg balancing, stepping, vertical jump, and grip strength performed by 900 Japanese volunteers aged 60 and above. For illustration purposes, calculated raw scores are transformed as index with the score of age group 60–64 equals 100.

Source: Kimura et al. (1989).

Figure 6.21: Cognitive Ability by Age Group Based on Psychometric Tests

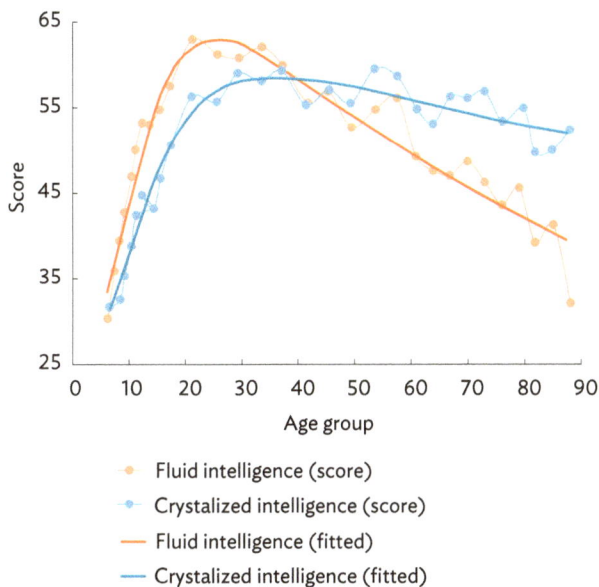

Notes: Scores are based on a battery of 15 psychometric tests from the Berlin Aging Study conducted to 356 participants aged 6–89 randomly drawn from a parent sample of 1,920 individuals provided by the Berlin City Registry. Fluid intelligence refers to the composite scores of psychometric tests involving (i) mental mapping, (ii) memory, and (iii) reasoning. Crystalized intelligence is a composite score of tests involving verbal knowledge and fluency. Higher scores indicate higher level of intellectual abilities.

Source: Li et al. (2004).

age, suggesting that the older population are more at risk to skills-related job disruptions (Figure 6.22). Even after controlling for factors that might overestimate differences across age, such as gender, education, and socioeconomic background, the skills gap between the prime age (25–44) and older (45–65) cohorts remains persistent (Paccagnella 2016).

Aging populations may adversely affect innovation and technology adoption of an economy.

As a society ages, the speed of innovation and technology adoption may decline (Weinburg 2004). It is often argued that a healthy share of the young population is favorable to innovation considering the longer investment horizon over their lifetimes, and characteristics relating to risk behavior, creativity, and interactivity (Derrien, Kecskes, and Nguyen 2018). Meyer (2007, 2011) and Wasiluk (2014) show that firms in Germany with a higher share of younger employees are more likely to adopt new technologies, while the older the workforce, the less likely it is that new technologies are adopted. One recent research

Figure 6.22: Literacy and Numeracy Skills by Age Group

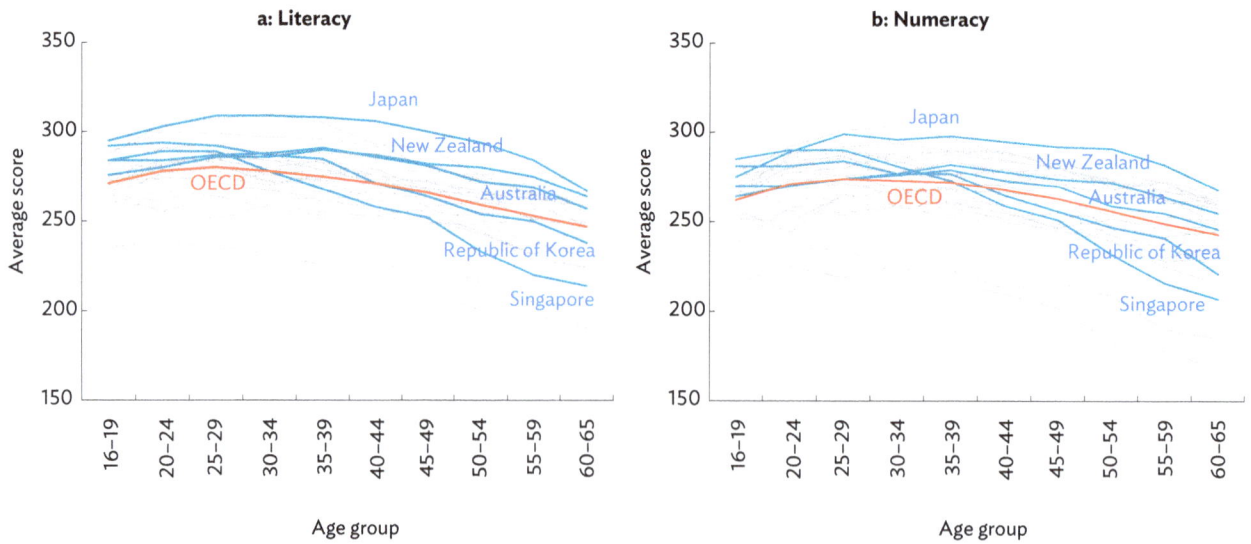

a: Literacy

b: Numeracy

OECD = Organisation for Economic Co-operation and Development.

Notes: Both scores are derived from the direct assessment of 5,000 respondent individuals age 16–65 in each participating country. Literacy evaluates adults' ability to read digital texts (e.g., texts containing hypertext and navigation features, such as scrolling or clicking on links) as well as traditional print-based texts. Numeracy evaluates the ability to use, apply, interpret, and communicate mathematical information and ideas.

Source: ADB calculations using data from Organisation for Economic Co-operation and Development. 2014–2015 Survey of Adult Skills of the Programme for the International Assessment of Adult Competencies. http://www.oecd.org/skills/piaac/data/ (accessed May 2019).

Figure 6.23: Walking Speed of Older Persons—Japan (meters per minute)

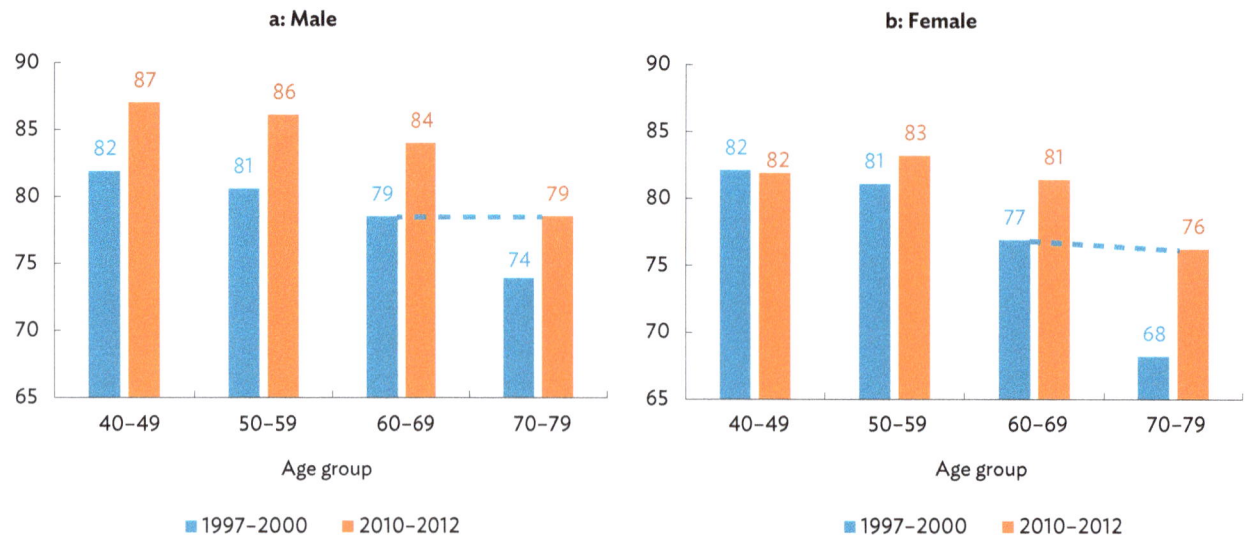

a: Male

b: Female

Source: ADB calculations using data from National Center for Geriatrics and Gerontology (Japan). http://www.ncgg.go.jp/cgss/english/department/nils-lsa/index.html (accessed July 2019).

points out that, in aging economies, innovation is depressed because young people lack opportunities to boost entrepreneurship. The chances for youth to learn and acquire business and management skills become slimmer in an aging society where older people linger in senior posts (Liang, Wang, and Lazear 2018).

But today's elderly are different from seniors in the past.

Longitudinal data in Japan suggests that elderly people today may be as much as 10 years younger in biological age as far as walking speed is concerned (Figure 6.23).

Healthy life spans among Asian economies have expanded 6.6 years from 57.2 in 1990 to 63.8 in 2017 (Figure 6.24). A comparative study that translates the improved health status of elderly people into their capacity for work shows that extended years of working life, among men of ages 55–69 can be as much as 8 years and 5.5 years on average among Organisation for Economic Co-operation and Development (OECD) countries, when comparing that cohort between 1977 and 2010 (Coile, Milligan, and Wise 2017).

Figure 6.24: Extension of Healthy Life Span in Asian Economies (number of years)

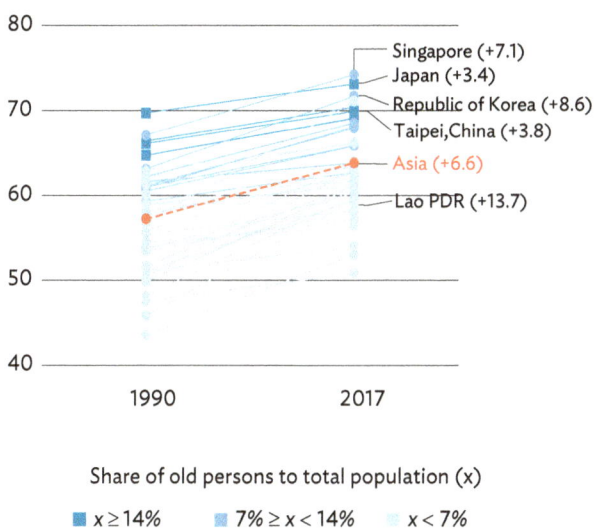

Singapore (+7.1)
Japan (+3.4)
Republic of Korea (+8.6)
Taipei,China (+3.8)
Asia (+6.6)
Lao PDR (+13.7)

Share of old persons to total population (x)

■ x ≥ 14%   ■ 7% ≥ x < 14%   ■ x < 7%

Lao PDR = Lao People's Democratic Republic.

Notes: Numbers in parentheses refer to the additional years of healthy life span from 1990 to 2017. The color gradient refers to the share to total population of people of ages 65 and above in 2019.

Source: GBD 2017 DALYs and HALE Collaborators (2018).

In addition to improvements in health, the extension in schooling years observed since 1980 (see Figure 6.17) makes today's new older cohorts better educated and therefore, more likely to be equipped with the foundational skills to learn new and emerging skills. Rapid improvement in the human capital of older groups presents an opportunity for society to revisit the conventional definition of "an old person," now

benchmarked at ages 65 or above. Box 6.3 discusses how to redefine and quantify the new "old" population.

Longevity and a longer working life will likely induce greater investment in education and skills acquisition among both the younger and older cohorts.

The returns from education are greater when working lives are longer (Bloom, Canning, and Sevilla 2003). Moreover, longer working lives mean skills acquired at a younger age will likely become obsolete at a later age, requiring more adult education and continuous learning. The rapid pace of technological change will also render many of current skills obsolete in the near future (ADB 2018).

Workforce aging can influence the firms' investment decision on the quantity and quality of complementary factors such as capital and resources.

Labor shortages and scarcity of prime age workers can prompt labor-saving capital investment, ultimately raising the productivity of older workers. In the PRC, firms with an aging or declining supply of workers due to the declining working age population are likely to adopt machinery and equipment that strengthen and complement human labor (Ge and Zhang 2019). In Japan's agriculture sector, manual and physical intensive tasks such as plowing, planting, harvesting, processing, and transferring are being automated, allowing old workers to remain in the fields. The average age of farmers in the country was 66.8 years in 2018.[54] Merging of information technology and artificial intelligence has led to further automation (smart agriculture) in the last few decades.

More generally, for countries in the advanced stage of aging, labor-saving (complementing) robots and artificial intelligence are increasingly being adopted. However, such phenomena may be more pronounced in specific

---

[54]   Data from the Government of Japan, Ministry of Agriculture, Forestry, and Fisheries. Agriculture and Forestry Census. http://www.maff.go.jp/j/tokei/sihyo/data/08.html (accessed July 2019).

Box 6.3: How Do We Define the "Old Age" Group?

There is a growing debate about how we define "old age" group. An individual is often classified "old" when he/ she turns the age of 65, just above the working age of 15 to 64. But when the new cohort of older adults are getting healthier, more educated, and less prone to severe age-related disabilities than the same cohort in the earlier periods, the use of a fixed benchmark to identify the old age group can be questioned.

Sanderson and Scherbov (2007) and Balachandran et al. (2017) bring light to this issue by defining "old" based on "prospective age" in lieu of the chronological age. Individuals should not be considered old just because he or she reached a certain number. Instead, the concept of old should evolve and shift as life expectancy extends and the physical and cognitive functions of older persons improve over time. Sanderson, Scherbov, and Gerland (2017) redefine the "old" applying the "prospective" concept, that is, based on the expected remaining years of life. Accordingly, old persons are those with the remaining life expectancy (RLE) of 15 years

or less, which was derived from the observed life expectancy at age 65 from low mortality countries in 1970. With sustained extension of life expectancy, the threshold age at which to consider individuals old will eventually move up over the years.

The Box Figure presents the population shares of "old" persons based on chronological and prospective age along with the threshold old-age in selected Asian economies. In 1970, old persons in the PRC, Sri Lanka, and Thailand are those at around aged 65 and above. In 2019, the threshold old-age increased to as high as 75 in Thailand, 73 in Sri Lanka, and 71 in the PRC. With relatively low life expectancy, 60-year-olds are considered old in Bangladesh in 1970, but improved to 71 in 2019. The share of the "old" to the total population based on prospective age are significantly smaller than what is expected using a fixed chronological age of 65. The charts suggest that countries that will successfully capitalize on longevity through encouraging older persons to remain active and stay employed may undergo a more gradual and possibly smoother transition towards aging society.

Redefining the Old

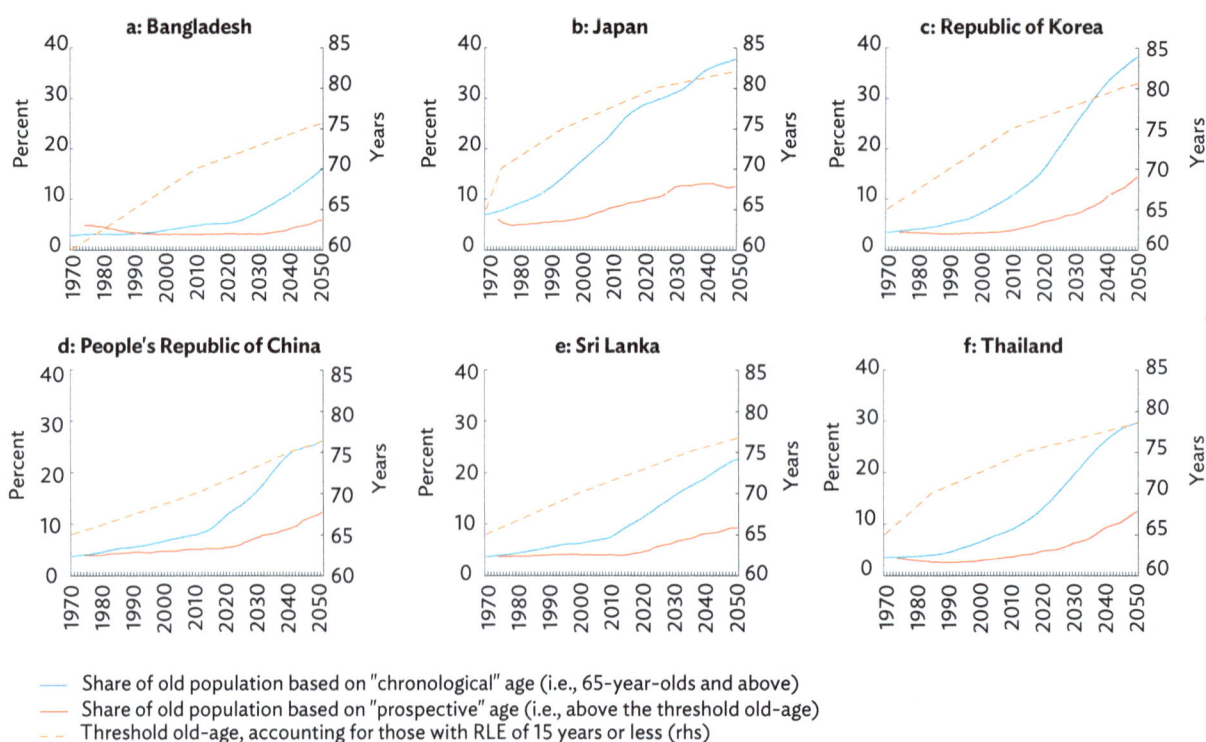

Share of old population based on "chronological" age (i.e., 65-year-olds and above)
Share of old population based on "prospective" age (i.e., above the threshold old-age)
Threshold old-age, accounting for those with RLE of 15 years or less (rhs)

RLE = remaining life expectancy

Note: Five-year data series on average remaining life expectancy by age group are used in the calculation, and the resulting share of redefined old is smoothed using 5-year moving averages.

Source: ADB calculations using data from United Nations Department of Economic and Social Affairs, Population Division. https://population.un.org/wpp/ Download/Standard/Population/ (accessed October 2019).

Sources: Balachandran, et al. (2017); Sanderson and Scherbov (2007); and Sanderson, Scherbov, and Gerland (2017).

industries (such as labor-intensive sectors) or in firms that increasingly rely on older workers, as the decline in saving rates and returns to capital associated with aging generally dampen economy-wide effects.

Population aging may incentivize firms to invest in technology adoption.

More innovation will arise to meet the needs of growing elderly consumers. Workforce aging (or contraction) may encourage firms to invest in innovative technologies that can boost the productivity of the scarce young workforce while accommodating a growing number of elderly workers (Hayami and Ruttan 1984).

Aging Effects on Economic Growth in Aggregate

If age and aging have both positive and negative effects on productivity by impacting the supply of labor, capital, and technology in production, what are the economy-wide net effects on productivity and growth in aggregate? The rich pool of macroeconomic literature presents mixed evidence.

A strand of existing macroeconomic literature finds that a growing elderly population slows down growth.

For example, Lindh and Malmberg (1999) use OECD country data from 1950 to 1990 and find that the increasing share of people of ages 65 and above reduces real per worker GDP growth. Similarly, Aiyar, Ebeke, and Shao (2016) find that growth in the share of workers of ages 55–64 reduces labor productivity growth in Europe. Using US data, Maestas, Mullen, and Powell (2016) find the same negative relationship between aging and state per capita output—a 10% increase in the population of ages 60 and above is associated with a 5.5% decline in the GDP per capita growth rate. Further decomposition analysis shows that only a third of this decline is attributable to a shrinking labor force, while the remaining two-thirds is explained by slower growth

of labor productivity. Table 6.1 summarizes related literature.

But another strand of literature notes the positive effect arising from a maturing workforce.

Feyrer (2007) found that a 5% increase in the age 40–49 cohort over 10 years is associated with a 1% to 2% increase in annual productivity over that period. In contrast, an increase in the younger age 15–39 cohort was associated with lower productivity. Results are mostly insignificant and mixed for the older age groups of 50 and above. Liu and Westlius (2017) also find, using prefectural data from Japan, that an increase in the age 40-49 cohort affects total factor productivity (TFP) positively. Where aging is still in progress and workforce growth is not occurring at the extreme end of the age distribution, having a greater share of the workforce in the resourceful, mid-career cohort boosts growth.

This mixed evidence may be partly explained by the fact that despite population aging, the projected demographic change will likely be accompanied by a stable share of workforce in some economies.

The growing share of older population will coincide with a period of continued expansion in the share of working age population if fertility falls rapidly in a short time span (Lee and Shin 2019). For example, the share of working age population in the Republic of Korea has expanded, though at a much slower rate, at the same time as the share of elderly to total population increases toward a more advanced stage of aging (Figure 6.25). This pattern can also be observed in other aging economies of Asia, such as the PRC, Bangladesh, Sri Lanka, Thailand, and Viet Nam. Under this scenario, countries will have at least some time (longer for some than others) to benefit from a healthy supply of economically active workers, even as the elderly population grows. These countries still have an opportunity for increased shares of these productive cohorts to propel economic growth and to make necessary adjustments before they decline.

Table 6.1: Aging and Productivity: A Literature Review

Study	Economy and Data Coverage	Productivity Indicator	Demographic or Aging Indicator	Main Results
Lindh and Malmberg (1999)	OECD economies 1950–1990	Real GDP per worker	Change in share to total population of the four age groups: 15–29, 30–49, 50–64, and 65 and above.	• Labor productivity growth declines as share to total population of people ages 65 and above rises. • A 1-percentage point increase in share to total population of ages 50–64 is associated with a 25 to 50 basis-point increase in labor productivity growth. • Labor productivity effects of rise in share of ages 15–29 and 30–49 are ambiguous.
Feyrer (2007)	87 economies 1960–1990	Real GDP per worker	Change in age composition of the labor force at 10-year age intervals: 10–19, 20–29, 30–39, 40–49 (benchmark group), 50–59, and 60–above.	• A 5% shift of 30–39 age group to 40–49 group is associated with 15% increase in labor productivity. • Labor productivity lowers as share of workforce ages 15–39 rises. • Insignificant and mixed results for the older age groups of 50–59 and 60–above.
Liu and Westlius (2017)	Japanese prefectures 1990–2007	Prefectural total factor productivity	Share to total working age population (ages 20–69) of 10-year age intervals: 20–29, 30–39, 40–49 (benchmark group), 50–59, and 60–69.	• The association of productivity and age follows an inverted U-shaped pattern, peaking at ages 40–49. • A 1-percentage point shift of people in their 30s to 40s increases total factor productivity by 4.4%. • Total factor productivity drops by 1.3% if people in their 40s get older to their 50s.
Maestas, Mullen, and Powell (2016)	US states 1980–2010	State level GDP per capita	Change in share of individuals ages 60 and above to the total population (considers only individuals aged 20 and above)	• A 10% increase in the share to state population of individuals aged 60 and above is associated with 5.5% (IV estimates) to 8.3% (OLS estimates) decline in state per capita GDP growth.
Aiyar, Ebeke, and Shao (2016)	EU28 economies 1950–2014	Real output per worker	Share to the total workforce of ages 55–64	• Labor productivity decreases as share of workers age 55–64 rises. • Main channel identified through which aging workforce dampens growth is lower total factor productivity growth.
Acemoglu and Restrepo (2018)	27 EU economies (19 industries) 1995–2007	Real value added per worker at the industry level	Change in the ratio of workers age above 56 to workers of ages between 21 and 55 from 1990 to 2025.	• A 10-percentage point increase in aging is associated with a 14.5%–17.3% decline in value added per worker. • Adoption of automation technologies helps industries gain higher productivity in the face of aging workforce.
Liang, Wang, and Lazear (2018)	57 economies (31 non-OECD) 2001–2010	Entrepreneurship rate	(i) Cohort shrink rate (derived by relating the size of ages 45 to another cohort), and (ii) Median age (20–64)	• Aging slows entrepreneurship when older workers limit skills acquisition among younger workers. • One standard deviation decrease in median age increases new business formation by 2.5 percentage points.

EU = European Union, GDP = gross domestic product, IV = instrumental variable, OECD = Organisation for Economic Co-operation and Development, OLS = ordinary least squares, US = United States.

Source: ADB compilation.

Figure 6.25: Population and Dependency Ratios—Selected Asian Economies (%)

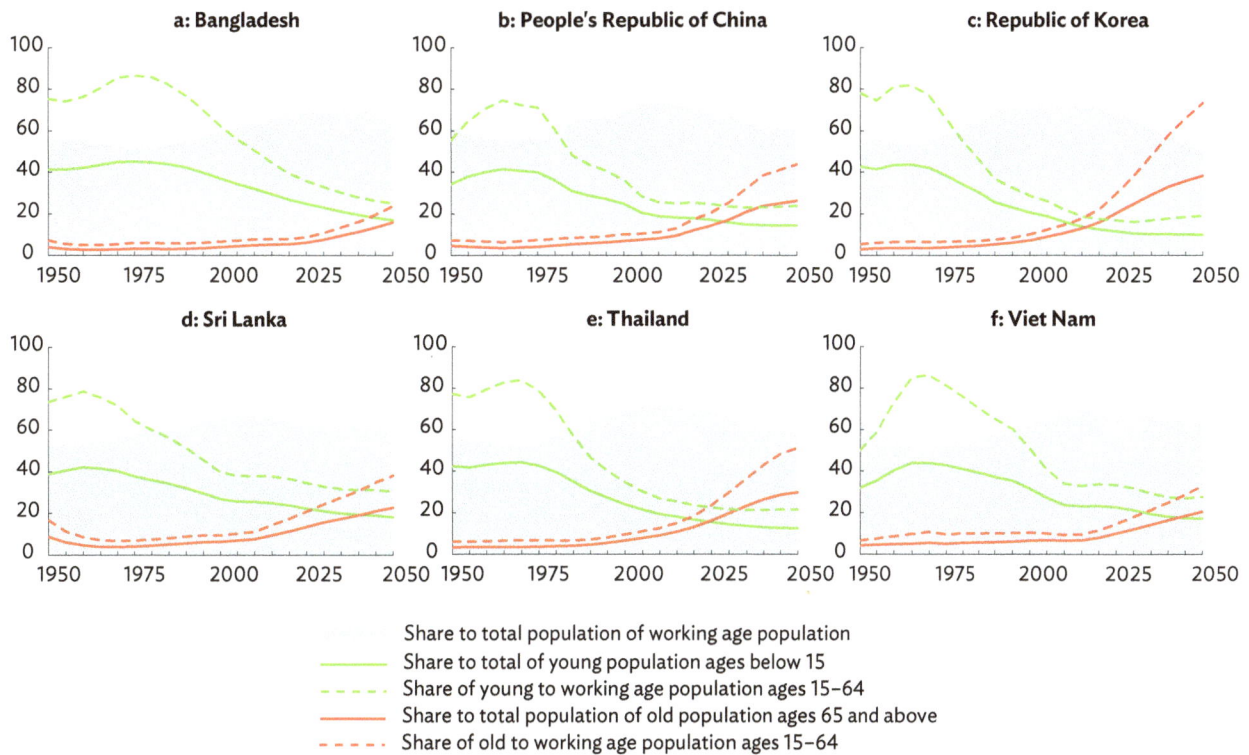

a: Bangladesh
b: People's Republic of China
c: Republic of Korea
d: Sri Lanka
e: Thailand
f: Viet Nam

Share to total population of working age population
—— Share to total of young population ages below 15
---- Share of young to working age population ages 15–64
—— Share to total population of old population ages 65 and above
---- Share of old to working age population ages 15–64

Source: ADB calculations using data from United Nations Department of Economic and Social Affairs, Population Division. Population Database. https://population. un.org/wpp/Download/Standard/Population/ (accessed June 2019).

In addition, recent literature offers new insight into how technology can alter the ways population aging affects productivity.

Recent literature argues that the relative scarcity of a productive age workforce can prompt technological innovation and adoption that sustains productivity growth. Figure 6.26 suggests that the growing share of more mature workers (ages 50–74) relative to younger workers (ages 25–49) during the past decade is accompanied by increasing use of industrial robots in manufacturing.

Acemoglu and Restrepo (2018) claim that population aging can promote productivity growth by encouraging more active adoption of robot technology. Theoretical and empirical evidence shows that aging leads to more intensive use and development of robots. Using US data, they find that robots substitute for middle-aged workers

Figure 6.26: Workforce Aging and Industrial Robot Adoption, 2007–2017

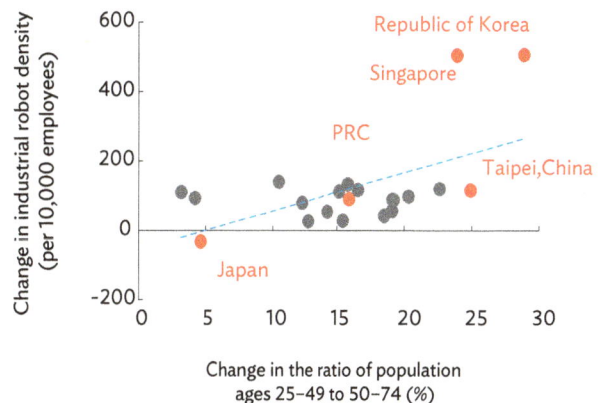

PRC = People's Republic of China

Note: Red dots refer to Asian economies with available data; gray dots to non-Asian economies.

Sources: International Federation of Robotics. Statistics. https://ifr.org (accessed July 2019); and United Nations Department of Economic and Social Affairs, Population Division. https://population.un.org/wpp/Download/Standard/ Population/ (both accessed June 2019).

while industries amenable to automation witness rising productivity. Abeliansky and Prettner (2017) provide a theoretical model that predicts countries with low population growth will introduce automation technologies earlier than those with high population growth, with supporting empirical evidence from 60 countries over 1993–2013. They find that a percentage-point increase in population growth is associated with a 2% reduction in the growth of robot density. In a study of robot adoption in 17 countries from 1993 to 2007, Graetz and Michaels (2018) find that increased robot use contributes to labor productivity and TFP and lowers output prices. Aiyar, Ebeke, and Shao (2016) find that government investment in research and development offsets the negative effect of a percentage-point increase in workforce aging by about 0.35 percentage points (i.e., from a roughly 0.7 decrease in TFP growth).

The Age Cohort Effects on Growth

Population aging can trigger a mixture of positive and negative impacts on growth depending on the stage of aging and the age distribution of the population.

Following the estimating equation from Fair and Dominguez (1991) using the whole age-distribution of the population of a country as a regressor, relative age group contribution to per capita GDP growth is derived from a panel of 170 countries in years 1965–2015 (Annex 6a details the methodology based on Park, Shin, and Kikkawa 2019b).

Figure 6.27 illustrates the estimated relative contribution of different age groups to per capita GDP growth. The results suggest that the increase in the share of the age cohorts of 10 to 54 push up a country's economic growth, with incremental contribution plateauing at 25–34 age brackets. The contribution to growth then slows down and becomes negative for cohorts of ages 55 and above. Overall, a change in age distribution that increases the elderly population and decreases the working age population is expected to dampen economic growth. In this estimation, expansion of age cohorts below age 10 will also have negative impact on

Figure 6.27: Relative Contribution to Per Capita GDP Growth by Age Cohorts

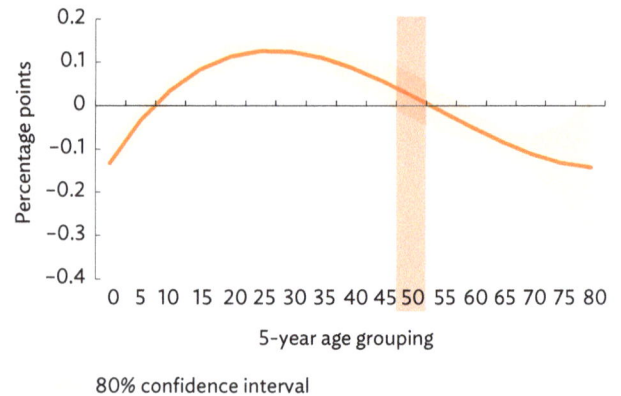

80% confidence interval

GDP = gross domestic product.

Notes: Derived from the fixed effects estimates (see Annex 6a for details on the methodology). In the horizontal axis, 0 represents the age group (0,4), 5 represents the age group (5,9) and so on. Shaded area in red represents the threshold old-age cohort that positively contributes to growth.

Source: Park, Shin, and Kikkawa (2019b).

growth. This implies that with a sharp fall in fertility, the effects aging will have on growth can be positive at the early stage. The inverted U-shape relationship between age cohorts and growth mirrors that of worker's age and productivity presented in earlier section.

Can Technology Mitigate the Effect of Aging on Growth?

Simulation analysis shows that technology helps extend productive contributions of older workers.

An extended version of the above analysis is used to examine whether the degree of technological adoption in a country alters the way population aging affects economic growth. Two proxies for technological progress are used: life expectancy, which extends with the advances in medical sciences and biotechnology, and the level of TFP, reflecting the degree of technological adoption. Each of these variables are interacted with aging indicators to evaluate if they can help mitigate the negative effects of population aging.

Figure 6.28 shows the relative contribution of different age cohorts to growth under two scenarios: low life

Figure 6.28: Relative Contribution to Per Capita GDP Growth by Age Cohorts with Interactions: Life Expectancy

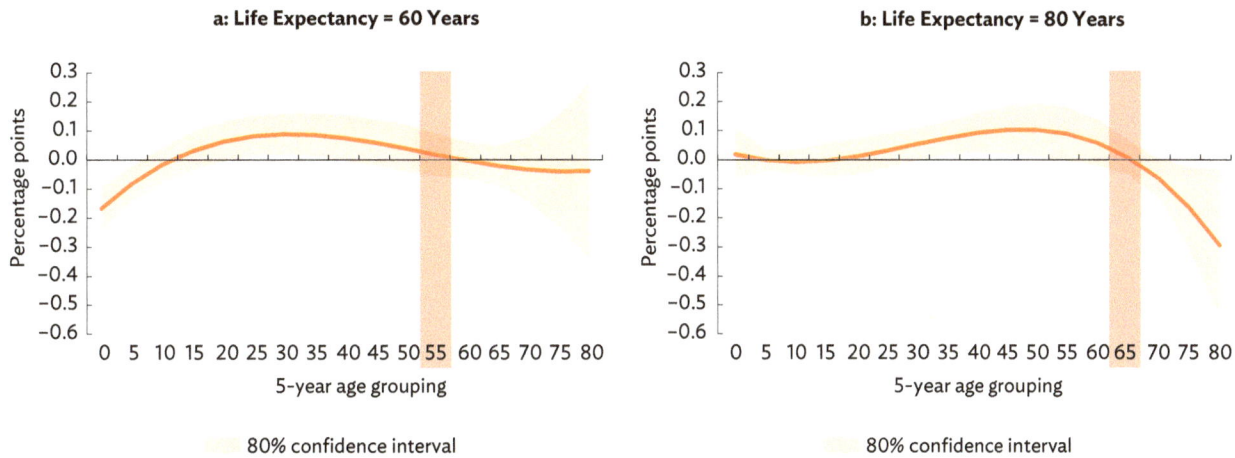

GDP = gross domestic product.

Notes: Derived from the fixed effects estimates (see Annex 6a for details on the methodology). In the horizontal axis, 0 represents the age group (0,4), 5 represents the age group (5,9) and so on. Shaded area in red represents the threshold old-age cohort that positively contributes to growth.

Source: Park, Shin, and Kikkawa (2019b).

expectancy of 60 years and high life expectancy of 80 years. The contributions to growth across the range of age cohorts in both cases show an inverted U-shape. But under the low life expectancy scenario, the productive cohorts are between ages 15 and the late 50s while an extension of life expectancy to 80 years shifts the curve further to the right, generating a positive contribution of workers as old as those in the 65–69 age group. In addition, growth contribution stays positive for old workers until their early 60s under the extended life expectancy compared with a negative contribution to growth by workers of age 55 and above in the shorter life expectancy scenario. In other words, the extension of healthy life span and longer working life will allow countries with growing shares of relatively older cohorts in their 60s to maintain growth.

The degree of technological adoption of a country proxied by TFP also seems to affect the relative contributions to growth by different age cohorts (Figure 6.29). Comparing the scenarios between low TFP (in log) at −0.5 and high TFP at 0.5, the difference is visible in the growth contribution of the age group between the 30s to the 60s. A percentage increase in the share of these age cohorts can boost their contributions to growth up to 20 times larger in high technology

adoption scenario than in low adoption case. Like the case of life expectancy, the high TFP scenario extends the productive years by 5 years. Interestingly, in the high TFP scenario, the age threshold for one to make positive contribution to growth will also be raised. This implies that more years of education would be needed for the youth to be productive in such scenario.

Country Case Studies and Policy Implications

Whether technology adoption mitigates the negative consequences of population aging depends on factors such as labor intensity of industry, types of technologies, private sector responses, and policy environment.

Country-specific cases from the Republic of Korea, Japan, and the PRC suggest more granular interplays between aging, technology adoption, and productivity (Ge and Zhang 2019; Kawaguchi and Muroga 2019; and Park, Shin, and Kikkawa 2019b). Whether and how technology adoption helps sustain growth amid an aging population depend, among other factors, on (i) specific characteristics of the industry such as the labor intensity of the sector, (ii) the types of technologies to be

Figure 6.29: Relative Contribution to Per Capita GDP Growth by Age Cohorts with Interactions: TFP

a: TFP (expressed in logs) = -0.5

b: TFP (expressed in logs) = 0.5

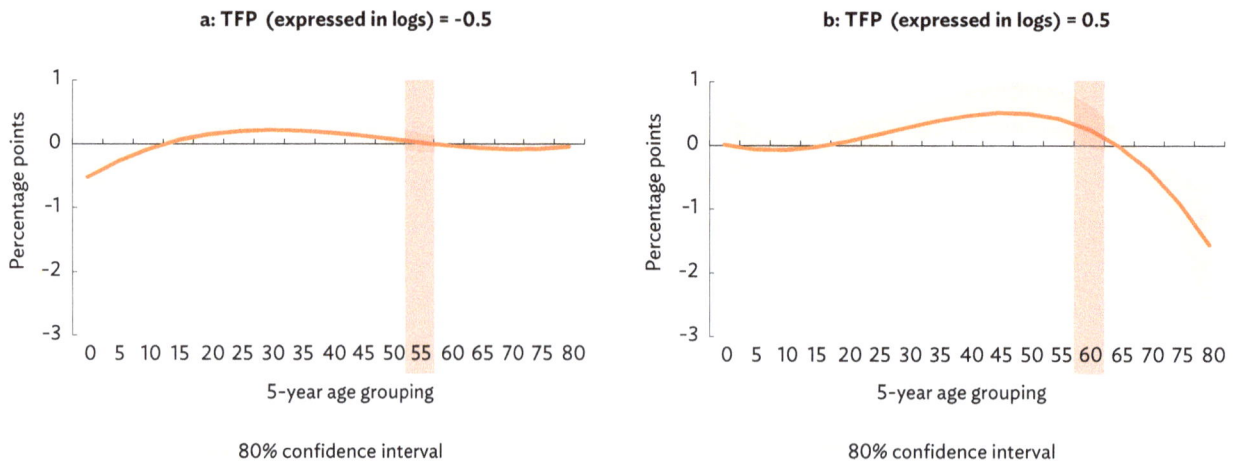

80% confidence interval

80% confidence interval

GDP = gross domestic product, TFP = total factor productivity.

Notes: Derived from the fixed effects estimates (see Annex 6b for details on the methodology). In the horizontal axis, 0 represents the age group (0,4), 5 represents the age group (5,9) and so on. Shaded area in red represents the threshold old-age cohort that positively contributes to growth.

Source: Park, Shin, and Kikkawa (2019b).

adopted, (iii) responses from the private sector, and (iv) the policy environment. Box 6.4 summarizes the main findings of the three case studies.

In the Republic of Korea, the relatively high labor intensity in textiles and construction enables these sectors to benefit from robot adoption by boosting the productivity of older workers. In the PRC, aging-induced technology adoption is evident only in labor-intensive sectors, not in capital-intensive ones.

Adoption of industrial robots helps improve the productivity of older workers in selected industries in the Republic of Korea, but that effect is not significant in Japan and the PRC. Interestingly, the mitigating role of technology on aging-induced productivity slowdown holds true in the PRC among relatively low-tech capital, such as machinery and equipment and also in research and development (R&D) expenditures. In Japan, the adoption of information and communication technology equipment showed a very small but significant association with the degree of workforce aging.

Varying firm responses also influence the mitigating role of technology adoption. Industries dependent on older workers react differently: they may either install industrial and service robots or move operation to countries with relatively young population. In Japan, the latter case possibly explains why the intensive technology adoption is not met with an equivalent increase in domestic productivity. Data show that Japan's robot exports are growing and are reportedly shipped to overseas manufacturing plants of Japanese companies in developing countries.

The policy environment shaping labor market conditions and technology adoption also matter if countries want to capitalize on technology's potential to mitigate the aging effect. The case of the Republic of Korea suggests how labor market rigidities partly explain the rapid adoption of automation and robots in some industries. These rigidities also seem to explain why some industries are unable to capitalize on certain technologies.

Box 6.4: Technology Adoption and Its Implications on Economic Growth in Aging Asia: Case Studies for Japan, the People's Republic of China, and the Republic of Korea

Using firm or industry-level data of Japan, the Republic of Korea, and the People's Republic of China (PRC), country-specific case studies attempted to answer the following questions (see Annex 6b summarizing the data and methodology):

- What is the effect of aging on productivity growth?
- What is the effect of aging on technology adoption?
- What is the effect of aging and technology adoption on productivity growth?

Republic of Korea

Using industry-level information on productivity (from the Bank of Korea and Korea Productivity Center) and robot adoption (from the International Federation of Robotics dataset), Park, Shin, and Kikkawa (2019a) find that aging is negatively associated with labor productivity or TFP growth. Evidence also points that the mitigating role of robot technology adoption applies strongly on labor-intensive or non-automobile industries. Further, results show how labor market rigidity can limit the interplay anticipated between technology adoption, the age distribution of the workforce, and productivity.

The study finds no evidence that robots are more heavily adopted in industries with an older workforce. While robot technology does not directly contribute to higher productivity growth, findings suggest that robot adoption can alleviate the negative impact of aging by reducing the adverse impacts on productivity growth from workers in their fifties and sixties, possibly by complementing their abilities.

Japan

Using the Japan Industrial Productivity database to capture labor productivity and the Cabinet Office's Survey of Orders Received for Machinery to capture technology adoption, Kawaguchi and Muroga (2019) find that an aging workforce is negatively associated with labor productivity growth—a

10% increase in the older workforce is associated with a 3% reduction in labor productivity growth. The study also finds no association between an aging workforce and industrial robot purchases, indicating that an aging workforce does not promote industry-wide technology adoption. Although the purchase of electronic machines is positively associated in a statistically significant way, the magnitude is limited.

Interestingly, the study finds no evidence of the mitigating role of technology adoption (proxied by shipments of industrial robots or computers) in Japan despite the country being at the forefront of robot technology and population aging. One possible explanation, which deserves more empirical inquiry, is the influence of Japanese companies' active foreign direct investment, especially the relocation of production sites in neighboring Asian countries with ample young and cost-efficient labor and growing market. Growth of robot exports are anecdotally destined to Japanese-owned plants located in Asian countries.

People's Republic of China

Using the Annual Survey of Industrial Firms and population censuses, Ge and Zhang (2019) find positive effect of population aging on GDP per capita, possibly capturing the benefit of the increased share of mature and experienced workers. Considering the extremely low density of robot use in many industries and minute cross-industry variation in aging, the study could not identify any relationship between adoption of robotics and population aging in the PRC.

Using firm-level capital–labor ratio and research and development (R&D) spending to capture technology adoption, the study finds systematic evidence that population aging has significant and sizable positive effects on firm-level economic outcomes. Evidence also indicates that technology adoption in the form of increases in capital–labor ratio and R&D investment offset the potential negative effects of population aging on productivity.

Sources: Ge and Zhang (2019); Kawaguchi and Muroga (2019); and Park, Shin, and Kikkawa (2019a).

Technology Options for Graying Asia

Technology could play a key role in sustaining productivity growth amid population aging by enabling countries and firms to mitigate the challenges posed by a shrinking and aging workforce. Technologies historically

have been labor-saving and making production more efficient, but recent studies also point to population aging as a factor inducing the adoption of new and advanced technologies. These "age-conducive" technologies can be broadly classified into five categories—technologies that (i) substitute labor and skills; (ii) complement labor and skills; (iii) aid education, skills development, and lifelong learning; (iv) improve matching workers with jobs and tasks; and (v) extend life and healthy life expectancy. This section provides in-depth, real-world examples of technologies under each category and examines their contribution to productivity and growth.

Interactions of Technology with Aging

Aging population induces technology adoption, which enhances capital accumulation and productivity.

Growing literature since the seminal work of Abeliansky and Prettner (2017) and Acemoglu and Restrepo (2017, 2018) incorporate workforce aging as an endogenous factor in directing technological changes (Figure 6.30). An aging population induces technology adoption, which in turn improves human and physical capital efficiency and productivity—and therefore future economic growth.[55]

Five Ways Technology Enhances Productivity

There are a wide range of technologies that can enhance productivity of labor and capital amid population and workforce aging. These can be classified into five groups based on its purposes.

Tech Group 1 addresses a shrinking workforce by substituting labor and skills with automation capital to save on labor inputs and reduce human error (Figure 6.31). These are supported by key innovations such as artificial intelligence (AI) or internet connectivity that boosts productivity of existing capital in many businesses. *Tech Group 2* can complement labor and skills by providing tools and platforms to perform tasks more efficiently, as exemplified by physical augmentation, remote office, and online collaboration tools. *Tech Group 3* includes online learning platforms and communities, which improve human capital by

Figure 6.30: Framework on Aging and Growth

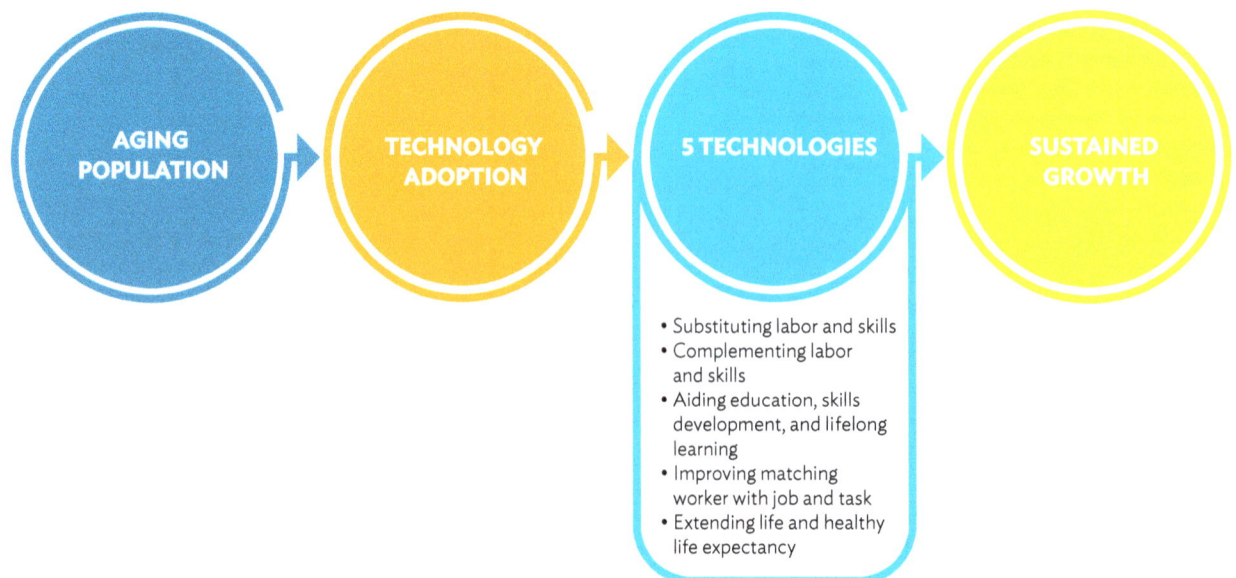

- Substituting labor and skills
- Complementing labor and skills
- Aiding education, skills development, and lifelong learning
- Improving matching worker with job and task
- Extending life and healthy life expectancy

Source: Asian Development Bank, expanding the framework of Acemoglu and Restrepo (2018).

[55] More precisely, Acemoglu and Restrepo (2018) states that productivity growth is expected in industries where the involved tasks and the age profile of the workforce is amenable to automation.

Figure 6.31: Ways Technology Enhances Factors of Productivity

1

TECH SUBSTITUTING
LABOR AND SKILLS

- Automation
- Industrial and service robots
- Robotic process automation

2

TECH COMPLEMENTING
LABOR AND SKILLS

- Physical augmentation
- Virtual office and remote work
- Collaboration tools

3

TECH AIDING EDUCATION,
SKILLS DEVELOPMENT, AND
LIFELONG LEARNING

- Online learning courses
- Education management systems
- Lifelong learning platforms

4

TECH IMPROVING MATCHING
WORKER WITH JOB AND TASK

- Job portals
- Social networking job or career sites
- Cloud platform for specific tasks
- Career guidance

5

TECH EXTENDING LIFE AND
HEALTHY LIFE EXPECTANCY

- Digital therapeutics
- Remote patient monitoring
- Bioinformatics

Source: Asian Development Bank.

facilitating education and skills development and promoting lifelong learning. *Tech Group 4* uses Big Data algorithms to improve the match between workers and jobs or tasks. *Tech Group 5* are devices and advances in health and medical science that contribute to extending longevity and healthy life spans.

The first group of technologies, exemplified by AI-powered industrial and service robots, can minimize the input requirement for scarce labor and skills and help sustain productivity.

Technologies that save on scarce labor bring substantial benefits where the workforce is contracting and aging. Emerging automation technologies such as industrial robots help substitute labor not only for physical and routine tasks but also for the types of works that involve cognitive tasks thanks to the advancement in AI and the applications tools (Box 6.5).

Industrial and Service Robots

Robot adoption is high among aging economies in the region, contributing to increased productivity by automating tasks and allowing workers to concentrate on tasks that require human presence and intelligence.

Automation of production and service provision is an essential solution for countries and firms facing a contracting and aging workforce, and an industrial robot[56] is one of the most sophisticated forms of automation capital. Aging Asia, as the supply chain hub of the world, has the largest number of industrial robots at 262,000 units as of 2017 (equivalent to 70% of world's total), and

---

[56]   The definition of industrial robots as per International Federation of Robotics (IFR), based on the International Organization for Standardization (ISO), is an "automatically controlled, reprogrammable multipurpose manipulator programmable in three or more axes."

Box 6.5: Artificial Intelligence and Its Application in the Workplace

Artificial intelligence (AI) is the ability of computers or computer-controlled robots to simulate intelligent human behavior, which includes the ability to adapt to changing circumstances (Marr 2018). AI is a versatile technology that is adopted in all five types of "age-conducive" technologies to automate business processes and boosts workforce productivity. Generally, the use of AI in routine tasks allows a company to focus on other success drivers, such as creativity and collaboration.

Office tasks, such as information gathering, analysis, and reporting processing are increasingly being automated through robotics process automation (RPA), which uses software with AI and machine learning capabilities. RPA automates repetitive human tasks, thereby reducing human error, increasing efficiency, and freeing employee time for higher-value work (IBM). Deloitte's global survey of organizations that use RPA showed improved compliance (92%), improved quality or accuracy (90%), improved productivity (86%), and reduced costs (59%) (Wright, Witherick, and Gordeeva 2018). The data also showed that returns on RPA investment can be seen in less than a

year and average to an additional 20% full-time equivalent capacity. Other major applications of AI at the workplace include image recognition and language translation or processing (e.g., chatbots).

For agriculture and aquaculture, AI use has had a significant impact on productivity. AI is used to make predictions about the environment, determining the best times to harvest, fertilize, and irrigate using sensors that gather vital farming information such as soil moisture, leaf wetness, light, wind, and rain (Ho 2018). In Asia, these technologies are timely, considering the rising average age of farmers.

Autonomous vehicles, another key application of AI, provide the mobility that most seniors need by enabling them to visit family, meet friends, or continue working (see Box 6.8). Lastly, in industries such as manufacturing, where older workers accumulate skills and precision, AI can facilitate the transfer of advanced skills from experienced older workers to younger ones by offering mentorship and apprenticeship programs (Schwartz et al. 2018).

Sources: Ho (2018); IBM. What is Big Data Analytics? https://www.ibm.com/analytics/hadoop/big-data-analytics (accessed July 2019); Marr (2018); Schwartz et al. (2018); and Wright, Witherick, and Gordeeva (2018).

is expected to grow further to 463,000 units by 2021.[57] The PRC tops with 137,900 units in 2017, followed by Japan (45,600 units), and the Republic of Korea (39,700 units)(Figure 6.32). In robot density (i.e., for every 10,000 employees), the Republic of Korea leads the region with 710 units, while Singapore has 658 units.

The economic benefit of robot adoption is large. Arbulu et al. (2018) estimate productivity gains of 10% to 50% amid adoption of robots in six countries of the Association of Southeast Asian Nations: Indonesia, Malaysia, the Philippines, Singapore, Thailand, and Viet Nam.[58] Overall equipment effectiveness, the standard in measuring manufacturing productivity which accounts for quality (i.e., good parts), performance (i.e.,

as fast as possible), and availability (i.e., no stop time), increased by 10% to 20%. Huge gains can be expected in electronics, chemicals (including oil and gas, and mining), consumer goods, food, and pharmaceuticals through reduction in equipment downtime, improvement in equipment lifetime, and reduced maintenance costs leading to quality products.

Service robots[59] are revolutionizing business processing, construction, and care facilities.

Equipped with AI and other innovations such as mobile technologies, Global Positioning System (GPS), and improved computer processing power, service robots

---

[57] As shown in Figure 6.26, the intensity of robot installation is high in the economies with a rapidly aging workforce.

[58] These gains were across five of the largest manufacturing industries: (i) electronics; (ii) chemicals, oil and gas, and mining; (iii) consumer goods; (iv) food; and (v) pharmaceuticals.

[59] A service robot defined based on ISO is a robot "that performs useful tasks for humans or equipment excluding industrial automation applications."

Figure 6.32: Robot Adoption in Selected Economies, 2017

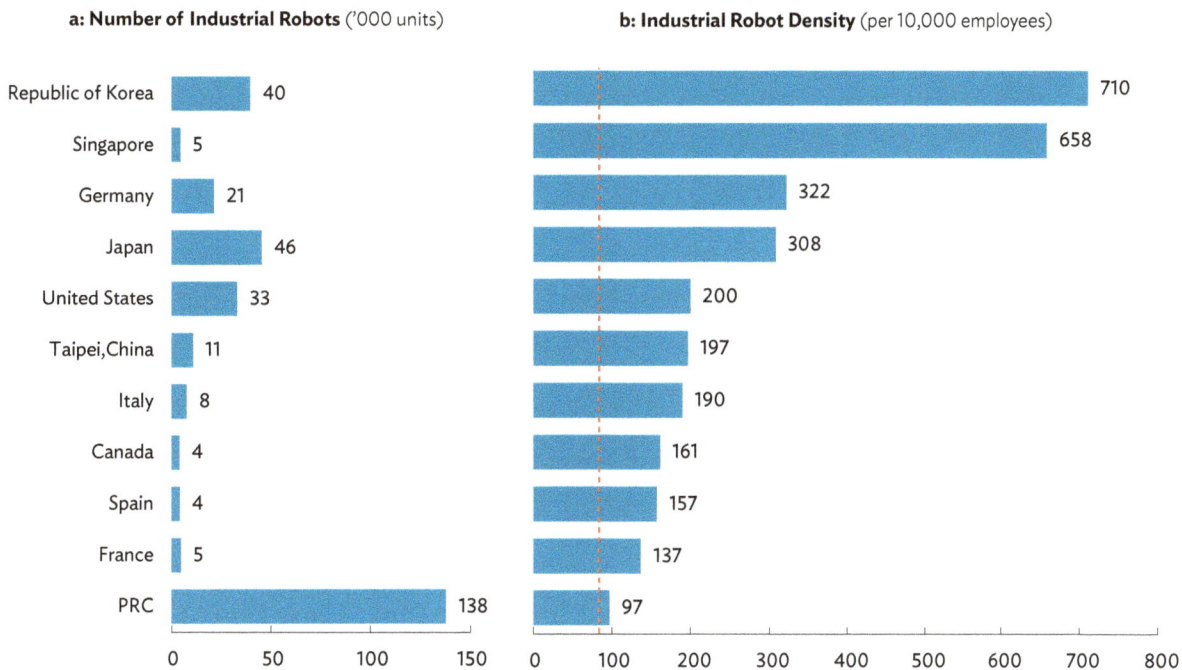

a: Number of Industrial Robots ('000 units)   **b: Industrial Robot Density** (per 10,000 employees)

Economy	Number ('000 units)	Density (per 10,000)
Republic of Korea	40	710
Singapore	5	658
Germany	21	322
Japan	46	308
United States	33	200
Taipei,China	11	197
Italy	8	190
Canada	4	161
Spain	4	157
France	5	137
PRC	138	97

PRC = People's Republic of China.

Note: Red dashed line refers to the world average of 85 installed industrial robots per 10,000 employees.

Source: International Federation of Robotics (2018).

perform highly sophisticated tasks. Japan's construction industry is one industry whose workforce is rapidly aging, and it is shifting gear toward increased adoption of robots not only to save on labor and reduce the physical intensity of task, but also to improve precision (Box 6.6). Robots are meeting some of the increasing demand for professional caregiving. Nursing homes in Japan are experimenting with different types of robots—from voice recognition systems to wearables and devices that reduce physically demanding tasks such as transferring and bathing. Socially assistive robots are found to improve elderly well-being such as positive emotions and an increase in social interactions (Matuszek 2017, and Kachouie et al. 2014).

The second group of technologies complements the application of labor and skills to improve productivity.

While the first technology group substitutes human labor, the second group are technologies that work side-by-side with workers, allowing them to stay in jobs and perform better, while at the same time assisting them in maintaining life-work balance.

Physical Augmentation

An aging workforce can remain productive with physical augmentation technologies aiding mobility and endurance.

Physical ability declines with age but technology can help older workers maintain their performance. Robotic exoskeletons are wearable electromechanical devices designed to enhance the physical ability of the user or provide locomotive support (Sirlantzis et al. 2019). One of the latest developments is an exoskeleton-type wearable robot designed to help with bending and stretching movements and give elderly people a natural walking experience by incorporating wire-type walking assistance technology. For example, HIMICO produced by ATOUN Inc. can provide as much as 30.7% assistance in rough terrain walking, 19% in hill walking, and 17.8% in stairs climbing (Panasonic 2018).

Box 6.6: Case Study of Japan's Shimizu Corporation's Adoption of Industrial Robots

One-third of Japan's construction workers are over the age of 54, and only around 10% are below 30. This construction labor pool is expected to decrease, especially with the 20% reduction of Japan's workforce from 2017 to 2040 projected by the Ministry of Health, Labour, and Welfare (Fleming 2019).

This is one of the major reasons why Shimizu, one of Japan's biggest construction companies, is increasing the number of robots on site. Shimizu has invested $179 million in construction robots from 2015, and it has reduced staffing needs for specific tasks by between 70% and 80%.

Shimizu Corporation (2018) tested three autonomous construction robots in the Shimizu Smart Site. These robots, specially designed for welding, ceiling installation, and transport, are equipped with artificial intelligence and building information modeling, allowing them to operate and decide on their own. They were designed to work with humans at a job site, reducing strenuous and repetitive tasks while increasing productivity. Trials show labor-savings

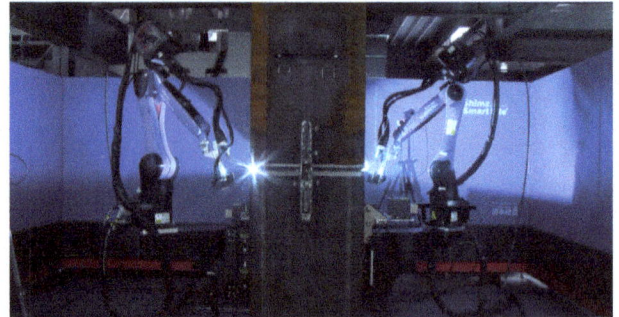

Coworking with autonomous robots. The robo-welder is among the three autonomous robots, equipped to operate on their own and work alongside people in Shimizu's Smart Sites (photo provided by Shimizu Corporation).

equivalent to 2,700 staff days on lifting and carrying, 2,100 days on ceiling and floor installation, and 1,150 days on column welding.

Sources: Fleming (2019) and Shimizu Corporation (2018).

Industrial exoskeletons and wearable robots also help workers meet agility and ergonomic requirements for specialized production tasks while minimizing physical injury. This feature is especially helpful for older workers more at risk of injuries during physical work. Box 6.7 summarizes the adoption of exoskeletons, especially in vehicles production, that reduces strain on overhead assembly tasks. Commonly known physical augmentation techniques such as prosthetics and bionics are introducing new features. For example, robotic gloves by Nuada help users who have lost control of hand movements to regain a strong grip, allowing them to pickup, carry, or maneuver heavy objects (Kolodny and Petrova 2017).

Remote Work Platforms

Technologies allowing workers to perform tasks remotely help retain older and younger talent.

Remote work platforms and cyber office space are gaining ground in the workplace by allowing tasks to be performed from a remote location, for example, from home or other sites away from an office. Telecommuting is a widely known working arrangement, replacing a traditional office commute with "commuting" by phone or computer (Reynolds 2018). It is often tagged as a business strategy to retain talented staff who may prefer flexibility. By cutting commuting time, remote work raises productivity as it creates more time to spend on productive tasks and encourages elderly people experiencing difficulty in commuting to continue using their skills.[60]

Remote work platforms include collaboration software, new teleconferencing technologies, and 5G-powered offices that make working in teams seamless. Telework/information and communication technology (ICT)-mobile work is largely being adopted in Europe and is used by 32% of employees in Sweden and 28% in Finland (Figure 6.33). In Asia, quite substantive shares are observed in India (19%) and Japan (16%).

---

[60]   For old workers facing challenges in commuting to work, the autonomous vehicle is a promising alternative to remote work (Box 6.8).

Box 6.7: Exoskeleton Use in Vehicle Manufacturing

Wearable robotics have been widely used by automotive companies and others—including BMW, Ford, and Hyundai— are using or testing exoskeletons. The main reasons automotive companies report for using exoskeletons are to improve efficiency and reduce or prevent work-related injuries.

Hyundai, the multinational auto manufacturing company from the Republic of Korea, developed two wearable industrial robots to be used in production. First, the Hyundai Chairless Exoskeleton (H-CEX) is a knee-joint protective device to help workers who sit for long periods and can withstand weight of up to 150 kilograms. The other is Hyundai Vest Exoskeleton (H-VEX), which adds 60 kilograms to the weight workers can lift, and so relieves pressure on their necks and backs.

Exoskeletons at work. Hyundai's Chairless Exoskeleton (H-CEX) is among the first to be used in car manufacturing, reducing strain on the workers (photo provided by Hyundai Motor Company).

Sources: Hyundai (2018) and Marinov (2019).

Figure 6.33: Rates of Telework or ICT-Mobile Work in Selected Countries (% of all workers)

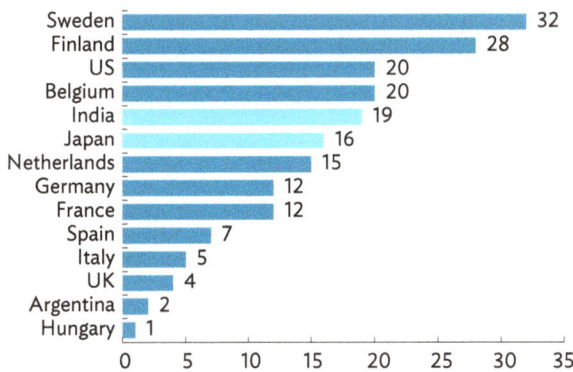

Sweden	32
Finland	28
US	20
Belgium	20
India	19
Japan	16
Netherlands	15
Germany	12
France	12
Spain	7
Italy	5
UK	4
Argentina	2
Hungary	1

ICT = information and communication technology, UK = United Kingdom, US = United States.

Notes: Telework or ICT-mobile work refers to work done outside the employer's premises in a variety of locations. Latest available data vary across countries: 2011 for Argentina, Belgium, and Spain; 2012 for France, Sweden, and the US; 2013 for Finland and Italy; 2014 for Germany, Hungary, Japan, and the Netherlands; and 2015 for India and the UK. Lighter blue bars refer to Asian economies.

Source: Eurofund and the International Labour Office (2017).

In the PRC, Ctrip, a 16,000-employee online travel agency saw productivity increase by as much as 30% when over half of its staff worked from home (Bloom et al. 2015). In an initial experiment where employees were randomly assigned to either work from home or continue in the office for 9 months, the former group performed 13% better, with more minutes per shift and more calls per minute. The group also exhibited a 50% lower attrition rate, suggestive of higher work satisfaction.

Collaboration Tools

A new generation of virtual offices is arriving with 5G technologies and facilitating better work collaboration.

The increasing preference for remote work requires interconnected devices ranging from e-mails and digital documents to more advanced technologies such as the internet of things and virtual and augmented reality to maintain collaborative efforts. The smooth transition to 5G, or fifth-generation, cellular wireless that has greater speed, lower latency, and allows more devices to be connected simultaneously, has a key role in achieving better synergies and synchronization (Segan 2019). In the Republic of Korea, SK Telecom, Samsung, and Cisco have collaborated to build 5G smart offices, that allows

Box 6.8: Autonomous Vehicles: Steering Technology in Favor of Seniors

The advancement of technology drove self-driven vehicles out of science fiction and into the streets in a matter of a decade. The development of autonomous vehicles is at the stage where the vehicle can manage all safety-critical functions under certain conditions, with driver taking over when alerted. Full automation, where the vehicle is completely capable of self-driving in every situation, is not expected until 2025.

The many benefits from using autonomous vehicles include improved traffic safety, convenience, and cheaper operation costs. For the elderly, autonomous vehicles provide a viable mobility option that may keep them economically active.

Japan, with its aging population, is experimenting with the idea in its rural communities, like Nishikata (Chakraborty 2017). In this community, a third of the population is age 65 and over, total population has contracted, and transport services are insufficient as the workforce has also shrunk. The experiment will use a driverless shuttle bus to take elderly passengers to hubs where medical, retail, and banking services are available. Should the trials succeed, self-driving services will be made available in 2020. It should be noted that other countries fully supporting this technology are those that are less populated and have orderly traffic, e.g., Australia, France, New Zealand, and Singapore.

Autonomous driving technology, however, is not for everyone. Aside from the prohibitive cost, densely populated countries with chaotic traffic situations will not find autonomous driving a viable transportation alternative. The adoption of autonomous vehicles will depend a lot on societies' need for such a solution, road readiness, and government backing through laws and infrastructure support.

Sources: Chakraborty (2017).

workers from different locations to hold meetings and watch visual materials altogether (Jun 2019).

Existing online collaboration tools range from e-mails and instant messaging, to working on documents simultaneously. Slack, with millions of users globally, is a well-integrated platform that allows users to collaborate between different departments of their company, to work with other companies, and to use other applications such as Asana for task assignments, or Dropbox for seamless file sharing. Slack lets users organize conversations, share files and documents, find archived information, integrate tools, and even talk face-to-face (Slack).

The third group of technologies builds professional and foundational skills by aiding education, skills development, and lifelong learning.

Exponential growth has occurred in technologies that build occupational and foundational skills through the use of devices (i.e., personal computers, smartphones, tablets, and Virtual Reality [VR] headsets) and online platforms, such as Coursera offering customized and interactive learning opportunities. Some of these technologies cater specifically for lifelong learning and for mature workers to update their skills (Kapoor 2019).

Online Professional Skills Learning

The rise of massive open online courses enable learners, including older workers, to access customizable and often free education from leading educational providers and institutions.

The United States (US)-based Coursera offers more than 2,700 courses from over 150 university partners, allowing over 35 million learners from 200 countries to create a curriculum tailored to their schedules and career needs.[61] Coursera's Skills Graph links learners to contents they plan to learn using skill nodes from a library of skills. Based on Coursera's 2017 Learner Outcomes Survey, users of the platform, from students seeking to advance their education to professionals upskilling for their current or future jobs, reported benefits such as being able to start new careers, getting a pay raise, or completing credits toward a degree (Levin 2017). Other major international and English-based massive open online courses (MOOCs) include edX, Udemy, Khan Academy, and Udacity. In many Asian countries, MOOCs in the local language help connect learners to domestic and international online learning resources.

Access to skills development technologies in local communities is growing in developing Asia.

One of the most interesting large-scale educational technology efforts in the world is led by EkStep, a philanthropic effort in India that builds open source platforms for government use. These technologies enable developing content and tools locally (Box 6.9). This is particularly important as one of the main challenges in the use of ICT in remote, low-income communities is that most products, services, usage models, expertise, and research come from high-income contexts and environments, with languages that are not used by local learners, and not fit in the context of developing countries.

In the Philippines, the Technical Education and Skills Development Authority (TESDA) Online Program

---

Box 6.9: Skills Development Technologies in Developing Asia

Technologies have been increasing access to education in different ways—creating content available in local or native languages and creating learning experiences that can be accessed virtually.

EkStep is an open learning platform in India with over 34,000 resources about literacy and numeracy and can be accessed on smartphones or other mobile devices. Since it allows for crowd-sourced collaboration and the creation of learning content in multiple languages, EkStep significantly increases the reach of students across the country.

Virtual Reality and Augmented Reality (VR/AR) have been used in higher education for learning the human anatomy or medical training for surgery across most developed nations. In developing Asia, VR/AR for education is still in its infancy. In the Philippines, as of 2017, only 13% of schools have science laboratories. Haraya Labs, a science and technology education platform, fills this gap by making experiential

VR/AR for education. Haraya Labs enables Philippine schools without physical laboratories to access science and technology education through VR/AR laboratories (photo provided by Paolo Espiritu).

learning affordable and more accessible. It offers laboratories in subjects such as biology, physics, robotics, chemistry, and even aerospace engineering (Haraya Learning Innovations).

Sources: EkStep. https://ekstep.in/ (accessed July 2019); and Haraya Learning Innovations. https://haraya.xyz/ (accessed July 2019).

(TOP) is providing free online technical education to advance skills and increase the income potential of workers. Over a million Filipinos, in the Philippines and abroad, have accessed the 59 available online courses teaching business, ICT, and electronics-related skills. Among users, only 4.4% are ages 45 and over (Dumaua-Cabauatan et al. 2018). People in this age group, representing 12.6% of the total unemployed in January 2019, can be encouraged to use TOP to improve their employability.

Organizations are exploring Virtual Reality technologies to educate and train the workforce.

Krokos, Plaisant, and Varshney (2018) found improvement in memory recall upon using Virtual Reality (VR) instead of traditional computers. In the field of medicine, VR has been increasingly used for surgical training and assessment. Osso VR provides the platform, content, and tools to address the training gap for surgeons by providing objective assessments. A pilot study showed that surgeons trained using Osso VR performed twice as well as those who used traditional means.

Benefits are enhanced when online learning is combined with face-to-face learning.

Blended learning is an approach where students learn using electronic or online media and traditional face-to-face teaching. This is considered more effective than just face-to-face learning for problem-solving skills and for recalling facts. Blended and e-learning broadens teaching and learning by providing a venue to explain complex issues and retain student attention. Replacing some traditional classroom time with online interactive content helps reduce instruction costs, especially when curriculums are more standardized. It has grown in developed countries and is now gaining traction in developing countries. Box 6.10 goes over examples of blended and e-learning in India and Thailand.

Box 6.10: Education and Information and Communication Technology in India and Thailand

In India, the Tata Institute of Social Sciences and the Massachusetts Institute of Technology (MIT) together launched the Connected Learning Initiative (CLIx), a program which integrates technology to create new learning experiences, such as active learning for secondary school students. The international collaboration included working on pedagogy, teacher development, school systems, and course technology (MIT Open Learning 2018). CLIx provides access to interactive, hands-on learning experiences from English, science, and mathematics, to instilling professionalism and related values among young people, mostly from lower- to middle-income rural areas (MIT Open Learning 2016). From its launch in 2016, CLIx now offers 15 science, technology, engineering, math, and English courses, which are also available in Hindi and Telugu, to 460 schools, 2,000 teachers, and 35,000 students in 2017. It has also received a United Nations Educational, Scientific and Cultural Organization award for its use of information and communication technology in education.

With India short of over a million trained and qualified teachers in primary and secondary schools, Teacher Education through School-based Support (TESS)–India offers a solution through freely available and easily adaptable Open Educational Resources. These resources, aimed at pre- and in-service teachers, focus on a more learner-centered, inclusive, participatory, and engaging classroom pedagogy. TESS-India was initiated in 2012 across seven key states and has already reached over a million teachers and teacher educators (The Open University).

Social entrepreneurs are also active in distributing the promise of technology to all. Learn Education from Thailand is a social enterprise that uses innovative learning platforms to help teachers provide better quality education with technology. They similarly use blended learning, which involves integrated content, real-time assessments, and school implementation. As of 2016, they have reached 100 schools and 25,000 students, and achieved better performance in science and mathematics compared with the national average.

Sources: Learn Education. https://www.learneducation.co.th/ (accessed July 2019); MIT Open Learning (2016, 2018); TESS-India. http://www.tess-india.edu.in/ (accessed July 2019); and The Open University. Projects and Programmes: TESS-India. http://www.open.ac.uk/about/international-development/projects-and-programmes/tess-india. (accessed July 2019).

Education Management System

The delivery of education can be improved using technologies that monitor teaching and learning outcomes.

Formal education that builds foundational skills like literacy, numeracy, communication, and digital literacy is ever more important in preparing the youth and adult workforce for future jobs. Digital learning materials and devices, teacher training programs, communication tools between teacher or among classmates, and data-driven evaluation of education outcomes are all part of education management systems, rapidly introduced in schools, contributing to raising the quantity and quality of education.

The Republic of Korea has laid out an extensive program for building an information technology (IT)-based school management and learning system to foster digital skills from primary to higher education across 891 pilot schools throughout the country (Korean Education and Research Information Service). E-textbook access is being launched, together with the installment of a wide range of hard and soft infrastructure in those schools. Infrastructure includes internet connectivity, IT devices, learning materials and trainings for teachers, and students, and cyberspace that facilitates communication among students, teachers, and parents.

Integrating ICT in education management improves the accessibility of quality education in developing economies.

Using and integrating ICT in the teaching and learning process are becoming increasingly important to improve education quality. For example, Bridge International Academies has introduced a comprehensive technology-based education management system and succeeded in upgrading the quality of education, as suggested by improved scores from children in underserved and low-income communities. Bridge uses technology to upskill teachers with extensive and continuous training, and provides tools (for example, "teacher guides" with detailed and step-by-step instructions to deliver lesson

content for each subject) through teacher tablets, which can be also used to monitor both the teaching pace and students' progress.

Lifelong Learning

Education technology helps overcome constraints on pursuing lifelong learning.

Financial constraints – A segment of the elderly population is unable to afford training. Online learning courses and webinars such as MOOCs often offer free or cost-effective learning opportunities, eliminating both tuition and transportation costs. Many of these modules are easily accessible through mobile phones, tablets, television, or computers. Singapore allows its citizens to access over 1,000 courses at Udemy for free through its lifelong learning support program, SkillsFuture.

Time constraints – Finding time is a major constraint for adult learners faced with work and family obligations. MOOCs have become increasingly accessible and provide a wide array of self-learning courses that can be followed at a person's own pace. Still, some may be longer than necessary to meet the needs of adult and senior learners (Lee, Czaja, and Sharit 2009). This preference, along with cognitive decline over time, suggests a demand for succinct and specific courses using creative technologies. One example is Singapore's National Silver Academy (NSA), which developed short duration active e-learning courses and "bite-sized" 3-hour courses on employable fields such as finance, business, IT, and science, which seniors could complete quickly.

Motivation – Several technology-based strategies can be implemented with lifelong learning initiatives to retain seniors' motivation to learn. Learn@50+, a platform of the American Association of Retired Persons provides interactive workshops to improve elderly technology use, especially in searching for jobs. The United Kingdom's University of the Third Age utilizes social media to encourage seniors to pursue skills or courses they are interested in, and to engage other people with similar interests. Singapore's NSA has an Intergenerational Learning Programme (ILP), which matches the youth and seniors to facilitate knowledge sharing, such as learning how to use social media (NSA). Another strategy to motivate learning is to track and reward learnings. The Republic of Korea's National Institute of Lifelong Learning runs K-MOOC, which links the institute's online Academic Credit Bank Systems. The system tracks formal and nonformal learning experiences of citizens and converts these to certificates and equivalent degrees.

The fourth kind of technologies underpins a supportive labor market infrastructure by improving the matching of workers to jobs and tasks.

A range of emerging technologies are contributing to better functioning of labor markets by closing information asymmetry among workers, employers, and providers of skills training and education services. This includes online job portals and cloud-sourcing platforms, and they use big data and machine learning to better match workers to jobs and tasks to workers, including the older ones. Alongside these matching tools are technologies providing career counseling and guiding skills development.

Job Portals and Job Matching

Cyber job portals and social network sites match jobs with potential candidates.

For most jobseekers, acquiring the skillsets needed for specific types of jobs is not enough. They need information source and a strong social network that connects them to jobs. Online job portals and cloud-sourcing platforms are now using big data and machine learning to better match workers to jobs and tasks to workers. These services make finding jobs easier for older workers who possess special skills and experiences and prefer to work at specific times or hours.

The portal Indeed is one of the leading job sites in the world. It has over 250 million unique monthly visitors, over 120 million resumes, 500 million salary data points, and 9.8 jobs added per second. The website offers features such as company reviews from previous employees and salary trends for different positions and

locations. All types of companies post jobs on *Indeed*, from tech giants such as Amazon and Facebook to government agencies, including the US Army. SkyHive, a skills-based work matching and training platform, automates job searching for candidates by extrapolating skills based on their background, work experience, and other preferences, and matches them with opportunities that fit their skills (SkyHive 2018).

Job-matching technologies allow for efficiently screening thousands of applicants and help employers to directly reach the talent they need. AI and machine learning can aid gathering, extracting, and processing information from jobseekers such as skills and experience and help translate these into compatible opportunities, interviews, and hires (Strauss 2018). Such technologies allow firms to identify top candidates for a position then prompt companies to reach out to them (Box 6.11).

Given the infancy of the industry, independent evaluations of impacts on job-matching remain scant. Online job portals have been widely studied and have shown positive results. In Germany, results of a large-scale field experiment showed that individuals who had access to information, which included job search strategies, had increased employment and increased earnings by around 4% (Altmann et al. 2018).

Social Networking Career Sites

Digital technology makes networking easier, allowing jobseekers to expand their networks virtually.

Estimates show that in the US, 70% to 85% of jobs are found through networking (Harden 2016 and Adler 2016). LinkedIn, a social network for businesses and professionals, has over 630 million members across 200 countries, 30 million companies represented, 20 million job openings, 90,000 schools, and 35,000 skills listed (LinkedIn Newsroom). It allows employers to quickly identify potential candidates based on the skills they need, and for jobseekers to find jobs. Although these platforms are effective, it may be that more effort is needed to reach out to the older workforce. Pew Research Center found in a survey

Box 6.11: Digital Interviews and Artificial Intelligence-Powered Human Resources

In addition to simple video platforms such as Skype or Google Hangouts, artificial intelligence (AI) technologies have made possible interviewing hundreds of potential hires in a short time. These new hiring technologies eliminate transportation costs for both recruiter and potential employee, and reduce the time required to hire. These tools are particularly helpful for senior workers doing remote work and for those in charge of human resources, as they improve worker productivity and efficiency.

Several platforms offer advanced software that uses AI and machine learning for talent acquisition, which includes audio, text, on-demand, and live video interviewing. On-demand video interviews allow firms to choose or create questions, the format they prefer the answers to be in (i.e., audio, text, or video), set time limits for answering, and allow managers to skip to specific portions of the interview in evaluating candidates. Some platforms allow for video and feedback sharing, for panel evaluations. For candidates, especially those working fulltime, on-demand interviews allow them to select their interview schedule and not have to spend time traveling. Such platforms include Montage, HireVue, Interview Stream, and GreenJob Interview. Montage says that its platform to date has resulted in a 30% increase in recruiter efficiency, a 70% reduction in the interview-to-hire ratio for their clients, and 97% of candidates having felt better represented. HireVue assessments involve using AI to assess facial expressions and body language, and it has been used to filter up to 80% of candidates for Unilever, while being able to feedback in multiple languages, saving time for candidates and recruiters.

Sources: HireVue. Unilever + HireVue: Unilever Finds Top Talend Faster with HireVue Assessments. https://www.hirevue.com/customers/global-talent-acquisition-unilever-case-study (accessed July 2019); and Montage. https://www.montagetalent.com/ (accessed July 2019).

of online users in the US that among the one in four who used LinkedIn, 29% were ages 18 to 29, 33% were 30 to 49, 24% were 50 to 64, and just 9% were ages 65 and over (Smith and Anderson 2018). LinkedIn's personalized job recommendation system uses a machine learning framework in its candidate selection model, incorporating user data, and returns the top-ranked job recommendation results. This feature, in preliminary testing experiments, increased the engagement of LinkedIn users for underserved jobs by 6.5% (Kenthapadi, Le, and Venkataraman 2017).

Crowdsourcing Platforms

Online platforms in the sharing economy let individuals offer their skills, create businesses, and access clients and finance.

Elderly workers can take advantage of crowdsourcing platforms to market their skills as experts, take on flexible jobs, or create businesses. Different types of platforms cater to specific needs of a firm or an individual, and account for, among other attributes, the quality and number of responses needed and the preferred level of expertise (Deloitte LLP 2016). Freelance work, for example, is growing in different areas across Asia. In India, one of the fast-growing platforms involves the provision of home services. India-based UrbanClap links over 100,000 skilled workers in home maintenance and repair, beauty and wellness services, and even fitness and yoga instruction, to over 32 million customers (Sharma 2019). To ensure a smooth customer experience, UrbanClap uses AI and machine learning to gather historical data from professionals, assess their performance, and provide training needed. The module determines when a worker lags in skills, then sends alerts to make sure the training is completed before taking up a job (Team YourStory 2019). This feature is especially relevant for the older workers who need to update their skills given advances in their specializations. To make these task sourcing services available to the older workforce, it is important that the platform, including job search functions and training modules, are accessible to older workers and serve their needs. Box 6.12 examines job-matching systems for older workers in Japan.

Career Counseling and Guidance

Technology can also be leveraged to understand what skills employers need, tackling gaps and mismatches.

Box 6.12: A Cloud Job-Matching System for Elderly Workers in Japan

Negative perceptions of elderly workers make it harder for them to access employment. This tendency for unemployment perpetuates social isolation and financial problems. However, aging societies are increasingly recognizing the potential of healthy senior workers and are tapping them for simpler tasks through crowdsourcing.

Gathering Brisk Elderly in the Region (GBER), is a web application, accessible through personal computers, tablets, and smartphones, that matches tasks and jobs with active seniors in Japan. In addition to skills-based matching, GBER features calendar-based and location-based matching capabilities (Arita, Hiyama, and Hirose 2017). The platform,

supported by a groupware function, allows retired people to maintain good health and socialize by working on community-based projects with other seniors. In the area of Kashiwa, it has resulted in 2,300 job placements (University of Tokyo 2018).

A pilot study in Kashiwa of 92 users with an average age of 67, showed that GBER was easy to use even for seniors with limited information and communication technology experience and that it promoted their engagement in local activities (Arita, Hiyama, and Hirose 2017). Given its success, GBER will expand to other cities. Its developers also plan to implement a recommendation system that will evaluate the platform's skills-matching functions.

Sources: Arita, Hiyama, and Hirose (2017); GBER. http://gber.jp/ (accessed July 2019); and University of Tokyo (2018).

Workforce and prospective labor market entrants will benefit from having access to information on the types of skills potential employers need or the skills that fit their employment or earning prospects. However, it is more often the case that students and jobseekers depend on advice from parents and peers who may not have up-to-date information about particular careers (ADB 2019). Emerging technologies help solve that information asymmetry.

Big data analytics and AI help identify skills in demand using data from professional job portals, company, and government databases. Such information, along with analysis of emerging and dying occupations, helps to establish dynamic labor market intelligence systems that provide real-time labor market information, including for elderly jobseekers and the providers of education and training. AI-powered career guidance is becoming essential to extending working life, which requires workers to continually upskill and reskill to stay employed.

A career development platform in Singapore, JobKred, uses AI in providing digital career guidance, skills gap analysis, and training recommendations. Real-time labor market information from multiple sources, such as job boards, resume sites, and government sites helps their

AI to understand current demand for skills and jobs. Based on platforms such as this, students can be guided effectively to the careers of the future, while employees are given ideas about the skills they should develop to fit their companies' direction. The technology possesses promising benefits if applied more systematically to guide the career and skills development of older workers.

The fifth type of technologies boosts health and healthy life expectancy by improving mental and physical health.

Emerging technologies that help maintain mental and physical wellness and other digital health services bode well for an aging population and workforce. These technologies include biotechnology, new drugs and treatments developed through medical science, and other innovative forms of health service delivery that integrate ICT, such as automated diagnosis and wearable devices.

Wearables, nonwearable smart devices, and mobile applications can help monitor and improve personal health.

New smart devices and mobile applications can obtain and track vital signs and monitor physiological responses to activities. The wearables deliver patients' diagnostic information to health providers to monitor symptoms, and help them refine and optimize treatment. There are also digital products that help manage chronic and noncommunicable diseases.

Digital therapeutics are evidence-based medical interventions that make use of high-quality software to help prevent, manage, or treat a medical disorder or disease (Digital Therapeutics Alliance 2018). These typically involve the online transmission of data to alert healthcare professionals to potential problems and emergencies, enabling a quicker medical response. Feedback on physical conditions is sent through smartphones, encouraging patients to be more engaged in their health status. Some clinical trials even found wearables efficient in treating people with metabolic syndrome. A pilot study in the Republic of Korea used wearable devices to patients with metabolic syndrome. Throughout 12 weeks, patients received feedback from a trained nurse on their physical activity, to provide encouragement and improve self-monitoring. Researchers found that feedback via wearable device was able to increase physical activity and resolve the metabolic syndrome for 45% of the participants who completed the trial (Huh et al. 2019).

Mental health is just as important as physical health, with older people facing higher risks of conditions such as dementia, Alzheimer's disease, depression, and anxiety attacks. The World Health Organization (WHO) (2017) estimates over 20% of people of ages 60 or over suffer from mental or neurological disorders, while 6.6% of older people's disability is mental or neurological. A number of digital therapeutic products are designed to address mental health, replacing conventional medications or used in conjunction with them to produce direct clinical benefit.[62]

VR has also been increasingly used as a tool to improve care of seniors who are especially at risk of dementia, depression, and isolation.

With VR headsets, custom software, and a tablet, seniors could travel the world virtually, attend sports games or even family gatherings. Other relevant features include cognitive therapy and early diagnosis of dementia. Residents of a senior community in Massachusetts with access to the VR-based services are reported happier by 40% (Matheson 2017). Similarly, robotic pets have been found to reduce loneliness among the elderly by providing canine or feline companionship (Dawson 2019). A study of patients suffering from dementia showed that the group that interacted with Paro, a robotic furry seal that responds to touch and provides companionship, had decreased stress and anxiety and needed less psychoactive and pain medications (Petersen et al. 2017). Pepper, a humanoid robot, leads group exercises for senior citizens, among its other features (Foster 2018).

Technology for Easier Access to Healthcare

Remote patient monitoring, or telemedicine, uses technology to deliver certain healthcare services remotely.

This entails using remote monitoring devices in nonclinical environments, such as in the home, to enable patients to consult their doctors, or for medical professionals to communicate and arrive at decisions on how to treat patients without needing to be physically present. Remote patient monitoring (RPM) increases access to healthcare and potentially decreases delivery costs, which can significantly improve the quality of life for patients, especially those with chronic diseases, who are often seniors. Globally, Dexcom, Honeywell Life Sciences, *and* Philips Healthcare are among the top RPM solution providers.

---

[62]   For example, in the US, FDA approved the prescription of a number of digital therapeutics targeting at treating opioid use disorder, mental illness, and major depressive disorder.

Box 6.13: Digital Interventions in Healthcare

Early diagnosis with technology

Early diagnosis can be achieved through two mechanisms. The first mechanism is through improvements in technologies for early disease detection. Identifying and detection of biomarkers, which refers to a broad subcategory of medical signs that can be measured accurately and reproducibly (Strimbu and Tavel 2010), for life-threatening diseases like cancer offer a wider range of treatment options, vastly improving diagnosis, prognosis, and survival rates. Developments in nanotechnology-enhanced biochips and computer-aided software based on artificial intelligence (AI) which utilizes big data in healthcare, enable automated diagnosis of conditions leading to early detection of malaria, tuberculosis, various types of cancer, Parkinson's disease, Alzheimer's, schizophrenia, and blindness.

The second mechanism is through genomic profiling—which involves the study of all of a person's genes (i.e., the genome), including interactions of those genes with each other and with a person's environment. This genetic information is examined to determine the likelihood of certain types of diseases, which allow for both preventative medicine and precision or customized treatment. Foundation Medicine, a molecular information company founded in 2010, is at the forefront of genomics. In 2012, it launched the first commercially available comprehensive genomic profiling test for cancer diagnosis. In 2018, its genomic profiling procedures for all solid tumors were approved for Medicare and Medicaid services coverage in the United States (US). Japan's Ministry of Health, Labour and Welfare has also approved the test for individuals living with advanced cancer (Foundation Medicine 2018). In Asia, a joint venture between Japan's Canon Medical Systems Corporation and Taipei,China's ACT Genomics formed ACTmed to offer precision cancer medicine, treatment for cancer relapse, drug resistance monitoring, cancer risk assessment, and immunotherapy evaluation using AI-powered bioinformatics database integrated with Asia-specific genome profiling.

Electronic management of health data

Electronic management of health data, which includes patients' electronic health records, staff information, stock levels of medicine or other commodities, has several benefits. Digitized records allow health workers to track and follow-up on patients' health status, enables telemedicine and targeted client communication, augments health workers' decisions through digitized job aids, and allows for better management of stocks and commodities (World Health Organization 2019). Adoption of electronic medical records in the US achieved an estimated net cumulative saving of $371 billion from 2004 to 2018 because of improved efficiency and increased safety (Hillestad et al. 2005). Kaiser Permanente, a US-based health plan provider, saved about $1 billion in reduced visits and lab tests and improved health outcomes. The implemented computer system encouraged use of electronic health records and ensured data exchange across medical facilities (Groves et al. 2013).

Big data analysis for healthcare

Big data analytics can transform the healthcare landscape. Some of its uses range from prevention to cure and cover everything else in between such as better-informed strategic planning and integrating medical imaging for broader diagnosis. Applications of big data analytics to health data, or bioinformatics could have a large benefit on patients and the general population by enhancing quality care, offering more precise treatment, and reducing healthcare costs. For healthcare providers, it could mean identifying people and populations at high risk for particular diseases, or improving accuracy in diagnosis based on evidence-based medicine. Around 40% of direct health interventions have been geared toward predictive capabilities (Groves et al. 2013). For example, advanced analytics used by Dignity Health, the largest hospital provider in California, have predicted sepsis, a fatal inflammatory response to infection, and so reduced the mortality rate by 5% (Beall 2019). For healthcare insurers, it could mean more efficiency and cost saving. For example, insurers can reduce costs by being able to streamline processes, preventing fraud and theft, and creating more appropriate coverage for their plan holders.

Sources: Beall (2019); Foundation Medicine (2018); Groves et al. (2013); Hillestad et al (2005); Strimbu and Tavel (2010); and WHO (2019).

In Asia, the lifting of regulatory restrictions on the use of devices on medical consultations has paved the way for telemedicine/telehealth companies to expand their services. In Japan, around 560 medical institutions have made use of remote medical consultations since 2014. *Ping An Good Doctor*, a one-stop healthcare ecosystem in the PRC, provides its 265 million users 24/7 online consultation services using AI technology—an AI-assisted chatbot routes a patient to a doctor. In early 2019, it rolled out its One-Minute Clinics across eight provinces and cities and signed service contracts for nearly 1,000 units, providing healthcare services to more than 3 million users (Koh 2019). In the Philippines, medical practitioners can diagnose patients from underserved and geographically isolated provinces through the Philippine Research, Education and Government Information

Network (PREGINET), a multiplatform delivery that provides accessible, affordable, and quality healthcare services. In Singapore, a fee of S$20 (about $14) entitles a registered user to a video consultation with one of Doctor Anywhere's pool of doctors.

Telehealth and telemedicine companies aiming for maximum reach have to contend with both regulations and their absence. In Southeast Asia, the lack of clear laws and regulations surrounding RPM-type medical services is an issue to growth-oriented companies that could be confronted by future laws and regulations. Another issue is that in many of the geographically inaccessible areas that stand to benefit most from remote healthcare delivery, people are not so trusting of technology and still prefer face-to-face consultation with doctors.

Aside from the telemedicine, a wide range of digital health systems make medical services more accessible, timely, and accurate, especially for the elderly.

Longer life expectancy means higher incidences of chronic conditions, and digitalization helps make health systems more responsive and sustainable (WHO 2019). Box 6.13 highlights other important applications of digital health interventions.

Assessing the Technology Needs of Countries Based on Age-Education Profiles

Population aging may be largely irreversible, but the economic consequences depend, in part, on how well countries adapt to the changes.

Looming scarcity of a productive workforce and a corresponding increase in the share of older workers can add downward pressure to aggregate productivity. With rapid technological advances, there is a need to take full advantage of new technologies, such as increasingly

sophisticated automation, and much-improved robots and versatile uses of digital technologies, to halt an age-related slowdown in productivity.

Economies in Asia are undergoing varying stages of demographic transition. The identification of technological solutions to labor market challenges in the economies of Asia demands a tailored approach. This section lays the ground for policy recommendations by assessing (i) the course of progression of the age and education profile of the region's economically active population, and (ii) the pattern of labor demand highlighting the evolution of tasks.

The section begins by mapping the transformation of age and educational attainment distribution in the region that can be classified into four broad types. The pattern of employment and labor market demand within each group is then assessed using information from labor force surveys.

Aging and Educational Attainment in Asia

Distribution of the economically active population is projected using trends in aging and the level of educational attainment since 1950.

Country-specific past (1980), current (2015), and projected (2050) population distribution by age and the level of educational attainment are gathered from the Wittgenstein Centre for Demography and Global Human Capital (Box 6.14 provides a brief note on the dataset). With formal qualifications easily and readily observable, these are often used as a satisfactory if not perfect proxy for actual skills (Massing and Schneider 2017).

Using a radar chart, the economically active population disaggregated by age and education level are fitted on six axes with the upper portion referring to the older (50–74) age group while the younger (25–49) age group occupies the bottom part.[63] The education level of the two broad age groups is mapped with the share of economically active population completing at most primary education

---

[63]   In this exercise, economically active population of ages 25 to 74 is used, which is different from the standard working age population of 15 to 64. For one, youth may still be in school up to early twenties so their educational attainment level may deviate substantially from the final attainment. Upper bound of working age is also extended to 75, given the rapid expansion of healthy life expectancy in the region (Figure 6.24).

Box 6.14: Future Aging and Educational Attainment Profile

Historic and projected level of human capital by age and level of educational attainment is gathered from the Human Capital Data Explorer (version 2.0) made available by the Wittgenstein Centre for Demography and Global Human Capital, a collaboration among the World Population Program of the International Institute for Applied Systems Analysis (IIASA), the Vienna Institute of Demography of the Austrian Academy of Sciences (VID/ÖAW), and the Demography Group of the Vienna University of Economics and Business.

The database includes historical and projected population by age, sex, and educational attainment for the period 1950–2100 for 201 economies, of which 42 are from Asia.[a]

It uses register and census data from national statistical institutes as the main data source to build historical data and others such as the Demographic and Health Surveys or Multiple Indicator Cluster Surveys where needed (Speringer et al. 2019).

The construction of database benefited from the large global expert inquiries which set assumptions on future fertility, mortality, migration, and education for all parts of the world (KC et al. 2018). One important feature of the Wittgenstein Centre's population projections is its alignment to the narratives in the context of Shared Socioeconomic Pathways, a forecasting model offering trajectories of society and economy for coming decades, and broadly used in development-related issues such as climate change mitigation and adaptation (KC and Lutz 2017).

[a] The 42 Asian economies are Afghanistan; Armenia; Australia; Azerbaijan; Bangladesh; Bhutan; Brunei Darussalam; Cambodia; the Federated States of Micronesia; Fiji; Georgia; Hong Kong, China; India; Indonesia; Japan; Kazakhstan; Kiribati; the Kyrgyz Republic; the Lao People's Democratic Republic; Malaysia; Maldives; Mongolia; Myanmar; Nepal; New Zealand; Pakistan; Papua New Guinea; the People's Republic of China; the Philippines; the Republic of Korea; Samoa; Singapore; Solomon Islands; Sri Lanka; Taipei,China; Tajikistan; Thailand; Timor-Leste; Tonga; Uzbekistan; Vanuatu; and Viet Nam.

Sources: KC et al. (2018); KC and Lutz (2017); and Speringer et al. (2019).

occupying the left-most part (*Low Edu*), those attaining at most secondary education in the middle part (*Medium Edu*), and those with post-secondary education, including ones attending short-cycle and post-secondary non-tertiary programs in the right-most portion (*High Edu*).

Using the People's Republic of China (PRC) as an example in Figure 6.34, in 1980, the younger age group attaining at most primary education comprises about 47% of the total economically active population in the PRC, while the older age group with similar level of educational attainment was about 30%. The distribution is shaped almost like a "compass," where it points to the age-education demography accounting for the largest proportion. As citizens age and receive more education, the age-education compass changes shape over time. The same figure swung to the right in 2015, suggesting that much of the population had improved educational attainment, and by 2050, the projection shows that a large portion of the population will be considered high-educated after receiving at least a post-secondary education. It is also interesting to note how the shape gravitates toward the upper portion of the chart. Broadly speaking, the potential labor force in the PRC is shifting gradually from largely a young low-educated labor force to one that will be older but more educated.

Figure 6.34: Population Distribution by Age and Education—People's Republic of China (%)

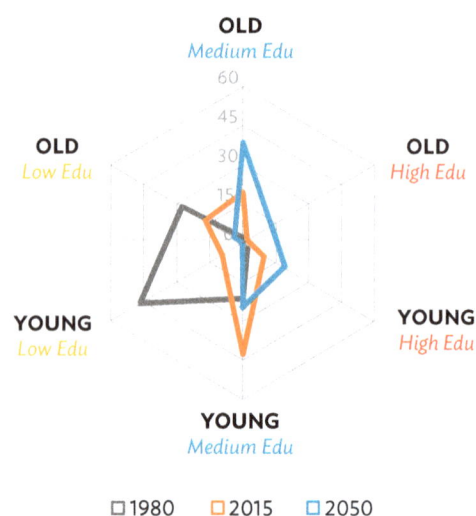

Notes: Young refers to the economically active population ages 25–49, while old are ages 50–74. Horizontal dashed line delineates the young (lower half) and old (upper half) population. *Low Edu* denotes completion of at most primary education, *Medium Edu* attains secondary education, and *High Edu* has post-secondary education including attendance to short-cycle non-tertiary programs.

Source: ADB calculations using data from Wittgenstein Centre for Demography and Global Human Capital. Wittgenstein Centre Data Explorer Version 2.0. www.wittgensteincentre.org/dataexplorer (accessed June 2019).

Four Types of Aging and Education Attainment Trajectories in Asian Economies

Using the available age and educational attainment information from 42 Asian economies, varying demographic trajectories are classified into four broad types.

Applying the calculated median from the 42 Asian country-observations as thresholds defining aging and improvements in human capital (in terms of education) outlined in Table 6.2, four representative age-education demographic patterns are derived.

First, the aging of economies is described as "Fast" if the share of economically active population ages 50–74 by 2050 exceeds the calculated median share of 44% (Box 6.15 contains a discussion on the choice between level and rate of aging). Economies below the median are otherwise classified as "Slow-Aging." Second, there is favorable human capital development if the proportion of the economically active population that completed post-secondary education (tertiary and non-tertiary

training/short courses) exceeds the median of 27.1% by 2050. Using the two distinctions, demographic patterns follow four broad types: (i) Fast-Aging, Above Median Education; (ii) Fast-Aging, Below Median Education; (iii) Slow-Aging, Below Median Education; and (iv) Slow-Aging, Above Median Education. The population characteristics of each types are described in the table below.

Type-1 (Fast-Aging, Above Median Education) represents a group of countries seeing a radical shift from young low-educated workers to older and more educated workers.

Rapid aging is visible with the share of older economically active population increasing from 29.4% in 1980 to 42.9% in 2015. This pattern is also apparent with its compass demographic chart (Figure 6.35) steadily moving upward over time. On average, a typical Type-1 economy, such as Japan and the Republic of Korea, would have the largest share of older economically active population by 2050, at around 53.3%, although the growth rate is slower at 0.6%.

Table 6.2: Description of Criteria Used to Classify Selected Economies in Asia

Criteria	Type-1 Fast-Aging, Above Median Education	Type-2 Fast-Aging, Below Median Education	Type-3 Slow-Aging, Below Median Education	Type-4 Slow-Aging, Above Median Education
a. The share of older economically active population or those ages 50–74 by 2050.	Above the median share of 44% by 2050.	Above the median share of 44% by 2050.	Below the median share of 44% by 2050.	Below the median share of 44% by 2050.
Average share of older population	**53.3%**	**50.5%**	**39.4%**	**39.0%**
b The share of post-secondary (high) educated economically active population by 2050.	Above the median share of 27.1% by 2050.	Below the median share of 27.1% by 2050.	Below the median share of 27.1% by 2050.	Above the median share of 27.1% by 2050.
Average share of population by educational attainment:				
• Post-secondary education *(High Edu)*	**48.4%**	**18.5%**	**15.6%**	**31.6%**
• Secondary education *(Medium Edu)*	**48.0%**	**58.1%**	**65.1%**	**61.6%**
• Primary education *(Low Edu)*	**3.6%**	**23.3%**	**19.3%**	**6.9%**

Source: ADB calculations using data from Wittgenstein Centre for Demography and Global Human Capital. Wittgenstein Centre Data Explorer Version 2.0. www.wittgensteincentre.org/dataexplorer (accessed June 2019).

Figure 6.35: Type-1 Population Distribution by Age and Education—Selected Asian Economies (%)

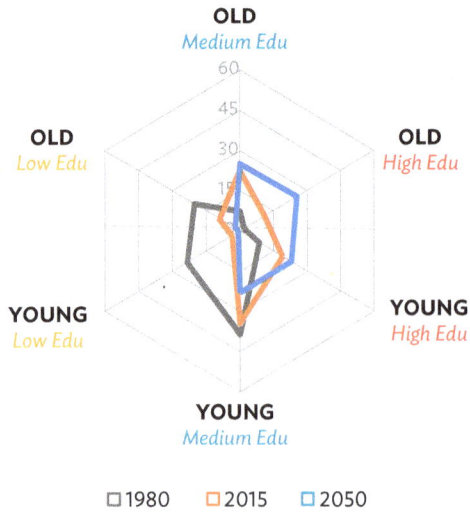

OLD
Medium Edu

OLD
Low Edu

OLD
High Edu

YOUNG
Low Edu

YOUNG
High Edu

YOUNG
Medium Edu

□ 1980   □ 2015   □ 2050

Notes: Young refers to the economically active population ages 25–49, while old are ages 50–74. Horizontal dashed line delineates the young (lower half) and old (upper half) population. *Low Edu* denotes completion of at most primary education, *Medium Edu* attains secondary education, and *High Edu* has post-secondary education including attendance to short-cycle non-tertiary programs.

Source: ADB calculations using data from Wittgenstein Centre for Demography and Global Human Capital. Wittgenstein Centre Data Explorer Version 2.0. www.wittgensteincentre.org/dataexplorer (accessed June 2019).

In the 1980s, the younger age group with at most secondary education qualification represented most of the population. There was also a large representation of the less educated population from both old (20.2%) and young (23.4%) age groups who achieved only up to primary education. By 2015, the educational attainment of the overall population improved markedly, with an outward distribution of young and old age groups achieving post-secondary education.

Many of the older cohort in 2015 completed post-secondary education and the younger ones achieved post-secondary education; therefore, the population distribution in the lower portion of the compass moves further to the right. By 2050, as the high-educated cohort gets older, further educational attainment backed by higher budget allocation per child leads to a majority of the population having had a post-secondary education. A typical country under Type-1 is expected to have a large pool of high-skilled workers as far as educational attainment is concerned by 2050, benefiting from their aggressive education and human

capital interventions during their early development and demographic transitions.

Type-2 (Fast-Aging, Below Median Education) has had historically low levels of education, especially among the younger economically active population.

While aging demography is showing a similar pattern with Type-1, the improvement in educational attainment in Type-2 in 2015 is not as quick, thus the younger population remains largely with a primary education. However, the proportion of those primary school educated has decreased significantly from 1980 resulting in a large movement toward the middle spectrum of education level (Figure 6.36).

Figure 6.36: Type-2 Population Distribution by Age and Education—Selected Asian Economies (%)

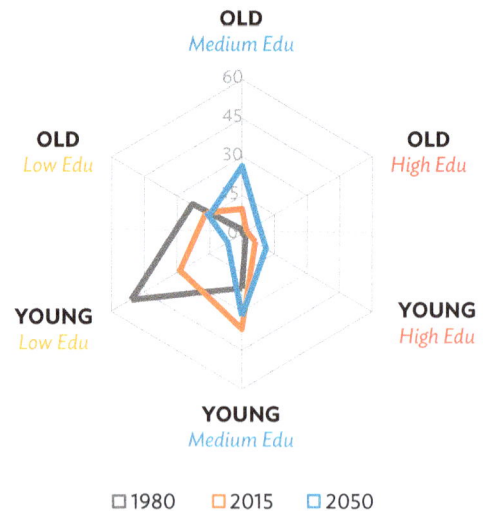

OLD
Medium Edu

OLD
Low Edu

OLD
High Edu

YOUNG
Low Edu

YOUNG
High Edu

YOUNG
Medium Edu

□ 1980   □ 2015   □ 2050

Notes: Young refers to the economically active population ages 25–49, while old are ages 50–74. Horizontal dashed line delineates the young (lower half) and old (upper half) population. *Low Edu* denotes completion of at most primary education, *Medium Edu* attains secondary education, and *High Edu* has post-secondary education including attendance to short-cycle non-tertiary programs.

Source: ADB calculations using data from Wittgenstein Centre for Demography and Global Human Capital. Wittgenstein Centre Data Explorer Version 2.0. www.wittgensteincentre.org/dataexplorer (accessed June 2019).

Unlike Type-1's rightward movement, in a typical Type-2 country, such as Bangladesh and Maldives, only a slight improvement in education can be expected in the younger age group if the current slow momentum persists, so that by 2050 there will be a large representation of the older population with at most a secondary education qualification. Correspondingly, there is a stable large share of young workers with secondary education. These patterns create an upward stretched population distribution compass toward the center. On average, the share of the older economically active population is expected to reach 50.5% by 2050, accompanied by a less favorable education demography, in which the share of the high-educated economically active population by 2050 is projected only at 18.5%.

Type-3 (Slow-Aging, Below Median Education) shares a similar historic demographic shift with Type-2, with a slower pace of societal aging and progression of education attainment, leading to a predominance of younger and middle-educated group in the workforce.

In the 1980s, almost 90% of the older population and over two-thirds of the younger population had achieved just the minimum education level (Figure 6.37). By 2015, the younger cohort dramatically shifts toward more completing secondary education. The share of the older population with primary education decreases slightly during the period, accompanied by a growing number in the older age group having secondary education. Improved educational attainment among the new, younger cohort shifts the distribution toward the middle, and is accompanied by very little increases in post-secondary education.

By 2050, the trajectory in a typical Type-3 country is leading toward a modest increase in the proportion of population with at least post-secondary education, which is more apparent among the younger age group. Government expenditure on tertiary education (as a proportion to total government expenditure on education) in economies following this type of age-education demographic pattern, such as Cambodia and Nepal, is generally lower than their other Asian counterparts. Relative to economies following the Type-2 pattern, both private and public spending on basic education and health per children is higher, which allows a stronger rightward pivot toward higher educational attainment, especially among the younger

Figure 6.37: Type-3 Population Distribution by Age and Education—Selected Asian Economies (%)

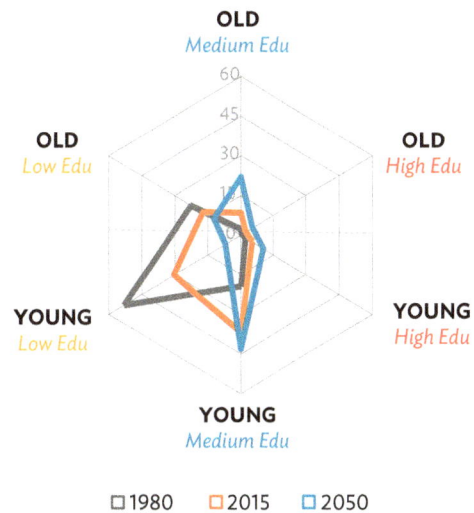

Notes: Young refers to the economically active population ages 25–49, while old are ages 50–74. Horizontal dashed line delineates the young (lower half) and old (upper half) population. *Low Edu* denotes completion of at most primary education, *Medium Edu* attains secondary education, and *High Edu* has post-secondary education including attendance to short-cycle non-tertiary programs.

Source: ADB calculations using data from Wittgenstein Centre for Demography and Global Human Capital. Wittgenstein Centre Data Explorer Version 2.0. www.wittgensteincentre.org/dataexplorer (accessed June 2019).

economically active population. On average, the share of older population in Type-3 economies will reach 39.4% by 2050, while the share of high-educated economically active population is projected to approach 15.6%, two-thirds of which is accounted for by the younger age group.

Type-4 (Slow-Aging, Above Median Education) experiences a strong rightward movement by 2050, as more and more of their younger population completes tertiary education.

Economies following this age-education demographic pattern expect the share of the older economically active population by 2050 to reach 39.0%. They are also expected to exhibit favorable human capital as the share of high educated population by 2050 is projected around 31.6%, almost two-thirds of which are ages 25–49 (Figure 6.38). It is interesting, however, that the government expenditure on both the secondary and post-secondary education (a percentage of total government expenditure in education) in these countries was relatively smaller than those following a Type-3 demographic pattern, although, private investment in human capital per children is particularly high in some countries typically classified as Type-4, such as Mongolia and the Philippines. Other factors seem to be playing a critical role for these countries to experience improved human capital despite education having low priority in state budgets.

Figure 6.38: Type-4 Population Distribution by Age and Education—Selected Asian Economies (%)

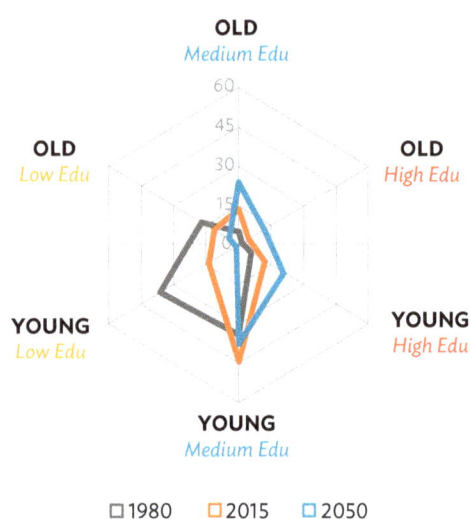

Notes: Young refers to the economically active population ages 25–49, while old are ages 50–74. Horizontal dashed line delineates the young (lower half) and old (upper half) population. *Low Edu* denotes completion of at most primary education, *Medium Edu* attains secondary education, and *High Edu* has post-secondary education including attendance to short-cycle non-tertiary programs.

Source: ADB calculations using data from Wittgenstein Centre for Demography and Global Human Capital. Wittgenstein Centre Data Explorer Version 2.0. www.wittgensteincentre.org/dataexplorer (accessed June 2019).

One important factor that could perhaps explain the rightward shift, but deserves further investigation for empirical evidence, would be cultural differences and how conducive the economic and policy environment are for women. Compared with the young economies in Type-3, Type-4 economies such as Kazakhstan and Mongolia are among the economies lauded for facilitating women's empowerment through improved access to education and participation in the labor market. If this is validated, then gender-sensitive or at least gender-neutral and more inclusive initiatives would indeed complement human capital development efforts.

Labor Market Momentum by Age and Tasks Across Different Types of Demographic Pattern

Understanding the patterns of evolving labor demand by age and tasks helps match appropriate groups of technologies to the demographic trajectory.

Adding insights on labor demand dynamics to the age/education analysis above will provide a more holistic view on the technologies appropriate for addressing potential challenges and take advantage of opportunities arising from societal aging.

Changing patterns of labor demand within the types are assessed based on information gathered for employment across three types of tasks—routine, nonroutine manual, and nonroutine cognitive—by younger and older age groups.

Disaggregated employment information sourced from labor force survey data in multiple economies are gathered within the types that stretch over several years to decades.[64] Age-occupation groups were created using that information. The age category follows the demographic compasses, with the younger group referring to ages 25–49 and the older group ages 50–74.

For occupation category, following the guidelines of the International Labour Organization (2015), the nine major groups of International Standard Classification of Occupations 2008, excluding armed forces occupations under code [0], are categorized into three different

---

[64]   This analysis uses labor force survey data for Japan (2007, 2017), the Republic of Korea (2010, 2017), and Australia (2000, 2018) which are readily downloadable from their respective statistical agencies. For other economies, labor force survey microdata from Bangladesh (2006, 2013); the People's Republic of China (2000, 2015); India (2000, 2012); Indonesia (2000, 2014); Mongolia (2002, 2016); Nepal (1999, 2008); Pakistan (2002, 2013); the Philippines (2001, 2016); Sri Lanka (2004, 2014); Taipei,China (2000, 2013); Thailand (2000, 2010); and Viet Nam (2007, 2013) are used. The sample economies represent more than 90% of the total employment of workers of ages 25 and above in Asia.

Box 6.15: Level of Aging versus Rate of Aging

The representative demographic types are determined by looking at the share of older economically active population (ages 50–74) by 2050. If the economies are above the median in share, they are listed as "Fast-Aging" and below the median as "Slow-Aging." An alternative distinction would be to generate types by how quickly the population was aging between now and 2050, or the annual growth rate of the elderly population from 2015 to 2050. In this case, if the economy's growth rate were above the median, it would be considered "Fast-Aging." The Box Figure shows the different composition of economies amid the aging definition.

On the right side are economies listed by the level of their population that will be older by 2050. The median share is 44.2%, and economies above this level are considered "Fast-Aging." On the left side are economies ordered by growth rate. If classified by growth rate, a typical profile of Types 1 and 2 would have been quite different, as several economies with rapidly aging populations, such as Mongolia and the Lao People's Democratic Republic, still would not have large elderly populations by 2050. Similarly, many economies have slower rates of aging, but will have a significant elderly population by 2050. Among them are Japan and Singapore. Given that the primary objective of this chapter is to discuss economies with large elderly population, the share of older population is used as the metric.

Defining Aging—Speed and Level (%)

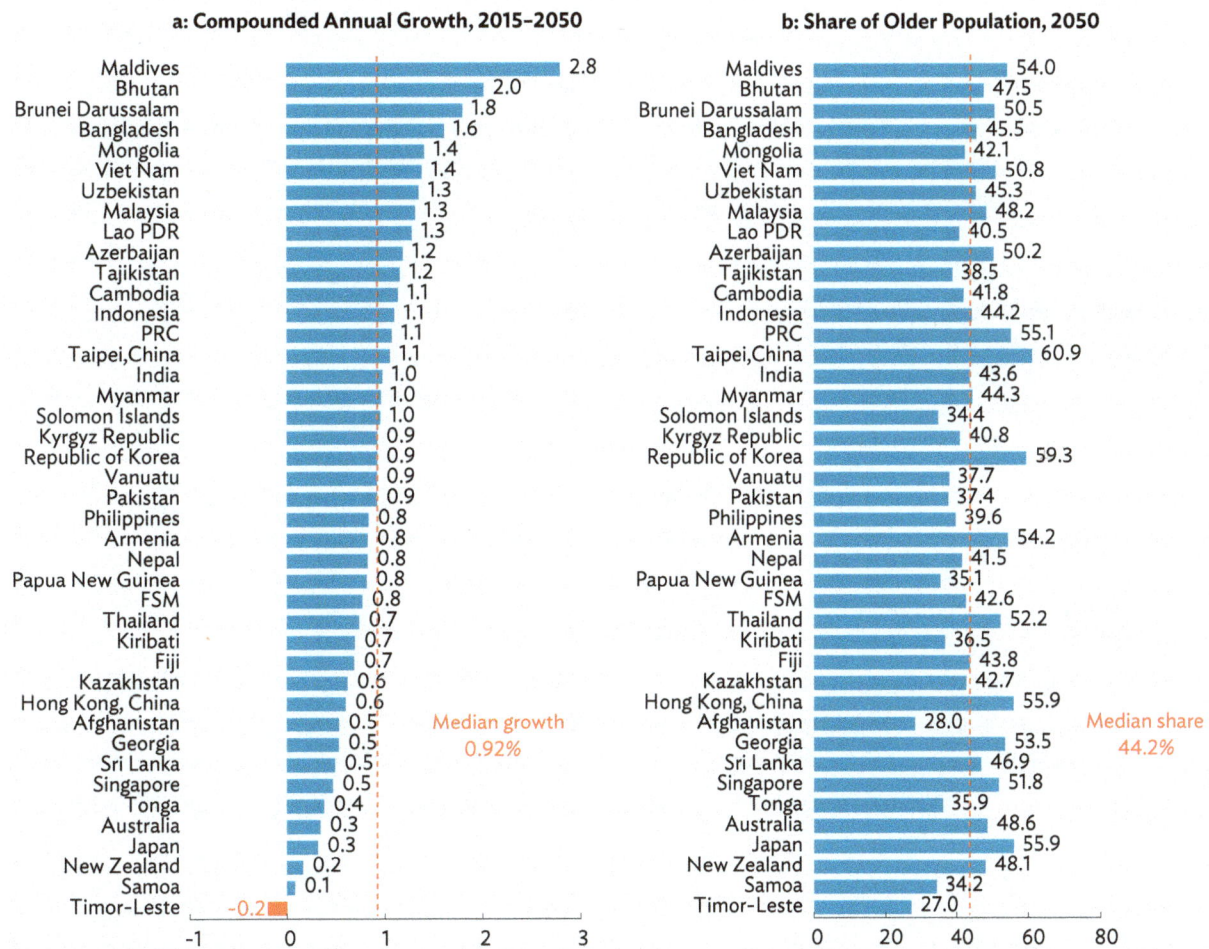

a: Compounded Annual Growth, 2015–2050

Economy	Growth
Maldives	2.8
Bhutan	2.0
Brunei Darussalam	1.8
Bangladesh	1.6
Mongolia	1.4
Viet Nam	1.4
Uzbekistan	1.3
Malaysia	1.3
Lao PDR	1.3
Azerbaijan	1.2
Tajikistan	1.2
Cambodia	1.1
Indonesia	1.1
PRC	1.1
Taipei,China	1.1
India	1.0
Myanmar	1.0
Solomon Islands	1.0
Kyrgyz Republic	0.9
Republic of Korea	0.9
Vanuatu	0.9
Pakistan	0.9
Philippines	0.8
Armenia	0.8
Nepal	0.8
Papua New Guinea	0.8
FSM	0.8
Thailand	0.7
Kiribati	0.7
Fiji	0.7
Kazakhstan	0.6
Hong Kong, China	0.6
Afghanistan	0.5
Georgia	0.5
Sri Lanka	0.5
Singapore	0.5
Tonga	0.4
Australia	0.3
Japan	0.3
New Zealand	0.2
Samoa	0.1
Timor-Leste	-0.2

Median growth
0.92%

b: Share of Older Population, 2050

Economy	Share
Maldives	54.0
Bhutan	47.5
Brunei Darussalam	50.5
Bangladesh	45.5
Mongolia	42.1
Viet Nam	50.8
Uzbekistan	45.3
Malaysia	48.2
Lao PDR	40.5
Azerbaijan	50.2
Tajikistan	38.5
Cambodia	41.8
Indonesia	44.2
PRC	55.1
Taipei,China	60.9
India	43.6
Myanmar	44.3
Solomon Islands	34.4
Kyrgyz Republic	40.8
Republic of Korea	59.3
Vanuatu	37.7
Pakistan	37.4
Philippines	39.6
Armenia	54.2
Nepal	41.5
Papua New Guinea	35.1
FSM	42.6
Thailand	52.2
Kiribati	36.5
Fiji	43.8
Kazakhstan	42.7
Hong Kong, China	55.9
Afghanistan	28.0
Georgia	53.5
Sri Lanka	46.9
Singapore	51.8
Tonga	35.9
Australia	48.6
Japan	55.9
New Zealand	48.1
Samoa	34.2
Timor-Leste	27.0

Median share
44.2%

FSM = Federated States of Micronesia, Lao PDR = Lao People's Democratic Republic, PRC = People's Republic of China.

Note: Both figures refer to the old population ages 50–74.

Source: ADB calculations using data from Wittgenstein Centre for Demography and Global Human Capital. Wittgenstein Centre Data Explorer Version 2.0. www.wittgensteincentre.org/dataexplorer (accessed June 2019).

Source: Asian Development Bank.

tasks: (i) *routine* involve occupations such as clerical support workers [4], craft and related trades workers [7], plant and machine operators and assemblers [8], and elementary occupations [9]; (ii) *nonroutine manual* involve occupations such as services and sales workers [5], skilled agricultural, forestry, and fishery workers [6]; and (iii) *nonroutine cognitive* include those of managers [1], professionals [2], and technicians and associate professionals [3].

The concordance of occupations into tasks is straightforward, simple and intuitive, though not perfect. People employed in elementary occupations perform mainly routine tasks, although some tasks of helpers or cleaners can be considered nonroutine manual jobs. After deriving employment distribution by age and task component, the country-specific average annual change of each age-task is calculated and then averaged, depending on where economies fall in the type of demographic pattern.[65] Figure 6.39 presents the type-specific changes in employment distribution by age and tasks, which proxy for labor market employment trends.

Asian economies' rapid structural transformation shifts employment patterns from routine to nonroutine tasks in all groups.

Much of the contraction in routine employment can be attributed to the gradual reallocation of jobs from low-skill agriculture toward modern industries and services-oriented sectors that require different skills. Figure 6.39 shows that the contraction in employment share involving routine activities is more pronounced among younger workers. Economies following the Type-2 (Fast-Aging, Below Median Education) pattern exhibit large declines with the share to total employment lower, on an annual average, by 1.53 percentage points.

With population aging, the share of employment of older workers increases across varied task types, especially among fast-aging groups.

Demographic patterns of Type-1 and Type-2 countries show a rise in the (net) share of employment by older workers across most tasks. The slow-aging demographic types also see moderate increase in the share of elderly employment in some tasks, while the share of younger workers is increasing, especially in jobs that requires nonroutine cognitive skills. However, the substantial decline in routine jobs among younger workers (or nonroutine manual jobs in Type-4) stymie the overall growth of the group's employment.

The increasing share of employment for nonroutine cognitive tasks bodes well for the expansion in schooling years and technological advancement occurring in many Asian economies.

Figure 6.39 also shows, across all types of demographic pattern, that the share of employment handling nonroutine cognitive-oriented tasks increases for both younger and older workers. Economies following a Type-4 demographic pattern have seen the largest expansion in nonroutine cognitive employment.

Changing patterns of jobs and tasks amid rapid advancement and permeation of technologies also explain some contraction and expansion in employment.

Most obviously, mechanization and automation contribute to the reduction of routine jobs, shifting the workforce to perform more sophisticated tasks. According to an ADB report, 43%–57% of new job titles in selected countries of the region in the past 10 years are related to ICT, including specialized technicians needed to work with computer-controlled machines (ADB 2018). In this category, employment for young workers is growing at a faster pace than for older workers. Demand for workers to handle nonroutine cognitive tasks is growing among the above median education Type-1 and Type-4 at a similar rate to the below median education Type-2 and Type-3.

---

[65]   Country-specific average annual change in employment distribution by age and task can be denoted as $\Delta\varepsilon_{cyt} = \dfrac{\left(\varepsilon_{cyt, m=latest} - \varepsilon_{cyt, m=earliest}\right)}{m_{latest} - m_{earliest}}$ where c refers to country, y denotes age group (i.e., young and old), t refers to the task category, and m is the labor force survey year.

Figure 6.39: Average Annual Change in Employment Share by Age and Task—Selected Asian Economies
(percentage points)

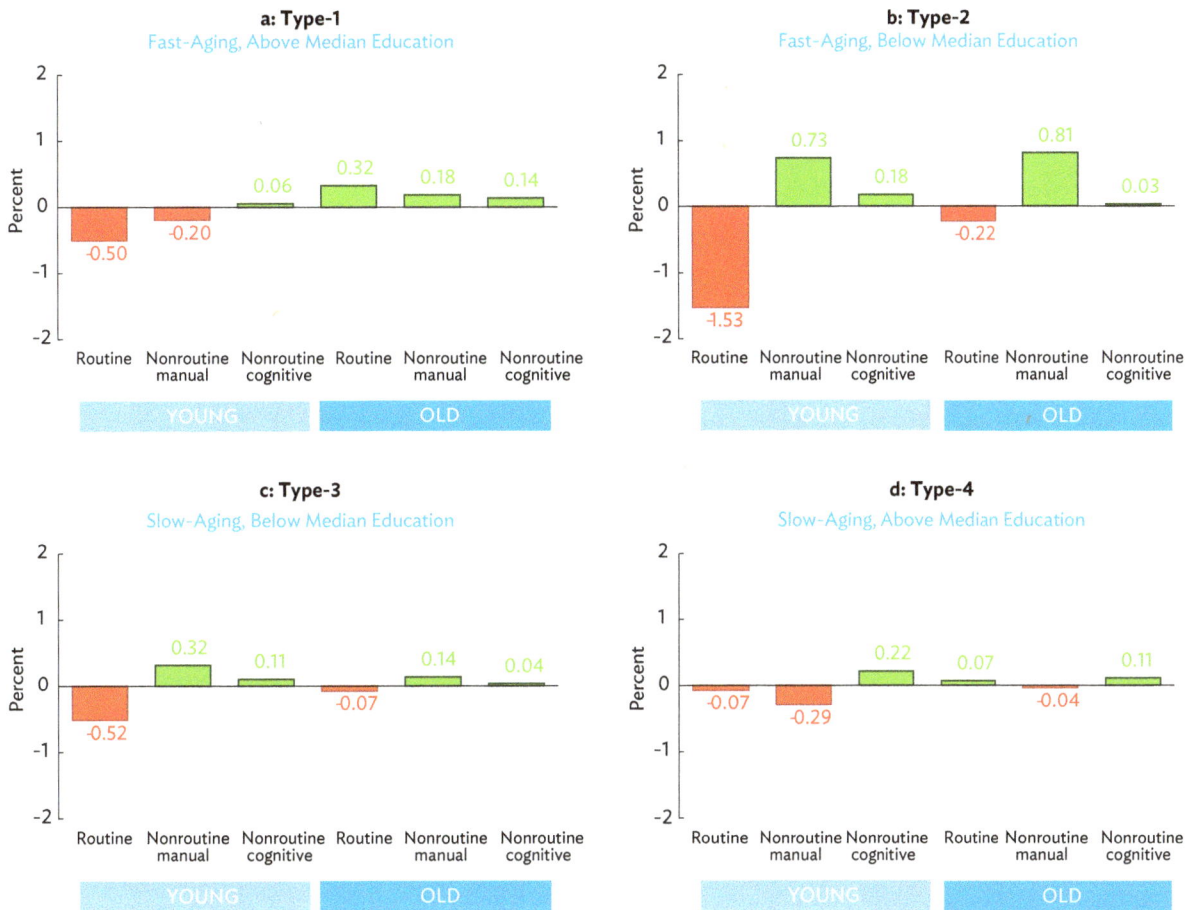

a: Type-1
Fast-Aging, Above Median Education

b: Type-2
Fast-Aging, Below Median Education

c: Type-3
Slow-Aging, Below Median Education

d: Type-4
Slow-Aging, Above Median Education

Note: Young refers to economically active population ages 25–49, while old are ages 50–74.

Sources: ADB calculations using data from respective country labor force surveys: Japan (2007, 2017); the Republic of Korea (2010, 2017); Australia (2000, 2018); Bangladesh (2006, 2013); the People's Republic of China (2000, 2015); India (2000, 2012); Indonesia (2000, 2014); Mongolia (2002, 2016); Nepal (1999, 2008); Pakistan (2002, 2013); the Philippines (2001, 2016); Sri Lanka (2004, 2014); Taipei,China (2000, 2013); Thailand (2000, 2010]; and Viet Nam (2007, 2013).

Increasing demand for handling nonroutine manual tasks will require medium- to high-skilled workers.

Over time, there has been a reallocation of employment toward nonroutine manual employment, for both younger and older workers. But nonroutine manual tasks, especially in service-oriented industries, are also at high risk of automation given advances in artificial intelligence, robotics, and the internet of things. The timing of this technology adoption, however, will vary across the four types, depending on the economic viability and technical feasibility of particular technologies in different countries (ADB 2018).

A changing labor market landscape can be expected amid further aging in Asia, altering the nature of work in the region.

Growing dependence on an older workforce will greatly influence the region's search for viable technology solutions to sustain productivity, and therefore growth. It is likely that job disruption caused by automation will hit the older workers more (Box 6.16). As discussed in the next section, both older and younger workers will need to gain foundational skills that help them pursue lifelong learning to adapt to the rapidly changing environment, especially given the expected longer working life.

Box 6.16: Technology and Older Workers

With the rapid adoption of technology at the workplace, a larger share of older workers who now handle routine tasks will need to learn nonroutine manual tasks, such as in manufacturing and retail trade industries. These conditions make older workers vulnerable as shown by estimates for higher potential job displacement rates (Box Figure 1).

Estimates show that older workers are more likely performing activities in industries that are at higher risk of automation. In the Philippines, for example, 53% of workers of ages 55 and above face automation-related risk, 1.5 percentage points higher than the median of all age groups, and 2 percentage points higher than workers of ages 30–54. Such a trend is shared across Asia.

Complicating the situation is the existing "gray divide" (Box Figure 2), where older cohorts remain less familiar with technologies that are often created with youth as primary users. The coverage and depth of use of these technologies remains significantly lower among the elderly than other age groups. In Singapore, the rate of internet access among people ages 60 and above was 68 percentage points lower than for ages 25–34 in 2016. Growing familiarity lowered the gap to 45 percentage points by 2018. Similar trends are evident in the Republic of Korea and Japan. The gray divide has narrowed over time but remains apparent. Governments and the private sector can do more to narrow the gap.

1 : Potential Automation-Related Job Displacement by Age Group—Selected Asian Economies (% of total)

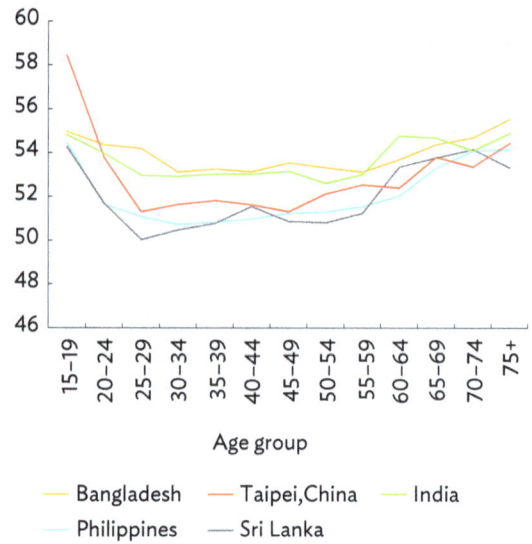

Sources: ADB calculations using data from labor force surveys of Bangladesh (2013); India (2012); the Philippines (2016); Sri Lanka (2014); and Taipei,China (2013); and McKinsey Global Institute (2017)'s technical automation potential by sector.

2: Internet Usage Among Older Cohorts (% of age-specific population)

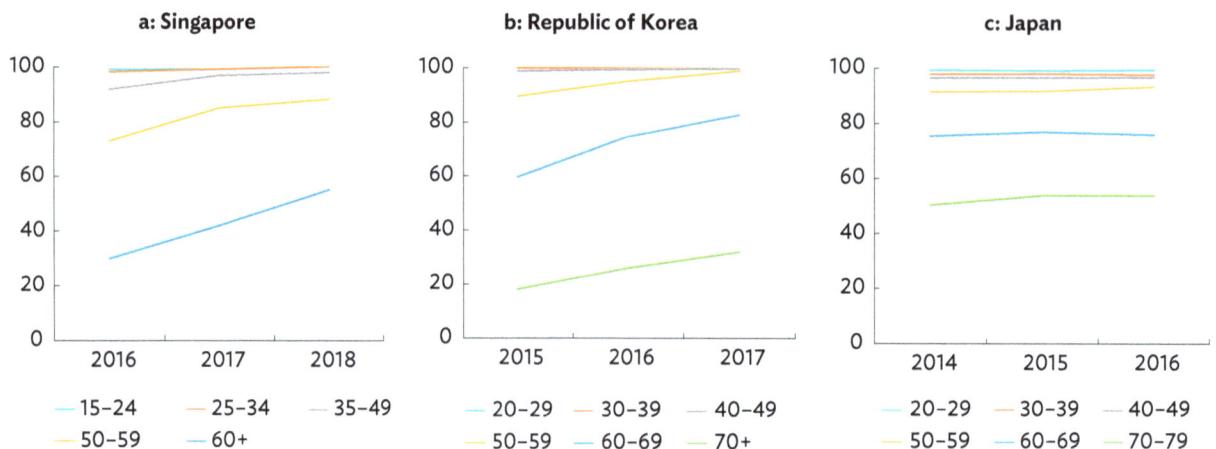

Sources: Infocomm Media Development Authority (Singapore). Annual Survey on Infocomm Usage in Households and by Individuals. www.imda.gov.sg; Ministry of Internal Affairs and Communications (Japan). Information & Communications Statistics Database. http://www.soumu.go.jp/johotsusintokei/whitepaper/h30.html; and Ministry of Science and ICT (Republic of Korea). http://english.msip.go.kr/english/main/main.do (all accessed May 2019).

Source: Asian Development Bank.

Turning the Demographic Headwind to a Tailwind–Policy Considerations

The role of technology for economies with aging populations and workforces has been discussed, and different technologies are systemically presented to show how they can help achieve sustained growth. This last section turns to the question of how government policies can encourage and catalyze technology adoption, in particular grouping these policies for each of the type of economies described in the previous section.

Based on each demographic pattern and corresponding labor market conditions described in the previous section, the first part of this section describes potential challenges and technology opportunities, focusing on where government intervention would be beneficial. Identification of specific technologies to tackle looming labor market challenges for different labor demographic types may help better provide a customized policy approach. In the second part, technology and related labor and social policies are identified that would need to be implemented across the region, along with the adoption of specific technologies. The section concludes with a discussion about how policies that help across the labor demographic types can be introduced.

Analysis of varying patterns of the demographic transition and employment evolution can help identify labor market opportunities and challenges for each type.

An opportunity may arise if demographic patterns are moving in concert with employment patterns. For example, an increase in the workforce as a share of total population by 2050 is accompanied by an increase in employment, balancing labor supply and demand. On the other hand, if these two forces to balance labor markets move in opposite directions or in a noncomplementary manner, then policy makers may have to step in to deal with the imbalances or challenges.

The benefit of using this approach might be that the patterns of mismatch between labor supply and demand for each type can suggest strategic directions about how technologies should be guided (focusing either on supporting the workforce or on modifying and adjusting work and the workplace) given the changing demographic pattern and employment conditions for that type. The caveat is that employment patterns are based on historic trends, which may not be the benchmark for future change. The exercise is to help countries understand how the changing age and education profile of their workforces may be aided by different types of technology.

Type-1: Fast-Aging, Above Median Education

Improved human capital and fast aging suggest Type-1 economies can benefit from all five technology groups.

The dynamics of labor demographics from 1980 to 2050 overlaid with task-disaggregated employment trends in Figure 6.40 reveal two potential opportunities. The first is the relatively large supply of older medium- and high-educated workers by 2050 coinciding with expanding employment opportunities for these segments. Governments in Type-1 countries should place high policy priority on promoting the adoption and application of technologies that complement labor and skills, aid education and skills development throughout one's working life; facilitate job search and match workers to jobs and tasks; and, last, help extend the healthy life expectancy of the aging population. Such types of technologies are particularly suited to support older workers with skills in the middle to high spectrum.

The second opportunity is on expanding supply of younger high-educated workers, given the historic expansion in employment of younger workers performing nonroutine cognitive tasks. A priority should be to take advantage of this opportunity by adopting technologies that complement labor and skills; aid education, skills development, and lifelong learning; and match educated younger jobseekers in work performing relevant nonroutine cognitive tasks.

Figure 6.40: Opportunities and Challenges in Type-1 (Fast-Aging, Above Median Education) Pattern

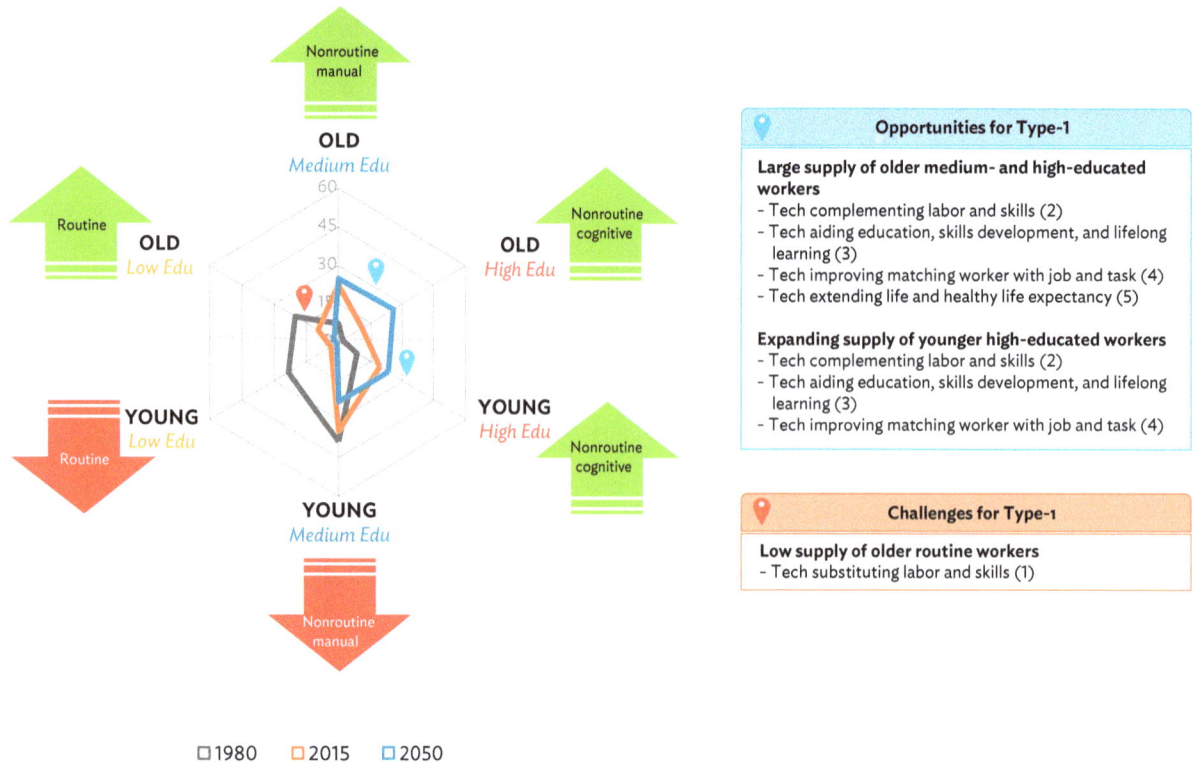

Opportunities for Type-1

Large supply of older medium- and high-educated workers
- Tech complementing labor and skills (2)
- Tech aiding education, skills development, and lifelong learning (3)
- Tech improving matching worker with job and task (4)
- Tech extending life and healthy life expectancy (5)

Expanding supply of younger high-educated workers
- Tech complementing labor and skills (2)
- Tech aiding education, skills development, and lifelong learning (3)
- Tech improving matching worker with job and task (4)

Challenges for Type-1

Low supply of older routine workers
- Tech substituting labor and skills (1)

□ 1980   □ 2015   □ 2050

Notes: Young refers to the economically active population ages 25–49, while old are ages 50–74. Horizontal dashed line delineates the young (lower half) and old (upper half) population. *Low Edu* denotes completion of at most primary education, *Medium Edu* attains secondary education, and *High Edu* has post-secondary education including attendance to short-cycle non-tertiary programs. Numbers in parentheses refer to the technology groups as classified.

Source: Asian Development Bank.

One potential challenge can be gleaned from Type-1 labor demographic and employment patterns. By 2050, the supply of older, low-educated workers will contract even as employment for routine tasks performed by older workers may expand. This mismatch would necessitate implementing technologies that substitute labors and skills, where possible. This could involve automating tasks previously undertaken by manual labor, and use of industrial or service robots. Because of fast aging, a Type-1 country likely faces a contraction of working age population, which calls for the adoption of labor-saving technologies in a wide range of industries. Table 6.3 summarizes the policies that are outlined in this section for all four types of labor demographic pattern.

An appropriate mix of technology and policy support should be designed to aid elderly employees performing routine and/or manual tasks, who are vulnerable to disruptive technologies.

The less educated older cohort may face more challenges given their limited ability to switch careers once their routine manual tasks become obsolete or redundant. However, it is encouraging that the relative increase in employment in other age-task components indicates that skills enhancement could benefit these workers.

Type-2: Fast-Aging, Below Median Education

With delayed improvement in education, the Type-2 pattern suggests that policy be directed to promote technologies toward building skills and job matching.

The primary opportunity for the Type-2 labor demographic pattern will come from an expanding supply of the older medium- and high-educated workforce, provided the relative expansion in employment of nonroutine tasks conducted by older workers continues (Figure 6.41). To harness this opportunity, countries can prioritize technologies that complement workers and their skills, aid skills development and lifelong learning, match workers to appropriate tasks and jobs, and extend healthy life expectancy. A similar set of technologies can benefit the moderately increasing supply of high-educated younger workers as well. A challenge facing a Type-2 country is the persistently high share of low-educated older workers. Routine tasks conducted by low-educated older workers are contracting. Therefore, the challenge is how to train this segment of the labor force to acquire appropriate skills. Adoption of education-related technologies targeting this group is recommended. Another challenge is the undersupply of young middle-educated workers. This can be partly offset by the growing older middle-educated workforce, but technologies that substitute labor or complement existing labor and skills would be also helpful.

With the early stage of technological adoption, Type-2 may be at risk of deindustrialization unless its challenges are properly addressed.

Figure 6.41: Opportunities and Challenges in Type-2 (Fast-Aging, Below Median Education) Pattern

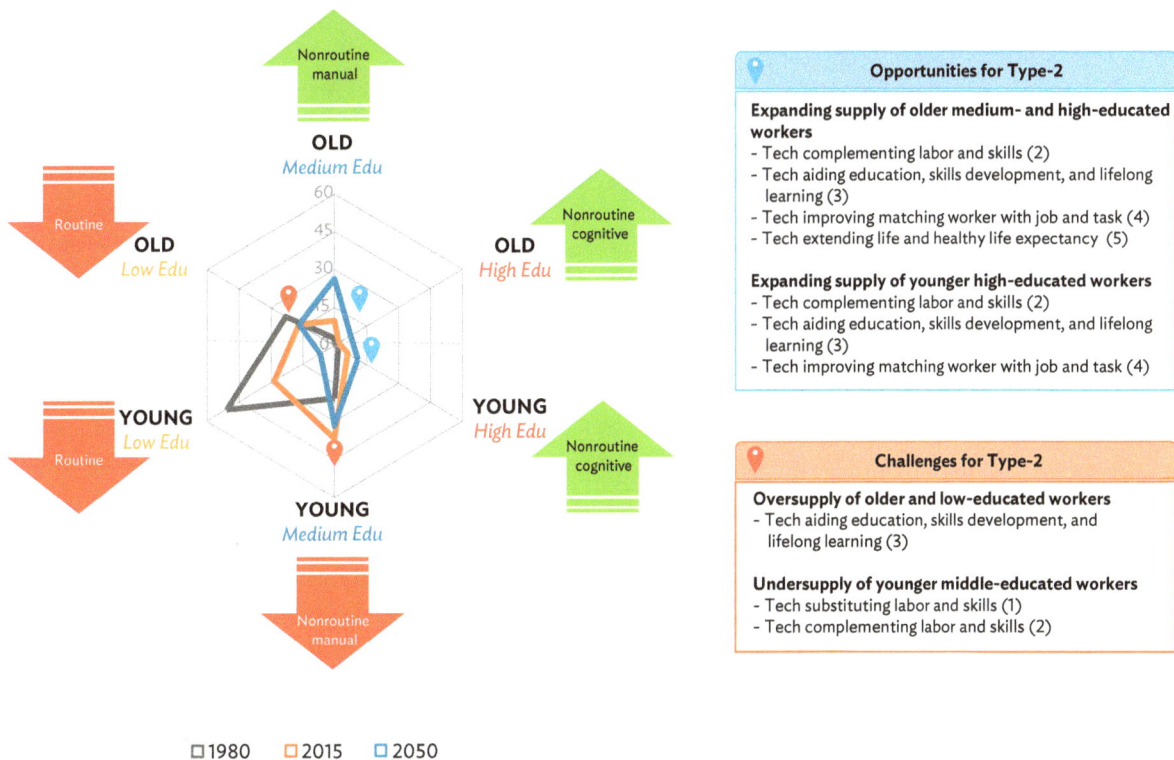

Notes: Young refers to the economically active population ages 25–49, while old are ages 50–74. Horizontal dashed line delineates the young (lower half) and old (upper half) population. *Low Edu* denotes completion of at most primary education, *Medium Edu* attains secondary education, and *High Edu* has post-secondary education including attendance to short-cycle non-tertiary programs. Numbers in parentheses refer to the technology groups as classified.

Source: Asian Development Bank.

With gradual progress in educational achievement, the development of the manufacturing sector, which largely employs workers performing routine tasks, remains a potential vulnerability. As the labor demographic structure shifts toward more medium-educated workers, expansion in employment performing nonroutine tasks will be helpful. Type-2 countries risk premature deindustrialization if less-educated older workers do not get opportunities to improve their skills and health to continue their contribution to the workforce.

Type-3: Slow-Aging, Below Median Education

The Type-3 pattern of age and education demography should prioritize policies to promote technologies that enhance education and skills for both young and old.

There are two opportunities for the Type-3 economies. The first is an expanding supply of older medium-educated workers and a moderate increase of high-educated older workers to match the relative expansion in nonroutine task employment (Figure 6.42). The second opportunity is when the expanding supply of younger medium-educated workers and young high-educated workers are met with increase in employment. Policy makers should pay attention to the types of technology that can complement and develop skills and enhance lifelong learning, and boost job-matching, along with the efforts to adopt technologies that extend healthy working lives. One challenge facing the Type-3 economy is the limited growth in the supply of high-educated workers, be it younger or older, which calls for particular attention to education and skills development technologies as well as those that complement the skilled workforce.

Past structural transformation in Type-3 economies, often characterized by shrinking agriculture sectors,

Figure 6.42: Opportunities and Challenges in Type-3 (Slow-Aging, Below Median Education) Pattern

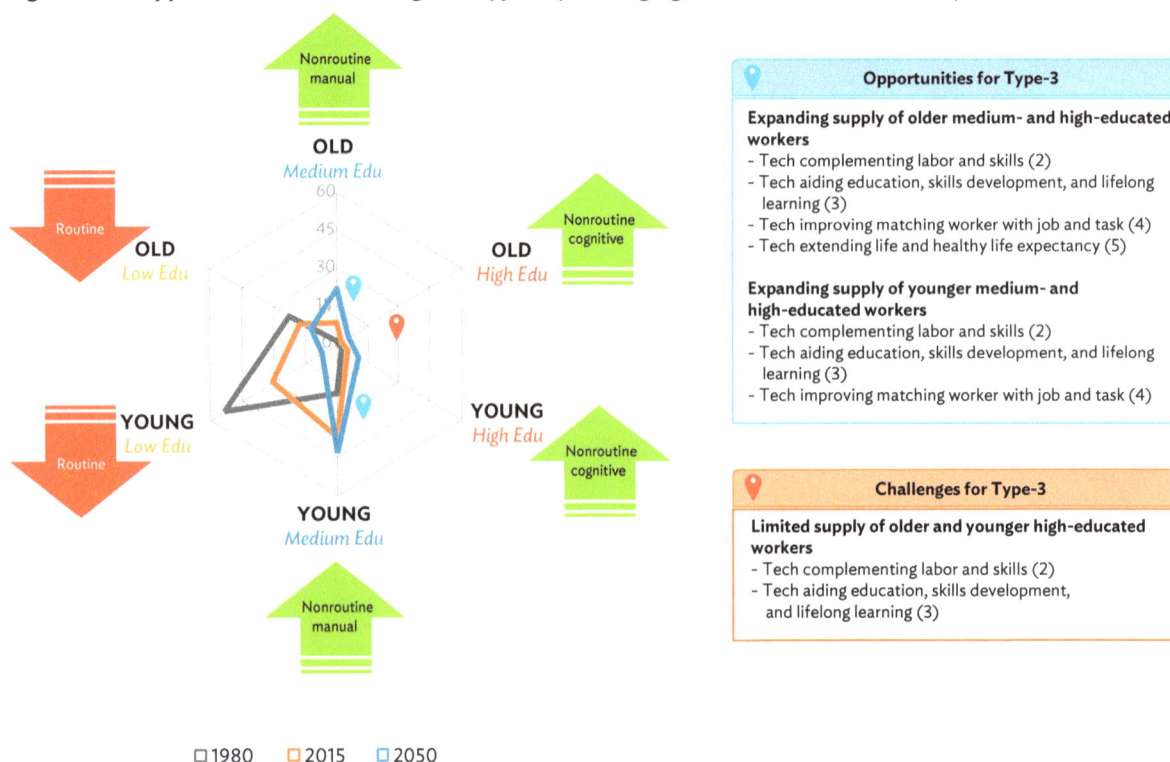

Opportunities for Type-3

Expanding supply of older medium- and high-educated workers
- Tech complementing labor and skills (2)
- Tech aiding education, skills development, and lifelong learning (3)
- Tech improving matching worker with job and task (4)
- Tech extending life and healthy life expectancy (5)

Expanding supply of younger medium- and high-educated workers
- Tech complementing labor and skills (2)
- Tech aiding education, skills development, and lifelong learning (3)
- Tech improving matching worker with job and task (4)

Challenges for Type-3

Limited supply of older and younger high-educated workers
- Tech complementing labor and skills (2)
- Tech aiding education, skills development, and lifelong learning (3)

☐ 1980   ☐ 2015   ☐ 2050

Notes: Young refers to the economically active population ages 25–49, while old are ages 50–74. Horizontal dashed line delineates the young (lower half) and old (upper half) population. *Low Edu* denotes completion of at most primary education, *Medium Edu* attains secondary education, and *High Edu* has post-secondary education including attendance to short-cycle non-tertiary programs. Numbers in parentheses refer to the technology groups as classified.

Source: Asian Development Bank.

explains much of the decline of largely routine employment. In addition, although not apparent in the analysis, both Type-3 and Type-4 economies show low labor force participation by young, educated women. Technology that helps with career counseling and job-matching could help bring these untapped talents to the labor market. Absent proper technologies and policies to build skills, these economies will end up having a large share of the workforce that are willing to work but do not have skills that match the tasks in demand.

Type-4: Slow-Aging, Above Median Education

Type-4 with rapid improvement in educational attainment may face a crunch in middle educated positions.

The opportunity here is that, given the strong human capital development, the supply of both older and younger high-educated workers is expanding (Figure 6.43). Simultaneously, employment for nonroutine cognitive tasks has increased over time. Policy support to adopt technologies that augment skills, improve job market efficiency, and enhance career counseling will be especially important to make the most of this opportunity. Increasing healthy working lives also hold a promise for the technology policy area. The challenge for Type-4 involves an oversupply of older medium-educated workers along with a severe contraction in employment of nonroutine manual tasks. Policy that prioritizes technology adoption for building skills and guiding lifelong learning will be useful to deal with such population and employment trends. Type-4 economies may also experience an undersupply of older low-educated workers to supplement younger workers who often perform routine manual tasks in early stages of their

Figure 6.43: Opportunities and Challenges in Type-4 (Slow-Aging, Above Median Education) Pattern

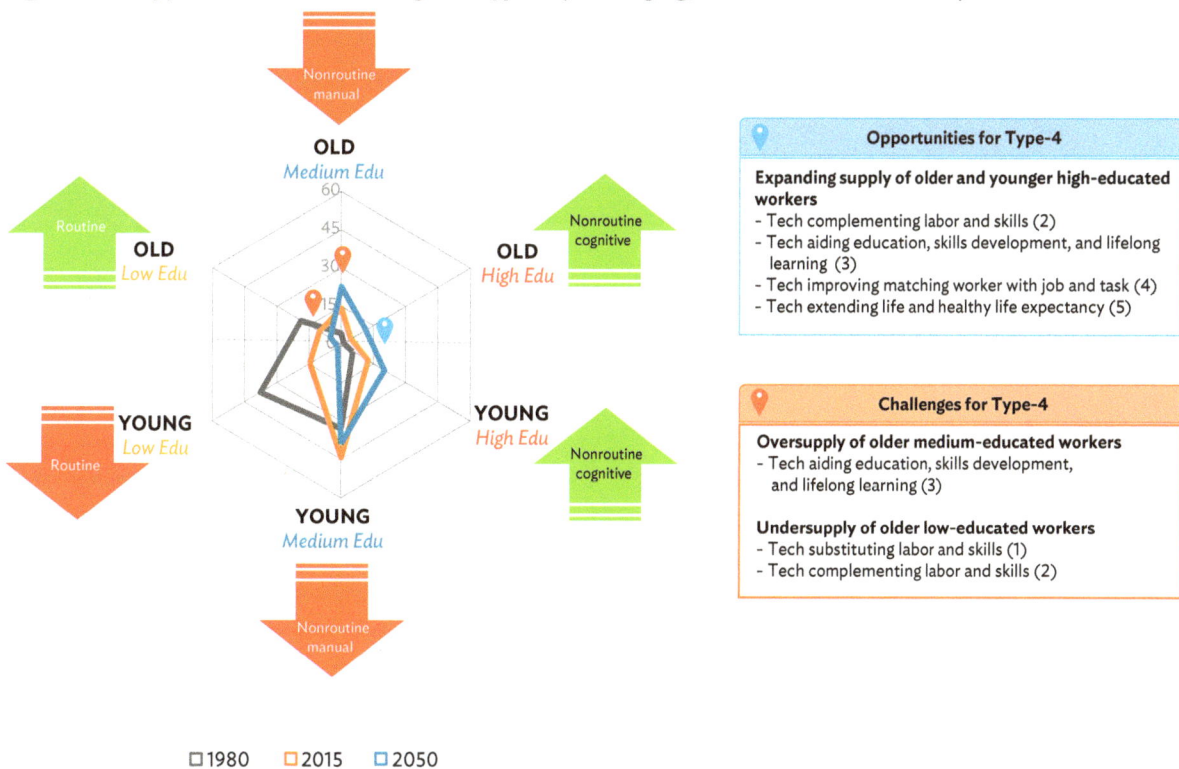

□ 1980   □ 2015   □ 2050

Notes: Young refers to the economically active population ages 25–49, while old are ages 50–74. Horizontal dashed line delineates the young (lower half) and old (upper half) population. *Low Edu* denotes completion of at most primary education, *Medium Edu* attains secondary education, and *High Edu* has post-secondary education including attendance to short-cycle non-tertiary programs. Numbers in parentheses refer to the technology groups as classified.

Source: Asian Development Bank.

careers. The adoption of automation capital or technologies that substitute scarce labor to deal with the shortage may be needed.

While Type-4's high education seems advantageous for rapid technological advances, increased labor market pressure for medium-educated workers remains a concern. Without policies to build skills, unemployment tensions will arise among medium-educated workers. Shifting resources from low productivity traditional sectors toward productive, modern ones is already happening in Type-4 countries. Without this, underemployment could persist. Type-4 economies should leverage technologies that reskill and boost employment and labor productivity. Without such

efforts, middle-skilled workers can be squeezed between job replacement by adoption of automated industrial processes, and demand for a highly educated or well-trained workforce along with advanced technologies.

In sum, Table 6.3 summarizes the different technology needs identified for each labor demographic type that help to harness the unique opportunities and challenges of the varied age/education patterns. Across all four types, fostering professional and foundational skills is important. Last, and importantly, individual countries need to examine their own economic and technological circumstances as well as their unique labor market opportunities and challenges to establish where they should place their priority among varied types of technologies.

Table 6.3: Summary Policy Matrix—Technology Needs by Type of Demographic Pattern and Priority

Type of Age-Education Demographic Pattern	Opportunities and Challenges	Tech Group 1 Substitutes labor and skills	Tech Group 2 Complements labor and skills	Tech Group 3 Aids education, skills development, and lifelong learning	Tech Group 4 Improves matching worker with job and task	Tech Group 5 Extends life and healthy life expectancy
Type-1 Fast-Aging, Above Median Education	Large supply of older medium- and high-educated workers					
	Expanding supply of younger high-educated workers					
	Low supply of older routine workers					
Type-2 Fast-Aging, Below Median Education	Expanding supply of older medium- and high-educated workers					
	Expanding supply of younger high-educated workers					
	Oversupply of older and low-educated workers					
	Undersupply of younger middle-educated workers					
Type-3 Slow-Aging, Below Median Education	Expanding supply of older medium- and high-educated workers					
	Expanding supply of younger medium- and high-educated workers					
	Limited supply of older and younger high-educated workers					
Type-4 Slow-Aging, Above Median Education	Expanding supply of older and younger high-educated workers					
	Oversupply of older medium-educated workers					
	Undersupply of older low-educated workers					

Note: Shaded cells indicate priority consideration.

Source: Asian Development Bank.

Technology Policy Considerations Across Demographic Types

Changing demographics and employment patterns require a major rethinking of education and skills training policies, with an acknowledgment of the necessity of lifelong or adult learning for all.

Technology may make skills of older workers depreciate rapidly, but it can also support workers by providing access to lifelong learning.

In the fast-transforming world of work, it is imperative for workers to acquire the proper skills needed for their jobs and to maintain them. Appropriate technology policy can help countries foster proper skill mixes for future jobs, like strong cognitive skills, including literacy and numeracy, basic ICT skills, analytical skills, and a range of noncognitive skills like creativity, problem-solving, and critical thinking. Interpersonal and communication skills, as well as emotional skills like self-awareness and the ability to manage stress and change, are also increasingly important.

A recent report of the Organisation for Economic Co-operation and Development (OECD) identifies technology, globalization, and aging as leading to widening disparities among workers in OECD countries (OECD 2019). It finds that younger workers without post-secondary education especially have experienced deteriorating labor market conditions (similar to the findings in this report). The report argues that all workers should have access to adequate employment protections, among which collective bargaining continues to be a flexible tool. In addition, advocating for policies that strengthen adult learning is crucial to help workers navigate a changing labor market. The concept of adult learning should be extended here by looking at technologies that support learning to adults, and technologies that support lifelong learning across populations.

Enhancing productivity with a longer working life necessitates regular upgrading of skills in various careers. For effective lifelong learning, governments will need to encourage behavioral change among workers and employers. On the workers' side, older workers face time constraints and a need for repetition and practice (Knowland and Thomas 2014). They also need to recognize the commitment required to acquire the desired skills and make the time to practice (or play out or repeat) what is learned. To maximize the gain from adult learning, it is important to build fundamental skills for learning, unlearning, and relearning of skills, i.e., developing a "learner's mindset." Government policy can help create broader learning ecosystems, where learning environments (teachers, peers, pedagogy along with technology) and a culture of learning (community, gender, age stereotypes) are fostered both internally and across countries in the region.

On the employers' side, firms will need to be incentivized to invest more in employee skills development that is age-neutral. This would imply instituting pedagogy that suits adults and seniors. Neuroscience finds that adults can learn just as well as children when the entire spectrum of learning elements are compared—adults can make better use of reason and learn based on their experiences (Knowland and Thomas 2014). Countries can help bridge the "gray divide" (see Box 6.16) by incentivizing firms to account for elderly workers' specific needs and concerns on technology usage.

Although the previous section highlighted specific policy areas for technology, significant work is still needed to identify all the ways that technology can help encourage lifelong learning in the workplace. Box 6.17 outlines potential directions for policy, given the economic literature. Technology policy that supports lifelong learning will be a common need in all Asian countries, and finding methods to apply the learning across all age groups and skill types will be critical.

Supportive Policies for Technology Adoption in Asia

To gain from increasingly available new technologies, countries will need to put in place policies that are wider in scope and can connect the technology to the workforce.

These include policies that (i) enhance diffusion, adoption, and application of technologies; (ii) adjust

Box 6.17: Setting New Directions Toward Lifelong Learning

In the paper, New Directions in Policies for Lifelong Learning, Kim and Park (2019) address issues to effectively capitalize on digital and new technologies especially in the era of lifelong learning.

Following is a set of new directions for policies drawn based on the review of existing literature:

- **Early childhood learning.** Although advocates on lifelong learning usually emphasize learning in old age, efficient lifelong learning should start from the early years. The effectiveness of human capital investment in later years of a worker's life depends critically on whether the worker was equipped with cognitive skills in early childhood. It is possible to compensate for exposure to adverse environments in early childhood if policy interventions are made sufficiently early in children's lives. Policies directed toward families and their children at early ages may improve the children's later school performance more effectively than expenditure on teacher salaries or new computers. A childcare facility well-staffed with qualified teachers can be a good alternative investment for lifelong learning.

- **Quality of formal education.** A new direction to take in formal education can focus on quality rather than quantities like schooling years. Educational

expenditure should be spent wisely because supply-side policies like spending on educational equipment are not typically effective. Instead, teacher quality should be an area for active policies. Hiring and monitoring high-quality teachers will be essential. This can be accomplished by maintaining high standards of curriculum design and teacher performance and recognizing the significance of retraining and regular assessments of educators.

- **Job training.** Job training before and after market participation has been an important policy arena for lifelong learning. However, these programs do not seem to be effective for improving the socioeconomic performances of trainees. New evidence suggests that job training in the private sector, with government subsidies to firms for worker training, can be more effective.

- **Enhance the role of local governments.** Lifelong learning policies can better achieve goals when tailored to the specific needs of people across age groups and regions. Emphasis should be placed on community-based learning because local facilities in easy reach of the public can play a vital role in creating learning environments as people are more motivated to visit these centers in their spare time.

Source: Kim and Park (2019).

labor markets to allow more flexible work styles; and (iii) reform social security/pension programs to incentivize longer working life.

Firstly, countries can support technological diffusion, adoption, and application across industries and for the aging workforce.

This can be promoted through sufficient funding for research and development and subsidies and tax incentives targeting firms, along with the development of human capital and resources in targeted sectors and industries. Government spending on research and development is a good indicator of technology adoption and has been shown to affect the productivity of aging populations (Aiyar, Ebeke, and Shao 2016).

Strong intellectual property protection also promotes technological application and should be put in place and strengthened, especially in countries with quickly aging populations.

The diffusion and adoption of technological innovation is an important avenue for countries to help technology connect to the workforce. Great inventions such as the internet, Global Positioning System (GPS), and artificial intelligence (AI) provide companies and individuals platforms to use these inventions for different purposes. For technologies to benefit users, such as firms and the elderly workforce, it is very important to create mechanisms that make them accessible. Typically, private companies or institutions have done this connecting, but governments can also take a role.

For example, the Massachusetts Institute of Technology in the US has created an ecosystem for academics, businesses, and workers to test recently created products (e.g., AgeLab, http://agelab.mit.edu/). Business incubation models that address the needs of an aging workforce in Europe (e.g., Active Assisted Living (AAL) Programme, http://www.aal-europe.eu/), and platforms that connect innovators to capital and networks of older workers (e.g., Aging2.0, https://www.aging2.com/) are good examples of projects that can be implemented (Box 6.18 highlights these initiatives).

A second area for wider policies is to create more flexible labor market conditions.

Labor laws should adapt to diverse and flexible working styles that go beyond the present dichotomy of full-time or part-time, employed or self-employed. So-called "gig" economies and workers that earn from it must be also covered by standard labor protection and benefits. Many times, the digital workforce is imaged and framed as "young" creators, but elderly workforce participants that prefer part-time and task-specific employment

with accumulated experience and specific skill sets can equally benefit from flexible work arrangements.

Governments can institute policies that incentivize firms, and promote flexible hiring, retention, and retirement practice by encouraging and subsidizing such reform in mid- and late-career employment, work sharing, and gradual retirement options. By encouraging the matching of older workers to jobs, these policies can create better employment outcomes, as elderly workers can retain familiarity with the workplace, tasks to perform, people and networks, or the community they are in, even if they are not in full-time positions.

The third area for broader policy support is for countries to restructure their social security pension system, and tax systems so as not to penalize or disincentive the elderly to take part in the workforce.

Statutory retirement age can be made more flexible so that individuals can decide when and how to retire. The concept of "pensionable age" as opposed to "retirement

---

Box 6.18: Initiatives That Promote Business and Academic Collaboration and Business Incubators on Aging Technologies

Developments in aging technologies are amplified when academia partners with businesses and the government. One example is the Active Assisted Living (AAL) Programme, where the European Commission and 17 countries fund projects by small and medium-sized enterprises that create information and communication technology (ICT)-based products and services for the elderly in home, community, and workplace. These projects aim to enhance the mobility and autonomy of elderly people, either through improving health or promoting more active lifestyles.

Aging2.0 is another large-scale initiative. It works with over 40,000 innovators across over 20 countries to address "grand challenges" facing older populations, such as engagement and purpose, financial wellness, mobility and movement, daily living and lifestyle, caregiving, care coordination, brain health, and end of life. Members

conduct forums to build awareness and hold global startup competitions to encourage innovation in solving issues about aging.

Since 1999, the Massachusetts Institute of Technology (MIT) AgeLab has been researching and working on projects about caregiving and well-being, retirement and longevity planning, home services and logistics, and transportation and livable communities. MIT works with businesses, governments, and nongovernment organizations to develop ideas and technologies for people to optimize their longer life spans. One of their research tools includes Age Gain Now Empathy System (AGNES), a suit that simulates the physical limitations of the elderly body, such as more fatigue, less flexibility, and sight problems. With the help of its partners and other tools, such as data studio and innovation studios, the lab has released over 280 publications.

Sources: Active Assisted Living (AAL) Programme. http://www.aal-europe.eu/ (accessed July 2019); Aging2.0. https://www.aging2.com/ (accessed July 2019); and Massachusetts Institute of Technology. Agelab. About Agelab. http://agelab.mit.edu/about-agelab (accessed July 2019).

Table 6.4: Early and Normal Retirement Ages by Type of Pension Scheme, 2016

Economy		Scheme	Early	Normal
East Asia/Southeast Asia				
People's Republic of China	men	DB/DC	–	60
	women	DB/DC	–	50/55
Malaysia		DC	50	55
Singapore		DC	–	65
Viet Nam	men	DB	55	60
	women	DB	50	55
South Asia				
India		DB	50	58
		DC		55
Sri Lanka	men	DC	–	55
	women	DC	–	50
OECD				
Australia		DC	60	
Japan		Basic/DB	60	65
Republic of Korea		DB	60	65
United States		DB	62	67
France		DB	62	63

– = early retirement or deferral of pension is not available; DB = defined benefit; DC = defined contribution, OECD = Organisation for Economic Co-operation and Development.

Notes: The normal retirement age is calculated assuming labor market entry at age 20. Where pension ages for men and women differ, they are shown as *men/women*.

Source: OECD (2017).

age" can be further promoted. For some countries undergoing rapid expansion of healthy life spans, revising the statutory retirement age may be needed (Table 6.4). Tax systems that give undue preferential treatment to people of working age who are not in full-time employment should be revisited.

Studies have shown that training offered for at least 1 year and on a flexible schedule has the most impact on earnings. The social security system can also be revisited to promote lifelong learning; for example, by allowing individuals to take breaks from work to upgrade and learn new skills, rather than doing so only when they lose jobs. This "gap year" approach can be encouraged where feasible and more clearly distinguished from frictional unemployment or conditions of mismatch or exit from labor markets.

Efforts can be strengthened to counter ageism in hiring, remuneration, retention, and dismissal procedures, as well as in accessing benefits and skills training.

So far, countries such as the US, Canada, Australia, and in Europe have banned discrimination based on age. There is significant variation in the provision, however. For example, the Age Discrimination in Employment Act of 1967 of the US is applicable to workers of ages 40 and above, whereas the European Commission directive is a comprehensive law prohibiting age and other discrimination across all working ages.[66] In many parts of Asia, where firms make recruitment, promotion, and retirement decisions based on seniority, comprehensive bans on workplace age discrimination

---

[66]   Council Directive 2000/78/EC of 27 November 2000 establishing a general framework for equal treatment in employment and occupation bans workplace discrimination based on age, belief, disability, and sexual orientation.

have been considered potentially disruptive to business. Experience from countries with anti-age discrimination law, especially in Europe, shows legal provisions can curtail age-based discrimination while accommodating customary employment practices if the rationale behind differential treatment is legitimate and justifiable.

Regional Cooperation in the Era of Workforce Aging

Turning to Asia, policies to promote regional cooperation and tackle issues related to aging can help leverage diverse regional demographic trends.

To determine regional policies, two broad areas can be examined: demographic change and employment patterns, and technology adoption. Examining the demographic and employment momentum for the region overall, Figure 6.44 shows balanced growth in the population in 2050, and that relatively equal employment of tasks will be available across the six categories. There is a shift in demographics toward more high-educated workers, but there will still be workers with at most a primary education available. Also, employment shows a slight overall contraction in routine tasks, but expansion in other areas. This balanced growth of population and equal employment of tasks would imply that regional cooperation in Asia can help meet future needs from aging.

The level of technology adoption is an important indicator of how willing countries will be to adopt technology to aid the elderly population in future. Using an innovation capability score as a proxy for technology adoption, it is clear that adoption varies significantly across Asia. Categorizing the region's countries into the four types, the economies undergoing a Type-1 pattern are in a more advanced stage, with the rest at early stages of technological adaption and capacity (Figure 6.45).

The regional picture on demographics, employment, and technology adoption would imply that labor, capital, and technology movement across Asia could help alleviate particular challenges facing certain types and expand on

Figure 6.44: Regional Demographics and Task Employment—Asia

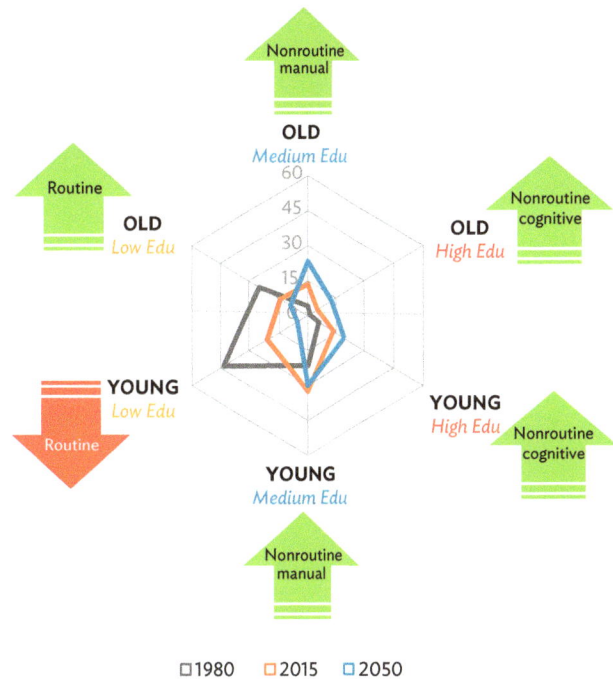

☐ 1980   ☐ 2015   ☐ 2050

Notes: Young refers to the economically active population ages 25–49, while old are ages 50–74. Horizontal dashed line delineates the young (lower half) and old (upper half) population. *Low Edu* denotes completion of at most primary education, *Medium Edu* attains secondary education, and *High Edu* has post-secondary education including attendance to short-cycle non-tertiary programs.

Source: Asian Development Bank.

particular opportunities (Figure 6.46). Specifically, three movements can be encouraged.

First, promoting foreign direct investment from Type-1 to three other types of labor demographic patterns can help tap a large supply of middle-skilled workers in the region.

An ADB study finds that greenfield foreign direct investment (FDI) alone generated almost a million jobs in 2018 (See Chapter 2: Cross-Border Investment). Around half these jobs were created through intraregional FDI. The potential of job generation through FDI from Type-1 fast aging countries remain large. The surge in FDI to Asia has been largely linked to the expansion of global value chains in manufacturing as multinationals relocated parts of the production process in search of lower labor costs.

Figure 6.45: Technology Adoption by Archetype—Asia

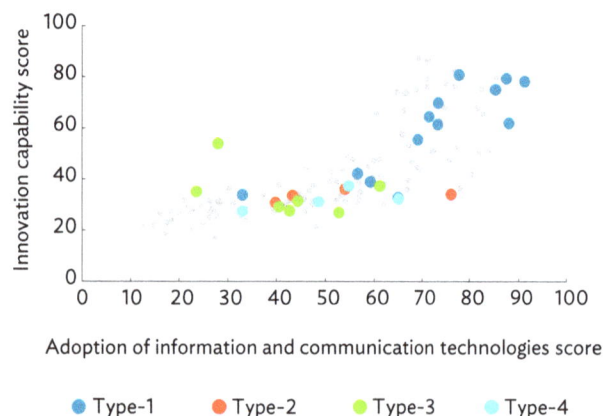

Adoption of information and communication technologies score

● Type-1   ● Type-2   ● Type-3   ● Type-4

Notes: Score on adoption of information and communication technologies (ICTs) refers to the Pillar 3 of Global Competitiveness Index (GCI) 4.0 and captures the degree of diffusion of specific ICTs. Score on innovation capability is the Pillar 12 of the GCI 4.0 and captures quantity and quality of formal research and development; the extent to which a country's environment encourages collaboration, connectivity, creativity, diversity and confrontation across different visions and angles; and the capacity to turn ideas into new goods and services. Asian economies are the colored dots, and are differentiated by archetypes. Type-1 includes the fast aging and high education economies. Type-2 includes the fast aging and low education economies. Type-3 includes the slow aging and low education economies. Type-4 includes the slow aging and high education economies. In gray dots are non-Asian economies.

Source: ADB calculations using data from World Economic Forum (2018).

Type-2 and Type-3 countries can continue to leverage their comparative advantage of abundant low- and middle-educated workers to create manufacturing jobs in labor-intensive industries. More recently, however, services FDI accounted for almost 40% of the total in 2017, most notably in ICT-enabled services. Almost 30% of greenfield jobs in the region were also created in services that employ the more educated workforce.

FDI promotion depends on several factors, including comparative advantage, economic integration, the quality of institutions, and policy factors.

Business environment and the quality of governance are important policy determinants of FDI, particularly from Asian source economies. Improving the business environment—through better ease of doing business such as ease of registering property or obtaining credit—can complement governance quality, which is often more time consuming to reform. Industrial policy such

as the creation of economic zones and investment liberalization that gives investors protection through dispute settlement mechanisms are all important tools for Type-2, Type-3, and Type-4 countries to create an investor-friendly environment.

Second, facilitating the international migration of workers from Type-3 to Type-1 economies, and from Type-4 to Type-3, can alleviate challenges associated with a lack of low-educated routine workers in Type-1 economies, and the limited supply of high-educated workers in Type-3.

Of the three recommendations for capital, technology, and labor movement across the types, capital and technology are already flowing between countries. The more challenging problem is to improve cross-country labor mobility. Two general solutions are promoting portability of skills and strengthening mechanism to bring transparency in the process of hiring and employing overseas workers. Both are increasingly important and regarded as promising forms of regional public goods in aging Asia.

Mutual skills recognition such as one adopted in a few Association of Southeast Asian Nations economies has the potential to catalyze increased mobility of labor across borders.

Facilitation of labor mobility requires a framework that recognizes skills and qualification, as well as a program that links those skills to jobs. Association of Southeast Asian Nations (ASEAN), for example, have mutual recognition agreements (MRAs) for several occupations such as architecture, engineering, medicine, nursing, and tourism, and some occupations have started issuing ASEAN licenses. These initiatives can lay a groundwork for creating mechanism to recognize qualifications covering a larger number of countries in the region. In addition, a lesson from the implementation of MRAs in ASEAN is that the establishment of qualification recognition system alone may not promote the skill mobility (Kikkawa and Suan 2019). It is therefore important that acquired recognition is linked to existing

Figure 6.46: Entry Points for Regional Cooperation Strategies

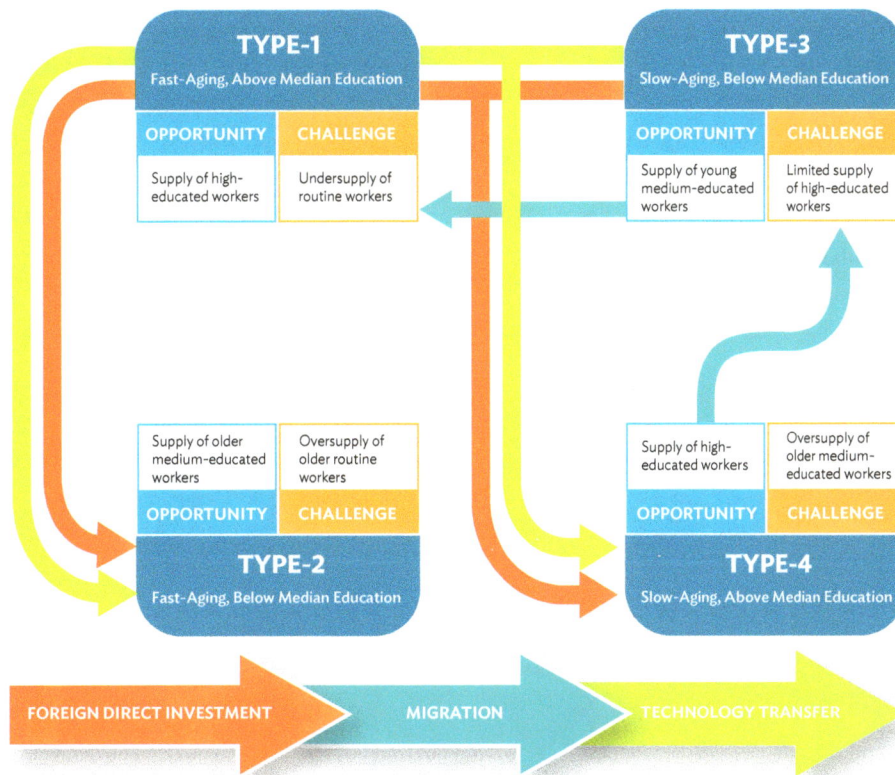

Source: Asian Development Bank.

or new channels of a skill migration program to encourage and promote the use, for example, by providing priority in various immigration-related verification and visa processing. In addition to MRA, a bilateral social security agreement that provides for mutual recognition of pensions and other contributions can reduce the barriers and cost to cross-border labor mobility, especially among the mature and older workforce.

Another solution, which is particularly important in the context of facilitating the mobility of workers with vocational skills is to strengthen mechanisms to bring transparency in the labor market of overseas workers and build an effective monitoring system to ensure that recruitment, placement, and employment of workers follow the stipulated rules and regulations. Collaboration among source and destination countries are needed to guide placement agencies and employers and help promote orderly and safe cross-border movement of migrant workers.

Benefits gained from labor mobility liberalization far exceed anticipated gains from removing barriers to trade or capital flow.

Estimated global gains from 1984 (Hamilton and Whalley 1984) were as large as $3.4 trillion, and even without full migration, they were estimated in 2004 at worth up to $1.97 trillion a year (Clemens 2011, Moses and Letnes 2004). Eliminating global restrictions resulted in efficiency gains of 15%–67% of world GDP, according to Iregui (2003). Moses and Letnes (2004) also show that a 10% increase in international migration corresponded to an efficiency gain of about $774 billion. Whether Asia as a region can seize this opportunity depends partly on whether its countries can create an enabling regional mechanism to encourage cross-border labor mobility.

Third, encouraging cross-border technology transfer can facilitate greater adoption and diffusion of technology to the elderly and poorer populations.

As seen from Figure 6.45, countries in the Type-1 demographic pattern typically have higher rates of technology adoption and diffusion. For countries of other types, where such technologies are not as widespread, companies or governments may be able to create forums for technology transfer. For example, Wi-Fi provision in rural and poorer populations is usually difficult because, given the expected return, private providers do not want to make the necessary infrastructure investments. To increase public Wi-Fi coverage, countries may make Wi-Fi provision a public good—which would enhance the use of other technologies to help the elderly and low-skill populations.

Background Papers

Chomik, R., and J. Piggott. 2018. Population Ageing and Technology: Two Megatrends Shaping the Labour Market in Asia. *ARC Centre of Excellence in Population Ageing Research Working Paper*. No. 2018/10.

Ge, S., and J. Zhang. 2019. Population Aging, Technological Change, and Productivity: Case Study of People's Republic of China. Background paper for the *Asian Economic Integration Report 2019/2020* Theme Chapter on "Demographic Change, Productivity, and the Role of Technology in Asia." Manuscript.

Kapoor, R. 2019. Tapping Technology to Harness the Demographic Dividend in Asia. Background paper for the *Asian Economic Integration Report 2019/2020* Theme Chapter on "Demographic Change, Productivity, and the Role of Technology in Asia." Manuscript.

Kawaguchi, D. and K. Muroga. 2019. Population Aging, Productivity, and Technology in Japan. Background paper for the *Asian Economic Integration Report 2019/2020* Theme Chapter on "Demographic Change, Productivity, and the Role of Technology in Asia." Manuscript.

Kim, J., and C.Y. Park. 2019. New Directions of Economic Policies in the Era of Lifelong Learning. Background paper for the *Asian Economic Integration Report 2019/2020* Theme Chapter on "Demographic Change, Productivity, and the Role of Technology in Asia." Manuscript.

Park, C. Y., K. Shin, and A. Kikkawa. 2019a. Aging, Automation and Productivity: A Case of Korea. Background paper for the *Asian Economic Integration Report 2019/2020* Theme Chapter on "Demographic Change, Productivity, and the Role of Technology in Asia." Manuscript.

———. 2019b. Demographical Change, Technological Advance, and Growth: A Cross-Country Analysis. Background paper for the *Asian Economic Integration Report 2019/2020* Theme Chapter on "Demographic Change, Productivity, and the Role of Technology in Asia." Manuscript.

References

Abeliansky, A., and K. Prettner. 2017. Automation and Demographic Change. *Center for European, Governance and Economic Development Research Discussion Papers.* No. 310. University of Goettingen.

Active Assisted Living (AAL) Programme. http://www.aal-europe.eu/ (accessed July 2019).

Acemoglu, D., and P. Restrepo. 2017. Secular Stagnation? The Effect of Aging on Economic Growth in the Age of Automation. *American Economic Review.* 107 (5). pp. 174–179.

——— 2018. Demographics and Automation. *NBER Working Paper.* No. 24421. Cambridge, MA: National Bureau of Economic Research.

Adler, L. 2016. New Survey Reveals 85% of All Jobs are Filled Via Networking. 29 February. *Linkedin.com.* https://www.linkedin.com/pulse/new-survey-reveals-85-all-jobs-filled-via-networking-lou-adler/.

Aging2.0. https://www.aging2.com/ (accessed July 2019).

Aiyar, S., C. Ebeke, and X. Shao. 2016. The Impact of Workforce Aging on European Productivity. *IMF Working Paper.* No. 16/238. Washington, DC: International Monetary Fund.

Altmann, S., A. Falk, S. Jäger, and F. Zimmermann. 2018. Learning about Job Search: A Field Experiment with Job Seekers in Germany. *Journal of Public Economics.* 164 (C). pp. 33–49.

Asian Development Bank (ADB). 2018. *Asian Development Outlook 2018: How Technology Affects Jobs.* Manila.

———. 2019. *Youth Education Investment and Labor Market Outcomes in the Philippines.* Manila.

Arbulu, I., V. Lath, M. Mancini, A. Patel, and O. Tonby. 2018. *Industry 4.0: Reinvigorating ASEAN Manufacturing for the Future.* Singapore: McKinsey & Company.

Arita, S., A. Hiyama, and M. Hirose. 2017. GBER: A Social Matching App which Utilizes Time, Place, and Skills of Workers and Jobs. In Proceedings of CSCW '17 Companion of the 2017 ACM Conference on Computer Supported Cooperative Work and Social Computing. 25 February–1 March. Portland, Oregon. pp. 127–130.

Badurashvili, I., and M. Nadareishvili. 2012. *Social Impact of Emigration and Rural-Urban Migration in Central and Eastern Europe: Final Country Report–Georgia.* Brussels. European Commission.

Balachandran, A., J. de Beer, K.S. James, L. van Wissen, and F. Janssen. 2017. Comparison of Ageing in Europe and Asia: Refining the Prospective Age Approach with a Cross-Country Perspective. *NIDI Working Paper.* 2017/01. The Hague: Netherlands Interdisciplinary Demographic Institute.

Beall, A. 2019. Big Data in Health Care: How Three Organizations Are Using Big Data to Improve Patient Care and More. SAS. https://www.sas.com/en_us/insights/articles/big-data/big-data-in-healthcare.html.

Becker, G. 1960. An Economic Analysis of Fertility. In G. S. Becker, ed. *Demographic and Economic Change in Developed Countries.* Princeton: Princeton University Press.

Belbase, A., G. Sanzenbacher, and C. Gillis. 2015. Does Age-Related Decline in Ability Correspond with Retirement Age? *CRR Working Paper.* 2015-24. Chestnut Hill, MA: Center for Retirement Research at Boston College.

Bell, D. and D. Blanchflower. 2011. Young People and the Great Recession. *Oxford Review of Economic Policy.* 27 (2), Summer. pp. 241–267.

Bloom, D., and D. Canning. 2004. Global Demographic Change: Dimensions and Economic Significance. *NBER Working Paper*. No. 10817. Cambridge, MA: National Bureau of Economic Research.

Bloom, D., and J. Williamson. 1998. Demographic Transitions and Economic Miracles in Emerging Asia. *The World Bank Economic Review*. 12. pp. 419–455.

Bloom, D., D. Canning, and J. Sevilla. 2003. *The Demographic Dividend: A New Perspective on the Economic Consequences of Population Change*. Santa Monica: RAND.

Bloom, N., J. Liang, J. Roberts, and Z. Ying. 2015. Does Working from Home Work? Evidence from a Chinese Experiment. *The Quarterly Journal of Economics*. 130 (1). pp. 165–218.

Cancho, C., S. Facusse, and T. Berenice. 2019. *Armenia International Outmigration: An Exploration on the Effects on Armenian Households' Welfare*. Washington, DC: World Bank Group.

Center for Retirement Research at Boston College. Susceptibility Index. http://crr.bc.edu/wp-content/uploads/2016/04/Susceptibility-Index_April-2016.pdf (accessed July 2019).

Chakraborty, A. 2017. Japan's Elderly Are Banking Heavily on Driverless Cars. *NewsBytes*. 14 September. https://www.newsbytesapp.com/timeline/Science/11009/59150/japan-embracing-self-driving-technology-wholeheartedly.

Chesnais, J. C. 1992. *The Demographic Transition: Stages, Patterns, and Economic Implications*. Oxford University Press.

Clemens, M. 2011. Economics and Emigration: Trillion-Dollar Bills on the Sidewalk? *Journal of Economic Perspectives*. 25 (3). pp. 83–106.

Coile, C., K. Milligan, and D. Wise. 2017. Health Capacity to Work at Older Ages: Evidence from the United States. In *Social Security Programs and Retirement around the World*, edited by D. Wise. Chicago: University of Chicago Press.

Coursera. https://blog.coursera.org/about/ (accessed June 2019).

Dawson, H. 2019. How Robotic Pets Can Help the Elderly in Care Homes Be Happy and Mingle More (Without Needing to Feed and Walk Them). *Daily Mail*. 9 May. https://www.dailymail.co.uk/news/article-7008589/How-robotic-pets-help-elderly-care-homes-happy-mingle-more.html

Deloitte LLP. 2016. *The Three Billion: Enterprise Crowdsourcing and the Growing Fragmentation of Work*. Deloitte: London.

Derrien, F., A. Kecskes, and P. A. Nguyen. 2018. Labor Force Demographics and Corporate Innovation. *HEC Research Paper Series*. No. 1243. HEC Paris.

Digital Therapeutics Alliance. 2018. *Digital Therapeutics: Combining Technology and Evidence-Based Medicine to Transform Personalized Patient Care*. https://www.dtxalliance.org/wp-content/uploads/2018/09/DTA-Report_DTx-Industry-Foundations.pdf.

Dumaua-Cabauatan, M., S. Calizo, F. Quimba, and L. Pacio. 2018. E-Education in the Philippines: The Case of Technical Education and Skills Development Authority Online Program. *PIDS Discussion Paper Series*. 2018–08. Manila: Philippine Institute for Development Studies.

East-West Center. 2017. Sharing the Demographic Dividend: Findings from Low and Middle Income Countries in Asia. *National Transfer Accounts Bulletin*. 12 (December). pp. 1–4. Honolulu.

EkStep. https://ekstep.in/ (accessed July 2019).

e-Stat (Portal Site of Official Statistics of Japan). https://www.e-stat.go.jp/ (accessed August 2019).

Eurofund and the International Labour Office. 2017. *Working Anytime, Anywhere: The Effects on the World of Work*. Luxembourg: Publications Office of the European Union, and Geneva: International Labour Office.

Fair, R., and K. Dominguez. 1991. Effects of the Changing U.S. Age Distribution on Macroeconomic Equations. *American Economic Review*. 81 (5). pp. 1276–1294.

Feyrer, J. 2007. Demographics and Productivity. *The Review of Economics and Statistics*. 89 (1). pp. 100–109.

Fleming, S. 2019. Japan's Workforce Will be 20% Smaller by 2040. *World Economic Forum: Regional Agenda*. 12 February. https://www.weforum.org/agenda/2019/02/japan-s-workforce-will-shrink-20-by-2040/.

Foster, M. 2018. Aging Japan: Robots May Have Role in Future of Elder Care. *Reuters*. 27 March. https://www.reuters.com/article/us-japan-ageing-robots-wideimage/aging-japan-robots-may-have-role-in-future-of-elder-care-idUSKBN1H33AB.

Foundation Medicine. 2018. Foundation Medicine Announces Regulatory Approval of FoundationOne CDx in Japan. News Release. 27 December. http://investors.foundationmedicine.com/news-releases/news-release-details/foundation-medicine-announces-regulatory-approval.

Gale, A. 2018. Japan to Accept More Foreign Workers in a Break from Its Historical Stance. *The Wall Street Journal*. 7 December. https://www.wsj.com/articles/japan-to-accept-more-foreign-workers-in-a-break-from-its-historical-stance-1544215014?mod=searchresults&page=1&pos=1&ns=prod/accounts-wsj.

GBD 2017 DALYs and HALE Collaborators. 2018. Global, Regional, and National Disability-Adjusted Life-Years (DALYs) for 359 Diseases and Injuries and Healthy Life Expectancy (HALE) for 195 Countries and Territories, 1990–2017: A Systematic Analysis for the Global Burden of Disease Study 2017. *Global Health Metrics*. 392 (10159). pp. 1859–1922.

GBER: Gathering Brisk Elderly in the Region. http://gber.jp/ (accessed July 2019).

Government of the People's Republic of China, Ministry of Human Resources and Social Security. 2016. China Labour Statistical Yearbook 2016. http://www.mohrss.gov.cn/2016/indexeh.htm (accessed June 2019).

Graetz, G., and G. Michaels. 2018. Robots at Work. *The Review of Economics and Statistics*. 100 (5). pp. 753–768.

Groves, P., B. Kayyali, D. Knott, and S. Van Kuiken. 2013. *The 'Big Data' Revolution in Healthcare: Accelerating Value and Innovation*. https://www.mckinsey.com/insights/health_systems/~/media/7764A72F70184C8EA88D805092D72D58.ashx.

Hamilton, B. and J. Whalley. 1984. Efficiency and Distributional Implications of Global Restrictions on Labour Mobility: Calculations and Policy Implications. *Journal of Development Economics*. 14 (1). pp. 61–75.

Haraya Learning Innovations. https://haraya.xyz/ (accessed July 2019).

Harden, P. 2016. How to Land a Job by Networking. 23 May. *The Washington Post*. 23 May. https://jobs.washingtonpost.com/article/how-to-land-a-job-by-networking/.

Hayami, Y., and V. Ruttan. 1984. Toward a Theory of Induced Institutional Innovation. *The Journal of Development Studies*. 20 (4). pp. 203–223.

Hillestad, R., J. Bigelow, A. Bower, F. Girosi, R. Meili, R. Scoville, and R. Taylor. 2005. Can Electronic Medical Record Systems Transform Health Care? Potential Benefits, Savings, And Costs. *Health Affairs*. 24 (5). pp. 1103–1117.

HireVue. Unilever + HireVue: Unilever Finds Top Talend Faster with HireVue Assessments. https://www.hirevue.com/customers/global-talent-acquisition-unilever-case-study (accessed July 2019).

Ho, V. 2018. The Yield: How to Feed the World Without "Wrecking the Planet." Microsoft: Transform. 23 August. https://news.microsoft.com/transform/videos/yield-feed-world-without-wrecking-planet/.

Huh, U., Y.J. Tak, S. Song, S.W. Chung, S.M. Sung, C.W. Lee, M. Bae, and H.Y. Ahn. 2019. Feedback on Physical Activity Through a Wearable Device Connected to a Mobile Phone App in Patients with Metabolic Syndrome: Pilot Study. *JMIR Mhealth Uhealth*. 7 (6). e13381.

Hyundai. 2018. Hyundai Motor Group Ventures Further into New Robotics Industry of the Future. News Release. 22 October. https://www.hyundainews.com/en-us/releases/2631.

IBM. What is Big Data Analytics? https://www.ibm.com/analytics/hadoop/big-data-analytics (accessed July 2019).

Infocomm Media Development Authority (Singapore). Annual Survey on Infocomm Usage in Households and by Individuals. www.imda.gov.sg (accessed May 2019).

International Federation of Robotics (IFR). 2018. Presentation at the IFR Press Conference. Tokyo. 18 October. https://ifr.org/downloads/press2018/WR_Presentation_Industry_and_Service_Robots_rev_5_12_18.pdf.

———. Statistics. https://ifr.org (accessed June 2019).

International Labour Organization. 2015. *World Employment Social Outlook Trends 2015*. Geneva.

———. ILOSTAT. https://www.ilo.org/ilostat (accessed June 2019).

Indeed. About Indeed. https://www.indeed.com/about (accessed July 2019).

Ip, G. 2019. How Aging Japan Defied Demographics and Revived Its Economy. *The Wall Street Journal*. 11 January. https://www.wsj.com/articles/how-aging-japan-defied-demographics-and-turned-around-its-economy-11547222490.

Iregui, A. 2003. Efficiency Gains from the Elimination of Global Restrictions on Labour Mobility: An Analysis Using a Multiregional CGE Model. *WIDER Working Paper Series*. No. 027. Helsinki: World Institute for Development Economic Research (UNU-WIDER).

Jun, J. 2019. SK Telecom Creates 5G-based Smart Office. *TheKoreaTimes*. 13 February. https://www.koreatimes.co.kr/www/tech/2019/02/133_263616.html.

Kachouie, R., S. Sedighadeli, R. Khosla, and M. T. Chiu. 2014. Socially Assistive Robots in Elderly Care: A Mixed-Method Systematic Literature Review. *International Journal of Human-Computer Interaction*. 30 (5). pp. 369–393.

KC, S., and W. Lutz. 2017. The Human Core of the Shared Socioeconomic Pathways: Population Scenarios by Age, Sex and Level of Education for All Countries to 2100. *Global Environmental Change*. 42. pp. 181–192.

KC, S., W. Lutz, M. Potančoková, G. Abel, B. Barakat, J. Eder, A. Goujon, S. Jurasszovich, T. Sobotka, M. Speringer, E. Striessnig, M. Wurzer, D. Yildiz, S. H. Yoo, and K. Zeman. 2018. Chapter 2: Approach, Methods, and Assumptions. In W. Lutz, A. Goujon, S. KC, M. Stonawski, and N. Stilianakis, eds. *Demographic and Human Capital Scenarios for the 21st Century: 2018 Assessment for 201 Countries*. Luxembourg: Publications Office of the European Union.

Kenthapadi, K., B. Le, and G. Venkataraman. 2017. Personalized Job Recommendation System at LinkedIn: Practical Challenges and Lessons Learned. In *Proceedings of RecSys '17*. 27–31 August. Como, Italy. pp. 346–347.

Kikkawa, A. and E. B. Suan. 2019. Trends and Patterns in Intra-ASEAN Migration. In E. Gentile, ed. *Skilled Labor Mobility and Migration: Challenges and Opportunities for the ASEAN Economic Community*. Manila: Asian Development Bank and UK: Edward Elgar.

Kimura, M., K. Hirakawa, T. Okuno, Y. Oda, T. Morimoto, T. Kitani, D. Fujita, and H. Nagata. 1989. An Analysis of Physical Fitness in the Aged People with Fitness Battery Test. *Jpn J Phys Fitness Sports*. 38. pp. 175–185.

Knowland, V. C. P., and M. S. C. Thomas. 2014. Educating the Adult Brain: How the Neuroscience of Learning Can Inform Educational Policy. *International Review of Education*. 60. pp. 99–122.

Ko, P. C., and K. Hank. 2014. Grandparents Caring for Grandchildren in China and Korea: Findings from CHARLS and KLoSA. *Journals of Gerontology*. Series B: Psychological Sciences and Social Sciences. 69 (4). pp. 646–651.

Koh, D. 2019. Ping An Good Doctor Launches Commercial Operation of One-Minute Clinics in China. *MobiHealthNews*. 7 January. https://www.mobihealthnews.com/news/asia-pacific/ping-good-doctor-launches-commercial-operation-one-minute-clinics-china.

Kolodny, L., and M. Petrova. 2017. This Robotic Glove Will Give You Bionic Hands. *CNBC*. 23 September. https://www.cnbc.com/2017/09/23/nuada-robot-glove-will-give-you-bionic-hands.html.

Korea Education and Research Information Service (KERIS). http://www.keris.or.kr/english/index.jsp (accessed June 2019).

Korean Statistical Information Service. https://kosis.kr/eng/ (accessed June 2019).

Krokos, E., C. Plaisant, and A. Varshney. 2018. Virtual Memory Palaces: Immersion Aids Recall. *Virtual Reality*. 23 (1). pp. 1–15.

Learn Education. https://www.learneducation.co.th/ (accessed July 2019).

Lee, C., S. Czaja, and J. Sharit. 2009. Training Older Workers for Technology-based Employment. *Educational Gerontology*. 35 (1). pp. 15–31.

Lee, H. H., and K. Shin 2019. Nonlinear Effects of Population Aging on Economic Growth. *Japan and the World Economy*. 51 (100963).

Levin, R. 2017. 2017 Learners Outcomes Survey: Online Learners Report Benefits from Advancing their Careers to Discovering a Field of Study to Gaining Confidence. *Coursera Blog*. 26 April. https://blog.coursera.org/online-learners-around-world-report-benefits-ranging-advancing-careers-discovering-field-study-gaining-confidence/.

Li, S. C., U. Lindenberger, B. Hommel, G. Aschersleben, W. Prinz, and P. B. Baltes. 2004. Transformations in the Couplings Among Intellectual Abilities and Constituent Cognitive Processes Across the Life Span. *Psychological Science*. 15 (3). pp. 155–163.

Liang, J., H. Wang, and E. Lazear. 2018. Demographics and Entrepreneurship. *Journal of Political Economy*. 126 (1). pp. 140–196.

Lindh, T. and B. Malmberg. 1999. Age Distributions and the Current Account–A Changing Relation? *Uppsala Working Paper Series*. 21. Uppsala University, Department of Economics.

LinkedIn. Newsroom: Statistics. https://news.linkedin.com/about-us#statistics (accessed June 2019).

Liu, Y., and N. Westlius. 2017. The Impact of Demographics on Productivity and Inflation in Japan. *Journal of International Commerce, Economics and Policy*. 8 (2). pp. 1–16.

Maestas, N., K. Mullen, and D. Powell. 2016. The Effect of Population Aging on Economic Growth, the Labor Force and Productivity. *NBER Working Paper*. No. 22452. Cambridge, MA: National Bureau of Economic Research.

Marinov, B. 2019. Passive Exoskeletons Establish A Foothold in Automotive Manufacturing. *Forbes.com*. 15 May. https://www.forbes.com/sites/borislavmarinov/2019/05/15/passive-exoskeletons-establish-a-foothold-in-automotive-manufacturing/#3a65392434ce.

Marr, B. 2018. The Key Definitions of Artificial Intelligence (AI) That Explain Its Importance. *Forbes.com*. 14 February. https://www.forbes.com/sites/bernardmarr/2018/02/14/the-key-definitions-of-artificial-intelligence-ai-that-explain-its-importance/#44ebd01c4f5d.

Mason, A., and R. Lee. 2011. Population Aging and the Generational Economy: Key findings. In R. Lee and A. Mason, eds. Population Aging and the Generational Economy. London: Edward Elgar Publishing.

Massachusetts Institute of Technology. Agelab. About Agelab. http://agelab.mit.edu/about-agelab (accessed July 2019).

Massing, N., and S. L. Schneider. 2017. Degrees of Competency: The Relationship between Educational Qualifications and Adult Skills across Countries. *Large-scale Assessment in Education*. 5 (6).

Matheson, R. 2017. Virtual-Reality System for the Elderly Wins Health Care Prize. *MIT News Office*. 24 February. http://news.mit.edu/2017/virtual-reality-elderly-sloan-health-care-innovations-prize-0224.

Matsukura, R., S. Shimizutani, N. Mitsuyama, S-H Lee, and N. Ogawa. 2018. Untapped Work Capacity among Old Persons and their Potential Contributions to the "Silver Dividend" in Japan. *The Journal of the Economics of Ageing*. 12 (November). pp. 236–249.

Matuszek, C. 2017. How Robots Could Help the Elderly Age in Their Homes. *Smithsonian.com*. 29 August. https://www.smithsonianmag.com/innovation/how-robots-could-help-elderly-age-in-their-homes-180964650/.

McKinsey Global Institute. 2017. *A Future that Works: Automation, Employment, and Productivity*. McKinsey&Company. https://www.mckinsey.com/~/media/mckinsey/featured%20insights/Digital%20Disruption/Harnessing%20automation%20for%20a%20future%20that%20works/MGI-A-future-that-works-Full-report.ashx.

Meyer, J. 2011. Workforce Age and Technology Adoption in Small and Medium-Sized Service Firms. *Small Business Economics*. 37 (3). pp. 305–324.

———. J. 2007. Older Workers and the Adoption of New Technologies. *ZEW Discussion Paper*. No. 07-050. Mannheim: Center for European Economic Research (ZEW).

Ministry of Internal Affairs and Communications (Japan). Information & Communications Statistics Database. http://www.soumu.go.jp/johotsusintokei/whitepaper/h30.html (accessed May 2019).

Ministry of Science and ICT (Republic of Korea). http://english.msip.go.kr/english/main/main.do (accessed May 2019).

MIT Open Learning. 2016. MIT Joins Collaboration to Bring Connected Learning Experiences to Indian Students and Teachers. *MIT News*. 27 January. http://news.mit.edu/2016/collaboration-connected-learning-experiences-indian-students-teachers-0127.

———. 2018. CLIx Project Receives UNESCO Award. *MIT News*. 13 March. http://news.mit.edu/2018/mit-clix-project-receives-unesco-award-0313.

Montage. https://www.montagetalent.com/ (accessed June 2019).

Moses, J., and B. Letnes. 2004. The Economic Costs to International Labor Restrictions: Revisiting the Empirical Discussion. *World Development*. 32 (10). pp. 1609–1626.

Munnell, A., S. Sass, and M. Soto. 2006. Employer Attitudes Towards Older Workers: Survey Results. *Work Opportunities for Older Americans Series*. 3 (June). Chestnut Hill, MA: Center for Retirement Research at Boston College.

Nagase, N. 2018. Has Abe's Womanomics Worked? *Asian Economic Policy Review*. 13 (1). pp. 68–101.

National Center for Geriatrics and Gerontology (Japan). http://www.ncgg.go.jp/cgss/english/department/nils-lsa/index.html (accessed July 2019).

National Silver Academy. https://www.nsa.org.sg/ (accessed September 2019).

National Transfer Accounts. www.ntaccounts.org (accessed June 2019).

———. Data Sheet 2016. https://www.ntaccounts.org (accessed July 2019).

Organisation for Economic Co-operation and Development (OECD). 2017. *Pensions at a Glance 2017*. Paris: OECD Publishing.

———. 2019. *OECD Employment Outlook 2019: The Future of Work*. Paris: OECD Publishing.

———. OECD.Stat Database. https://stats.oecd.org/ (accessed June 2019).

———. 2014–2015 Survey of Adult Skills of the Programme for the International Assessment of Adult Competencies. http://www.oecd.org/skills/piaac/data/ (accessed May 2019).

Oshio, T. 2018. Health Capacity to Work and Its Long-term Trend among the Japanese Elderly. *RIETI Discussion Paper Series*. 18-E-079. Tokyo: Research Institute of Economy, Trade and Industry.

Oshio, T., E. Usui, and S. Shimizutani. 2018. Labor Force Participation of the Elderly in Japan. *NBER Working Papers*. 24614. Cambridge, MA: National Bureau of Economic Research.

Osso VR. The Osso Story. https://ossovr.com/the-osso-story/ (accessed July 2019).

Paccagnella, M. 2016. Age, Ageing and Skills: Results from the Survey of Adult Skills. *OECD Education Working Papers*. No. 132. Paris: OECD Publishing.

Panasonic. 2018. ATOUN to Make CES Debut with 'MODEL Y' Exoskeleton. News Release. 28 December. https://news.panasonic.com/global/topics/2018/64460.html.

Park, R. Nisbett, and T. Hedden. 1999. Aging, Culture, and Cognition. *Journals of Gerontology*: Series B Psychological Sciences and Social Sciences. 54. pp. 75–84.

Petersen, S., S. Houston, H. Qin, C. Tague, and J. Studley. 2017. The Utilization of Robotic Pets in Dementia Care. *Journal of Alzheimer's Disease*. 55 (2). pp. 569–574.

Reynolds, B. 2018. What is a Remote Job? *FlexJobs*. 9 January. https://www.flexjobs.com/blog/post/what-is-a-remote-job/.

Rones, P. 1983. The Labor Market Problems of Older Workers. *Monthly Labor Review*. May. pp. 3–12.

Sanderson W.C., and S. Scherbov. 2007. A New Perspective on Population Aging. *Demographic Research*. 16(2). pp. 27–58.

Sanderson, W.C., S. Scherbov, and P. Gerland. 2017. Probabilistic Population Aging. *PLoS ONE*. 12 (6).

Sato, H. 2019. Foreign Workers in Japan Double in 5 Years, Hitting Record. *Nikkei Asian Review*. 25 January. https://asia.nikkei.com/Spotlight/Japan-immigration/Foreign-workers-in-Japan-double-in-5-years-hitting-record.

Schwartz, J., K. Monahan, S. Hatfield, and S. Anderson. 2018. No Time to Retire: Redesigning Work for Our Aging Workforce. *Deloitte Insights*. https://www2.deloitte.com/content/dam/Deloitte/at/Documents/human-capital/at-workforce-longevity.pdf.

Segan, S. 2019. What is 5G? *PC Mag*. 16 April. https://www.pcmag.com/article/345387/what-is-5g.

Sharma, B. 2019. UrbanClap Launches Operations in Abu Dhabi. *The Urban Guide*. 24 June. https://www.urbanclap.com/blog/company-updates/urbanclap-launches-operations-in-abu-dhabi/.

Shimizu Corporation. 2018. The Shimizu Smart Site Autonomous Robots Can Transform a Job Site! 26 April. https://www.shimz.co.jp/en/topics/construction/item12/index.html.

Sirlantzis, K., L. Larsen, L. Kanumuru, and P. Opera. 2019. 11-Robotics. In D. Cowan and L. Najafi, eds. *Handbook of Electronic Assistive Technology*. London: Academic Press.

SkyHive. 2018. SkyHive Launches the World's First Skills Matching Recruitment Training Platform. *Medium.com*. 31 May. https://medium.com/@iskyhive/skyhive-was-established-in-2016-with-a-simple-mission-help-people-get-work-they-love-fast-a21650988162.

Slack. https://slack.com/ (accessed June 2019).

Smith, A., and M. Anderson. 2018. *Social Media Use in 2018*. Washington, DC: Pew Research Center.

Speringer, M., A. Goujon, S. KC, M. Potančoková, C. Reiter, S. Jurasszovich, and J. Eder. 2019. Global Reconstruction of Educational Attainment, 1950 to 2015: Methodology and Assessment. *Vienna Institute of Demography Working Papers*. 02/2019. Wien: Austrian Academy of Sciences.

Statistics Bureau of Japan. Employment Status Survey 2018. https://www.stat.go.jp/english/data/index.html (accessed June 2019).

Strauss, K. 2018. The Role of Artificial Intelligence in The Future of Job Search. *Forbes*. 2 February. https://www.forbes.com/sites/karstenstrauss/2018/02/02/the-role-of-artificial-intelligence-in-the-future-of-job-search/#1709ff2a4cb0.

Strimbu, K., and J. Tavel. 2010. What are Biomarkers? *Current Opinion in HIV and AIDS*. 5(6). pp. 463–466

Team YS. 2019. FromBbeauty to Home Repairs, How UrbanClap Leverages AI to Serve Over 2 million Workers. *YourStory.com*. 4 January. http://yourstory.com/2019/01/urbanclap-leverages-ai-serve-2-million-customers.

TESS-India (Teacher Education through School-based Support). http://www.tess-india.edu.in/ (accessed July 2019).

The Open University. Projects and Programmes: TESS-India. http://www.open.ac.uk/about/international-development/projects-and-programmes/tess-india. (accessed July 2019).

United Nations Department of Economic and Social Affairs, Population Division. https://population.un.org/wpp/Download/Standard/Population/ (both accessed June 2019).

University of the Third Age (U3A). https://u3a.org.uk/ (accessed September 2019).

University of Tokyo. 2018. Turning Aging Society on Its Head: Web App Helps Seniors Find Jobs, Stay Connected. Features. 14 September. https://www.u-tokyo.ac.jp/focus/en/features/z0508_00007.html.

Wasiluk, K. 2014. Technology Adoption and Demographic Change. *Working Paper Series*. 2014-05. Konstanz: University of Konstanz Department of Economics.

Weinburg, B. 2004. Experience and Technology Adoption. *IZA Discussion Paper Series*. 1051. Bonn: Institute of Labor Economics (IZA).

Wittgenstein Centre for Demography and Global Human Capital. Wittgenstein Centre Data Explorer Version 2.0. www.wittgensteincentre.org/dataexplorer (accessed June 2019).

World Bank. World Development Indicators. https://databank.worldbank.org/source/world-development-indicators (accessed July 2019).

World Economic Forum. 2018. *The Global Competitiveness Report 2018*. Geneva.

World Health Organization (WHO). 2017. Mental Health of Older Adults. 12 December. https://www.who.int/news-room/fact-sheets/detail/mental-health-of-older-adults.

———. 2019. What You Need to Know about Digital Health Systems. 5 February. http://www.euro.who.int/en/health-topics/Health-systems/pages/news/news/2019/2/what-you-need-to-know-about-digital-health-systems.

Wright, D., D. Witherick, and M. Gordeeva. 2018. *The Robots Are Ready. Are You?* London: Deloitte Development LLC. London.

ANNEX 6a: Demographical Change, Technological Advance, and Growth: A Cross-Country Analysis

A Methodological Note

I. Revisiting the Impact of Aging Population on Macroeconomic Growth

The empirical specification below follows the methodology of Fair and Dominguez (1991) allowing to investigate the economic growth effect of aging considering country i at time t's entire population age distribution represented by $p1_{it}, p2_{it}, ..., pJ_{it}$ over J-age groups:

$$y_{it} = \lambda + X_{it}\beta + \alpha_1 p1_{it} + \alpha_2 p2_{it} + \cdots + \alpha_J pJ_{it} + u_{it} \quad (1)$$

where y_{it} refers to the 5-year average growth of real gross domestic product (GDP) per capita, λ is a constant term, X_{it} denotes k-column vector of control variables, α_j is age-group j's coefficient, and u_{it} is the error term. To minimize cyclical fluctuations, t refers to the 5-year subperiods between 1965 and 2015. With a constant term included, the sum of age-group coefficients is restricted to equal to zero such that $\sum_{j=1}^{J} \alpha_j = 0$. Further, to reduce the number of coefficients to be estimated, age-group coefficients are restricted to lie on a third-order polynomial, i.e., $\alpha_j = \gamma_0 + \gamma_1 j + \gamma_2 j^2 + \gamma_3 j^3$, thereby transforming the specification in equation (1) as follows (see Higgins [1998] for the derivation):

$$y_{it} = \lambda + X_{it}\beta + \gamma_1 D1_{it} + \gamma_2 D2_{it} + \gamma_3 D3_{it} + u_{it}$$

where $D1_{it} = \sum_{j=1}^{J} j \cdot pj_{it} - \frac{1}{J}\sum_{j=1}^{J} j$, $D2_{it} = \sum_{j=1}^{J} j^2 \cdot pj_{it} - \frac{1}{J}\sum_{j=1}^{J} j^2$,

and $D3_{it} = \sum_{j=1}^{J} j^3 \cdot pj_{it} - \frac{1}{J}\sum_{j=1}^{J} j^3$. $\quad (2)$

Before estimation, outliers are removed by excluding extreme growth observations, i.e., 5-year annual average growth less than −5% or over 15%, and extremely young countries with old dependency rate less than 4%. Real GDP information refers to the GDP at constant prices in local currency unit from the version 9.0 of the Penn World Table. Dividing it by the total population gives the per capita terms. The age distribution of population (on

a 5-year age groupings, i.e., 0–4, 5–9,..., 80+) is derived from the World Population Prospects 2017 published by the Population Division of the United Nations.

Annex Table 6a.1 presents the results of several estimates of equation (2). Columns 1-3 report the pooled OLS regression estimates. Column 1 is estimated without control variables, while Columns 2 and 3 control for the initial per capita GDP, with the latter adding region dummies. Columns 4 and 5 are panel FE estimates, with the latter involving only OECD samples. Age group-specific coefficients α_j ($j = 1, ... 17$) are retrieved from the transformation: $\alpha_j = \gamma_0 + \gamma_1 j + \gamma_2 j^2 + \gamma_3 j^3$ and mapped in Figure 6.27. While there are some differences across different specifications, one common feature is that age groups between 15 and 40 (or 45) have positive and age groups below 10 and above 60 have negative contributions to the future growth.

II. Investigating the Effect of Technological Advancement on the Relation between Demographic Change and Growth

The exercise requires adding an interaction term between measures of technological advancement T_{it} and age-group distribution to the regressors while maintaining the restriction that age-group coefficients lie on a third-order polynomial, such that:

$$y_{it} = \lambda + X_{it}\beta + \gamma_1 D1_{it} + \gamma_2 D2_{it} + \gamma_3 D3_{it} +$$

$$[T_{it} \times (\sigma_0 + \sigma_1 D1_{it} + \sigma_2 D2_{it} + \sigma_3 D3_{it})] + u_{it} \quad (3)$$

Four proxies attempt to capture technological advancement: (i) life expectancy reflecting technological improvement in providing healthcare, (ii) labor productivity, (iii) robot density measuring technological progress narrowly by degree of automation, and (iv) total factor productivity. Life expectancy at birth information is gathered from the United Nations' World Population Prospects: The 2017 Revision. Labor productivity is calculated from the GDP and employment data from the Penn World Table 9.0. Robot density is derived from information on the country-specific operational stock of industrial robots available from 1993–2015 reported by the International Federation of Robotics. Total factor productivity (TFP), known for capturing development of production and process technologies, is based from the calculated series of the Penn World Table version 9.1 expressed as levels relative to the United States.

Annex Table 6a.2 presents estimation results of equation (3). Transformation to age-specific coefficients finds that expansion in life expectancy widens the range of age groups that have positive impact on future growth including the older ones (see Figure 6.28). Similar case is found when technological advancement leads to higher labor productivity. Meanwhile, higher automation adoption does not move the range of age groups that have positive impacts on economic growth. Higher robot density nevertheless enables the old population to remain growth contributors. Last, technological adoption enhances the growth contribution of productive age groups from 30s to 60s when one compares low (−0.5) to high (0.5) TFP (in log) scenarios (see Figure 6.29).

Annex Table 6a.1: Impact of Age Distribution on GDP Per Capita Growth

Variables	(1)	(2)	(3)	(4)	(5)
Log initial GDP per capita		-0.006***	-0.006***	-0.019***	-0.032***
		(0.001)	(0.001)	(0.004)	(0.006)
D1	0.110***	0.170***	0.147***	0.139***	0.099
	(0.029)	(0.032)	(0.031)	(0.045)	(0.068)
D2	-0.011**	-0.019***	-0.017***	-0.015**	-0.005
	(0.005)	(0.005)	(0.005)	(0.007)	(0.009)
D3	0.000	0.001***	0.001***	0.000	-0.000
	(0.000)	(0.000)	(0.000)	(0.000)	(0.000)
Pooled OLS estimates	Yes	Yes	Yes		
Panel FE estimates				Yes	Yes
Region dummies			Yes		
OECD sample					Yes
No. of observations	1,454	1,454	1,445	1,454	321
R-squared	0.065	0.089	0.127	0.100	0.347
p-value of joint test	0.000	0.000	0.000	0.000	0.004
No. of countries	167	167	167	167	35

*** = significant at 1%, ** = significant at 5%, * = significant at 10%. Robust standard errors in parentheses. The p-value is for the joint hypothesis that the coefficients of D1, D2, and D3 are all zero.

FE = fixed effects, GDP = gross domestic product, OECD = Organisation for Economic Co-operation and Development, OLS = ordinary least squares.

Note: The tenth sub-period refers only to the four years from 2010 to 2014 due to the data availability in the Penn World Table 9.0.

Source: Park, Shin, and Kikkawa (2019b).

Annex Table 6a.2: Technological Advancements and Impact of Age Distribution on GDP Per Capita Growth

Variables	Life Expectancy		Labor Productivity		Robot Density (in logs)		Total Factor Productivity (in logs)	
	Pooled OLS	Panel FE	Pooled OLS	Panel FE	Pooled OLS	Panel FE	Pooled OLS	Panel FE
Log initial GDP per capita	-0.008***	-0.021***	-0.005	-0.053***	-0.011***	-0.038***	-0.011***	-0.030**
	(0.001)	(0.004)	(0.004)	(0.012)	(0.003)	(0.012)	(0.003)	(0.014)
D1	0.567***	0.612**	1.672***	2.355***	0.197	0.572	0.171	0.072
	(0.200)	(0.307)	(0.269)	(0.404)	(0.224)	(0.351)	(0.164)	(0.236)
D2	-0.081***	-0.078*	-0.230***	-0.324***	-0.017	-0.067	-0.014	0.007
	(0.031)	(0.047)	(0.042)	(0.066)	(0.032)	(0.054)	(0.023)	(0.032)
D3	0.003***	0.003	0.009***	0.012***	0.000	0.002	0.000	-0.001
	(0.001)	(0.002)	(0.002)	(0.003)	(0.001)	(0.002)	(0.001)	(0.001)
Technological advancement (T)	-0.003***	-0.001	-0.021***	0.016	0.002	0.000	-0.046*	-0.141***
	(0.001)	(0.001)	(0.007)	(0.018)	(0.003)	(0.012)	(0.026)	(0.047)
D1 x T	-0.007**	-0.008*	-0.158***	-0.226***	-0.002	-0.053	-0.023	-0.559*
	(0.003)	(0.005)	(0.028)	(0.040)	(0.037)	(0.059)	(0.349)	(0.296)
D2 x T	0.001**	0.001	0.022***	0.032***	0.000	0.006	0.009	0.086*
	(0.000)	(0.001)	(0.004)	(0.007)	(0.005)	(0.008)	(0.051)	(0.043)
D3 x T	-0.000***	0.000	-0.001***	-0.001***	0.000	0.000	-0.001	-0.004**
	(0.000)	(0.000)	(0.000)	(0.000)	(0.000)	(0.000)	(0.002)	(0.002)
No. of observations	1,439	1,439	1,324	1,324	183	183	252	252
R-squared	0.129	0.115	0.158	0.161	0.442	0.402	0.286	0.343
p-value of joint test: level terms	0.000	0.074	0.000	0.000	0.060	0.094	0.000	0.102
p-value of joint test: interaction terms	0.000	0.131	0.000	0.000	0.846	0.600	0.187	0.027
No. of countries	165	165	167	167	65	65	63	63

*** = significant at 1%, ** = significant at 5%, * = significant at 10%. Robust standard errors in parentheses. The p-value is for the joint hypothesis that the coefficients of D1, D2, and D3 are all zero.

FE = fixed effects, GDP = gross domestic product, OLS = ordinary least squares, T = Technological advancement.

Note: The tenth sub-period refers only to the 4 years from 2010 to 2014 due to the data availability in the Penn World Table 9.0.

Source: Park, Shin, and Kikkawa (2019b).

ANNEX 6b: Data and Methodology Used in Country Case Studies

Country	Japan	People's Republic of China	Republic of Korea
Growth indicator	Value added per hours worked	(i) Gross domestic product per capita, and (ii) Value added per worker at the firm level	(i) Value added per hours worked, and (ii) Total factor productivity growth
Aging indicator	(i) Share of workers over age 65 to ages 15–64, and (ii) Alternatively, share of age 55 and above	Share of population above the age of 55 to ages 21–55	(i) Share of workers in their sixties and seventies, and (ii) Median working age
Technology indicator	(i) Industrial robots, and (ii) Electrical computation machines	(i) Industrial robots, and (ii) Capital–labor ratio, (iii) Research and development expenditure	(i) Industrial robots, and (ii) Capital–labor ratio
Period of analysis	1990 to 2010 5-year growth	1998 to 2007 (and to 2016 for industrial robots)	2006 to 2015 5-year growth
Unit of analysis	Industry level	Prefecture and firm level	Industry level
Empirical method	Pooled ordinary least squares	Pooled ordinary least squares	Pooled ordinary least squares
Other controls	Industry fixed effects Capital–labor ratio, labor capital ratio, time fixed effects	Firm-level characteristics, wage level, prefecture and time fixed effects	Capital–labor ratio, time fixed effects
Instrumental variables	No	Yes, fine for unauthorized birth	Yes, 3-year growth rate

Sources: Ge and Zhang (2019); Kawaguchi and Muroga (2019); and Park, Shin, and Kikkawa (2019a).

7 Statistical Appendix

The statistical appendix comprises 12 tables of selected indicators on economic integration for the 49 regional members of the Asian Development Bank (ADB). The succeeding notes describe the country groupings and the calculation procedures undertaken.

Regional Groupings

- Asia consists of the 49 regional members of ADB.
- Developing Asia refers to Asia excluding Australia, Japan, and New Zealand.
- European Union (EU) consists of Austria, Belgium, Bulgaria, Croatia, Cyprus, Czech Republic, Denmark, Estonia, Finland, France, Germany, Greece, Hungary, Ireland, Italy, Latvia, Lithuania, Luxembourg, Malta, the Netherlands, Poland, Portugal, Romania, Slovak Republic, Slovenia, Spain, Sweden, and the United Kingdom.

Table Descriptions

Table A1: Asia-Pacific Regional Cooperation and Integration Index

The Asia-Pacific Regional Cooperation and Integration Index (ARCII) is a composite index that measures the degree of regional cooperation and integration in Asia and the Pacific. It comprises six dimensional indices based on 26 indicators to capture the contributions of six different aspects of regional integration: (i) trade and investment, (ii) money and finance, (iii) regional value chains, (iv) infrastructure and connectivity, (v) free movement of people, and (vi) institutional and social integration. The construction of ARCII follows two steps: first, the

26 indicators have been weight-averaged in each of the six dimensions to produce six composite dimensional indices; second, these six dimensional indices are weight-averaged to generate an overall index of regional integration. In each step, the weights are determined based on principal component analysis. For more details on the methodology and to download the data, please see Asia-Pacific Regional Cooperation and Integration Index Database. https://aric.adb.org/database/arcii.

Table A2: Regional Integration Indicators—Asia (% of total)

The table provides a summary of regional integration indicators for three areas: movement in trade and investment, movement in capital, and people movement (migration, remittances, and visitors); for Asian subregions, including Association of Southeast Asian Nations (ASEAN) plus 3 (including Hong Kong, China). Cross-border flows within and across subregions are shown as well as total flows with Asia and the rest of the world. Table Descriptions of Tables A3 and A9 (movement in trade and investment), Tables A7 and A8 (movement in capital), and Tables A10, A11 and A12 (people movement), provide additional description for each indicator.

Table A3: Trade Share—Asia (% of total trade)

It is calculated as $(T_{ij}/T_{iw})*100$, where T_{ij} is the total trade of economy "i" with economy "j" and T_{iw} is the total trade of economy "i" with the world. A higher share indicates a higher degree of regional trade integration.

Table A4: Free Trade Agreement Status—Asia

It is the number and status of bilateral and plurilateral free trade agreements (FTAs) with at least one of the Asian economies as signatory. FTAs only proposed are excluded. It covers FTAs with the following status: Framework agreement signed—the parties initially negotiate the contents of a framework agreement, which serves as a framework for future negotiations; Negotiations launched—the parties, through the relevant ministries, declare the official launch of negotiations or set the date for such, or start the first round of negotiations; Signed but not yet in effect—parties sign the agreement after negotiations have been completed, however, the agreement has yet to be implemented; and Signed and in effect—provisions of the FTA come into force, after legislative or executive ratification.

Table A5: Time to Export and Import—Asia (number of hours)

Time to export (import) data measures the number of hours required to export (import) by ocean transport, including the processing of documents required to complete the transaction. It covers time used for documentation requirements and procedures at customs and other regulatory agencies as well as the time of inland transport between the largest business city and the main port used by traders. Regional aggregates are weighted averages based on total exports (imports).

Table A6: Logistics Performance Index—Asia (% to EU)

Logistics Performance Index scores are based on the following dimensions: (i) efficiency of border control and customs process; (ii) transport and trade-related infrastructure; (iii) competitively priced shipments; (iv) ability to track and trace consignments; and (v) timeliness of shipments. Regional aggregates are computed using total trade as weights. A score above

(below) 100 means that it is easier (more difficult) to export or import from that economy compared with the EU.

Table A7: Cross-Border Portfolio Equity Holdings Share—Asia (% of total cross-border equity holdings)

It is calculated as $(E_{ij}/E_{iw})*100$ where E_{ij} is the holding of economy "i" of the equity securities issued by economy "j" and E_{iw} is economy i's total holdings of cross-border equity securities. Calculations are based solely on available data in the Coordinated Portfolio Investment Survey (CPIS) database of the International Monetary Fund (IMF). Rest of the world (ROW) includes equity securities issued by international organizations defined in the CPIS database and "not specified (including confidential) category". A higher share indicates a higher degree of regional integration.

Table A8: Cross-Border Portfolio Debt Holdings Share—Asia (% of total cross-border debt holdings)

It is calculated as $(D_{ij}/D_{iw})*100$ where D_{ij} is the holding of economy "i" of the debt securities issued by economy "j" and D_{iw} is economy i's total holdings of cross-border debt securities. Calculations are based solely on available data in the CPIS database of the IMF. ROW includes debt securities issued by international organizations defined in the CPIS database and "not specified (including confidential) category". A higher share indicates a higher degree of regional integration.

Table A9: Foreign Direct Investment Inflow Share—Asia (% of total FDI inflows)

It is calculated as $(F_{ij}/F_{iw})*100$ where F_{ij} is the foreign direct investment (FDI) received by economy "i" from economy "j" and F_{iw} is the FDI received by economy "i" from the world. Figures are based on net FDI inflow data. A higher share indicates a higher degree of regional integration. The bilateral FDI database was constructed using data from the United Nations Conference on Trade and Development, ASEAN Secretariat, Eurostat, and national sources. For missing data from 2017 to 2018, bilateral FDI estimates derived from a gravity model are used. All bilateral data available from 2001–2018 from the data sources were utilized to estimate the following gravity equation: $\ln FDI_{ijt} = \alpha + \beta_1 \ln GDP_{it} + \beta_2 \ln GDP_{jt} + \gamma \cdot X_{ijt} + \delta_i \cdot F_i + \delta_j \cdot F_j + \delta_t \cdot F_t + v_{ijt}$, where FDI_{ijt} is the FDI from economy "j" (home) to economy "i" (host) in year t, GDP_{it} is the gross domestic product (GDP) of economy "i" in year t, GDP_{jt} is the GDP of economy "j" at year t, X_{ijt} are the usual gravity variables (distance, contiguity, common language, colonial relationship) between economies "i" and "j", and F_i, F_j, F_t, are home, host, and year fixed effects, and v_{ijt} is the error term. Data on distance, contiguity, common language, colonial relationship are from the Centre d'Études Prospectives et d'Informations Internationales (the French Research Center in International Economics) and data on GDP are from the World Development Indicators of the World Bank. For more details on methodology and data sources, please see *Asian Economic Integration Report 2018* online Annex 1: http://aric.adb.org/pdf/aeir2018_onlineannex1.pdf

Table A10: Remittance Inflows Share—Asia (% of total remittance inflows)

It is calculated as $(R_{ij}/R_{iw})*100$ where R_{ij} is the remittance received by economy "i" from partner "j" and R_{iw} is the remittance received by economy "i" from the world. Remittances refer to the sum of the following: (i) workers' remittances which are recorded as current transfers under the current account of the IMF's Balance of Payments (BOP); (ii) compensation of employees which includes wages, salaries, and other benefits of border, seasonal, and other nonresident workers and which are recorded under the "income" subcategory of the current account; and (iii) migrants' transfers which are reported under capital transfers in the BOP's capital account. Transfers through informal channels are excluded.

Table A11: Outbound Migration Share—Asia (% of total outbound migrants)

It is calculated as $(M_{ij}/M_{iw})*100$ where M_{ij} is the number of migrants of economy "i" residing in economy "j" and M_{iw} is the number of all migrants of economy "i" residing overseas. This definition excludes those traveling abroad on a temporary basis. A higher share indicates a higher degree of regional integration.

Table A12.a: Inbound Visitor Share—Asia (% of total inbound visitors)

It is calculated as $(TR_{ij}/TR_{iw})*100$ where TR_{ij} is the number of nationals of economy "i" that have arrived as visitors in destination "j" and TR_{iw} is the total number of nationals of economy "i" that have arrived as visitors in all international destinations. A higher share indicates a higher degree of regional integration.

Table A12.b: Outbound Visitor Share—Asia (% of total outbound visitors)

It is calculated as $(TR_{ij}/TR_{iw})*100$ where TR_{ij} is the number of nationals of economy "i" that have traveled as visitors in destination "j" and TR_{iw} is the total number of nationals of economy "i" that have traveled as visitors abroad. A higher share indicates a higher degree of regional integration.

Table A1.a: Overall Asia-Pacific Regional Cooperation and Integration Index and Dimensional Subindexes—Asia

		Dimensional Subindexes					
	Overall Index	Trade and Investment	Money and Finance	Regional Value Chain	Infrastructure and Connectivity	Movement of People	Institutional and Social Integration
2006	0.495	0.527	0.440	0.517	0.473	0.479	0.313
2007	0.485	0.478	0.460	0.529	0.473	0.482	0.315
2008	0.485	0.504	0.405	0.512	0.482	0.484	0.323
2009	0.482	0.526	0.392	0.513	0.482	0.486	0.331
2010	0.499	0.533	0.432	0.514	0.487	0.483	0.334
2011	0.496	0.562	0.412	0.505	0.495	0.482	0.335
2012	0.497	0.522	0.396	0.507	0.489	0.489	0.336
2013	0.491	0.514	0.404	0.501	0.489	0.490	0.339
2014	0.500	0.515	0.405	0.495	0.491	0.481	0.341
2015	0.496	0.579	0.398	0.496	0.494	0.480	0.341
2016	0.515	0.547	0.416	0.502	0.528	0.482	0.340
2017	0.495	0.541	0.334	0.492	0.536	0.487	0.343

Table A1.b: Asia-Pacific Regional Cooperation and Integration Index—Asia Subregions and Subregional Initiatives

	Central Asia	East Asia	Southeast Asia	South Asia	Oceania	ASEAN	CAREC	GMS	SASEC
2006	0.363	0.558	0.554	0.417	0.555	0.554	0.408	0.547	0.429
2007	0.350	0.530	0.567	0.432	0.531	0.567	0.417	0.571	0.435
2008	0.350	0.535	0.550	0.431	0.532	0.550	0.408	0.550	0.443
2009	0.361	0.534	0.551	0.423	0.540	0.551	0.412	0.550	0.433
2010	0.338	0.541	0.551	0.447	0.558	0.551	0.424	0.553	0.456
2011	0.363	0.537	0.558	0.443	0.540	0.558	0.419	0.552	0.456
2012	0.353	0.543	0.554	0.429	0.537	0.554	0.428	0.548	0.428
2013	0.369	0.544	0.560	0.412	0.544	0.560	0.427	0.557	0.418
2014	0.379	0.556	0.567	0.423	0.540	0.567	0.442	0.566	0.425
2015	0.374	0.546	0.564	0.428	0.522	0.564	0.434	0.564	0.435
2016	0.362	0.583	0.571	0.453	0.537	0.571	0.440	0.574	0.469
2017	0.375	0.558	0.553	0.435	0.520	0.553	0.438	0.548	0.441

ASEAN = Association of Southeast Asian Nations, CAREC = Central Asia Regional Economic Cooperation, GMS = Greater Mekong Subregion, SASEC = South Asia Subregional Economic Cooperation.

Notes:
(i) The Asia-Pacific Regional Cooperation and Integration Index (ARCII) for each subregion (subregional initiative) for each year is calculated by averaging the ARCII scores for all the economies in each subregion (member economies in each subregional initiative).
(ii) ASEAN and Southeast Asia include Cambodia, Indonesia, the Lao People's Democratic Republic (Lao PDR), Malaysia, the Philippines Singapore, Thailand and Viet Nam. CAREC includes Georgia, Kazakhstan, the Kyrgyz Republic, Mongolia, Pakistan, and the People's Republic of China (PRC). Central Asia includes Georgia, Kazakhstan and the Kyrgyz Republic. East Asia includes Hong Kong, China; Japan; Mongolia; the PRC; and the Republic of Korea. GMS includes Cambodia, the Lao PDR, the PRC, Thailand, and Viet Nam. Oceania includes Australia and New Zealand. SASEC includes Bangladesh, India, Nepal and Sri Lanka. South Asia includes SASEC and Pakistan.

Sources: ADB. Asia Regional Integration Center. Asia-Pacific Regional Cooperation and Integration Index Database. https://aric.adb.org/database/arcii (accessed October 2019); and methodology from C. Y. Park and R. Claveria. 2018. Constructing the Asia-Pacific Regional Integration Index: A Panel Approach. *ADB Economics Working Paper Series*. No. 544. Manila: Asian Development Bank (ADB); and H. Huh and C. Y. Park. 2018. Asia-Pacific Regional Integration Index: Construction, Interpretation, and Comparison. *Journal of Asian Economics*. 54. pp. 22–38.

Table A1.c: Regional Integration Index—Asia versus Other Regions

	Asia	European Union	Latin America	Africa
2006	0.428	0.376	0.567	0.382
2007	0.419	0.362	0.568	0.366
2008	0.424	0.383	0.568	0.377
2009	0.418	0.394	0.576	0.371
2010	0.432	0.382	0.564	0.376
2011	0.429	0.380	0.563	0.370
2012	0.431	0.385	0.566	0.384
2013	0.428	0.395	0.553	0.383
2014	0.437	0.404	0.586	0.409
2015	0.433	0.363	0.552	0.384
2016	0.449	0.392	0.602	0.419
2017	0.436	0.369	0.562	0.389

Note: The regional integration index for each region is calculated in the same method as the Asia-Pacific Regional Cooperation and Integration Index calculation, but is based on worldwide normalization, i.e., normalizing raw indicator values using global minimum and maximum values.

Sources: ADB. Asia Regional Integration Center. Asia-Pacific Regional Cooperation and Integration Index Database. https://aric.adb.org/database/arcii (accessed October 2019); and methodology from C. Y. Park and R. Claveria. 2018. Constructing the Asia-Pacific Regional Integration Index: A Panel Approach. *ADB Economics Working Paper Series*. No. 544. Manila: Asian Development Bank (ADB); and H. Huh and C. Y. Park. 2018. Asia-Pacific Regional Integration Index: Construction, Interpretation, and Comparison. *Journal of Asian Economics*. 54. pp. 22–38.

Table A2: Regional Integration Indicators — Asia (% of total)

	Movement in Trade and Investment		Movement in Capital		People Movement		
	Trade (%)	FDI (%)	Equity Holdings (%)	Bond Holdings (%)	Migration (%)	Visitors (%)	Remittances (%)
	2018	2018	2018	2018	2017	2017	2017
Within Subregions							
ASEAN+3 (including HKG)[a]	46.5 ▼	48.9 ▼	15.1 ▲	11.1 ▲	38.3 ▼	71.6 ▲	32.6 ▼
Central Asia	7.6 ▲	2.9 ▼	0.0 ▲	0.4 ▲	9.2 ▼	60.7 ▲	6.7 ▲
East Asia	35.5 ▼	46.4 ▼	10.4 ▼	7.6 ▲	33.1 ▼	65.2 ▼	35.5 ▼
South Asia	6.3 ▲	0.1 ▼	0.4 ▲	1.7 ▼	23.4 ▼	26.2 ▲	9.4 ▼
Southeast Asia	23.1 ▲	16.5 ▼	7.1 ▲	7.3 ▼	32.4 ▼	38.7 ▲	12.4 ▼
The Pacific and Oceania	5.9 ▼	4.5 ▼	4.6 ▲	3.3 ▲	56.7 ▲	31.1 ▼	28.9 ▲
Across Subregions							
ASEAN+3 (including HKG)[a]	11.3 ▲	3.8 ▲	3.6 ▲	6.0 ▼	8.6 ▼	9.1 ▲	3.0 ▼
Central Asia	25.7 ▲	33.6 ▲	11.1 ▼	17.9 ▲	0.4 ▼	2.6 ▼	0.7 ▼
East Asia	20.0 ▲	6.3 ▼	3.1 ▼	7.8 ▲	13.9 ▼	15.3 ▼	15.4 ▲
South Asia	33.7 ▼	45.7 ▲	36.4 ▲	5.4 ▼	5.7 ▼	23.2 ▼	5.8 ▲
Southeast Asia	46.2 ▲	34.8 ▲	33.8 ▲	17.6 ▼	14.5 ▼	43.4 ▲	13.8 ▲
The Pacific and Oceania	65.8 ▲	20.0 ▼	8.5 ▼	10.3 ▼	5.5 ▼	42.1 ▼	13.8 ▼
TOTAL (within and across subregions)							
Asia	**57.5** ▼	**48.2** ▼	**18.0** ▼	**16.8** ▲	**34.7** ▼	**78.4** ▲	**27.7** ▼
ASEAN+3 (including HKG)[a]	57.8 ▼	52.7 ▼	18.8 ▲	17.1 ▲	47.0 ▼	80.8 ▲	35.6 ▼
Central Asia	33.3 ▲	36.5 ▲	11.1 ▼	18.3 ▲	9.6 ▼	63.3 ▲	7.3 ▲
East Asia	55.5 ▼	52.7 ▼	13.5 ▼	15.4 ▲	47.0 ▼	80.5 ▲	50.9 ▼
South Asia	40.0 ▼	45.9 ▲	36.8 ▲	7.1 ▼	29.1 ▲	49.4 ▲	15.2 ▼
Southeast Asia	69.3 ▲	51.3 ▲	40.8 ▲	24.9 ▼	46.9 ▼	82.0 ▲	26.2 ▼
The Pacific and Oceania	71.7 ▲	24.5 ▼	13.1 ▼	13.7 ▼	62.2 ▲	73.2 ▼	42.8 ▼
With the rest of the world							
Asia	**42.5** ▲	**51.8** ▲	**82.0** ▲	**83.2** ▼	**65.3** ▲	**21.6** ▼	**72.3** ▲
ASEAN+3 (including HKG)[a]	42.2 ▲	47.3 ▲	81.2 ▼	82.9 ▼	53.0 ▲	19.2 ▼	64.4 ▲
Central Asia	66.7 ▼	63.5 ▼	88.9 ▲	81.7 ▼	90.4 ▲	36.7 ▼	92.7 ▼
East Asia	44.5 ▲	47.3 ▲	86.5 ▲	84.6 ▼	53.0 ▲	19.5 ▼	49.1 ▲
South Asia	60.0 ▲	54.1 ▼	63.2 ▼	92.9 ▲	70.9 ▲	50.6 ▼	84.8 ▲
Southeast Asia	30.7 ▼	48.7 ▼	59.2 ▼	75.1 ▲	53.1 ▲	18.0 ▼	73.8 ▲
The Pacific and Oceania	28.3 ▼	75.5 ▲	86.9 ▲	86.3 ▲	37.8 ▼	26.8 ▲	57.2 ▲

▲ = increase from previous period; ▼ = decrease from previous period.

ASEAN = Association of Southeast Asian Nations; FDI = foreign direct investment; HKG = Hong Kong, China.

[a] Includes ASEAN (Brunei Darussalam, Cambodia, Indonesia, the Lao People's Democratic Republic, Malaysia, Myanmar, the Philippines, Singapore, Thailand, and Viet Nam) plus Hong Kong, China; Japan; the People's Republic of China; and the Republic of Korea.

Trade—no data available on the Cook Islands and Niue.

Equity and Bond Holdings—based on investment from Australia; Bangladesh; Hong Kong, China; India; Indonesia; Japan; Kazakhstan; Malaysia; Mongolia; New Zealand; Pakistan; Palau; the Philippines; the Republic of Korea; Singapore; and Thailand.

Migration—share of migrant stock to total migrants in 2017 (compared with 2015).

Visitors—share of outbound visitors to total visitors in 2017 (compared with 2016).

Remittances—share of inward remittances to total remittances in 2017 (compared with 2016).

Sources: ADB calculations using data from ASEAN Secretariat. ASEANstats Database. https://www.aseanstats.org (accessed July 2019); CEIC; Eurostat. Balance of Payments. http://ec.europa.eu/eurostat/web/balance-of-payments/data/database (accessed July 2019); International Monetary Fund (IMF). Coordinated Portfolio Investment Survey. http://cpis.imf.org (accessed September 2019); IMF. Direction of Trade Statistics. http://imf.org/en/data (accessed September 2019); Department of Economic and Social Affairs, United Nations. Trends in International Migrant Stock. http://www.un.org/en/development/desa/population/migration/data/estimates2/estimates15.shtml (accessed July 2018); United Nations Conference on Trade and Development. Bilateral FDI Statistics. http://unctad.org/en/Pages/Home.aspx (accessed July 2019); United Nations World Tourism Organization. Tourism Satellite Accounts. http://statistics.unwto.org (accessed April 2019); World Bank. World Bank Migration and Remittances Data. http://www.worldbank.org/en/topic/migrationremittancesdiasporaissues/brief/migration-remittances-data (accessed April 2019); and World Investment Report 2019 Statistical Annex Tables. https://unctad.org/en/Pages/DIAE/World%20Investment%20Report/World_Investment_Report.aspx (accessed June 2019).

Table A3: Trade Shares—Asia, 2018 (% of total trade)

| | Partner | | | | | |
| | | of which | | | | |
Reporter	Asia	PRC	Japan	EU	US	ROW
Central Asia	**33.3**	**15.8**	**1.7**	**31.0**	**2.3**	**33.3**
Armenia	18.4	10.4	1.3	24.9	3.1	53.7
Azerbaijan	18.9	4.2	1.3	41.7	2.8	36.6
Georgia	29.8	8.2	0.7	26.8	4.1	39.2
Kazakhstan	27.9	12.5	2.2	40.6	2.6	28.9
Kyrgyz Republic	50.3	30.5	0.7	15.7	2.0	31.9
Tajikistan	38.5	11.1	0.4	5.9	0.5	55.1
Turkmenistan	79.2	64.9	0.2	6.9	0.4	13.6
Uzbekistan	47.5	20.0	2.4	10.5	1.1	40.8
East Asia	**55.5**	**15.3**	**5.8**	**12.2**	**12.4**	**19.8**
China, People's Republic of	46.2		7.1	14.8	13.7	25.3
Hong Kong, China	78.6	49.7	4.3	7.6	6.5	7.3
Japan	55.2	21.0		11.3	14.8	18.7
Korea, Republic of	58.4	23.6	7.5	10.5	11.6	19.5
Mongolia	76.1	65.7	4.6	6.4	1.7	15.8
Taipei,China	72.9	31.1	9.7	8.5	10.5	8.1
South Asia	**40.0**	**12.0**	**2.4**	**14.0**	**9.4**	**36.6**
Afghanistan	74.0	14.4	5.0	1.8	0.7	23.5
Bangladesh	45.5	15.4	3.0	22.8	6.6	25.1
Bhutan	94.7	0.7	0.5	1.6	2.5	1.1
India	37.0	10.8	2.1	13.3	10.2	39.5
Maldives	63.1	15.5	0.7	11.5	2.1	23.3
Nepal	81.2	9.9	0.6	4.7	1.1	13.0
Pakistan	40.6	19.3	3.0	16.1	7.9	35.3
Sri Lanka	54.6	13.1	5.7	16.4	10.6	18.4
Southeast Asia	**69.3**	**17.3**	**8.3**	**10.3**	**8.8**	**11.5**
Brunei Darussalam	92.3	17.4	22.8	2.9	3.9	0.9
Cambodia	64.8	24.4	5.2	17.1	9.6	8.5
Indonesia	71.4	19.5	10.1	8.4	7.7	12.5
Lao PDR	92.3	26.6	2.2	3.7	1.1	2.9
Malaysia	74.8	17.7	7.5	10.4	5.1	9.7
Myanmar	84.1	32.5	5.8	9.5	2.2	4.1
Philippines	72.4	17.1	11.3	9.7	10.4	7.4
Singapore	67.2	12.8	5.4	11.0	9.4	12.3
Thailand	66.4	16.0	12.0	9.4	8.6	15.5
Viet Nam	66.0	22.4	7.9	11.7	12.6	9.6
The Pacific	**79.6**	**16.5**	**8.5**	**12.6**	**3.0**	**4.8**
Cook Islands	–	–	–	–	–	–
Fiji	84.0	13.8	5.6	4.2	6.8	4.9
Kiribati	82.3	2.8	1.9	1.4	3.3	12.9
Marshall Islands	72.4	16.6	10.1	22.1	2.3	3.2
Micronesia, Federated States of	48.1	5.0	5.0	0.2	12.8	38.9
Nauru	74.0	1.6	3.3	0.5	2.6	22.9
Niue	–	–	–	–	–	–
Palau	37.7	8.8	12.2	2.0	30.0	30.3
Papua New Guinea	87.9	16.7	9.0	7.6	1.3	3.2
Samoa	82.3	10.7	4.6	1.3	10.1	6.3
Solomon Islands	90.7	44.5	1.8	5.9	1.4	2.0
Timor-Leste	80.0	20.5	2.6	6.7	2.8	10.4
Tonga	82.7	5.9	5.6	2.1	13.6	1.6
Tuvalu	79.3	0.7	9.4	2.2	5.3	13.2
Vanuatu	83.7	7.7	2.2	5.4	5.0	5.8
Oceania	**71.2**	**28.3**	**11.1**	**11.7**	**7.4**	**9.6**
Australia	72.6	29.4	11.9	11.4	7.0	9.0
New Zealand	63.2	21.8	6.5	13.6	10.0	13.2
Asia	**57.5**	**16.0**	**6.2**	**12.2**	**11.1**	**19.1**
Developing Asia	**57.2**	**14.8**	**6.8**	**12.4**	**10.8**	**19.7**

– = unavailable, EU = European Union, Lao PDR = Lao People's Democratic Republic, PRC = People's Republic of China, ROW = rest of the world, US = United States.

Notes: Calculations use bilateral trade data. The mirror trade approach was used to fill in missing data.

Source: ADB calculations using data from International Monetary Fund. Direction of Trade Statistics. https://www.imf.org/en/Data (accessed September 2019).

Table A4: Free Trade Agreement Status—Asia

Economy	Under Negotiation		Signed but Not Yet In Effect	Signed and In Effect	Total
	Framework Agreement Signed	Negotiations Launched			
Central Asia	**0**	**7**	**2**	**47**	**56**
Armenia	0	5	2	11	18
Azerbaijan	0	0	0	9	9
Georgia	0	0	0	13	13
Kazakhstan	0	7	2	11	20
Kyrgyz Republic	0	5	2	11	18
Tajikistan	0	0	0	8	8
Turkmenistan	0	0	0	5	5
Uzbekistan	0	0	0	9	9
East Asia	**0**	**29**	**4**	**61**	**94**
China, People's Republic of	0	11	2	17	30
Hong Kong, China	0	1	1	7	9
Japan	0	8	0	17	25
Korea, Republic of	0	13	1	16	30
Mongolia	0	0	0	1	1
Taipei,China	0	1	0	8	9
South Asia	**1**	**26**	**2**	**24**	**53**
Afghanistan	0	0	0	2	2
Bangladesh	0	2	1	3	6
Bhutan	0	1	0	2	3
India	1	16	0	13	30
Maldives	0	1	2	1	4
Nepal	0	1	0	2	3
Pakistan	0	7	1	10	18
Sri Lanka	0	3	0	6	9
Southeast Asia	**3**	**32**	**6**	**49**	**90**
Brunei Darussalam	0	1	0	10	11
Cambodia	0	1	0	7	8
Indonesia	0	7	4	10	21
Lao PDR	0	1	0	9	10
Malaysia	1	6	1	16	24
Myanmar	1	2	0	7	10
Philippines	0	3	0	9	12
Singapore	0	8	1	24	33
Thailand	1	9	0	14	24
Viet Nam	0	3	1	12	16
The Pacific	**0**	**0**	**1**	**8**	**9**
Cook Islands	0	0	1	3	4
Fiji	0	0	1	4	5
Kiribati	0	0	1	3	4
Marshall Islands	0	0	1	4	5
Micronesia, Federated States of	0	0	1	4	5
Nauru	0	0	1	3	4
Niue	0	0	1	3	4
Palau	0	0	1	3	4
Papua New Guinea	0	0	1	5	6
Samoa	0	0	1	3	4
Solomon Islands	0	0	1	4	5
Timor-Leste	0	0	0	0	0
Tonga	0	0	1	3	4
Tuvalu	0	0	1	3	4
Vanuatu	0	0	1	4	5
Oceania	**0**	**9**	**4**	**21**	**34**
Australia	0	5	4	13	22
New Zealand	0	6	1	12	19
Asia	**4**	**83**	**13**	**159**	**259**
Developing Asia	**4**	**73**	**12**	**150**	**239**

Lao PDR = Lao People's Democratic Republic.

Notes:
(i)   Framework agreement signed: The parties initially negotiate the contents of a framework agreement, which serves as a framework for future negotiations.
(ii) Negotiations launched: The parties, through the relevant ministries, declare the official launch of negotiations or set the date for such, or start the first round of negotiations.
(iii) Signed but not yet in effect: Parties sign the agreement after negotiations have been completed. However, the agreement has yet to be implemented.
(iv) Signed and in effect: Provisions of free trade agreement come into force, after legislative or executive ratification.

Source: ADB. Asia Regional Integation Center. https://aric.adb.org (accessed August 2019).

Table A5: Time to Export and Import—Asia (number of hours)

	Time to Export		Time to Import	
	2017	2018	2017	2018
Central Asia	**195**	**162**	**78**	**81**
Armenia	41	41	5	5
Azerbaijan	62	50	68	47
Georgia	8	8	17	17
Kazakhstan	261	233	8	8
Kyrgyz Republic	41	26	108	108
Tajikistan	141	117	233	233
Turkmenistan	–	–	–	–
Uzbekistan	286	208	285	285
East Asia	**32**	**26**	**91**	**50**
China, People's Republic of	47	35	158	72
Hong Kong, China	2	2	20	20
Japan	25	25	43	43
Korea, Republic of	14	14	7	7
Mongolia	230	230	163	163
Taipei,China	22	22	51	51
South Asia	**157**	**103**	**311**	**160**
Afghanistan	276	276	420	420
Bangladesh	315	315	360	360
Bhutan	14	14	13	13
India	145	81	326	126
Maldives	90	90	161	161
Nepal	99	99	109	109
Pakistan	130	130	263	263
Sri Lanka	91	91	120	120
Southeast Asia	**66**	**61**	**99**	**99**
Brunei Darussalam	272	272	180	180
Cambodia	180	180	140	140
Indonesia	115	115	206	206
Lao PDR	73	69	74	71
Malaysia	55	38	79	43
Myanmar	286	286	278	278
Philippines	78	78	168	216
Singapore	12	12	36	36
Thailand	62	55	54	54
Viet Nam	105	105	132	132
The Pacific	**132**	**132**	**145**	**145**
Cook Islands	–	–	–	–
Fiji	112	112	76	76
Kiribati	96	96	144	144
Marshall Islands	84	84	144	144
Micronesia, Federated States of	62	62	91	91
Nauru	–	–	–	–
Niue	–	–	–	–
Palau	174	174	180	180
Papua New Guinea	138	138	192	192
Samoa	75	75	109	109
Solomon Islands	170	170	145	145
Timor-Leste	129	129	144	144
Tonga	160	160	98	98
Tuvalu	–	–	–	–
Vanuatu	110	110	174	174
Oceania	**43**	**43**	**40**	**40**
Australia	43	43	43	43
New Zealand	40	40	26	26
Asia	**48**	**40**	**112**	**72**
Developing Asia	**51**	**42**	**119**	**76**

– = unavailable, Lao PDR = Lao People's Democratic Republic.

Notes: Time to export (import) data measures the number of hours required to export (import) by ocean transport, including the processing of documents required to complete the transaction. It covers time used for documentation requirements and procedures at customs and other regulatory agencies as well as the time of inland transport between the largest business city and the main port used by traders. Regional aggregates are weighted averages based on total exports (imports).

Source: ADB calculations using data from World Bank. Doing Business Database. https://doingbusiness.org (accessed May 2019).

Table A6: Logistics Performance Index—Asia (% to EU)

	2014	2016	2018
Central Asia	**66.5**	**64.1**	**68.9**
Armenia	69.2	55.9	67.0
Azerbaijan	63.4	–	–
Georgia	64.9	59.7	62.8
Kazakhstan	69.8	69.8	72.2
Kyrgyz Republic	57.2	54.7	65.5
Tajikistan	65.4	52.3	60.1
Turkmenistan	59.6	56.1	61.9
Uzbekistan	62.0	61.0	66.3
East Asia	**94.8**	**95.8**	**95.5**
China, People's Republic of	91.4	92.9	92.7
Hong Kong, China	99.0	103.2	100.8
Japan	101.3	100.7	103.5
Korea, Republic of	94.9	94.3	92.9
Mongolia	61.0	63.6	61.0
Taipei,China	96.2	93.8	92.5
South Asia	**77.5**	**83.1**	**77.8**
Afghanistan	53.5	54.3	50.1
Bangladesh	65.9	67.6	66.2
Bhutan	59.3	58.9	55.8
India	79.7	86.7	81.7
Maldives	71.1	63.7	68.5
Nepal	67.0	60.3	64.6
Pakistan	73.1	74.1	62.2
Sri Lanka	69.7	–	66.8
Southeast Asia	**90.8**	**86.0**	**87.7**
Brunei Darussalam	–	72.8	69.6
Cambodia	70.9	71.0	66.3
Indonesia	79.7	75.7	81.0
Lao PDR	61.8	52.4	69.4
Malaysia	92.9	86.9	82.8
Myanmar	58.2	62.4	59.1
Philippines	77.7	72.4	74.6
Singapore	103.6	105.1	102.7
Thailand	88.7	82.6	87.7
Viet Nam	81.6	75.5	84.2
The Pacific	**63.8**	**62.5**	**57.5**
Cook Islands	–	–	–
Fiji	65.9	58.7	60.5
Kiribati	–	–	–
Marshall Islands	–	–	–
Micronesia, Federated States of	–	–	–
Nauru	–	–	–
Niue	–	–	–
Palau	–	–	–
Papua New Guinea	62.9	63.7	55.9
Samoa	–	–	–
Solomon Islands	67.0	61.3	66.1
Timor-Leste	–	–	–
Tonga	–	–	–
Tuvalu	–	–	–
Vanuatu	–	–	–
Oceania	**98.0**	**94.7**	**96.9**
Australia	98.6	96.2	96.4
New Zealand	94.3	85.9	99.6
Asia	**92.3**	**92.5**	**92.2**
Developing Asia	**90.8**	**91.3**	**90.5**

– = unavailable, EU = European Union, Lao PDR = Lao People's Democratic Republic.

Source: ADB calculations using data from World Bank. Logistics Performance Index. https://lpi.worldbank.org (accessed August 2019).

Table A7: Cross-Border Equity Holdings Share—Asia, 2018 (% of total cross-border equity holdings)

Reporter	Asia	PRC	Japan	EU	US	ROW
Central Asia	**11.1**	**0.0**	**7.9**	**23.1**	**56.0**	**9.8**
Armenia	–	–	–	–	–	–
Azerbaijan	–	–	–	–	–	–
Georgia	–	–	–	–	–	–
Kazakhstan	11.1	0.0	7.9	23.1	56.0	9.8
Kyrgyz Republic	–	–	–	–	–	–
Tajikistan	–	–	–	–	–	–
Turkmenistan	–	–	–	–	–	–
Uzbekistan	–	–	–	–	–	–
East Asia	**16.1**	**7.3**	**1.0**	**14.9**	**22.9**	**46.1**
China, People's Republic of	44.4		2.6	13.8	26.7	15.1
Hong Kong, China	24.6	20.8	0.9	11.4	3.7	60.3
Japan	5.9	0.8		16.0	29.9	48.1
Korea, Republic of	17.9	3.9	5.7	22.7	48.5	10.9
Mongolia	61.7	0.4	0.2	15.7	15.3	7.3
Taipei,China	–	–	–	–	–	–
South Asia	**36.8**	**26.1**	**1.0**	**15.8**	**32.5**	**15.0**
Afghanistan	–	–	–	–	–	–
Bangladesh	100.0	0.0	0.0	0.0	0.0	0.0
Bhutan	–	–	–	–	–	–
India	39.5	28.3	1.0	16.5	34.8	9.2
Maldives	–	–	–	–	–	–
Nepal	–	–	–	–	–	–
Pakistan	0.0	0.0	0.0	7.2	4.7	88.1
Sri Lanka	–	–	–	–	–	–
Southeast Asia	**40.8**	**11.4**	**5.6**	**11.4**	**23.2**	**24.6**
Brunei Darussalam	–	–	–	–	–	–
Cambodia	–	–	–	–	–	–
Indonesia	56.6	13.0	0.2	0.5	38.4	4.4
Lao PDR	–	–	–	–	–	–
Malaysia	47.0	2.9	0.9	11.0	37.3	4.6
Myanmar	–	–	–	–	–	–
Philippines	12.5	0.2	0.1	49.6	28.8	9.1
Singapore	40.8	12.7	6.4	10.0	21.8	27.4
Thailand	24.8	1.3	1.1	47.1	18.2	9.9
Viet Nam	–	–	–	–	–	–
The Pacific	**–**	**–**	**–**	**–**	**–**	**–**
Cook Islands	–	–	–	–	–	–
Fiji	–	–	–	–	–	–
Kiribati	–	–	–	–	–	–
Marshall Islands	–	–	–	–	–	–
Micronesia, Federated States of	–	–	–	–	–	–
Nauru	–	–	–	–	–	–
Niue	–	–	–	–	–	–
Palau	–	–	–	–	–	–
Papua New Guinea	–	–	–	–	–	–
Samoa	–	–	–	–	–	–
Solomon Islands	–	–	–	–	–	–
Timor-Leste	–	–	–	–	–	–
Tonga	–	–	–	–	–	–
Tuvalu	–	–	–	–	–	–
Vanuatu	–	–	–	–	–	–
Oceania	**13.1**	**0.1**	**4.7**	**18.3**	**46.1**	**22.5**
Australia	10.3	0.0	4.8	19.2	47.2	23.2
New Zealand	35.1	0.8	3.8	10.6	37.2	17.1
Asia	**19.6**	**7.0**	**2.2**	**14.8**	**26.0**	**39.6**
Developing Asia	**31.2**	**13.3**	**3.2**	**13.1**	**18.0**	**37.7**

– = unavailable, EU = European Union, Lao PDR = Lao People's Democratic Republic, PRC = People's Republic of China, ROW = rest of the world, US = United States.

Source: ADB calculations using data from International Monetary Fund. Coordinated Portfolio Investment Survey. http://cpis.imf.org (accessed September 2019).

Table A8: Cross-Border Debt Holdings Share—Asia, 2018 (% of total cross-border debt holdings)

Reporter	Partner					
	Asia	of which		EU	US	ROW
		PRC	Japan			
Central Asia	**18.3**	**1.2**	**5.5**	**20.0**	**48.1**	**13.5**
Armenia	–	–	–	–	–	–
Azerbaijan	–	–	–	–	–	–
Georgia	–	–	–	–	–	–
Kazakhstan	18.3	1.2	5.5	20.0	48.1	13.5
Kyrgyz Republic	–	–	–	–	–	–
Tajikistan	–	–	–	–	–	–
Turkmenistan	–	–	–	–	–	–
Uzbekistan	–	–	–	–	–	–
East Asia	**16.4**	**4.4**	**1.5**	**28.0**	**37.8**	**17.8**
China, People's Republic of	31.1		1.3	10.7	26.3	32.0
Hong Kong, China	45.6	22.9	7.2	15.1	23.3	15.9
Japan	8.0	0.4		32.9	42.2	16.9
Korea, Republic of	15.0	2.5	3.4	25.8	39.8	19.3
Mongolia	19.6	1.0	0.0	6.7	18.9	54.9
Taipei,China	–	–	–	–	–	–
South Asia	**7.1**	**1.0**	**1.3**	**27.7**	**57.0**	**8.2**
Afghanistan	–	–	–	–	–	–
Bangladesh	13.9	2.1	2.7	59.3	15.2	11.7
Bhutan	–	–	–	–	–	–
India	0.0	0.0	0.0	0.5	98.2	1.3
Maldives	–	–	–	–	–	–
Nepal	–	–	–	–	–	–
Pakistan	17.9	0.0	0.0	0.1	22.8	59.2
Sri Lanka	–	–	–	–	–	–
Southeast Asia	**24.9**	**5.7**	**0.4**	**11.2**	**31.0**	**32.9**
Brunei Darussalam	–	–	–	–	–	–
Cambodia	–	–	–	–	–	–
Indonesia	9.3	1.0	0.8	60.7	6.1	23.9
Lao PDR	–	–	–	–	–	–
Malaysia	55.8	2.2	1.7	7.5	21.8	14.9
Myanmar	–	–	–	–	–	–
Philippines	37.0	3.8	0.8	7.0	39.3	16.8
Singapore	22.2	5.4	0.0	10.5	32.7	34.6
Thailand	59.1	19.0	9.2	6.7	9.5	24.7
Viet Nam	–	–	–	–	–	–
The Pacific	**0.0**	**0.0**	**0.0**	**0.0**	**100.0**	**0.0**
Cook Islands	–	–	–	–	–	–
Fiji	–	–	–	–	–	–
Kiribati	–	–	–	–	–	–
Marshall Islands	–	–	–	–	–	–
Micronesia, Federated States of	–	–	–	–	–	–
Nauru	–	–	–	–	–	–
Niue	–	–	–	–	–	–
Palau	0.0	0.0	0.0	0.0	100.0	0.0
Papua New Guinea	–	–	–	–	–	–
Samoa	–	–	–	–	–	–
Solomon Islands	–	–	–	–	–	–
Timor-Leste	–	–	–	–	–	–
Tonga	–	–	–	–	–	–
Tuvalu	–	–	–	–	–	–
Vanuatu	–	–	–	–	–	–
Oceania	**13.7**	**0.0**	**5.6**	**28.7**	**29.0**	**28.7**
Australia	12.3	0.0	5.5	31.1	32.3	24.4
New Zealand	25.7	0.0	6.1	8.8	0.0	65.5
Asia	**17.5**	**4.2**	**1.7**	**25.4**	**36.2**	**20.9**
Developing Asia	**31.3**	**10.2**	**3.3**	**14.4**	**29.4**	**24.9**

– = unavailable, EU = European Union, Lao PDR = Lao People's Democratic Republic, PRC = People's Republic of China, ROW = rest of the world, US = United States.

Source: ADB calculations using data from International Monetary Fund. Coordinated Portfolio Investment Survey. http://cpis.imf.org (accessed September 2019).

Table A9: Foreign Direct Investment Inflow Share—Asia, 2018 (% of total FDI inflows)

Reporter	Asia	of which PRC	of which Japan	EU	US	ROW
Central Asia	**36.5**	**20.9**	**4.6**	**133.4**	**59.1**	**(128.9)**
Armenia	5.3	4.7	0.0	33.8	3.4	57.5
Azerbaijan	6.3	1.4	1.1	20.2	3.4	70.2
Georgia	28.6	5.3	0.4	46.4	8.4	16.6
Kazakhstan	65.6	39.0	10.6	294.9	140.0	(400.6)
Kyrgyz Republic	805.6	719.3	0.9	219.3	12.2	(937.1)
Tajikistan	9.8	5.8	0.0	25.2	6.6	58.4
Turkmenistan	1.4	0.7	0.0	5.9	1.4	91.3
Uzbekistan	14.6	5.2	3.5	31.0	8.1	46.3
East Asia	**52.7**	**5.9**	**3.6**	**14.1**	**7.3**	**25.9**
China, People's Republic of	77.4		2.7	7.5	1.9	13.1
Hong Kong, China	27.7	12.9	3.3	9.1	5.5	57.7
Japan	49.0	8.1		110.1	59.9	(118.9)
Korea, Republic of	32.2	8.1	9.0	27.9	40.6	(0.7)
Mongolia	0.0	0.0	0.0	0.0	0.0	100.0
Taipei,China	36.3	3.3	21.8	70.7	3.8	(10.8)
South Asia	**45.9**	**4.0**	**5.4**	**16.9**	**0.9**	**36.3**
Afghanistan	5.5	3.4	0.0	11.2	3.9	79.4
Bangladesh	10.7	2.0	1.3	8.0	1.9	79.4
Bhutan	229.8	0.0	0.0	45.8	0.0	(175.6)
India	48.9	0.9	6.0	17.2	0.4	33.5
Maldives	8.2	2.8	2.2	16.9	4.6	70.3
Nepal	12.3	6.3	2.9	14.6	4.7	68.5
Pakistan	85.1	64.9	3.8	32.0	6.1	(23.2)
Sri Lanka	6.4	1.6	1.2	8.8	2.3	82.5
Southeast Asia	**51.3**	**6.9**	**14.3**	**14.4**	**5.5**	**28.9**
Brunei Darussalam	160.7	0.5	12.4	(68.0)	0.0	7.2
Cambodia	84.3	25.7	6.4	5.7	1.9	8.1
Indonesia	94.4	9.7	22.5	(5.5)	4.9	6.2
Lao PDR	100.6	79.2	3.6	0.2	0.4	(1.2)
Malaysia	40.7	2.2	14.8	27.6	20.1	11.6
Myanmar	93.5	13.1	3.5	6.2	0.1	0.1
Philippines	26.9	3.1	3.4	5.3	2.5	65.4
Singapore	23.9	4.8	6.4	22.3	5.6	48.2
Thailand	100.6	4.9	53.9	17.7	6.0	(24.3)
Viet Nam	85.3	7.0	24.2	5.1	1.6	8.0
The Pacific	**113.4**	**22.1**	**33.4**	**115.3**	**101.3**	**(230.0)**
Cook Islands	917.6	55.6	0.0	1,349.1	0.0	(2,166.7)
Fiji	1.4	0.2	0.0	1.0	1.5	96.0
Kiribati	3,725.4	0.0	0.0	6,040.7	0.0	(9,666.1)
Marshall Islands	–	–	–	–	–	–
Micronesia, Federated States of	–	–	–	–	–	–
Nauru	–	–	–	–	–	–
Niue	–	–	–	–	–	–
Palau	48.5	9.9	27.8	0.0	47.7	3.8
Papua New Guinea	56.2	5.6	7.4	32.5	19.6	(8.3)
Samoa	570.3	69.2	94.4	255.0	365.6	(1,090.8)
Solomon Islands	155.8	0.0	37.5	156.2	115.1	(327.2)
Timor-Leste	0.0	0.0	0.0	0.0	0.0	100.0
Tonga	95.0	15.2	0.0	100.5	101.1	(196.5)
Tuvalu	253.3	0.0	0.0	470.0	540.0	(1,163.3)
Vanuatu	42.2	5.6	7.4	9.6	0.0	48.2
Oceania	**23.3**	**4.4**	**8.9**	**10.6**	**5.0**	**61.1**
Australia	19.6	4.3	8.8	9.8	4.5	66.1
New Zealand	184.0	8.4	13.0	42.3	26.8	(153.1)
Asia	**48.2**	**6.1**	**7.2**	**16.2**	**7.0**	**28.5**
Developing Asia	**51.4**	**6.3**	**7.2**	**15.1**	**6.2**	**27.4**

( ) = negative, – = unavailable, EU = European Union, FDI = foreign direct investment, Lao PDR = Lao People's Democratic Republic, PRC = People's Republic of China, ROW = rest of the world, US = United States.

Sources: Association of Southeast Asian Nations Secretariat. ASEANstats Database. https://www.aseanstats.org (accessed July 2019); CEIC; Eurostat. Balance of Payments. http://ec.europa.eu/eurostat/web/balance-of-payments/data/database; United Nations Conference on Trade and Development. Bilateral FDI Statistics. http://unctad.org/en/Pages/Home.aspx (all accessed July 2019); and World Investment Report 2019 Statistical Annex Tables. https://unctad.org/en/Pages/DIAE/World%20Investment%20Report/World_Investment_Report.aspx (accessed June 2019).

Table A10: Remittance Inflows Share—Asia, 2017 (% of total remittance inflows)

Reporter	Partner				
	Asia	Middle East	EU	US	ROW
Central Asia	**7.3**	**1.1**	**8.0**	**2.6**	**81.0**
Armenia	4.4	0.4	10.5	13.8	70.8
Azerbaijan	24.1	4.0	3.4	2.0	66.4
Georgia	9.2	2.7	16.8	2.4	69.0
Kazakhstan	4.2	0.7	22.2	0.8	72.2
Kyrgyz Republic	4.7	0.9	12.8	0.6	80.9
Tajikistan	12.8	0.4	4.2	0.9	81.7
Turkmenistan	0.0	0.0	0.0	0.0	100.0
Uzbekistan	0.0	0.0	0.0	0.0	100.0
East Asia	**50.9**	**0.1**	**9.0**	**27.4**	**12.6**
China, People's Republic of	52.7	0.1	9.0	25.3	12.9
Hong Kong, China	22.6	0.0	11.6	30.8	35.0
Japan	39.7	0.3	13.1	34.8	12.1
Korea, Republic of	43.4	0.0	4.5	44.8	7.3
Mongolia	45.1	0.4	20.0	0.3	34.3
Taipei,China	–	–	–	–	–
South Asia	**15.2**	**58.6**	**9.5**	**12.0**	**4.6**
Afghanistan	31.6	56.5	8.0	2.1	1.8
Bangladesh	36.2	54.1	5.5	3.3	0.9
Bhutan	97.0	0.0	1.8	0.2	1.0
India	13.0	55.8	8.7	17.0	5.5
Maldives	58.0	1.3	12.7	0.0	28.0
Nepal	21.4	70.4	3.0	4.8	0.4
Pakistan	5.4	70.2	14.0	6.7	3.7
Sri Lanka	17.0	51.3	19.1	3.1	9.5
Southeast Asia	**26.2**	**23.8**	**10.3**	**32.4**	**7.3**
Brunei Darussalam	–	–	–	–	–
Cambodia	68.8	0.0	7.4	20.8	3.0
Indonesia	40.0	51.6	4.6	2.8	1.1
Lao PDR	74.6	0.0	4.2	19.5	1.8
Malaysia	89.3	0.0	4.3	3.8	2.6
Myanmar	66.4	27.1	0.7	5.4	0.4
Philippines	18.3	31.6	7.1	33.8	9.1
Singapore	–	–	–	–	–
Thailand	37.1	4.1	25.2	27.6	6.0
Viet Nam	19.6	0.0	15.6	56.1	8.6
The Pacific	**59.3**	**0.0**	**1.9**	**26.1**	**12.6**
Cook Islands	–	–	–	–	–
Fiji	59.7	0.0	3.2	23.1	14.1
Kiribati	50.7	0.0	0.8	46.5	2.0
Marshall Islands	2.5	0.0	0.2	94.3	3.0
Micronesia, Federated States of	1.6	0.0	0.0	71.8	26.5
Nauru	–	–	–	–	–
Niue	–	–	–	–	–
Palau	7.1	0.0	0.4	56.0	36.5
Papua New Guinea	89.3	0.9	1.1	7.7	0.9
Samoa	64.3	0.0	0.2	12.5	23.0
Solomon Islands	88.8	0.1	2.1	4.4	4.5
Timor-Leste	93.7	0.0	5.9	0.0	0.4
Tonga	57.1	0.0	0.3	39.3	3.3
Tuvalu	77.2	0.2	1.3	5.1	16.1
Vanuatu	21.2	0.0	10.2	2.1	66.6
Oceania	**38.5**	**1.4**	**37.5**	**13.4**	**9.2**
Australia	31.5	1.6	41.8	14.9	10.2
New Zealand	84.1	0.1	9.2	3.9	2.7
Asia	**27.7**	**30.9**	**9.7**	**20.8**	**11.0**
Developing Asia	**27.4**	**31.7**	**9.4**	**20.6**	**10.9**

– = unavailable, EU = European Union, Lao PDR = Lao People's Democratic Republic, ROW = rest of the world, US = United States.

Source: ADB calculations using data from World Bank. World Bank Migration and Remittances Data. http://www.worldbank.org/en/topic/migrationremittancesdiasporaissues/brief/migration-remittances-data (accessed April 2019).

Table A11: Outbound Migration Share—Asia, 2017 (% of total outbound migrants)

Reporter	Asia	of which PRC	of which Japan	EU	US	ROW
Central Asia	**9.6**	**0.0**	**0.0**	**14.8**	**2.3**	**73.4**
Armenia	19.4	0.0	0.0	8.7	9.7	62.2
Azerbaijan	14.7	0.0	0.0	3.6	1.8	80.0
Georgia	11.8	0.0	0.0	20.0	3.2	65.0
Kazakhstan	1.4	0.0	0.0	26.2	0.7	71.8
Kyrgyz Republic	3.7	0.0	0.0	12.4	0.8	83.1
Tajikistan	5.9	0.0	0.0	5.7	0.8	87.6
Turkmenistan	2.5	0.0	0.0	4.2	0.9	92.3
Uzbekistan	21.7	0.0	0.0	3.7	3.0	71.6
East Asia	**47.0**	**3.3**	**9.2**	**9.4**	**29.1**	**14.5**
China, People's Republic of	51.5		7.4	10.0	24.0	14.5
Hong Kong, China	40.8	25.1	0.0	9.3	22.3	27.6
Japan	22.7	0.8		17.1	44.3	15.9
Korea, Republic of	40.1	7.6	23.7	4.0	48.0	7.9
Mongolia	39.0	0.0	0.0	25.8	0.0	35.2
Taipei,China	0.0	0.0	0.0	0.0	0.0	0.0
South Asia	**29.1**	**0.1**	**0.2**	**8.4**	**8.0**	**54.4**
Afghanistan	32.5	0.0	0.0	6.4	1.5	59.6
Bangladesh	48.9	0.1	0.1	5.1	2.9	43.1
Bhutan	89.1	0.0	0.0	4.0	0.0	7.0
India	19.7	0.1	0.2	7.5	13.5	59.4
Maldives	75.3	0.0	0.0	14.9	0.0	9.8
Nepal	50.8	0.0	0.0	5.4	6.1	37.7
Pakistan	24.3	0.1	0.2	14.0	6.2	55.5
Sri Lanka	20.8	0.3	0.6	21.4	3.1	54.7
Southeast Asia	**46.9**	**0.8**	**2.0**	**7.7**	**21.3**	**24.1**
Brunei Darussalam	77.0	0.0	0.0	12.1	0.0	11.0
Cambodia	71.0	0.0	0.3	6.6	16.2	6.1
Indonesia	42.8	1.0	0.7	4.3	2.4	50.4
Lao PDR	79.5	0.0	0.0	3.8	16.2	0.5
Malaysia	89.1	0.3	0.5	4.7	3.7	2.6
Myanmar	84.5	0.0	0.0	0.7	4.6	10.2
Philippines	15.8	1.3	4.2	8.7	36.8	38.7
Singapore	65.3	0.0	0.8	18.2	10.9	5.6
Thailand	34.5	1.7	5.2	26.7	29.2	9.5
Viet Nam	24.6	1.1	3.1	15.0	51.9	8.6
The Pacific	**64.7**	**0.0**	**0.0**	**2.8**	**19.1**	**13.4**
Cook Islands	99.9	0.0	0.0	0.0	0.0	0.0
Fiji	62.4	0.0	0.0	2.8	21.4	13.4
Kiribati	94.4	0.0	0.0	3.4	0.0	2.2
Marshall Islands	1.8	0.0	0.0	0.1	94.2	3.9
Micronesia, Federated States of	3.1	0.0	0.0	0.7	38.2	58.0
Nauru	96.3	0.0	0.0	1.2	0.0	2.5
Niue	99.3	0.0	0.0	0.0	0.0	0.7
Palau	12.2	0.0	0.0	7.4	0.0	80.4
Papua New Guinea	49.5	0.0	0.0	30.8	0.0	19.7
Samoa	69.9	0.0	0.0	0.7	15.7	13.8
Solomon Islands	91.3	0.0	0.0	8.4	0.0	0.3
Timor-Leste	89.7	0.0	0.0	10.1	0.0	0.2
Tonga	62.7	0.0	0.0	0.7	32.1	4.6
Tuvalu	78.1	0.0	0.0	1.9	0.0	20.0
Vanuatu	23.0	0.0	0.0	11.5	0.0	65.5
Oceania	**61.3**	**0.4**	**1.0**	**23.7**	**8.8**	**6.2**
Australia	26.9	1.0	1.9	45.5	16.2	11.4
New Zealand	83.6	0.0	0.4	9.6	4.0	2.7
Asia	**34.7**	**0.8**	**2.1**	**9.4**	**14.1**	**41.7**
Developing Asia	**34.4**	**0.8**	**2.1**	**9.1**	**13.9**	**42.6**

– = unavailable, EU = European Union, Lao PDR = Lao People's Democratic Republic, PRC = People's Republic of China, ROW = rest of the world, US = United States.

Source: ADB calculations using data from United Nations. Department of Economic and Social Affairs, Population Division. International Migrant Stock 2017. http://www.un.org/en/development/desa/population/migration/data/index.shtml (accessed July 2018).

Table A12.a: Inbound Visitor Share—Asia, 2017 (% of total inbound visitors)

Destination	Asia	of which PRC	EU	US	ROW
Central Asia	**63.3**	**0.8**	**3.3**	**0.8**	**32.7**
Armenia	9.2	1.1	21.0	17.5	52.3
Azerbaijan	25.3	0.4	4.0	0.6	70.2
Georgia	46.2	0.3	4.7	0.6	48.6
Kazakhstan	70.6	1.2	2.9	0.4	26.1
Kyrgyz Republic	86.1	0.8	1.0	0.3	12.6
Tajikistan	57.8	1.5	3.0	0.7	38.6
Turkmenistan	–	–	–	–	–
Uzbekistan	91.9	0.6	0.8	0.0	7.2
East Asia	**80.5**	**14.1**	**2.8**	**2.6**	**14.1**
China, People's Republic of	76.9		2.1	1.5	19.5
Hong Kong, China	88.3	66.0	4.4	3.1	4.2
Japan	87.6	25.7	4.7	4.8	2.9
Korea, Republic of	82.9	31.9	4.6	6.7	5.9
Mongolia	60.1	30.4	9.6	3.6	26.7
Taipei,China	90.8	25.8	2.4	5.3	1.5
South Asia	**49.4**	**6.5**	**24.5**	**10.8**	**15.3**
Afghanistan	–	–	–	–	–
Bangladesh	–	–	–	–	–
Bhutan	54.0	10.3	21.9	14.8	9.3
India	48.5	2.5	21.5	13.8	16.3
Maldives	44.7	22.1	36.4	2.8	16.0
Nepal	64.8	11.8	20.3	8.9	6.0
Pakistan	–	–	–	–	–
Sri Lanka	50.4	12.8	32.7	2.7	14.2
Southeast Asia	**82.0**	**21.0**	**9.1**	**3.4**	**5.5**
Brunei Darussalam	88.9	20.5	7.7	1.6	1.7
Cambodia	77.3	21.8	13.0	4.6	5.0
Indonesia	80.7	17.4	12.7	2.9	3.7
Lao PDR	94.8	16.7	3.2	1.0	1.0
Malaysia	93.2	8.8	3.7	0.8	2.3
Myanmar	90.6	29.6	6.3	2.2	1.0
Philippines	69.0	15.1	8.6	15.0	7.4
Singapore	85.3	19.1	8.3	3.4	3.1
Thailand	74.0	29.1	12.9	3.0	10.1
Viet Nam	80.0	32.7	8.7	5.0	6.3
The Pacific	**82.7**	**8.6**	**5.1**	**8.4**	**3.8**
Cook Islands	85.3	0.5	6.3	5.3	3.1
Fiji	81.5	6.4	5.6	10.7	2.2
Kiribati	51.0	3.3	9.8	36.7	2.5
Marshall Islands	35.6	–	0.7	61.0	2.6
Micronesia, Federated States of	–	–	–	–	–
Nauru	–	–	–	–	–
Niue	95.7	0.0	1.7	2.6	0.0
Palau	89.9	47.6	2.9	6.2	1.1
Papua New Guinea	85.6	8.1	6.9	6.3	1.2
Samoa	77.5	1.8	1.9	7.5	13.2
Solomon Islands	86.8	5.9	4.4	7.9	0.9
Timor-Leste	82.3	13.0	12.9	3.5	1.2
Tonga	81.4	2.7	3.8	14.1	0.8
Tuvalu	76.7	6.4	6.2	14.5	2.6
Vanuatu	82.3	4.0	1.2	0.0	17.7
Oceania	**67.0**	**14.2**	**16.4**	**8.9**	**7.7**
Australia	66.1	15.4	17.1	8.9	7.9
New Zealand	69.1	11.4	14.7	9.0	7.2
Asia	**78.4**	**15.0**	**5.9**	**3.2**	**12.5**
Developing Asia	**78.1**	**14.2**	**5.6**	**2.9**	**13.4**

– = unavailable, EU = European Union, Lao PDR = Lao People's Democratic Republic, PRC = People's Republic of China, ROW = rest of the world, US = United States.

Source: ADB calculations using data from United Nations World Tourism Organization. Tourism Satellite Accounts. http://statistics.umwto.org (accessed April 2019).

Table A12.b: Outbound Visitor Share—Asia, 2017 (% of total outbound visitors)

		Destination			
		of which			
Origin	Asia	PRC	EU	US	ROW
Central Asia	**56.1**	**1.3**	**0.9**	**0.2**	**42.8**
Armenia	64.2	0.3	1.3	0.6	34.0
Azerbaijan	35.0	0.3	0.7	0.2	64.1
Georgia	17.7	0.3	2.6	0.1	79.6
Kazakhstan	55.2	2.5	0.9	0.3	43.6
Kyrgyz Republic	76.7	1.5	0.1	0.1	23.1
Tajikistan	70.5	1.6	0.1	0.1	29.3
Turkmenistan	30.3	2.5	0.4	0.2	69.1
Uzbekistan	86.2	0.9	0.4	0.2	13.2
East Asia	**74.9**	**35.2**	**5.8**	**3.6**	**15.7**
China, People's Republic of	61.1		8.2	3.2	27.6
Hong Kong, China	92.5	85.6	0.3	0.2	7.0
Japan	59.2	11.6	14.9	15.6	10.3
Korea, Republic of	71.9	12.7	8.9	7.7	11.5
Mongolia	82.4	74.5	0.1	0.5	17.0
Taipei,China	84.4	32.8	4.7	2.7	8.3
South Asia	**49.2**	**5.4**	**8.0**	**6.3**	**36.4**
Afghanistan	18.2	1.3	1.1	0.2	80.5
Bangladesh	85.5	2.8	0.5	1.0	13.0
Bhutan	96.2	1.4	1.1	1.1	1.7
India	48.6	6.2	12.7	9.7	28.9
Maldives	94.3	3.0	0.2	0.1	5.3
Nepal	86.8	24.6	0.7	5.9	6.6
Pakistan	12.5	3.3	3.1	2.4	82.0
Sri Lanka	85.3	6.9	1.3	2.5	10.8
Southeast Asia	**92.5**	**24.5**	**1.3**	**1.0**	**5.2**
Brunei Darussalam	99.4	0.4	0.0	0.1	0.5
Cambodia	98.5	4.7	0.1	0.4	1.1
Indonesia	79.9	6.2	1.6	1.0	17.5
Lao PDR	99.9	30.4	0.1	0.0	0.1
Malaysia	91.1	9.8	2.0	0.6	6.3
Myanmar	99.7	91.5	0.0	0.1	0.2
Philippines	80.9	17.2	2.5	4.6	12.0
Singapore	95.9	4.7	1.5	0.7	1.9
Thailand	92.6	7.2	1.6	1.0	4.8
Viet Nam	97.9	56.1	0.1	1.0	0.9
The Pacific	**84.1**	**4.0**	**0.3**	**3.5**	**12.0**
Cook Islands	95.7	0.0	0.2	0.4	3.7
Fiji	88.5	4.3	0.4	6.4	4.7
Kiribati	90.9	31.7	0.4	2.9	5.7
Marshall Islands	42.9	12.9	0.8	4.4	52.0
Micronesia, Federated States of	9.6	1.8	0.4	2.8	87.2
Nauru	92.1	3.9	1.6	1.8	4.5
Niue	95.7	0.0	0.2	0.9	3.2
Palau	11.5	1.7	0.6	3.2	84.7
Papua New Guinea	96.4	2.3	0.1	1.1	2.4
Samoa	77.9	4.2	0.1	0.0	22.0
Solomon Islands	91.2	6.4	1.0	1.7	6.1
Timor-Leste	93.7	6.9	0.9	1.1	4.3
Tonga	89.1	3.5	0.2	9.3	1.4
Tuvalu	81.0	10.3	1.1	2.6	15.4
Vanuatu	81.6	3.1	0.4	0.6	17.4
Oceania	**58.2**	**4.4**	**23.5**	**8.2**	**10.2**
Australia	54.7	4.5	26.3	8.2	10.8
New Zealand	73.4	3.9	11.2	8.0	7.4
Asia	**75.1**	**27.7**	**5.5**	**3.2**	**16.2**
Developing Asia	**76.9**	**29.9**	**4.0**	**2.2**	**16.9**

– = unavailable, EU = European Union, Lao PDR = Lao People's Democratic Republic, PRC = People's Republic of China, ROW = rest of the world, US = United States.

Source: ADB calculations using data from United Nations World Tourism Organization. Tourism Satellite Accounts. http://statistics.umwto.org (accessed April 2019).

www.ingramcontent.com/pod-product-compliance
Lightning Source LLC
Chambersburg PA
CBHW050041220326
41599CB00045B/7247